American Poetry of the Twentieth Century

Longman Literature in English Series

General Editors: David Carroll and Michael Wheeler
University of Lancaster

For a complete list of titles see pages viii–ix

American Poetry of the Twentieth Century

Richard Gray

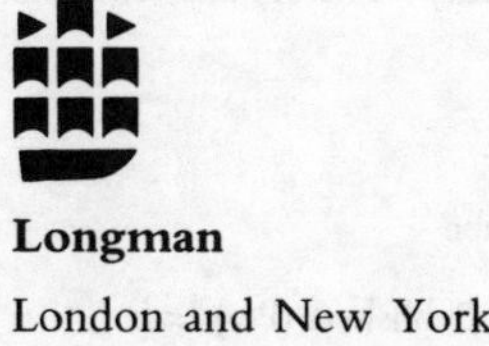

Longman

London and New York

Longman Group UK Limited,
Longman House, Burnt Mill, Harlow,
Essex CM20 2JE, England
and Associated Companies throughout the world.

Published in the United States of America
by Longman Inc., New York

First published 1990
Second impression 1991

BRITISH LIBRARY CATALOGUING IN PUBLICATION DATA

Gray, Richard, *1944–*
American poetry of the twentieth century. –
(Longman literature in English series).
1. Poetry in English. American writers, 1900 –
Critical studies
I. Title
811′52′09

ISBN 0-582-49437-0 CSD
ISBN 0-582-49444-3 PPR

LIBRARY OF CONGRESS CATALOGING IN PUBLICATION DATA.

Gray, Richard J.
American poetry of the twentieth century / Richard Gray.
p. cm. – (Longman literature in English series)
Bibliography: p.
Includes index.
ISBN 0-582-49437-0. – ISBN 0-582-49444-3
1. American poetry – 20th century – History and criticism.
I. Title. II. Series.
PS323.5.G73 1989
811′.5′09 – dc19 88-38543
CIP

Set in Linotron 202 $9\frac{1}{2}$/11pt Bembo

Produced by Longman Singapore Publishers (Pte) Ltd.
Printed in Singapore.

Contents

Longman Literature in English Series viii

Editor's Preface x

Author's Preface xi

Acknowledgements xiii

1 Backgrounds: America, The Poem, and The Twentieth Century 1

America the poem: ideas of America and its writing 1
America's poets: formative figures for the twentieth century 19
America and modernism: new readings of reality 29
America and 'revolution': new frontiers for art 38

2 The Modernist Experiment: Imagism, Objectivism, and some Major Innovators 49

Imagism: the social and cultural situation 49
The significance of Imagism 52
From Imagism to Objectivism or Dream: H. D., Zukofsky, Oppen, Reznikoff, Niedecker, Fletcher, Aiken 57
From Imagism to the redemption of history: Pound 73
From Imagism to contact and community: Williams 82
From Imagism to discovery of the imagination: Stevens 88

3 In Search of a Past: the Fugitive Movement and the Major Traditionalists 101

Traditionalism: the social and cultural situation 101
The significance of the Fugitives 106
Traditionalism and the South: Ransom, Tate, Davidson, Warren, J. P. Bishop, Berry, Dickey 109

Traditionalism outside the South: Winters, Cunningham, Eberhart 125
Traditionalism, scepticism, and tragedy: Frost 131
Traditionalism, quiet desperation, and belief: Robinson 138
Traditionalism, inhumanism, and prophecy: Jeffers 145

4 **The Traditions of Whitman: Other Poets from between the Wars 157**

The language of crisis and the language of Whitman: other aspects of the social and cultural situation between the wars 159
Whitman and the shape of American poetry 161
Whitman and American populism: Sandburg, Lindsay, Masters 162
Whitman and American radicalism: Rexroth, MacLeish, Fearing, Patchen 168
Whitman and American identity: Hughes, Johnson, Cullen, Tolson, Hayden, Brooks, and the question of black poetry 176
Whitman and American individualism: Moore, Wylie, Millay, Miles, Bogan, Adams 184
Whitman and American experimentalism: cummings 194
Whitman and American mysticism: Rukeyser, Riding, Crane 199

5 **Formalists and Confessionals: American Poetry since the Second World War 214**

From abundance to anger: the social and cultural tendencies of the first two decades after the war 214
From the mythological eye to the lonely 'I': a progress of American poetry since the war 218
Varieties of the personal: the self as dream, landscape, or confession 225
From formalism to freedom: a progress of American poetic techniques since the war 231
The imagination of commitment: a progress of American poetic themes since the war 238
The uses of formalism: Bishop, and others 243
The confessional 'I' as primitive: Roethke 247
The confessional 'I' as historian: Lowell 251
The confessional 'I' as martyr: Berryman 256
The confessional 'I' as prophetess: Plath 260
New formalists, new confessionals: recent departures 264

6 **Beats, Prophets, and Aesthetes: American Poetry since the Second World War 273**

From the public to the personal: social and cultural tendencies of the Sixties and after 273
Rediscovering the American voice: the Black Mountain poets (Olson, J. Williams, Levertov, Blackburn, Wieners, Creeley, Dorn, Duncan) 279
Restoring the American vision: the San Francisco poets (Ferlinghetti, Everson, Spicer, Lamantia, Whalen, McClure, Snyder) 291
Re-creating American rhythms: the Beat poets (Ginsberg, Corso) and Bukowski 299
Resurrecting the American rebel: black poetry (Baraka, Kaufman, Joans, Evans, Sanchez, Giovanni, Mahubuti, Karenga, Nelson) 307
Reinventing the American self: the New York poets (O'Hara, Guest, Schuyler, Berrigan, Koch, Ashbery) and Merrill 315
Postscript: America a poem 328

Appendix: The problem of literary nationality: the case of T. S. Eliot 336

Chronology 347

General Bibliographies 366

(i) Bibliographies and reference guides 366
(ii) Literary, historical and cultural backgrounds 367
(iii) History and criticism 372
(iv) Some useful anthologies 379

Individual Authors 381

Notes on biography, major works, and criticism 381

Index 420

Longman Literature in English Series

General Editors: David Carroll and Michael Wheeler
University of Lancaster

Pre-Renaissance English Literature

* English Literature before Chaucer *Michael Swanton*
English Literature in the Age of Chaucer
* English Medieval Romance *W. R. J. Barron*

English Poetry

* English Poetry of the Sixteenth Century *Gary Waller*
* English Poetry of the Seventeenth Century *George Parfitt*
English Poetry of the Eighteenth Century 1700–1789
* English Poetry of the Romantic Period 1789–1830 *J. R. Watson*
* English Poetry of the Victorian Period 1830–1890 *Bernard Richards*
English Poetry of the Early Modern Period 1890–1940
English Poetry since 1940

English Drama

English Drama before Shakespeare
* English Drama: Shakespeare to the Restoration, 1590–1660 *Alexander Leggatt*
* English Drama: Restoration and Eighteenth Century, 1660–1789 *Richard W. Bevis*
English Drama: Romantic and Victorian, 1789–1890
English Drama of the Early Modern Period, 1890–1940
English Drama since 1940

English Fiction

* English Fiction of the Eighteenth Century 1700–1789 *Clive T. Probyn*
* English Fiction of the Romantic Period 1789–1830 *Gary Kelly*
* English Fiction of the Victorian Period 1830–1890 *Michael Wheeler*
* English Fiction of the Early Modern Period 1890–1940 *Douglas Hewitt*
English Fiction since 1940

English Prose

English Prose of the Renaissance 1550–1700
English Prose of the Eighteenth Century
English Prose of the Nineteenth Century

Criticism and Literary Theory

Criticism and Literary Theory from Sidney to Johnson
Criticism and Literary Theory from Wordsworth to Arnold
Criticism and Literary Theory from 1890 to the Present

The Intellectual and Cultural Context

The Sixteenth Century
* The Seventeenth Century, 1603–1700 *Graham Parry*
* The Eighteenth Century, 1700–1789 *James Sambrook*
The Romantic Period, 1789–1830
The Victorian Period, 1830–1890
The Twentieth Century: 1890 to the Present

American Literature

American Literature before 1880
* American Poetry of the Twentieth Century *Richard Gray*
American Drama of the Twentieth Century
* American Fiction 1865–1940 *Brian Lee*
American Fiction since 1940
Twentieth-Century America

Other Literatures

Irish Literature since 1800
Scottish Literature since 1700

Australian Literature
Indian Literature in English *William Walsh*
African Literature in English: East and West
Southern African Literature in English
Caribbean Literature in English
* Canadian Literature in English *W. J. Keith*

* *Already published*

Editors' Preface

The multi-volume Longman Literature in English Series provides students of literature with a critical introduction to the major genres in their historical and cultural context. Each volume gives a coherent account of a clearly defined area, and the series, when complete, will offer a practical and comprehensive guide to literature written in English from Anglo-Saxon times to the present. The aim of the series as a whole is to show that the most valuable and stimulating approach to literature is that based upon an awareness of the relations between literary forms and their historical context. Thus the areas covered by most of the separate volumes are defined by period and genre. Each volume offers new informed ways of reading literary works, and provides guidance to further reading in an extensive reference section.

As well as studies on all periods of English and American literature, the series includes books on criticism and literary theory, and on the intellectual and cultural context. A comprehensive series of this kind must of course include other literature written in English, and therefore a group of volumes deals with Irish and Scottish literature, and the literatures of India, Africa, the Caribbean, Australia, and Canada. The forty-seven volumes of the series cover the following areas: pre-Renaissance English Literature, English Poetry, English Drama, English Fiction, English Prose, Criticism and Literary Theory, Intellectual and Cultural Context, American Literature, Other Literatures in English.

David Carroll
Michael Wheeler

Author's Preface

The title of this book is, I hope self-explanatory: I have tried to offer a reasonably comprehensive account of the development of American poetry since the early years of this century. In doing so, I have also attempted to take account of the historical and cultural forces that have helped shape that poetry and to utilise recent theories concerning the relationship between text and context, literature and other dimensions of experience. I am painfully aware, as I write this, that there are many good poets who receive only passing mention or even no mention at all. Names like William Bronk, Maxine Kumin, and Audre Lord spring to mind immediately; the reader will undoubtedly think of many others. In extenuation of this, all I can plead is that any account of American poetry has to stop somewhere, to exclude a number of distinct and distinguished writers, if it is not to degenerate into a simple list of names. I am also aware, much less painfully, that my ambition first and last has been to concentrate on the individual poet and poem. It is the experience of reading the single poem, after all, and encountering the voice of a singular poet, that fires the reader's imagination into life; and so it is to this that any study of poetry must eventually return, no matter how detailed or protracted its investigation may be of poetry's social and ideological underpinnings.

I have accumulated many debts in the course of writing this book. I would like to thank the University of Essex for its generosity with sabbatical leave, and the many students at Essex – particularly those in the M.A. course in American poetry – from whom I have learned over the years. I would also like to express my gratitude for the financial assistance I have received from the university, which has enabled me to pursue at least part of my research in the United States. Above all, there are the personal debts. I would like to thank Sylvia Sparrow for patiently typing the several drafts of this book and, in the process, having to decipher my almost illegible script. I would like to thank Arthur Terry for his informed advice and the loan of many useful books, Joe Allard for helping me to understand just how complex a fate it is to be an American, and George Dekker and Lindajo Bartholomew for their kindness and hospitality. I would, finally, like to thank Gordon Brotherston, Herbie Butterfield, Cherry Good, Jack Hill, Haytham Mahfoud, Dennis Reid, Kate Rhodes, Tjebbe Westendorp and Dudley Young for the many conversations I have had with them: conversations that have given me whatever insights I now enjoy into literature in general and poetry in particular. Good friends all, these and many others have made the writing of this book an education and an almost unequivocal pleasure.

Richard Gray
Wivenhoe, Essex

Acknowledgements

We are grateful to the following for permission to reproduce poems:

Atheneum Publishers, an imprint of Macmillan Publishing Co, the author & the author's agents for an extract from 'The Morning' in *The Compass Flower* by W. S. Merwin, copyright © 1977 by W. S. Merwin; Elizabeth Barnett, Literary Executor of Edna St Vincent Millay, for 'First Fig', 'Second Fig' and extracts from 'Passer Mortuus Est', 'What lips my lips have kissed, and where, & why' and 'Thursday' by Edna St Vincent Millay in *Collected Poems* (Harper & Row, Inc), Copyright 1921, 1922, 1923, 1948, 1950, 1951 by Edna St Vincent Millay & Norma Millay Ellis; the author, Gwendolyn Brooks for 'We Real Cool' in *Blacks* (The David Co, Chicago), copyright 1987; The University of California Press for an extract from 'The Pattern' by Robert Creeley in *The Collected Poems of Robert Creeley, 1945–1975*, © 1983 The Regents of the University of California; Jonathan Cape Ltd on behalf of the Estate of Robert Frost and Henry Holt & Co, Inc for extracts from 'The Pasture', 'Stopping by Woods on a Snowy Evening' and 'Design' by Robert Frost in *The Poetry of Robert Frost* edited by Edward Connery Lathem, US copyright © 1969 by Holt, Rinehart & Winston, Inc. Copyright © 1962 by Robert Frost. Copyright © 1975 by Lesley Frost Ballantine; Carcanet Press Ltd and New Directions Publishing Corporation for 'Oread' by HD in *Collected Poems 1912–1944*, copyright © 1982 by the Estate of Hilda Doolittle and an extract from 'Young Sycamore' by William Carlos Williams in *Collected Poems 1909–1939*, US copyright 1938 by New Directions Publishing Corporation; Carcanet Press Ltd and Viking Penguin, a division of Penguin books USA, Inc for extracts from 'Paradoxes & Oxymorons' in *Shadow Train* by John Ashbery, US title *Selected Poems*, copyright © John Ashbery, 1985; City Lights Books for extracts from 'Revolutionary Letter' in *Revolutionary Letters* by Diane DiPrima, copyright © 1971, 1974, 1979 Diane DiPrima and 'The Day Lady Died' in *Lunch Poems* by Frank O'Hara, copyright © 1964 by Frank O'Hara; Cid Corman, Literary Executor for the Lorine Niedecker Estate, for extracts from 'You are my friend', 'There's a better shine' and 'Paul', copyright

© Cid Corman; Faber & Faber Ltd and Doubleday, a division of Bantam, Doubleday, Dell Publishing Group, Inc, for extracts from 'Open House' and 'Cuttings (later)' in *The Collected Poems of Theodore Roethke* by Theodore Roethke, copyright 1941, & 1948 Theodore Roethke; Faber & Faber Ltd and Farrar, Straus & Giroux, Inc for 'The Death of the Ball Turret Gunner' in *The Complete Poems of Randall Jarrell* by Randall Jarrell, copyright © 1945, 1969 by Mrs Randall Jarrell, copyright renewed © 1972 by Mrs Randall Jarrell and extracts from 'Epilogue' in *Day By Day* by Randall Jarrell, Copyright © 1977 by Robert Lowell; Faber & Faber Ltd and Harcourt Brace Jovanovich, Inc for extracts from 'Children of Light' in *Poems 1938–1949* by Robert Lowell, US title *Lord Weary's Castle*, copyright 1946 and renewed 1974 by Robert Lowell; Faber & Faber Ltd and Alfred A. Knopf, Inc for extracts from 'Metaphore of a Magnifico' in *The Collected Poems of Wallace Stevens* by Wallace Stevens, copyright 1923, 1951 by Wallace Stevens; Faber & Faber Ltd and Macmillan Publishing Co for extracts from 'Poetry' in *The Complete Poems of Marianne Moore* by Marianne Moore, US title *Collected Poems*, copyright 1935 by Marianne Moore, renewed 1963 by Marianne Moore & T. S. Eliot; Faber & Faber Ltd and New Directions Publishing Corporation for 'In a Station of the Metro' and 'The Jewel Stairs Grievance' and extracts from 'A Pact', 'The Return' and 'The Garden' in *Collected Shorter Poems* by Ezra Pound, US title *Personae*, copyright 1926 by Ezra Pound; Farrar, Straus & Giroux, Inc for extracts from 'The Map' in *The Complete Poems 1927–1979* by Elizabeth Bishop, copyright © 1979, 1983 by Alice Helen Methfessel and extracts from 'Portrait' & 'Simple Autumnal' in *Collected Poems: 1923–1953* by Louise Bogan, copyright © 1954 by Louise Bogan, renewal copyright © 1981 by Madie Alexander Scannell; Elizabeth Friedman on behalf of the author, Laura (Riding) Jackson for 'Incarnations' and 'Beyond'; Grafton Books, a division of William Collins Sons & Co Ltd, and Liveright Publishing Corporation for extracts from 'In Just-' in *Tulips & Chimneys* by e. e. cummings, edited by George James Firmage, copyright 1923, 1925 and renewed 1951, 1953 by e. e. cummings, copyright © 1973, 1976 by the Trustees for the e. e. cummings Trust, copyright © 1973, 1978 by George James Firmage, 'IN)/all those who got' in *No Thanks* by e. e. cummings, edited by George James Firmage, copyright 1935 by e. e. cummings, copyright © 1968 by Marion Morehouse Cummings, copyright © 1973, 1978 by the Trustees for the e. e. cummings Trust, copyright © 1973, 1978 by George James Firmage & 'enter no (silence is the blood whose flesh' from *Complete Poems, 1913–1962* by e. e. cummings, © 1923, 1925, 1931, 1935, 1938, 1939, 1940, 1944, 1945, 1946, 1947, 1948, 1949, 1950, 1951, 1952, 1953, 1954, 1955, 1956, 1957, 1958, 1959, 1960, 1961, 1962 by the Trustees of the e. e. cummings Trust, copyright ©

1961, 1963, 1968 by Marion Morehouse Cummings; Harcourt Brace Jovanovich, Inc for extracts from 'Chicago' in *Chicago Poems* by Carl Sandburg, copyright 1916 by Holt, Rinehart & Winston, Inc, and renewed 1944 by Carl Sandburg; Harper & Row, Inc for extracts from 'Looking Into A Face' in *Light Around The Body* by Robert Bly, copyright © 1967 by Robert Bly and 'At the Bomb Testing Site' in *Stories That Could Be True* by William Stafford, copyright © 1960, 1977 by William Stafford; Houghton Mifflin Co for extracts from 'You, Andrew Marvell' in *New & Collected Poems 1917–1982* by Archibald MacLeish, copyright © 1985 by the Estate of Archibald MacLeish; the author's agents and Alfred A. Knopf, Inc for 'The Cat & the Saxophone' in *Selected Poems of Langston Hughes* by Langston Hughes, US title *The Weary Blues*, copyright 1926 by Alfred A. Knopf, Inc and renewed 1954 by Langston Hughes; the author's agents for extracts from 'Black Art', 'Leroy', '20th Century Fox' in *Black Magic Poetry* by Leroi Jones (Amiri Baraka), (Bobs-Merrill), copyright © 1969 by Amiri Baraka, 'The Insidious Dr Fu Man Chu', 'The New Sheriff' and 'Notes for a speech' in *Preface to a 20 Vol. Suicide Note* by Leroi Jones (Amiri Baraka), (Totem Press/Corinth Books, 1961), copyright © 1961 by Leroi Jones (Amiri Baraka); the author, Robert Kelly for '(Prefix:' in *Finding A Measure* (Black Sparrow Press); Alfred A. Knopf, Inc and Random House, Inc for extracts from 'Divinely Superfluous Beauty Lines', 'To the Stone-Cutters', 'Continents End', 'My Burial Place' in *The Selected Poetry of Robinson Jeffers* by Robinson Jeffers (Random House, Inc), 'Still Here', 'I, Too' in *Selected Poems of Langston Hughes* by Langston Hughes (Alfred A. Knopf, Inc), 'Music' & 'My Heart' in *The Collected Poems of Frank O'Hara* by Frank O'Hara (Alfred A. Knopf, Inc); Liveright Publishing Corporation for extracts from 'From the Corpse Woodpiles, from the Ashes' in *Angle of Ascent, New & Selected Poems* by Robert Hayden, copyright © 1975, 1972, 1970 & 1966 by Robert Hayden; New Directions Publishing Corporation for extracts from 'Often I Am Permitted To Return To A Meadow' in *The Opening of the Field* by Robert Duncan, copyright © 1960 by Robert Duncan, 'Bad Times', Sarah in her Father's Arms' & 'Psalm' in *Collected Poems of George Oppen* by George Oppen, copyright © 1974 by George Oppen, 'Requiem for the Spanish Dead' in *Collected Shorter Poems* by Kenneth Rexroth, copyright 1940 by Kenneth Rexroth & 'O City, City' in *Selected Poems: Summer Knowledge* by Delmore Schwartz, copyright 1938 by New Directions Publishing Corporation; North Point Press for extracts from 'Stay Home' & 'Below' in *A Part* by Wendell Berry, copyright © 1980 by Wendell Berry; W. W. Norton & Co, Inc & the author, for extracts from 'Aunt Jennifer's Tigers' in *Poems, Selected & New, 1950–1974* by Adrienne Rich, copyright © 1975, 1973, 1971, 1969, 1966 by W. W. Norton & Co, Inc, copyright © 1967,

1963, 1962, 1961, 1960, 1959, 1958, 1957, 1956, 1955, 1954, 1953, 1952, 1951 by Adrienne Rich; Ohio University Press/Swallow Press for extracts from 'Epigram No 43', 'Epigram No 19', 'To What Strangers What Welcomes, Poem 1' by J. V. Cunningham in *The Collected Poems & Epigrams of J. V. Cunningham* (Swallow Press, 1971) and 'The Realization' by Yvor Winters in *The Collected Poems of Yvor Winters* (Swallow Press, 1978); Oxford University Press, Inc and the author, Richard Eberhart for 'For a Lamb' and extracts from 'Anima', 'If Only I Could Live at the Pitch that is Near Madness', 'The Incomparable Light' and 'Centennial for Whitman; Sect III' in *Collected Poems 1930–1976*; Persea Books, Inc for extracts from 'The Continuity' by Paul Blackburn in *The Collected Poems of Paul Blackburn* edited by Edith Jarolim, copyright © 1985 by Joan Blackburn; the author's agents and Alfred A. Knopf, Inc for an extract from 'Dead Boy' in *Selected Poems* by John Crowe Ransom (Methuen London, Ltd/Alfred A. Knopf, Inc), copyright 1945 by Alfred A. Knopf, Inc; the author's agents for extracts from 'This Place in the Ways' in *The Collected Poems of Muriel Rukeyser* by Muriel Rukeyser (McGraw Hill); Charles Scribner's Sons, an imprint of Macmillan Publishing Co, for Bishop's epitaph for himself in *Collected Poems* by John Peale Bishop, copyright 1948, and renewed 1976, by Charles Scribner's Sons; the author, Gary Snyder for extracts from 'Riprap' and 'Hunting' in A Range of Poems; Wesleyan University Press for extracts from 'Waiting Inside' in *Poems 1934–69* by David Ignatow, originally published in *The Nation*, copyright © 1970 by David Ignatow, 'Reunion' & 'Spider Crystal Assension' in *China Trace: Selected Early Poems* by Charles Wright, copyright © 1977 by Charles Wright and 'Lying in a Hammock at William Duffy's Farm in Pine Island, Minnesota' in *Collected Poems* by James Wright, copyright © 1961 by James Wright; the author, Jonathan Williams for an extract from 'Dirge for Seer-Scrivener, Prince Plangent for Gormenghast'; Mr Paul Zukofsky for 'Ferry' in *The Collected Shorter Poems of Louis Zukofsky* by Louis Zukofsky.

We have been unable to trace the copyright holder in 'Vive Noir!' in *I am a Black Woman* by Marie Evans Phemster (William Morrow & Co, Inc) & would appreciate any information that will enable us to do so.

TO
BEN AND CATHARINE
AND
MY FATHER AND MOTHER

Chapter 1

Backgrounds: America, The Poem, and The Twentieth Century

America the poem: ideas of America and its writing

'America is a poem in our eyes: its ample geography dazzles the imagination, and it will not wait long for metres'. The words are those of Ralph Waldo Emerson, from an essay entitled 'The Poet' published in 1844, and they sum up that desire to turn the New World into words which has seized the imagination of so many Americans. The wilderness of North America had seemed strange from the beginning, the first days of white colonisation. This was a 'silent country', observed one settler (conveniently ignoring the Indians) and it seemed positively to need language to fill the void, to give it identity and shape. After the founding of the republic, language was called on to perform another task as well, which was to help the infant American nation articulate its destiny. 'We have yet had no genius in America', declared Emerson:

> . . . which knew the value of our incomparable materials, and saw, in the barbarism and materialism of the times, another carnival of the same gods whose picture he so much admired in Homer . . . [1]

That genius would come, Emerson and others believed, to turn the disparate facts of American historical experience into a coherent story, a heroic narrative with a beginning, middle, and a millenial end. In creating this epic of the new republic such a genius would, it was hoped, do something still further, perhaps more pressing and certainly more personal: he, or she, would tell Americans something about their individual selves. 'The American is a new man', St. Jean de Crèvecoeur proclaimed in 1782, 'who acts upon new principles; he must therefore entertain new ideas, and form new opinions.'[2] The idea was simple, radical, and surely true: in committing themselves to what they perceived as a 'Promised Land', each and every single person had been altered by that commitment; they might change the land, certainly, but the land in turn would change them. An additional purpose of the new poetry followed from this: it would describe this change, this process of psychic transformation. It would show each reader how, why, and in what manner he or she had become 'an American'.

So, according to this vision of things, the American landscape was a text that could be read, and understood, with the help of the American poem; American history was a series of disparate facts waiting for the American poet to give them narrative shape; and the American people, collectively and individually, were morally embryonic beings whose birth into full knowledge of themselves depended on both the poem and the poet. The vision was undoubtedly an apocalyptic one but it was widely shared; and it could be seen as a natural extension of the utopian dreams that accompanied the early settlement, the millenial visions of the Puritans, and the idealism of the founding fathers of the republic. If America was a New Eden, or, alternatively, a new Canaan, then it surely required its own prophetic voices to announce it. If the United States of America was a new phenomenon, a nation deliberately founded by a few people at a particular moment in time and according to certain specific principles, then it positively demanded someone who could articulate those principles in a measured and memorable way. The American poet was to tell the tale of the tribe: not, perhaps, in the primitive sense of preserving myths of origin but to the extent that he was to offer his readers some intimation of who they were and where they stood. The prophetic voice is not, of course, peculiar to American poetry, even in modern times, but it has sounded more frequently and resonantly there than elsewhere. From the early celebrations of Divine Providence in allowing the colonisers to come safe to land, through Walt Whitman's annunciation of a manifest destiny, to the visionary speech of Hart Crane and then, later Allen Ginsberg: through all these and many other metamorphoses, the millenary impulse has survived. This passage from a poem called 'The Rising Glory of America', published at the end of the eighteenth century, offers one crude but clear example:

> And when a train of rolling years are past . . .
> A new Jerusalem, sent down from heaven,
> Shall grace our happy earth . . .
>   . . . Paradise anew
> Shall flourish, by no second Adam lost,
> No dangerous tree with deadly fruit shall grow,
> No tempting serpent to allure the soul
> From native innocence. – A Canaan here,

Another Canaan shall excel the old,
And from a fairer Pisgah's top be seen . . .

The fiercer passions of the human breast
Shall kindle up to deeds of death no more,
But all subside in universal peace. –
Such days the world,
And such America at last shall have
When ages, yet to come, have run their round
And future years of bliss alone remain.[3]

From the first, however, the millenary impulse in American poetry has had to do battle with something else that grows directly out of the national inheritance – or, to be more accurate, derives immediately from the freight of cultural assumptions that many of the colonists brought with them across the Atlantic. That 'something' is a distrust of fiction, of the 'made' and 'made up' quality of literature in general and poems in particular. 'Be not so set upon poetry', warned the New England Puritan Cotton Mather, 'as to be always poring on the passionate and measured pages'. Verse fed the sensuous appetites, no matter what its ultimate, higher aims might be, and besides it told tales; it depended – at least in the first instance – on human invention, on men's lies rather than God's truth. And to the Puritan injunction against fiction-making could subsequently be added a distrust of anything that was not immediately useful, functional, that did not help in the clearing of woods or the building of farms, shops, schoolhouses, and churches. 'To America', insisted Benjamin Franklin:

> one schoolmaster is worth a dozen poets, and the invention of a machine or the improvement of an implement is of more importance than a masterpiece of Raphael . . . . Nothing is good or beautiful but in the measure that it is useful . . .[4]

Admittedly, Franklin looked forward to a more 'refined state of society' when 'poetry, painting, music (and the stage as their embodiment)' might be 'necessary and proper gratifications'. But his demotion of such activities to the level of the elegantly decorative hardly implied that they would, even then, be very central, vital to the life of the culture; and many other commentators, lacking Franklin's intelligence and wit, have somehow contrived to suggest that to be a poet is not to be useful in any conceivable circumstances, and that not to be useful is not to be American. So to the roles of prophet and teller of tribal tales are added those of misfit and trickster: much of what is fruitful and energetic – as well as much of what is confusing and self-contradictory – grows out of the tensions created by this plethora of roles.

There are, basically, two possible answers to this charge of uselessness. One is illustrated, in the early history of American poetry, by Edgar Allan Poe, who took the scarlet letter of shame and turned it into an emblem of pride. Poe not only accepted the charge of uselessness, he positively revelled in it. Playing the part of elegant dandy, the aristocrat born out of his due time and into a crass, bourgeois culture, he chose to insist that it was the special merit of poetry that it was useless. It could not, in any way, be employed as a means to a worldly end; it had no moral or intellectual application; it had to do with matters and experiences "out of SPACE – out of TIME". The poet was concerned with the 'circumscribed Eden' of his own dreams, not the new Eden of America; and the poem was simply a tapestry of talismanic signs and sounds designed to draw, or rather subdue, the reader into sharing that circumscribed Eden for a moment. 'It is the desire of the moth for the star', Poe said of the poetic impulse:

> . . . Inspired by an ecstatic prescience of the glories
> beyond the grave, we struggle, by multiform
> combinations among the things and thoughts of Time, to
> attain a portion of that Loveliness whose very elements,
> perhaps, appertain to eternity alone.[5]

The ideal poem, Poe implies, would be one in which the words efface themselves, disappear as they are read, leaving only a feeling of significant absence, of no-thing. This is about as far from the world of use, the realm of pulpits, schoolmasters, 'barbarism and materialism', as one could go. Yet as an aim to be pursued, or perhaps a temptation to be feared, 'the desire of the moth for the star' has remained as seminal in American poetry as those other, more substantial and tangible urges described by Mather, Franklin, and Emerson.

The other response to the charge that poetry makes nothing happen is illustrated, in the nineteenth century, by the figure who is rightly seen as the founding father of the American poetic tradition: Walt Whitman. For to the charge that a poem was an object far less useful than an axe or shovel, Whitman responded, again and again, that it performed essentially the same function as those implements. It cleared the ground; it broke the new wood; it helped, significantly, in the making of the new nation. Others had more or less said this before Whitman, of course, but never with such passion and conviction: with Whitman it came to dictate everything he did, not only what he said but how he said it. His poetry was 'a language experiment', Whitman claimed. The aim of such experiment was:

> to give the spirit, the body, the man, new words,
> new potentialities of speech – an American, a cosmopolitan
> (the best of Americanism is the best cosmopolitanism)
> range of expression. The new world, the new times, the
> new peoples, the new vistas, need a tongue according . . .[6]

As Whitman saw it, poetry could play a vital part in the process of creating a new nation. It was really use-full. For it could enable Americans to celebrate their release from the Old World and the colonial yoke: to describe, in other words, the condition from which they had freed themselves. And it could help them, also, to understand their new status: to define, even if only in a provisional way, the positive forms their freedom had assumed.

Which brings us back to the prophetic function of American poetry, and to the nature of its prophecies. What, precisely, was the character of 'the new times, the new peoples, the new vistas', as Whitman and others saw them? What were the 'new words, new potentialities of speech' to be unravelled by the American Homer? Perhaps as succinct an answer as any was given by Alexis de Tocqueville in his *Democracy in America*, which was first published in two volumes in 1835 and 1840. 'In democracies', Tocqueville declared, 'men never stay still: a thousand random circumstances continually make them move from place to place, and there is almost always something unexpected, something . . . provisional about their lives.'[7] More to the point, he argued, 'each man is for ever driven back upon himself alone'; for whereas 'aristocracy brings everyone together, linking peasant to King in one long chain', one thoroughly articulated, hierarchical framework, 'democracy breaks the chain and separates each link'. As a result, people 'become accustomed to thinking of themselves in isolation, and imagine that their entire fate is in their own hands'.

This was a theme to which Tocqueville returned more than once in his account of the infant republic. 'Each citizen in a democracy', he insists at one point, 'usually spends his time considering the interests of a very insignificant person, namely, himself'; 'there is a danger', he adds elsewhere, 'that he may be shut up in the solitude of his own heart'.[8] Solitude or isolation, self-reliance or egotism, freedom or loneliness, self-sufficiency or pride: the terms may vary – and, indeed, do so throughout American writing – but they can all be traced back to the structure of feeling that Tocqueville perceived, a structure that has as its keystone the idea of the individual, the simple, separate self.

It does not take a great deal of ingenuity, to see how this idea had assumed such importance. For it was and is the initial assumption in American ideology, the country's image of itself, that the American was someone who had opted out of society in all but its most elemental and inescapable forms. He had left Europe behind, and its relatively sophisticated social framework, to light out for a territory in which he could determine his own fate: where he could act as his own judge and jury, and his own witness. He had, in a sense, repudiated the past ('Practically', declared Thoreau, 'the old have no very important advice to give the young . . . Every child begins the world again' . . .)[9]. Or, as later, more Freudian commentators would have it, he had denied the image of the father. Either way, he had, in the process, rejected those institutions, the products of history, which at once burdened the European and gave him a reassuring sense of purpose and identity. And he had discovered or devised a neutral territory, where his principal task became the invention of himself.

No series of cultural assumptions occur in a vacuum, and it is worth pausing for a moment to consider how this particular series had come about. There was, of course, in the first place the simple, historical fact that, when the first waves of white emigration to North America began, Europeans were looking for somewhere that might answer their need for a neutral space: somewhere where the burden of the actual past could be shrugged off and the lost innocence – or, rather, the lost possibilities – of some mythological past might be recovered. People usually find what they are looking for, and what they found in their new home was precisely:

> a Virgin Countrey so preserved by Nature out of a desire to show mankinde fallen into the Old Age of Creation, what a brow of fertility and beauty she was adorned with when the world was vigorous and youthfull.[10]

Once things were perfect, the argument runs: before history started, before adulthood and shades of the prison-house began to close in, before time and the past and other people imposed their burden. Things can be perfect again, this argument continues, the past and otherness can be obliterated; the lost perfection and possibility of times gone by can be recovered in times to come. Longing for an idealised yesterday and hope for an imagined tomorrow form the basic ingredients of what has become known as 'the American Dream'. This strange but compelling mixture of elegiac and optimistic feeling characterised early European writing about America, and it has coloured

American writing ever since – as these memorable, closing lines from *The Great Gatsby* by F. Scott Fitzgerald illustrate:

> Gatsby believed in the green light, the orgiastic future that year by year recedes before us. It eluded us then, but that's no matter – tomorrow we will run faster, stretch out our arms farther . . . And one fine morning –
>
> So we beat on, boats against the current, borne back ceaselessly into the past.[11]

After the first waves of emigration, the frontier West with all its enthralling possibilities became the site of such nostalgic utopianism: 'I reckon I got to light out for the Territory ahead of the rest', declares Huckleberry Finn, 'because Aunt Sally she's going to adopt and civilize me, and I can't stand it. I been there before'. And when the frontier disappeared as an historical fact, towards the end of the nineteenth century, the *idea* of the frontier survived – as *The Great Gatsby* indicates – as an appropriate space or place, a field for individual activity limited only by the demands of the imagination.

It is almost impossible to exaggerate this, the formative influence of the West and the frontier: as an historical experience that many people lived through, learning lessons of self-reliance and enduring long periods of isolation, and, even more important, as an idea shaping aims and images of the self both before and after the actual frontier vanished. Not everyone could light out for the Territory during the first few centuries of settlement, or even perhaps wished to; nobody can now. Nevertheless, Americans have habitually perceived themselves in pioneering terms – through the language of open spaces, new horizons, personal mobility and endless opportunity. They continue to do so, and not only themselves but the nation as a whole. As the pioneer rapidly advanced across the continent in the nineteenth century, for instance, poets like Whitman were only too eager to see the frontier gradually stretched out until it encompassed the globe:

> I chant the world on my Western sea . . .
> I chant the new empire, grander than ever before – As in
> a vision it comes to me;
> I chant America, the Mistress – I chant a greater
> supremacy . . .[12]

At such moments, ideas of individual freedom and opportunity begin to shade, in a rather sinister fashion, into notions of personal power: without impugning Whitman's own motives, it is possible to trace a connection here between the American pioneering spirit and American imperialism – something that more recent writers, like Robert Lowell and Norman Mailer, have been not at all reluctant to do. Which is not to say that those writers have not, in turn, been touched by that spirit, quite the contrary. The ideal of the frontier may now be secreted in, say, an urban location, with the anonymity of the city supplying a convenient site, the moral vacuum in which the individual can choose his identity and so re-create himself. Or it may be dislodged into the notion of inner space, a purely mental, internal freedom that survives the proximity of others and, even, living within a closed system. It may find refuge in the aim of perpetual mobility, a journey without destination that becomes an outward and visible sign of an inward quest. Alternatively, it may be transformed into a matter of creative attitude: the writer, in other words, may take upon *himself* the role of pioneer pursuing, as Hart Crane put it, 'new thresholds, new anatomies' – new frontiers of vocabulary and imagination. Whatever its transmutations, though, the ideal remains alive, both in American thought and in its writing. The imagery of the pioneer and the frontier, the idea of a world elsewhere in which self-emancipation is attainable: all still exert their pressure as sources of inspiration, difficult and sometimes troubling myths.

While it is almost impossible to exaggerate the importance of the frontier, however, it is possible to make the mistake of seeing it in isolation, as if it alone were responsible for the 'new vistas', the fresh ideologies Whitman described. In a sweeping and memorable passage in his essay on the significance of the westward movement, for instance, the great historian Frederick Jackson Turner suggests as much: when he declares that the frontier was 'the line of most rapid and effective Americanization' and was almost entirely responsible for creating 'a new product that is American'. Some literary critics have been quick to take up Turner's suggestion and argue that what makes American writing, in turn, characteristically American is the consciousness of the frontier – that, as Van Wyck Brooks puts it, American literature is a 'sublimation of the frontier spirit' or that, more simply, all American books are really Westerns. The flaw in this argument is, of course, that it ignores the existence of other historical factors. It suppresses all acknowledgement that what Turner calls, at one point, 'the American mind', was formed out of a dialectical interplay between various, and often quite separate, events and systems of belief. As Lewis Mumford puts it, in his classic study of American culture *The Golden Day*, 'ideas . . . nurtured in Savoy, in the English lake country, and on the Scots moors' wedded themselves to 'a new set of experiences'[13] to help form those habits of language and belief that we recognise as distinctively American. The culture of the New World, and even the frontier spirit itself, were profoundly affected by certain distinctively European notions – not all of them from the places that Mumford cites.

What were these notions, and how did they help to shape America's consciousness of itself? There were many, of course, far too many to be itemised here. But at least a number of them were related to three major intellectual movements that have been mentioned in passing already. First of all, there was Puritanism: the religious system that dominated the early history of New England and that continued to exert a powerful influence on the hearts and minds of Americans long after the Puritan hegemony ceased to exist. For the Puritan, every material fact was an emblem, a symbol of some deeper, spiritual truth: every human experience could be seen as part of a moral fable, an epic narrative devised by God. An event as trivial as a mouse gnawing away a Bible, left by accident in a barn, could be interpreted allegorically – and was. For by looking at what was left in the Bible the good Puritan could read the message sent by the Divine Being through one of HIS messengers; he could study the events of history – even the most inconsequential and apparently absurd events – and then turn them into myth.[14] Few Americans after the early Puritans were willing to push the allegorical habit quite so far, or to interpret things in such straightforward, moralistic terms. But possibly one reason why American *writers* in particular are so prone to symbolism, and so intent on endowing those symbols with an ethical dimension, is that they are part of a culture still haunted by the Puritans. Like a ghost, a familiar spirit, the Puritan tendency to emblematise and moralise is still there, in however elusive, shadowy a form.

Dostoevsky once observed that the American spirit is at once fantastical and 'strangely "material"': which, while being a paradox, is surely true. There is a curious combination of idealism and materialism in a great deal of American thought; and there is a tendency, noticeable in American writing especially, to de-materialise the material while rendering the spiritual dimension in all too solid a way. Part of this paradox must be attributed to Puritanism, with its willingness to see the physical world as a series of signs (which serves to dematerialise it) but easily interpretable, chiefly moral signs (which serves to bring matters back to the realm of action, to concrete experience). Part, however, has its source in the second movement that exerted significant pressure on American intellectual and cultural life, the philosophy of the Enlightenment. For Enlightenment thinking – responsible for such cornerstones of the American state as the Declaration of Independence and the Constitution – proclaims its allegiance to the concrete, tangible world while nevertheless building up all knowledge from self-awareness, the certainty of one's own existence.

As Bertrand Russell has suggested, it is at once 'objective' and 'subjective':[15] 'objective' in the sense that it directs attention to empirical experience and demonstrable proof, and 'subjective' in that its criteria of judgement – clearness, distinctness, agreement or disagreement – have an internal, individualistic, subjectivist basis, so making life contingent upon mind. Alert to this startling combination of idealism and materialism in the people they knew, Charles Eliot Norton declared that Walt Whitman united 'the characteristics of a Concord philosopher with those of a New York . . . fireman', while James Russell Lowell observed of Emerson that he had 'A Greek head on right Yankee shoulders, whose range/ Has Olympus for one pole, for t'other the Exchange'. Emerson was a 'Plotinus-Montaigne', Lowell went on, in whom 'the Egyptian's gold mist/ And the Gascon's shrewd wit cheek-by-jowl coexist'.[16] Similar remarks have been made about their American characters by (among others) Nathaniel Hawthorne, Herman Melville, Henry James, F. Scott Fitzgerald, and William Faulkner: for example, Ahab in Melville's *Moby Dick*, Jay Gatsby, and Thomas Sutpen in Faulkner's novel, *Absalom, Absalom!* – all of them confuse power in the material world with the fulfilment of an intangible and very personal dream. It would be wrong, of course, to put all this down to the influence of the Enlightenment, or even the combined effects of the Enlightenment and Puritanism – Emerson and Whitman were more than just cultural descendants of Cotton Mather and Benjamin Franklin. But it would surely be right to say that one reason why American thinking brings together 'gold mist' and 'shrewd wit' has to do with the mixed heritage of Descartes, Locke, and the founding fathers of the republic.

The other, shaping ideas the Enlightenment offered to the American tradition were those of Use and Progress. Use, the utilitarian attitude, has been touched upon already, but the notion of Progress is perhaps worth pausing over since it has had such an impact on the way Americans, including American poets, perceive themselves. Obviously, the Puritans, when they first arrived in the New World, believed in progress of a kind but it was primarily *personal* and *spiritual* progress. They hardly believed in *social* progress, the – potentially unending – improvement of an entire society; and they claimed, at least, not to be interested in *material* progress as an end in itself – material rewards, so the doctrine went, were important only in so far as they could be seen as a sign of God's grace. There was a certain amount of casuistry or self-deception implicit in this last claim, of course: it was here, perhaps, that the seeds of that confusion between the spiritual and the material, mentioned just now, were sown most profusely and dangerously. But the way in which a culture perceives itself *is* important; it has a profound effect upon its life and development. So it is worth emphasising the fact that the Puritans did see themselves in this way, and that, by contrast, the body of thought that the Enlightenment offered to the United States set the idea of Progress with a capital 'P' upon a pedestal. A person like Franklin was sure that the good life could be realised here and now upon earth; he was sure that individuals could go on bettering themselves and that society could go on improving; and he was sure, finally, that all this could be done best of all in America. He, and others like him, gave to the country the concepts of limitless growth, of dynamic development and almost inevitable self-improvement, that have been responsible, equally, for the historical doctrine of Manifest Destiny, the visionary optimism of a Walt Whitman or a Hart Crane, and, on a less exalted level, for these rather creaking lines from an utterly typical nineteenth-century poet:

> What strength! what strife! what rude unrest!
> What shocks! what half-shaped armies met!
> A mighty nation moving west,
> With all its steely sinews set
> Against the living forests.[17]

As such lines illustrate, the Enlightenment doctrine of Progress could fit in perfectly here with the ideology of the westward movement: they seem to derive force and energy from each other, as each thrusts into the light a vision of total possibility, an open road, a boundless future.

Of almost equal relevance, as far as this vision is concerned, is the third major intellectual movement that contributed to the development of American thought: Romanticism. Romanticism has a particular significance for American poetry, because American poetry, on the whole, is poetry written during or after the Romantic Revolution. Of course, a considerable body of poetry was produced during the colonial period, and there were one or two impressive poets, notably Anne Bradstreet and Edward Taylor. But no distinctive poetic tradition ever emerged; there was no sign of a characteristically American 'voice'. There were various reasons for this, including the mainly theological bent of New England, the primacy of politics and the public life in the states to the South, and the cultural as well as political dependence of the colonies on the mother country across the Atlantic. Whatever the reasons, though, the fact remained the same: that the distinctiveness of American poetry, and indeed of American literature generally, only began to emerge in the early nineteenth century. Here it is worth noting a nice paradox, which brings us back to the specific impact of Romanticism. For one major reason why a distinctive, self-conscious and articulate literary tradition did begin to emerge in the United States was precisely because of lessons learned from old Europe – and, in particular from its poets and philosophers. Certainly, the political break with England helped focus minds upon such questions as 'What is an American?' and 'What is an American poet?' But such questions came to seem especially pressing, for people like Emerson, because they had learned about the importance of national character and national culture from British and German writers: 'the spirit of the nation', 'the folk', the idea of a national epic – all these were part of the currency of European Romanticism, which Americans willingly adopted as their own.[18]

The particular forms American literary nationalism took – and, to some extent, has taken ever since – betray a similar debt. Along with the ideology of westward expansion and the progressive tendencies in Enlightenment thought, the visionary dimension in Romanticism spurred Americans on to think of their destiny as an open one, their horizons as limitless. Along with other strains in the national heritage, it promoted that nostalgic utopianism mentioned earlier: Shelley's memorable lines, 'We look before and after,/ And pine for what is not,' could almost be taken as an epigraph for the American Dream. Romanticism also encouraged Americans to find consolation in nature for their alleged lack of culture; or, to be more accurate, it prompted them to celebrate nature as the true embodiment of their culture – its openness, its air of possibility, and its innocence. As one historian has commented, nineteenth-century Americans 'if challenged to produce some present sign of American greatness . . . could always expatiate on nature . . . . Nature meant many things – the sheer bigness of the country, the novelty of its fauna and flora, the abundance of life, the sense of room to spare'.[19] The landscape thus became the American equivalent of the Pyramids, the Acropolis, or the Colosseum. Combining the idea of America as the world's newly recovered garden with a Romantic interest in preserving idyllic and primitive natural conditions. American poets recorded their surroundings seen as if for the first time, a country untouched by European sensibility, let alone settlement.

And, then, there was and is Romanticism's most important contribution of all to American poetry in particular: the idea of an American epic, some great work that would enshrine in verse the achievements and promise of the new world. There had been evident during the colonial period a fairly widespread desire for such a work; several attempts were made to present God's way with His Chosen People in epic terms. The greatest of these, although not a poem, is Cotton Mather's *Magnalia Christi Americana*, a learned and vastly documented history of New England which begins by echoing Virgil's *Aeneid*: 'I write the Wonders of the CHRISTIAN RELIGION', Mather announces, 'flying from the Deprivations of Europe, to the American

Strand . . .'. But it was not until the nineteenth century, really, that the appropriate form for an American epic began to emerge; and it began to do so partly under the pressure of republican feeling and partly responding to the inspiration of Romanticism. 'I should hope', wrote the statesman and second American President John Adams, 'to live to see our young America in Possession of an Heroick Poem, equal to those the most esteemed in any Country'.[20] And, although Adams was not to live to see it, one example of such an heroic poem did appear by the middle of the century, in 1855 to be precise: 'Song of Myself' in Walt Whitman's *Leaves of Grass*. 'Song of Myself' illustrates the true shape of the American epic: a shape that was to be imitated by, among many others, Ezra Pound, William Carlos Williams, and Hart Crane. It is, essentially, the shape of the Romantic epic: like Blake's *Jerusalem*, it is more concerned with spiritual possibility than historical attainment, and like Wordsworth's *Prelude* it has the poet himself at its centre and the growth and development of the poet's mind as its narrative substance. The great American epics, 'Song of Myself' indicates, would follow the great Romantic epic in being plotless and without a conventional protagonist; for their strategy would be to create a hero rather than celebrate one and to make rather than record the history that surrounds him. They would, in effect, jettison the third-person hero of traditional epic, the prince or aristocratic warrior whose deeds are itemised as a way of articulating and fixing the values of a culture; and in his place they would put the poet himself as a representative, democratic man who discovers his identity and values in the course of writing, on his own and on our behalf. The essential form of such epics would have to be open because the process of self-discovery would be perceived as a continuous one: the poet could never cease exploring until the end of his life and, besides, each reader could and should continue such explorations for himself, following the paths the poet had signposted. And like most great long poems in the Romantic tradition, they would appear to exist in space rather than time, since they would not so much progress in a conventional, logical way as circle back and forth, supplying workings of form and language on which the reader could bring his own imagination to bear – making connections, establishing priorities and collaborating with the poet in the creation of meaning.

Puritanism, the philosophy of the Enlightenment, Romanticism: these three great intellectual and cultural movements all contributed in their own way to the formation of the national culture. During the course of the two centuries following the establishment of white colonies in North America, they were brought over the Atlantic and there, by means of interaction with one another, by cross-fertilisation with native ideas and experiences, in short by a process that involved the dreams of the Old World coming into contact and dialectical conflict, both with each other and with the facts of the New: by means of all these things, there grew up a body of ideas which can be called definitively American. Of course, these three movements were utterly different in many ways: one can hardly imagine a meeting of minds between, say, Cotton Mather, Benjamin Franklin, and Edgar Allan Poe. But one thing they shared in common, and offered to the country collectively as it were, was that one thing that Tocqueville chose to emphasise when he contemplated American democracy: which is to say, a preoccupation with the individual. The Puritan might talk about the individual soul, the light of the conscience, the philosopher of the Enlightenment might prefer to think in terms of the reason, the power latent in each individual mind, and the Romantic might swear his allegiance to the individual imagination. But all three took their stand on this idea of an original, a direct and personal relationship with the ground of reality. All of them helped to sow the seeds of a culture in which, to repeat that phrase from Tocqueville, 'each man is for ever driven back upon himself alone'.

What were the immediate literary consequences of this individualism? In what ways did and does this cult of the personal, the idea of a unique self, inform and shape American writing? In answering such questions, Tocqueville is helpful once again, because he was one of the first to consider them and came up with some useful answers. 'On the whole', Tocqueville argued:

> the literature of a democracy will never demonstrate the order, regularity, skill and art characteristic of aristocratic literature; formal qualities will be ignored or despised. The style will often be bizarre, incorrect, overburdened, loose, and almost always strong and bold . . . There will be rough and untutored energy of thought with great variety and extraordinary fecundity. Authors will attempt to astonish more than please, and excite passions rather than charm taste.[21]

What Tocqueville was saying, in effect, was that the American writer, seeing himself as a unique individual, could not depend on established forms and precedents, the literary 'rules' created by other people in and for other situations. He could not, except with considerable reluctance or qualification, put himself and his beliefs within the strait-jacket of conventional verse and traditional structures – particularly in view of the fact that many of these structures were meant to 'communalise' experience, to some extent, to render it less individualistic and idiosyncratic. He had, somehow, to invent, to unravel a form that would adequately express his own special vision of life, his personal place in the scheme of things; he had to find a way of saying, as Whitman said, '*I* am the man, *I* suffer'd, *I* was there'. And he had to do all this at the risk of appearing eccentric or bizarre: which, if it did happen, would at least mean that he had remained true to the anarchic, splintering tendencies of his culture and had not committed the cardinal sin for a democrat – he had not, that is, simply conformed.

Tocqueville was surely right about the formal literary consequences of American individualism, and not least for verse: the tradition of American poetry *is* a tradition of the new. It is a tradition of radical experiment, the personal address and frequently eccentric innovation. Even less obviously experimental poets like Robert Frost or Edwin Arlington Robinson seem to speak to us from out of the depths of their solitude; even the distanced, hieratic tone of a John Crowe Ransom or the elaborate patternings of a Marianne Moore cannot disguise the fact that they too are engaged in a lonely confrontation with the real, largely unmediated by social or literary convention. In this sense, every major American poem could be called 'song of myself', for each is the utterly unrepeatable expression of the author, the isolated 'man alive', in a particular place and at a particular point in time; and to every American poet of any consequence could be applied a remark once made about Emily Dickinson – that he, or she, writes as if nobody else had ever written before.

But the experimentalism and eccentricity that Tocqueville anticipated has not, in the event, turned out to be a matter of literary form alone: it has embraced style as well as structure, the particular vocabulary that American poets have felt compelled to devise. For, as people like Emerson and Whitman recognised, nobody can be an American poet unless they can write as an American – until, that is, they can arrive at a satisfactory type of speech. This is not simply a matter of using American words and expressions (although it is perhaps worth pointing out that the first two truly great American poets, Whitman and Dickinson, were innovators in this respect). It is a case, too, of unearthing a *personal* language: an idiom that seems to grow out of and imitate the contours of the individual poet's life. Language, as semioticians never tire of telling us, exists in a state of mutual dependence with consciousness, shaped by it and helping to shape it in turn. So to have a language of one's own is to have something which is at once a demonstration and, to some extent, a means to self-definition; to possess a 'voice' is to make a giant step towards the discovery of identity. Here, the American poet is faced with a special problem. For he has to create a language that is true to himself but at the same time comprehensible to his audience. He cannot lapse into rhetoric, naturally, the language of the person talking entirely to and for others:

but he cannot lapse into obscurity either, the language of the person talking entirely to and for himself. He has to build a bridge of words to his audience; to a certain extent, he has actually to build or create that audience, since he has to create the taste for his own individual type of speech, his own particular 'song of myself'. And he has to do all this while remembering that, like everyone else's, his is a developing identity, and so his language must change just as he and his sense of life do.

With some reservations, a lot of this is true of the European poet: but it is precisely those reservations that are important here – and that reveal the special nature of the problems confronted by the American poet – from the moment he began to think of himself as an American. Whatever the degree of his inventiveness or originality, the European does, even now, appear to start from *something*. There is the sense of a staple idiom to which he is giving his own inflections and which endows his work with a substance, a sense of belonging, which it would not otherwise have. The American, on the other hand, seems to start almost from scratch. Despite particular debts that one writer may owe to another, the debt that William Carlos Williams and Wallace Stevens owe to Walt Whitman, for instance, or the one that Hart Crane has acknowledged to both Whitman and Poe, each of them seems to be evolving his own means of expression as he goes along. And despite the fact that the degree of audience awareness may vary – Whitman, for example, is much more openly conscious of his readers than Poe and Dickinson are, while William Carlos Williams addresses his with far greater intimacy than either Stevens or Robinson Jeffers care to – there is still the feeling of a gap, or absence. There is still the sense of an abyss yawning between the poet and the reader that it is up to the poet to bridge – or, if not that, then, sadly or triumphantly, to accept.

Some of the larger problems posed by the gap between the American poet and his audience can be left until later, however. For the moment, it is worth returning to Tocqueville and his meditations on the possible character of American writing. Even while considering the forms – or rather, as he saw it, formlessness American literature might assume, Tocqueville raised the question of its potential subjects: which would not, he believed, include the 'legends . . . traditions, and memories of distant times'. The future poet of American democracy, Tocqueville argued:

> will not try to people the universe again with supernatural creatures in whom neither his audience nor he believes any longer, nor will he coolly personify virtues and vices more appropriately seen in their natural state. All these

> resources fail him, but there remains man, and the poet needs nothing else. Human destiny, man himself, freed from time and place, and brought face to face with nature and with God, with his doubts, his unexpected good fortune, and his incomprehensible miseries, will for these peoples be the chief and virtually the only subject of poetry.[22]

The familiar themes and stories would be lost to the American poet, perhaps, but something else patiently awaited his contemplation: what was previously referred to as representative, democratic man seen most clearly in the poet's own mirror, in his own consciousness, personality, and experiences. This would be enough to supply an infinite variety of narratives, ideas and plots peculiar to each work; in terms of subject, too, the American poet could, as Ezra Pound once put it, 'make it new'.

At this point, it is worth considering an important objection that might be made to Tocqueville's argument, or to any account of American poetry which sees that poetry primarily as a drama of the self. The notion of the self, it is now often insisted, is just that – a notion, which has its source in a particular system of language rather than anything that can properly be called reality. It is a matter of idiom rather than fact, epistemology rather than ontology; it is just what it appears to you now, a word, a group of letters, a particular written (and, of course, in other cases spoken) code. This objection sounds radical, since at first sight what it appears to do is demote the drama of the self to mere shadow-play, a conflict of signs that never inheres in the real. But, when looked at more closely, it does something quite different: it enriches our knowledge and appreciation of such drama, rather than undermining it – it offers another way of understanding what we mean when we say that the American poet pursues self-discovery and self-expression. To speak tautologically for a moment, a writer writes: that is, he always deals, in the first instance, with epistemology, matters of perception and communication. In more local terms, he always deals with the language possibilities of his own culture; and, as far as the American writer is concerned at least, 'the self' is so much a part of those possibilities that even if he tries to dissociate himself from it – as, say, Robinson Jeffers or Charles Olson do – he is, in a sense, only confirming its importance. Something that the American linguist Benjamin Lee Whorf said is worth quoting here. 'We dissect nature', Whorf argued, 'along lines laid down by our native language':

> . . . the world is presented in a kaleidoscopic flux of impressions which has to be organized in our minds – and

> this means largely by the linguistic systems in our minds. We cut nature up, organize into concepts, and ascribe significances as we do, largely because we are parties to an agreement to organise it in this way – an agreement that holds throughout our speech community and is codified in the patterns of our language. The agreement is, of course, an implicit and unstated one, BUT ITS TERMS ARE ABSOLUTELY OBLIGATORY: we cannot talk at all except by subscribing to the organisation and classification of data to which the agreement subscribes.[23]

It is not necessary to accept the authoritarian implications of this; in fact, it would be unwise to do so, since it would leave anyone's room for verbal manoeuvre, including the American poet's, drastically limited. Without doing so, however, one can see how this restores the drama of the self to a central place in American poetry even for those who question the validity of the very idea of a self, an individual, coherent identity – which is to say, its basis in empirical fact.

Accepting, then, that such a thing as the drama of the self is possible, what narrative shapes did this drama assume? If, as Tocqueville was surely right to claim, the story of 'human destiny, man himself' was metamorphosed into the stories of American poetry, then how, in the event, were these stories told? Obviously, there are as many answers to these questions as there are significant American poets: but certain areas of concern and possibility, first mapped out in the nineteenth century, should be mentioned. For what the poets of the first hundred years of the American republic did, often without knowing it, was establish a foundation on which those of the twentieth century could build; they identified problems and established strategies that subsequent poets have had to accept and develop – not, of course, because they are under any tangible obligation to do so but quite simply because they are Americans. In his poetic tribute to Walt Whitman, Ezra Pound concluded with these words:

> It was you that broke the new wood,
> Now it is a time for carving.
> We have one sap and root
> Let there be commerce between us.[24]

The tone is a little grudging and patronising, perhaps, giving Whitman less than his due: but the pioneering metaphor is, as Pound must have recognised, an apt one. It was and is precisely in this way that the earlier generations have helped the later ones: by clearing the ground and planting the seeds – supplying 'new wood' in terms of material *and* example.

America's poets: formative figures for the twentieth century

Of all American poets prior to the twentieth century, the one who has been crucial in this way is, of course, Whitman: a fact that not only Pound acknowledged but other people as otherwise different as Wallace Stevens and William Carlos Williams. Whitman saw himself as the fulfilment of Emersonian prophecy: the Homer of the New World who would realise its poetic possibilities, find metres for its 'ample geography'. 'Read these leaves', he urged in the Preface to the first edition of *Leaves of Grass* (1855), 'in the open air of every season of every year of your life, re-examine all you have been told at school or church or in any book, dismiss whatever insults your own soul.' Openness, freedom, above all individualism: Whitman's aim was nothing less than to initiate a poetic tradition in which the one recognition shared is a recognition of difference, one of the few precedents accepted is the rejection of precedent, and Truth and Beauty are identified with a procedure of constant metamorphosis. The only genuine way in which the American *could* acknowledge his participation in a common cultural effort, he believed, was by behaving as a supreme individualist. He would pay his greatest respect to his past in rebelling from it, and the finest compliment he could to his nation by denying its authority over him.

However – and this is an important point – Whitman did not feel that in doing all this he would be rejecting contact with others: those he lived with, those whom he observed and addressed in his poems. On the contrary, his essential purpose was to identify his ego with the world, and more specifically with the democratic 'en-masse' of America. This identification on which all his poems depend, or to be more accurate the dialectic from which they derive their energy, is established in the opening lines of 'Song of Myself';

> I celebrate myself, and sing myself,
> And what I assume you shall assume
> For every atom belonging to me as good belongs to you.

Two people, Whitman believed, could be 'twain yet one': their paths could be different, and yet they could achieve a kind of transcendent contact. Equally, many people could realise a community while remaining individuals: their lives could be enriched by maintaining a dynamic equilibrium, a dialectical relationship, between the needs of the self and the demands of the world. As the lines just quoted illustrate, it was Whitman's intention to state this again and again: like many subsequent American poets, he was not afraid of the pedagogical role, and he tried to tell his fellow citizens about this dialectical process on which, as he saw it, their lives depended. His aim, though, was not merely to tell but to show. He wanted to dramatise the process of contact: to make his audience aware of the fact that they could be many yet one by compelling them to feel it, to participate in a series of reciprocal relationships in the course of reading his poems.

The most obvious way in which Whitman dramatises the process of contact has to do with self-presentation. In 'Song of Myself', the poetic 'I' is presented as being capable of sympathetic identification with all kinds of people without any loss of personal identity, 'I am the hounded slave', Whitman declares at one point:

> I wince at the bite of the dogs,
> Hell and despair are upon me, crack and again crack the
>   marksmen,
> I clutch the rails of the fence, my gored ribs,
>   thinn'd with the ooze of my skin,
> I fall on the weeds and stones;
> The riders spur their unwilling horses, haul close,
> Taunt my dizzy ears and beat me violently over
>   the head with whipstocks.
>
> Agonies are one of my changes of garments.[25]

The hunted slave, a lonely woman, a bridegroom, a trapper, a bereaved wife, an 'old artillerist': in the course of the poem, Whitman becomes all these people and many more, and yet still remains 'Walt Whitman . . . of Manhattan the son'. He can, he convinces the reader, empathise, achieve sympathetic identification with others while retaining his own distinctive voice with its dynamic patterns of speech and its predilection for the 'fleshy, sensual' aspects of experience. This is not just 'negative capability', in Keats's famous phrase: a loss of the self in the being of another, an act of total immersion or projection. It is, as Whitman presents it, a *discovery* of the self in the other: like many American poets after him, Whitman was firm in his belief that the individual is most himself when honouring and imagining – and, perhaps, re-creating – the individualism of someone else.

The direct address to his audience with which 'Song of Myself' opens, however, suggests that the relationship Whitman is dramatising is a triangular one: the poet is there, obviously, the subjects of the poem – the slave, the woman, the bridegroom, and so on – are there, but so too is the reader, the 'you' to whom the poet turns in the third line of his poem. In a manner that, again, was to become characteristic of American poetry, Whitman invites us, as we read his lines, to participate in the process of sympathetic identification; we are asked to share the experiences and the consciousness of the poet, and the beings he presents, while nevertheless remaining 'the readers' – people standing outside this world of words. 'Closer yet I approach you', says Whitman in another of his poems, 'Crossing Brooklyn Ferry?':

> What thought you have of me now, I had as much
> of you – I laid in my stores in advance,
> I consider'd long and seriously of you before you were
> born.
>
> Who knows, for all the distance, but I am as good as
> looking at you now, for all you cannot see me?[26]

An intimate contact between the 'I' and 'you' of the poem, the abolition of gaps temporal, spatial, and cultural between poet and audience, an encounter between author and reader through the filmy gauze of language: such things are yearned for in these haunting lines, and Whitman's *oeuvre* as a whole – and, perhaps, achieved for a transitory, enchanted moment. At such times, the dilemma of people shut up in the solitude of their own hearts seems to be temporarily forgotten, or rather transcended because the poem itself has become an act of communion.

Whitman, then, attempts to solve the problems of isolation and audience confronting the American poet by turning his poem into a gesture of relationship, a bridge between 'I' and 'you'. And it is a relationship that is essentially open, the arc described by this bridge is *intended* at least to span past, present, and future. This comes out most strikingly in the closing moments of 'Song of Myself'. 'I bequeath myself to the dirt to grow from the grass I love', Whitman declares:

> If you want me again look for me under your boot-soles.
>
> You will hardly know who I am or what I mean,
> But I shall be good health to you nevertheless,
> As filter and fibre to your blood.
>
> Failing to fetch me at first keep encouraged,
> Missing me one place search another,
> I stop somewere waiting for you.[27]

Whitman identifies himself, in these lines, with the 'spear of summer's grass' that, at the beginning of the poem, offered him a medium of mystical insight: a means of achieving a sense of transcendent unity with the given world. The implication is clear: Whitman and his 'Song' will, ideally, act as a source of continuing inspiration and contact for the reader each time he or she reads this poem; it will be an agent of vision and communion quite as inexhaustible as the leaf of grass was for the poet. This is that open-endedness of American poetry mentioned earlier, whereby the reader is required to continue the journey on which the poet embarked: to continue the poem in his or her own terms and so, in effect, reinvent it. Each reading consequently becomes an act of co-production, joint creation – in a way, a fresh making of the text. And not only of the text. 'The Poet', Wordsworth insisted in his Preface to the *Lyrical Ballads* 'is . . . an upholder and preserver, carrying everywhere with him relationship and love'. To which Whitman might well have added that, in an American setting, the reader is this as well. Under the pressure of the lessons learned while reading such things as 'Song of Myself', he joins with the poet in the making of *community* – or, to use Wordsworth's term 'relationship and love'.

The open-ended, provisional nature of Whitman's, and of much of American, poetry is not simply the product of a few, brave closing lines, however. On the contrary, it grows out of the entire conception of the poem – and of life, where, to borrow a phrase from Charles Olson, 'What does not change/ is the will to change.'[28] The point is made over and over again by American poets of otherwise different persuasions: that their aim is to restore and renew things for us because, in the act of resurrecting their own habits of perception, they resurrect ours as well. Each time the poem is read, ideally, the world is freshly seen and fully discovered as it was once, presumably and continually, by the writer; things are lifted out of their greasy contexts and new, more personal and changeable, ways of seeing and naming are released. There is an element in all this of what the Russian formalist critic, Victor Shklovsky, called 'defamiliarisation'. 'As perception becomes blurred by habit', Shklovsky suggested, 'it becomes automatic', and 'we see the object as though it were hidden in a sack. We know what it is by its configuration, but we see only its silhouette'. Gradually, the machinery of habitualisation devours everything: 'objects, clothes, furniture, one's wife, and the fear of war'. We begin to lose our sense of things, and it could be added (although Shklovsky does not say so) our sense of ourselves, our own separate identities, too. As Shklovsky perceives it, the aim of art is to oppose all this, to reverse the desensitising process; art, he says:

> exists to help or recover the sensation of life, it exists to enable us to feel things, to make the stone stony. The purpose of art is to give a sensation of the object as something seen, not something recognised. The technique of art is to make things unfamiliar.[29]

It is not hard to see how Shklovsky's remarks apply with special force to American poetry. After all, both Emerson and Whitman say very similar things. 'All around', declared Emerson in one of his essays, 'what powers are wrapped up under coarse mattings of custom, and all wonder prevented . . . the wise man wonders at the usual'. 'Make the aged eye sun-clear', he pleads elsewhere, in a poem – a theme on which Whitman expanded in the following lines:

> You shall no longer take things at second or third
> hand . . . nor look through the eyes of the dead . . .
> nor feed on the spectres in books,
> You shall not look through my eyes either, nor take
> things from me,
> You shall listen to all sides and filter them for
> yourself.
> . . .
> Long enough have you dreamed your contemptible
> dreams,
> Now I wash the gum from your eyes,
> You must habit yourselves to the dazzle of the
> light and of every moment of your life.[30]

Rejecting the tutelage of other people, past and present, the American poet becomes, in these terms, the ideal agent of defamiliarisation. He realises his own individuality in and through a passionate acceptance of the individual phenomena around him; and he encourages his readers to realise their own personal identities, to wash their own eyes and imaginations clean. 'Poets are thus liberating gods', declared Emerson: a point on which Whitman and many subsequent American poets would clearly agree. For they try, fiercely, 'to turn upon things' (to quote Whitman again) 'with wonder and love', and unlock their particularity; and they aim, with equal ferocity, to endow each member of their audience with a similar capacity for wonder – 'the power', to use Emerson's phrase, 'to fix the momentary eminency of an object'. As Whitman's reference to 'the spectres in books' illustrates, however, there is an interesting paradox at work here. The poem is seen as a potentially liberating force, certainly, but also, it may be, as an imprisoning one. It is a stratagem for being, a medium for, or prologue to, knowing, not a body of ready-made knowledge; it requires the reader to actively engage with it, to use it. If he does not – if he accepts it passively, as a product rather than a process – then he becomes confined within its terms, its vocabulary and vision; he resigns himself to looking 'through the eyes of the dead'.

This idea of the poem as a beginning for the reader, as a passionate gesture of attention, is crucial to a good deal of American poetics.

Among other things, it helps to explain Whitman's own evolution of a line the main characteristic of which is its flexibility. As Whitman recognised, 'free verse' is a perfect medium for American poetry because it can be varied to register the inflections of individual speech or the nature of a particular vision or occasion. Free verse, when properly used, has a dynamic and provisional quality to it; it turns the poem into an open field, an area of vital possibility where the reader can allow his own imagination to play. It seems to be asking each member of the audience to 'complete' it: to resolve doubts about such things as pace, rhythm, and intonation and, in the process, re-write it in his or her own terms. Not only free verse can achieve this, of course: as Emily Dickinson's work illustrates, and Robert Lowell's, a highly disruptive use of more traditional metres can produce similar effects – a feeling of surprise, a series of stimulating discords out of which each of us must evolve our own harmonies. But at such points, and with such poets, the traditional metres are being stretched to approximate to the condition of the 'free'. They are being rendered more plastic, more malleable and open, in response to a highly personal – one might say, idiosyncratic and anarchic notion of the poem's purpose that is not very different from Whitman's.

Nor do the poetics of American individualism stop there, with the evolution of the free verse line and/or the disruption of conventional metres. Again, as Whitman illustrates, a looser, more open-ended syntactical structure is frequently favoured. Lines and sentences are left lying side by side just as things are, undisturbed and separate. There are few compound sentences to draw objects and experiences into a net of theory, an elaborate plan or hierarchy; the reader is offered a sequence in which each thing, each experience, each person observed is valued in and for itself – there was this, we are told, and this, and then this. The poet's eye establishes a democracy of objects, and the poetic syntax arranges a democracy of words and statements, linked only by a minimal 'and', perhaps, a semi-colon, a dash, or a series of dots. To do more than that, to absorb things into complex intellectual or grammatical structures, would – the assumption is – lead to blindness and betrayal; for it would be to interject the meddlings of the mind between the eye and the pressure of reality, and to deny the gospel of individualism. A language as varied and polyglot as the melting-pot character of America allows, metaphors that call attention to the minute particulars of experience, an active grammar in which the present participle is preferred to other verb forms in order to underline the belief that life is a continuous, never-ending process: all these, too, are preferred by Whitman and many poets who have come after him – and under their influence a special voice is created, as multiform and individualistic as the self that is the object of celebration. On a number of occasions during his life, when he was discussing this voice, Whitman insisted that it was the most appropriate medium for the 'American bard'. The claim had a characteristic touch of arrogance to it but, like so many of Whitman's more arrogant statements, it also contained a great deal of truth. For the poetic voice of which Whitman was so proud supplied, at its very best, the most effective expression possible of the belief that there was no necessary conflict between the needs of the self and the demands of the world. To the question, 'what is an American?', Whitman clearly replied that he or she, was an individual and a supreme individualist who could nevertheless *make* a community – build a comfortable and comforting human universe.

Not everyone agreed with Whitman, however, and, to the extent that they did not, helped to mark out the further boundaries of the American poem. The poet creating a community for himself was one possibility, as Whitman indicated. But still others were located by two significant figures in nineteenth-century American poetry with whom Whitman had little in common: Edgar Allan Poe and Emily Dickinson. Some reference has been made already to Poe's rejection of American culture: his denial of utilitarianism and the whole ethic of getting and spending. With Poe, though, it is important to stress that it was not just the world of use he denied but the whole world outside of the self, whatever form it might assume; the entire thrust of his work is centripetal, away from ordinary, phenomenal experience, in and down towards the deepest levels of consciousness. Poe's metaphysics and his aesthetic are inextricably woven together here. The self, he believed, creates its own world, inviolable and intangible; and the poem, ideally, makes a supreme version of that world – it is self-contained, fixed, and perfect. Each word, as he saw it (or, for that matter, each note in a musical composition, or each brushstroke in a painting) should become a talismanic sign, a locus of feeling, association and suggestion; and each work of art should become a 'pure' or 'closed' field, as autonomous and impalpable as the reality it imitates. 'O! nothing earthly', begins one of Poe's earliest pieces:

save the ray
(Thrown back from flowers) of Beauty's eye,

. . .

O! nothing earthly save the thrill
Of melody in woodland rill –
Or (music of the passion-hearted)
Joy's voice so peacefully departed
That, like the murmur in the shell
Its echo dwelleth and will dwell –

Oh, nothing of the dross of ours –
Yet all the beauty – all the flowers
That list our love, and deck our bowers –
Adorn yon world afar, afar –
The wandering star.[31]

This is poetry as incantation: a rejection, not just of society, but of anything that violates selfhood. It is as if Poe had read Tocqueville's warning about the isolating possibilities of American democracy and turned them upon their head. For, in his work, solipsism becomes the *aim*: the poet seeks not community but solitude, the sanctuary of the disengaged soul.

With Dickinson, too, the solitude is there: but in her case it is not something she necessarily wants. For her, the self is not so much a circumscribed Eden as a prison-house from which it seems impossible to escape. 'Nature is a stranger yet', she observes in one of her poems (most of which were published after her death):

The ones that cite her most
Have never passed her haunted house,
Nor simplified her ghost.

To pity those that know her not
Is helped by the regret
That those who know her, know her less
The nearer her they get.[32]

Pushed back from nature, and from the people around her, by their irredeemable other-ness, she turns to her internal geography in the belief that it is all she can ever really know. Her self and her feelings tend to encompass her world, and her recognition of this explains the extraordinary intensity with which she describes pleasure, melancholy, or despair: the eruption of pain, when it comes, becomes an apocalyptic event and exultation seems to irradiate all existence. Only *seems* to, however: as Dickinson is only too acutely aware, her self may be her world but that world is in no way coextensive with reality. This awareness shadows all her work, but it comes out with particular force in those poems about the one experience that marks a definite conclusion to her world: which is, of course, death. In the best of these poems, death is an experience that is approached with a strange mixture of desire and fear, because it might, as Dickinson sees it, lead to a 'title divine', the final escape of the self from its imprisonment – or it might simply be a prelude to annihilation and nothingness. All that she can be sure of is the simple fact that she cannot be sure; on this, as on all other matters, the verdict must be left open. The self,

Dickinson intimates, is fragile, evanescent, dwarfed by its surroundings; and the worlds it creates, the knowledge it articulates must – by the very nature of their source – remain arbitrary, temporary, and incomplete.

This sense of the circumscriptions imposed on the isolated self, and the consequently random, truncated nature of all human knowledge dictates Dickinson's poetic practice. Unlike Poe's, Dickinson's poems are 'open': but 'open' in a way that is interestingly different, in turn, from the poetry of Walt Whitman. What Dickinson's work tends to do is to emphasise its own arbitrariness, its own dislocated, disjunctive nature: a point that is brought out, in particularly high profile, by her disruptive use of rhythm and her frequent use of discords or half-rhymes. Whitman's poems may not end in the conventional sense, but at least they usually achieve an emotional resolution – the feeling that the ideas and impulses behind them have been given an adequate shape, appropriately full expression. With Dickinson, even this is denied us. One of her most famous poems about death, for example, ends with these lines:

> And then a Plank in Reason, broke,
> And I dropped down, and down –
> And hit a World, at every plunge,
> And finished knowing – then – [33]

Finished knowing then – and then, what? The closing lines, and indeed all the preceding ones, subvert any claims Dickinson may make to understand her subject, to define and know the experience that is the poem's occasion. As a result, this is not so much a poem about death in the conventional sense as a poem about the impossibility of ever writing such a poem – and, more generally, about the impossibility of doing much more in any event than measuring one's own limits. As Dickinson put it in one of her lyrics, she dwells in the 'fairer House' of possibility where the most she can do is offer a series of provisional names for the furniture. The names must be provisional because she is, she feels, a prisoner caught within the circumference of her own consciousness: she is therefore not describing the world as it is, or even as it might be, but merely constructing a language-system, and by implication a system of values, acceptable to her individual soul. The self in Dickinson's work may be an adventurer, certainly, pushing out from the centres of her being: but it is an adventurer engaged in a quest that it can never really complete. 'I could not see to see – ' ends another of her poems: ultimate vision is invariably denied her, an adequate vocabulary is never attained, the need to understand things remains just that – a need.

Emily Dickinson marking out the limits of her prison-house, peering through the bars and considering the possibility of escape; Edgar Allan Poe turning inward upon the circumscribed Eden of his dreams, an inner world where his desires could receive entire satisfaction; Walt Whitman venturing the idea of a dialectic between the individual consciousness and the world and turning that idea into action, into the making of an exemplary audience for his poetry: together, these three nineteenth-century figures defined an area of concern that subsequent American poets were to explore. They established parameters within which others, in the twentieth century, were to undertake their own charting of the country's ample geography, their own attempts to translate the landscape of America into verse. Their example was not a restrictive one, of course. It did not, and does not, limit American poets to a narrow set of alternatives beyond which they are forbidden to go. It offers not a prescriptive grammar but a transformational one: a range of options on which each writer can build, structures that are generative, susceptible to change and development, a series of opportunities rather than rules. 'Poets to come!' wrote Whitman:

> Not to-day is to justify me and answer what I am for,
> But you, a new brood, native, athletic, continental, greater
> than before known,
> Arouse! For you must justify me.
>
> I myself but write one or two indicative words for the
> future,
> I but advance a moment only to wheel and hurry back
> in the darkness.
>
> I am a man who, sauntering along without fully
> stopping, turns a casual look upon you
> and then averts his face,
> Leaving it to you to prove and define it,
> Expecting the main things from you.[34]

If he were able to return now, Whitman would surely find his expectations satisfied. Looking over a body of poetry that, during the past seventy or eighty years, has found its inspiration in the ideas and experiences of America, he would surely feel that his 'one or two indicative words' have borne fruit: that his own work has been justified, proved and defined, by a great and continuing tradition that has, as at least one of its unacknowledged aims, the forging of the uncreated conscience of the nation.

America and modernism: new readings of reality

Before turning to the details of that tradition, however, it is worth saying a little about some of the other factors that helped initiate it, and that served to make modern American poetry not only *American* but *modern*. The America that Poe lived in, and that Emerson, Whitman, and Dickinson began at least to write about, was very different from the one into which Pound, Williams, and Frost were born. A few, cold facts and figures will perhaps serve to register the differences: the radical transformations of social and economic structure that the first generation of modern American poets were required to confront, whether they liked it or not, and to respond to, somehow, in their work. In the early 1860s, the United States was still a predominantly rural, agricultural society and it extended, economically speaking, only as far as the Missouri River. It did not manufacture any steel; it had very few railways; and it had an industrial investment of only one and a half billion dollars. All that changed very quickly. Within twenty years after the end of the Civil War, for instance, it had developed the most extensive railway system in the world, binding East and West together in one great economic unit. It had become one of the giants of the international steel industry; the number of factories within its borders had more than doubled, and it had an industrial investment of over four million dollars. With frightening speed, America was changing, and continued to change, from a country of smallholdings and trading-posts into a country of great industries and business corporations; and inexorably, at the same time, it was changing from a country of farms and villages into a country dominated by the town and the city. By as early as 1880, for example, over half the population of the Eastern United States lived in towns of more than 4,000 people; while places like New York, Philadelphia, and Boston, which had once been provincial market-places, were turning into urban, metropolitan centres. At the beginning of the nineteenth century, the United States had only just come into existence as a nation: but by the end, such was the pace of technological advance, that it was rapidly outstripping Great Britain and Germany in urban development and industrial production.

One sensitive observer of these changes was the American historian (and, incidentally, grandson of the second American President, quoted earlier) Henry Adams. In 1893, Adams attended the World's Columbian Exposition in the bustling, skyscraper city of Chicago. Chicago itself served as a measure of the alterations that had taken place in the

American landscape: a village of 200–300 people in 1833, it had become the country's second largest city, a junction for the great railway systems of the nation and 'Hog Butcher for the World' (to use Carl Sandburg's later description), with a population of well over a million. And the Exposition, in turn, offered a celebratory account of the technological developments that had made such alterations possible – and that were, in Adams's view, seducing people into 'the habit of thinking a steam-engine or a dynamo as natural as the sun'. Looking at both city and exhibition in an attitude of what he termed 'helpless reflection', Adams felt, he declared (using the third person for himself here, as he does throughout his autobiography), that 'his education spread ever chaos'. 'Indeed', he added, 'it seemed to him as though, this year, education went mad'. The reasons for this feeling were not far to seek. 'Chicago' Adams suggested, 'asked in 1893 for the first time the question of whether the American people knew where they were driving'; and 'Adams answered, for one, that he did not know'. What was more, 'he decided that the American people probably knew no more than he did'.[35] However, he went on, both for his own sake and other people's, he would try at least to find out.

Strictly speaking, finding out occupied most of the remainder of Adams's life: but a crucial moment of discovery occurred, he tells us, when visiting another exhibition, the Great Exposition in Paris in 1900. In the seven intervening years, the new order of things anticipated in Chicago had come even closer: x-rays and radium 'that metaphysical bomb' had been discovered, while the automobile 'since 1893 . . . had become a nightmare at a hundred kilometres an hour'. Standing in the Gallery of Machines at the Great Exposition, Adams felt, he says, 'his historical neck broken by the irruption of forces totally new'. In particular, he began to see the forty-four dynamos on display there 'as a moral force, much as the early Christians felt the cross', as 'a revelation of mysterious energy'. 'The planet itself seemed less impressive', he insists, 'in its old-fashioned, deliberate, annual or daily revolution, than this huge wheel, revolving within arms-length at some vertiginous speed and barely murmuring'. The message it murmured to Adams was that 'in . . . seven years man had translated himself into a new universe which had no common scale of measurement with the old'. Along with the old modes of production, the old modes of feeling had been demolished too. 'The child born in 1900', Adams suggested:

> would . . . be born into a new world which would not be a unity but a multiple. Adams tried to imagine it, and an education that would fit it. He found himself in a land where no one had ever penetrated before; where

> order was an accidental relation obnoxious to nature; artificial compulsion imposed on motion; against which every free energy of the universe revolted; and which, being merely occasional, resolved back into anarchy at last.[36]

Instead of unity, there would be proliferation and change, what Adams christened 'the law of the multiverse'; in place of order, religious or otherwise, there would be 'a supersensual world' in which man could 'measure nothing except by chance collisions of movements imperceptible to his senses, perhaps even imperceptible to his instruments, but perceptible to each other, and so to some known ray at the end of the scale'. Such alterations, Adams felt, would affect all cultures, but particularly those strongly committed to the new 'anarchical' forces – and, above all, a 'twenty-million-horse-power-society' like America. Just because the American had embraced the 'occult mechanism' of the dynamo so fiercely, he would be especially susceptible to the consequences – whatever, as it turned out, those consequences might be. He might become part of a new evolutionary cycle or part of a new, radically dehumanising system; he might become 'the child of new forces', energetic and liberating, or he might equally be transformed into 'the chance sport of nature', reduced to one more helpless atom in a random universe. Adams was not sure, although on the whole he seemed predisposed towards the latter, gloomier series of possibilities. However, one thing he was perfectly certain about, the process of accelerating technological change would lead to an alteration of consciousness, vitally affecting every American's structure of perception, the way he thought about himself and the world – and new forms of education, new epistemological and aesthetic structures would be needed to grasp the conditions of contemporary life, to register and at least try to understand the 'multiverse'.

Henry Adams's apocalyptic prophecies about the direction of American history have proved only too accurate. The material culture (which is to say, towns, factories, and so on) has radically altered over the past hundred years; and, at almost the same time, the non-material culture (that is, beliefs, customs, and institutions) has altered too, in ways that are quite as unprecedented and far-reaching. Darwinism, with its new view of human nature and society, was one of the first movements to threaten the non-material fabric of American culture: not only because it challenged the religious inheritance of places like New England and the fundamentalist South but because it called into question the humanist legacy of nineteenth-century intellectual America. By offering an exhaustively documented and entirely plausible pattern of cause and effect, based on the slow processes of sexual and natural selection and the reductive results of environmental factors, Darwin left little place either for metaphysical notions of Original Sin and Redemption or for Emerson's, and Whitman's, belief in the potential divinity of man. As science and Darwinism undermined the old religious and ethical order, so Marxism and socialism placed a large question mark over the liberal orthodoxies of America. The collectivist ideologies that proliferated in the late nineteenth century and early twentieth seemed to deny the individualistic tenets on which the nation had been founded. They were 'un-American', perhaps, and yet for many people they seemed a more appropriate response to the urban ghettoes and sweatshops of the emergent economy than the Jeffersonian, and frontier, ethic of self-help. 'Those who labour in the earth are the chosen people of God', Jefferson had written:

> if ever he had a chosen people, whose breasts he has made his peculiar deposit for substantial and genuine virtue . . . Corruption of morals . . . is the mark set on those, who not looking . . . to their own soil and industry, as does the husbandman, for their subsistence, depend for it on the casualties and caprice of customers . . .[37]

Noble sentiments these might be, but in the face of the historical upheaval that both Adams and Marx observed, they appeared just a little anachronistic. 'The husbandman' might have seemed an admirable figure to Jefferson – just as, for that matter, the frontiersman did to the celebrants of the West – but it was difficult to imagine him ambling down the streets of Chicago or living in a tenement apartment in New York.

While Marx provided Americans with a different perspective on their society, and the transformations it was experiencing, Albert Einstein – whose ideas, in a necessarily popularised form, gradually became current in the earlier part of the twentieth century – offered them nothing less than a new view of reality. Einstein's theory of relativity implied a multiple perspective on the universe: there was no absolute view, the theory suggested, no 'God's view' of events in the universe. The relationships of before and after, and simultaneous with, depend on the observer's position in relation to events. This emphasis on the part played by the observer gradually permeated the experimental sciences generally. Niels Bohr, for example, and de Broglie, discussed it with reference to quantum theory, pointing out that the object of investigation altered by being investigated, and that the outcome of the investigation depended on the standpoint that was originally taken. It culminated in Werner Heisenberg's formulation of the indeterminacy or uncertainty principle, according to which it is impossible to determine both the position and the velocity of an object at a given moment. If you know exactly where an object is, Heisenberg argued, you cannot tell how fast it is moving; to tell how fast it is moving, you have to consider its movement over a given distance, that is, an indefinite number of possible positions. So, once again, things are determined by the viewpoint of the observer or spectator; our knowledge of reality becomes contingent on the particular perspective or perspectives assumed.

It is difficult to measure accurately the impact that the theories of relativity or indeterminacy – or, for that matter, the ideas of Darwin or Marx – had on the arts generally, and American poetry in particular. Quite apart from anything else, it is dangerous anyway to think in terms of specific *influence*. It was quite possible for writers like Ezra Pound or Wallace Stevens to inhabit the same intellectual ground as Einstein without having read a word of his work, or even perhaps having heard of him, because ideas about what Adams termed the 'multiverse' were, as Adams himself indicates, part of the intellectual currency of the time. Poets, scientists, political theorists: all were exploring new terrain in often analogous or parallel ways but without necessarily affecting one another directly. That being said, however, it is clear that some notion of relativity feeds into both the forms and the arguments of a great deal of twentieth-century poetry: something that is registered, among other ways, in the use of discontinuous styles, multiple levels of allusion, and aggressively non-linear structures. In a work like Pound's *Cantos*, for instance, traditional American ideas about the character of epic, the dispensability of narrative, and the poet as exemplary are wedded to more recent, modernist notions about the nature of knowledge, the inter-dependent relationship between the perceiver, the medium of perception, and the thing perceived. And the result is a poem more radically disjunctive and rapidly associative – and more alert to the possibilities latent in the triangular relationship between author, subject, and reader – than anything Whitman could ever have imagined.

Mention of the associative character of a great deal of twentieth-century American poetry suggests another figure and body of thought that was immensely important: Sigmund Freud and the science of psychology. Freud's naming of the 'Unconscious' supplied a focus for a variety of intuitions in the later part of the nineteenth century to the effect that the psyche contains an unwitting domain by which the patterns of past experience, both personal and racial, affect involuntarily the conscious self. It helped to demolish the notion of unitary personality, the solidity of the social and moral self – what D.H. Lawrence scornfully referred to as 'the old stable *ego* of the character'; and, in its place, it substituted a duality, the idea of *two* levels in the mind which may be not only discrete but at odds. By extension, Freud and Freudianism also tended to subvert any belief in free will. 'Many people . . . contest the assumption of psychic determinism', Freud declared:

> by appealing to a special feeling of conviction that there is a free will . . . But so far as I can observe, it does not manifest itself on great and important decisions of the will: on these occasions the feeling that we have is rather one of psychical compulsion ("Here I stand: I can do no other"). On the other hand, it is precisely with regard to the unimportant, indifferent decisions that we would like to claim that . . . we have acted of our free – and unmotivated – will . . . But what is thus left free by the one side receives its motivation from the other side, from the unconscious; and in this way determination in the psychical sphere is still carried out without any gap.[38]

Along with Darwin's biological determinism, and Marx's social and historical determinism, this 'psychic determinism' of Freud's issued a challenge to those assumptions of individual choice, the self's capacity to choose its own fate and even reinvent itself, that are situated at the heart of the American Dream. As such, it required an answer even from those who cherished these assumptions; it became no longer possible (as it had been, to some extent, in the earlier part of the nineteenth century) to hold on to that Dream uncritically – without considering those forces, psychic as well as social, that appeared to shadow it, to demote it to the status of irrelevant fantasising.

Freudianism was important in more than just this respect, however. For, as Lionel Trilling has observed:

> of all mental systems, the Freudian psychology is the one which makes poetry indigenous to the very constitution of the mind. Indeed, the mind, as Freud sees it, is in the greater part of its tendency exactly a poetry-making organ . . . Freud has not merely naturalised poetry; he has discovered its status as a pioneer settler, and he sees it as a method of thought.[39]

Freud's concern with dreaming suggested new possibilities for the poem, whereby it is released from its obligations to some compressed attenuation of the syntactic conventions governing prose. The transitions in, say, Hart Crane's *The Bridge* or William Carlos Williams's *Paterson* are stark, unpredictable, confusing, but never without a purpose: in Kenneth Burke's phrase, they oblige us to see the 'poem as dream' – not as any particular dream but as the product of a communicative process governed by its own types of coherence, associative laws and processes of the kind Freud had observed. In his own way, together with people like Einstein, Freud opened the door to the freeing of language from the normal demands of logical progression as they are embodied in our syntactic conventions, and to the development of forms, patterns of nuance and suggestion, that could accommodate the multiple activities of the human mind. Without him, poets such as Pound and Williams would still almost certainly have dispensed with even the minimal commitment to narrative demonstrated by the traditional lyric, and pursued imagery that could attain to the numinous particularity we associate with the products of the unconscious. Neither Freud, in other words, nor even the popular notion of Freudianism current in the earlier part of the twentieth century, is solely responsible for such things as Imagism. But Freud, too, assisted on the voyage into strange seas of thought; he also was part of that general intellectual upheaval that encouraged modern American poets to re-shape, not just their subject matter, but their language, their arts of consciousness and expression.

American poets, along with other writers, found their attention in any case called to their medium of language by the developing science of linguistics. The scientific study of language that had grown up in the eighteenth and nineteenth centuries had been primarily historical in its emphasis: the nature of language was investigated through its putative origins in primitive life. In the early decades of the twentieth century, however, this historical approach tended to lose favour; and what supplanted it was an approach, largely associated with Ferdinand de Saussure, that examined language in terms of its internal structure. The established view of language had been that it was an aggregate of separate units, called 'words', each of which constituted a referential reflection of an object, idea, or feeling, the whole existing within a *diachronic* or historical dimension which makes it subject to observable and recordable laws of change. But Saussure argued that language should be studied not only in terms of its individual parts, and not only diachronically, but also in terms of the relationship between those parts, and *synchronically*: that is, in terms of its current adequacy. In short, he proposed that a language should be studied as a unified field as we actually experience it now; for it was strictly an autotelic system with structures, in themselves largely arbitrary, that govern our most intimate construction of the world, individually and collectively – and only the more significantly for working, on the whole, at a subliminal level. Some of the wheels Saussure set in motion are suggested by the passage from the writings of Benjamin Lee Whorf that was quoted earlier. Or, again, they are indicated by these remarks made by another American linguist, Edward Sapir:

> Human beings do not live in the objective world alone, but are very much at the mercy of the particular language which has become the medium of expression for their society. It is quite an illusion to imagine that one adjusts to reality essentially without the use of language and that language is merely an incidental means of solving specific problems of communication and reflection. The fact of the matter is that the 'real world' is to a large extent built up on the language habits of the group. No two languages are ever sufficiently similar to be considered as representing the same social reality. The worlds in which different societies live are distinct worlds, not merely the same world with different labels attached . . . We see and hear and otherwise experience very largely as we do because the language habits of our community predispose certain choices of interpretation . . .[40]

What were the literary implications of the linguistic revolution that Saussure initiated? In what ways, more specifically, did American poets betray the fact that they breathed the same air, shared a similar climate of thought and feeling? In the first place, it might be said that the reflections of Saussure and the linguists who came after him would tend to confirm American poets in their 'Americanness': that the noticeable differences between the American language and others, even the mother tongue of English, implied or indeed necessitated a difference between 'worlds'. The American perception of social reality, according to this argument, would be distinct from the perceptions of any other culture simply because its language habits were distinct; and the American poet would be obliged, by the very nature of the tools he used, to articulate this distinctiveness. And, in the second place, it could be argued that the new linguistics encouraged poets to think of language in a way to which they were in any event predisposed: as an end as well as a means, an object as well as a medium, with its own intrinsic substance and symmetry. 'The function of poetic language', wrote the linguist Jan Mukarovsky, 'consists in the maximum of foregrounding of utterance . . . in order to place in the foreground the act of expression . . . itself' – a sentiment echoed and expanded upon in this statement by the formalist critic, Roman Jakobson:

> The distinctive feature of poetry lies in the fact that a word is perceived as a word and not merely as a proxy

> for the denoted object or an outburst of emotion, that words and their arrangement, their meaning, their outward and inward form acquire weight and value of their own.[41]

According to this formulation, words might be used in a transitive way, as a mode of signification, a way of organising and describing phenomena: but they could also be used in an intransitive fashion, drawing attention to the act of writing – the shape of a vowel, perhaps, the sinuous pattern described by a sentence, the 'breath' of a line. In essence, what Jakobson is saying here is no different from what Wallace Stevens says when he declares in 'The Man with the Blue Guitar': 'Poetry is the subject of the poem. From this the poem issues and/ To this returns'. Whatever else it may be, the poem is 'about' itself, Stevens – and Jakobson and Mukarovsky – suggest: its subject, among other subjects, is the language or 'materia poetica' out of which it is created.

The impact of the new linguistics was felt not only in poetry but in philosophy as well; for, although Aristotle, Aquinas, Locke, and Kant had all been aware of the importance of language, it was not until the early part of the twentieth century that philosophers began to grasp its full implications. A representative, and seminal, figure in this respect is Ludwig Wittgenstein, whose attitude towards the structuring tendencies inherent in our vocabularies is summed up by these four propositions from *Tractatus Philosopho-Logicus*, which he wrote while serving as a soldier in the Great War:

> 1. The world is all that is the case.
> 1.1 The world is the totality of facts, not of things.
> 1.115 A *picture* held us captive. And we could not get outside it, for it lay in our language and language seemed to repeat it to us inexorably.
>
> . . .
>
> 5.62 What the solipsist *means* is quite correct; only it cannot be *said*, but makes itself manifest. The world is *my* world . . .[42]

The world, Wittgenstein argued, is the sum of what we take to be true and believe that others take to be true. We construct our world from the inside out; we do not merely adjust ourselves to a given world outside, even though outside circumstances impose certain constraints on our constructing. We build our 'picture', our totality of 'facts' or version of reality, which will be significantly related to but never quite the same as the configurations, the pictures built up by others. And a crucial factor in these configurations, these patternings of things is the system of language we have at our disposal; for, as Wittgenstein puts it, the picture we create – the world that is '*my* world' that we build – lies inevitably in our language.

As far as the matter of influence is concerned, it is probably necessary to move forward in time as far as the last two or three decades in order to appreciate the full implications of the new linguistic philosophy. For it is then that the idea of the poem as verbal process comes into its own: with writers like James Merrill and John Ashbery producing works that very often read like glosses on Wittgenstein's first proposition – 'lexical playfields'[43] (to use Vladimir Nabokov's handy phrase) that in their fluidity, gaiety of language, and gamesomeness seem designed to remind us that 'The world is all that is the case'. However, it is worth repeating the point that we are not primarily concerned with the vexed question of influence here. In response to Henry Adams's 'multiverse', parallel revolutions were occurring in all kinds of fields, including those of philosophy and poetry. So it is hardly surprising that, even while Wittgenstein was composing his *Tractatus*, American poets were concentrating their minds just as fiercely on problems of language, thought, and reality; and they were discovering and defining – in their own ways, just as Wittgenstein was – what they saw as the personal, creative nature of all three. They were not being easily or thoughtlessly subjective. On the contrary, their approach was, like Wittgenstein's, a toughly objective one. For they wanted as much as he did to understand how we construct a notion of personal identity, how we create a version of the world, and how we relate the 'I' to the 'thou', the self to otherness, using (and, perhaps, being used by) the patterns of language. In addition to being objective, their approach was also a modernist one. Certainly, they were returned to the bedrock idea of American culture, the isolated individual and the realities he or she invents, just as so many American poets had been before them. But they were returned, with a difference: in ways that betrayed their kinship, not merely with Poe, Whitman, and Dickinson but with people like Yeats, Joyce, and Lawrence, Darwin, Marx, and Einstein, Freud, Wittgenstein, and Saussure.

America and 'revolution': new frontiers for art

'The revolution/ is accomplished', wrote William Carlos Williams in one of his poems. Three things, in particular, mark the beginnings of the revolution Williams is referring to here – a revolution that saw the emergence of a poetry at once genuinely *American* and significantly *modern*. One is Imagism, which will be discussed in the next chapter; the others are the founding of *Poetry: A Magazine of Verse* in 1912, and the opening of the great Armory Show of the visual arts since Impressionism in 1913. *Poetry*, published by Harriet Monroe in Chicago, became a focus for the new movement in poetry. This was basically because it found room within its pages for an immense, and various, amount of significant work: within a few years of its founding, it had published such diverse and radical experimenters as William Carlos Williams and Wallace Stevens, Ezra Pound (who acted as a sort of roving editor in London, collecting the right material to send back to Harriet Monroe), Carl Sandburg, H. D., Marianne Moore, T. S. Eliot, Vachel Lindsay, and Hart Crane. Gradually, it acquired a reputation, but only gradually; its early issues were greeted with suspicion, especially by the literary establishment and particularly in view of the fact that it took no special 'stand'. All it asked of its contributors was that they should write good, distinctive verse. Harriet Monroe herself tended to prefer writers like Sandburg and Lindsay, but she instinctively recognised the essence of the American tradition: which is to be different. As Thoreau put it, in a seminal passage in *Walden* (1854):

> If a man does not keep pace with his companions, perhaps it is because he hears a different drummer. Let him step to the music which he hears, however measured or far away.[44]

The best of the new poets who began to appear in the pages of *Poetry* all seemed to have heeded Thoreau's injunction: to step to the music of a different drummer – to respond to the rhythms of American life as each person's ear heard and understood them.

Quite apart from its individual importance, *Poetry* was and is the progenitor of all the 'little magazines' that have proliferated over the past seventy or so years, and that have probably had more to do with the promotion of modern American poetry than any other medium. In New York, there was *Others*, founded in 1913 by Walter Arensberg and (more importantly) Alfred Kreymborg, which, according to William Carlos Williams, 'published enough to put a few young men and women on their feet'. 'It was individually useful to many of us', added Williams, 'it gave a hearing to us in the face of the universal refusal to publish and pay for available new work by young poets'.[45] There was also *Seven Arts*, inaugurated in 1916 by James Oppenheim, and *The Masses*, which began publication in 1911. *Seven Arts* lasted only a year, before being absorbed into the *Dial*, the famous review for which Emerson had written, but in that brief time it managed to publish people like Sandburg, Robert Frost, and Amy Lowell. *The Masses* lasted longer, until 1917, linking its original, socialist and pacifist, ideas with a strong interest in the arts, and in 1926 it was resurrected as *New Masses*. Other influential magazines included Margaret Anderson's *Little Review*, which began publication in Chicago in 1914 and then eventually moved to Paris, and *Contact*, which William Carlos Williams helped to found in 1920, along with Robert McAlmon. Nor were these new flagships for the arts confined to the big cities of the Northeast and Midwest. In the South, *The Double-Dealer* appeared in New Orleans between 1921 and 1926, publishing the work of John Crowe Ransom, Allen Tate, and Hart Crane, and *The Fugitive* (of which more will be said in chapter three) was produced in Nashville, Tennessee from 1922 until 1925. The West, meanwhile, saw the publication of *Midland* and *Prairie Schooner*, with a strong regional emphasis; and from 1927 until 1934 academic Harvard weighed in with the *Hound and Horn*, which drew its title from two lines of Ezra Pound's:

> Tis the white stag, Fame we're a-hunting
> Bid the world's hounds come to horn![46]

Mention of Pound, and indeed the reference to the *Little Review* earlier, brings to the foreground another important aspect of the little magazines: as many young American writers migrated to Europe, and particularly to Paris, in the second or third decade of this century, they either took their reviews with them or founded new ones over there. Their reasons for becoming expatriates were many, and included the simple fact that, due to a very favourable exchange rate, Americans could live reasonably well and cheaply in Europe just after the Great War. But one common, deeper reason was suggested by Gertrude Stein when she declared:

> . . . writers . . . have two countries, the one where they belong and the one in which they live really. The second one is romantic, it is separate from themselves, it is not real but it is really there.[47]

Developing this a little further, it could be said that for many young American poets the first country Stein refers to here was the place where they had been born: an urban, industrial culture in which, as one contemporary observer put it, 'each citizen functions with pride in the . . . conspiracy against the individual'. The second country, on the other hand, was the place where they might have been born. It was another America entirely, that land of perfect freedom which was and is as much a product of the mind as a geographical location. And it was in order to realise this second America, in their individual imaginations and then in their work, that many poets felt compelled to detach themselves from their given, native land. They had to leave the America they had known because, more than ever before, it appeared to have betrayed the American Dream. They had to travel abroad, not because they wished to abandon their inheritance, but because they wanted to keep a firm grasp on it, and cope dispassionately with the problems it had created. Like so many others before them the American poet-exiles were in effect living out a paradox, never closer to home than when asserting their (physical or moral) distance from it.

Anyway, whatever their individual reasons, many poets did travel abroad and in the process their little magazines took on a more internationalist flavour. In Italy, Alfred Kreymborg and Harold Loeb founded *Broom*, which from 1921 until 1924 published American and European experimentalists side by side. More to the point, Paris became the source of a whole host of important little magazines: *Secession*, started in 1922 by Gorham B. Munson, *This Quarter*, which lasted from 1925 until 1932, *Transition*, which under Eugene Jolas published people like Hart Crane, Allen Tate, and Archibald MacLeish between 1927 and 1938 and promoted what was called the 'Revolution of the Word', Pound's *Exile, Tambour*, and the *New Review*. The list could go on and on; and it could be extended still further by mentioning just a few of the innumerable little magazines published in the United States as the expatriate movement faded and American poets returned, with reluctance or enthusiasm, across the Atlantic. On the more established side, there have been liberal publications such as *Partisan Review*, periodicals associated with particular universities like the *Southern Review*, the *Kenyon Review*, and the *Chicago Review*, and magazines like the *Paris Review* and *Transatlantic Review* that continue the expatriate traditions. On the more experimental side, there has been *Evergreen Review*, which published the work of many of the Beat poets, *Black Mountain Review*, which provided an outlet for poets like Charles Olson and Robert Creeley, Robert Bly's *The Sixties* (formerly called *The Fifties*), and *Art and Literature* edited by John Ashbery among others. And on the still more experimental side there have been countless smaller magazines and broadsheets whose adventurous, and sometimes subversive, nature may even be suggested by their titles: *Journal for the Protection of All Beings, C Magazine, Angel Hair, Adventures in Poetry, Some Thing, Floating Bear, Six-Pack, The San Francisco Earthquake*. But it would be invidious to go on mentioning titles, since the point of such publications is their apparently inexhaustible variety and evidently unstoppable growth. As the authors of a history of little magazines argue, the movement *Poetry* helped to start has 'stood, since 1912 to the present, defiantly in the front rank of the battle for a mature literature.'[48] The review that Harriet Monroe founded, and which is still alive today, helped establish a medium without which it would have been difficult, if not impossible, for the new poets to reach their audiences – to tell them in dramatic detail about the measures they had heard, beaten out by a different drummer.

Shortly after *Poetry* began publication in Chicago, another event of the first importance to the arts, including poetry, occurred in New York: the Armory Show – so called because it was held in the Sixty-ninth Regiment Armory on Lexington Avenue – opened its doors to the public. Those who organised the show had little doubt about the probable effects of the exhibition. 'It will be like a bomb shell', wrote one:

> . . . Everybody is electrified . . . We have a great opportunity in this show, and must try to make it truly wonderful . . . We want this old show of ours to mark the starting point of the new spirit in art, at least as far as America is concerned.[49]

As these remarks suggest, the Armory Show was intended to deliver an educative shock. More specifically, it was meant to make Americans aware, whether they liked it or not, of what had been happening in European painting since Impressionism: movements like Fauvism, Cubism, Expressionism, and Pointillism, painters such as Van Gogh, Cézanne, Picasso, and Duchamp. Nor were the organisers of the show disappointed, at least as far as its general impact was concerned. After it opened on 17 February, 1913, some 70,000 people paid admission to see what were estimated to be 1,600 works, including sculpture, groups of drawings and prints. Individual reactions varied, of course: but the commonest one was illustrated by Theodore Roosevelt, who was reported to have wandered about the exhibition shaking his head and muttering occasionally, 'But is it art? But is it art?' Later, in an article entitled 'A Layman's View of an Art Exhibition', Roosevelt modified his views sufficiently to concede that 'real good . . . is coming out of the new movements'. But he continued to ridicule the 'Cubists, Futurists, or Near-Impressionists', and he persisted in lumping all the more experimental artists together and entitling them 'the lunatic fringe'. Roosevelt's theme was taken up by others. The gallery of the Cubists became popularly known as 'the chamber of horrors'; American *Art News* offered a prize of ten dollars to anyone who could find the nude in Marcel Duchamp's 'Nude Descending a Staircase'; and, as the exhibition moved on to Chicago, it became the target of both would-be wits and self-appointed custodians of the nation's morals. Ridiculed, parodied, vilified, dismissed as a joke or labelled a symptom of degeneracy: whatever the response, it could not be ignored. And, after it was all over, all those who had participated in the organising and holding of the show held a party that was at once a wake and a jubilee, in recognition of the fact that what they had done marked the end of one era and the beginning of another. As one contemporary newspaper put it, 'American art will never be the same again'.

American art, and American poetry: among those who jostled with the crowds at the Armory Show was William Carlos Williams. 'There was at that time a great surge of interest in the arts generally before the First World War', he recalled later, in his *Autobiography*:

> New York was seething with it. Painting took the lead. It came to a head for us in the famous "Armory Show" of 1913. I went to it and gaped along with the rest at a "picture" in which an electric bulb kept going on and off; at Duchamp's sculpture (by "Mott & Co."), a magnificent cast-iron urinal, glistening of its white enamel . . . The "Nude Descending a Staircase" is too hackneyed for me to remember anything clearly about it now. But I do remember how I laughed out loud when I first saw it, happily, with relief.[50]

The relief Williams, and others, felt was the relief of liberation: here, at last, was something that would help to free them from tradition, the tyranny of conventional, representational art. Ideas that had come to them, impulses they had felt, were, they suddenly realised, not peculiar to them: they were shared by many others, in Europe and perhaps elsewhere. Wandering around the exhibits at the Armory Show, budding American poets, among others, could feel that they were part of an international community of experiment: a new generation for whom – to borrow a famous remark of D. H. Lawrence's – the old world had ended. The aim of such poets was not, of course, to copy Duchamp or anyone else (even supposing that such direct imitation of the visual arts might be possible); nor would it be right to suggest that, without the Armory Show, they would never have had the nerve to experiment in the way they did. Still, the new frontiers being opened up by European painters did encourage people like Williams to continue their own individual explorations of rhythm and language. As Williams himself put it:

> Whether the Armory Show in painting did it or whether it was no more than a facet – the poetic line, the way the

> image was to lie on the page was our immediate concern.[51]

Certain poets, like Ezra Pound, wanted to push the connection a little further than that. Pound himself had not visited the Armory Show. However, based as he was in London at the time, he had ample opportunity to acquaint himself with the latest developments in the visual arts and to meet some of the new painters and sculptors. And what he saw and learned convinced him that certain, fairly precise analogies could be drawn between what he, and a few kindred spirits, were trying to do in poetry and what was happening in the visual field. In 1912, for instance, he made this criticism of his friend Ford Madox Ford's poetry:

> His flaw is the flaw of impressionism . . . The *conception* of poetry is a process more intense than the *reception* of an impression. And no impression, however carefully articulated, can, recorded, convey that feeling of sudden light which the works of art should and must convey.[52]

Ford, he insisted, went wrong because 'nearly everything he says applies to things *seen*. It is the exact rendering of the visible image'. 'The organization of forms is a much more energetic and creative action than the copying or imitating of light on a haystack', Pound argued, but Ford, unfortunately, did not seem to understand this: he was 'not an *imagiste,* but an impressionist'. 'Expressionism, neo-cubism, and imagism' were for Pound, all 'gathered together in one camp' in that, unlike impressionism, they were all concerned 'with the specific gravity of things, with their nature': 'Their nature *and* show, if you like', he went on, 'with the relation between them, but not with the show alone'. Their aim was intensive, whereas impressionism was 'a spreading, or surface art', registering little more than the data 'the cinematograph records'. Compared to Ford's 'impression of a moment', the dispassionate perception of superficial appearances, what he himself was after, Pound claimed, was an epiphanic experience, 'the sense of the "special moment"', of intense contemplation. And, he felt, he had come pretty close to achieving it in a poem like his famous *haiku*, 'In a Station of the Metro':

> The apparition of these faces in the crowd;
> Petals on a wet, black bough.

In such lines, Pound declared, he was 'trying to record the precise instant when a thing outward and objective transforms itself, or darts into a thing inward and subjective'. 'This particular sort of consciousness', he added, 'has not been identified with impressionist art'.

The further details of Pound's poetry, and his ideas about poetry, can be left until the next chapter, however, What matters here is that, like Williams and many others, he sensed a parallel between poetry and other arts. In response to the crisis of the times, he saw that many people in different fields were embarking on their own kinds of revolution, their own investigations not merely into the content of experience but into the way human beings have habitually structured it. They were conducting their own personal inquiries into the grounds of knowledge and being: inquiries that, of necessity, went further than those of their predecessors – in the poets' case, further even than the language experiments of Poe, Whitman, and Dickinson. 'The process of definition is the intent of the poem', Robert Creeley has said. True in particular of American poetry, it has become truer than ever before during this century: in the hands of its finest practitioners, modern American verse is never less than an act of discovery – discovery of the self, that is, and of the priorities to which that self committed. No fixed conclusion is reached, nor even hinted at. Instead, poets evolve a passing sense of order out of the sheer dynamics of their work. And they weave an identity out of the entire fabric of their language, a geometry of the self that is purely temporary because, as they alter from moment to moment, the speech that serves to define them must alter too. Nor is this personal voice woven out of words *just* personal. 'America is a poem in our eyes', Emerson had written and Emerson's successors have taken him at his word: their geometries of the self have, accordingly, been maps of the country's 'ample geography' – its contours, physical and moral, its lights and its shadows. Whatever their differences, in fact (and there are many), their shared aim, the one thing American poets of the twentieth century have had in common is the impulse to imitate the shape of the nation in rhythm, word, image, and line: to change 'America . . . a poem' into an American poem.

Notes

1. Ralph Waldo Emerson, 'The Poet'. See also: William Byrd of Westover, letter to Charles Boyle, Earl of Orrery, July 5, 1726, cited in *The London Diary and Other Writings*, edited by Louis Booker Wright and Marion Tinling (New York, 1958), p. 77.

2. St. Jean de Crèvecoeur, 'What is an American?', letter 3 in *Letters from an American Farmer* (1793). See also, William Strachey, *The Historie of Travaile into Virginia*, edited by Louis Booker Wright and Virginia Freund, Hakluyt Soc. Reprint (London, 1953), pp. 30–31.
3. Philip Freneau, 'The Rising Glory of America', lines 437–39, 443–49, 466–72.
4. Cited in Constance Rourke, *The Roots of American Culture* (New York, 1942), p. 3. See also, Cotton Mather, *Manuductio ad Ministerium* (1726), in Perry Miller and Thomas Johnson (eds.), *The Puritans: A Sourcebook of Their Writings* (1938; New York, 1963 edition), p. 686.
5. Edgar Allan Poe, 'The Poetic Principle'. See also, 'Dream-Land', line 8.
8. Walt Whitman; 'An American Primer'.
7. Alexis de Tocqueville, *De la Democratie en Amérique* (1835–40), II, Ch. 15 (My translation). See also, II, Ch. 2.
8. Ibid., II, Ch. 2. See also, II, Ch. 18.
9. Henry David Thoreau, *Walden*, Ch. 1.
10. Edward Williams, 'Virginia, more especially the South Part thereof Richly and Truly Valued' (1650), p. 19 in Peter Force (ed.), *Tracts and Other Papers Relating Principally to the Origin, Settlement, and Progress of the Colonies in North America* (1836–46; New York, 1947 edition), III.
11. F. Scott Fitzgerald, *The Great Gatsby* (1925), Ch. 9. See also Mark Twain. *The Adventures of Huckleberry Finn*, 'Chapter the Last'.
12. Walt Whitman, 'A Broadway Pageant', section II. See also, Hart Crane, 'The Wine Menagerie', line 29.
13. Lewis Mumford, *The Golden Day: A Study in American Literature and Culture* (1926; New York, 1968 edition), p. 20. See also, Frederick Jackson Tuner, 'The Significance of the Frontier in American History', in F. J. Turner (ed.), *The Frontier in American History* (New York, 1963), pp. 3–4, 37; Van Wyck Brooks, cited in Jay B. Hubbell, 'The Frontier', in Norman Foerster (ed.), *The Reinterpretation of American Literature (1929*; New York, 1959 edition), *p. 5.*
14. For a fuller discussion of the Puritan tendency to locate the visible by reference to the invisible, see Perry Miller, *The New England Mind from Colony to Province* (Cambridge, Mass., 1953).
15. Bertrand Russell, *History of Western Philosophy* (London, 1946), p. 513.
16. James Russell Lowell, 'A Fable for Critics', lines 552–53. See also lines 548–49; Charles Eliot Norton, letter to James Russell Lowell, 23 Sept., 1855, in Milton Hindus (ed.), *Walt Whitman: The Critical Heritage* (London, 1971), p. 30.
17. Joaquin Miller, 'Westward Ho!', lines 1–5.
18. On the 'spirit of the time' and the 'spirit of the nation' see J. C. Herder, *Outlines of a Philosophy* translated by T. Churchill (London, 1800).
19. Marcus Cunliffe, *The Nation Takes Shape 1789–1837* (Chicago, 1959), p. 135. See also, Percy Bysshe Shelley, 'To a Skylark', lines 86–7.
20. John Adams, cited in B. T. Spencer, *The Quest for Nationality* (Syracuse. N.Y., 1953), p. 61.

21. Tocqueville, *De la Democratie en Amérique*, II, Ch. 13. See also, Walt Whitman, 'Song of Myself', section 33.
22. Tocqueville, *De la Democratie en Amérique*, II, Ch. 17.
23. Benjamin Lee Whorf, *Language, Thought, and Reality: Selected Writings of Benjamin Lee Whorf* edited by John B. Carroll (Cambridge, Mass., 1950), p. 213.
24. Ezra Pound, 'A Pact', lines 6–9.
25. Whitman, 'Song of Myself', section 33. See also, section 24.
26. Walt Whitman, 'Crossing Brooklyn Ferry', section 7.
27. Whitman, 'Song of Myself', section 52.
28. Charles Olson, 'The Kingfishers', section I.
29. Victor Shklovsky, 'Art as Device' in *On the Theory of Prose* (Moscow-Lenigrad, 1925), p. 12. I am indebted to Dr. Leon Burnett of the Department of Literature, University of Essex, for providing me with a literal translation and advice.
30. Whitman, 'Song of Myself', section 2. See also, Emerson, 'The Poet'; Tony Tanner, *The Reign of Wonder: Naivety and Reality in American Literature* (Cambridge, 1965), pp. 17, 30–1.
31. Edgar Allan Poe, 'Al Aaraaf', lines 1–2, 5–15.
32. Emily Dickinson, 'What mystery pervades a well!', lines 13–20. See also, 'Title Divine – is Mine!'.
33. Emily Dickinson, 'I felt a Funeral in my Brain' lines 17–20. See also, 'I dwell in Possibility', 'I heard a Fly buzz – when I died –'.
34. Walt Whitman, 'Poets to Come', lines 1, 2–9.
35. Henry Adams, *The Education of Henry Adams* (1918), Ch. 22. See also, Carl Sandburg, 'Chicago', line 1.
36. Adams, *Education*, Ch. 31. See also, Ch. 25.
37. Thomas Jefferson, *Notes on the State of Virginia* (1784), query 19.
38. Sigmund Freud, *The Psychopathology of Everyday Life*, in *The Standard Edition of the Complete Psychological Works of Sigmund Freud* edited by James Strachey (London, 1957–74), v, pp. 253–54. See also, D. H. Lawrence, letter to Edward Garnett, 5 June, 1914, in *Selected Literary Criticism* edited by Anthony Beal (London, 1955), p. 18.
39. Lionel Trilling, 'Freud and Literature', in *The Liberal Imagination* (New York, 1950), p. 32. See also, Kenneth Burke, 'Freud – and the Analysis of Poetry', reprinted in R. Ruitenbeck (ed.), *Psychoanalysis and Literature* (New York, 1964), p. 121.
40. Edward Sapir, *Selected Writings in Language, Culture and Personality* edited by David G. Mandelbaum (Berkeley, Calif., 1949), p. 162. See also, Ferdinand de Saussure, *Cours de linguistique générale* edited by Charles Dally, Albert Sechehaye with Albert Reidlinger (1915) translated by Wade Baskin as *Course in General Linguistics* (New York, 1959).
41. Roman Jakobson, cited in Victor Erlich, *Russian Formalism: History – Doctrine* (1955; The Hague, 1965 edition), p. 183. See also, Jan Mukarovsky, 'Standard language and poetic language', in *A Prague School Reader on Aesthetics, Literary*

Structure and Style selected and translated by Paul L. Garvin (Washington D.C., 1964), pp. 43–4; Wallace Stevens, 'The Man with the Blue Guitar', section 22, lines 1–3.

42. Ludwig Wittgenstein, *Tractatus Logico-Philosophicus* translated by D. F. Pears and B. F. McGuiness (London, 1961).

43. Vladimir Nabokov, *Pale Fire* (London, 1962), p. 260.

44. Thoreau, *Walden*, Ch. 18. See also. William Carlos Williams, 'A Poem for Norman MacLeod', lines 1–2.

45. William Carlos Williams, *The Autobiography of William Carlos Williams* (1951; London, 1968 edition), p. 141.

46. Ezra Pound, 'The White Stag', lines 6–7. See, Mitzi Berger Hanovitch (ed.), *The 'Hound and Horn' Letters* (Athens, Ga., 1982), p. 1.

47. Gertrude Stein, *Paris, France* (London, 1940) p. 20. See also, Frederick J. Hoffman, *The Twenties: American Writing in the Postwar Decade* (New York, 1949), Ch. 1.

48. Frederick J. Hoffman, Charles Allen, and Carolyn F, Ulrich, *The Little Magazine: A History and a Bibliography* (Princeton, N.J., 1947), p. 1.

49. Cited in Richard McLanathan, *The American Tradition in the Arts* (New York, 1968), p. 400. See also, p. 402–6.

50. Williams, *Autobiography*, p. 135.

51. Ibid., p. 138.

52. Ezra Pound, 'The Book of the Month', *Poetry Review*, 1 (March 1912), 133. See also 'Vorticism' (Sept. 1914), reprinted in *Gaudier – Brzeska: A Memoir* (1916; New York 1970 edition), pp. 89, 90, 92; *Selected Prose 1909–1965* edited by William Cookson (London, 1978), p. 402.

Chapter 2
The Modernist Experiment: Imagism, Objectivism and some Major Innovators

Imagism: the social and cultural situation

By the second decade of the twentieth century, the United States had become the most powerful industrialised nation in the world, outstripping Britain and Germany in terms of industrial production. Accompanying this growth of industry, there was a rapid expansion of urban centres. The ten largest cities in the United States in 1910 – New York, Chicago, Philadelphia, St. Louis, Boston, Cleveland, Baltimore, Pittsburgh, Detroit, and Buffalo – had experienced an almost three-fold increase in population in the previous thirty years; while, over the same period, new cities like Los Angeles, Minneapolis, and Seattle had sprung into existence. Perhaps the main agencies for disseminating urban life-styles, however, were the smaller cities: in the last decade of the nineteenth century and the first one or two of the twentieth, thousands of quiet little townships with their few services for the surrounding farming population were transformed into small urban centres, each with its own paved streets, bank, cinema, department store, hospital, shops, factories, and warehouses. There was a radical alteration in the material landscape, as more and more people crowded into the towns: the national census indicated that by 1920 the urban population exceeded the rural population – and it is quite likely that this change of balance had in fact occurred five or six years earlier. America was no longer a nation of happy farmers, even if it ever had been; and, regardless of where they lived, Americans found themselves a part of the emergent technological culture. The telephone ceased to be a curiosity and became commonplace: by 1915, the ratio of telephones to population was one to ten. And the radio, along with other agencies of mass communication, began imposing its own imagery of the new normalcy on the nation at large: in 1926 the National Broadcasting Company, and the following year the Columbia Broadcasting Service, confirmed this trend, when they hooked together hundreds of local radio stations in two giant national networks. So, along with the changes in the material landscape came changes in the non-material, systems of belief and behaviour; along with alterations in the national economy came alterations in the national consciousness.

Perhaps nothing symbolises this change in the direction of American energy so clearly and vividly as the automobile. In 1925, a woman in Muncie, Indiana, remembered that, as she put it:

> In the nineties we were all much more together. People brought chairs and cushions out of the house and sat on the lawn evenings. We rolled out a strip of carpet and put cushions on the porch steps to take care of the unlimited overflow of neighbours that dropped by. We'd sit out so all evening.[1]

The citizens of Muncie were different now, she lamented: assaulted by advertising urging them to buy cars and 'Increase Your Weekend Touring Radius'. 'A man who works six days a week', a banker was quoted as saying in one such advertisement, 'and spends the seventh on his own doorstep certainly will not pick up the extra dimes on the great thoroughfare of life'. Mobility had completely supplanted stability. In 1891, on July 4th, a Muncie merchant had noted in his diary that the town was 'full of people' celebrating Independence Day: by contrast, some twenty-nine years later, two observers found the streets deserted – all the inhabitants had apparently left town for the day and taken to the road. Some of those in authority might occasionally denounce the Model-T Ford, as one judge memorably did, by describing it as 'a house of prostitution on wheels', but 1,000,000 models of the 'Tin Lizzie' were sold each year, and there were 26,500,000 vehicles on the road by 1929. Others might lament, as that Muncie woman did, the passing of the old folkways. But those ways were irrecoverable now: cars, along with radios, vacuum cleaners, record players and other consumer goods, had become the foundation stones of a new economy – and the precipitants of a new consciousness. Listening to network radio shows, seduced by the imagery of advertising and the cinema, encouraged to ride out of familiar, stable locations in search of the unfamiliar or for the sheer experience of movement, Americans became part of a distinctively modern, discontinuous and anonymous culture: a culture that was, and is, not specifically tied down to any individual locality, state, or region – or, indeed, to any particular nation.

The changes in culture and consciousness sketched out here were confirmed by the experience of the First World War. The United States emerged from involvement in global conflict with an altered economic relationship with the rest of the world: from a debtor nation it had been transformed into a creditor nation, with loans to Europe worth $13,000,000,000. For a while, under the leadership of Woodrow

Wilson, it tried to assume the status of a moral and cultural creditor as well: in 1918, while war was still being waged, Wilson formulated his Fourteen Points, which outlined the need for a peaceful world and provided a 'guarantee' of continued peace through a 'general assembly of nations'. It was this League of Nations that was rejected by Congress in 1919, after which American foreign policy seemed to move decisively towards isolationism. But while it is true that the United States did tend to withdraw from active political involvement in world affairs – at least, involvement to the extent that Wilson had hoped for – it was too deeply implicated now, economically and culturally, in what happened outside its borders, and particularly in Europe, ever to recapture the isolation, the sheer sense of apart-ness, that it had experienced in the previous century. Mass immigration from Europe, the memories of servicemen returning from war, a mass communication system and a system of culture that both ultimately denied national boundaries: all these, among other things, ensured that America was involved with Europe regardless of whether or not its political leaders wanted it to be.

The most immediate and obvious sign of this withering away of cultural boundaries between the United States and Europe was the expatriate movement. After the First World War was over, hundreds of writers or would-be writers invaded Europe in a literary migration that has had no equal either before or since. A favourable rate of exchange was perhaps the immediate precipitant; other motivating factors included a possible desire to escape from provincialism and puritanism and as one expatriate, Gertrude Stein, put it, to be 'all alone with English and myself'.[2] But whatever the reason, these writers soon found themselves involved with other, European novelists and poets who shared their hunger for new modes of thought and expression and absorbed into literary and artistic movements that ignored the existence of national boundaries. The revolt against earlier norms of belief and behaviour was not, people like Ernest Hemingway and Hart Crane discovered, a purely American prerogative; the anxious need to have the emergent culture, and the new sensations it engendered, adequately explained, was not the monopoly of either side of the Atlantic. So, while remaining American poets, they began to participate in the international experiments of Symbolism, Surrealism, and Dadaism; the resources of language they carried with them from the New World were added to, and enriched, by their encounter with the Old. Whether they ventured to Europe only for a while, as, say, Hart Crane, e.e. cummings, or William Carlos Williams did; whether they stayed away most of their lives, like T.S. Eliot and Ezra Pound; or whether, for that matter, their venturings abroad were imaginative and intellectual rather than literal, in the manner of Marianne Moore or Wallace Stevens: whatever the case, these writers were affected, however circuitously, by the alterations of vision and vocabulary that characterised Europe as well as the United States – and they became the enthusiastic disciples, many of them, of literary movements that denied the traditional categories of history and geography. These movements that answered to the newer, mobile and discontinuous culture were invariably different, ranging in attitude from the hostile to the hospitable: but easily the most important and influential, as far as poetry is concerned, was that movement known as Imagism.

The significance of imagism

'The *point de repère* usually and conveniently taken as the starting-point of modern poetry', declared T.S. Eliot, 'is the group denominated 'imagists' in London about 1910'.[3] Actually, the beginnings of the Imagist movement can be traced to an earlier date than this, and to the feeling common among young writers in the first few years of the twentieth century that poets were for the most part playing for safety and sentimentality. 'The common verse . . . from 1890', remarked Ezra Pound with characteristic brusqueness, 'was a horrible agglomerate compost, not minted, most of it not even baked, all legato, a doughy mess of third-hand Keats, Wordsworth, heaven knows what, fourth-hand Elizabethan sonority blunted, half-melted, lumpy'. In reaction against all this, a group began to gather around T.E. Hulme and F.S. Flint in London dedicated, among other things, to the aim of reproducing 'the peculiar quality of feeling which is induced by the flat spaces and wide horizons of the virgin-prairie' – and to the belief that 'poetic ideas are best expressed by the rendering of concrete objects'. They were joined, in April 1909, by the young expatriate Pound whose own ideas about poetry had been outlined in a letter to William Carlos Williams approximately six months earlier:

1. To paint the thing as I see it.
2. Beauty.
3. Freedom from didacticism.
4. It is only good manners if you repeat a few other men to at least do it better or more briefly.[4]

Some while after this, in 1911, Pound renewed acquaintances with Hilda Doolittle, newly arrived from the United States and already calling herself H.D. By now, Pound was looking around for good poetry to send to Harriet Monroe in Chicago and found it both in the work of H. D. and in that of a young British writer, Richard

Aldington. He was in the habit of meeting H.D. and Aldington in a tea shop in Kensington, to discuss their verse with them; and it was at one such meeting in 1912 that he informed them, apparently to their surprise, that they were Imagistes. H.D., Pound insisted, was even to sign herself 'H.D. Imagiste', and in writing to Harriet Monroe about her he forced the point home. 'I've had luck again', Pound exulted:

> and am sending you some *modern* stuff by an American. I say modern, for it is in the laconic speech of the Imagistes, even if the subject is classic. This is the sort of American stuff that I can show here and in Paris without its being ridiculed. Objective – no slither; direct – no excessive use of adjectives, no metaphors that won't permit examination. It's straight talk, straight as the Greek![5]

Pound did not explain it, but evidently the French version of the word was chosen to suggest a connection with modern French poetry. Whatever the reason, he and his colleagues eventually thought better of it and reverted to the English word: the new group of poets were to be called Imagists.

The obvious step after this announcement of a phenomenon called Imagism was the publication of an anthology, and in 1914 that anthology duly appeared. It included in its pages the work of William Carlos Williams, Amy Lowell, F.S. Flint and Ford Madox Ford (or Ford Madox Hueffer as he then called himself), but H.D. and Aldington were the centre-pieces. Pound later declared, in fact, that the whole business of Imagism and the Imagist anthology 'was invented to launch H.D. and Aldington before either had enough stuff for a volume'. This seems, at most, only partially true: Pound's interest in the *ideas* behind Imagism antedated and clearly survived his enthusiastic pioneering on behalf of those two young poets. As far as the Imagist movement itself was concerned, however, Pound soon lost interest. The 1914 anthology was poorly received, and Pound moved on to Vorticism, a stricter form of Imagism that emphasised the dynamic nature of the image. 'The image is not an idea', he declared while campaigning on behalf of Vorticism:

> It is a radiant node or cluster; it is what I can, and must perforce, call a VORTEX, from which, and through which, and into which ideas are constantly rushing.[6]

With Pound abandoning Imagism, the way was left clear for the American writer and heiress Amy Lowell to assume control of the movement. Under her auspices, two more anthologies were published in 1916 and 1917. 'There will be no more volumes of *Some Imagist Poets*', Lowell announced shortly after the 1917 book appeared, 'The collection has done its work. These three little books are the germ, the nucleus, of the school: its spreading out, its amplifications, must be sought in the unpublished work of the individual members of the group'. And as far as Pound was concerned, the announcement came none too soon. For him, Imagism had already become 'Amy-gisme', an excuse for brief, mediocre descriptive pieces, written in free verse and modulating into pleasant fancy: something like Amy Lowell's own poem, 'Meeting-House Hill'.

The further history of Imagism need not detain us, however. As even Amy Lowell sensed, and Pound illustrated, what matters about Imagism is not so much the movement itself as the beliefs it articulated. It provided a focus: not, like *Poetry*, a practical focus but an ideological one. It served to crystallise certain tendencies, certain notions about the nature of poetic experiment, which had been developing in a rather piecemeal fashion over the previous decade – to organise, to define, and so to promote them. The nature of these tendencies can be glimpsed in two essays about Imagism published in *Poetry* in 1913, one written by Pound and the other by F.S. Flint. Pound's essay begins with this:

> An Image is that which presents an intellectual and
> emotional complex in an instant of time . . .
> It is the presentation of such a 'complex' instantaneously
> which gives that sense of sudden liberation; that sense of
> freedom from time limits and space limits; that sense of
> sudden growth, which we experience in the presence of
> the greatest works of art.
> It is better to produce one Image in a lifetime than to
> produce voluminous works.[7]

Flint's essay, in turn, announces three 'rules' that all Imagists, and by implication all good poets, were to follow:

1. Direct treatment of the 'thing' whether subjective or objective.
2. To use absolutely no word that did (*sic*) not contribute to the presentation.
3. As regarding rhythm: to compose in sequence of the musical phrase not in sequence of the metronome.[8]

'The point of Imagisme', Pound wrote in 1914, 'is that it does not use images as ornaments. The image itself is the speech. The image is the word beyond formulated language'.[9] This statement, corresponding to his own opening remarks in the *Poetry* essay and to the first of Flint's 'rules', suggests the primary Imagist objective: to avoid rhetoric and moralising, to stick closely to the object or experience being described and hardly ever, if at all, to move from this to *explicit* generalisation. Poetry, the feeling was, had for too long relied upon expansive verbal gestures, the ethereal and the abstract. It had to be brought back to fine particulars. The poet might very well (as the philosopher of the Imagist movement, T.E. Hulme put it) 'glide through an abstract process', but he had to make it seem inevitable, a natural result of his meditation on particulars; and, in any event, it would be far better if he left it to the reader to intuit those abstractions, to gather up what is commonly called the 'meaning' of the poem, from the resonance, the reverberations of the image. Several things could be said about this primary tenet of Imagism. In the first place, it reveals the links between Romanticism, Symbolism, and Imagism. Whatever the differences between these movements (and there are, of course, many) all three had this in common: a belief in the primacy of a condensed, intense, and above all intuitive form of communication, in imaginative rather than rational discourse. In the second, it exposes some of the specifically American roots of Imagist thinking: for this observation of the concrete that Pound and Flint talk about, that allows the observer to catch the wonder, the aura that surrounds simple, particular things is a stance towards reality that characterises many earlier American writers – people like Emerson, say, or Whitman. And, in the third place, the *representative* nature of Imagism is clear when we note how omnipresent this belief in the concrete is in twentieth-century American poetry. There are the obvious examples like Robert Frost, whose own brand of subtle, playful pragmatism is expressed in lines like, 'The fact is the sweetest dream that labour knows',[10] or William Carlos Williams who, in one of his most famous and repeated statements, insisted that there should be 'No ideas but in things.'[11] But – and this is the crucial point – we need not necessarily confine ourselves to such immediate and self-evident cases. Even Hart Crane, who is surely one of the most unworldly and mystical of modern American writers, wanted to anchor his mysticism in mundane experience. His favourite metaphor for the speculative flight was, in fact, the bridge: something that crosses another element (water), reaches towards heaven, yet keeps both feet firmly planted on earth. He would never have dreamed of simply rejecting the ordinary as earlier followers of the Ideal had done; and the fact that he would not have done so testifies to the strength, the almost incalculable impact of an idea to which Pound, Flint, and their companions were among the first (in this century at least) to give memorable expression.

'Use no superfluous word', insisted Pound in his 1913 *Poetry* essay, 'no adjective, which does not reveal something'. This, the second of Flint's 'rules', was perhaps what Amy Lowell had in mind when she said that the Imagist principles 'are not new; they have fallen into desuetude. They are the essentials of all great poetry'. Be that as it may, this 'ridding the field of verbiage' became one of the central activities in modern American poetry. 'Cut and cut again whatever you write', William Carlos Williams advised Denise Levertov ' – while you leave by your art no trace of your cutting – and the final utterance will remain packed with what you have to say'. 'The test of the artist', he added later, 'is to be able to revise without showing a seam . . . It is quite often no more than knowing what to *cut*'.[12] Williams, as we shall see, demonstrated an almost ferocious enthusiasm in following such advice; and so too did poets as otherwise different, from Williams and each other, as Carl Sandburg and Wallace Stevens. Superficially, at least, the diction of Sandburg or of Stevens bears little resemblance to that of Williams; yet fundamentally their concern – or, one might say, their obsession – is the same. Sandburg's robust colloquialism and Stevens's precious, meticulous language, both issue out of a preoccupation with functional speech: which is to say, a speech that achieves a maximum effect with the minimum possible resources. 'Precision, economy of statement, logic employed to means that are disinterested, drawing and identifying . . . liberate the imagination',[13] said Marianne Moore. Her statement of faith was echoed by scores of other American poets, many of whom had no direct connection with Imagism – and, in fact, would have stoutly resisted the suggestion that they had any sympathy with its principles.

And then there is the third 'rule' promulgated by Flint and expanded upon by Pound in this fashion:

> Don't chop your stuff into separate *iambs*. Don't make each line stop dead at the end, and then begin every next line with a heave. Let the beginning of the next line catch the rise of the rhythm wave, unless you want a definite longish pause.
> In short, behave as a musician, a good musician, when dealing with the phase of your art which has exact parallels in music. The same laws govern, and you are bound by no others.[14]

'Rhythm MUST have meaning', Pound wrote to Harriet Monroe. 'It can't be merely a careless dash off, with no grip and no real hold to the words and sense, a tumty tum tumty tum tum ta'. The *vers libre* of the Imagists was one aspect of their work to which contemporary critics took particular exception. John Livingstone Lowes, for example, claimed to see no difference between Amy Lowell's free verse and George Meredith's prose: to which Lowell herself replied, '. . . there is no difference . . . Whether a thing is written as prose or verse is immaterial'. Pound would not have put things as categorically as Lowell. As he saw it, poetry should be at least '*as well written as prose*' but there *was* a difference: because in poetry, he believed, words are infused with something more than their prose meaning – with a musical quality that gives them a further dimension, an additional substance and thrust. 'To break the iamb, that was the first heave', as he put it in the *Cantos*: the poet should first shake off the tyranny of predetermined verse forms. Having done this, however, his aim should not be mere looseness or licence, the 'fluid, fruity, facile stuff' of an Amy Lowell, but movements and melodies intrinsic to the occasion: tough, sinuous, sharply etched rhythms that described the contours of an individual experience – a hidden but nevertheless clearly audible music that captured the pace, poise, and tone of the personal voice. In this sense, Imagism was building on the innovations, not only of an obvious *vers libriste* like Walt Whitman, but of idiosyncratic rhythmists like Poe and Dickinson. And to this extent, the Imagist belief in a flexible verse form (which was in turn the symptom of a broader commitment to an open, unpremeditated structure) was to find expression, both in the language experiments of e.e. cummings, Theodore Roethke, and Marianne Moore, and in the less extreme but no less original, musical shapes of John Crowe Ransom, Robinson Jeffers, and Hart Crane.

From Imagism to Objectivism or Dream: H. D., Zukofsky, Oppen, Reznikoff, Niedecker, Fletcher, Aiken

Among the poems included in the 1915 Imagist anthology was 'Oread' by H.D. Cited by Pound as the supreme example of an Imagist poem, it is besides a perfect illustration of what Richard Aldington referred to as the 'accurate mystery'[15] of H.D.'s work. For both these reasons (and because it is, in any case, characteristically terse), it is well worth quoting in its entirety:

Whirl up, sea –
Whirl your pointed pines,

Splash your great pines
On our rocks,
Hurl your green pine over us,
Cover us with your pools of fir.

Perhaps the first thing that strikes a reader about a poem like this is the absence of certain familiar elements. There are no similes, no symbols, no generalised reflections or didacticism, no rhymes, no regular metre, no narrative. One might well ask what there is, then; and the answer would be a great deal. There is a pellucid clarity of diction, and a rhythm that is organic, intrinsic to the mood of the poem; there is a vivid economy of language, in which each word seems to have been carefully chiselled out of other contexts, and there is a subtle technique of intensification by repetition – no phrase is remarkable in itself, perhaps, but there is a sense of rapt incantation, an enthralled dwelling on particular cadences that gives a hermetic quality, a prophetic power, to the whole. It is the entire poem that is experienced, not a striking line, a felicitous comparison, or an ingenious rhyme; the poem has become the unit of meaning and not the word, so each single word can remain stark, simple, and unpretentious. In 'Oread', the image that constitutes the poem becomes not merely a medium for describing a sensation but the sensation itself. The sea *is* the pinewood, the pinewood *is* the sea, the wind surrounds and inhabits both; and the Greek mountain-nymph of the title comprehends and becomes identified with all three elements. There is a dynamic and unified complex, an ecstatic fusion of natural and human energies; and the image represents the point of fusion, 'the precise instant' (to quote that remark of Pound's again) 'when a thing outward and objective transforms itself, or darts into a thing inward and subjective'.

'Oread' is typical of H.D.'s work in many ways. 'I would be lonely', she once admitted, while living at the heart of literary London, 'but for the intensity of my . . . inner life'.[16] And this became the subject of her work, from the early Imagist verse to the later, more oracular poems: the secret existence that cast her, in the midst of company, into permanent but willing exile, the ecstatic sense of inhabiting a borderline between land and ocean, outer world and inner, time and eternity. The earlier work (of which, of course, 'Oread' is an example) is what she is, perhaps, most well known for. Here, greatly influenced by classical Greek poetry, H.D. speaks in a taut and suggestive manner, omitting everything that is inessential, structurally or emotionally unimportant. But the later poems, although less well known, are just as notable; since they represent a far more open, and frequently moving, attempt to discover what H.D. called 'the finite definition / of the infinite'. In making this attempt, she drew on Greek and Egyptian mythology, her own Moravian heritage, astrology, psychoanalysis, and numerology, and then fashioned out of those diverse sources a poetry that is at once crystalline and prophetic: a tough, muscular and yet mystical verse to which she gave the title 'spiritual realism'.[17]

Some critics have chosen to dwell on the differences in tone and idiom between this later writing and the earlier; however, the continuities are far more important. All through her life, she retained an intense belief in the religious possibilities of art – or, to be more exact, in the mystical nature of the creative process, the act of turning experience into words. 'Writing . . . trains one to a sort of yogi or majic (*sic*) power', she insisted, 'it is a sort of contemplation, it is living on another plane'. In her eyes, poetry tended to become an equivalent of prayer. It was a way of communicating with another world, of using the idiom of what she termed once 'passionate grave thought' to enter into a higher level of consciousness. Her great war trilogy makes this especially clear. Written in London during the Second World War the three books that comprise the trilogy – *The Walls Do Not Fall, Tribute to the Angels*, and *The Flowering of the Rod* – represent a search for 'ancient wisdom', the still, generative centre at the heart of the contemporary turbulence. '*We are voyagers*', she declares:

discoverers
of the not-known
the unrecorded;
we have no map;
possibly we will reach heaven,
haven.[18]

Firm in the belief that 'every concrete object / has abstract value', she attempts to fathom the mystery of personality, to re-create her own identity – in a sense, to write herself by reinventing her life in the process of remembering and rehearsing it. The activity hauntingly recalls Whitman's in 'Song of Myself' as, indeed, does H.D.'s firm denial of egocentricity: 'my mind (yours)', she insists, '/your way of thought (mine)'. Each individual imagination has its 'intricate map', we are told, but each map charts the same 'eternal realities'; as in all great American epics, to sing and celebrate oneself is also to sing and celebrate others.

H.D.'s trilogy is an American epic, then, but it is also an Imagist epic: it does not, even in its form, represent a departure from her poetic beginnings. The reason is simple. Like Whitman, H.D. dispenses with narrative; far more than Whitman, however, she depends on what

Pound called the ideogrammic method – which involves, essentially, a rapid association of images. Images are, in H.D.'s own words, 'superimposed on one another like a stack of photographic negatives': one image or perception leads into another and the reader's imagination is actively engaged, making the connections, discovering the point of intersection. Instead of a story, in which events occur in time, or a process of logical argument, there is a juxtaposing or overlaying of different images and impressions; and their inter-action, the energy that passes between them, constitutes the 'argument' of the poem. In her trilogy, H.D. characteristically uses an image to describe this Imagistic technique – of the many colours which, at their point of intersecting, become one colour:

> And the point in the spectrum
> where all lights become one,
> is white and white is not no-colour
> as we were told as children
> but all-colour;
> where the flames mingle
> and the wings meet, when we gain
> the arc of perfection,
> we are satisfied, we are happy,
> we begin again; [19]

In this sense, Robert Duncan is entirely right to suggest that H.D.'s trilogy stands, along with Pound's *Cantos* and William Carlos Williams's long poem *Paterson*, as 'a major work of the Imagist genius in full'.

As H.D.'s work suggests, Imagism – or, to be more exact, the impulses that brought Imagism into existence – could lead off in a number of different directions. One of these directions was Objectivism, associated in particular with William Carlos Williams, George Oppen, Louis Zukofsky, and Charles Reznikoff. In February, 1931, *Poetry* brought out a special Objectivist issue edited by Zukofsky, who specified as required reading Pound's *xxx Cantos*, Williams's *Spring and All*, Eliot's *The Waste Land* and Marina, e.e. cumming's *Is 5*, Marianne Moore's *Observations* and Wallace Stevens's *Harmonium*. A press was founded, financed by George Oppen, and in 1932 under the name of 'To Publishers' it brought out *An 'Objectivists' Anthology*. Edited by Zukofsky, it included work by Williams, Oppen, Reznikoff, Carl Rakosi and Kenneth Rexroth. Pound was represented by his 'Yittischer Charleston' and Eliot by 'Marina'. Shortly after this, 'To Publishers' became the Objectivist Press, under the general editorship of Zukofsky and Williams. Recollecting this period, what Williams chose to emphasise were the differences, as he perceived them, between Objectivism and Imagism. 'We had had Imagism', he said

> which ran quickly out. That, though it had been useful in ridding the field of verbiage, had no formal necessity implicit in it. It had already dribbled off into so called 'free verse' which, as we saw, was a misnomer. There is no such thing as free verse! Verse is a measure of some sort . . . But, we argued, the poem, like every other form of art, is an object, an object that in itself formally presents its case and its meaning by the very form it assumes. Therefore, being an object, it should be so treated and controlled – but not as in the past. For past objects have about them past necessities – like the sonnet – which have conditioned them and from which, as a form itself, they cannot be freed. The poem being an object (like a symphony or a cubist painting) it must be the purpose of the poet to make of his words a new form: to invent, that is, an object consonant with his day. This is what we wished to imply by Objectivism, an antidote, in a sense, to the bare image haphazardly presented in loose verse.[20]

Persuasive as Williams's account may sound, however, it does not take much investigation to see that the gap between Imagism and Objectivism was not nearly as wide as he suggests. Of course, there were differences: a greater emphasis on the formal structure of the poem, its physical contours, and a more intense interest in its musical properties, the aural dimension as compared with the visual. 'In contemporary writing', Zukofsky wrote in 1931, 'the poems of Ezra Pound alone possess objectivication to a most constant degree; his objects are musical shapes';[21] and it is clear that for him, as for the other Objectivists, those words, 'objects', 'musical', and 'shapes' were invested with far more significance than they generally were for the Imagist group. Having said that, though, it has to be added that, just like the Objectivists, the Imagists had been concerned with precision, exactitude, with rendered experience rather than statement, and that the best of them at least believed in organic form – not the kind of flabby 'free verse' that Williams talks about here, but rhythms and cadences that are the necessary product of a particular moment and voice. In effect, it seems fairly obvious that Objectivism grew dialectically out of Imagism – not in opposition to it but in fruitful tension with it – and that what Williams and his fellow Objectivists were most at odds with was, as this passage suggests, not so much Imagism as 'Amy-gism'.

The poet associated with Objectivism in whom the concern with music, sound, is at its strongest is Louis Zukofsky. 'The order of all poetry', he insisted, 'is to approach a state of music wherein the ideas present themselves sensuously and intelligently and are of no predatory intention'. For him, and in his work, meaning is subordinated to sound. In his literary essays, for instance, he has spoken of his own poetry as a 'process of active literary omission,' involving a conscious rejection of crude metaphor and symbolism and an exploitation of typography in order to demonstrate 'how the voice should sound'. The individual word becomes an object, its sound and look more important than its meaning, and the poem becomes a score: a score investigating the possibility that the order and movement of sound in a poem might itself create a flux and reflux of emotions underlying the literal significance of the words. At its most extreme, Zukofsky's commitment to the physical shape and the aural dimension leads him to declare that:

> it is possible in imagination to divorce speech of all its graphic elements, to let it become a movement of sounds. It is this musical horizon of poetry . . . that permits anybody who does not know Greek to listen and get something out of Homer: to 'tune in' to the human tradition, to its voice which has developed among the sounds of natural things, and thus escape the confines of time and place, as we hardly ever escape them in studying Homer's grammar. In this sense, poetry is international.[22]

However, Zukofsky admits, 'poems perhaps never reach' this 'musical horizon'. Like the actual, geographical horizon it may be something that of its very nature remains a goal, a line receding even as the poet-voyager pursues it.

All of this may make Zukofsky's work seem intolerably abstract. In fact, the opposite is true. A poem like 'Ferry', for instance, uses a vivid verbal texture to make the reader share the experience, feel the cold night, the water, the fog, the silence punctuated by the sound of the siren:

> Gleams, a green lamp
> In the fog:
> Murmur, in almost
> A dialogue
>
> Siren and signal
> Siren to signal

Parts the shore from the fog,
Rise there, tower on tower,
Signs of stray light
And of power.

Siren to signal
Siren to signal.

Hour-gongs and the green
Of the lamp

Plash. Night. Plash. Sky[23]

Other poems, such as 'During the Passaic Strike of 1926', can convey fierce political passion through the use of hissing sibilants and harsh gutturals, and others, like 'To my baby Paul' employ gentle labials and soft consonants melting into one another to suggest delicate but deep personal emotions. Many use typography as well as verbal pattern to re-create a particular moment: in 'Ferry', for instance, Zukofsky deploys the blank spaces between each verse paragraph to imitate, or suggest, the foggy emptiness within which the lights and sounds of the ferry are forced to operate – and, perhaps, the vacuum that we must all try to negotiate with our signs and signals.[24]

Nor was Zukofsky just a composer of vignettes. In 1927, he began writing a long poem entitled *'A'*. *'A' 1–12* was published in 1959, *'A' 13–21* in 1969, and *'A' 22 & 23* in 1977, shortly before his death. Zukofsky described the poem as an autobiography. 'The words are my life', he explained:

> The form of the poem is organic – that is, involved in history and a life that has found by contrast to history something like perfection in the music of J. S. Bach . . . Or to put it in other words, the poet's form is never an imposition of history but the desirability of projecting some order out of history as it is felt and conceived.[25]

The poem opens, in fact, with memories of a performance of Bach's St. Matthew Passion; and then, with characteristic frugality of speech, precision of cadence, and warmth of feeling, Zukofsky considers the injustices and inequalities of contemporary America, personal memories and affections, and aesthetic experience. Bach jostles alongside Henry Ford; the Chinese and Chinese poetry are celebrated for their clarity and brevity of utterance; and, despite the size of the work, there is the feeling that each word has been chosen, and each line chiselled with scrupulous care. Zukofsky's aim, essentially, is to evolve something shapely, rhythmic, and structured out of experience: something with its own intrinsic life, its own capacity for change and surprise.

One critic has called it a continuous day-book. Perhaps it would be more accurate to call it an Objectivist epic: which, like other great epics in the American tradition, was and is destined never to end.

A poet who was perhaps more aware of growing out of the Imagist movement, as well as the Objectivist, is George Oppen. 'What I felt I was doing was beginning from imagism as a position of honesty', he said once, 'The first question at that time in poetry was simply the question of honesty, of sincerity'.[26] 'At that time' was the time of writing the poems in his first book, *Discrete Series*, which was published in 1934. These early poems are remarkable for their attention to the word as the primary unit of meaning and to the relationships between words and images and things. They slow down the mind, concentrating it on words and things one at a time and so quicken it, eventually, into a new sense of the relations between them. A poem like 'Bad Times' is exemplary, in this respect:

> Bad times:
> The cars pass
> By the elevated posts
> And the movie sign.
> A man sells post-cards.

Oppen's language is stark, stripped ('What I couldn't write I scratched out ' he said, 'I wrote what I could be sure of . . .'), but in its starkness it positively requires us to be alert. This is a *constructed* world, Oppen suggests, in which a word of great value ('elevated') has been so devalued as to be associated only with posts, and where 'cars pass' as if their mechanism had taken over the city completely. The only human activity involves dehumanisation: a man is reduced to a marketing activity, less important than a 'post' (the repetition of the word is intentional) or a machine.

In a very negative way, a poem like 'Bad Times' illustrates Oppen's sense that human beings at once encounter and structure their world. Another poem, clearly concerned with America, puts it even more succinctly:

> The edge of the ocean,
> The shore: here
> Somebody's lawn,
> By the water.

The non-human otherness of the 'ocean', with the shore as its 'edge' here leads us into the astonishing discovery of an attempt to domesticate and possess that otherness ('Somebody's lawn'): to settle the wilderness, to convert it to human need – which is, after all, the history of the New World. Oppen's stance is less critical in this poem than in 'Bad times' – he is, after all, concerned with what he sees as the definitively human activity – and in still other, sometimes more personal and sometimes more philosophical poems, his attitude comes close to being celebratory. 'Sara in her Father's Arms', for example, begins with a sense of wonder at the making of a human being ('Cell by cell the baby made herself, the cells / Made cells'); and then modulates into an attentive meditation on the making of a human order:

> the little seed eyes
> Moving, trying to see, smile for us
> To see, she will make a household
> To her need of rooms . . .
> . . . this seed will speak
> Max, words! . . .
> . . . What will she make of a world
> Do you suppose, Max, of which she is made.[27]

As these lines suggest, the act of making a human order depends on seeing and speech. The baby sees the world and in seeing it forms a relationship with otherness *and* becomes a separate, conscious self; she speaks the world and in speaking it places herself within it *and* apart from it, in her own structure, her own network of relationships – her own 'household'.

'Sara in her Father's Arms' is from *The Materials*, published in 1962, and it illustrates how Oppen gradually extended his 'position of honesty' from the instant of perception to sometimes complex processes of thought. The result is philosophical poetry that retains what Oppen himself has termed 'the imagist intensity of vision': that explores the sometimes problematical relationship between language, thought, and things. 'Psalm', for instance, presents us with an intensely realised vision of deer in a forest that nevertheless subtly reminds us of their otherness:

> Their eyes
> Effortless, the soft lips
> Nuzzle and the alien small teeth
> Tear at the grass.[28]

Nature is a stranger yet, here as it is in Dickinson; and this portrait of an 'alien small' world is juxtaposed with the words naming it:

The small nouns
Crying faith
In this in which the wild deer
Startle, and stare out.[29]

'This in which' the deer occur is at once 'the small beauty of the forest' and the poem made out of 'small nouns': two utterly separate objects that are, all the same, vitally attached. Oppen's allegiance is to them both, to the language human beings have made and the world they have not made but share with other creatures; and it is to the relationship between the two – the bridge built between world and language, earth and 'household', out of seeing and speaking.

Two other notable poets who illustrate the various directions in which the imagist intensity of vision could lead are Charles Reznikoff and Lorine Niedecker. In Reznikoff's case, a general indebtedness to Pound was combined with an almost uninterrupted residence in New York to produce what has been called 'urban imagism': a poetry that alerts us to the loneliness, the small ironies and amusements, and the numbness of the immigrant in the urban tenement. In the best of these earlier, shorter poems Reznikoff refuses to moralise, to withdraw from the experience in order to comment on it or 'place' it; the lives of the poor in the city possess an integrity that he chooses simply to respect and record – as this poem, entitled 'Scrubwoman', illustrates:

One shoulder lower,
with unsure steps like a bear erect
the smell of the wet black rags that she cleans
with about her.
Scratching with four stiff fingers her half-bald head,
smiling.

Not that these poems are without their personal or political dimension. A work like 'Depression', for instance, leaves us in no doubt of Reznikoff's sympathy for the victims of society, the dispossessed:

in the drizzle
four in a row
close to the curb
that passers-by might pass,
the squads stand
waiting for soup
a slice of bread
and shelter –
grimy clothes
their uniform:[30]

It is just that, here as elsewhere in Reznikoff's work – and, for that matter, in Williams's, Zukofsky's, and Oppen's – the social comment is all the more powerful for remaining implicit: the politics issues directly out of the urgency, the intensity with which the poet attends to the scene.

At some point in the 1950's, Reznikoff began to dedicate himself to a larger enterprise. He had been working for a publisher of law books between the Wars, 'reading cases', he wrote later, 'from every state and every year (since this country became a nation)'. Reading such material, he came to feel that out of it 'the century and a half during which the United States has been a nation could be written up': not, he explained, 'from the standpoint of the individual, as in diaries', nor 'from the angle of the unusual, as in newspapers' but rather 'from every standpoint – as many standpoints as were provided by the witnesses themselves'.[31] The result of these speculations was a projected four-volume history of the nation between 1885 and 1915, to be written in free verse, and consisting entirely of the testimony, the cases Reznikoff encountered in the law books. The first two volumes were published in 1965 and 1968; and a complete edition, including previously unpublished material, appeared in 1978–79. *Testimony*, as this epic history is called, has as its epigraph Ephesians IV. 31: 'Let all bitterness, and wrath, and anger, and clamour, and railing, be put away from you, will all malice'; and this registers the poet's stance towards his voluminous material. Reznikoff clearly chose the period 1885–1915 because he felt that a kind of social and psychic crisis occurred in the nation between those years: but he is careful not to allow this, or indeed any explicit judgement to intrude, to interfere with his simple recording of individual cases. Personal cases, examples of racial violence, accidents in factories, petty crimes and major incidents are all registered without comment in the characteristically American assumption that every life is worth remembering, the testimony of every person is worth attending to in and for its own sake. This, in fact, is another American epic that draws its energy from its omnivorousness: the poet's refusal to exclude anything from his unselective eye, his attitude of wonder.

Unlike Reznikoff, Lorine Niedecker was born and spent most of her life in rural surroundings, in the region of the lakes in Wisconsin; like him, however, the sense of place has clearly and indelibly imprinted itself on her poetry. Her work communicates the vastness of American geography, the simple fact of wide, open spaces and the feelings of loneliness and exile that fact can instil. Faced with that vastness, though, Niedecker herself looks back at it without flinching – with a steady, determined optimism issuing from the recognition that loneliness is not to be feared and is, in any case, never total: 'How impossible', she says in one poem, 'it is / to be alone.'[32] The familiar site of her work is a wide, watery terrain: 'Fish / fowl / flood / Water lily mud / My life', as she puts it in 'Paean to Place'. But it is a terrain that nevertheless allows for, even encourages, human intimacy, the pleasures and affections of family life, as the characteristically titled 'You are my friend' illustrates. The *human* context is warmly established in poems that reveal American speech, whittled down to its essentials:

> Remember my little granite pail?
> The handle of it was blue.
> Think what's got away in my life –
> Was enough to carry me thru.

And it is revealed, too, in poems that clearly define the continuity between the human and the natural:

> in the leaves and on water
> My mother and I
> born
> in swale and swamp and swarm
> to water[33]

A work like 'Lake Superior', for instance, which begins 'In every part of every living thing / is stuff that once was rock / In blood the minerals / of the rock', Niedecker draws a series of cryptic but powerful connections between human history, archaeology, and etymology, so as to suggest the continuities of existence. For her, the story of human beings, the story of their words, and the story of the rocks are all inextricably interwoven.

'Lake Superior' is unusual, however, in being a long poem. Most of her work is vividly, intensely brief: 'I learned / to sit at desk / and condense', she says in 'Poet's work'. And all her poems are pared down to their essentials, depending for their effect on the force of each word – on puns, pauses, calculated repetitions and delicate tonal melodies:

> There's a better shine
> on the pendulum
> than is on my hair
> and many times
> . . .
> I've seen it there.[34]

Comparisons could be made with the Japanese *haiku* (at which

Niedecker did, in fact, try her hand), with an earlier poet like Dickinson, or with the two poets she has acknowledged as influences, Williams and Zukofsky. In the end, though, she must be seen as her own person and poet. Such a poem as 'Paul', for example, could only have been written by her:

> Paul
>   when the leaves
>   fall
>
> from their stems
>   that lie thick
>   on the walk
> . . .
> playing
>   to leaves
>   when they leave
>
> the little
>   thin things
>   Paul[35]

The words here turn in a slow descent and, apart from the double meaning in 'leaves', they attain their effect by putting the sound of 'fall', its rhyme 'Paul' and isophone 'play' against opposite sounds like 'thick', 'thin', and 'thing'. The plangency, the recognition of inevitable loss, concerns equally the shedding of a tree and the corresponding human situation: but it is a plangency beautifully contained within a tiny structure, representing emotion stored and shaped a long time. 'What would they say', asks Niedecker of the people she once worked with, 'if they knew / I sit for two months on six lines / of poetry?' With luck, what they might have said was that the long process of meditation, revision, and compression was worthwhile, producing as it did work of undistractable clarity – and fidelity to what Niedecker herself termed 'My life / by water'.

If the work of Lorine Niedecker marks out one extreme towards which the impulses expressed in Imagism could move, that of John Gould Fletcher and Conrad Aiken marks out another. In his essay, *As For Imagisme*, Pound suggests that the image 'can be of two sorts':

> It can arise within the mind. It is then "subjective".
> External causes play upon the mind perhaps; if so, they
> are drawn into the mind, fused, transmitted, and emerge
> in an Image unlike themselves. Secondly, the Image can be
> "objective". Emotion seizing upon some external scene or

> action carries it in fact to the mind; and that vortex purges
> it of all save the essential or dominant or dramatic
> qualities, and it emerges like the external original.[36]

The distinction may seem a little artificial, perhaps, because in either case what Pound emphasises here, as elsewhere, is the reciprocity of the relationship between the external and the internal. Nonetheless, it does point to the fact that Pound and others were well aware of the connection between their own interest in the image and contemporary interest in the subconscious. Freud had described a process whereby a dream image was constellated by a large number of unconscious complexes: the complexes combined and interacted and, as a result, a single image emerged into consciousness. One function of the image, it was felt, might be to reverse this process: to plumb the depths and register the vagaries of the unconscious through the agency of figurative language. John Gould Fletcher clearly believed this. An associate of Pound and Amy Lowell, he used an impressionistic and often undisciplined free verse in his early years, blending intoxicating colours with a prodigality of imagery in an attempt to capture the wanderings of his sensibility. With Amy Lowell, he also invented 'polyphonic prose' which, according to Lowell herself, made use of 'the "voices" of poetry, namely metre, vers libre, assonance, alliteration, rhyme and return': in effect, it was an even more capacious medium than free verse designed, like the stream-of-consciousness fiction of the time, to accommodate all the haphazard movements of the subconscious. Fletcher subsequently turned from experimentalism to regionalism, and to more traditional forms, but even here there is a sense of the half-accomplished. As a poet, he is in fact more interesting for what he represents than what he achieved, since he went further than most in search of what H.D. once called 'the rare intangible thread . . . the dream parallel'.[37]

Conrad Aiken is a different matter. Influenced by the Imagists, and for a while a friend of Fletcher, Aiken was also deeply affected by a number of other, not always related figures, including Poe and Eliot. Above all, though, there was the example of Freud. Poetry, Aiken once declared, is 'the vanguard of man's consciousness' and, in his opinion, Freud had contributed more to the understanding of that consciousness, its workings and its vagaries, than anyone else in modern times. Not that Aiken was inclined to set Freud apart: as he saw it, 'Know thyself' had always been 'the theme' of all significant intellectual activity. 'Freud had merely picked up the magic words', he said 'where Socrates, the prototype of the highest man, had let them fall '. Freud had done something especially important for his contemporaries, however. He had opened up the road for 'the only religion that was any longer tenable or viable, a poetic comprehension of man's position in the universe, and of his potentialities . . . through self-knowledge and love'. He had made it possible to see that the final, and by definition unending, stage of human evolution was 'an ever more inclusive consciousness'. And he had offered people, not a philosophy of life, but a methodology – a way of coming to grips with:

> that perennially fascinating problem of personal identity which perplexes each of us all his life: the basic and possibly unanswerable question, *who and what am I*, how is it that I am I . . . and not someone else?[38]

Committing himself to this 'quest for the knowable', and bearing in mind the techniques and hypotheses of Freud, Jung, and Adler among others, Aiken then devised a poetic form that reflected his own deep love of music: in which lines, words, and images come together and separate with a gentle fluidity, like a stream following the poet's consciousness. Aiken had, he said, 'a strong bias towards an architectural structure analogous to that of music' and had from the first been seeking 'some way of getting contrapuntal effects in poetry – the effects of contrasting and conflicting tones and themes, a kind of underlying simultaneity in dissimilarity'. The *Preludes*, published in two books, represent a relatively early venture in this direction. 'Planned', Aiken tells us, 'to be an all-out effort at a probing of the self-in-relation-to-the-world' and written generally in pentameters, they are, by turns, opulently figurative, melodic, evocative, mistily vague, diffuse, and narcissistic. Ideas or themes are introduced, dropped, reintroduced and then developed in conjunction with other themes; images appear, wandering and elusive, and then just as elusively slip from our attention. 'Here are the bickerings of the inconsequential'. Aiken says at one point:

> The chatterings of the ridiculous, the iterations
> Of the meaningless. Memory, like a juggler,
> Tosses its coloured balls into the light, and again
> Receives them into darkness . . .[39]

'You are *you*?' asks the poet in one of the *Preludes*:

> But what is you? What is this thing called you?
> A seed, a leaf? a singing congregation
> Of molecules? an atom split in two?
> Electrons dancing in a magic circle?[40]

The poem does not pretend to answer such questions. What it does, instead, is offer us the mysteries of 'A world, of which self-knowledge is the centre': the adventurings of a mind that is never finally at rest.

Aiken's development of musical forms and 'exploration of the fragmented ego' led him to the composition, over several years, of what is perhaps his most ambitious work: *The Divine Pilgrim*. Not published until 1949, its constituent poems were, in fact, written between 1915 and 1925. Here, Aiken seems to have been aiming at the musical equivalent of a symphony: the natural culmination, as he saw it, of his pursuit of 'contrapuntal effects'. 'By using a large medium', he explained, 'dividing it into several main parts, and subdividing those parts into short movements in various veins and forms' there would be 'no limit to the variety of effects obtainable'. The repetition of phrases and images or groups of lines, juxtapositions and combinations in various sequences would produce something that was 'no less a matter of emotional tone than of form'. 'Such a poetry', he added, '. . . will not so much present an idea as use its resonance. It is the apotheosis of the poetic method which we have called implication'. In *The Divine Pilgrim*, as in his other poems, there is no systematic quest, only a circuitously conducted inquiry: an inquiry that is not so much stated as demonstrated, alluded to in innumerable, indirect ways. As in a tone-poem by Richard Strauss or Schoenberg, themes are offered that conflict, are resolved and developed to tragedy or serenity through disharmony or harmony. And, as in so many American poems, there is no ultimate conclusion. 'Who am I?' asks a figure named Forslin:

> Tired of change I seek the unmoving centre
> But is it moveless, or are all things turning?[41]

All things *are* turning, it seems; the still centre, the point of balance and certainty continues to elude him; like other figures in the poem, the most he can know is his own complexities. Admittedly, in the concluding moments of *The Divine Pilgrim* there appears to be finality of a kind, as the poet spirals down through concentric layers of human experience to his own consciousness. Appearances are deceptive, however. In its conclusion, the poem starts the mind's journey outward again from the grounds of self-knowledge: in its end, really, is its beginning. Our first duty to ourselves and others, Aiken has said, is 'to begin by *understanding*, or trying to understand'; and, from the evidence of his own often rich, mellifluous poetry, this is our last duty as well.

From Imagism to the redemption of history: Pound

Of all the poets closely involved with the Imagist movement, the outstanding figure is (as the number of references that have been made to him already suggest) Ezra Pound. For Pound, however, even more than for people like Oppen and Zukovsky, Imagism was just one chapter in a varied and distinguished career. Pound's commitment to poetry was total: to poetry as a craft, as a moral and spiritual resource, and eventually as a means of salvaging culture, redeeming history. 'It is tremendously important that great poetry be written', he declared once, 'it makes no jot of difference who writes it'; and this disinterested belief in the poem – a belief that, not coincidentally, he shared with his great American predecessor, Whitman – was proved by his dedicated support of other poets. 'Il miglior fabbro', Eliot called him, borrowing the phrase from Dante, 'the better artist', in recognition of Pound's help in transforming *The Waste Land* into the dense, allusive, and elliptical poem that we have today. Pound also assisted Frost, despite the obvious differences in the two poets' attitudes towards their craft, H.D. (as we have seen) and William Carlos Williams. He helped Yeats in his metamorphosis from the poet of Celtic twilight into one of the great voices in modernist verse and, in later years, he became an inspiration for people like Ginsberg and Olson. Pound was the great evangelist for poetry, and he was also the great assimilator: absorbing and, in the best sense, imitating the work of other imaginations so as to make it available for his own audiences. Starting from the premise that the state of art in a culture, and the state of poetry and language in particular, is a gauge or symptom of its health, he attempted to mediate the achievements of other, earlier periods – to offer the best that had been thought and said in the past as an example and agent of recovery for the present. This was not an antiquarian enterprise; Pound was not simply trying to write 'like' earlier poets, to borrow their idiom. His aim, rather, was to reclaim the *principles* implicit in the work of other people: principles that were expressed, and could only be expressed (for Pound was an Aristotelian, not a Platonist), in specific, material terms, according to the language and conditions of an individual culture. 'Poetry is a sort of inspired mathematics', Pound said, 'which gives us equations . . . for human emotions. If one has a mind which inclines to magic rather than science, one will prefer to speak of these equations as spells or incantations'.[42] Human emotions, for Pound, remained the same, but the equations or spells used to uncover them altered with time and place. Each poet, in this sense, had to contrive his own mathematics or magic; no matter how much he might derive from others, he had ultimately to forge his own style – a voice that was more than just the sum of the myriad voices he echoed.

Pound's early poetry is saturated in the kind of *fin-de-siècle* romanticism he was later to abjure. There are the familiar poetic subjects: songs in praise of a lady ('Praise of Ysolt', 'Ballatetta'), songs concerning the poet's craft ('Mesmerism', 'And Thus In Nineveh'), love and friendship ('The House of Splendour', 'The Altar'), death ('For E. McC.'), the transience of beauty and the permanence of art ('No Audiart'). Not unrelated to these, there are some of the subjects that Pound was to make peculiarly his own: the pain of exile ('In Durance'), metamorphosis ('The Tree'), the 'delightful psychic experience', the ecstatic moment that is nonetheless perfect for being just that, a moment ('Erat Hora'). There are elaborate conceits, images that call attention to their own *bravura*, poetic inversions, self-conscious archaisms of word and phrasing. What saves these poems, however, is Pound's consummate sense of rhythm. From first to last, Pound was blessed with the gift of what he called 'melopeia': 'wherein the words are charged, over and above their plain meaning, with some musical property, which directs the bearing or trend of that meaning'.[43] Most of these early poems are written according to an established metrical pattern, some traditional form that is often notable for its complexity, the challenge it offers to the skill of the poet. 'Sestina: Altaforte' is a good example, where the poet uses the same six rhyme words in each stanza. Usually, though, as in 'Sestina: Altaforte', Pound more than meets the challenge. He turns the form into an instrument on which he can play his own music: an apparently inevitable medium for his own speaking or singing voice.

The other important aspect of this early poetry is Pound's use of antiquity. Many of these poems are imitations of earlier verse or adopt the voice of an earlier poet; and, even when this is not the case, Pound very often speaks from behind an assumed character, a mask. The reasons for this return us to the heart of his beliefs. As a passage quoted just now indicates, Pound saw the poem as an objective verbal equation for an emotional, and basically incommunicable, experience. Imagism or vorticism was, he felt, one way of finding such an equation; and the use of personae was another. The poet, he argued, cannot relate a delightful psychic experience by speaking out directly in the first person: he must 'screen himself' and speak indirectly through 'an impersonal and objective story'.[44] The story, and in particular the stories of myth and earlier literature, can supply the modern poet with luminous details which he can array to adumbrate certain moods or perceptions of his own; they can provide him with the means not only of expressing his own ecstatic encounter with fundamental principles but of relating that encounter to the common stock of human experience. A poem like 'The Seafarer' illustrates how Pound turned these ideas into action. A translation of an Anglo-Saxon poem, it does two things. First, it communicates a sense of the past in all its past-ness: the use of the Anglo-Saxon alliterative verse form, the stylistic tessellation, the gnomic phrasing excite a sense of strangeness, as if the narrator were calling to the reader across the chasms of history. But, secondly, it explores certain common human feelings that Pound himself experienced with peculiar intensity: feelings of exile, distance, loss, separation not only from the world of the 'Burgher' but from other, more comforting domesticities that can never be known to the poet-wanderer – feelings, too, of nostalgic stoicism, that have little to do with the Christian elements in the original but have been highlighted by Pound, not least through the vigorous, muscular quality of the language. The eventual result of all this is a perfect example of what Pound called 'criticism in new composition'. Pound captures here something of what he termed the 'permanent basis in humanity': the common principles, the moral order that survives through the flux of experience. At the same time, however, he honours the thing as it was: the particular historical shapes, the very specific human and physical ways in which such forms necessarily manifest themselves.

'The Seafarer' appeared in *Ripostes*, published in 1912; and, apart from Pound's subtle use of antiquity, this collection is remarkable because it reveals the poet's discarding of metrically regular unrhymed verse in favour of free verse. A poem like 'The Return' shows this; and it also illustrates Pound's growing ability to write pieces that are not necessarily 'about' anything in any traditional sense but are, rather, equations for a mood or an emotion:

See, they return; ah, see the tentative
Movements, and the slow feet,
The trouble in the pace and the uncertain
Wavering!
See, they return, one, and by one
With fear, as half-awakened . . .[45]

The placing of 'tentative' makes it hover in mid-air, as it were, while the monosyllabic 'and the slow feet' actually re-creates a plodding movement – which is then quickened into uncertainty by the solitary positioning of the word 'Wavering'. After the pause, the next lines creep forward again, but with an even stealthier tread now, 'With fear, as half-awakened'. Pound's mastery of free verse here is complete: because, essentially, it is the rhythm that is extending sensibility, creating meaning. 'I made poems like "The Return"', Pound declared, 'which is an objective reality and has a complicated sort of significance like Mr. Epstein's 'Sun God' or Mr. Brezska's "Boy with a Coney"'. The comparison is an apt one because, as with modern, abstract sculpture, Pound's aims in such a poem are strictly non-representational: in the sense that it is impossible to tell just who 'they' are and exactly what 'they' are about. 'The Return' refers to nothing outside itself. Instead, it presents a series of images in rhythmic movement; and it is this series and movement that constitute the meaning of the poem – or, to use Pound's own phrase, its 'inspired mathematics'.

As Pound's work grew in authority, he retained this understanding of the possibilities of rhythm and image but coupled it with a growing distinctiveness of voice and a greater alertness to the problems of modern culture. A poem like 'The Garden', for instance, published in *Lustra* (1916) shows Pound becoming distinctly 'modern', using unromantic similes drawn from contemporary life. More to the point, it shows him developing his own language: a combination of the mandarin and the demotic, the passionate, the satirical, and the vividly self-critical, that serves to express both his own deracination and the precarious, polyglot character of the society through which he moves:

Like a skein of loose silk blown against a wall
She walks by the railing of a path
      in Kensington Gardens,
And she is dying piece-meal
            of a sort of emotional anaemia.[46]

As these lines indicate, the heterogeneous nature of contemporary society is more than just a matter of voice in such poems; it is also a subject, an obsession. Already, in fact, we see emerging that idea that was to dominate more and more of Pound's time, thought, and work: the lack of an organising centre in the modern world – that diffuseness and multiplicity Henry Adams had noted, which led to 'emotional anaemia', apathy and confusion.

So, in effect, Pound gradually added to his gift of 'melopoeia' the two other necessary constituents of good poetry, as he saw it: 'phanopoeia' which he described as 'a casting of images upon the visual imagination' and 'logopoeia', 'the dance of the intellect among words'.[47] As far as 'phanopoeia' is concerned, Pound was helped, not only by his formulation of 'do's, and 'dont's' for Imagists, but by his interest in Japanese and Chinese poetry. His *haiku*, 'In a Station of the Metro', quoted and discussed in the first chapter, illustrates the Japanese influence and how it helped Pound pursue brevity and imagistic indirection. And the poems collected in *Cathay* (1915) reveal the importance of Chinese verse for him. They were written after he had read the work of a distinguished Chinese scholar, Ernest Fenollosa. Fenollosa pointed out that the Chinese language is made up of characters, each simple character representing a 'particular', an image. Each complex character is then made by combining simple characters and, in this sense, Chinese remains anchored in concrete, perceptual reality; it can never lose itself in vague abstraction. Not surprisingly, Pound with his hatred of abstract discourse jumped at this; and, without knowing a word of the language, he began working on a set of versions from the Chinese which, as Eliot has said, have made him 'the inventor of Chinese poetry for our time'. The very brief, and intense poem, 'The Jewel Stair's Grievance', illustrates Pound's achievement:

> The jewelled steps are already quite white with dew,
> It is so late that the dew soaks my gauze stockings,
> And I let down the crystal curtain
> And watch the moon through the clear autumn.

Certain virtues of this piece will be obvious even from a first reading: the utter clarity and limpidity of diction, the parallelism of line and rhythm, the technique of intensification by repetition whereby no phrase or image is memorable in itself but instead the sad, slow dwelling on a dying cadence makes all for the memorableness of mood. In a note to the poem, however, Pound himself points out what else it does that requires perhaps a little more attentiveness from the reader. The lines are a lament, evidently, uttered by a lady ('gauze stockings') who has been kept waiting a long time ('the dew soaks') for her lover who has no excuse on account of the weather ('clear autumn'). But the lament is implied, not stated; the narrative is there but just beneath the surface, as it were, caught in a subtle arrangement of images. As Pound says, 'the poem is especially prized' because its speaker 'utters no direct reproach'. To which one might well add that the emotion generated by the piece is especially powerful because it is a matter of voice rather than statement. What it says, its drama, is a product of movement and metaphor; once again, the medium of a poem *is* its meaning.

Taken together, the poems in *Cathay* are not just a reinvention of a particular language and culture, however, and more than new chapters in the story of Imagism. Their pervasive themes are loneliness, loss, exile: absence from home and from loved ones through some accident, it may be, from human choice or historical necessity. Which is as much as to say that the voice of 'The Seafarer' is recalled, albeit in a different key; although Pound himself hardly begins to acknowledge it, these pieces offer further impersonal and objective stories through which the poet can express his feelings of uprootedness and isolation. In her own, quiet way, the lady in 'The Jewel Stair's Grievance' is a mask, a persona: just as, for that matter, the multiple voices in another, very different poem are – *Hugh Selwyn Mauberley*, published in 1920. *Mauberley* has been variously described as Pound's departing address to England and his farewell to aestheticism. But it could be more accurately described as a packed, allusive, and notably modernistic look both at his own plight and the plight of modern culture. The opening lines of the first section suggest something of the approach and the tone:

> For three years out of key with his time,
> He strove to resuscitate the dead art
> Of poetry; to maintain the "sublime"
> In the old sense. Wrong from the start –
>
> No, hardly, but seeing he had been born
> In a half-savage country, out of date;
> Bent resolutely on wringing lilies from the acorn;
> Capaneus; trout for factitious bait . . .

The section is entitled 'E.P. Ode Pour L'Election De Son Sepulcre'; and, in this poetic epitaph, an anonymous narrator cryptically and wittily dismisses a rather anachronistic figure who is at once Mauberley and a part of Pound himself ('E.P.'). In this respect, it is an act of exorcism: stripping Mauberley / E. P. of his aesthetic pretensions, his attempts to 'maintain the "sublime" / In the old sense', mockingly comparing him to Capaneus, the hero who defied the gods of *his* time and paid the penalty, reminding us that Mauberley / E.P. was 'out of date' in his aims not least because he was born in the 'half-savage country' of America. As an act of exorcism, it effectively frees Mauberley / E.P. to write a different kind of poetry: something like *Mauberley* itself, perhaps, which is more responsive to, more in 'key' with the times. A comparison could be made here with other great works of Modernism, like James Joyce's *Ulysses*, since on this level *Mauberley* would seem to be about its own writing – or, at least, the processes preliminary to its writing, and the necessary preconditions for creativity. One should be wary in saying all this, however, of identifying Pound's stance in the lines just quoted with that of the narrator. Mauberley / E.P. may be criticised but so too, implicitly, is the author of these criticisms – he is just a little too breezily self-confident, dismissive, and reductive. In the context of the entire poem, in fact, we can say that if Mauberley / E.P. offers us the mask of aestheticism, then the narrator of the section offers us the equally debilitating mask of pragmatism, opportunism, and imaginative literalism – a simple capitulation to the demands of the age.

In effect, the dance of the intellect in *Mauberley* is at once lively and complicated. Writing in the aftermath of the Great War (which is very much a presence in the poem), Pound analyses the plight of modern society in and through an investigation of the plight of its writers: who are tempted, he suggests, either to give in to society's claims, offering it 'an image / Of its accelerated grimace', or to withdraw from it completely into 'the obscure reveries / Of the inward gaze'.[48] Going back into the previous century, focussing powerfully on recent symptoms of cultural decline, moving like quicksilver between different personae and poetic forms, he offers us the poetic equivalent of Henry Adams's *Education*: an ironic, self-critical, third-person account of a multiple, modern personality that is also a radical dissection of the miscellaneousness of modern culture – its restlessness, its variety, and its lack of a centre. There are no answers in *Mauberley*: except in the sense that the poem itself is an answer, suggesting a way out from the constricting alternatives of surrender or solipsism, a mask other than those of the pragmatist or aesthete. Instead, the reader is offered a kaleidoscopic series of questions: a creative analysis that follows Pound's customary route from the state of the language to the state of the culture.

In its own way, this route is also the route of the *Cantos*, which Pound began very early on in his career and was still writing at the time of his death. Only here the route is a far more complex and labyrinthine one because Pound is openly concerned, not just with contemporary cultural decay, but with the possible sources of cultural renewal. The *Cantos* are Pound's epic. Following in the tradition of Whitman, he attempts to tell the 'tale of the tribe'[49] in and through the story of an epic hero or wanderer who is, first and last, the poet himself. In doing so, however, his poetic imagination ranges a good deal further than Whitman's, to embrace multifarious examples of humanity, multiple ideas of order. There is a quest at the basis of the *Cantos* which, as Pound suggests from time to time, can be likened to Odysseus's ten-year quest in search of his home. The difference – and it is a crucial one – is that this quest is unending: involving as it does the human being's perpetual search for civilisation, his constant attempts to rediscover the springs of skill or delight. The content of the *Cantos* stretches out far and wide, in pursuit of appropriate models of language, thought, and conduct, taking in, among many others, the Provençal and early Italian poets, founders of modes of government and codes of behaviour like Confucius and Jefferson, and some of the examples of primitive religious feeling recorded in Ovid's *Metamorphoses*. And as it does so, Pound constantly reminds us of his Imagist background, just as H. D does in *Trilogy*: by relying, not on an argument or a narrative in the traditional sense, but on a series of instances and images that take fire from their placing – that quicken the reader's mind into a new sense of awareness by virtue of rhythm, phrasing, and juxtaposition.

Although there is no conventional narrative and relatively little abstract argument in the *Cantos*, there are certain beliefs that surface throughout the poem and that help to explain the shapes, voices, and movement it assumes. There is a kind of logic at work here: but it is a logic of the imagination, and a very American, very modern imagination at that. As a result, the beginning, middle, and end of the tale Pound has to tell appear simultaneously as it were: story in the *Cantos* is quite separate from chronology. Abstracting from the poem, however, we can say that the story begins from Pound's sense of present disorder: the so-called 'Hell' Cantos (XIV and XV), for instance, detail the moral and social chaos of the modern world, which is then characteristically linked to the modern artist's dilemma (XLV, LXXV). From this perception of things stems the poet's search for order. This involves, by implication, a search for the principles on which the poet's craft is based. For, as 'Kung' (Confucius) tells us in Canto XIII, 'If a man have not order within him / He can not spread order about him'; the attainment of such personal order depends upon self-definition; this, in turn, depends upon precise verbal definitions, having the correct language; and *this*, in its turn, is the poet's responsibility. Digressing from the 'tale' of the *Cantos* for a moment, we could say that this is the crucial reason why Pound was concerned with its indirect, imagistic discourse, its avoidance of generalised, abstract statement: because right principles were for him founded on right language. Exact terminology, what he once called 'sorting things into organic categories',[50] was, he saw it, the basis of all order and therefore his epic's *raison d'être*. As with his earlier poetry then, though in a far more radical sense, vocabulary and vision are inseparable.

But to return to the tale Pound has to tell: the principles that the poet / hero seeks are to be found in historical experience. To use Aristotelian terms, they are the 'forms' separable only in logic from the historical 'matter', the particular terms of time and place in which they manifest themselves. The poet / hero can only learn about those forms or principles in and through their historical manifestations, since they cannot be said to exist otherwise (Canto XC). It therefore becomes his task to explore other cultures in which they have been realised. This involves a descent into the past, of the kind that is the subject of Canto I, where Odysseus summons up the ghosts from Hades in order that they may speak to him, reveal their wisdom. In making this descent, the poet / hero – who is at once Odysseus, the protagonist of the Canto, and Pound, its author – must make some effort simultaneously to capture the constant element in the flux and yet to honour the thing *as it was*: which Pound himself does in Canto I, just as he does in 'The Seafarer', by using the taut, Anglo-Saxon alliterative verse form that sounds to modern ears like a primitive chant. The ghosts or exempla of the past consequently seem to speak to the poet / hero, and to us, through the mists of time. And, in hearing them and reporting their message, the poet / hero becomes a founder or 'inventor', at one with the other heroes – artists, statesmen, mythical warriors – who have sailed after knowledge and, for a moment, released the 'god . . . inside the stone',[51] the absolute principles immanent in human and natural life.

It is not difficult to see how the *Cantos* grew out of Pound's earlier work. The imagistic form of discourse, the linking of ethics, politics, and aesthetics, the founding of correct principles on correct language, and, not least, the belief that poetry can offer a verbal equation for those moments when, metaphorically at least, the human encounters the divine: all these are as basic to his poetic beginnings as they are to his tale of the tribe. Nor is it difficult to see the connections with American epic: a language experiment more radical than anything Whitman ever dreamed of, the *Cantos* set within their open-ended structure a poet who is at once a representative person, a prince, and a pedagogue, a voyager and a visionary, who tells us about good citizenship and offers us its appropriately heroic model. Whether the *Cantos* are a great, single poem or a series of magnificent fragments is open to debate. Pound himself seems to have been undecided: 'I am not a demigod / I cannot make it cohere', he admitted in Canto CXVI but then added, 'it coheres all right / even if my notes do not cohere'. What is indisputable, is that if there is coherence here it is of a different kind than that to be found in traditional epics, and that, even if there is not, there is still poetry like the following that is the fruit of a lifetime's experience and among the very finest in the language:

> What thou lovest well remains,
>   the rest is dross
> What thou lov'st well is thy true heritage
> Whose world, or mine or theirs
>   or is it of none?
> First came the seen, then thus the palpable
>   Elysium, though it were in the halls of hell,
> What thou lovest well is thy true heritage
> What thou lov'st well shall not be reft from thee[52]

From Imagism to contact and community: Williams

A poet with similarly close connections to the Imagist movement is William Carlos Williams, whom another poet, Marianne Moore, described as a person supremely 'able to fix the atmosphere of a moment'.[53] In Williams's work, as a remark of his quoted earlier indicates, there are 'no ideas but in things': attention is concentrated on the individual object or emotion or event, caught at a particular time and a particular point in space. The object does not stand for anything; it is not a symbol, nor is there even a great deal of figurative language. Instead, we are asked to attend to the thing in itself: its *hacceitas* or 'this-ness' – what makes the object or moment *this* and no other. 'So much depends', says Williams in *Spring and All*,

upon
a red wheel
barrow
glazed with rain
water
beside the white
chickens

In some ways, this is a little joke of reversed expectations: the deliberately vague and enormously suggestive opening leads the reader more accustomed to traditional poetry to expect some grandiose statement (such as 'Beauty is Truth, Truth Beauty'), whereas all he gets is a simple portrait, an image. But in other ways, it is intensely serious, since as usual Williams is quietly checking our yearning towards the abstract, what might be, and reminding us of the homely beautiful of the actual, what *is*.

Williams, then, is one of the great populists in American poetry, for whom the world is a democracy of objects. There are no hierarchies, no one thing is more important than another, each is to be valued for itself. And there are no allegories; no one thing is to be used as a tool, a vehicle to refer to another thing – it does not mean, it simply exists. Whether it is a woman lamenting the loss of her husband ('The Widow's Lament in Springtime'), a natural object ('Sea-Trout and Butterfish'), a strange moment of happiness ('The Revelation'), a street scene ('Proletarian Portrait'), or an instance of intimacy ('This Is Just to Say'), whatever it may be Williams's purpose remains the same: to empathise or identify with the thing, not just to describe it but to imitate it in words, to allow it to express itself, to give it verbal shape, a voice. And the immediate consequence of this aim is, not surprisingly, a commitment to free verse: rhythms that follow the shape of the object and that respond to the exigencies of a specific occasion. 'I must tell you', begins Williams in 'Young Sycamore': the address is characteristically urgent and intimate, as if the poet were speaking under the pressure of immediate experience. And, having grabbed our attention, he then directs it to the object, whose contours are caught in the curve, pitch and sway of the free verse lines:

this young tree
whose round and firm trunk
between the wet

pavement and the gutter
(where water is trickling) rises
bodily

into the air with
one undulant
thrust half its height –

The use of tactile references here is characteristic: in a sense, the poet is trying to 'touch' the tree and make us touch it – to achieve contact (an important word for Williams) and, for a moment, live the life of another thing. And equally characteristic is the pattern of verbs and verbals: Williams, like Whitman, sees life as process, constant motion. As in a painting by Van Gogh, there is a sense of the tree as animate life, thrusting towards the sky and continuing to grow long after the artist's imitation of it is finished.

Not that it is ever definitively finished: like so many of Williams's poems, 'Young Sycamore' does not end, it simply stops short without a full stop or even any punctuation mark:

hung with cocoons
it thins
till nothing is left of it
but two

eccentric knotted
twigs
bending forward
hornlike at the top[54]

Excitedly, our attention has been drawn up the tree, from its base to its topmost twigs, and we are left gazing at what will be: alteration, new growth requiring new poems. The sense of possibility with which the poem leaves us is quietly accentuated by the fact that the sentence with which it begins is never completed. All of the poem from the third line on ('whose round and firm trunk . . .') is a subordinate clause; Williams never returns to the main clause of the first two lines; the reader is consequently left (whether he is consciously aware of the reasons for it or not) with feelings of openness and incompleteness – utterly appropriate in a world governed by change.

'The poem is made of things – on a field', declared Williams. A statement like this helps explain his patience and care with language. There is reverence for the individuality of words in his poems, as well as of objects. And it alerts us to the intense *inner* activity of his verse. Like a series of particles on a magnetic field, the words in 'Young Sycamore' and other good Williams poems insist on their status as separate entities, engaged in an active relationship with their context. Individualism of word, object, and person: it is a very American concept, and it will probably come as no surprise to hear that Williams was among the most self-consciously American of modern poets. This was not a matter of narrow nationalism. It was simply because of his firm belief in the particular and local. 'Place is the only reality', he insisted:

> the true core of the universal. We live in one place at one time, but far from being bound by it, only through it do we realize our freedom . . . ., only if we make ourselves sufficiently aware of it, do we join with others in other places[55]

To be an individualist meant, for Williams, to attend to one's individual locality: not to turn away from even its most alienating or inhibiting features but to try to understand and achieve communion with it. The aim, Williams argued, was not to 'run out – / after the rabbits' as Pound and Eliot did, deserting American nature in search of European culture. It was to stay as and where one was, as Poe and Whitman had: to 'return to the ground' in order truly to know the 'new locality' of America, the particulars of the here and now – which, in Williams's own case, meant his hometown of Rutherford, New Jersey.

There was a potentially debilitating side to this approach to poetry, of which Williams himself was well aware. Poems might resolve themselves into a series of isolated instances, fragments that could not develop beyond the pressure of the immediate moment nor comment beyond the demands of the singular experience. One should not exaggerate this danger, of course. Even a poem written during Williams's

'Objectivist period' like 'Young Sycamore' is hardly imprisoned in its occasion; and it is shaped by feelings of tenderness and generosity that suggest an appropriate stance towards reality. Reaching out towards the life of another thing, it is in no sense a cold or constricted piece; its humanity, its warm moral values are there in what it does, its responsiveness to experience, even if what it says is strictly contained. Nevertheless, Williams clearly did begin to feel that he wanted more opportunity to comment and a chance, too, to develop his poems beyond the moment, eliciting and perhaps quietly stating principles that had only been implicit in the earlier work. Sometimes, in his later poetry, the desire to comment issues is just that, comment. 'Asphodel, That Greeny Flower' illustrates this. Addressed to the poet's wife, it weaves a lyric meditation out of the flower of its title: a meditation on love, empathy, and memory and on the human being's destructive and creative capacities – 'the bomb' and the 'grace of the imagination'. Certainly, the bright, particular asphodel supplies the occasion for all this: the poet never strays very far from it, or from the sphere of domestic affection. But there is a degree of generalisation springing from the occasion, and the experience of affection, that the younger Williams would probably never have allowed himself:

What power has love but forgiveness?
        In other words
                by its intervention
what has been done
        can be undone.[56]

There are other ways in which these later poems begin to comment and expand, though. One, also illustrated by 'Asphodel, That Greeny Flower' or, for that matter, by the opening poem in *Spring and All* ('By the road to the contagious hospital') is symbolism, or something very close to it. The poet concentrates upon a particular thing – a flower or, in the case of the *Spring and All* poem a day in early spring – and by the sheer intensity of his concentration, the degree of imaginative responsiveness he brings to bear, that thing begins to assume additional meanings, new dimensions. By the end of 'By the road to the contagious hospital', for example, the poet and the reader are still gazing at something specific and mundane: the 'waste of broad, muddy fields' that Williams saw on his way to work at the hospital (he was, by profession, a doctor). The descriptive detail is such, however, that many other things have been suggested: the babies in the hospital wards who, like plants, 'enter the new world naked / cold, uncertain of all', the quickening of the individual imagination ('One by one objects are defined – / It quickens: clarity, outline of leaf'), the revival of all life, material and moral, caught up in the 'contagion' of Spring. 'That is the poet's business', Williams insisted, 'Not to talk in vague categories but to write particularly, as a physician works upon a patient, upon the thing before him, in the particular to discover the universal'.[57] The particularity is still there in such poems, as it was in earlier work, but the universality is just a little less implicit, a fraction closer to the surface. It is a small difference, perhaps, but a significant one.

The third and probably the crucial way in which Williams allowed his later poetry to expand has to do with his growing concern with structure. 'It is a design', concludes 'The Orchestra' published in *The Desert Music* (1954), and that precisely is what many of the later poems are. They are, in the first instance, aural designs that permit radical variations of rhythm within coherent, and often quite complex musical patterns and, in the second, imaginative designs, verbal tapestries or mosaics that allow within their framework for significant combinations of detail. The developing interest in aural structures is perhaps best illustrated by Williams's invention, for some of his later poetry, of the 'variable foot'. One problem, in particular, vexed him through much of his later career: how to create a rhythmic pattern welded to 'the American idiom', that would enable its users to combine the maximum flexibility with the discipline necessary to place the pauses and emphases where they were required. And with the 'variable foot', he believed, he had discovered a possible solution to that problem. The principle behind the 'variable foot' is very simple: it is a metrical pattern in which, as Williams himself put it, 'time is the real matter of measure, and not stress. Elapsed time is the whole story'.[56] Measure, that is, becomes a relative quantity and a matter of duration, with each foot taking up the same amount of time in the reading regardless of whether it consists of seven or eight words read quickly or one syllable followed by a long pause. The opening lines of 'The Descent', the poem in which Williams claimed to have invented the 'variable foot', will serve to illustrate how the principle worked in practice:

The descent beckons
          as the ascent beckoned.
                    Memory is a kind
of accomplishment,
          a sort of renewal
                    even
an initiation . . .

In this poem, each line is divided into three feet, which are indicated by typographical arrangement. The third foot in the second line consists of one word, 'even'. Obviously, in order to let it take up the same amount of time in the reading as the previous two feet, the reader has to make an immense pause after it: which effectively reproduces the voice of the poet, reaching out tentatively for a further definition, a deeper understanding of the 'descent' into memory. The structure of such lines may be 'open' in the sense that no particular system of stresses is predicated, nor even any specific length of line; nevertheless, so Williams intends, it prescribes pace, pause, and tone, it follows the 'breath' of the poet, the movement of his diaphragm and his mind, with the sort of fidelity that is not always possible in free verse.

As far as imaginative design is concerned, the exemplary instance is Williams's epic poem, *Paterson*. Like so many American epics, *Paterson* is unfinished: Book One was published in 1946, and Williams was still working on Book Six at the time of his death in 1963. Long before he died, though, Williams had anticipated this. There would never be an end to the poem, he explained, because it had to remain open to the world of growth and change. This was something his epic shared with all his work. and so too was its general approach; for, in its own way, *Paterson* is as much concerned with a reverent investigation of the particular as Williams' other poems are. The basic particulars in this case are Paterson the town, an imaginative space or place not unrelated to Rutherford, New Jersey, and Paterson the man who is, like other protagonists in American epic, at once the poet himself and all people, all democratic individualists. The two identities of Paterson are, in any case, related; since from the very beginning of his career Williams had insisted that personality was inextricable from place – that the human being and his activities were 'an extension of nature's processes . . .. transfused with the same forces which transfuse the earth'.[59] 'A man himself is a city', declared Williams in his 'Author's Note' to the poem, 'beginning, seeking, achieving and concluding his life in ways which the various aspects of a city may embody – if imaginatively conceived'. To descend into locality, in this case Paterson was consequently also to descend into character; to investigate the city, with the help of the imagination, was necessarily to investigate the man.

The notion of 'design', however, is not so much a matter of subject as of form, the terms in which this investigation is conducted. 'To make a start, / out of particulars', *Paterson* begins:

> and make them general, rolling
> up the sum . . .
>   . . . rolling up out of chaos,
> a nine months' wonder, the city
> the man, an identity . . .
> Rolling up, rolling up heavy with
> numbers.[60]

In his later years, Williams was attracted by the example of the Bayeux tapestry and the paintings of Pieter Bruegel: because in such works, he felt, great mosaics of life were constructed out of a multitude of cherished particulars. *Paterson*, as he saw it, was to be a verbal equivalent of such visual adventures. During the course of his epic, Williams uses verse, prose, drama, dialogue, excerpts from books, letters, interviews, anecdotes. history, and fable. Every experience recorded, every event or person re-created, is studied closely, permitted the dignity of close attention. Yet out of this conglomerate of individual moments and objects, Williams manages to fashion a total pattern of meaning, a vision of life that draws its energy and its coherence from the poet's reverence for simple things, the pleasures, pains, and the dreams of ordinary people. 'This is a POEM!' Williams insists cheerfully at one point in Book Four. *Paterson* is that, although it should perhaps be added that it is a poem set firmly within the twin traditions of American epic and Imagist method. 'Unless there is / a new mind there cannot be a new line', says Williams elsewhere, in Book Two, 'the old will go on / repeating itself with recurring deadliness'. *Paterson* is a testament to that, as well: Williams's life-long belief in the necessity of personal experiment. Perhaps the final emphasis, though, should be on something else characteristic of the poet that this great personal epic of his reveals: which is, quite simply, his sympathy, his capacity for imaginative understanding. More than any other American poet of this century, Williams was possessed of what Keats called 'negative capability', the ability to bridge the gap between the perceiving subject and the perceived object. For some reason, he was able to feel a sense of kinship with any particular thing, to appreciate and to imitate its particularity: which makes him, after his great predecessor Whitman, the finest American celebrant of the democratic impulse.

From Imagism to discovery of the imagination: Stevens

Wallace Stevens was personally acquainted with several of those involved in the Imagist movement; and many of the short poems in his first volume *Harmonium* (1923) owe something to the principles of Imagism, in that they attempt to capture the exact curve of thing in rhythms unhampered by conventional metre. A poem like 'Metaphors of a Magnifico' reveals Stevens's Imagist connections: but it also shows where he and the Imagists parted company. In the poem, the narrator presents us with an event, 'Twenty men crossing a bridge / Into a village', which he attempts to explain by using different types of abstract statement. The attempt fails. Abstraction cannot help. And the narrator falls back on what Stevens called 'the veritable ding an sich' – the thing in itself, the irreducible concrete reality of the event: 'The boots of the men clump/On the boards of the bridge. / The first white wall of the village / Rises through the fruit-trees'.[61] The desires of the abstracting mind are effectively put aside, and we are required to gaze at the bare fact; to this extent, 'Metaphors of a Magnifico' is an Imagist poem. Only to this extent, however, for Stevens clearly asks us to see this concentration on the thing in itself as a beginning. The poem ends expectantly, with two unfinished lines ('The first white wall of the village . . . / The fruit-trees . . .') as if to remind us that this is just the first stage of understanding. What is more, the dismissal of the abstract in the poem and the introduction of the victorious concrete is clearly undertaken as a quasi-metaphysical task. Even while Stevens is defending 'the veritable ding an sich', he is tempting us into speculative thought, inviting us to meditate on and generalise from specific experience. Here as elsewhere in Stevens's poetry, in fact, the mind and its needs are not really suppressed for very long; because for him, unlike the Imagists, they were of equal importance with the world and its demands. Forever separate, mind and world still depend on each other eventually: in that, as Stevens saw it, they create the dialectic from which the knowledge and pleasure of our lives must spring.

This is all by way of saying that Stevens, like the great Romantics, believed in the power of the imagination. Reality, Stevens felt, was not something given to us, which our minds receive passively, but is on the contrary something made, the product of an interchange between our minds and our given circumstances. We, or more accurately our consciousnesses, are not simply blank pieces of paper on which the world writes its messages, not just mirrors that reflect our environment; rather, they are lamps, active, creative things which illuminate that environment, helping to give it form and perspective and so making it adequate, even if only temporarily, to ordinary human desires. 'The imagination' declared Stevens echoing Blake and Coleridge, 'is the power of the mind over the possibilities of things', 'like light, it adds nothing, except itself'.[62] In a way, Stevens argued, our world is always an imagined one because our senses start to arrange things almost as soon as they perceive them, and whenever we think about experience we begin to structure it according to some law – such as the scientific law of cause and effect. We start to 'read' and interpret the world in the same manner that, instinctively, we read and interpret a written text. For Stevens, however, the supreme example of this shaping, structuring capacity, is the artistic imagination: those acts of the mind whereby people attempt quite consciously to give significance to life – to devise some moral or aesthetic order, however fragile or provisional, which can give coherence and a sense of purpose to things. This kind of order was what Stevens called a 'supreme fiction', and for him, as for Coleridge, the prime creator of such fictions was the poet. The poet, according to Stevens, strives for a 'precise equilibrium' between the mind and its environment at any given moment in time; and then creates a fiction which is at once true to our experience of the world and true to his and our need for value and meaning.

It is worth emphasising the fact that, as Stevens perceived it, the imaginative faculty does not so much impose designs *on* the world as discover designs inherent *in* it: hence, the constant need to return to 'the veritable ding and sich'. And it is also worth adding that he saw the act of the imagination as a continuous, theoretically unending one: that he insisted on the primacy of change. We are always altering, Stevens believed, our given circumstances alter too, and the fictive world created out of the synthesis or union of the two must invariably respond to this. We must be reassessing our personal needs and given circumstances continually so as to devise new ideas which do full justice to the dynamic nature of both mind and world; and the poet, in turn, must be writing new poems, new fictions all the time so as to pay his tribute to the metamorphic nature of things. Stevens's analogue for this process was the seasons, with winter seen as the bare, icy reality void of all fictive covering ('The Snow Man'); spring as the moment when the imagination and the world meet together, 'embrace / And forth the particulars of rapture come' (*Notes Toward a Supreme Fiction*, II. iv); summer as the period of fruition when the marriage between the desires of the mind and the things of the world is complete and harmonious ('Credences of Summer'); and autumn as the moment when the fiction no longer suffices because the imagination that created it, and the world it was created for, have altered, requiring new fictions, fresh identities and relationships ('The Death of a Soldier'). As this rather bare outline indicates, perhaps, the imagery of sexual congress and conflict mingles with that of natural growth and decay to describe what Stevens, in one of his poems, termed the imagination's 'ancient cycle'.[63] Mind and world, 'flesh and air', male and female: life is seen as a marriage of opposites ('Life is Motion'). Joy, or a sense of meaning, is the offspring of this marriage (*Notes*, I, iii). And what Stevens called 'poverty' or 'the malady of the quotidien' ('The Ordinary Women', 'The Man Whose Pharynx Was Bad') – a sense of melancholy and futility – comes when the marriage fails; when, for example, the world is too much with us and the mind becomes a passive instrument ('Depression Before Spring') – or, alternatively, when the mind escapes from the pressures of the world altogether and withdraws into solipsism and day-dreaming ('Esthétique du Mal', xv).

'A poet looks at the world as a man looks at a woman'. This, from the 'Adagia', offers a variation on the sexual metaphor; and it is also a reminder of just how seductive, for Stevens, was the figure of the poet. For Stevens was no less of a Romantic in this, his tendency to see the fabulator, the maker of poems as a latter-day prophet: someone who creates the myths that give meaning to people's lives and so enables them to survive – and who also offers an example to his audience, by showing them how to devise their own myths as well as listen to his. The poet's function, Stevens insisted, 'is to help people live their lives'. In effect, he returned the poet to his ancient role of bard or myth-maker, offering purpose and a sense of meaning to his tribe. And to this he added another, more peculiarly Romantic and American dimension: which was that of hero. For the poet, Stevens suggested, is his own hero because his mind, his representative imagination, is the catalyst of events. Instead of a third person protagonist, the poet, the 'I' of the poem, occupies the centre of the stage; there, 'like an insatiable actor, slowly and / with meditation', he speaks words and acts out a drama to which

> an invisible audience listens,
> Not to the play, but to itself, expressed
> In an emotion as of two people, as of two
> Emotions becoming one.[64]

Just what, in detail, the poet / actor spoke of, and what his audience attended to, was explained elsewhere in Stevens's work. 'Poetry', he declared in 'The Man with the Blue Guitar', '. . . must take the place / Of empty heaven and its hymns'. Like so many of his great, nineteenth-century predecessors – and, in particular, like his mentor, the philosopher George Santayana – Stevens was convinced that the old religious myths had crumbled into irrelevance. So poetry had to act now as an agent of redemption. The poet had to replace the priest. Art had to replace the liturgy of the church. Imaginative belief – 'belief . . . in a fiction, which you know to be a fiction' – had to replace religious faith. And a possible earthly paradise, created here and now out of the marriage between mind and world, had to replace the vision of a heavenly paradise, situated in some great hereafter. 'The great poems of heaven and hell have been written', said Stevens, 'and the great poem of earth remains to be written'.[65] The opposition this announces is at once the motive and the subject of much of his work. It is, for example, central to 'Sunday Morning', one of the finest pieces in *Harmonium*. In it the poet conducts a meditation through a woman whose mind is the scene, which has as its focus the choice between two alternatives. One alternative is the vision of paradise proposed to us by the Christian faith, 'The holy hush of ancient sacrifice': a vision founded upon the belief that since this is a universe of death, never answering to our desires, then we must look for our satisfactions in another dimension. The other alternative is the vision of an earthly paradise. The universe, the poet admits, may well be a universe of death when looked at in its pristine state: but it can perhaps be transformed into a living, constantly changing 'mundo' with the help of the active imagination. It is, of course, the second alternative that is ultimately preferred. Believing that 'The greatest poverty is not to live / In a physical world', the poet ends his meditation with a magnificent hymn to the earth:

> Deer walk upon our mountains, and the quail
> Whistle about us their spontaneous cries;
> Sweet berries ripen in the wilderness;
> And, in the isolation of the sky,
> At evening, casual flocks of pigeons make
> Ambiguous undulations as they sink,
> Downward to darkness, on extended wings.[66]

Beautifully poised between motion and rest, the perfect stillness of an artefact, a thing of the mind, and the movement, the restlessness and changeableness (and the odour of death) which belong to the things of this world, lines like this illustrate why Stevens is commonly regarded as one of the modern masters of blank verse.

The particular spot of earth that Stevens hymned in 'Sunday Morning' and elsewhere was almost exclusively American: an important point because, as Stevens put it in one of his very last poems, 'a mythology reflects its region'. 'The gods of China', he insisted, 'are always Chinese': that is, the world the imagination embraces is always a specific, local one and the fictions created out of that embrace must bear the stamp of their locality. 'One turns with something like ferocity toward a land that one loves', he said elsewhere, '. . . to demand that it surrender, reveal, that in itself which one loves'. As Stevens saw it, this consummation devoutly to be wished, this marriage between a particular person and place, was 'a vital affair, not an affair of the heart . . ., but an affair of the whole being, a fundamental affair of life'.[67] It was not simply a matter of idiom and gesture, in other words, but of identity and vision. Of course, the paraphernalia of American culture is there in Stevens's poems – things like coffee, saxophones, and large sombreros – and, like Whitman, Stevens uses a rich, polyglot language that shows he has fallen in love with American names. But these things matter less, as a mark of origin, than the fact that Stevens chose as his starting-point what he called 'human loneliness / A part of space and solitude'.[68] Like every great American poet, in fact, he began with the isolated consciousness – Whitman's 'essential Me' – and then progressed from there to the new dimensions, the moments of self-assertion or communion, which that consciousness struggles gamely to create.

Here, however, we are confronted with a crucial paradox in Stevens's work. Like other American writers, Stevens began with the isolated self, the separate mind and its world. Unlike most of them, however, he then moved in two quite different directions. One direction is centripetal and recalls that arch-egotist and solipsist, Edgar Allan Poe. The self, Stevens insists, devises its own world, which the poem then imitates in that it is closed and autonomous, a durable integration of experience. The other recalls Emily Dickinson. For Stevens can be quite as insistent that the self is limited, transient, and that the worlds or works it creates must carry the imprint of their creator in being tentative, provisional, and unfinished. In some respects, Stevens's poems resemble Poe's. 'Pure' or closed poems in a way, they are as self-sufficient and intangible as the realms of experience they describe; they seem to exist in their own special dimension or, as Stevens himself put it once, 'beyond the compass of change / Perceived in a final atmosphere'. In other respects, though, they edge out tentatively towards the boundaries of experience just as Dickinson's poetry does. 'Impure' or open poems of a kind, they tend to emphasise their own arbitrariness, to offer themselves up to re-invention – and so to remind us that they are (to quote Stevens again) 'inconstant objects of inconstant cause / In a universe of inconstancy'.[69]

Just how Stevens manages to walk this tightrope between open and closed structures is illustrated by one of his most famous earlier pieces, 'Anecdote of the Jar'. The animating conception here is very simple: the jar serves as a point which orders all that surrounds it. It performs the function of the imagination just as its surroundings, organised for a moment into a series of significant relationships, perform the function of reality. What complicates things, however, and gives an additional dimension to the poem is its form, the way Stevens fleshes out this conception. The poem begins with a series of unrhymed couplets, continues with them to the eighth line; and then suddenly presents the reader with two end-stopped lines, set off for the first time by rhyme:

> It took dominion everywhere.
> The jar was gray and bare.

It sounds for a moment as if the argument is completed, the poem rounded off. But then, it turns out, it is not; and the premature finality of the lines just quoted gives an air of *un*finality to the two lines which follow, and which form another unrhymed couplet. Even this, the feeling that things have not quite been rounded off, is not left unqualified, however, because the last line returns us to a word used in the first line, 'Tennessee'. Joining the end to the beginning, the poet still seems to be trying to round the poem off, to seal it; and we, the readers, cannot really be sure that he has failed. So we are made to feel that the work is at once complete *and* incomplete, that the argument has been concluded and yet that something has been missed out, left hanging loose. 'Anecdote of the Jar' is, in effect, made to imitate in its form, as well as describe in its content, the continuing act of the imagination, by which worlds are created that are complete in themselves and yet subject to alteration. The mind behind the poem has apparently composed things for a moment, achieved an order 'beyond the compass of change'; and yet it intimates that it must give that order up soon and – casting aside 'the rotted names', obsolete forms and vocabulary – submit itself to 'a universe of inconstancy'.

'Anecdote of the Jar' is exemplary in several ways. The same essential structure, for instance, is used with a difference in many of Stevens's longer poems. In 'Thirteen Ways of Looking at a Blackbird', it is the blackbird mentioned in the title that serves as a focal point, a means of bringing out the significance of the context in which it is involved. The meaning of the bird depends on each context, just as the meaning of the context depends upon it, with the result that there is exactly the same condition of interdependence between the bird and each of its settings as there is between the jar and its surroundings: a condition which (it need hardly be added) Stevens felt to be characteristic of the relationship between the imagination and its surroundings. In the first section of the poem, for example, the blackbird provides a focal point for the landscape it composes in the same way that a compositional centre composes a landscape painting; and, in doing so, it provides a paradigm of the way the mind orders reality by discovering significant relations in it:

> Among twenty snowy mountains
> The only moving thing
> Was the eye of the blackbird.

In this case, the snowy surroundings are static, and the eye / I of the blackbird offers the only motion. By contrast, in the final section the terms are reversed:

It was evening all afternoon.
It was snowing
And it was going to snow.
The blackbird sat
In the cedar-limbs.

Now the blackbird has become a still point. The imagination is, apparently, at rest; and the poet, making the last lines echo the first. seems to be bringing things full circle. Everything appears to be completed; that is, until we are reminded that, for Stevens, winter was a beginning as well as an end. This section concludes 'Thirteen Ways', certainly; but by reminding us of the process of decreation – what Stevens called 'getting rid of the paint to get at the world itself'[70] – it also acts as a prelude to further imaginative activity, an opening to poems as yet to be written. Once again, things are complete and yet somehow incomplete, closed and at the same time open.

Quite apart from the structure, the tone and idiom of 'Anecdote of the Jar' are also characteristic. The tone is serio-comic as with so many of Stevens's poems, especially the earlier ones; here as in, say, 'Bantams in Pinewoods' or 'Le Monocle de Mon Oncle' the poet uses wit and irony to qualify and complicate matters further, and so prevent the reader from coming to too simple or final a conclusion. And the idiom, in turn, is characterised by repetition and echo ('round . . . Surround . . . around . . . round . . . ground'), a series of significant if often subterranean connections. This repetitive pattern becomes far more elaborate in some of the longer pieces, with the result that poems like, say, 'The Idea of Order at Key West' resemble mosaics, in which the poet seems to be trying to construct his own personal version of the imaginative fictions he celebrates. Complex designs of word, sound and image, they offer the reader a special world, in this case a verbal one, which may be abstracted from and so depend upon our given surroundings – but which has its own innate structure and system of cross-reference.

It would be wrong, however, to dwell on 'Anecdote of the Jar' as if it summed up the whole of Stevens's work, even in its paradoxes and ambiguities. No one poem could do that. One reason is that the later poetry is, on the whole, less spry and balletic than the earlier – more meditative and austere, more discursive and openly philosophical. And another is that Stevens rarely allowed himself to be contained by a particular idiom even within the space of one poem. Each of his pieces is complexly layered, moving almost casually and without warning between high rhetoric and the colloquial, book-words, foreign borrowings, and native slang. As a result, each seems unique, with its own particular rhythms and adjustments, its own special way of turning the world into words. One of the finest of Stevens's later poems, for example *Notes Toward a Supreme Fiction* (1942), explores his familiar subject: 'The imagination, the one reality / In this imagined world'.[71] But it creates its own separate 'mundo', full of noise, colour, and movement; and, rather than any argumentative structure, it is this 'mundo', strange, illogical, and quite unpredictable, which enables us to see the world in a new light. This passage, from the poem that concludes the third section of *Notes*, will perhaps illustrate its quality. Like the concluding lines to 'Sunday Morning', it is a hymn to the earth: the 'fat girl' of the opening line who, Stevens suggests, can only be understood through an act of the imagination, a poem or fiction of some kind – something in which her changeableness, her extraordinary vitality and and variety, can be caught for a moment in a single, crystalline image:

> Fat girl, terrestrial, my summer, my night . . .
> . . .
> . . . when I think of you as strong or tired,
> Bent over work, anxious, content, alone,
> You remain the more than rational figure. You
> Become the soft-footed phantom, the irrational
>
> Distortion, however fragrant, however dear.
> That's it: the more than rational distortion,
> The fiction that results from feeling. Yes, that.
>
> They will get it straight one day at the Sorbonne.
> We shall return at twilight from the lecture
> Pleased that the irrational is rational.
>
> Until flicked by feeling, in a gildered street,
> I call you by name, my green, my fluent mundo.
> You will have stopped revolving except in crystal.[72]

The image of the revolving crystal is, essentially, an image of an image: a fictional embodiment of the kind of imaginative fiction that can at once recover the world about us, in all its brightness, plenitude, and vitality, and raise it to a higher power, a superior dimension of reality. With this image we are back, really, at the centre of the Romantic-Symbolist tradition: of which the Imagist movement – for all its, often justified, protestations of novelty – was itself a part. For the forms of knowledge and vision that Stevens celebrates here are significantly connected to those celebrated by many of the other poets discussed in this chapter. When H.D. talked about 'spiritual realism' and, for the purposes of understanding, superimposed one image on another 'like a stock of photographic negatives', she was showing that she was driven by motives and impulses fascinatingly similar to those which drove Wallace Stevens. So was William Carlos Williams, when he spoke of an imaginative 'design' that might liberate the meanings of people, events, and objects; and so, even more, was Ezra Pound, when he referred to poetry as a sort of inspired mathematics or investigated the ideogrammic method. This is not to imply, of course, that all these poets were saying precisely the same thing; such an idea would be hopelessly myopic and reductive. But it is to say that their writing was initially fired into life by a belief in the image, whatever the circuitous routes on which that belief might subsequently take them. Each one of them was animated by the conviction that, to quote Stevens again, 'All poetry is experimental poetry' and that 'The poem reveals itself only to the ignorant man'.[73] Each one of them sought personal ways of knowing things, and perhaps reconciling the contradictions of experience, not by relying on narrative or logic but with the help, and under the 'miraculous influence' of the imagination. For Stevens, in particular, that led to the awareness, even while he sought knowledge, that 'always there is another life / A life beyond this present knowing.'[74] So his introspective voyages could never be finished. But it led equally to the sense that, in the absence of God, the mind could perhaps achieve its own redemption: by working with the world it might abstract something out of that world, and so (as Stevens himself put it once) build a bridge between fact and miracle.

Notes

1. Cited in Lawrence E. Levine, 'Progress and Nostalgia: The Self Image of the Nineteen Twenties', in *The American Novel in the Nineteen Twenties* edited by Malcolm Bradbury and David Palmer (London, 1971), p. 45.
2. Gertrude Stein, *The Autobiography of Alice B. Toklas* (London, 1933).
3. T. S. Eliot, 'American Literature and the American Language', in *To Criticise the Critic* (London, 1965), p. 58. See also, Michael Reck, *Ezra Pound: A Close-Up* (London, 1968), pp. 14–15; Michael Roberts, *T. E. Hulme* (London, 1938), p. 266; Ford Madox Ford, 'Those Were the Days', in *Imagist Anthology 1930*, p. xiii.
4. Ezra Pound, *The Letters of Ezra Pound 1907–1941* edited by D. D. Paige (New York, 1950), p. 6. Letter dated 21 October, 1908.
5. Ibid., p. 11. Letter dated October, 1912.
6. Pound, 'Vorticism', p. 92. See also, *Letters*, pp. 113, 213. Letters dated August, 1917 and 26 September, 1927; Amy Lowell, *Tendencies in Modern American Poetry* (New York, 1927), p. 255.

7. Ezra Pound, 'A Few Don'ts by an Imagiste', *Poetry* (Chicago), March 1913. See also, 'A Retrospect', in *Literary Essays of Ezra Pound* edited by T. S. Eliot (London, 1954), p. 4.
8. F. S. Flint, 'Imagisme', *Poetry* (Chicago), March 1913. See also. Pound, 'A Retrospect', p. 3.
9. Ezra Pound, *The Fortnightly Review* (London), September 1914, p. 466.
10. Robert Frost, 'Mowing', line 13.
11. William Carlos Williams, *Paterson*. Book I, section i: 'The Delineaments of Giants'. See also, *Autobiography*, p. 390.
12. William Carlos Williams, Letters, *Stony Brook* (New York), (1/2 Fall, 1968). Letters dated 23 August, 1954 and 13 June, 1956. See also Pound, 'A Few Don'ts by an Imagiste'; Amy Lowell, Preface to *Some Imagist Poets 1915*, p. vi.
13. Marianne Moore, *Predilections* (New York, 1955), p. vii.
14. Pound, 'A Few Don'ts by an Imagiste'. See also, *Letters*, p. 101. Letter dated January, 1915; Canto LXXXI; John Livingstone Lowes, review in *Nation*, 24 February, 1916; Amy Lowell, interview in *New York Times*, 26 March 1916; Richard Aldington, *Life for Life's Sake* (London, 1968), pp. 123–24.
15. Richard Aldington, 'A Young American Poet', *The Little Review* (Chicago), March 1915.
16. Barbara Guest, *Herself Defined: The Poet H.D. and Her World* (London, 1985), p. 81.
17. *The Walls Do Not Fall* (1944), reprinted in *Trilogy*, section 35. See also, section 31.
18. Ibid., section 43. See also, sections 15, 38; Guest, *Herself Defined*, p. 269.
19. *Tribute to the Angels* (1945), reprinted in *Trilogy*, section 43. See also, H.D., *Bid Me To Live* (New York, 1963), p. 89; Robert Duncan, review in *Poetry* (Chicago), January 1958.
20. Williams, *Autobiography*, pp. 264–65.
21. Louis Zukofsky, 'An Objective', in *Prepositions: The Collected Critical Essays of Louis Zukofsky* (London, 1967), p. 24.
22. Louis Zukofsky, 'A Statement for Poetry', in *Prepositions*, p. 28. See also, 'An Objective', p. 26.
23. Louis Zukofsky, 'Ferry', lines 1–4, 11–15.
24. See also Louis Zukofsky, '9' in '29 Poems', lines 4–6.
25. Louis Zukofsky, 'Preface' to *'A' 1–12* (1959). See also, sections 6, 12.
26. George Oppen, interview with L. S. Dembo, *Contemporary Literature* (Spring 1969), 160. See also, L. S. Dembo, *Contemporary Literature* (Spring 1969), 160. See also, L. S. Dembo, 'Oppen on his Poems: a Discussion', in *George Oppen: Man and Poet* edited by Burton Hatlen (New York, 1981), p. 204.
27. George Oppen, 'Sarah in her Father's Arms', lines 4–7, 9–10, 11–12. See also, lines 1–2.
28. George Oppen, 'Psalm', lines 4–7. See also Dembo, interview with Oppen, p. 161.

29. Oppen, 'Psalm', lines 16–19. See also, line 1.
30. Charles Reznikoff, 'Depression', lines 42–51.
31. Charles Reznikoff, *Testimony* (New York, 1934), p. xiii. The passage quoted in the text is from a letter Reznikoff wrote to Kenneth Burke. The book published in 1934 is a prose volume, and represents Reznikoff's first attempt to utilise the material he had found; it was in the 1950s that he decided free verse was a more appropriate medium.
32. Lorine Niedecker, 'T. E. Lawrence', lines 1–2. See also, 'Paean to Place', lines 1–3.
33. Niedecker, 'Paean to Place', lines 5–9.
34. See Ed Dorn's comments on such a poem's 'undistractable clarity' of word and welding of that word 'to a freely sought, beautifully random instance' in 'Introduction', in *The Full Note: Lorine Niedecker* edited by Peter Dent (Budleigh Salterton, Devon, 1981), p. 23.
35. Lorine Niedecker, 'Paul', lines 1–2, 4–5. See also, 'In the great snowfall before the bomb', lines 22–24.
36. Ezra Pound, 'As for Imagisme', *The New Age* (London) (28 January, 1915), 349.
37. H.D., *The Walls Do Not Fall*, section 15.
38. Conrad Aiken, 'Gehenna', in *Collected Short Stories* (1934; New York, 1960 edition), p. 128.
39. Conrad Aiken, *Preludes for Memnon*, section 1. See also, 'Counterpoint and Implication', *Poetry* (Chicago) 1917 reprinted as an appendix to *The Divine Pilgrim*, in *Collected Poems*, second edition (New York, 1970), pp. 1026–28.
40. Aiken, *Preludes for Memnon*, section ix.
41. Conrad Aiken, 'The Jig of Forslin', section 6. See also, 'Counterpoint and Implication', pp. 1026–28.
42. Ezra Pound, *The Spirit of Romance* (London, 1910), p. 14. See also, Pound, 'A Retrospect', p. 10.
43. Ezra Pound, 'How to Read', in *Literary Essays*, p. 25. See also, *Spirit of Romance*, p. 92.
44. Ezra Pound, 'Arnold Dolmetsch', in *Literary Essays*, p. 431. See also, *Spirit of Romance*, p. 92; 'The Critic as Artist', in *Intentions* (London, 1909), p. 188.
45. Ezra Pound, 'The Return', lines 1–6. See also, Pound, *Gaudier-Brzeska*, p. 85.
46. Ezra Pound, 'The Garden', lines 1–3.
47. Pound, 'How to Read', p. 25. See also T. S. Eliot, 'Introduction' to *Ezra Pound: Selected Poems* (London, 1948), p. 14.
48. Ezra Pound, *Hugh Selwyn Mauberley*, II, lines 1–2, 5–6.
49. Ezra Pound, *Guide to Kulchur* (London, 1938), p. 194.
50. Ezra Pound (translation and commentary), 'Ta Hio: The Great Digest' in *Confucius: The Great Digest and the Unwobbling Pivot* (London, 1952), p. 31.
51. Ezra Pound, 'Cavalcanti', in *Literary Essays*, p. 152.
52. Ezra Pound, Canto LXXXI.

53. Marianne Moore, review in *Contact* IV (Summer 1921), reprinted in *William Carlos Williams: A Collection of Critical Essays* edited by J. Hillis Miller (Englewood Cliffs, N.J., 1966), p. 37.
54. William Carlos Williams, 'Young Sycamore', lines 17–24.
55. Linda W. Wagner, *The Poems of William Carlos Williams: A Critical Study* (Middletown, Conn., 1963), p. 8. See also, William Carlos Williams, *Autobiography*, p. 333; *Paterson*, 'Preface' to Book I.
56. William Carlos Williams, 'Asphodel, That Greeny Flower', Book III.
57. Williams, *Autobiography*, p. 391.
58. William Carlos Williams, 'Letter on Pound', *Quarterly Review of Literature*, V (Autumn 1950), 301.
59. William Carlos Williams, *Spring and All* (Dijon, 1923), p. 50.
60. Williams, *Paterson*, 'Preface' to Book I. See also, Book II, section i: 'Sunday in the Park'; Book IV, section i: 'The Run to the Sea'.
61. Wallace Stevens, 'The Comedian as the Letter C', section i: 'The World without Imagination'.
62. Wallace Stevens, 'Imagination as Value', in *The Necessary Angel: Essays on Reality and the Imagination* (London, 1960), p. 136; 'The Figure of the Youth as Virile Poet', ibid., p. 37.
63. Wallace Stevens, *Notes Toward a Supreme Fiction*, section I, poem ii.
64. Wallace Stevens 'Of Modern Poetry', lines 15–18. See also, lines 11–12, in 'Adagia' *Opus Posthumous* edited by Samuel French Morse (London, 1957), p. 165; 'The Noble Rider and the Sound of Words', in *Necessary Angel*, p. 12.
65. Wallace Stevens, 'Imagination as Value', p. 142. See also, 'The Man with the Blue Guitar', poem V; 'Adagia', p. 163.
66. Wallace Stevens, 'Sunday Morning', poem viii. See also, poem i; 'Esthètique du Mal', section XV.
67. Wallace Stevens, 'John Crowe Ransom. Tennessean', in *Opus Posthumous*, p. 257. See also, 'A Mythology Reflects its Region', line 1; 'Two or Three Ideas', in *Opus Posthumous*, p. 211.
68. Wallace Stevens, 'The Sail of Ulysses', section ii.
69. Wallace Stevens, *Notes Toward a Supreme Fiction*, section II, poem i. See also, 'The Man with the Blue Guitar', poem vi.
70. Wallace Stevens, *Letters of Wallace Stevens* edited by Holly Stevens (London, 1967), p. 402. Letter dated Feb. 18, 1942.
71. Wallace Stevens, 'Another Weeping Woman', lines 8–9.
72. Wallace Stevens, *Notes Toward a Supreme Fiction*, section III, poem x, lines 1, 9–21.
73. Wallace Stevens, 'Adagia', p. 160. See also, p. 161; 'Final Soliloquy of the Interior Paramour', line 9.
74. Wallace Stevens, 'Sail of Ulysses', section v.

Chapter 3
In Search of a Past: The Fugitive Movement and the Major Traditionalists

Traditionalism: the social and cultural situation

In 'Echoes of a Jazz Age', the novelist F. Scott Fitzgerald remembered how, in 1927:

> something bright and alien flashed across the sky. A young Minnesotan who seemed to have had nothing to do with his generation did a heroic thing, and for a moment people set down their glasses in country clubs and speak-easies and thought of their best dreams.

Fitzgerald was referring to the solo flight of Charles Lindbergh across the Atlantic, which seemed to bring America and Europe closer together than ever before. The imaginations of Americans were stirred by what they saw as an epic event: but, as John Ward has pointed out, they were stirred in two significantly contradictory ways. On the one hand, Lindbergh became in the popular mind the living embodiment of the pioneer spirit, the 'spirit of St. Louis', the young, independent and individualistic American, unaffected by public institutions and pressures. Yet, on the other, his achievement was also seen as a witness to the miracle of technology, what was possible with the help of team-work, organisation, and commitment to the production economy. Lindbergh had done it alone, it was pointed out. 'No kingly plane for him', one very minor American poet declared:

> No endless data, comrades, moneyed chums;
> No boards, no councils, no directors grim –
> He plans Alone . . . and takes luck as it comes.[1]

As such, his heroic flight could be seen as a gesture of defiance to the anonymity of the urban, mechanical present, a recovery of true American values, the self-sufficiency of the frontier. Lindbergh himself, however, gave at least equal credit to his plane, 'that wonderful motor', and to team spirit: something clearly acknowledged in the title he chose for the book describing his flight, *We*. President Coolidge himself pointed out that Lindbergh's aeroplane was his 'silent partner', that 'in every particular represented American genius and industry'. And despite their odes to individualism, Americans in general could never really ignore the fact that Lindbergh had been borne to success in a product of the city, industry, and technology. 'All day I felt the pull / Of the Steel Miracle', another minor American poet observed when celebrating Lindbergh's flight: in some, fairly crucial respects, this was a triumph of modernity.

This dual response to the achievement of Charles Lindbergh is significant because, as Ward has pointed out, it indicates just how much, in the first few decades of this century, Americans were torn between conflicting notions of their own experience. The same groups or individuals could and did respond to Lindbergh's achievement as an anticipation of future technological miracles and as an affirmation of the values of the past. Committed to the power, leisure, and wealth of the new, urban world, they nevertheless felt irresistibly drawn towards what they saw as the simpler, purer, and more individualistic values of the old. At the end of the Twenties, two American sociologists observed that 'we today are probably living in one of the eras of greatest rapidity of change in the history of human institutions'; 'any people are in a process of change', they acknowledged but the pace of transition now was radical and unique. Whether they were right about this or not, this was a feeling widely shared among Americans: as one politician observed, 'We live in a new creation. Literally, the old things have passed away and all things have become new'. The conviction of newness and uniqueness mattered to Americans of this period, profoundly affecting their thought and language; and while, as their reaction to Lindbergh showed, part of them was inspired by it, an equal part was clearly frightened. Compelled towards the horizons of tomorrow they were also drawn to the golden landscapes of yesterday. As the anthropologist Ralph Linton has pointed out:

> Even in the most progressive and forward-looking community changes in culture produce some individual discomforts. At least some of the members of the group will develop nostalgic attitudes towards a past which appears rosy in the light of present difficulties. The more intense and widespread the discomfort due to change, the more widespread the attitudes are likely to be.[2]

This struggle between what one historian has termed progress and nostalgia was at a notably acute stage in the earlier part of this century; and it made most Americans of this period, at some point or other, look back with yearning to times that seemed simpler, morally more certain and socially more stable – to the quietude and contentment of a more pastoral age.

This yearning or nostalgia for apparently simpler and better times assumed many forms: in 1920, the newly elected President Warren Harding caught some of it when he told his fellow Americans that theirs was a period for 'not heroics but healing; not nostrums but normality; not resolution but restoration'. In institutional terms, it was perhaps most powerfully reflected in the prohibition movement and the gradual reaction against mass immigration from Europe. In 1920, the Eighteenth Amendment to the Constitution was passed, prohibiting the sale of alcoholic beverages in the United States. Many groups were involved in promoting this amendment, including some progressives who believed that it was as legitimate to preserve a person from the consumption of alcohol as it was to protect him or her against unhealthy or dangerous factory conditions. But undoubtedly the major impetus towards prohibition came from rural, protestant America; and its principal opponents were the urban, industrial, immigrant populations who neither believed in this enshrining of fundamentalist values in law, nor, like the rich, could afford to evade that law by buying bootleg liquor. As one historian has put it, prohibition was in effect a 'symbolic reform',[3] which gave institutional legitimacy to the norms and values of the old America. It transformed at least one crucial aspect of the American Protestant ideal of the good life into a legal requirement. As such, it represented an attempt to hold back the tides of cultural change; it was an exercise, and for a while a reasonably successful exercise, in political nostalgia.

Shortly after the passing of the prohibition amendment, laws were passed restricting immigration from Europe. As with prohibitionism, the motives for this alteration in the law were several: but one significant one was fear – and behind that, again, a desperate need to recover what a Southern newspaper editor called 'The Old America, the America of Jackson and of Lincoln'. At its most extreme, and worst, this fear of the new found its expression in the Ku Klux Klan-whose leader, Hiram Wesley Evans, complained in 1926 that 'the Nordic American today is a stranger in large parts of the land his fathers gave him'. 'When the Klan first appeared', Evans recalled, 'the nation was in the confusion of sudden awakening from the lovely dream of the melting pot'. Traditional Americans had 'decided that even the crossing of salt water did not dim a single spot on a leopard: that an alien usually remains an alien no matter what is done to him . . . They decided that the melting pot was a ghastly failure'. Plagued by confusion and a general breakdown of moral standards, they found that 'those who maintained the old standards did so only in the face of constant ridicule'. 'The sacredness of our Sabbath', Evans continued, 'of our homes, of chastity, and finally even of our right to teach our own children in our own schools fundamental facts and truths' had been 'torn away'. So, he argued, Americans had turned to organisations like the Klan, in the belief that nothing else could save them other than 'a return of power into the hands of the everyday, not highly cultured, not overly intellectualized, but entirely unspoiled and not de-Americanized average citizen of the old stock'.[4]

The terms in which the Imperial Wizard of the Ku Klux Klan put his beliefs were invariably and unusually violent: but they found an echo in the hearts of many Americans who would never dream of joining Evans's movement. Large numbers of people, from the President down, reacted against what were popularly known as 'hyphenated Americans': they longed to return from what they perceived as an anonymous and confusingly heterogeneous mass society to the pieties and coherence of an older culture. Quite apart from the laws containing immigration – which, it was hoped, would help America preserve or recover Anglo-conformity, a traditional Anglo-American community – the laws passed at this time prohibiting the teaching of evolution in schools were symptomatic of the unease and desperate nostalgia felt by so many sections of the community. In 1925, for instance, the Tennessee legislature passed an Anti-Evolution Act which the Governor of the state, after signing it into law, described as 'a distinct protest against an irreligious tendency to exalt so-called science, and deny the Bible in some schools and quarters . . .'. Despite the Governor's belief that the act would never be implemented, only a short while after a young teacher named John Scopes was put on trial in Dayton, Tennessee for violating the law. The reasons why Scopes had been brought to trial are in themselves significant evidence of the psychic divide, the pull between past and future, experienced by so many Americans. Scopes had been approached by the American Civil Liberties Union to defend a test case: he was to teach evolution to his pupils so as to provoke the authorities into enforcing the new law which would, in turn, enable opponents of that law to test its validity. Scopes was reluctant to do so at first: but then something strange occurred. A group of civic boosters, people who wanted to put Dayton on the map and encourage investment in the town, came to see Scopes, to persuade him to accept the offer made by the Civil Liberties Union. In effect, they wanted to exploit their community's commitment to its inherited values in order to enhance its business status. They wanted to use the principles of the old order to advance the interests of the new, and so turn the ambiguities of their culture to their advantage.

The trial of John Scopes was itself a showpiece, attracting national media attention. The politician and former Presidential candidate William Jennings Bryan acted for the prosecution while Clarence Darrow, perhaps the most famous lawyer of his day, appeared for the defence. Journalists poured into Tennessee in their hundreds to report on events: what matters more in retrospect, though, is not what they said, the variously nostalgic or satirical portraits they drew of small-town life in Dayton and the so-called Bible Belt in general, but the tensions and ambiguities that even they, and those involved in the legal process, felt. A general anxiety about the way in which American culture was progressing created the anti-evolution law, whereas a more specific desire to accelerate that process occasioned the trial. The ambivalent loyalties of Americans, to both past and future, set the scene, and this ambivalence was suitably reflected in the final verdict: Scopes was found guilty, but the fine imposed on him as a punishment was then overruled by the Tennessee Supreme Court on a legal technicality. In effect, the legal system found the accused guilty and then refused to punish him. 'America is not yet dominated by its great cities', one newspaper proudly asserted, 'Control of its destinies still remains in the small communities and rural regions, with their traditional conservatism and solid virtues'. As the 'Monkey trial' in Dayton showed, however, this was possibly more an expression of hope than of fact; and the hope itself was profoundly qualified, tempered by a yearning towards progress.[5]

The nostalgic impulses that found convoluted expression in such things as the Scopes trial, prohibition, or immigration quotas also helped generate varieties of artistic traditionalism. There was a new interest in the recovery of the American past among both writers and critics. Observers of the cultural scene, like Van Wyck Brooks and Matthew Josephson, began constructing the idea of an American literary tradition. Writers from the previous century, like Walt Whitman and Emily Dickinson, were rediscovered. More to the point, perhaps, novelists and poets alike began an imaginative exploration of what one of them, Willa Cather, termed 'the precious, the incommunicable past'. This passage, from Cather's novel, *My Antonia*, captures something of that feeling shared by so many of these writers. The words are attributed to Jim Burden, the narrator, but they clearly express Cather's own views, the impulses that fired her narrative into life:

> While I was in the very act of yearning towards the new forms . . . brought up before me, my mind plunged away from me, and I suddenly found myself thinking of the places and people of my own infinitesimal past. They stood out strengthened and

> simplified now . . . They were all I had for answer to the new appeal.[6]

'The past is never dead. It's not even past', observes a character in one of William Faulkner's novels: which is another way of expressing this obsession with yesterday, the desire to remember or even reinvent past times. Other ways, many of them, were offered by the poets between the wars as they sought sure anchorage, moral and perhaps also formal; and not least among these poets was a group associated with the South who were known, for a while, as the Fugitives.

The significance of the Fugitives

In 1915, a group of writers, students, and amateur men of letters, many of them associated with Vanderbilt University, began meeting in Nashville, Tennessee. Their meeting-place was the home of a local dilettante called Sidney Hirsch; and, although theoretically they met to discuss matters of philosophy and metaphysics, they spent much of the time simply listening to their host expounding his latest opinions. Hirsch was a bizarre and impressive figure. A former athlete and artist's model, an amateur playwright and etymologist, a world traveller and friend of Gertrude Stein, he claimed to be one of the seven sages, alive in the world at any time, on whom humanity depends for its wisdom and progress. It was perhaps inevitable that young university students – people like Donald Davidson, for instance, fresh from the Southern countryside – found him intimidating; and, partly as a defence, they asked their English instructor, John Crowe Ransom, to accompany them. Ransom, although only a few years older than his students, was already an imposing character. He readily agreed, and with his arrival the meetings grew more open, more popular, and more specifically literary. They were halted for a while, when the United States entered the First World War and many members of the group enlisted, but they resumed soon after the Armistice. By now, Ransom had published his first book of poetry, called *Poems About God*; and then in 1921 the group was joined by Allen Tate, a fiercely intelligent undergraduate who introduced his companions to the intricacies of modern poetry and in particular to work of T. S. Eliot. Gradually, under the influence of people like Ransom, Tate, and Davidson, the group spent more and more time discussing their individual literary efforts; and it was out of such discussions that the idea of producing a magazine grew.

It was, in fact, Hirsch (otherwise something of a marginal figure by now) who suggested starting a magazine and who provided a name: *The Fugitive*. What was initially implied by that title was later explained by Tate. 'A Fugitive', he said, 'was quite simply a Poet: the Wanderer, . . . the Outcast, the man who carries the secret wisdom of the world.'[7] This certainly fitted in with Hirsch's own prophetic, cabalistic notion of poetry. However, when the first edition of the magazine appeared, it was not so much this connotation that was stressed as a more regional and contemporary one. 'THE FUGITIVE flees from nothing faster than from high-caste Brahmins of the Old South', the opening statement declared. The common theme was alienation from a particular tradition: 'a tradition', as the editors of the magazine put it, 'that may be called a tradition only when looked at through the haze of a generous imagination.' The Fugitives saw themselves fleeing, in fact, from Southern romanticism, nostalgia for the region's past. And they saw themselves fleeing, too, from contemporary society: finding refuge in brotherhood from the dehumanising environment that they saw all around them – in Nashville, in the *modern* South, and in the newly industrialised United States. Something of both their distaste for regional atavism and the disdain they felt for modern, urban culture was reflected in the pseudonyms they adopted for the first two issues. Ransom called himself Roger Prim, Tate was Henry Feathertop, and Davidson Robert Gallivant. Names like these suggested a *coterie* of elegant dandies who, like Poe, had little affection either for utilitarian culture or for the sentimentality of the 'moonlight and magnolias' school. And even when the pseudonyms were dropped, the alienation, the sense of distance remained: for the Fugitives, it seemed, to be conscious of their age meant to be conscious of their isolation from it.

The Fugitive magazine lasted for three years: coinciding with what R. P. Blackmur called the *Anni Mirabiles*, when suddenly an 'explosion of talent took place' in the Western world that has dwarfed everything since – 'crystallizing between 1922 and 1925 in *Ulysses, The Waste Land, The Magic Mountain, The Tower, The Counterfeiters*, and a great deal more'.[8] During that period others joined the group, notably Robert Penn Warren and Laura Riding, but apart from one or two poems each by Tate, Warren, Riding, and Davidson, and Ransom's contributions, the actual quality of the poetry in the magazine was not especially high. There are, in fact, few poems produced by Fugitive writers during the Fugitive period, apart from those of Ransom, which can be described as major; and yet this little periodical, never selling more than five hundred copies, is of considerable importance to the story of modern American verse. Why? In some respects, the answer to this question suggests a parallel with the Imagists. Like the Imagist movement, the Fugitives did not produce very much significant work immediately;

they could not even be called a movement, really, since they never had anything that could properly be called a programme or manifesto, only a few 'do's and don'ts.' But like the Imagists, the Fugitives did supply a nursing-ground for a number of quite exceptional poets; and they did develop together certain ideas about poetry that were to be crucial both to them individually and to many other American poets during this century, whether directly influenced by them or not.

That, however, is about as far as the resemblance between the Fugitives and the Imagists goes. In most other ways, in terms of precisely what they believed and practised, they offer a profound contrast to each other. Allen Tate, in fact, when he was trying to explain what was special about the Fugitive group, used this contrast as a means of definition. 'I would call the Fugitives', he declared, 'an intensive and historical group as opposed to the eclectic and cosmopolitan groups that flourished in the East.'[9] As far as literature was concerned, the Imagists were experimentalists and internationalist. They believed, like Pound, in making it new, and they saw themselves as part of a larger, cosmopolitan, cultural community. The Fugitives, by comparison, were traditionalists and regionalists. With the occasional exception of Tate, who liked to pose as the modernist gadfly of the group (although, as his poems show, he was not that much of a modernist in practice), they subscribed to the traditional forms, metres, and diction. And with the exception only of Riding, they belonged to the South: they were born in the South, raised in the South and – for all their attacks on the nostalgic habits of the region – they saw themselves primarily in terms of their 'Southern-ness'. Nor does the contrast end there. The Imagists were, for the most part, optimists, rationalists, creatures of the Enlightenment: Pound is again the exemplary figure here, believing in the innocence and perfectibility of the individual, the possibility of progress, and the improvement or even perfecting of an entire society. The Fugitives were very different. Classical humanists or, alternatively, typical products of the Bible Belt, they believed in the reality of evil: inherited and tested forms and principles were necessary, they instinctively felt, to support the individual in his weakness, to focus his vision and prevent him from wandering into error. Perhaps the Imagists could be called a 'movement' in the loose sense: innovative, enthusiastic, revolutionary in impulse, and alive with the unexpressed possibilities and the mobility of the present. If so, the Fugitives should be called a 'school': disciplined, cautious, deliberate, and aware above all of an immense debt to the past.

Another possible way of seeing the two groups is in terms not so much of contrast as of balance or dialectic. John Gould Fletcher, the only poet to participate in both, tended to see them in this way. For in an essay published after *The Fugitive* magazine had ceased to exist, he claimed that the Fugitive movement had been a necessary reaction to the Imagists. His argument was that the 'free verse' school under Pound had run its course and that a new 'Classical' school had emerged in the early Twenties, initiated by Eliot but best represented by the Fugitives. This school, Fletcher insisted, was more subtle and sophisticated than its predecessor:

> It takes the innovations of form of the free-verse school . . . for granted; what it quarrels with is fundamentally their attitude towards art. It begins by challenging the importance of emotion in poetry; it asserts that intellect and not emotion is the true basis of poetic art; and it proposes a return to classicism as the only possible remedy for the common looseness and facility of much present-day poetic art.[10]

Some of the terms Fletcher uses may seem rather questionable. Are the austere, epigrammatic poems of H.D., for instance, any less 'classical' than the tortured introversions of Tate? Or is Pound any less aware of the function of the intellect than Ransom? But his argument does, at least, offer another useful way of looking at the relationship between the Imagists and the Fugitives. The Imagist emphasis on freedom and the Fugitive interest in form; the Imagist concentration on the spiralling suggestiveness of metaphor, and the Fugitive preference for wit, irony, and ambiguity; the Imagist commitment to density of texture, the subtleties of associational thought, the disjunctive power of the ideogram, and the Fugitive adoption of more traditional forms of articulation, of rational, discursive argument. Such distinctions are necessarily simplified and need to be qualified in individual cases. Nevertheless, they suggest the poles between which most American poetry of the past sixty or so years has been written: most of the writers we are concerned with have operated somewhere within the territory they define.

Traditionalism and the South: Ransom, Tate, Davidson, Warren, J. P. Bishop, Berry, Dickey

Of all the poets nurtured by the Fugitive movement, John Crowe Ransom is perhaps the most interesting. Consistently, in his critical work Ransom pushed the Fugitive commitment to traditionalism about as far as it could go: defending the world of myth, ritual, and above all art against what he saw as the arrogant assumptions of science. Science, he argued, is partial because it supplies us with abstract knowledge only: it, and its language, satisfy no more than the rational sense. Myth and the arts, on the other hand, bring order into life without ever denying contingency or the particular – or the strangeness and ultimate intractability of the universe. Combining and qualifying abstractions with a firm sense of the concrete, they satisfy the whole person: the intellect, the emotions, *and* the senses. In a traditional society, the entire personality is thereby developed; since the myths and ritual that underpin it foster the sensibility as well as the reason – a sense of mystery, of what human beings *cannot* do, as well as a sense of possibility, what they *can*. In an un-traditional society such as our own, however, such wholeness is impossible. There is no real place for the feelings, the imagination; everything is judged in terms of use. The reason has been developed at the expense of sensibility; and people assume that nothing is beyond their scope, or the power of scientific rationalism. As a result, their personalities are fragmented, they are only half-developed. We are left, in fact, with that recurrent phenomenon in Ransom's poetry, the dissociated sensibility, the divided man.

As Cleanth Brooks has observed, the desperation of many of Ransom's poetic characters springs from the fact that they cannot achieve unity of being. They are like the narrator of 'Winter Remembered' who, separated off from his beloved, comes to typify the sense of fragmentation, estrangement, and sheer vacuum which all those who have failed to attain wholeness of being must experience. Lonely old spinsters ('Emily Hardcastle, Spinster'), young scholars ('Persistent Explorer'), old eccentrics ('Captain Carpenter'), thwarted lovers ('Parting at Dawn', 'The Equilibrists'), abstract idealists and optimists ('Man Without Sense of Direction'): they all illustrate that 'old illusion of grandeur' which Ransom explores in one of his later poems, 'Painted Head' – the belief, that is, that the mind can exist apart, 'play truant from the body bush.'[11] This, certainly, is one of Ransom's favourite themes: that 'cry of Absence, Absence in the heart' which charts out a more general situation of emptiness and loss. Others are death and the world of the child, which are often treated together: as in 'Dead Boy', 'Bells for John Whiteside's Daughter', and 'Blue Girls'. 'Death is the greatest subject for poetry', Ransom insisted, '. . . there's no recourse from death, except that we learn to face it.' As such, it provides modern man in particular with a timely reminder of his limitations: the most powerful example possible of all that the reason cannot encompass or control. And when that subject is the death of a child then, for Ransom, a further dimension is added: because, in a fragmented society such as our own, only the child's world is whole. Only this world does not suffer from dissociation, Ransom believed, and a consequent feeling of spiritual absence; and even so it presents a less than satisfying possibility because – as the very facts of transience and mortality indicate – it is innocent, limited, and frail.

Ransom's aim is not simply to describe such characters and situations, however. He tries to place them, most often with the help of a peculiar quality of language and tone. 'Winter Remembered', for instance, ends with these lines:

> Dear love, these fingers that had known your touch,
> And tied our separate forces first together
> Were ten poor idiot fingers not worth much,
> Ten frozen parsnips hanging in the weather.[12]

This mundane image, contrasting sharply with the romantic framework of the rest of the poem, brings together the conflicting figures of heat and cold that characterise the rest of the poem: the parsnips, normally capable of warmth and growth, have been frozen into lifelessness just as, in a way, the narrator and his limbs have. The peculiar tone or attitude engendered by this comparison is characteristic of Ransom, and has been variously described as 'acid gaiety', 'wrinkled laughter', or 'detached, mock-pedantic, wittily complicated.' Perhaps the best description is Ransom's own, though. For when he refers in his essays to that 'irony' which, by combining the dream of the ideal with the dismay of the actual, becomes 'the rarest of the states of mind, because . . . the most inclusive', he is implicitly describing the strategy of his own work. In such lines, in fact, the poet himself seems to step forward, to establish the kind of 'mellow wisdom' (to use Ransom's own phrase) of which the narrator-lover himself is incapable: the ironic inclusiveness of vision that somehow eludes most people in an un-traditional world.

Irony is just one of the weapons in Ransom's poetic armoury: in most of his work, he also tries to suggest wholeness of vision through the general idioms of his verse. Poetry at its best, according to Ransom, should devote equal stylistic attention to what he calls 'structure' and 'texture': that is, to the totality of the work, the 'logical object or universal' that appeals to the reason, and to 'the tissue of irrelevance' and particularity that caters more to the demands of the sensibility. 'A beautiful poem', according to these criteria, 'is one that proceeds to the completion of a logical structure, but not without attention to the local particularity of its components.'[13] This, precisely, is the kind of beauty Ransom aims for. Almost from the beginning of his poetic career he tried to articulate a form which involves the simultaneous evocation of contradictory responses, catching the complex and yet unified reaction of the complete personality to experience. And where this attempt has been successful, the result has been a type of poetic discourse that demonstrates its positives in its methods of expression: in which manner, as a whole, offers a definitive comment on matter.

'Dead Boy' is a good illustration of this. Its occasion is a simple one, the death of a young child known to the narrator. With the help of radical alterations of diction, metaphor, and metrical effect, however, Ransom suggests a response that is far from simple:

> The little cousin is dead, by foul subtraction,
> A green bough from Virginia's aged tree,
> And none of the county kin like the transaction,
> Nor some of the world of outer dark, like me.
>
> A boy not beautiful, nor good, nor clever,
> A black cloud full of storms too hot for keeping.
> A sword beneath his mother's heart – yet never
> Woman bewept her babe as this is weeping.
>
> A pig with a pasty face, so I had said,
> Squealing for cookies, kinned by poor pretence
> With a noble house. But the little man quite dead,
> I see the forbears' antique lineaments.[14]

The feelings aroused by this portrait are labyrinthine. The ornate, Latinate diction of the first three lines, and the elevated image in the second, suggest one reaction to the death, which is to distance it with the help of ceremonious language and gesture. But this is hastily qualified by phrases that echo the King James version of the Bible ('outer dark', 'black cloud full of storms') and consequently help to place the event in a larger, religious context, where it seems part of a universal process. And it is flatly contradicted by lines such as the ninth, in which the staccato rhythm combines with a dismissive image and harsh alliterative effects to suggest the intrusion of a more realistic assessment. Throughout the poem archaisms jostle with a more colloquial idiom, and the mellifluous cadences of one line are denied by the eruptive movement of the next. And all these reactions, we are led to infer, belong, not to different people, but to one complex personality, who can love the dead boy and yet recognise his frailty; regret his death but know that his world was doomed in any case; realise the 'poor pretence' involved in talk of 'forbears' and in the funeral rites, while acknowledging the value of the beliefs, in tradition and ceremony, so illustrated. The style of the poem, in effect, dramatises the personality of the narrator; and that personality defines for us that unity of being, the marriage of thought and feeling, which Ransom's un-traditional people so conspicuously lack.

Not that it is always left to the style to perform this positive function in Ransom's poetry: just occasionally he is more explicit. This is the case with one of the few poems where he is directly concerned with the Southern tradition, 'Antique Harvesters'. Set on the banks of the Mississippi, the poem presents Ransom's native region as a place where wholeness of being is still available. This is not, it should be emphasised, because the poet indulges in that easy nostalgia that the Fugitives criticised. On the contrary, it is because he invites us into the myth-making process. He observes the river, the land, the harvesters, the old men who watch them, and 'the hunters, keepers of a rite'[15] who ride by. And, as he does so, he gradually and consciously associates all these things with the notions of ceremony and chivalry, the belief in a usable past and an inheritable pattern of living. What seemed at first little more than 'A meager hill of kernels, a runnel of juice' is transformed during the course of the poem into a spiritual resource, a setting that evidently furnishes roots and identity; and that process of transformation, whereby an anonymous and apparently unpromising environment becomes an heroic land, is as much a matter for the reader's attention as the purported subject is. The earth becomes 'our Lady'; the hunters become 'archetypes of chivalry', the hunted fox a 'lovely ritualist'; the harvesters become *antique* harvesters, participating in time-honoured ceremonies and expressing through their work a religious devotion to the land. Yet all this is done without any rejecting or minimising of the original facts in the case of the farm labourer, or in the case of any person destined to work and then die. 'Antique Harvesters' is, in fact, not so much a portrait from life as a minor historical myth: in which the process of creation, the act of making a landscape and then attaching to it the idea of unity of consciousness is the intent of the poem – and constitutes a vital part of its *content* too.

In some ways, Allen Tate bears a haunting resemblance to Ransom. He, too, is preoccupied with the radical discontinuities of modern existence; he, too, longs for a traditional society in which moral unity is the norm. But Tate was also affected by the verse experiments of Eliot and Hart Crane – he even defended *The Waste Land* against Ransom's dismissive criticisms – and this is reflected in the tone, and sometimes the structure, of his work. Freer forms alternate with formal patterns. Logical connectives are omitted, sentences inverted, scenes changed rapidly. Like Eliot, Tate exploits references to, or quotations from, earlier literature (Ransom's poetic world is certainly soaked in the classics, but he does not allude to them in this way). Like Eliot, too, he uses images to animate abstractions ('And abnegation folds hands'), builds metaphor within metaphor, and uses images that grow incrementally from one poem to another: the figure of the idiot, for example, appears in at least three poems, 'Subway', 'Idiot', and 'Epistle (to W.W.)'. Like Crane, he employs a strained, extraordinarily dense vocabulary in which, as one critic has put it, 'almost every adjective . . . challenges the reader's imagination to follow it off at a tangent'. And like Crane, as well, this often leads to verbal violence, to extraordinary mixing of metaphors:

> The day is a loud grenade that bursts a smile
> Of serious weeds in a comic lily plot.[16]

The result is that while Ransom's tone is, as a rule, courtly, poised, and mannered, Tate's is intense, over-wrought. The environment he describes is dark and doomed ('broken', 'fractured', 'blind' are favourite adjectives, and favoured nouns include 'iron', 'stone', 'winter', 'bone', 'night' and 'cold'). The approach he adopts is characterised by a chilly passionateness, an icy despair. Unlike Ransom, Tate is never the measured observer; he is himself a desperate part of the desperate world he creates.

The distance between Tate and Ransom is measured with particular force in Tate's most famous poem, 'Ode to the Confederate Dead'. In some ways, 'Ode' operates within the same series of assumptions as 'Antique Harvesters'. It, too, is a profoundly traditionalist poem which attempts to create a myth, an ideal version of the past, as a corrective to the present. It, too, is a poem that dramatises the mythologising process, the creation of an idea, a complex of possibilities, out of historical fact. The narrator, a man who characterises the modern failure to live according to principle (or what Tate, in his essay on his own work, calls 'active faith'), stands by the monuments raised to those killed fighting for the South during the Civil War; and as he describes their lives, or rather what he imagines their lives to have been, the description is transmuted into celebration. The past is reinvented, just as place, landscape is in 'Antique Harvesters'; the soldiers being remembered are transformed into an heroic alternative to the plight of the person remembering them. That is the drama of the poem, accounting for the poignancy of lines like the following:

> Turn your eyes to the immoderate past,
> Turn to the inscrutable infantry rising
> Demons out of the earth – they will not last.
> Stonewall, Stonewall, and the sunken fields of hemp,
> Shiloh, Antietam, Malvern Hill, Bull Run,
> Lost in that orient of the thick-and-fast
> You will curse the setting sun.

Cursing only the leaves crying
Like an old man in a storm
You hear the shout, the crazy hemlocks point
With troubled fingers to the silence which
Smothers you, a mummy, in time.[17]

And yet these lines suggest how unlike Ransom Tate is, even while he appears to echo him. The voice of 'Antique Harvesters' is the voice of all Ransom's poems: accomplished, witty, serene – the voice of someone who can, apparently, fathom and perform his nature. The voice of 'Ode' is, by contrast, uncertain, feverish, disoriented – the voice of the 'locked-in ego' as Tate puts it elsewhere, of a man unable to liberate himself from a sense of his own impotence and fragmentation. The narrator of Ransom's poem remains triumphantly detached: sometimes helping to gauge the failure of his subjects and sometimes, as in 'Antique Harvesters', helping to endow his subjects' achievements with articulate shape. The narrator of the 'Ode', however, is like the narrator of most of Tate's poetry: a person obsessed with his failure to attain unity of being, whose introversions, tortured idiom, clotted imagery, and convoluted syntax register what Tate has called 'the modern squirrel cage of our sensibility, the extreme introspection of our time.'

For all its nervous intensity, though, 'Ode to the Confederate Dead' does not degenerate into hysteria: a measure of control is retained, so as to give dramatic force to the narrator's feelings of isolation and waste. Tate remains a traditionalist in this respect, too, that his poems are tightly organised; his narrators may disperse their energies, scattering themselves piecemeal, but he tries to ensure that his poetic forms never do. 'Ode' is, in fact, structured according to classical precepts, with a Strophe (establishing the themes of the poem), an Anti-strophe (answering the themes of the Strophe), and an Epode (gathering up the opposing themes). In addition, it is carefully arranged into verse paragraphs, separated by a refrain that provides (to use Tate's phrase) 'occasions of assimilation';[18] it demonstrates a cunning use of rhyme; and there is a dominant metre of iambic pentameter with varying six, four, and three stressed lines. The result is a constant tension between texture and structure: the language, packed and disruptive, the multiple levels of allusion and bitter ironies of feeling, are barely kept in control by the formal patterns of the verse. Like the narrator who turns his eyes to the immoderate past, the poet seems to be trying to will himself into a discipline, to force upon himself the rigours of an inherited form; and on this level, at least, the level of manner rather than matter, the pursuit of traditionalism is not entirely unsuccessful.

Tate's search for a traditional order, with its associated idea of wholeness of being, eventually led him away from the South and into religious faith. From the first, he had been a little sceptical about the claims of his region: even at its finest, before the Civil War, it was, he declared, 'a feudal society without a feudal religion' and to that extent was fatally incomplete. And he gradually turned, for the promise of moral unity, to the Roman Catholic church. Out of the actual process of conversion came poems like 'Seasons of the Soul', a powerful and often pained sequence that ends with a prayer to a mysterious 'mother of silences' who, recalling both the 'Lady of Silences' in Eliot's 'Ash Wednesday' and Baudelaire's 'maitresse de maitresses', seems to combine intimations of the spiritual and the sensual, the Virgin Mary and the carnal knowledge that concludes in death:

> Speak, that we may hear;
> Listen, while we confess
> That we conceal our fear;
> Regard us, while the eye
> Discerns by sight or guess . . .
>
> . . .
>
> Whether your kindness, mother
> Is mother of silences.[19]

After the conversion, in turn, came poems like 'The Swimmers'. Relaxed, fluent, idiomatic, although capable of allusion and even moments of apocalypse, such poems reveal a new willingness to submit to the material rather than force it into a mould – and, in particular, to submit to the sanctions of memory and the compulsions of personality:

> I see again
> The shrill companions of that odyssey:
>
> Bill Eaton, Charlie Watson, "Nigger" Layne
> The doctor's son, Harry Duèsler who played
> The flute; and Tate, with water on the brain.
>
> Dog-days: the dusty leaves where rain delayed
> Hung low on poison-oak and scuppernong,
> And we were following the active shade
>
> Of water that bells and bickers all night long[20]

Tate found ultimate salvation for the traditionalist, then, in religion. Ransom found salvation, of a kind, elsewhere: after he had lost faith in the possibility of resurrecting traditional principles on a formal, social basis, he turned to art. 'The arts are expiations', he declared rather dolefully, 'but they are beautiful . . . They seem worth the vile welter through which homeless spirits must wade between times.'[21] The paths of the two other notable Fugitive poets, Donald Davidson and Robert Penn Warren, were different in turn from these and from each other. Davidson's is the simpler case. Uppermost in the mind of his group, Davidson later claimed:

> . . . was a feeling of intense disgust with the spiritual disorder of modern life . . . We wanted a life which through its own conditions . . . would engender . . . order, leisure, character, stability . . . What history told us of the South . . . drove us straight to its tradition . . .[22]

Partially true of Ransom, Tate, and Warren, this is almost entirely true of Davidson himself: disgust with the present precipitated a turning in on the past, revulsion from the machine age bred an attachment to a time when factories were still the exception rather than the rule. *The Tall Men*, a long poem first published in 1927, reveals the beliefs and allegiances to which Davidson remained true throughout his life. The poem is divided into eight sections, and the connecting link is a dramatised narrator, a representative man whose life the reader shares for one day – from the moment when he is 'Flung up from sleep against the breakfast table / Like numb and helpless driftwood' to the hour when he lies half asleep, trying to devise an escape from his situation. During the day, the poem ranges back and forth in time, although the place is nearly always Nashville, and through this process we are supplied with a means of assessing the evidence: the present is judged in terms of a past articulated in dream, in memory – or more simply by means of a contrast between locations in Tennessee then and now.

Some portions of the poem demonstrate Davidson's particular talent for launching powerful assaults on the 'mechanical age'. A passage like the following, for instance, dehumanises the narrator by presenting him as a series of dissociated elements whose functions have been usurped by the machine:

> The modern brain . . .
> Requires the aid of mystical apparatus
> (Weights, levers, motor, steel rods, black boy)
> And pyramiding dollars nicely invested
> To float in boredom up to the cool fifth floor . . .[23]

Other portions show an equally characteristic ability to capture the routines of the rural South, in dramatic and nicely particularistic terms:

. . . A boy's hands thrusts
Insistent swords of corn-leaves from his face,
. . . The field
Waits where the mower clicks its teeth . . .
. . . Here are the teams.
Waggons rattle and halt. The haft of a pitchfork
Presses hickory into a youngish palm.[24]

The problem is that, when *The Tall Men* is looked at as a whole, no clear picture of the past emerges. The function of the Old South in the poem is simple: it is there to supply a notion of the Great Good Place to which 'the modern brain' longs to flee. As such, it has little to do with either the facts of the case or the kind of mythologising process to be found in the work of Ransom and Tate. Like anywhere that is the product of wish fulfilment, it is a world in which all is possibility, where the limitations of the actual disappear and nothing is frustrated by circumstance. So it is variously portrayed, in terms of primitive vigour and feudal munificence; Davy Crockett jostles alongside a planter described as 'the finest gentleman / That ever lived'; and passages like the one just quoted are followed by others that talk of 'old tremulous histories / Of slender hands, proud smiling lips and halls / Peopled with fragile beauty.' At one point in his poem, Davidson refers to 'the motley splendours' of the past; and, lost amid the maze of quite different associations inspired by this portrait of old Tennessee, the reader may feel tempted to agree, while placing additional emphasis upon the word 'motley'.

So, unlike Ransom's and Tate's forms of traditionalism, Davidson's is largely uncritical: he takes different aspects of the past, apotheosises each of them in turn, and insists that they are all somehow typical – without recognising, apparently, that the notion of typicality involves an acceptance of the principle of consistency. Unlike Ransom and Tate, also, Davidson never moved very far from his original stance. Times changed, but he did not. His later work is little more than a less flexible version of the earlier, with opinions hardened into prejudices to the point where 'reactionary' seems a more appropriate term than 'traditional'. Perhaps the starkest contrast here, however, is not with Ransom and Tate but with Warren. Consider, for example, this passage from Warren's long dramatic poem, *Brother to Dragons*:

JEFFERSON: One day I wrote to Adams . . .

I wrote, and said
That the dream of the future is better than the
dream of the past.
Now could I find hope to find courage to say

That without the fact of the past, no matter
how terrible,
We cannot dream the future?[25]

As this passage implies, Warren believes in the reality of evil. Nobody can escape that reality; and the best way of acknowledging it is to dwell on the past and foster the historical sense. 'History', says Warren in one of his later poems, 'is what you can't / Resign from';[26] nor should you try, since what the 'dream of the past' can develop is a healthy awareness of human limits – a sense of the sheer 'massiveness of experience' bearing down on the human personality and drastically circumscribing the capacity for action. Looking at what has gone before, people can learn from their mistakes and also begin to understand the nature of that fallible human community to which they belong. That is not the entire story, though: as Warren indicates, there is the dream of the future as well as the dream of the past. 'Of the brute creation' people may be, but they are also, potentially, 'a little lower than the angels.' Consequently, while they require an adequate definition of terror to remind them of their monstrous origins, they need at the same time to find some way of 'accommodating flesh to idea' so as 'to be able to frame a definition of joy.' Tradition, the stored wisdom of the past, is certainly crucial in suggesting appropriate values, principles by which to live. But values, according to Warren, are actually formulated by individuals out of the experience of living and, even as they develop, qualify and enrich that experience. Past and future, fact and idea, the traditionalist sense of what has been and the utopian feeling for what might be: the process is a dialectical one and there is no end to it, and so no end to the growth and discovery of the self, other than that offered to each of us individually by death.

Some of Warren's poetry is concerned with the failure to realise this dialectic, the 'process whereby pain of the past in its pastness / May be converted into the future tense / Of joy.' Like Ransom, Warren has his own gallery of betrayed idealists, and many of his poems offer secular versions of the Fall. The closing lines of 'Picnic Remembered', for instance, rehearse characteristic themes of disillusioned innocence and vanished dreams:

Or is the soul a hawk that, fled
On glimmering wings past vision's path,
Reflects the last gleam to us here
Though sun is sunk and darkness near
– Uncharted Truth's high heliograph?[27]

At its worst, the fall into experience then provokes nihilism, surrender to the brute materiality of things: the so-called 'realist' is, in Warren's eyes at least, no more adequate – that is, just as blind to the dialectic of past and future – as the idealist is. But, at its best, it leads on to a kind of redemption, expressed sometimes in terms of a rediscovery of the father. Seeing his father properly, the narrator/protagonist of Warren's poems begins to see himself; accepting and embracing him, warts and all, he starts to accept his own limitations and embrace the human community. 'Man can return to his lost unity,' Warren has insisted, 'and . . . if the foliage and flower of the innocent garden are now somewhat browned by a late season, all is the more precious for the fact, for what is now achieved has been achieved by a growth of moral awareness.[28]

The figure of the garden or clearing – 'browned by a late season', perhaps, yet not without a sense of serenity – recurs throughout Warren's work, and it brings together the two patterns of the fall followed by redemption and the return to the father. For it is at once the familiar home of Adam and the old homestead, somewhere in western Kentucky, to which Warren and his protagonists, born in just such a place, dream of returning. Quite apart from that, it also offers a reminder of that equipoise so vital to Warren's work, since it is neither utterly savage nor completely subdued. Just as the human personality, according to Warren, operates best in the space between fact and idea, tradition and opportunity, so the various clearings he describes exist in a border territory between forest and town, the energies of the wilderness and the structures of civilisation. They are not necessarily cultivated spots. For example, the place where the protagonist in *Audubon: A Vision* has his first mystical experience is simply an open space created by nature:

> October: and the bear
> Daft in the honey-light, yawns.
>
> The bear's tongue, pink as a baby's, outcrisps
> to the curled tip.
> It bleeds the black blood of the blueberry.
>
> . . .
>
> He leans on his gun. Thinks
> How thin is the membrane between himself and
> the world.[29]

They are always, though, as this passage suggests, both outer landscapes and inner ones: they are products partly of history and Warren's own experience and partly of myth, his fictive powers.

Given that Warren is so committed, in principle, to the notion of change, it is hardly surprising that his work bears witness to some remarkable alterations of language and tone – and even, to a certain extent, of vision. His early poetry tended towards the highly wrought and frigidly impersonal: crabbed, allusive, and sometimes rather too knowingly ironic, it seemed to be borrowing a manner – from Ransom and Tate, in particular – instead of shaping one in response to personal needs. The later work, by contrast, has been more expansive and open: a richer, more variable idiom has combined with fluent, muscular rhythms to create a sense of energetic composure, disciplined ease. At the same time, the preoccupation with failure or chilly forms of redemption that characterised the early writing has given way to an interest in existential humility, the possible sources of courage and awe. Above all, Warren has begun to seek the springs of well-being more fiercely than ever before: to search for an identity forged out of a passionate and positive engagement with the world. 'Tell me a story of deep delight',[30] *Audubon* concludes, and that line articulates the impulse that prised the poet loose from his earlier habits. Traditionalist Warren remains, but a traditionalist seeking poetic narratives that release the glory of life – or, as he put it once, enable him to 'frame a definition of joy.'

Ransom, Tate, Warren: together these three major figures suggest the various possibilities of traditionalism, and in particular of Southern traditionalism. But they are not alone in doing this even within the context of their region. Another, unjustly neglected figure suggests other possibilities: John Peale Bishop. Born in West Virginia, a close friend to F. Scott Fitzgerald and Edmund Wilson, Bishop thought of himself as a Southerner to the end of his life. The epitaph that he dictated to his wife three days before he died gives some indication of his position, and his voice:

> Long did I live
> Consistent, lonely, proud.
> Not death, but fear of death
> Restores us to the crowd.

As Tate put it, this 'could have been the epitaph of a Roman under Augustus.'[31] More than any other poet, Bishop reveals the neo-classical strain in the Southern tradition: the feeling is stoical, the sense of honour is fierce, the form of expression laconic, chiselled. Many Southerners, especially in the eighteenth century, liked to model themselves on republican Rome; and Bishop developed this tendency, perceiving himself as a patrician republican confronted with the corruption of empire. He saw a parallel between the decline of Rome and the decadence of the United States; and he felt the necessity of withdrawing into the exercise of private virtue. Convinced of the necessity of order, personal and public, totally committed to the ideas of duty and ceremony, he was perhaps more single-mindedly traditionalist than even Ransom or Tate – as these lines, from 'Speaking of Poetry', suggest:

The ceremony must be found
that will wed Desdemona to the huge Moor . . .

. . .

The ceremony must be found

Traditional, with all its symbols
ancient as the metaphors in dreams;
strange, with never before heard music; continuous
until the torches deaden at the bedroom door.[32]

At once precise and resonant, these words pick out one of Bishop's most insistent themes: elegance must be married to force, art to magic, order to impulse – married, not merely yielded up to the kind of unceremonious possession that turns inevitably to destruction. It is 'ceremony' that makes of a passionate attachment a true marriage, as it makes of passionate perception a true poem; it is tradition, ritual issuing from our deepest level of being ('ancient as the metaphors in dreams') that enables us to give articulate form to our emotions, coherent shape to our lives.

But ceremony was lost in America, Bishop felt: the pursuit of the future excluded any honouring of the past. One of his finest poems, 'Experience in the West', explores this failure:

The long man strode apart
In green no soul was found,
In that green savage clime
Such ignorance of time.

The green parrot's scream
Clung to the wild-tree fruit.
The wild foot tracked a stream.
What anger could confute
Green crowns of crashing bough
When every day dawned Now?[33]

These are lines that hauntingly reverse the westward myth since, for

Bishop, it is precisely the tragedy of America that it supplanted culture with nature. Striding apart from the human community, the pioneer made for himself a world without 'soul': that is, without those dimensions and resonances that only ritual and ceremony can offer. Lighting out to a place without memory, where 'every day dawned Now', the American stripped his life of the meanings that 'time', a sense of the past and inherited forms, can give. Other poets celebrate the openness of America, its substitution of geography for history; in Bishop's opinion, however, this is something to be lamented. As he sees it, there is a seamless, sad connection between the literal wilderness, 'that green savage clime' into which 'the long man' strode centuries ago, and the moral wilderness that is America now.

Bishop was roughly a contemporary of the Fugitives, but other, more recent Southern poets have continued to testify to the vitality and variety of traditionalism. Most notable, in this respect, and very different from each other, are Wendell Berry and James Dickey. Berry has developed what might be called the ecological tendency in traditionalist writing: the attachment to one dear, particular place that blossoms out into a recognition of kinship with nature. 'I will wait here in the fields', begins a poem with the characteristic title, 'Stay Home':

> to see how well the rain
> brings on the grass.
> In the labour of the fields
> longer than a man's life
> I am at home. Don't come with me.
> You stay home too.

The affection for home expressed here is typical, as is the quiet, idiomatic speech, the mastery of rhythm and pause, the delicate use of tonality and repetition. Simple though these lines are, they allow for a subtle allusion to Frost's poem, 'The Pasture' ('I shan't be gone long', Frost says, ' – You come too') that helps underline Berry's 'stay-at-home' message. Berry wishes to 'stay home' and invites us to do the same, in the midst of nature which is our true homeplace. Elsewhere, he develops this allegiance into a celebration of the ecological cycle ('The Hog Killing'), precise, unpatronising scenes from rural life ('The Adze'), and portraits of the simplicity and self-possession of animals ('The Watchers'). Always, the animating conviction is that 'slowly we return to earth.' And always the enemies are those familiar *bêtes noires* of the traditionalist, mechanism and abstraction – a world in which people are turned into products in the name of certain insubstantial theories concerning nature, human nature, and power:

Above trees and rooftops
is the range of symbols:
banner, cross, and star:
air war, the mode of those
who live by symbols; the pure
abstraction of travel by air . . .

. . .

But I aspire
downward . . .
All my dawns cross the horizon
and rise, from underfoot.
What I stand for
is what I stand on.[34]

Dickey is as preoccupied with nature and the past as Berry is, but his preoccupations take very different forms. For his major interest is in the primeval bases of existence – that storehouse of energies and imagery, the series of remembered and recurring experiences which belong almost entirely to the sub-rational levels of life. Hunting provides the framework for many of Dickey's poems: its incidents are frequently his subject, its rituals supply him with a language, and its code prescribes the nature and scope of his perceptions. It is, in effect, during and by means of the hunt that many of Dickey's narrators achieve contact with the subliminal dimensions of experience – go down into the ground, as it were, to commune with the inhuman. 'Listening to Foxhounds', for instance, starts in this way:

When in that gold
Of fires, quietly sitting
With the men whose brothers are hounds

You know which man has heard

A thing like his own dead
Speak out in a marvellous, helpless voice . . .[35]

The accumulative, nervously expectant movement of the syntax, the finely nerved energy of the rhythms, the fluidity of expression and sense of hidden melody: all help dramatise the atavistic burden of this piece, in which the hunters discover a kinship with the hunted. The scene is Southern but less specifically so, perhaps, than in poems like 'The Slave Quarters' and 'Hunting Civil War Relics at Nimblewill Creek'. The latter reveals a particularly astute use of Southern motifs. It seems like a typical traditionalist work at first: the scene is a battlefield, where Dickey and his brother are using a mine detector to hunt for 'the buried battle / Of Nimblewill.' Gradually, however, it becomes clear that the past haunting these lines is not the historical past, re-created in memory, but the collective psychic past, stretching back to pre-human times, which exists for us now in our subconscious selves:

> I choke the handle
> Of the pick . . .
>
> . . .
>
> Like a man who renounces war
> Or one who shall lift up the past,
> Not breathing "Father",
> At Nimblewill
> But saying, "Fathers! Fathers!"[36]

For writers like Ransom and Tate, there is a single past, identified with a singular historical figure or culture: for Dickey, however, there are many pasts, battalions of dead who exist within us whether we like it or not. Of late, Dickey has become more interested in what he calls 'the conclusionless poem, . . . the un-well made poem', but the thrust of his work has not changed. His best writing remains that in which the protagonist falls into the otherworld of the unconscious ('Falling') – where the dead speak, not only to us but through us.

Traditionalism outside the South: Winters, Cunningham, Eberhart

Outside of the South, the convictions to which the Fugitives gave such spirited expression animated many poets, among them Yvor Winters. Best known, perhaps, for his criticism, Winters is a poet of distinction whose attitude towards the writing of poetry is summed up by his advice 'To a Young Writer':

> Write little; do it well.
> Your knowledge will be such,
> At last, as to dispel
> What moves you overmuch.[37]

'What I did', he says elsewhere, 'was small but good': for him, poetry is considered utterance. To achieve 'the final certitude of speech', the poet must reflect and select: he must use a rigorously disciplined form, containing concise and rationally controlled reflections on experience of moral significance. Winters constantly attacked romantic vagueness and 'immorality' and praised the logical and logically spoken poem: the poem, that is, that uses a logic so refined, so resolutely purified beyond prose logic, as to be final. At first, his pursuit of precision, his hatred of unfocussed or effusive subject-matter, led him towards Imagism: some of his earlier pieces, like 'Jose's Country' or 'April' are considered poems of the moment, mixing Imagist instantaneity with Winters's own special brand of rational reflection. But Winters soon felt that Imagism lacked intellectual backbone and convincing structure; so he moved away from it towards more traditional forms, through which he could comment lucidly and concisely on experience. 'The fine indignant sprawl', he wrote, ' / Confuses all.' Far better was 'corrosion and distrust': a healthy scepticism, a mistrust of large gestures, a keen eye for cant, and a willingness to refine and then refine again. As 'On Teaching the Young' puts it:

> The poet's only bliss
> Is in cold certitude –
> Laurel, archaic, rude.[38]

For Winters, this exacting austerity of approach was absolutely necessary because it offered the only way to understand; and understanding, knowledge of experience, was the ultimate goal. The understanding might be of death:

> Death. Nothing is simpler. One is dead.
> The set face now will fade out; the bare fact,
> Related movement, regular, intact,
> Is reabsorbed, the clay is on the bed.[39]

It might be of the *malaise* of modern times:

> Fool and scoundrel guide the State.
> Peace is whore to Greed and Hate.
> Nowhere may I turn to flee:
> Action is security.
> Treading change with savage heel,
> We must live or die by steel.[40]

Whatever, it was facilitated by a precise formal structure, metrical severity, and accurate phrasing. The aim was, in fact, not merely to find certitude but to present it. Such severity did not deny pleasure or passion; on the contrary, it enhanced or more accurately refined appreciation of them. Nor did it involve a denial of simpler sensory enjoyment, as these lines in praise of California wine amply demonstrate:

> It yields the pleasure of the eye,
> It charms the skin, it warms the heart;
> When nights are cold and thoughts crowd high,
> Then 'tis the solvent for our art

The praise here is really for two arts: those of the wine-maker and the poet. Through the careful practice of crafts learned from earlier generations, Winters suggests, both are able to enrich our lives, promoting pleasure and community. Out of the cultivation of grapes and the cultivation of poetry comes a distilled essence: something that helps to make life worth living.

There is a distinctly 'Roman' quality to Winter's verse, noticeable not least in his Virgilian *pietas* towards his adoptive home of California. True of Winters (and, as we have seen, of Bishop), it is equally true of another stern traditionalist, J. V. Cunningham: of whom Winters himself offered the highest praise when he declared that Cunningham's poems 'offer no solace unless clear understanding be solace.' 'The Roman voice', one critic has astutely observed, 'uttering its close-woven language, tends towards the lapidary, the epigrammatic'; and some of Cunningham's best work has consisted of epigrams. It is also a voice that rejects the urge towards transcendence, and dwells instead on the pleasures and the pains, the occasional joys and frequent absurdities, that a brief span of sixty or seventy years can bring. So many of Cunningham's epigrams poke sly fun at the posturings of the human animal – posturings that become particularly exaggerated whenever the abbreviated character of human life is ignored:

> This Humanist whom no beliefs constrained
> Grew so broad-minded he was scatter-brained.[42]

Other epigrams are affectionate, or elegiac, confronting death with stoic resignation but also with a sense of possible compensation. Knowledge of life's brevity can, after all, add intensity to the appreciation of life's beauty, as Cunningham's variations on the *carpe diem* theme testify. And the epitaph the poet wrote for himself illustrates another profoundly traditional way of dealing with the fact of mortality:

When I shall be without regret
And shall mortality forget,
When I shall die who lived for this,
I shall not miss the things I miss.
And you who notice where I lie
Ask not my name. It is not I.[43]

The poem is a characteristic blend of wit and sadness, metrical severity and verbal subtlety. Cunningham adopts the conventions of the classical epitaph here (the anonymity, the address to the passing stranger) and writes an *exegi monumentum* that acknowledges in a half-proud, half-sad way the consequences of his mortality. He has 'lived for this' and 'this' (his life, his talent, his work) has gone, but the better part of him will perhaps continue for a while in lines like these ones. Life has departed, but with it also regretfulness; death has arrived, uninvited, but with it also forgetfulness – a sly and sensible corrective to the usual Romantic notions ('Our birth is but a sleep and a forgetting').

The apparent simplicity of the last line asks us to consider the disappearance of the poet's 'name' and identity with death, the possible survival of that name elsewhere in the products of his craft, and the blending of this one ultimately insignificant individual personality into the company of the dead – and, in particular, into the company of the many other, long dead poets who composed their own epitaphs. In this sense, 'It is not I' is at once a humble acknowledgement of Cunningham's personal unimportance and an arrogant assertion of the power of his craft, the great tradition of poetry being invoked and imitated.

Even when Cunningham turns away from epigram, the voice remains laconic, the language pure to the point of austerity, the verse movements precise and poised. Sometimes, he makes his traditionalist, not to say aristocratic, leanings clear from his satirical thrusts at contemporary tastes in life and literature: his reference, for instance, to 'Ambitious boys / Whose big lines swell / With spiritual noise',[44] is an unambiguously sardonic comment on the influence of Whitman in American poetry. Sometimes, these leanings are acknowledged by his references to classical literature, his quotations and translations from Latin, or by his embracing of some distinctly conservative positions – 'Radical change', he declares in one of his poems, 'the root of human woe.' Most often and successfully, however, his belief that the best work is done 'By caution under custom's guide' emerges from the tone and texture of his verse. *To What Strangers, What Welcomes,* for example, is a set of poems on a theme familiar enough in American writing, the experience of driving westward. But the subject is given unfamiliarity by Cunningham's treatment, as the opening poem illustrates:

I drive Westward. Tumble and loco weed
Persist. And in the vacancies of need
The leisure of desire, whirlwinds a face
As luminous as love, lost as this place.

Other American poets have written about the emptiness of the western landscape; others have associated it with notions of mobility. Very few, though, have been quite so classically restrained in their approach to this subject, or attached it so closely to the traditional theme of *lacrimae rerum*. Spare and severe though these lines are, they manage to suggest something of the contradictory feelings that issue from solitude, the luminosity and the lost-ness, and something too of the melancholy attendant on the mere condition of being alive.

The wit and sadness, and the preoccupation with mortality, that characterise so many traditionalists like Cunningham, Bishop, and Ransom are also typical of another poet who has been important both in his own right and as an influence upon others, Richard Eberhart. 'We are / Betrayed by time, which made us mortal',[45] Eberhart declares in one of his poems; and nearly all of his work starts from this recognition. The structure of the world is 'hard'; we all fall from 'the pitch that is near madness', the 'violent, vivid' and 'immaculate' state of childhood, 'into a realm of complexity . . . / Where nothing is possible but necessity'; and only a willingness to see things 'in a hard intellectual light' can restore the 'moral grandeur of man.' These beliefs feed into Eberhart's writing, so that even his simpler poems become striking for their intellectual dexterity and rigour: ideas or experiences are introduced in a straightforward, even ingenuous, fashion and then cunningly extended, in ways that often rely on allusion or verbal or metaphoric tension for their impact. Eberhart's aim is not only to see things clearly, however, but also with 'the supreme authority of the imagination' as his guide. Consequently, an acknowledgement of what is never inhibits an awareness of what might be. 'The light beyond compare is the light I saw', he says in one of his finest pieces, 'I saw it in childhood . . . / I glimpsed it in the turbulence of growing up'; now, he adds, 'It is this strange light I come back to, / Agent of truth, protean, a radical of time.'[46] In effect, Eberhart sees no contradiction between the 'hard' light of the intellect and the 'strange' light of the imagination: on the contrary, the one is for him the precondition of the other. He uses wit and intellectual dexterity, not as a substitute for vision, but as a means of liberating it, of discovering what he calls 'The truth of the positive hour': which, for him, consists of 'love /

Concrete, specific', 'the grace to imagine the unimaginable' that 'Elevates man to an angelic state', 'the heart's holy rapture', and the 'Inescapable brotherhood of the living.'

'For a Lamb' offers a succinct illustration of Eberhart's approach. The opening is as apparently naive, and yet as full of guile, as the opening of any poem by Dickinson:

> I saw on the slant hill a putrid lamb
> Propped with daisies. The sleep looked deep.
> The face nudged in the green pillow
> But the guts were out for crows to eat.
> Where's the lamb? whose tender plaint
> Said all for the mute breezes.
> Say he's in the wind somewhere,
> Say, there's a lamb in the daisies.

The language of the first few lines is lucid and unfussy, the syntax plain, the rhythms regularly iambic apart from the occasional anapaest. Yet there is a touch of dry irony, malicious mischief in the use of that word 'putrid' and, on closer inspection, some of the descriptive detail is distinctly odd ('slant hill', 'Propped with daisies'). Rather like the phenomena Robert Frost comes across in his poem, 'Design', these things seem strangely yet deliberately arranged, a grotesque set-piece set up by some unknown hand with the intention of appalling anyone who comes near it. The sense of heterogeneous particulars yoked together by violence is exacerbated by the contrast between the decorous verbal melodies ('hills . . . lamb . . . sleep . . . looked', 'sleep . . . deep') and sylvan associations of the first three lines and the monosyllabic horror of the fourth. The disconcerting, even unnerving quality of the first stanza is then extended in the second, which opens with a question: 'Where's the lamb?' What has happened, the poet asks, to the creature and the qualities of innocence and simplicity traditionally associated with it? Do they survive somehow, carried on 'the mute breezes' just as its 'tender plaint' once was, metamorphosed from earth into air? Or is all that remains the putrefying corpse, the bare, concrete fact of extinction? Eberhart is content to leave us with the mystery, to respond to the initial question by offering both possible answers:

> Say he's in the wind somewhere,
> Say, there's a lamb in the daisies.[47]

Like so many of Eberhart's poems, 'For a Lamb' ends in a neatly articulated enigma, a recognition of 'hard' fact and an understanding of 'strange' possibilities. The apparent finality of death is accepted, but it is complicated by an awareness of the potential absorption of all things into a universal cycle. As his 'Centennial for Whitman' admits, Eberhart shares very little with the founding father of American verse as far as technique is concerned; he has little time, even, for Whitman's belief in human perfectibility. But he does meet with him in his 'knowledge of the changeless in birth and death', his glimmering sense of a process whereby 'Death is but a door' into other forms of living. 'What shall I say to Walt Whitman tonight?' asks Eberhart, then continues:

> I praise him not in loose form, not in outpouring
> Not in a positive acclamation of frenetic belief,
> Not in the simplicity of a brotherhood, such peace,
> And not in the dawn of an original compulsion,
> But speak to him in the universe of birth and death.[48]

There could hardly be a more measured, and therefore more honest, tribute from a traditionalist to one who was above all an experimentalist.

Traditionalism, scepticism, and tragedy: Frost

As we have seen, Whitman was not only the founding father of American poetry: he was also, and not just coincidentally, the first great practitioner of free verse. And the man who is probably the greatest traditionalist in twentieth-century American poetry has left his own, inimitable comment on free verse forms. 'I had as soon write free verse', Robert Frost declared, 'as play tennis with the net down.'[49] For Frost, traditional metres were a necessary discipline, something against which he could play off the urgencies of his own speaking voice, the chance movements of his emotions, the catch and tilt of his breath. 'I've wanted to write down certain brute throat noises', he said, 'so that no one could miss them in my sentences'; and those noises, he felt, acquired additional pungency and point from being placed in tension with established rhythms and rhyme. The very first poem in his first published volume suggests what he was after – it is the poem that Wendell Berry subtly alludes to in 'Stay Home':

> I'm going out to clean the pasture spring;
> I'll only stop to rake the leaves away
> (And wait to watch the water clear, I may);
> I shan't be gone long. – You come too.

There is musicality of a traditional kind here, certainly ('going . . .

only', 'clean . . . leaves . . . clear', 'wait . . . watch . . . water'): but already in this early poem musicality has begun to be displaced by emphasising the dramatic intonations and cadences of everyday speech. The thoughtful pause and colloquially awkward construction of the third line, the two heavy stresses on 'gone long' underlining the pause at the caesura in the abbreviated fourth line and endowing the last three assonanced monosyllables ('You come too') with additional urgency: such things are ample testimony to Frost's craft. Together with a deliberately simple (if subtly melodic) vocabulary, they make it clear what the poet meant when he admitted once, 'my nerves are so susceptible to sound.'

The play of speech and song that characterises all Frost's best work is not just a matter of voice, however, but of vision. By means of it, he explores the paradoxes implicit in one of his most famous lines: 'The fact is the sweetest dream that labour knows.' 'Stopping by Woods on a Snowy Evening' illustrates this. Its opening stanza establishes the ambivalent tone of the poem and the imaginative tension that constitutes its debate:

> Whose woods these are I think I know,
> His house is in the village though;
> He will not see me stopping here
> To watch his woods fill up with snow.

The duality of the narrator's response to the woods is caught in the contrast between the relaxed, conversational idiom of the first three lines (note the gentle emphasis given to 'think', the briskly colloquial 'though') and the dream-like descriptive detail and hypnotic verbal music ('watch . . . woods', 'his . . . fill . . . with') of the last. Clearing and wilderness, law and freedom, civilisation and nature, fact and dream: these oppositions reverberate throughout American writing. And they are registered here in Frost's own quietly ironic contrast between the road along which the narrator travels, connecting marketplace to marketplace, promoting community and culture – and the white silence of the woods, where none of the ordinary limitations of the world seem to apply. In a minor key, they are caught also in the implicit comparison between the owner of these woods, who apparently regards them as a purely financial investment (he lives in the village) and the narrator who sees them, at least potentially, as a spiritual one.

This contrast between what might be termed, rather reductively perhaps, 'realistic' and 'romantic' attitudes is then sustained through the next two stanzas: the commonsensical response is now playfully attributed to the narrator's horse which, like any practical being, wants to get on down the road to food and shelter. The narrator himself, however, continues to be lured by the mysteries of the forest just as the Romantic poets were lured by the mysteries of otherness, sleep and death. And, as before, the contrast is a product of tone and texture as much as dramatic intimation: the poem communicates its debate in how it says things as much as in what it says. So, the harsh gutturals and abrupt movement of lines like, 'He gives his harness bells a shake / To ask if there is some mistake', give verbal shape to the matter-of-fact attitude attributed to the horse, just as the soothing sibilants and gently rocking motion of the lines that follow this ('The only other sound's the sweep / Of easy wind and downy flake') offer a tonal equivalent of the strange, seductive world into which the narrator is tempted to move. 'Everything that is written', Frost once said, 'is as good as it is dramatic'; and in a poem like this the words of the poem become actors in the drama.

The final stanza of 'Stopping by Woods' does not resolve its tensions; on the contrary, it rehearses them in particularly memorable language.

> The woods are lovely, dark and deep,
> But I have promises to keep,
> And miles to go before I sleep,
> And miles to go before I sleep.[50]

Having paid tribute to the dangerous seductiveness of the woods, the narrator seems to be trying to shake himself back into commonsense reality by invoking his 'promises' or mundane responsibilities. The last line is repeated, however; and while at first it seems little more than a literal reference to the journey he has to complete (and so a way of telling himself to continue on down the road), the repetition gives it particular resonance. This could, after all, be a metaphorical reference to the brief span of human life and the compulsion this puts the narrator under to take risks and explore the truth while he can. Only a few 'miles' to go before 'I sleep' in death: such a chilling *memento mori* perhaps justifies stopping by the woods in the first place and considering the spiritual quest implicit in the vision they offer. Perhaps: the point is that neither narrator nor reader can be sure. 'The poem is the act of having the thought', Frost insisted; it is process rather than product, it invites us to share in the experiences of seeing, feeling, and thinking, not simply to look at their results. So the most a piece like 'Stopping by Woods' will offer – and it is a great deal – is an *imaginative* resolution of its tensions: the sense that its conflicts and irresolutions have been given appropriate dramatic expression, revelation and equipoise.

'It begins in delight and ends in wisdom', said Frost in his remarkable definition of 'the figure a poem makes':

> The figure is the same as for love . . . It begins in delight, assumes direction with the first line laid, it runs a course of lucky events, and ends in clarification of life – not necessarily a great clarification, such as sects and cults are founded on, but in a momentary stay against confusion.[51]

The incessant coupling of opposites, the felicitous, serious play that ends in 'a momentary stay against confusion' is precisely what characterises Frost's work. It makes all his best lyrics, like 'Stopping by Woods', essentially dramatic in that they enact internal conflicts, savage dualisms of thought and feeling. In turn, it makes all of his best dramatic poems, like 'The Death of the Hired Man' and 'West-Running Brook' essentially lyrical in that they reproduce, in beautifully individualised form, those same conflicts, turning them into intimate human communication. In 'The Death of the Hired Man', for example, the event that gives the poem its title is merely the occasion for a loving argument between husband and wife that brings out their differences of speech and approach. The husband's voice is abrupt, with many stops and few connectives, full of imperatives and wilful declarations, turning aside for brusque rhetorical or cross-examining questions. The seal of his tone is set by his caustic description of home: 'Home is the place where, when you have to go there, / They have to take you in.'[52] His character, clearly, is that of the maker of good bargains, the shrewd calculator of motives, the uncompromising champion of harsh truth. The wife is very different, as her definition of home suggests: 'I should have called it / Something you somehow haven't to deserve'. Far more hesitant, her speech has breaks for another kind from her husband's: of someone reaching for the right word, more sympathetic and imaginative, using emotion and a kind of lyric responsiveness to soften the hard edges of fact. Very different in character, and in their reactions to the hired man who returns to them after a long absence looking for work, they are nevertheless in intimate touch with each other; and they are drawn even closer together by the hired man's sudden death. They never entirely agree; their differences are no more resolved than the differences in 'Stopping by Woods' are. But, like 'Stopping by Woods', they suggest the possible coexistence of these differences, a marriage or, to use Frost's own phrase, 'happy-sad blend' of realism and romance.

Another, simpler way of describing the circuitous, serpentine character of Frost's work is to say that he is the supreme example of the sceptic in modern American poetry: the person who mistrusts categorical answers, utopian solutions, and who, for reasons he thoroughly articulates, cannot or will not make up his mind. In 'For Once, Then, Something', for instance, he plays on the traditional idea of looking down into a well in search of the truth. The narrator, we are told, once peered into the subterranean darkness and, for a moment, saw 'a something white, uncertain': but then a ripple in the water 'Blurred it, blotted it out.'[53] 'What was that whiteness?' the narrator asks himself, and can find an answer only in his own indecision: 'Truth? A pebble of quartz? For once, then, something.' 'Something' might be everything or nothing. Having wound, in slow, meditative hendecasyllabics, through the mysteries of exploration, the poem ends in a series of questions that only underline the difficulties of knowing. A comparison with an earlier New England poet, Emily Dickinson, is relevant here, for in 'What mystery pervades a well!' Dickinson pursues exactly the same theme. Dickinson, however, concludes that 'nature is a stranger yet': she is at least sure that she has seen nothing, or at least very little, and so measured the dimensions of what she called her 'magic prison.'[54] For Frost, even this radically limited degree of certainty is impossible. He cannot gauge the size or nature of his cell; he cannot be certain whether the 'something' he has seen is trivial or significant. Dickinson at least knows that she cannot know: Frost, by comparison, cannot know even this. The limits to perception, the nature and scope of knowing and naming, the accessibility of truth: all these things remain hidden from him, and so he falls back on the ultimate weapon of the impotent and irresolute, irony.

Irony is by no means Frost's only weapon, though. As his autobiographical poem, 'The Oven Bird', makes clear, he is a poet struggling to find 'what to make of a diminished thing.'[55] Transcendence is not available for him in the way it was for earlier writers like Emerson and Whitman. Consequently, he must do what he can with what Randall Jarrell has called 'a minimal case.' This sometimes involves ironic meditations on the human pursuit of knowledge, as it does in 'For Once, Then, Something' or 'Neither Out Far Nor In Deep'. But just as often it precipitates tentative inquiry into the mysteries that hover on the edges of experience, the possible sources of fear and wonder. The more unnerving results of such an inquiry emerge in poems like 'Out, Out – ' and 'Design'. 'Out, Out – ' begins with what seems like a gently nostalgic piece of rural portrait-painting:

> The buzz saw snarled and rattled in the yard
> And made dust and dropped stove-length sticks of wood,
> Sweet-scented stuff when the breeze drew across it . . .

From this, the poet moves slowly, in an almost relaxed fashion, into an account of an apparently minor accident: we are told, in quietly serio-comic terms, how one of the workers, a young boy, cut his hand on the buzz saw. Things grow more serious when the possibility emerges that the boy might lose his hand. Just the same, we are hardly prepared for the final lines:

> And then – the watcher at his pulse took fright.
> No one believed. They listened at his heart.
> Little – less – nothing! – and that ended it.
> No more to build on there. And they, since they
> Were not the one dead, turned to their affairs.[56]

'I think of Robert Frost as a terrifying poet', Lionel Trilling declared, and reading these lines we can see why. This is death stripped of any sense of occasion, denied preparation or ceremony. Unanticipated, greeted with incomprehension, stilted phrases and awkward reactions, and followed by numbness, together with the indelible feeling that the dead are gone while the living must continue, this is death as the terrifying, universal and in some sense inconsequential, fact that it is – and as very few writers have been willing to acknowledge it.

'Design' is a very different poem that arrives at similarly unnerving conclusions. In it, Frost uses the rigidity of the sonnet form to present a formal philosophical problem. We are introduced, in the course of the octave, to 'Assorted characters of death and blight', three things the narrator happened to come across once: 'a dimpled spider, fat and white', a white flower, and, held up by the flower, 'a moth / Like a white piece of rigid satin cloth.' The three are introduced separately, assembled in synthesis to demonstrate the incongruity of their relationship, and then re-described in the last two lines of the octave for emphasis:

> A snow-drop spider, a flower like a froth,
> And dead wings carried like a paper kite.

Up to this point, the scientist-poet has only permitted himself the emotional shock of the elements presented for his examination and he accepts them as specimens at random. In the sestet, however, he tries to solve the problems they pose and, as he does so, the tension suddenly breaks, along with the rhyme-scheme. In a series of negatives and outraged rhetorical questions, he demands reasons for the strange combinations of existence. What is the 'design' behind all this, he asks. All he can summon up, by way of an answer, is the following:

> What but design of darkness to appal? –
> If design govern in a thing so small.[57]

Far from solving the problem, this conclusion only exacerbates it. For the alternatives are either that the 'design' reflects some vast malevolent joke, or that the concept of 'design' is absurdly irrelevant – in which case, the process of questioning in the sestet is itself called into question. This, in effect, is the irresolution of 'For Once, Then, Something' returned with a vengeance, since on the borders of it now hovers a sense of fear. It is bad enough to believe that we are condemned to abide amidst uncertainties; it is even worse to suspect that those uncertainties harbour danger, that the universe is not only unknowable but treacherous.

However, like so much in Frost's poetry, this remains only a suspicion. Fear lurks beneath the surface of a poem like this, certainly: but, in other poems, Frost's playfulness, his willingness to entertain all kinds of doubts and possibilities leads him in the contrary direction – not to transcendence of facts, perhaps, but to a wondering, joyful apprehension of their potential, to the sense that nature might after all be whispering secret, sympathetic messages to us. 'The Most of It' belongs in this second group. It presents us with a situation familiar enough in Romantic literature, and one that American writers like Cooper, Emerson, and Whitman were particularly fond of exploring: the protagonist – the 'he' of the poem – stands looking across a lake towards some distant hills, seeking comfort and instruction from nature. In accord with the tradition, Frost's protagonist cries out to the hills, seeking what the poet calls 'counter-love, original response': some sign that nature sympathises and that he has not 'kept the universe alone'. But, in this case at least, there is no clear reaction. All he seems to get back is the 'mocking echo' of his own voice, confirming him in his isolation. Or does he? This, after all, is the concluding description of the echo:

> As a great buck it powerfully appeared,
> Pushing the crumpled water up ahead,
> And landed pouring like a waterfall.
> And stumbled through the rocks with horny tread,
> And forced the underbush – and that was all.[58]

If a symbol is, in Jung's phrase, 'the best possible expression of a relatively *unknown* fact', then this is the purest of symbols. Perhaps all the protagonist apprehends is the echo of his voice. However, that echo is described with such dramatic bite, such vitality, that perhaps he apprehends more: perhaps he has glimpsed, if not the Emersonian Over-Soul, then at least some of the strange, animistic forces that give life dimension and energy, that transform 'fact' into 'dream'. He, and we, cannot be sure, and it is the achievement of the poem that we cannot be: that we are left, in short, with a feeling of mystery.

A similar feeling is likely to issue from any reading of another of Frost's finest poems, 'After Apple-Picking'. On the simplest narrative level, the poem describes how, after a strenuous day of apple-picking, the speaker dreams dreams in which his previous activities return to him 'magnified', blurred and distorted by memory and sleep. On a deeper level, however, it presents us with an experience in which the world of normal consciousness and the world that lies beyond it meet and mingle. 'I cannot rub the strangeness from my sight', says the narrator, and this strangeness, the 'essence of winter sleep', is something he shares with the reader. The dreamy confusion of the rhythm, the curiously 'echoing' effect of the irregular, unpredictable rhyme-scheme, the mixing of tenses, tones, and senses, the hypnotic repetition of sensory detail: all these things promote a transformation of reality that comes, paradoxically, from a close observation of the real, its shape, weight, and fragrance, rather than any attempt to soar above it:

Magnified apples appear and disappear,
Stem end and blossom end,
And every fleck of russet showing clear.
My instep arch not only keeps the ache,
It keeps the pressure of the ladder-round.
I feel the ladder sway as the boughs bend.
And I keep hearing from the cellar bin
The rumbling sound
Of load on load of apples coming in.[59]

As usual, in this poem Frost hovers between the daylight world of commonsense reality and the dream world of possibility, the voices of sense and of song, the visions of the pragmatist and the prophet, the compulsions of the road and the seductions of the woods. This time, however, he appears to belong to both realms, rather than hold back from a full commitment to either. Dualism is replaced by an almost religious sense of unity here; and the tone of irony, quizzical reserve, completely disappears in favour of wonder and incantation.

Traditionalism, quiet desperation, and belief: Robinson

Robert Frost is a traditionalist poet, a New England poet, and an American poet: using traditional forms, he meditates with irony and uncertainty, fear and occasional wonder, on the nature of his own small plot of earth, the apparent absence of divinity, and the character of human isolation. The same could be said of a slightly earlier poet who had some influence on Frost, Edwin Arlington Robinson. Robinson's first and last love was what he called 'the music of English verse'. As he explained to a friend, he was 'a classicist in poetic composition', who believed that 'the accepted media for masters of the past' should 'continue to be used for the future'. However, he was far from being one of the 'little sonnet-men' as he contemptuously referred to them, mere imitators of English fashions and forms. On the contrary, he was deliberately local: many of his poems are set in Tilbury Town, a fictive place based on his boyhood home of Gardiner, Maine. And he was a genuine original, obsessed with certain personal themes: human isolation, the tormented introversions of the personality, the doubts and frustrations of lonely people inhabiting a world from which God appears to have hidden His face. 'No poet ever understood loneliness or separateness better than Robinson', James Dickey has observed, 'or knew the self-consuming furnace that the brain can become in isolation'. So his perennial subjects became what he termed 'the slow tragedy of haunted men' – those whose 'eyes are lit with a wrong light', illusions that at once cripple and save them – and 'The strange and unremembered light/That is in dreams' – the obsessive effort to illuminate and make sense of experience when there is perhaps no sense to be made. 'The world is not a "prison-house"', Robinson declared, 'but a kind of spiritual kindergarten, where millions of infants are trying to spell "God" with the wrong blocks'.[60] Robinson saw himself and his poetic characters as particularly notable members of that kindergarten: people whose minds and language, their 'words' can never quite encompass the truth about the universe, the 'Word', but who nevertheless keep on trying.

The bleakness of Robinson's vision, particularly in his earlier work, comes out in poems like 'The House on the Hill' and 'Richard Cory'. In 'The House on the Hill', the bleakness issues from the sense that, now that the house in question is in 'ruin and decay' and its inhabitants are departed, any comment seems a superfluous gesture. The opening lines announce this perception:

> They are all gone away,
> The House is shut and still,
> There is nothing more to say.

To try to attach words to vacancy, to clothe transience and loneliness in language, is a futile gesture, the poem suggests. More remarks are added to the opening ones: but the constant repetition of the first three lines, in varying sequence, gives the impression that nothing more is really being said. Perhaps there is indeed 'nothing more to say'. Nevertheless, Robinson keeps on trying to say more; and in 'Richard Cory' he explores the anonymous surfaces of life in another way – by suggesting, however cryptically, the contrast between those surfaces and the evident hell that lies beneath them. The character who gives the poem its title is described in admiring detail, from the perspective of his poorer neighbours. 'He was a gentleman from sole to crown', the reader is told, 'Clean favoured, . . . imperially slim' and 'rich – yes, richer than a king'. Comments like these hardly prepare us for the horror of the final stanza:

> So on we worked, and waited for the light,
> And went without the meat, and carved the bread;
> And Richard Cory, one calm summer night,
> Went home and put a bullet through his head.[61]

The irony of these lines, and the poem as a whole, depends on the contrast between the serenity of Cory's appearance and the violence of his death; its melancholy, upon our recognising that Cory – for all his privileges – is as acutely isolated and spiritually starved as anyone else. 'There is more in every person's soul than we think', Robinson observed once, 'Even the happy mortals we term ordinary . . . act their own mental tragedies and live a far deeper and wider life than we are inclined to believe possible in the light of our prejudices'. This is precisely the lesson that the 'we' of the poem, Cory's neighbours in Tilbury Town, never learn: the night on which Cory shoots himself remains 'calm' in their view, and the use of that word only underlines the distance between him and them.

Quiet desperation, the agony that Richard Cory's neighbours failed to notice, is a distinguishing feature of many of Robinson's characters. The despair may come, apparently, from emotional poverty ('Aaron Stark'), the pain of loss and bereavement ('Reuben Bright', 'Luke Havergal'), or the treadmill of life ('The Clerks'): whatever, it is palpably there in an awkward gesture, a stuttered phrase, a violent moment as in 'Richard Cory' or, as in 'The House on the Hill', the sense that behind the stark, simple words lies an unimaginable burden of pain. Many of Robinson's poems, in fact, derive their power from reticence, a positive refusal to expand or elaborate. In 'How Annandale Went Out', for example, the reader only gradually realises that 'Annandale' is the name of a man who has been reduced by some incurable disease, or accident, to the vegetable state, and that the narrator is a doctor who has evidently been merciful enough to relieve him of his life. Such is the cryptic indirection, the emotional austerity of lines like 'They called it Annandale – and I was there / To flourish, to find words, and to attend',[62] that the meaning is not immediately clear. New Englanders, Robinson observed, are not like 'those / Who boil elsewhere with such a lyric yeast', at least not on the surface. Their dramas, whatever they may be, are enacted within. So the power of many of his poems stems from the reader recognising just how much emotional pressure there is behind the spare diction, the poignant contrast between the enormity of feeling implied and the bare, stripped manner of implication. In effect, the reader is often asked to conjecture, just as so many of Robinson's narrators conjecture about the lives of those who have gone or those they hardly know except as inhabitants of the same town. The poem becomes an act of commemoration, in which the speaker recalls and rehearses a life with the discomfiting sense that he can only offer some provisional notes towards understanding it. 'We cannot have them here with us', admits the narrator of his departed friends in 'Calverly's', '/ To say where their light lives are gone'. He cannot say what has happened to them, what their lives were and their fates are; and because he cannot say – and because there is nothing and no way to find out – he cannot know what his own fate is, or its meaning. He can only know that he himself once spent his time at an inn called 'Calverly's', that the others were there and are now gone, and that he will follow them in due course. He cannot say what this means or if, in fact, it means anything. Although he can guess at what it might mean, all he really knows is what happened.

But perhaps Robinson's most powerful and memorable account of loneliness and its consequences is 'Eros Turannos'. Its title means 'the tyrant Love', but its subject is the distance separating man from man, or man from Nature, and the dreams and illusions to which imprisonment within the self makes one susceptible. Even love, the emotion commonly supposed to bind human beings together, is seen here as a product and symptom of separation. The woman in this poem may well be ruled by 'the tyrant Love' or, at least, by a mixture of need and antagonism which Robinson takes to be a potent illustration of love's tyranny. But, clearly, what she feels for her husband is limited by the 'engaging mask' he wears before her at all times; what attracts and repels her is much more a matter of appearance than anything else. Both husband and wife may well be dependent on one another, in other words, but they are nevertheless seen as two solitary people, together only in their shared isolation. Using a form that he found particularly congenial – a series of alternating tetrameter and trimeter lines, more or less regular but given an idiosyncratic touch by extensive feminine rhyme – Robinson explores the tragic implications of this relationship, and then arrives at a startling conclusion:

We tell you, tapping on our brows,
    The story as it should be, –
As if the story of a house
    Were told, or ever could be;
We'll have no kindly veil between
Her visions and those we have seen, –
As if we guessed what hers have been,
    Or what they are or would be.[63]

Suddenly, a further dimension is added to the themes of solitude and illusion: the poet, insisting on the 'otherness' of things, now admits that he may not be telling the whole truth. All he is doing, he says, is describing what he sees: and since, being human, he too is isolated he may be as much a victim of appearances and the eccentricities of personal vision as the man and woman who are his subjects. The admission comes, perhaps, as a surprise, but in fact it has been implicit from the beginning, in the poet's methods of expression. The incessant use of simile, for instance, high profile language and images that call attention to themselves, suggests that the narrator is trying to point to his limitations: that all he can do is describe what his subject *resembles* – not what, in essentials, it *is*. And the characteristically marmoreal language and cryptic phrasing make this poem, like so many of Robinson's others, sound like an epitaph, dedicated to people whom the narrator hardly knew and whom the reader can never know immediately. Once more, narrator and reader are on the outside looking in, trying to construct 'the story of a house' from externals; once again, Robinson adopts a strategy of guess and conjecture, the tentative arts of the memorialist.

In rehearsing the mute, inglorious lives of the inhabitants of Tilbury Town Robinson was, as he knew, rebelling against the orthodoxies of the pastoral tradition: that body of writing, particularly strong in the United States, that locates happiness, a kind of Edenic innocence and peace, in the rural world and village life. His sonnet addressed to the English poet, George Crabbe, establishes his allegiances. Like Crabbe, he implies, he is concerned with the loneliness of country people, the austerity and sheer poverty of their existence; and he tries to write about these things 'In books that are as altars where we kneel / To consecrate the flicker, not the flame.' The image measures the scope of Robinson's ambitions and the way, like Frost, he tries to place himself in terms of his Romantic predecessors. The flame is a traditional Romantic image for the transfiguring power of the imagination. Crabbe's work, and by implication his own, may not have this, Robinson admits: but traces of that flame, one or two 'flickers' of imaginative possibility, are discernible there nevertheless. A character like Miniver Cheevy, in Robinson's poem of that name, illustrates the point; for, while Miniver might not be capable of transforming his environment in the way a Romantic hero would be, he is not entirely determined by it either. 'Miniver', we are told:

> sighed for what was not
> And dreamed, and rested from his labours;
> He dreamed of Thebes and Camelot
> And Priam's neighbours.[64]

Lines like these, combining irony with a touch of sympathetic melancholy, at first invite us to see no resemblance between the dreamer and his dreams and then gradually, through their very poignancy, qualify this, just a little, by hinting that a 'flicker' of the heroic impulse is to be found in a man like Miniver – even though it may be too feeble ever to burst into 'flame'. At worst, Miniver Cheevy is dimly aware of the barrenness of his circumstances and finds refuge in what Robinson elsewhere calls 'the . . . / Perennial inspiration of his lies'; at best, he can perhaps dream better possibilities – his mind is actively engaged in a quest for meaning.

In his later years, Robinson tended to concentrate on the more positive implications of impulses like Miniver's, the human capacity for dreaming dreams of a better life. Something of this is suggested by the short poem, 'Mr Flood's Party', published eleven years after 'Miniver Cheevy'. Like 'Miniver Cheevy', it describes a pathetic figure who retreats from an intolerable present into dreams of the past; it, too, mixes irony with sympathy. But, whereas in the earlier poem the sympathy is relatively slight, peripheral and qualified, in 'Mr Flood's Party' it is central to our understanding of the protagonist. When, for instance, about midway through the poem Robinson compares Mr Flood to 'Roland's ghost winding a silent horn',[65] the comparison seems at once incongruous and just. In some ways, Mr Flood is quite unlike the bravest of Charlemagne's officers who, after most of his friends had gone, died blowing on his horn for help. Mr Flood's 'horn', after all, is not a horn at all but a jug full of liquor, and he is not so much a bold young adventurer as a tired old man. In other ways, though, the knight and the drunkard turn out to be very much alike. Both, for example, present types of endurance, as men who recall the past while preparing to meet their former companions in another world. Comic Mr Flood may be, but there is a touch of the hero to him as well: more than a touch, perhaps, when, towards the end of the poem, Robinson describes him 'amid the silver loneliness / Of night' lifting up his voice and singing 'Until the whole harmonious landscape rang.' By now, the jug has assumed a symbolic status roughly analogous to the jar in Wallace Stevens's 'Anecdote of the Jar': belonging to a world where 'most things break', it has nevertheless become the node around which the scene is momentarily harmonised. More important, Mr Flood's inebriated state now smacks of the divine drunkenness of the poet: the man who comes close to liberating himself, and metamorphosing his environment with the help of his vivid imagination.

It was in a series of longer poetic narratives, however, rather than in short pieces like 'Mr Flood's Party' that the later Robinson moved towards affirmation: poems such as the trilogy based on the legend of King Arthur and published between 1917 and 1927, *Merlin, Lancelot,* and *Tristram*. 'The Man Against the Sky', written at about the midpoint in Robinson's career, indicates the change; in a reflective poem over three hundred lines long, the poet sketches out the mature philosophical attitude implicit in later and even longer works. The opening lines establish the basic image, of a man making the upward climb over the hill of life to death, in a way that suggests both the man's diminutiveness and his possible grandeur. This image then leads the poet to speculate on the various attitudes of people as they face death. Representing different philosophies of life as well as death, they describe a scale of increasing negation, from faith to doubt to denial and seem, too, roughly chronological, moving from primitive religious belief to contemporary materialism. Having pushed the argument this far, the poet then develops it a little further. We no longer believe in the 'two fond old enormities' of heaven and hell, he acknowledges, but that is no reason for assuming that life is meaningless and death an annihilation. Perhaps there is order in the universe. Admittedly, we can never know whether there is or not because we are limited by the confines of the self. But it is surely better to believe that there is such an order, since life is otherwise reduced to 'a blind atomic pilgrimage', a pointless trek; better, and more reasonable. For our own continued will to survive, Robinson argues, and to perpetuate the race, suggests that we have some intuitive conviction implanted in us, something that tells us that life is worth living. We persist; and that, together with any further glimpses of the truth we may receive by means of dreams, hints and guesses, is the best possible evidence we can have of the existence of purpose. 'Where was he going, this man against the sky?' the poet asks, and then answers:

You know not, nor do I.
But this we know, if we know anything:
That we may laugh and fight and sing
And of our transience here make offering
To an orient Word that will not be erased,

Or, save in incommunicable gleams
Too permanent for dreams,
Be found or known.[66]

The argument is characteristically tentative, but clear. Perhaps, the suggestion is, the simple human will to live, and to look for meaning, provides a basis for belief. Despite their isolation, and the acute limitations imposed on them, people continue to search for value; they remain dreamers. And perhaps their dreams, together with the instinct to continue, bring them closer to the truth than they can ever know. The world may well be 'a spiritual kindergarten', Robinson concedes, but it can offer occasional lessons, moments of illumination however dim and inadequate. We, its members, may not be able to spell the 'orient Word' with the few words available to us: but the failure to spell it does not disprove its existence – it may still be lurking there, somewhere.

Traditionalism, inhumanism, and prophecy: Jeffers

Robinson's best poetry is the kind that, to use his own phrase, 'tells the more the more it is not told'; it derives much of its power from its stoicism, its cryptic nobility, and its respect for the more fundamental qualities of the human being, notably endurance. Robinson Jeffers, the major poet most closely associated with the Far West of the United States, shares some of these tendencies but with a difference. In many respects, Robinson is a humanist, concerned with unearthing and investigating what distinguishes the human animal from the rest of creation: the agonies that torture him, the dreams that captivate him, the will to live and believe that perhaps offers him a means of redemption. Jeffers, ultimately, is quite the opposite: his aim was, as he put it once, to 'uncentre the human mind from itself.'[67] He wanted his verse to break away from all the versions of experience which emphasised its exclusively human properties, and to rediscover our relationship with elemental nature. Man, Jeffers insisted, must acknowledge the superior value of the instinctive life, of natural action, simplicity, and self-expression. He must try to imitate the rocks in their coldness and endurance, the hawks in their isolation, and all physical nature in its surrender to the wild, primeval levels of being. This necessarily meant a repudiation of all humanistic philosophies in favour of what the poet liked to call 'Inhumanism'. It meant, he admitted, 'a shifting of emphasis and significance from man to not-man' with a consequent loss of those values which, for centuries, we have learned to cherish – among them, reason and self-restraint, urbanity and decorum. But, Jeffers hastened to add, it also meant the rediscovery of an older liberty, aligning us with the people of ancient cultures; and it involved, too, an escape from the involuted self-consciousness, the entanglements and dark internecine conflicts, which make our modern world such a painful one.

A poem like 'Divinely Superfluous Beauty' illustrates the means by which Jeffers tried to express his philosophy of Inhumanism. It opens with a vision of the spontaneous energy running through all things, 'The storm-dances of gulls, the barking game of seals', and then concludes with the wish to be identified with this energy, to become one with all that is 'divinely superfluous'. 'The incredible beauty of joy / Stars with fire the joining of lips', declares the poet:

> O let our loves too
> Be joined, there is not a maiden
> Burns and thirsts for love
> More than my blood for you, by the shore of
> seals while the wings
> Weave like a web in the air
> Divinely superfluous beauty.[68]

As in all of Jeffers's shorter poems, the impact of these lines depends upon perspective: human life is seen from an immense distance, as it were, placed within the larger dimensions of earth, sea, and sky. The poet-philosopher who speaks here helps to place the subject as well, for his voice, primitive and oracular, seems to align him with the older freedoms he is celebrating. This is largely the result of the style Jeffers developed, in which the tones of colloquial speech are re-created without weakening formal control of the line. Of great flexibility, hovering somewhere between free verse and iambic pentameter, the rhythms are precise and emphatic without being regular. Together with the unelaborate syntax, and comparatively simple diction, they help to give poems like this a feeling of rugged exactitude: to communicate what Jeffers himself termed 'power and reality . . ., substance and sense.'

As Jeffers was acutely aware, especially in his earlier poetry, there were certain paradoxes implicit in his philosophy of Inhumanism. Another poem, 'To the Stone-Cutters', brings these paradoxes out vividly; addressed, as its title suggests, to 'Stone-cutters fighting time with marble',[69] it plays a characteristically personal variation on the traditional theme of the conquest of Time by Art. Both the stone-cutters and the poet who describes them are trying to defy time: they are 'Challengers of oblivion', struggling to achieve permanence through their creations, and to some extent they are admired for this. Admired though they may be, however, they are clearly being mocked as well. They are, we are reminded, 'foredefeated / Challengers of oblivion', who are in error if they suppose that their work can equal the rocks and the hills in its enduring power or that they themselves can properly escape from the pain of being human and the plight of being mortal. They are cut off from nature by their own natures, their art is bound by the fact that it is a specifically human product, and no amount of effort on their part can ever alter this. 'The square-limbed Roman letters / Scale in the thaws, wear in the rain', Jeffers observes. The poet himself 'Builds his monument mockingly / ; For man will be blotted out.' Eventually, even the 'blithe earth' will perish, 'the brave sun / Die blind and blacken to the heart.' Everything will wither away, to return to primal matter, and none of us can dodge or ignore this however hard we may try. Jeffers may long to identify himself with 'divinely superfluous beauty' but usually, as here, he remains aware that total identification is impossible. The simple fact, which he must acknowledge, is that human beings cannot rid themselves of their humanity. They must remain caught between the demands of their instincts and the requirements of their consciousnesses and, caught there, their lives become the stuff of poetry. Sometimes, too, they themselves become poets.

If Jeffers was unlike Robinson, or for that matter Frost, in terms of his fundamental vision and voice – categorical where they were uncertain, rapt and bardic while they played in a quieter, more enigmatic key – he was nevertheless like them in his obsession with the past and his attachment to place. With Jeffers, though, the past that signified was not immediate, a matter of conscious memory and cultural history, but ancient, prehistorical, not so much a human as a subhuman inheritance. Traditionalist he might be, in the sense of looking backward for his allegiances, but one for whom the crucial traditions were beyond the scope of consciousness and community – incorporating the sense that, as he put it once, 'the universe is one being, all its parts are different expressions of the same energy.'[70] With him, too, the locality that mattered was not in the East, where he was born, but in the West, his adoptive home. It was, in fact, in California, where he built for himself and his wife a granite house and tower facing the sea, that he found an appropriate spirit of place. Its rugged scenery and way of life, its detachment from the civilised communities of the East and Europe, were to exercise a potent influence. It was only in 'the Monterey mountains', he insisted that he had ever found 'people living . . . essentially as they did in the Idyls or Sagas, or in Homer's Ithaca. Here was life purged of its ephemeral accretions. Here was contemporary life that was also permanent life.' In addition, the position of California, facing what he called 'the final Pacific', convinced him that here was 'the world's end.' With the conquest of the American continent, Jeffers believed, the westward movement of civilisation was completed. Human history was effectively over; although, of course, cosmic history would continue.

Among the many poems that explore Jeffers's own peculiar version of frontier legend, the mythology of the West, are 'The Torch-Bearer's Race' and 'Continent's End'. In the latter, the poet stands on the Californian coastline, watching the Pacific. As he watches, and meditates, it occurs to him that the sea represents a form of life much older than human history, a form from which human beings, in the progressive stages of their development, have moved ever further away. 'The long migrations meet across you', observes the poet, addressing the ocean:

and it is nothing to you,
you have forgotten us, mother.
You were much younger when we crawled out of the womb
and lay in the sun's eye on the tideline.[71]

Gradually, however, another perception occurs to him: that, despite evolution, there lurk within man ways of being and knowing that antedate even the sea. Both man and ocean, the poet recognises, evolved out of an 'older fountain', the primeval chaos that preceded the universe as we now know it, and both contain within them still a few traces of their origins. 'The tides are in our veins', he insists:

we still mirror the stars, life is your child,
but there is in me
Older and harder than life and more impartial, the eye
that watched before there was an ocean.[72]

As Jeffers put it elsewhere: 'The pasts change and pass . . ., people and races and rocks and stars; none of them seems important in itself, but only the whole.' At the 'continent's end', the poet can contemplate the passing of particular things and the survival of the whole, the primeval energies of existence. What is more, he can bear witness to the presence of those energies within himself, not least in the way he writes poems. For, as he concludes, still addressing the ocean:

Mother, though my song's measure is like your surfbeat's
ancient rhythm I never learned it of you.[73]

His line, he suggests, imitates movements that are fundamental to life, movements that are also recalled in the pulse of the sea, the beating of the heart. In this way, he taps into larger processes, the 'tides of fire' or rhythms of being of which human history and individual natural phenomena form only a part.

But perhaps the finest of Jeffers's pieces in which California is a visible, palpable presence is the longer, narrative poem, 'Roan Stallion'. Jeffers was frequently drawn towards longer forms. Most of his published volumes include one or two long narrative or dramatic poems. Among his dramatic pieces are adaptions of Greek legend, like 'The Tower beyond Tragedy', 'At the Fall of an Age', and *Medea* as well as his idiosyncratic version of the story of Jesus, 'Dear Judas'; while, over thirty years, he wrote fifteen narrative poems all located in California in the twentieth century. Not alone among these narratives, 'Roan Stallion' has its origins in local character and experience: at least some of its events, Jeffers later claimed, were 'part of . . . actual history.' Starting from there, however, the poem soon assumes the dimensions of myth: like so much of Jeffers's work, it belongs at once to a particular people and place and to a world of elemental human experience. Its central action suggests these larger dimensions; when the heroine rides a stallion by moonlight to a hilltop, and there falls upon the ground prostrating herself beneath its hooves. The stallion, the poet tells us:

backed at first; but later
plucked the grass that grew by her shoulder.
The small dark head under his nostrils: a small round
stone that smelt human, black hair growing from it;
The skull shut the light in: it was not possible
for any eyes
To know what throbbed and shone under the sutures
of the skull, . . . a shell full of lightning . . .

After this moment of brooding excitement, the poem quickly rises to a strange, mystical experience of union:

The atom bounds-breaking,
Nucleus to sun, electrons to planets, without recognition
Not praying, self-equalling, the whole to whole,
the microcosm
Not entering nor accepting entrance, more equally,
more utterly, more incredibly conjugate
With the other extreme and greatness; passionately
perceptive of identity . . .[74]

Reading lines like this in context, we cannot help being reminded of one of the most persistent of ancient legends, in which a god comes to a woman in the shape of a beast and there is sexual contact between them. This, in turn, encourages us to see the entire narrative as a symbolic one, with several different levels of meaning. One level is registered in the heroine's name, California, and the fact that she is one quarter Indian, one quarter Spanish, and one half Anglo-Saxon. On this level, the poem is clearly a myth of the American West: California represents a new land and a new breed of people, and her moment of communion with the horse figures the close contact with nature that land and those people enjoy – 'life', to recall Jeffers's description of the Monterey mountains, 'purged of its ephemeral accretions.' Another level invites a comparison with some of Ransom's work, and Tate's: on this level, 'Roan Stallion' is a kind of racial myth which has as its subject myths and the mythologising process in general. Jeffers presents us with a legendary union between a mortal woman and a god in the shape of a beast, and then proceeds to explain why, since the beginning of time, people have created such legends. After the passage just quoted, for instance, the poet connects the central incident of the poem to other mythical annunciations, and then connects every one of these in turn with what he calls:

> . . . the phantom rulers of humanity
> That without being are yet more real than what they
> are born of, and without shape, shape that which
> makes them.[75]

All of these legends, he is saying, exist because we need them. They serve to remind us of the power and the glory latent in us, which we share with the elements, and which can only find a partial expression in the lives that we lead, the societies we build.

This leads us to the third, and most significant, level of meaning in the poem. Above all, 'Roan Stallion', like all of Jeffers's work, is about the gospel of Inhumanism. The stallion, according to this reading, figures the power of nature just as the creatures in 'Divinely Superfluous Beauty' do; and, in surrendering to it, the woman momentarily identifies herself with that power, just as Jeffers always longed to. The identification is not easy, as the poet's description of the mystical experience at the heart of the poem indicates. A rapprochement between woman and nature begins to occur at the beginning of the lines quoted just now, suggested by the comparison of California's 'small dark head' to a 'small round stone'. But, at first, there is a gulf if only because the head is full of the 'lightning' of self-consciousness. More effort is required to bridge that gulf and turn rapprochement into union: 'lightning' in this sense could also refer to the power generated in the struggle to escape self-consciousness. And, at the lines beginning 'The atom bounds-breaking', the gulf is finally bridged. 'Humanity is the mould to break away from', Jeffers insists elsewhere in the poem, 'the crust to break through, . . ./ The atom to be split.'[76] Suddenly, in an experience that transcends and illuminates all that surrounds it, the atom *is* split and man assumes the status of 'not-man'. 'I think one of the most common intentions in tragic stories', Jeffers said, 'is to build up the strain for the sake of the explosion of its release – like winding up a ballista.' If this is true, then 'Roan Stallion' is certainly a tragic story. Its heroine may only be able to achieve union with inhuman nature for a while: at the end of the poem, in fact, she betrays the beast-god by shooting him. But, for a brief enchanted moment, she does experience that union, and in doing so provides narrator and reader alike with a very special version of tragic catharsis.

Towards the end of Jeffers's life, however, there was a distinct shift of emphasis away from the tragic and towards the mystical. The sense of an inescapable conflict between nature and human nature became of less concern; and the poet concentrated more than ever before on the possibility of union. Of course, union as an idea (as in 'Divinely Superfluous Beauty') or a momentary experience (as in 'Roan Stallion') is often present in his earlier work: but there it is normally qualified by a recognition of the needs and limits of the human character. In the work of Jeffers's last years, by contrast, this recognition tends to lose its power, and the poet is consequently left freer to contemplate those occasions when, as he put it once, there is 'no passion but peace'. In 'The Eye', for instance, the poet finds refuge from the horrors of the Second World War in a feeling of identification with 'the staring unsleeping / Eye of the earth': the poem is a perfect illustration of Jeffers's claim that Inhumanism is 'neither misanthropic nor pessimistic' but 'a means of maintaining sanity in slippery times', because it fosters 'reasonable detachment as a rule of conduct.' In 'My Burial Place', in turn, Jeffers anticipates the moment at which the union between himself and nature will be complete, when his body will be compounded into dust. 'Now comes for me the time to engage / My burial place', he insists:

put me in a beautiful place far off from men
No cemetery, no necropolis,

. . .

But if the human animal were precious
As the quick deer or that hunter in the night the lonely puma
I should be pleased to lie in one grave with 'em.[71]

Death, Ransom suggested, is the greatest subject for poetry; certainly, it has become the greatest subject for traditionalist poetry. Like Ransom himself and Tate, like Bishop and Winters, Frost and Robinson, Jeffers contemplates his own mortality here, in severe and immaculate lines that register how absurd and petty the human animal is, and how everything is dwarfed by the enigmatic beauty, the intrinsic perfection of nature. More, Jeffers reminds us, as the other major traditionalist poets do, that all our words are nothing more than a temporary bridge erected over a vacuum. Just as they do, he recalls us to the fact that all our ceremonies are mere shadow play: no more than fragile defences against the time when, as we inevitably must, we shed our humanity, returning to the earth, our origins.

Notes

1. See John William Ward, 'The meaning of Lindbergh's flight'. *American Quarterly*, X (1958), 3–16. This discussion is also indebted to Jacqueline Fear and Helen McNeil, 'The Twenties', in *Introduction to American Studies* edited by Malcolm Bradbury and Howard Temperley (London, 1981) and Lawrence W. Levine, 'Progress and Nostalgia: The Self Image of the Nineteen Twenties', in *The American Novel and the Nineteen Twenties* edited by Malcolm Bradbury and David Palmer (London, 1971).
2. Ralph Linton, 'The distinctive aspects of acculturation', in *Acculturation in Seven American Tribes* edited by Linton (New York, 1940), p. 517. See also, Robert S. Lynd and Helen M. Lynd, *Middletown: A Study of American Culture* (New York, 1929).
3. See Joseph Gosfield, *Symbolic Crusade: State Politics and the American Temperance Movement* (Urbana, Ill., 1963).
4. See David Chalmer, *Hooded Americanism* (Garden City, N.J., 1965); Hiram Wesley Evens, 'The Klan's Fight for Americanism', *The North American Review*, CCXXIII (March, 1926), 33–61.
5. See Ray Ginger, *Six Days or Forever? : Tennessee v. John Thomas Scopes* (Boston, 1958).
6. Willa Cather, *My Antonia* (1918; London, 1962 edition), p. 262.
7. Allen Tate, 'The Fugitive 1922–1925: A Personal Recollection Twenty Years After', *Princeton University Library Chronicle*, III (April, 1942), 79. I am indebted to William Pratt's Introduction to *The Fugitive Poets* (1965) for much of the substance of the extended comparison between the Imagist "movement" and Fugitive "school" and for the quotations from R.P. Blackmur and John Gould Fletcher. See also, Hoffman et al., *The Little Magazine*, p. 121; [Donald Davidson], 'Merely Prose', *The Fugitive*, II (1922), 1. The material on the Fugitives is quite extensive. Among the most useful discussions are John M. Bradbury, *The Fugitives: A Critical Account* (Chapel Hill, N.C., 1958); Louise M. Cowan, *The Fugitive Group: A Literary History* (Baton Rouge, La., 1959); Louis D. Rubin, *The Wary Fugitives: Four*

Poets and the South (Baton Rouge, La., 1978); and John L. Stewart, *The Burden of Time: The Fugitives and Agrarians* (Princeton, 1965). Another important source of information is Thomas D. Young, *Gentleman in a Dustcoat: A Biography of John Crowe Ransom* (Baton Rouge, La., 1976).

8. R. P. Blackmur, 'Anni Mirabiles 1921–25: Reason in the Madness of Letters', Four Lectures Presented Under the Auspices of the Gertrude Clarke Whittall Poetry and Literature Fund (Washington, 1956), p. 10.
9. Tate, 'The Fugitive 1922–1925', p. 83.
10. John Gould Fletcher, 'Two Elements in Poetry', *Saturday Review of Literature*, IV (August 27, 1927), 65–66.
11. John Crowe Ransom, 'Painted Head', line 8. See also, 'Winter Remembered', line 3: 'Arts and Philosophers', *Kenyon Review*, I (Spring 1939), 197–98; Cleanth Brooks, *Modern Poetry and the Tradition* (Chapel Hill, N.C., 1939), p. 88.
12. John Crowe Ransom, 'Winter Remembered', lines 17–20. See also, Bradbury, *Fugitives*, p. 33.
13. John Crowe Ransom, 'A Poem Nearly Anonymous', in *The World's Body* (New York, 1938), p. 28. See also, 'I. A. Richards: The Psychological Critic', in *The New Criticism* (Norfolk, Conn., 1941), p. 53.
14. John Crowe Ransom, 'Dead Boy', lines 1–12.
15. John Crowe Ransom, 'Antique Harvesters', line 19. See also, lines 3, 21, 22, 43.
16. Allen Tate, 'Credo in Intellectum Videntum', lines 9–10. See also, 'Retroduction to American History', line 9.
17. Allen Tate, 'Ode to the Confederate Dead', lines 44–55. See also, 'Narcissus as Narcissus', in *Essays of Four Decades* (London, 1970), pp. 596, 598, 599.
18. Tate, 'Narcissus as Narcissus', p. 601.
19. Allen Tate, 'Seasons of the Soul; Spring', lines 54–55, 59–60. See also, 'Remarks on the Southern Religion', in *I'll Take My Stand: The South and the Agrarian Tradition* (1930; New York, 1962 edition), p. 166.
20. Allen Tate, 'The Swimmers', lines 14–22.
21. John Crowe Ransom, 'Art and the Human Economy', *Kenyon Review*, VII (Autumn 1945), 685.
22. Donald Davidson, 'I'll Take My Stand: A History', *American Review*, V (Summer 1935), 307.
23. Donald Davidson, 'Geography of the Brain', book I of *The Tall Men*, sect. i, lines 1, 3–6.
24. Donald Davidson, 'Geography of the Brain', sect. iii, lines 9–10, 23–7. See also, sect. vii, lines 2–4; sect. viii, line 2.
25. Robert Penn Warren, *Brother to Dragons: A Tale in Verse and Voices (New Version)* (New York, 1979), p. 118.
26. 'Shoes in Rain Jungle', lines 24–25. See also, 'T. S. Stribling: A Paragraph in the History of Critical Realism', *American Review*, II (Feb., 1934), 476; *Segregation: The Inner Conflict in the South* (New York, 1953), p. 26: 'The

Great Mirage: Conrad and *Nostromo*', in *Selected Essays* (London, 1958), p. 54; 'A Note on Three Southern Poets', *Poetry*, XL (May, 1932), 110; *Who Speaks for the Negro?* (New York, 1965), p. 413.

27. Robert Penn Warren, 'Picnic Remembered', lines 45–49. See also, 'I Am Dreaming of a White Christmas: The Natural History of a Vision', section 12, lines 5–6.
28. Robert Penn Warren, 'Knowledge and the Image of Man', *Sewanee Review*, XLIII (Spring 1955), 18.
29. Robert Penn Warren, *Audubon: A Vision* (New York, 1965), section I (B), lines 1–4, 13–14.
30. Ibid., section VII (B), line 7.
31. Allen Tate, 'Introduction' to *The Selected Poems of John Peale Bishop* (London, 1960), p. ix.
32. John Peale Bishop, 'Speaking of Poetry', lines 1–2, 36–40.
33. John Peale Bishop, 'Green Centuries', section II of 'Experience in the West', lines 3–12.
34. Wendell Berry, 'Below', lines 1–6, 13–14, 17–20. See also, 'Another Descent', line 10.
35. James Dickey, 'Listening to Foxhounds', lines 1–3, 9–12.
36. James Dickey, 'Hunting Civil War Relics at Nimblewill Creek', lines 61–62, 68–72. See also, lines 10–11; Preface to *Falling, May Day Sermon, and Other Poems*, reprinted in *Night Hurdling: Poems, Essays, Conversation, Commencements, and Afterwords* (Columbia, S.C., 1983).
37. Yvor Winters, 'To a Young Writer', lines 9–12. See also, 'Two Old Fashioned Songs' 'II: A Dream Vision', line 10; 'For the Opening of the William Dinsmore Briggs Room', line 11.
38. Yvor Winters, 'On Teaching the Young', lines 10–12. See also, line 3; 'A Postcard to the Social Muse', lines 11–12.
39. Yvor Winters, 'The Realization', lines 1–4.
40. Yvor Winters, 'Before Disaster', lines 15–20.
41. Yvor Winters, 'In Praise of California Wines', lines 13–16.
42. J. V. Cunningham, Epigram No. 43. See also, Yvor Winters, *The Poetry of J. V. Cunningham* (Denver, Col., 1961), p. 39; Jack Hill, 'J. V. Cunningham's Roman Voices', in *Modern American Poetry* edited by R. W. (Herbie) Butterfield (London, 1984), p. 174.
43. J. V. Cunningham, Epigram No. 19.
44. J. V. Cunningham, 'For My Contemporaries', lines 6–8. See also, 'All Choice is Error', line 18; 'Fancy', line 12.
45. Richard Eberhart, 'Anima', lines 9–10. See also, 'The Hard Structure of the World', line 23; 'If Only I Could Live at the Pitch that Is Near Madness', lines 3, 14–15; 'In a Hard Intellectual Light', lines 1, 19; 'The Supreme Authority of the Imagination', line 17.
46. Richard Eberhart, 'The Incomparable Light', lines 1, 3–4, 13–14. See also, line 20; 'The Supreme Authority of the Imagination', lines 13–14; 'The Goal

of Intellectual Man', lines 13–14, 19; 'Centennial for Whitman', section IV, line 20.

47. Richard Eberhart, 'For a Lamb', lines 7–8.

48. Richard Eberhart, 'Centennial for Whitman', section III, lines 1, 7–11. See also, line 21; 'The Recapitulation', line 4.

49. For Frost's many comments on the 'sound of sense', the dramatic possibilities of traditional verse forms, see the relevant headings in the indices to Lawrance Thompson, *Robert Frost: The Early Years, 1874–1915* (New York, 1966); *Robert Frost: The Years of Triumph, 1915–1938*; Lawrance Thompson and R. H. Winnick, *Robert Frost: The Later Years, 1938–1963* (New York, 1976).

50. Robert Frost, 'Stopping by Woods on a Snowy Evening', lines 13–16.

51. Robert Frost, Preface to *Collected Poems* (New York, 1939), reprinted in *Selected Prose of Robert Frost* edited by Hyde Cox and Edward C. Lathem (New York, 1961), p. 18.

52. Robert Frost, 'The Death of the Hired Man', lines 118–19. See also, lines 119–20.

53. Robert Frost, 'For Once, Then, Something', line 14. See also, line 15.

54. Emily Dickinson, 'Of God we ask one favour', line 6. See also, 'What mystery pervades a well!', line 13.

55. Robert Frost, 'The Oven Bird', line 14. See also, Randall Jarrell, 'To the Laodiceans', in *Poetry and the Age* (London, 1955), p. 66.

56. Robert Frost, '"Out, Out –"', lines 29–34. See also, Lionel Trilling, 'A Speech on Robert Frost: A Cultural Episode', *Partisan Review*, XXVI (Summer 1959), 448.

57. Robert Frost, 'Design', lines 13–14. See also, lines 1, 2–3.

58. Robert Frost, 'The Most of It', lines 16–20. See also, lines, 1, 3, 8.

59. Robert Frost, 'After Apple-Picking', lines 18–26. See also, line 9.

60. For a fuller account of Robinson's philosophical development see, Estelle Kaplan, *Philosophy in the Poetry of Edwin Arlington Robinson* (New York, 1940); for the relevant literary influences see, Edwin Fussell, *Edwin Arlington Robinson: The Literary Background of a Traditional Poet* (Berkeley, Calif., 1954). The passage quoted here comes from a letter to *Bookman*, March, 1897. See also, Edwin Arlington Robinson, 'Oh for a poet – a beacon bright', line 1; James Dickey, 'Edwin Arlington Robinson: The Many Truths', 'Introduction' to *Selected Poems of Edwin Arlington Robinson* edited by Morton Zabel (London, 1965), p. xx.

61. Edwin Arlington Robinson, 'Richard Cory', lines 13–16. See also, lines 3, 4, 9; Wallace Anderson, *Edwin Arlington Robinson: A Critical Introduction* (Cambridge, Mass., 1968), p. 68.

62. Edwin Arlington Robinson, 'How Annandale Went Out', lines 1–2. See also, 'New England', line 4; 'Calverly's', lines 25–6.

63. Edwin Arlington Robinson, 'Eros Turannos', lines 33–40. See also, line 3.

64. Edwin Arlington Robinson, 'Miniver Cheevy', lines 9–12. See also, 'George Crabbe', lines 13–14; 'Uncle Ananias', line 20.

65. Edwin Arlington Robinson, 'Mr. Flood's Party', line 20. See also, lines 45–46, 48.

66. Edwin Arlington Robinson, 'The Man Against the Sky', lines 224–32. See also, lines 204, 217.

67. Robinson Jeffers, Letter to James Rorty, in S. S. Alberts, *A Bibliography of Robinson Jeffers* (New York, 1933), p. 38. See also, *The Selected Letters of Robinson Jeffers, 1897–1962* edited by Ann N. Ridgeway (Baltimore, Md., 1968), p. 116.

68. Robinson Jeffers, 'Divinely Superfluous Beauty', lines 7–12. See also, line 1.

69. Robinson Jeffers, 'To the Stone-Cutters', line 1. See also, lines 2, 4–6, 7–8.

70. Jeffers, *Letters*, p. 221. See also, 'Foreword' to *The Selected Poetry of Robinson Jeffers* (New York, 1938), p. xvi, 'The Torch-Bearer's Race,' line 1.

71. Robinson Jeffers, 'Continent's End', lines 7–8.

72. Ibid., lines 11–12. See also, line 16; *Selected Letters*, p. 132.

73. Robinson Jeffers, 'Continent's End', line 15. See also, line 16.

74. Robinson Jeffers, 'Roan Stallion', lines 225–58, 229–33. See also, *Themes in my Poems*, p. 71.

75. Robinson Jeffers, 'Roan Stallion', lines 234–45.

76. Ibid., lines 155–56.

77. Robinson Jeffers, 'My Burial Place', lines 6–8, 10–12. See also, 'The Eye', lines 13–14.

Chapter 4
The Traditions of Whitman: Other Poets from between the Wars

The language of crisis and the language of Whitman: other aspects of the social and cultural situation between the wars

The cultural history of the United States between the two World Wars is not, of course, simply the story of a conflict or tension between optimism and nostalgia, the pull towards the future and the backward glance towards the past, the urge to experiment and the search for more traditionalist norms. Other forces were at work; and Americans were inevitably and profoundly affected in the later part of this period by what seemed to be the crisis of capitalism. The Wall Street Crash of 1929 was a significant economic event: within four years of its occurrence, *per capita* income had dropped one hundred per cent and unemployment, which had been remarkably low in the Twenties, had risen from 500,000 to 13 million. Many of those who were unemployed had no economic assistance of any kind, and were forced to wander the country in search of work. They rode freight trains from one state to another, risking injury or even death, and erected shanty towns, ironically called 'Hoovervilles', after the then President Hoover. Farmers unable to meet mortgage payments were evicted from their holdings; beggars, street-corner orators demanding revolution, bread-lines and soup kitchens all became commonplace. Those in employment fared little better: in 1932, the average wage in several major industries ranged between 20 and 30 cents an hour and the average income of working Americans in general dropped back to what it had been at the beginning of three decades of technological revolution. Over all this chaos, Hoover presided with little sense of what to do: the measures he offered to alleviate or alter things were too little, too late. Farm relief, federal loans for business, public works, all these measures were tried half-heartedly because they went against Hoover's own cherished philosophy of 'rugged individualism'. He believed that the slump was a short-term affair, that would gradually correct itself. Others, including the vast majority of the American electorate, tended to disagree. Hoover had been elected as 'the Great Engineer' in 1928; in 1932 he was defeated by Franklin Roosevelt in a landslide. Even in his own home state of Iowa, Hoover was picketed during the election by two thousand men holding placards that said it all: 'In Hoover We Trusted, Now We are Busted'.

If the Crash and the Depression that followed it was a significant economic event, though, it was an even more significant cultural and psychological one, as those placards carried in Iowa indicated. For what it generated was a crisis of confidence: the ingrained American beliefs in the rewards due to hard-work, the central importance of self-help, the inevitability of progress – all were called into question by an occurrence for which the word 'panic' seemed precisely the right word because it was at once devastating in terms of the human suffering it caused and unpredictable, more or less totally unexpected. When the Crash came, most bankers and financiers were not only unprepared for it, they tried at first to deny its implications: what the economist J. K. Galbraith has termed the 'generally poor state of economic intelligence' at the time made them oblivious to the sheer scale of the collapse. And, as it worsened, many were inclined to treat it not as a *cultural* event, susceptible to analysis and explanation, but as a *natural* one: a natural disaster, like an earthquake or typhoon, for which little preparation was possible and which had to be endured for a while. The simple and terrible fact was that a failure of language occurred: Americans, to begin with, lacked the vocabulary, political, economic, or imaginative, adequately to confront and possibly to deal with what had happened. Even the most 'realistic' of the popular cinematic forms at this time, the gangster movie, was concerned as much with compensatory fantasy as it was with hard facts. For while it acknowledged that the urban-industrial surroundings, the cities of America had become oppressive, bewildering, and even terrifying places, it offered a series of dynamic, rebellious, and above all individualistic protagonists who seemed to have achieved temporary mastery over the urban jungle. Morally, these heroes might be subject to a disapproval that required them to be shot or electrocuted in the final reel: on another, subliminal level, however, they offered their audiences another version of the dream of freedom, the independence and mobility of the outsider – suitably darkened to reflect the darker times.[1]

'I like the Americans because they are healthy and optimistic', the novelist Franz Kafka once remarked, adding, when he was asked what he knew about America, 'I always admired Walt Whitman'.[2] The Crash and Depression may have provoked people in the United States to bewilderment and anger and compensatory fantasies of power: but it could never quite extinguish that belief in possibility, in reinventing the self and society however shattered, of which Kafka was thinking – and for which, as Kafka realised, the most memorable spokesman in earlier American writing had been the author of *Leaves of Grass*. The election of Roosevelt in 1932 foregrounded this belief: insisting that Americans had nothing to fear but fear itself, the newly elected President helped to restore popular confidence at least a little. In the first hundred days of his administration – the first hundred days of what he called the New Deal – Roosevelt pushed Congress into passing a mass of legislation designed to restore some health to a radically sick economy. In the following years came other measures. The three Agricultural Adjustment Acts of 1933, 1936, and 1938 were attempts to maintain farm prices by artifically created scarcity; the Social Security Act of 1935 was an important welfare-state measure, providing for a system of old-age retirement payments and unemployment pay; the Works Progress Administration was established to implement relief work on a vast scale and by 1939 had provided employment for 8,500,000 people in a whole variety of occupations. Historians continue to argue over the practical efficacy of this and other legislation – arguing, for instance, that it took the booming economy of war to restore full employment. What is unarguable, though, is that Roosevelt helped restore Americans' belief in their power to manage things, the solubility of the problems with which they were confronted. In an ideological sense, this meant that most of them never lost complete confidence in the system, the virtues of capitalism and free enterprise. And in a more specifically moral sense, this involved a recovery of the 'can do' philosophy, the conviction that everything is manageable, given hard work, pluck and luck, and the exercise of the independent, individual will.

In the area of the arts, this crisis of confidence and gradual recovery was reflected in many forms. There was, for instance, a renewed sense of the social responsibility of the artist. Ezra Pound, as we have seen, sought a solution to contemporary problems in the politicisation of poetry and the aestheticising of politics and, eventually, in commitment to Mussolini and the Fascists. The Objectivists, in turn, tried to take the measure of the times in hard, spare distillations of the urban scene. While many of the traditionalists, notably the Fugitives, attempted to prevent what they saw as the virtual inevitability of Marxist revolution by celebrating the values of an earlier, inherited American culture: a system that, as they saw it, was at once prior and superior to the confusions of urban capitalism. There were 'proletarian novels' – books, that is, written by working-class people – such as *The Disinherited* by Jack Conroy; there were novels of social protest like *The Land of Plenty* by Robert Cantwell and *The Grapes of Wrath* by

John Steinbeck; and there was fiction exposing the plight of the dispossessed urban minorities, such as *Call It Sleep* by Henry Roth or *Native Son* by Richard Wright. Writers like F. Scott Fitzgerald, William Faulkner, and Ernest Hemingway tried to secrete an awareness of contemporary problems into their narratives: Fitzgerald did so in *Tender is the Night* and Faulkner and Hemingway in, respectively, *The Wild Palms* and *To Have and Have Not*. Others turned directly to the techniques of journalism or documentary to make their point: as, say, James Agee did in his account of three poor Southern tenant-farming families, *Let Us Now Praise Famous Men*. A sense of apocalypse or annunciation, which had always come relatively easy to American writers, now became even more pronounced: apocalypse, for example, feelings of nightmare and catastrophe, are all clearly there in books like *The Day of the Locust* by Nathanael West while Hart Crane's poem *The Bridge* is, to some extent, one long annunciatory act.[3]

There is no one simple way of summing up the artistic response to crisis: crisis in general, that is, or the particular crisis encountered by the American people between the wars. Extraordinary things happened. For instance, in a radical departure from the traditional American belief that the artist, like every good citizen, should be self-reliant, government agencies were actually established to employ people in the creative arts. Among the most notable of these agencies was the Federal Theatre Project, sponsored by the Works Progress Administration: which was a national organisation of theatre groups that re-employed thousands of theatrical workers – by 1937, it was playing to weekly audiences of 350,000. Other projects included the financing of photographic accounts of the rural working class, popular America and American folk customs; the employment of painters under the Federal Art Project to decorate banks, post offices, and schools with murals developing themes of labour, agriculture, and history; and the federal support of books and films intended to reveal the essential nature of the United States, its human and natural resources, to its people. Impossible as it is to summarise this response, though, perhaps something of it can be caught by saying that, in reaction to crisis, American writers rediscovered their social and prophetic function: they were reawakened, more than ever before, to their responsibility as bards, telling what Ezra Pound had called the tale of the tribe. Poets, in particular, felt compelled to come to terms with their role as Americans, to confront the pressures and events that had helped shape the national identity and that seemed, for a while, to threaten its survival; they were driven to respond to the challenge the times threw down with an even greater commitment to self-definition, social and personal, than ever before. In a very specific way, that meant, for many of them, coming to terms with the poet who had made being an American, a private face in the public place of the New World, his subject and his inspiration: the one who had explored American character and investigated American forms at an earlier moment of imminent catastrophe and potential recovery – that author of a 'language experiment', whom Kafka admired so much, Walt Whitman.

Whitman and the shape of American poetry

'He *is* America. His crudity is an exceeding great stench, but it *is* America'. Ezra Pound's tribute to Walt Whitman is, perhaps, all the more convincing for being so barbed: like a number of other literary expatriates – Henry James, for instance – Pound tended to associate the author of *Leaves of Grass* with all that he hated, as well as all that he cherished or at least respected, about his native land. Pound, as we have seen, made his own 'pact' with Whitman eventually: which involved, among other things, coming to terms with Whitman's experiments with epic and free verse forms. Most other American poets of this century have had to do the same. Of course, the nature of that 'pact' has varied with each poet. 'Do I contradict myself?' asked Whitman in 'Song of Myself', then continued:

> Very well then I contradict myself,
> (I am large, I contain multitudes.)[4]

And it is this very multitudinousness, this willingness to embrace apparent opposites, that has helped make it possible for different people to learn different lessons from the founding father of American poetry. Whitman the singer of self and Whitman the democratic populist; Whitman the nationalist, the American bard, and Whitman the internationalist, the celebrant of mankind; Whitman the pragmatist and Whitman the idealist; Whitman the political orator and Whitman the prophetic visionary: these and other contradictions in this most omnivorous of poets have made it possible for those who have followed him to take quite different paths. Whether it is his commitment to American epic, or his formal experiments and interest in open poetic structures; whether it is his preoccupation with the creation of an American speech, or his transformation of autobiography into history and history into the stuff of myth; whether it is his concern with the possible usefulness of poetry, or with the antinomies of nature and culture, the wilderness and the clearing, freedom and law; whether it is one of these or something else entirely; whatever shape it assumes, the figure of the Good, Gray Poet hovers behind a whole variety of different texts. As far as it can be said of any one person, it can be said of the author of *Leaves of Grass* that, as Pound grudgingly admitted, he *is* America – or, at least, America in verse.

Whitman and American populism: Sandburg, Lindsay, Masters

The writers who owe the most conspicuous debt to Whitman, perhaps, are those who imitate his populism: who recall him principally as a poet of the common people, celebrating the spaciousness of the American continent and the vitality of American men and women in vigorous language, free verse, and open forms. Of these, the most remarkable, at roughly the time when Pound was making his own pact with Whitman, were a group gathered in Chicago. Much of their work was published in the earlier editions of *Poetry*, the magazine Harriet Monroe founded; and their very presence in the city testified to a remarkable 'renaissance', a sudden expansion of cultural activity, Chicago was experiencing at the time. The 'renaissance' was in part a consequence of Chicago being established as the unofficial capital of the Mid-West; as the economic and political importance of the city grew, so did its interest in the arts and culture. In quick succession, a new university and a new symphony orchestra were founded, both of them destined to acquire an international reputation. It acquired its own little theatre, and its own bohemian quarters. Finally, it was given its own bard: in 1916, *Chicago Poems* was published, its author the son of immigrants who had spent his youth travelling across the Middle West working in various menial jobs. His name was Carl Sandburg, and his poem addressed to 'Chicago' announced the nature of his vision:

> Hog Butcher for the World
> Tool Maker, Stacker of Wheat,
> Player with Railroads and the Nation's Freight Handler
> Stormy, husky, brawling,
> City of the Big Shoulders:
>
> . .
>
> . . . I turn once more to those who sneer

at this my city, and I give them back the sneer
and say to them:
Come and show me another city with lifted head singing
so proud to be alive and coarse and strong and cunning.
. . .
Laughing the stormy, husky, brawling laughter of Youth,
half-naked, sweating, proud to be Hog Butcher,
Tool Maker, Stacker of Wheat, Player
with Railroads and Freight Handler to the Nation.[5]

As these lines suggest, 'Chicago' is at once a description of the economic centre of the middle West and a celebration of the common people, its inhabitants. Its simple, unanalytical populism is reflected in the style, in which a rhetorical and flexible line, an idiomatic language and bold rhythms, all become part of the attempt to create a poetic equivalent of folk speech. Like Whitman, Sandburg uses a paratactical syntax: phrases and clauses are left lying side by side, linked only by an 'and', rather than arranged into an elaborate hierarchy of mains and subordinates. No particular person or impression is allowed to be more or less important than any other here: everything has an equal relevance for the innocent, unprejudiced and uninhibited, eye of the poet. Like Whitman, too, he habitually uses participles, so as to dramatise the idea of life as process, and his rhetoric is really a voice whose rhythms create a basic recurrent form; the introductory series of descriptive phrases, for instance, is linked together both rhythmically and phonetically (by the harsh gutturals) and then repeated in the last line quoted, which is also the last line of the poem. At certain points in the portrait, Chicago seems to be transformed into a folk hero, along the lines of Paul Bunyan or Mike Fink; and at certain points the portrayer seems something of a folk hero as well, responding to everything as he does with an equal feeling of wonder, a reverence for its power and particularity. This is a simple poem, perhaps, but it is also a remarkable one, because its celebration of the Middle West and America in general is a matter not only of vision but of voice. It is a song both in praise and in imitation of American energy, the sense of strength and possibility that an almost unlimited amount of living space can bring.

Sandburg's response to America was not uncritical, however; as M. L. Rosenthal has observed, his populism could make him 'hard as Bertolt Brecht is hard'. A poem like 'A Fence' illustrates this harder, more aggressive side. Here he turns from celebration of the innate energies of the people to an attack on those who would suppress such energies, or even worse divert them to their own ends. The fence that the rich man builds around 'his stone house on the lake front' is identified in this poem with the barriers behind which he and his special interests prefer to hide. Passing through its bars, the poet observes, 'will go nothing except Death and Rain and Tomorrow'; and that last word is clearly a symptom of unbounded confidence in the future – after today, evidently, the barriers *will* be penetrated, a freer, more open society *is* certain. Other poems, such as 'New Feet' and 'Gone' suggest, not so much the critical side of Sandburg, but a sadder, more ironic one. 'Gone', for example, is a poignant and regretful piece that captures the anonymity of urban life rather than (as in 'Chicago') its vitality. The subject of 'Gone' is a girl called Chick Lorimer who has left town without trace or explanation. Its theme is sounded in the closing lines:

> Everybody loved Chick Lorimer
> Nobody knows where she's gone.[6]

It is, after all, a sadly diminished form of affection that involves no real knowledge of its object's movements or intentions. 'Love' in this environment, it seems clear, means no more than casual intimacy, the ephemeral relationships of people who meet occasionally in the crowd. Chick Lorimer is hardly seen in this poem and, when she is, it is in significantly vague, deliberately trite terms. She is known, the reader infers, only as most people in towns and cities are known: as a fleeting, quite enigmatic presence, whose real personality must remain lost in the restlessness of her surroundings.

Few writers have matched Sandburg's understanding of the urban landscapes of the period or the characters who populated them. A parallel could be drawn with the Naturalists, novelists and muckraking journalists like Theodore Dreiser and Lincoln Steffens who – at roughly the same time as Sandburg – were writing about the vibrancy and corruption of city life. But perhaps a closer parallel can be found in the visual arts. Seven years before the Armory Show, a group called The Eight held an exhibition of paintings. Their leader was Robert Henri, born in the Mid-Western city of Cincinnati; and, as earlier artists had gone into the countryside to paint what they might find, so they went out into the streets to capture both the random gestures and the underlying truths of the people they met. These new realists had a Whitmanesque desire to embrace all types of existence. 'The ideal artist', one of them proclaimed, 'is he who . . . experiences everything, and retains his experience in a spirit of wonder'. And just as Whitmanesque was there longing to combine such largeness of vision with specificity of focus: 'I am looking at each individual', Robert Henri declared, 'with the eager hope of finding something of dignity of life there, the humour, the humanity, the kindness'. Sandburg, of course, shared both these traits. In some poems, such as 'Ice Handler', a conversational, even slangy idiom is used to voice his commitment to particular people, the humour and humanity of individuals, seen in the streets; while in others, such as 'Band Concert', a broader canvas, a more deliberately repetitive diction is exploited to convey the teeming life of the cities. 'Band concert public square Nebraska city', the latter poem begins:

> Flowing and circling dresses, summer-white
> dresses. Faces, flesh tints flung like sprays of cherry
> blossoms. And gigglers, God knows, gigglers, rivalling
> the pony whinnies of the Livery Stable Blues.

In order to convey their excitement, the new realists adopted sketchlike techniques in which brushstrokes acted as conductors of emotion. 'The brushstroke', Henri insisted, 'at the moment of contact, carries inevitably the exact state of being of the artist at that exact moment into the world'.[7] It is surely not too far-fetched to say that the abrupt language, the syncopated rhythm and impressionistic sweep of this one, packed line make this the verbal equivalent of just such a brushstroke. In its own way, it communicates the immediacy of mood, the heightened, excited response that Henri and his followers desired.

But Sandburg did not confine himself to the city scene; on the contrary, some of his finest poems are concerned with the signts, sounds, and the people of the prairies. In 'Sunset from Omaha Hotel Window', for example, he charts the geography of the particular moment mentioned in the title. The desolate quality of 'the blue river hills' and 'the long sand', the stillness and brooding silence, above all the sense of vast space that hits the narrator as the last rays of the sun stretch away over an open, scarcely peopled landscape: all these things are caught in the insistent, repetitive, chanting rhythm of the poem and its hard, spare, almost primitive style. 'More Country People' is primitive in a different sense. Here, Sandburg describes 'six pigs at the breast of their mother' in a poetic equivalent of a primitive, abstract portrait. A series of basic colour combinations and strictly proportioned shapes is used to supply a medium through which the creatures of the farm can be seen in a special way: in terms, that is, of a ritual which, although quite familiar and simple, seems fresh and new every day. As the title suggests, by calling these animals 'people' the poem acts in part as a fable, describing a pattern of behaviour which human beings would do well to imitate. 'Look once at us', declares the poet, giving a voice to the pigs, ' – today is the day we call today'.[8] The inhabitants of the farm are, in effect, made to express Sandburg's very American message that (as he put it elsewhere), 'The past is a bucket of ashes': each day must be lived without any conscious reference to its predecessors, evidently, as a unique occasion. Such a stance towards reality does not involve any neglect of history. As another poem, 'Still Life', indicates, Sandburg was acutely aware of the historical changes occurring all round him. 'Cool your heels on the rail of an observation car', the poem begins and then offers the reader a poignant mixture of continuity and change, the old and the new: the 'rolling land and new hay crops' and the express train that hurtles through them, the 'gray village' the poet passes and the shadow of Kansas City towards which he moves. Sandburg was also keen, however, to place such an awareness within a broader framework of populist values: that commitment to space, finally, rather than time and the future more than the past which is shared by all poets of the open road.

Just how total Sandburg's belief in populist values was can be gathered from two monumental works: his biography of Abraham Lincoln, begun in 1919 and not finished until 1939, and his re-working of folk song and idiom in *The People, Yes*, a long poem that appeared in 1936. In the biography, Lincoln appears as an embodiment of the American Dream; while, in the poem, Sandburg declares his faith in the democratic experiment – taking the word 'democracy' in the most literal sense possible, as a government of the people, by the people, for the people. 'The people will live on', Sandburg insists, towards the end of the poem:

> The people is a polychrome,
> a spectrum and a prism
> held in a moving monolith,
> a console organ of changing themes,
> a clavilux of colour poems . . .
>
> . . .
>
> In the darkness with a great bundle of grief
> the people march.
> In the night, and overhead a shovel of stars for
> keeps, the people march!
> "Where to? what next?"[9]

Using a frequently apocalyptic tone and an incantatory rhythm and language, Sandburg presents 'the people' as an indomitable force, dormant now but about to assert its rightful supremacy. This is American epic at its simplest and most straightforward: plotless, concentrating more on natural potential than on cultural attainment, and ending as these lines show on a note of hope. At its centre is 'a polychrome, / a spectrum and a prism': a mysterious, multifarious figure who is at once everybody and nobody in particular – nobody, that is, apart from that representative of his nation the poet knows best, himself.

'Oh, the great poem has yet to be written . . . Jeffersonian democracy as an art is a thing to be desired'. The words are those of another poet associated with Chicago, Vachel Lindsay. Like Sandburg, Lindsay was devoted to Abraham Lincoln: 'The prairie-lawyer', he called him, 'master of us all'. He was equally devoted to Andrew Jackson (a man for whom, as he saw it, 'Every friend was an equal'), and to William Jennings Bryan. Bryan, in particular, was a charismatic figure for him: the Democratic Presidential candidate of 1896 who, for a time, made it seem possible that the farming interests of the West might yet prevail over the cities and factories of 'the dour East'. Lindsay was, in fact, raised in Illinois during the period of agrarian and populist revolt against the emergent urban-industrial economy; and it left an indelible mark on him. So, too, did the walking tour of the United States that he undertook in 1912, without occupation or even prospects. Out of both experiences grew a determination to create an 'American' rhythm, related to the sounds of galloping herds and shrieking motors, black music and what he called 'vaudevilles' and 'circuses'. And out of this, in turn, came poems like 'General William Booth Enters Into Heaven' (which reveals his millenialism, his commitment to the social gospel of the underprivileged), 'In Praise of Johnny Appleseed' (the mythical American hero for whom, Lindsay suggests, 'the real frontier was his sunburnt breast'), and, perhaps his most famous work, 'Bryan, Bryan, Bryan, Bryan':

I brag and chant of Bryan, Bryan, Bryan,
Candidate for president who sketched a silver Zion,
The one American Poet who could sing outdoors,
He brought in tides of wonder, of unprecedented
splendour,
Wild roses from the plains, that made hearts tender,
All the funny circus silks
Of politics unfurled . . .[10]

As these lines indicate, Lindsay's poetry is heavily rhetorical, with a proliferation of heavy accents, emphatic rhymes and verbal melodies, repetition and chanting rhythms. It is, really, a poetry meant to be spoken: the later years of Lindsay's life were devoted to an exhausting programme of public performances, which had as its aim nothing less than what he termed 'an Art Revolution'. 'We must make this', he insisted, 'a *Republic of Letters*'; and, in order to establish such a republic, he hoped that at least ninety-nine other poets would follow in his wake. 'When I quit,' he said, 'I want the 99 to be *well started, singing.*'

Predictably, his hopes remained unrealised; less predictably, and more tragically, he committed suicide. Whatever may be thought of his work and aims, though, he remains a curiously noble figure: someone who took the populist fervour, the pedagogical and proselytising impulses implicit in the Whitman tradition to their logical and not entirely absurd extreme.

The third memorable poet associated with the Chicago 'renaissance' was a populist in a different sense: in that he wanted to record the real lives of people as they were lived in the Middle West, without heroic disguise or romantic decoration. Edgar Lee Masters aimed, he said, to write 'a sort of Divine Comedy' of small-town life: its minor tragedies, its melancholy and its frustrations. Like Sandburg and Lindsay, he received the encouragement of Harriet Monroe; and it was still quite early on in his career when the major fruit of his labours appeared, *Spoon River Anthology*. Using a loose verse form and spare, dry language, Masters presents the reader with a series of self-spoken epitaphs. The tone is sometimes elegiac, very occasionally lyrical and affirmative: but the major impression left by the book is one of waste. Men, women, and children reveal what happened to them and what happened was, for the most part, shame and disappointment. 'Why, a moral truth is a hollow tooth / Which must be propped with gold',[11] declares 'Sersmith the Dentist' at the conclusion of his epitaph; and the gaunt, bitter tone of this is characteristic. Gradually, the poems overlap to produce a composite picture of Spoon River: a picture that recalls Tilbury Town, but without the passion and the mystery, or Robinson's sense that perhaps something more lies beneath the monotonous surface. Masters is largely forgotten now, except as an example of what is commonly called 'the revolt from the village': that reaction against small-town values which characterised many American writers earlier on in this century. Perhaps it would be more useful, though, to remember him as someone who attempted to honour the stoicism of ordinary men and women, their laconic idioms and the harsh rhythms of their existence – and, in this sense at least, achieved one of Whitman's aims, of speaking not only to the people (Masters was immensely popular for a time) but for them.

Whitman and American radicalism: Rexroth, MacLeish, Fearing, Patchen

Implicit in the poetry of Sandburg, Lindsay, and even Masters is a kind of radicalism: the kind that Whitman gave voice to when he declared that 'our American republic' was 'experimental . . . in the deepest sense'. It was left to some other poets, however, to give free rein to this radicalism: with them, the populist strain was sometimes still evident but, even when it was, it was absorbed into a larger structure of feeling that anticipated political, social, and perhaps sexual change. Responding in part to the horrors of the Depression, in part to the wider economic pressures the United States was experiencing between the two World Wars, these poets, working quite separately from one another, were heirs of Whitman in a different way from the Chicago group: in that political activism, the notions of commitment and relevance, lay fairly close to the surface in much of their work. In short, they wanted America altered, and they said so in no uncertain terms. The finest of these poets was someone who was to exercise considerable influence on writers after the Second World War, and in particular on those associated with Black Mountain College: Kenneth Rexroth. The nature of his political commitment is perhaps clear from these lines, the conclusion to a poem called 'New Objectives, New Cadres':

> . . . see the arch dialectic satyriast;
> Miners and social workers
> Rapt in a bated circle about him;
> Drawing pointless incisive diagrams
> On a blackboard . . .
> . . . .
> We do not need his confessions.
> The future is more fecund than Molly Bloom –
> The problem is to control history,
> We already understand it.[12]

This has many of the familiar Rexroth trademarks: a cool, sardonic and yet passionate tone, a fierce commitment to the community of ordinary people and an equally fierce hatred of intellectuals ('spectacled men', as he calls them in another poem), the sense of a spirit as flinty and tenacious as the Western landscapes where the poet made his home. There is nothing strained or artificial about these lines: they have the power and the intimacy of measured conversation. 'Poetry', Rexroth insisted, is 'the living speech of the people', elsewhere adding, 'I have spent my life trying to write the way I talk'. Consequently, he disdained elaborate and elevated rhetoric in favour of clarity of speech, a poised syntax, and simple, lucid images. As William Carlos Williams observed of Rexroth, 'he is no writer in the sense of a wordman. For him words are sticks and stones to build a house – but it's a good house'.

Another way of putting it would be to say that poetry, for Rexroth, is not so much an imitation of life as a state of being alive. 'Poetry', he suggested, 'is vision, the pure act of sensual communion and contemplation'; it is 'the very link of significant life itself, of the individual to his society, of the individual to his human and nonhuman environment'. What he means by this is suggested by his 'Requiem for the Spanish Dead'. It begins as so many of his poems do, with a vision of the stars and the High Sierras:

> The great geometrical constellations
> Lift up over the Sierra Nevada,
> I walk under the stars, my feet on the
> known round earth.

Along with Robinson Jeffers, Rexroth is the finest poet of the Far West, presenting us with landscapes that seem to dwarf and diminish the invading human element. Standing on a quiet hilltop, contemplating the mountains, the sea and the stars, he often achieves a sense of mystical solitude, wonder and awe, that recalls the classic Chinese, Japanese, and Greek poets whom he admired so much. 'Ten thousand birds sing in the sunrise', he says in another poem that describes the Sierras, '/ Ten thousand years revolve without change': but, then, he adds there (thinking of one particularly memorable trip to the Sierras he took with his daughter) 'All this will never be again'.[13] That last, poignant observation measures the distance between him and Jeffers. For Rexroth, the Western landscape dwarfs human beings, certainly, making them look, as they are, tiny and temporary. Yet, it also makes their occasions of contact and community all the more precious: because they *are* only for a cherished moment and because, in so far as they are expressions of *natural* emotion, they are part of the continuity between human and nonhuman worlds.

The feeling of continuity begins to emerge in the second stanza of 'Requiem', after Rexroth has described the colossal landscape of mountains and sky, and observed a distant plane passing overhead. He thinks of another mountainous landscape where 'an unknown plane' may be passing over: in Spain where, at that time, there is Civil War. He imagines 'men waiting' in those other, Spanish mountains, 'clutched with cold and huddled together', tensing with fear as the plane 'flies southeast / Into the haze above the lines of the enemy', relaxing when it passes and then growing 'tense again as their own thoughts return to them'. He considers 'The unpainted pictures, the interrupted lives . . ./. . ./. . . the quick grey brains broken and clotted with blood'. Then suddenly, under the impact of these thoughts, he is 'caught up in the nightmare'. 'Alone on a hilltop in San Francisco', he feels 'the dead flesh / Mounting over half the world'[14] pressing against him. 'I am the man, I suffer'd, I was there', said Whitman, and Rexroth is saying almost exactly the same. Originating in personal vision, the poem has moved into interpersonal communication: an act of imaginative identification, between the poet who has certain beliefs and the many men and women suffering and dying for those beliefs in other parts of the world – in particular, the Spanish Republicans.

'Requiem' does not end with this experience of shared fear and suffering, however. The final stanza focusses upon the immediate scene:

> Then quietly at first and then rich and full-bodied,
> I hear the voice of a young woman singing,
> The emigrants on the corner are holding
> A wake for their oldest child . . .[15]

This is to remind us of the human community in another way. 'In the rites of passage', Rexroth argued, 'life at its important moments is ennobled by the ceremonious introduction of transcendence; the universe is focussed on the event in a Mass or ceremony that is itself . . . a work of art'. The wake being performed by the emigrant family is a humble illustration of Rexroth's argument. It is a ceremony that releases pain and ennobles experience because it links the particular with the universal, the death of a child with the continuities of past, present and future. It is also something that supplies another perspective on the suffering and death described in the previous stanzas. Terrible though it is, Rexroth intimates, such suffering is not meaningless because it too is part of the continuities; it, also, has its ritualistic significance, since it represents a sacrifice offered up in the name of the human community. Having quietly established this perspective, the poet then ends by returning us to the original vision of the wheeling stars:

> Voice after voice adds itself to the singing.
> Orion moves westward across the meridian,
> Rigel, Bellatrix, Betelgeuse, marching in order,
> The great nebula glimmering in his loins.[16]

Now that vision is seen with a difference, however. The first line here links 'voice after voice' together in one song, a specifically human moment of communion. But then the human is linked with the natural, the nonhuman: a link that is made all the more effective by giving the people in the scene a curiously anonymous, even substanceless quality (they have, after all, become voices rather than visible presences) and by anthropomorphising the stars in a profoundly traditional way. The constellations almost seem to be 'Marching in order' to the song sung by the mourners; certainly, voices and stars are moving together, responding to the same rhythms. And those rhythms move the poet too, he has become another part of the ritual. The poet and all those dying in distant countries, the emigrants and 'the great nebula', men, mountains, sea, and sky: all have become absorbed into what Rexroth elsewhere called 'the tragic unity of the creative process'. So has the reader: the poet's intimate form of communication has invited him into the process, made him a part of the ceremony. In this sense, the poem not only describes a sacrament, it also performs one; it functions, however briefly, as an act of holy union.

As Rexroth saw it, this, the sacramental nature of poetry had a peculiar significance for his contemporaries. 'The conviction that "nobody wants me, nobody needs me . . ." is coming to pervade all levels of modern society', he said. So the problem was how 'in the face of a collapsing system of values . . . to refound a spiritual family': how to heal the divisions that capitalism engendered, how to reclaim the humanity and restore the connection with nature that the city and the factory denied. Poetry was a part of the solution since it promoted 'the realization . . . of universal responsibility'. 'A kelson of the creation is love', Whitman had proclaimed; Rexroth agreed, and agreed too with Whitman that poets had a crucial role to play in the publication of this truth. They were indispensable, in fact, to the rediscovery of community. Sometimes, the community Rexroth celebrates and dramatises is with one particular person, as in 'A Letter to William Carlos Williams' or 'Delia Rexroth'; sometimes it is with many people, past and present, as in 'Autumn in California' or 'Wednesday of Holy Week, 1940'; sometimes, as in 'The Signature of All Things', it is with all created life, 'streaming / In the electrolysis of love'. Always, though, it involves a devoted attention to the particulars of the object, and a faithful re-creation of the voice of the subject: Rexroth's phrasing is organically determined by his own speaking and breathing, so a powerful sense of Rexroth the individual emerges from his work – humorous, honest, irascible, passionate, proud. William Carlos Williams called him 'a moralist with his hand at the trigger ready to fire at the turn of a hair'. To which could be added that he was also a poetic prophet whose prophecies were shaped by an indestructible optimism, an abiding hope: as these lines, from a poem written just before the start of the Second World War, amply suggest:

These are the last terrible years of authority.
The disease has reached its crisis.
Ten thousand years of power,
The struggle of two laws.
The rule of iron and spilled blood,
The abiding solidarity of living blood and brain.[17]

A similar; if less persuasive, optimism characterises another poet for whom the social role, the idea of the writer as agent of cultural change, was crucially important: Archibald MacLeish. Macleish's early work, written mostly while he was in Europe is preoccupied with the plight of the artist and is full of unassimilated influences: notably of Eliot, Pound, and the French Symbolistes. On his return to the United States, however, at about the time of the Depression, he became increasingly interested in social issues and began to work towards a poetic diction closer to common speech. A series of poems followed examining the problems and possibilities of his native country (*New Found Land*). These were followed, in turn, by an epic poem describing the attempted conquest of the Mexican Aztecs by the Spanish Cortés, (*Conquistador*) and by other poems satirising the excesses of American capitalism (*Frescoes for Mr. Rockefeller's City*) or chastising American poets for their withdrawal from what MacLeish saw as their social responsibilities (*The Irresponsibles*). 'Instead of studying American life', MacLeish declared of the writers of the Twenties, 'literature denounced it. Instead of working to understand American life, literature repudiated it'. His clearly stated aim was to reverse this trend: 'This is my own land', he announced in 'American Letter', 'It is a strange thing – to be an American'. For MacLeish, as for so many of his predecessors, this strangeness, the special quality of his native land resided in the idea of America rather than the historical fact: the New World as a place of freedom and solitude, a site of possibility. 'America is neither a land nor a people', he insisted,

America is West and the wind blowing
America is a great word and the snow.
A way, a white bird, the rain falling,
A shining thing in the mind and the gulls' call.[18]

These lines repeating a common theme illustrate a significant weakness in MacLeish's poetry. His most famous poetic statement comes from 'Ars Poetica', 'A poem should not mean / But be'; and its fame perhaps prevents us from registering that it *is* a statement. Paradoxically, it invites us to interpret its meaning even while it insists that a poem should not 'mean'. Too often, MacLeish comments rather than creates;

he offers us definitions ('America is . . . / America is . . .') not dramatic experiences; he presents us with the product, a precise formulation of an idea, rather than the process. What is missing from much of his work, in fact, is indicated by his occasional successes. His fine poem, 'You, Andrew Marvell', for instance, begins with an evocative description of the sunset, the 'always rising of the night', that carries with it intimations of mortality ('To feel . . . / The earthy chill of dusk . . .'). At first, this looks like a meditation on personal death, inspired perhaps by Andrew Marvell's famous lines, 'But at my back I always hear / Time's winged chariot hurrying near'. Imperceptibly, though, the poem moves into a meditation on cultural crisis and death, in the past and in the present:

> And straight at Ecbatan the trees
> Take leaf by leaf the evening strange
> The flooding dark about their knees
> The mountains over Persia change
>
> And now at Kermanshah the gate
> Dark empty . . .[19]

Then, in the final stanza, the poet returns to the immediate scene:

> And here face downward in the sun
> To feel how swift how secretly
> The shadow of the night comes on . . .[20]

This poem has a public dimension, certainly, but for once it is a dimension that draws its power from an acutely experienced moment of personal tension. The sense of cultural crisis is felt precisely because it is inextricable from a sense of individual, immediate crisis. The darkening of the evening sky, the shades of death, the shadow of social conflict: all are brought together in the one, long sentence that constitutes the poem – a sentence that is incomplete because, on the cultural, communal, and natural levels at least, this is a process that never ends. MacLeish did not always remember Frost's warning that a poem is 'drama or nothing' but, when he did, the results, as here, could be remarkable.

The need MacLeish felt to serve his society drew him into institutional life: eventually, he became something of an establishment figure, working as Assistant Secretary of State under Roosevelt and acting as a member of the delegation that founded U.N.E.S.C.O. The same could hardly be said of two other poets for whom the social dimension of poetry was crucial, Kenneth Fearing and Kenneth Patchen. Fearing, in particular, has almost been marginalised by his commitment to techniques and attitudes formed during the Depression. Discarding what he called 'the entire bag of conventions and codes usually associated with poetry', he adopted a documentary style, the eye of the camera, and abrupt, syncopated rhythms. The opening lines of 'King Juke' illustrate the result:

The juke-box has a big square face,
A majestic face, softly glowing with red
  and green and purple lights.
Have you got a face as bright as that?

BUT IT'S A PROVEN FACT, THAT A JUKE-BOX
  HAS NO EARS.

With its throat of brass, the juke-box eats live
  nickels raw . . .

Fearing's favourite subject, as here, is street life, the world of dime stores, cheap cafés, gangsters and hustlers; his approach, apart from the occasional attack on bourgeois stupidity, that of the reporter; city slang, disjunctive imagery, and an elastic free verse line are all used to capture what he calls, in one of his poems, 'the new and complex harmonies . . . of a strange and still more complex age'.[22] The range of his work may be limited, perhaps: but, taken on its own terms, it represents one very specific and successful response to Emerson's call for an American bard – someone, that is, who could mirror in some fashion 'the barbarism and materialism of the times'.

Patchen, while being even more of an anti-establishment figure than Fearing, is also a more varied and subtler poet. Influenced by the European surrealist tradition and committed to free verse forms, he has gravitated between haunting lyrics of personal emotion ('The Character of Love') and vitriolic social comment ('Nice Day for a Lynching'), sharp vignettes of city life ('Do the Dead Know What Time It Is?') and fierce jeremiads directed at 'the falsity, the smug contempt' of 'drugstore-culture' in America ('O Fiery River'). Sometimes, the social comment has what R. P. Blackmur called 'a kind of *excathedra* automatism' about it: the targets are too easy, the conclusions a little too pat. For instance, a poem with the eye-catching title, 'The Eve of St. Agony or, The Middleclass Was Sitting on its Fat', ends with the glib cry, 'Hey! Fatty, don't look now but that's a Revolution breathing down your neck'. Fortunately, this is rare. More characteristic are poems like 'Street Corner College' and 'The Fox'. In 'Street Corner College', Patchen speaks for the adolescent boys to be found on the corner of any city street. The poem is a mixture of the abrupt, abrasive, language of urban life ('Watching the girls go by; /

Betting on slow horses; drinking cheap gin') and a strange, surreal idiom ('solitude is a dirty knife at our throats'). Out of all this comes a powerful feeling of sympathy for such people: the contrast between their jazzy, streetwise exteriors and their jumpy inner selves, their vitality dimmed by the perception that they are 'Sleepwalkers in a dark and terrible land'. They are the dispossessed, the poet intimates: on the bottom rung of a society they cannot begin to comprehend, destined when the next war comes to die for a culture that has given them nothing – not even the courage to be themselves. 'The Fox' uses a rather more lyrical mode to arrive at equally stark conclusions. It opens with an evocative description of a snowscape, 'white falling in white air', into which the figure of a wounded, bleeding fox is introduced. Slowly, incrementally, the poem then builds towards the final lines: 'Because she [the fox] can't afford to die', the poet says:

> Killing the young in her belly
>
> I don't know what to say of a soldier's dying
> Because there are no proportions in death.[22]

In this bleak landscape of red and white, hunters and hunted, victimisers and victims, no one death is worse or better than another, nothing is morally quantifiable. No comparison need apply; all there is, is the simple, recurring fact of exploitation.

Whitman and American identity: Hughes, Johnson, Cullen, Tolson, Hayden, Brooks, and the question of black poetry

Nobody knows more about exploitation in the United States, of course, than black people: as James Baldwin observed, 'the Negro tells us where the bottom is because he is there'. Nobody, either, has been more involved in the search for roots and the assertion of identity: with black American poets of this century, in fact, Whitman's desire to sing self into being, to use poetry as an agent of self-discovery and cultural change, achieves a new intensity. One reason for this is that the problems confronting every American poet have been exacerbated in the case of black poets. Like other American poets, the black poet has been caught between his private self and his public role, isolation and community; the crucial difference is that, in his case, the sense of himself is that much more indefinite, the roles attributed to him are that much more fixed and restrictive, and the language available to him is often peculiarly 'foreign' – that is, the product of an exceptionally alien literary tradition. The contemporary black writer, Imamu Amiri Baraka (Leroi Jones), put this problem in the spotlight when he declared, 'I am inside / Someone who hates me'. The roles offered to a black in American society, Baraka suggests, are so very much the products of a strange culture – one that regards him as at best inferior and at worst an enemy – that he risks schizophrenia if he accepts them. This problem is, in turn, related to a second, more specific one: which W. E. B. DuBois was referring to when he said the black person in America is burdened with 'a double-consciousness . . . two souls, two thoughts, two unreconciled strivings, two warring ideals in one dark body'.[23] The Afro-American is, after all, American *and* African: and the question is, which is the more important? Should the primary impulse of Afro-American art be towards absorption into the dominant culture or towards assertion of a separate cultural identity? Is assimilationism the priority, or black nationalism?

One person who has tended towards nationalism, assertion of the separate and distinctive identity of black Americans, is the finest poet the Afro-American community has so far produced, Langston Hughes. 'To my mind', Hughes insisted:

> it is the duty of the young Negro
> artist . . . to change through the force of his
> art that old whispering "I want to be
> white" hidden in the aspirations of his people,
> to "Why should I want to be white? I
> am a Negro – and beautiful!"[24]

This did not mean, Hughes said, that the black writer should simply idealise black life: 'We know we are beautiful', he observed, 'And ugly too'. But it did mean that black writers should devote themselves to uncovering the power and glory of Afro-American traditions, the 'heritage of rhythm and warmth, [and] incongruous humour that, so often, as in the Blues, becomes ironic laughter mixed with tears'. Accordingly, Hughes has made black people his subject, especially 'low-down folks, the so-called common element'. He is more interested in the ordinary men and women of the fields and streets, and in particular of Harlem, than he is in the black bourgeoisie – who, on the few occasions when they do appear in his work, are "buked' and scorned'. Like Whitman, his aim is clearly identification, imaginative empathy with these people. He is, above all, a dramatic poet, speaking through a multiplicity of voices – a young schoolchild, perhaps

('Theme for English B'), a smart and sassy older woman ('Madam's Past History') or a dying man ('Sylvester's Dying Bed') – so as to capture the multiple layers, the pace, drive, and variety of black American life. Like Whitman, too, although in a much more specific sense, Hughes is a socially committed poet. 'The major aims of my work', he declared, 'have been to interpret and comment upon Negro life, and its relations to the problem of Democracy'.[25] This commitment is most evident in the work that permits itself overt social comment: some of the poems written within a Marxist frame in the Thirties, say ('Christ in Alabama'), or, more generally, his bitter attacks on 'The lazy, laughing South / With blood on its mouth'. But it is just as powerful a shaping force in works dramatising the petty frustrations and particular oppressions of individual black people ('Ballad of the Landlord'), their dreams of liberation ('Dream Variations') or their stony endurance ('Life is Fine'). 'I've been scarred and battered', admits the narrator of one poem, then adds, 'But I don't care! / *I'm still here*!'; and his one voice, defiant, resolute, even hopeful, speaks for a thousand others.

'Most of my . . . poems are racial in theme', Hughes said, 'In many of them I try to grasp and hold some of the meanings and rhythms of jazz'. The latter remark suggests another, crucial way in which consciousness of the black tradition enters into his work. Hughes may have learned a great deal about free verse from Sandburg, Lindsay, and above all Whitman: but he learned even more from Afro-American music, and what he called its 'conflicting changes, sudden nuances, sharp and impudent interjections, broken rhythms . . . punctuated by . . . rifts, runs, breaks, and distortions'. 'Jazz is a heartbeat', Hughes argued, 'its heartbeat is yours'. By 'jazz' Hughes nearly always meant black musical culture in general: jazz, as he saw it, was a vast sea 'that washes up all kinds of fish and shells and spume with a steady old beat, or off-beat'. That sea was the source of spirituals, work songs, field hollers, and shouts, as it was of blues, gospel, ragtime, and rock and roll. 'A few more years', he observed, 'and Rock and Roll will no doubt be washed back half forgotten into the sea of jazz'. In the meantime, it too could play its part in fostering an art of subversion: for the essence of jazz, Hughes believed, was that it was open-ended and improvisational and as such challenged the closed structures of the dominant white culture. Whether it assumed the shape of, say, jive or be-bop – offering 'a revolt against weariness in a white world, a world of subway trains and work, work, work' – or of blues – suggesting 'pain swallowed in a smile', resistance to the apparently irresistible – jazz for Hughes constituted an act of rebellion. Hughes's exploitation of black music takes many forms. Sometimes, he uses the classic, three-line blues form ('Seven Moments of Love'); sometimes, as in a poem quoted just now, 'Still Here', he employs fragments of blues themes and vocabulary; sometimes, as in 'The Weary Blues', he mixes classic with other forms:

Droning a drowsy syncopated tune,
Rocking back and forth to a mellow croon,
    I heard a Negro play . . .
        . . .
I heard that Negro sing, that old piano moan –
    "Ain't got nobody in this world,
    Ain't got nobody but ma self.
    I's gwine to quit ma frownin'
    And put ma troubles on the shelf".[26]

Elsewhere, he tries to imitate the energy, the frenetic excitement of instrumental jazz:

EVERYBODY
Half-pint –
Gin?
No, make it
LOVES MY BABY
corn. You like
liquor,
don't you honey?
BUT MY BABY
Sure. Kiss me
DON'T LOVE NOBODY
daddy.
BUT ME.[27]

One of Hughes's most impressive works, *Montage of a Dream Deferred*, employs the free associations and abrupt rhythms of boogie-woogie and 'street poetry', rapping and jive talk ('Oop-pop-a-da! / Skee! Daddle-de-do! / Be-bop!'), to create a verbal portrait of Harlem. His use of black religious music is less frequent and pervasive, but a poem like 'Fire' shows how he could turn to it to dramatise the spiritual side of his culture:

Fire,
Fire, Lord!
Fire gonna burn my soul!

I ain't been good,
I ain't been clean –
I been stinkin', low-down, mean.[28]

Spirituals or street poetry, be-bop or blues: whatever forms Hughes utilises, he demonstrates an intimate knowledge of its intricacies – 'The rhythm of life', he said, '/ Is a jazz rhythm' and this, in turn, is the rhythm of his poetry.

While emphasising his commitment to the black community and culture, though, Hughes was always willing to acknowledge his debt to certain white writers and, in particular, the author of *Leaves of Grass*. He saw no contradiction here, because what Whitman offered him above all was the example of self-emancipation and self-discovery. As another black writer of the period, Claude McKay, observed of poets like Whitman:

> I could feel their race, their class, their
> roots in the soil, growing into plants, spreading
> and forming the backgrounds against which
> they were silhouetted. I could not feel their
> reality without that. So likewise I could
> not realize myself writing without conviction.[29]

The way Hughes plays his personal variations on this American theme, singing his own 'Song of Myself', is suggested by two of his finest poems, 'I, Too' and 'The Negro Speaks of Rivers'. 'I, Too' involves a fairly clear echo of Whitman. 'I, too, sing America', it begins:

> I am the darker brother.
> They send me to eat in the kitchen . . .
> . . .
> Tomorrow,
> I'll sit at the table
> When company comes . . .
> . . .
> They'll see how beautiful I am
> And be ashamed, –
>
> I, too, am America.[30]

The poem plays beautifully on two themes. The first is the ancient, legendary theme of dispossession: the 'darker brother' is banished from the table of communion for a while but, growing strong, proud, confident of his beauty, he prepares to reclaim his rightful inheritance. And the second is the more recent American theme of the poet as democratic hero, the representative of his culture: not, however, in this case his culture as it is but as it might and should be. Even more firmly and fiercely than Whitman, Hughes seems to declare, 'I project the history of the future'.

'The Negro Speaks of Rivers' is more concerned with the past than the future, the heritage that is the black American's special privilege and strength. 'I've known rivers', its narrator reveals,

> I've known rivers ancient as the world and older
> than the flow of human blood in human veins.
>
> My soul has grown deep like the rivers.[31]

The poem then goes on to describe some of the rivers with which 'the Negro', or rather his spirit and his race, have been associated – the Euphrates, Congo, Nile, and the Mississippi – before returning, like the river, to its beginnings: 'My soul has grown deep like the rivers'. As with Whitman in some of his more elegiac works ('Out of the Cradle Endlessly Rocking', for instance), Hughes uses a sonorous, flowing line here to create a sense of meditation, and incremental repetition ('I bathed . . . I built . . . I looked . . . I heard') to suggest the tones of the prophet, the tongue of the seer. The vision unfolded is at once accurately historical and elemental, mythical: since the rivers, as they are named in order, recall some of the civilisations the black race has helped build, while rehearsing the ancient idea that the same deep forces run through the body of the earth and the bodies of men and women. Knowing the rise and fall of cultures, black people have known the tale of time; they have seen once proud civilisations pass away and will doubtless see others follow in due course. Participating in the flow of waters 'ancient as the world', however, they also know something of the story of eternity: through their veins and those of the world course the same ceaseless currents, endowing them with both strength, the capacity to endure, and a kind of magic and majesty. 'Consider me', one of Hughes's other dramatic voices asks, 'Descended also / From the / Mystery'. Hughes's poems are always asking the reader to consider this, the mysterious essences of black life as well as its jazzy surfaces. As in the best black music there is energy, sensuality, humour, certainly, but also that unique quality, soul.

Other poets roughly contemporary with Hughes showed a similar desire to voice the separateness of black culture. Most notable among these was James Weldon Johnson, who emphasised the need for what he termed 'a form that will express the racial spirit', and who tried to meet that need in poems addressed to the anonymous authors of blues and spirituals ('O Black and Unknown Bards') or written in imitation of black musical forms ('Sence You Went Away'). His most notable work is *God's Trombones*, a series of poems in which he attempts to re-create the passion and power of black sermons using polyrhythmic cadences, vivid diction and a technique of intensification by repetition. The results can be illustrated by the closing lines of one poem, 'The Creation':

This Great God
Like a mammy bending over her baby
Kneeled down in the dust
Toiling over a lump of clay
Till He shaped it in His own image;
Then into it He blew the Breath of life,
And man became a living soul.
Amen. Amen.[32]

Not everyone agreed with Hughes and Johnson, however. The black writer, George Schuyler spoke for these when he declared, 'The Aframerican is subject to the same economic and social forces that mould the actions and thoughts of the white American . . . it is sheer nonsense to talk about "racial differences"'. 'What is Africa to me . . .', begins a poem by Countee Cullen:

One three centuries removed
From the scenes his fathers loved,
Spicy grove, cinnamon tree,
What is Africa to me?[33]

Cullen wanted, he said, to be 'a poet, not a Negro poet', adding elsewhere, 'the individual diversifying ego transcends the synthesising hue'. Consequently, he chose as his models poets like Keats ('To John Keats, Poet, at Springtime') and, for the most part, sounded like any other pale imitator of Romantic verse. Occasionally, the pain involved in his struggle to become 'universal' breaks through the discreet surfaces of his work. 'My colour shrouds me', he admits in one poem and, in another, 'Yet do I marvel at this curious thing: / To make a poet black and bid him sing!' But, as a rule, he refused to think or write in terms of a distinctive ethnic heritage. In response 'To Certain Critics' who had apparently questioned this refusal, he was quite adamant: 'never shall the clan', he insisted, 'Confine my singing to its ways / Beyond the ways of man'. The problem was that, in trying to become 'universal', Cullen usually only succeeded in sounding vacuous; in attempting to engage with many traditions, he ended up embracing none. It is significant that, in each of his first three volumes, there is a section entitled 'Colour'; and equally significant that he should criticise one of Hughes's attempts to imitate black musical forms by saying, 'This creation is a *tour de force* of its kind, but is it a poem?' For Cullen, evidently, his identity as black could be cordoned off from the rest of his being and experience; and, in any event, it was more or less incompatible with his role as poet.

In the generation immediately following Hughes and Cullen, the most articulate spokesmen for Cullen's position were Melvin B. Tolson and Robert Hayden. Tolson insisted that, 'as a black poet', he had absorbed the 'Great Ideas of the Great White World' and that his roots were 'in Africa, Europe, and America'. The result of this polyglot perception of his own identity was poems like *Harlem Gallery*: dense, intricate, Eliotic exercises in literary allusion and cultural reference. Hayden said something similar: he was, he said, 'opposed to the chauvinistic and doctrinaire' and saw 'no reason why a Negro poet should be limited to 'racial utterances'' or why his writing should be 'judged by standards different from those applied to the work of other poets'. However, in his case the rejection of any attempt to reinvent black traditions or rehearse the particularities of black life has produced more memorable and moving poetry. He is essentially a traditional poet, even though he often uses free verse (a free verse that is, though, markedly iambic); and his subjects include the perennial ones of personal memory ('Those Winter Sundays') and the conflict between the impulses towards life and death ('The Swimmer'). He can, certainly, dramatise the sufferings of black people with clarity and power ('Night, Death, Mississippi') and their 'dream of the beautiful, needful thing' known as freedom ('Frederick Douglass'). But, even here, he is not slow to relate 'the news from Selma and Saigon', or to see a connection between the black victims of American history and the victims of history generally, of whatever complexion. 'From the corpse woodpiles, from the ashes / and staring pits of Dachau, / Buchenwald they come – ', he says:

> From Johannesburg, from Seoul,
> Their struggles are all horizons,
> Their deaths encircle me.[34]

There is little place here for the perception of a distinctive inheritance of suffering, or its transcendence.

Opposed to this position, in turn, in this next generation is Gwendolyn Brooks. In her early work, admittedly, she was rather like Tolson: for, while her main subject was black life, her style was mannered, academic, and sometimes difficult. Much of this poetry is traditional, with regular stanzas and rhyme schemes, archaic diction and inverted syntax. Even at its best, such writing often offers a disconcerting contrast between form and content, the elegant phrases and cadences and the violent, vivid experiences being described. A moment of sexual union, for instance, is presented in these terms:

Her body is like new brown bread
Under the Woolworth mignonette.
Her body is a honey bowl
Whose waiting honey is deep and hot,
Her body is like summer earth,
Receptive, soft, and absolute . . .[35]

Gradually, however, under the influence of younger poets, and in particular those, like Haki R. Mahubuti (Don Lee), associated with the Organization of Black American Culture in Chicago, Brooks developed freer, looser poetic forms, a tougher idiom, and a more unequivocal, committed stance. 'It is my privilege', she said, 'to present Negroes not as curios but as people'. Like Hughes, she often adopts the voice of the poor and dispossessed ('the mother'): but she can, just as easily, assume that of the more articulate and self-conscious ('Negro Hero'). There is an almost overwhelming sense of black suffering and anger in much of her work ('Riot'), and a sharp perception of the gap between black and white that sometimes leads to crafty satire at the expense of white liberals ('The Lovers of the Poor'). But her best work is simple to the point of starkness. A hard, stony idiom, taut syntax, and primitive, urgent rhythms are all harnessed to the re-creation of black street life: a re-creation that combines sympathy for the oppressed with a sardonic appreciation of the sources of their oppression – as in this poem, 'We Real Cool':

We real cool. We
Left school. We

Lurk late. We
strike straight. We

Sing sin, We
Thin gin. We

Jazz June. We
Die soon.

Whitman and American individualism: Moore, Wylie, Millay, Miles, Bogan, Adams

'We must have the courage of our peculiarities'.[36] The words are those of Marianne Moore; and they remind us of another way in which the fatherly presence of Whitman has hovered behind so much modern American poetry – as a formal influence, encouraging writers to conduct their own, often peculiar experiments in language and rhythm. Whitman was a populist, certainly, a radical and a man preoccupied with roots and ethnicity: but he was also a consummate craftsman, who devised an extraordinary and original verse form in order to express his own idiosyncratic vision. He had, to use Moore's phrase, the courage of his pecularities: the willingness to be different and to embody this difference in his poetry. This was the best way, he felt, in which he could act as an example to others, particularly other American poets: not by telling them *what* to do but *how* to do it. Moore herself was one of the poets to learn from this strictly formal example: what she gathered from Whitman was a stubborn determination to be herself – to risk eccentricity, if it meant the creation of her own measure. The results were original and inimitable. Just as in life she had her own vivid, odd presence, instantly recognisable because of the black cape and black tricorn hat she habitually wore, so, in her work, she had her own distinctive, unique voice, as this opening stanza from her poem, 'The Steeple-Jack', illustrates:

> Dürer would have seen a reason for living
>   in a town like this, with eight stranded whales
> to look at; with the sweet air coming into your house
> on a fine day, from water etched
>   with waves as formal as the scales
> on a fish.

The peculiar quality of lines like these, poised as they are between the controlled and the spontaneous, largely results from Moore's use of the medieval device of 'rime-breaking'. The formal outlines are severe: the stanzas based on syllable count, the lines so arranged on the page as to repeat specific and often quite complicated patterns. But these strict proportions are rendered much less strict by making the stanza, instead of the line, the basic unit. Rhymes are sparse, enjambement the rule, and the sense of run-on lines is increased by ending lines with unimportant words and hyphenations. There is a frequent use of internal rhyme, too, to break up the apparently formal pattern; and the pattern itself, which depends on such extreme differences in line-length (there are, for example, nine syllables in line five of this and every other stanza, only three syllables in line six), seems to participate in the liveliness of the material quite as much as to organise it or set it off. The mixed feelings of order and spontaneity generated by this complex verse structure are then underlined by Moore's special way with images and words. The descriptive detail is extraordinarily, almost gratuitously, specific ('eight stranded whales'), asking us to look closely at the object. Moore, like Williams, tried to capture the exact contours of things in a painterly, microscopic manner ('waves as formal as the scales / on a fish'): but not because, like Williams, she wished to be appropriated by them or live their life. On the contrary, her firm belief was that, by observing an object lovingly, she could discover significance *in* it which extended *beyond* it. Precision liberated the imagination, she felt; the discipline of close observation was, for her, a means of imaginative release. And precision also characterised her language. Some of the words in the stanza just quoted appear almost to have been picked out with a tweezer. In many of her poems, in fact, she behaves even more like a collector of verbal felicities or archaeologist of language: using quotations, placing them carefully in inverted commas, and then identifying them in the Notes – all on the grounds that, as she put it, 'if a thing has been said in the very best way, how can you say it better?' However, as that opening to 'The Steeple-Jack' indicates ('Dürer would have seen a reason for living / in a town like this'), the result does not smell of the museums; exact and allusive her poetry may be, but it is also perky, immediate, conversational. 'The accuracy of the vernacular!' Moore exclaimed, 'It's enviable! That's the kind of thing I am interested in'.[37] Like the measures and metaphors she uses, her language steers between the artfully arranged and the apparently casual: it is precise to the point of epigram, yet full of surprises and fresh insights – addressing the reader directly, even intimately, as so many of the best American poems do.

As another poet, Charles Tomlinson, has argued, there is a peculiar correspondence between Moore's voice and her vision: for the patterns of her verse, as Tomlinson puts it, 'embody and reinforce by technical means our sense' of 'a world where spontaneity and order are not at odds and where the marriage between them results in 'spiritual poise''. All Moore's poems start from a belief in discipline, the acceptance of boundaries. This acceptance was necessary, she felt, for two reasons. In the first place, the mind could discover a safeguard against danger by accepting limitations. A good deal of Moore's poetry, Randall Jarrell has pointed out, 'is . . . about armour, . . . protection, places to hide'; and it is so probably because Moore saw life in terms of risk, the threats our environment confronts us with, the menace likely to overcome us if ever we should lose control. The second reason is more significant, however: Moore also clearly believed that, in accepting limitations, the mind discovers fulfilment. Freedom and happiness, she felt, are to be found only in the service of forms: in an acknowledgement of the needs and restrictions of our natures, the scope of our particular world. For Moore, 'Contractility is a virtue / as modesty is a virtue' and just as "compression is the first grace of style": as poets, and as people, we need discipline – formal, moral, intellectual, or whatever – in order to realise our best possibilities. Something of this is suggested in 'The Steeple-Jack' by the character who gives the poem its title. From 'the pitch / of the church', the poet tells us:

> a man in scarlet lets
> down a rope, as a spider spins thread;
> he might be part of a novel, but on the sidewalk a
> sign says C. V. Poole, Steeple Jack,
> in black and white: and one in red
> and white says
>
> Danger.[38]

The steeple-jack may be dressed in a flamboyant colour, stand high above the town; he may even seem to be 'part of a novel'. But, after all, he is not a hero, epic or exotic. He is an ordinary man, performing his duties with the minimum of fuss and wasted effort: devoted to his craft and doing his best to avoid all the dangers he can during the course of his day. Within the limited space marked out by his signs, his words, he has created an area of freedom; he has devised his own humble example of spiritual – and, as it happens, physical – poise. The poem illustrates poise, spiritual balance, then, through characters like the steeple-jack and through the lively discipline of its style. Not only that, it supports it. It does so, in the sense that the world it describes is, without pretence, a *fictional*, invented one. The opening lines alert us to this: the town, Moore quietly reminds us, is like one of Dürer's water-etchings – an imaginative construct, as formal and right as the scales on a fish. What 'The Steeple-Jack' offers for our inspection, we the readers infer, is an *idea* of order: a place, and a plainly imaginary place at that, which, in its own special combination of the ordained and the haphazard, the regulated and the random, supplies the poet – and, potentially, us – with spiritual refuge.

On the subject of poetry, Moore declared, in one of her most famous poems, 'I, too, dislike it: there are things that are important beyond all this fiddle.' But, then, she added this:

> Reading it, however, with a perfect contempt for it,
> one discovers in
> it, after all, a place for the genuine.[39]

For Moore, as she goes on to explain, 'genuine' poetry is the absolute reverse of the 'high-sounding'; it is 'useful' just as Whitman believed it was – in the sense, that is, that all things necessary to the perpetuation of life are. Everything is the stuff of poetry, even '"business documents and / school-book"'. 'All these phenomena are important', she says; only 'half poets' make the mistake of thinking otherwise. So Moore can make her poetry out of the world of nature ('The Pangolin') and of art ('No Swan So Fine'), out of the activities of everyday life ('When I Buy Pictures') and special moments of meditation ('What Are Years?'), out of places ('England'), institutions ('Marriage'), or people ('The Student'). What matters is the *how* of poetry: how a thing is perceived, how it is felt, experienced, imagined. As Moore puts it towards the end of 'Poetry':

> nor till the poets among us can be
> "literalists of
> the imagination" – above
> insolence and triviality and can present
>
> for inspection, "imaginary gardens with real toads
> in them", shall we have
> it.[40]

A fresh subject matter is not enough, evidently. A poet must also imagine so exactly and astutely that he can perceive the visible at the focus of intelligence where vision and idea coincide, and where a fact is transformed into a truth. The phrase used to express this notion, 'literalists of the imagination', is borrowed from W. B. Yeats: but the other remark in quotation marks here was invented by Moore and apparently presented in this way for emphasis. 'Imaginary gardens with real toads in them' is a characteristically pungent symbol for the aesthetic order, the arrangement of 'these phenomena' in a modifying structure and texture. Without this, Moore concludes, the subject will not be assimilated into the poem and will acquire no new reality, while losing its original own. There will be no poem in short – nothing that offers what Moore elsewhere calls 'piercing glances into the life of things' – only a half poem.

The range of Moore's work shows how closely she followed her own prescription for 'genuine' poetry. Each of her best pieces constitutes an act of imaginary possession, in which she perceives an object carefully, and with reverence, and then attempts to absorb it – to grasp its significance in her mind. There is no imperialism of the intellect here. The essential properties of the object are not denied; on the contrary, it is precisely because the poet acknowledges them that she can then go on, in language that is all sinew, severe and pure, to discover ulterior meaning. Many of her poems concerned with inanimate objects, such as 'An Egyptian Pulled Glass Bottle in the Shape of the Fish', are what William Carlos Williams called 'anthologies of transit . . . moving rapidly from one thing to the next' and thereby giving 'the impression of a passage through . . . of . . . swiftness impaling beauty'. They depend, in effect, on their deftness of vision and lightness of touch, their absolute refusal to moralise in the conventional way. In turn, her animal poems are notable for the refusal to anthropomorphise. In 'The Frigate Pelican', for example, Moore first insists on the bird's remoteness from man, 'a less/ limber animal'. It has been difficult, we are told, to find 'the proper word' for this creature; furthermore, it is impossible to equate it with human standards of morality, because it lives in a way that we might well regard as makeshift and ruthless – by bullying other birds, the 'industrious crude-winged species', and forcing them to surrender what they have caught. Only when Moore has established this difference does she then go on to make the moral discovery. 'The unconfiding frigate bird', the poet tells us, 'hides / in the height and in the majestic / display of his art'.[41] The creature may exist apart from human concerns but in the very act of doing so he seems to offer what John Crowe Ransom called 'an exemplum of rightness and beauty': his capacity for going his own way can, after all, be translated into *strictly human terms*. He has the courage of his peculiarities: he follows the dictates, the truths and limitations, of his nature. So, paradoxically, the bird is 'like' the good man in being so 'unlike' him: like the good man and, Moore might have added, like the good poet too.

'Ecstasy affords / the occasion and expediency determines the form': Moore's memorable formulation could serve as an epigraph to her work. For that matter, it could serve as an epigraph to the work of a number of other writers who, like Moore, used formal structures to channel and so intensify feeling. Elinor Wylie, for instance, was a memorable practitioner of the classical lyric, using it to create an art that was, to use her own words, 'elaborate, neat, enamelled, elegant, perhaps exquisite'. 'Avoid the reeking herd' begins one of her poems; and this expresses one of the major impulses in her poetry – the longing to escape a malicious, stupid world, where 'The rumbling of the market-carts / The pounding of men's feet' bruise the soul, and to seek out some private realm where it may be possible to 'Live like that stoic bird / The eagle of the rock'. The realm may be a pastoral one ('Wild Peaches'); it may be one of pure artifice ('The Fairy Goldsmith'), or of sleep and death ('The Coast Guard's Nephew'). Whatever form it assumes, it is shaped by the rapt, hermetic nature of Wylie's vision, her peculiar ability to mingle sensuousness and spirituality. 'Velvet Shoes', for instance, proposes a dreaming yet dignified progress through a landscape of snow. 'We shall walk in velvet shoes', says the poet:

Wherever we go
Silence will fall like dews
On white silence below
We shall walk in the snow.[42]

In these strange, crystalline surroundings, even the natural elements assume a ghostly quality: everything is soundless, soft, above all white. The snow is new-fallen, virgin, eliciting in the walkers an emotion of sensuous tranquillity: feelings that are enhanced in the reader, in turn, by the controlled melodies of the lyric form Wylie uses, the subtle repetitions and word music. In some of her later work, Wylie became, at times, more frankly sexual (as in 'One Person', a series of autobiographical sonnets addressed to a lover) and, at other times, more openly visionary (as in 'Chimaera Sleeping', where the poet talks of pursuing a 'foreknown and holy ghost' that dissolves as she pursues it). Even these later poems, though, have that quality of dreamy sensuality, erotic mysticism that characterises 'Velvet Shoes' – and that sense of dark passions lurking beneath a bright, brittle surface that Wylie herself was probably thinking of when she declared, 'All that I /Could ever ask / Wears . . . / . . . a thin gold mask'.

Several of Wylie's poems are addressed to 'that archangel', Percy Bysshe Shelley; he is the subject of one of her novels; and members of her family tried to promote the legend that Wylie was a sort of female Shelley of the twentieth century. If Shelley's presence does indeed hover behind Wylie's writing then Lord Byron, in turn, is a ghostly presence in the work of another skilful manipulator of classic lyric forms, Edna St. Vincent Millay. Like Byron, Millay combined a lively iconoclasm, a positive desire to offend bourgeois sensibilities and mock bourgeois morality, with an astute understanding of traditional forms and metres. For a while, during the Twenties, she became the lyric voice for the lost generation. In poems that sang gaily of going 'back and forth all night on the ferry' or cavalierly acknowledged the death of a love affair ('Unremembered as old rain / Dries the sheer libation'), she attacked conventional notions of virtue – and, in particular, feminine virtue – with impudence, irreverence, and wit. 'What lips my lips have kissed, and where, and why, / I have forgotten', she announced, and elsewhere, in perhaps her most famous lines:

My candle burns at both ends;
It will not last the night;
But ah, my foes, and oh, my friends –
It gives a lovely light![43]

Several of her poems recall the bravura, the insouciance, and the sly grace of the Cavalier poets:

And if I loved you Wednesday,
　　Well, what is that to you?
I do not love you Thursday –
　　So much is true.[44]

While her rejection of utilitarian structures, standard measurements of use and value, echoes that first American bohemian, Poe:

Safe upon the solid rock the ugly houses stand:
Come and see my shining palace built upon the sand![45]

As the Twenties faded, the work Millay produced showed her branching out towards political commitment ('Justice Denied in Massachusetts') and, on the other hand, classical themes ('Oh, Sleep Forever in the Latmian Cave'). But she began losing much of her audience, like that other, greater poet laureate of the Jazz Age, Fitzgerald. It is, in any case, for the earlier work that she will be remembered – and, more especially, for her ability to capture both the rebelliousness and the romanticism of what Fitzgerald called 'the greatest, gaudiest spree in history'.

Three other poets whose work demonstrates a vivid contrast between the intensely personal, subjective nature of their subjects and the extraordinarily polished, objective character of the poetic forms they use are Josephine Miles, Louise Bogan, and Léonie Adams. The forms used by these three, however, are less obviously lyrical and romantic than the ones favoured by Wylie and Millay: they belonged to what Yvor Winters termed the 'reactionary generation' – poets, like Winters himself, who chose a strict impersonality of voice as well as tight disciplines of structure and metre. Of these, Josephine Miles is probably the least impressive. A teacher of English interested in the systematic use of literary language, she tends towards highly wrought intellectualism, a poetry that at its best is strenuous, witty, and abstruse. The closing lines of a poem called 'Grandfather' are typical:

And I think, Pater and my fine fathers,
Your rich prose taught and taught us at its knee,
And still thunders its cloud we argue under,
Yet now we argue barest daylight in the expanse of green.[46]

The interplay of concrete and abstract diction here, the ironic pun ''Pater''/''fathers'') and veiled allusion to Andrew Marvell's 'green thoughts in a green shade', the urgent rhythms and cunning use of repetition and verbal echo ('thunders . . . under'): all make for a verse that is as tense, nervously mobile, and as unnerving as anything written by Tate.

Louise Bogan is also a supreme technician, concerned with what she called (borrowing the phrase from Synge) 'the strong things of life'. In her case, though, clarity of image, exactitude of phrase and rhythm, and a measured, lucid diction make for poems that derive their emotional power from the poet's positive refusal to invite an easy, emotional response. 'Portrait', for instance describes a woman who has 'no need to fear the fall / of harvest', and no need either to 'hold to pain's effrontery / Her body's bulwark'. The reader is not told why, exactly. All the poet offers us (and it is a great deal) is lines that capture the larger paradoxes of life – its ebb and flow, losses and gains, passion and its ambiguous rewards:

What she has gathered, and what lost,
She will not find to lose again,
She is possessed by time, who once
        Was loved by men.[47]

The impassive, oracular tone, the balances and antitheses of the first three lines and the dying fall of the last, give an air of finality to the enigma posed by the poem. Is the poet talking about herself, perhaps? Or about a woman lost to men's love (cunningly linked with possession here) because of time or death? Or about both? It is not clear. For this is not only a valediction forbidding mourning, it is a valediction forbidding any simple, single definition of the person being mourned: everyone of us, after all, is 'possessed by time'. Elsewhere, Bogan uses other, similarly effective distancing techniques. In 'The Dream', for instance, the nightmare of a 'terrible horse' is used, in a way that is reminiscent of Edwin Muir, to dramatise and objectify the attraction, and the fear, of desire. In 'Stanzas', the dying away of desire itself is expressed in jewelled yet implicitly sensual imagery ('No longer burn the hands that seized / Small wreaths from branches scarcely green'): there is a personal inspiration here, certainly, but the hieratic treatment turns it into something separate from the poet, rounded and crystalline. In turn, 'Simple Autumnal' begins with an evocative portrait of Autumn ('The measured blood beats out the year's delay'), and then modulates into a subtle evocation of grief's longing, and failure, to find in the season a consoling mirror of its mood:

Because not last nor first, grief in its prime
Wakes in the day, and knows of life's intent.
Sorrow would break the seal stamped over time.
And set the baskets where the bough is bent.

Full season's come, yet filled trees keep the sky.
And never scent the ground where they must lie.[48]

Characteristically, Bogan makes 'grief in its prime' all the more moving by her rejection of the pathetic fallacy: because of the contrast she draws between 'sorrow' longing for fallen leaves to reflect its mood and the stubborn indifference of the 'filled trees' to such pressures.

The setting and theme that Bogan deals with so astutely in 'Simple Autumnal' are ones that Léonie Adams has made peculiarly her own. Adams's early poems are a little precious, perhaps, with their deliberate archaisms and invocations to 'Beauty'. Yet even here the preciousness is tempered and qualified by a harsh sense of what she calls 'the old cheating of the sun': the recognition that even the most beautiful of days must pass, even the most intense of experiences wither away. This harsher element grew as she and her poetry matured. Poems like 'Grapes Making' or 'Sundown' are exquisitely shaped, vividly sensuous portraits of rural America that, however, derive much of their colour and poignancy from the recollection that 'The careless autumn mornings come, / The grapes drop glimmering to the shears'. 'The faint leaf vanishes to light', Adams declares in 'Grapes Making': sunset, late summer, and early autumn are her favourite occasions, moments when everything in nature seems to be waiting, hushed with expectancy, for the ebb tide, the falling away of things. She is like Emily Dickinson and Robert Frost in this, her interest in what Dickinson called the 'spectral canticle' of late summer and Frost, 'that other fall we name the fall'. However, she is unlike them in that premonitions of mortality are rarely dwelt upon in her work, and the immediate, personal note struck even more rarely. 'Now straightening from the flowery hay', the final stanza of 'Country Summer' begins:

Down the still light the mowers look . . .

. . .

Yet thick the lazy dreams are born,
Another thought can come to mind,
But like the shivering of the wind
Morning and evening in the corn.[49]

This is the closest Adams comes in this poem to openly acknowledging what she elsewhere calls 'the immortal extinction, the priceless wound / Not to be staunched'. Transience, or rather awareness of it, is always there shaping her verbal landscapes, but it is all the more powerful for remaining in the background, an admonitory absent presence. Like Moore and the other formalists, Adams clearly believed that, as Moore herself put it, 'The deepest feeling always shows itself in silence; / not in silence, but restraint'.

Whitman and American experimentalism: cummings

'To be nobody-but-yourself in a world that is doing its best, night and day, to make you everybody else – means to fight the hardest battle which any human being can fight'. Marianne Moore would undoubtedly have approved of this remark of e.e. cummings's. Perhaps she knew of it, since the two were friends and not only liked but admired each other. Moore even wrote several warm reviews of cummings's work, one of which drew this delighted rejoinder:

Dear Miss Moore –
Thanks for your essay in the May
"Echo" . . .
. . .
You have (unlike many learned
"critics" of this obloquyflattery
unworld) a gift: appreciation.
You feel and you express your
feeling. That's miraculous[50]

Later, cummings was to tell Moore that not even a bouquet 'so big / that all Brooklyn might easily throb & / wander beneath its petals' would be large enough to express his admiration for her; and, after cummings died, Moore admitted that she approached writing about him with diffidence since he was 'too distinctive a person to be subjected to inapposite comment'. The reasons for this mutual warmth are not hard to seek: both Moore and cummings were poets individualistic to the point of eccentricity, in the great, idiosyncratic tradition of Whitman. This meant in turn, though, that, much as they admired each other, they were by definition very different from each other: each was unique, *sui generis*. Some of this difference came out in Moore's disapproval of the more erotic and scabrous sides of cummings's verse. The most she would concede on this score was that, as she put it, 'Mr. Cummings' obscenities are dear to him, somewhat as Esau's hairiness is associated with good hunting': the associations of poetry with obscenity and hunting with hairiness were erroneous, Moore thought, but if necessary in order to bring home the poem or the kill, then they could be accepted as useful fictions. Piquant though this area of difference is, however, it pales in comparison with something rather more fundamental. Moore's individualism led her, as we have seen, towards a firm (if idiosyncratic) belief in discipline, measure. cummings's individualism, on the other hand, led him towards a kind of imaginative anarchism. To be 'nobody-but-yourself', he felt, you had to achieve liberation from the 'unworld', the mind-forged manacles of society and culture. You would then become 'incorrigibly and actually alive', experiencing everything with a 'unique dimension of intensity'; and you could then begin to discover a world in which love transcends time, natural spontaneity prevails over the demands of habit and convention, and the dreams of each particular person are the supreme reality.

According to cummings, freedom was not easy: especially, freedom in poetry. 'As for expressing nobody-but-yourself in words', he declared, 'that means working just a little harder than anybody who isn't a poet can possibly imagine'. His aim was to create a unique, and where necessary eccentric, voice to express his unique, and sometimes eccentric, personality; and, in order to fulfil this aim he armed himself with a whole battery of technical effects – free verse or, on occasion, a highly original development of traditional verse forms, irregular typography, startling imagery, word coinages and syntactical or grammatical distortions. 'in Just – ' is a characteristic free verse poem, its opening lines suggesting what cummings meant when he said, 'I am abnormally fond of that precision which creates movement':

> in Just –
> spring when the world is mud –
> luscious the little
> lame balloonman
> whistles far and wee
>
> and eddieandbill come
> running from marbles and
> piracies and it's
> spring

The occasion for this poem is a personal memory: the poet's sister recalled that, for the Cummings children, 'the first and most exciting sign spring had really come was the balloon man. First you heard his whistle in the distance; then he would come walking down the street'. What cummings transforms this memory into, however, is a celebration of 'Just – / spring', the very moment when Spring arrives: the characteristically quirky hyphenating of the two words and capitalisation of 'just' emphasises the immediacy, the particularity of the moment – it is *just* this conjunctioning and no other. A world of Spring, this is also the world of the child, any child: seen through a child's eyes and expressed in a cunning imitation of a child's voice. There is childish wonder in that fifth line, for instance, where the spacing between the words helps capture the echoing, distant quality of the balloon man's whistle; and there is the breathless excitement of a child both in the running together of 'eddieandbill' and in the pun on 'wee', recreating exactly the kind of noise ('whee') children make as they run to express their exhilaration. Like Huckleberry Finn, the narrator of this poem does not want to be civilised because he inhabits a world of infinite possibility and hope, where the constraints of society hardly apply. And like Mark Twain, the creator of the poem does not want a civilised literature: the *appearance*, at least, of craft and cultivation. On the contrary, he uses his craft to create the effect of spontaneity, lively, unpremeditated speech – an innocent eye and an innocent voice. 'But our wiser years still run back to . . . childhood', Emerson declared, 'and always we are fishing up some wonderful article out of that pond'.[51] In his own idiosyncratic way, cummings fishes in that pond too: catching, so he hopes, something of that stage in life when all the necessities of life are answered, and the balloon man inevitably appears around the corner.

Whitman insisted, 'No shuttered room or school can commune with me / But roughs and little children better than they'. Like Whitman, cummings chooses 'roughs and little children' for his heroes: outsiders who, according to the Romantic and American notions of things, have achieved absolute selfhood. Among the roughs is Buffalo Bill, a typically Western hero associated with the careless energy of the frontier: 'he was a handsome man', cummings tells us, who used to 'break onetwothreefourfivepigeonsjustlikethat'. And among the other exceptional individuals and supreme individualists is cummings's own father, celebrated in one of his most famous poems, 'my father moved through dooms of love':

> my father moved through dooms of love
> through sames of am through haves of give
> singing each morning out of each night
> my father moved through depths of height[52]

The use of the lyric form is beautifully exact and traditional here. What renders the poem strange and individualistic is cummings's wily way with language: the grammatical functions of words are constantly being changed – an adjective ('same') or a verb ('am' / 'have' / 'give') being translated into a noun, perhaps – so as to produce quite magical, inimitable effects. The result is at once moving and witty, like some of the work of the Metaphysical poets. It is, in fact, this ability to give emotion a verbal edge that often saves cummings's poetry from sentimentality. He has written frequently about love: in part because, as he sees it, love offers access to that dimension of intensity needed to be 'incorrigibly and actually alive'. And his best love poems are precisely those that combine intense personal feeling with intelligence and verbal felicity. In 'since feeling is first', for instance, the poet wittily mocks the rules and regulations of language, the very disciplines he is using: 'who pays any attention / to the syntax of things', he insists, 'will never wholly kiss' the woman he is addressing. Similarly, in 'somewhere; have never travelled, gladly beyond', cummings alters the conventional word-order and employs a delicate mixture of adverbs, repetition, and nicely placed parentheses to create a gently ruminative tone. We are obliged to pause while we read this poem, and so experience that attitude of patient meditation which is, apparently, one of the special blessings of love:

> your slightest look easily will unclose me
> though i have closed myself as fingers,
> you open always petal by petal myself as Spring opens
> (touching skilfully, mysteriously) her first rose[53]

Closely related to cummings's poetry of love are his erotic poems, the ones that Marianne Moore found it so difficult to stomach. cummings's erotic verse is at its best when it is at its funniest, as in 'she being Brand / – new'. In fact, a lot of his poetry generally is at its best in this vein. He is probably the finest American comic poet of this century because his comedy issues from serious commitments: a dedication to Eros, the intensities of physical love, and a hatred of 'manunkind' – those people who reject such intensities in favour of stock reactions, the language and instincts of the crowd. Ogden Nash is probably as skilful as cummings when it comes to satirising particular social types or writing nonsense verse; Don Marquis is almost as adept in the use of verbal and typographical oddities to disturb and amuse the reader. Only cummings, however, can successfully fuse swingeing comic polemic and verbal jugglery, trenchant satire and typographical play. 'next to of course god america;', for instance, is a brilliant parody of patriotic cant that makes a powerful point about people who prefer to lose their identity in some anonymous nationalistic mass rather than discover an identity for themselves, and another, very brief poem presents us with a damning epitaph for 'manunkind':

IN)
    all those who got
    athlete's mouth jumping
    on&off bandwaggons
                    (MEMORIAM

The people memorialised here, who have worn their voices out ('got / athlete's mouth') expressing received opinions are so non-existent as individuals that they can be dismissed within the space of one parenthetical mark and the next. They do not deserve mention for themselves at all: but only for the fact that they are dead, either literally or (more probably) in the spiritual sense.

At its most extreme, cummings's interest in typographical play can lead to difficulties of interpretation. One highly idiosyncratic piece, for instance, begins in this way:

a –
float on some
?
i call twilight

Its subject is the moon, which is transformed as it is described into a symbol of the dream world of the liberated individual; and an appropriate quality of enigma is given to this symbol by the poet's radical innovations of technique. Here, for instance, he replaces the second syllable of 'something' with a question mark, the implication being that 'thing' is too solid and mundane a word to use in describing the shifting, delicate presence of the twilight. And, elsewhere, he uses a punctuation mark, the second half of a parenthesis, for its visual effect: because it traces the gentle curve of the moon. cummings sometimes referred to his work as 'poempictures', which perhaps alerts us to its visual quality: the impact of the typography on the blank, white page can be a primary part of its meaning. At its best, though, cummings's writing blends the visual dimension with the aural: as in this passage, which concludes a poem about death written towards the end of the poet's life:

O, come, terrible anonymity, enfold
phantom me with the murdering minus of cold
                    . . .
gently
            (very whiteness: absolute peace
never imaginable mystery)
                        descend[54]

Beautifully cadenced, these lines dramatise the gradual relaxation of consciousness, the slipping away of life. Left syntactically and grammatically unfinished, they also imply that the descent into death is rich in possibilities. Characteristically, cummings responded to death, with fear certainly, but also with wonder: to be enfolded in 'terrible anonymity', he felt, was a unique experience that nevertheless deserved comparison with other, unique moments of intensity in life.

Whitman and American mysticism: Rukeyser, Riding, Crane

It would be stretching things to say that, in his later poems, cummings was edging towards mysticism, but he was clearly picking up something else from Whitman here: that is, the idea of death as an adventure, a possible entry into new forms of experience – and the related notion that one could, as Whitman put it, 'troop forth' from death, 'replenish'd with supreme power, one of an average unending possession'. 'I launch all men and women forward with me into the Unknown', Whitman declared, and then added elsewhere, 'I am the poet of the Body and I am the poet of the Soul'. This is another, crucial and fruitful paradox in Whitman's work. He was a populist, 'no stander above men and women or apart from them'; he was a practical man, dedicated to solid pleasures – 'Turbulent, fleshy, sensual', as he put it, 'eating, drinking, and breeding'. But he was also a mystic, a visionary, whose faith was 'the greatest of faiths and the least of faiths / Enclosing worship ancient and modern and all between ancient and modern'. 'I am an acme of things accomplish'd', he insisted:

> and I am an encloser of things to be.
> My feet strike the apices of the stairs,
> On every step bunches of ages . . .
> . . .
> My rendezvous is appointed, it is certain,
> The Lord will be there and wait till I come
> on perfect terms,
> The great Camerado, the lover true for whom I
> pine will be there.[55]

And it is this intense, visionary quality that other American poets of this century have found most seductive, together with Whitman's clear belief that poetry itself is vision, an access to truth.

Among the writers who have been drawn by this visionary impulse are Muriel Rukeyser and Laura Riding (Jackson). Much of Rukeyser's early work is determinedly modernist, using a radically free verse line, allusive imagery, disruptive syntax and grammar, and an associative structure to capture something of the rapid, disjunctive movements of modern life. Even here, however, the concerns that were to dominate her poetry are quite clear: power and its betrayal, the immense possibilities latent in the human being, his 'dynamics of desire', and their denial by a society that 'makes thin the imagination and the bone'. The title poem from her first volume, for instance, 'Theory of Flight' contrasts Whitman's dreams of rapid movement through space now translated into a reality (Rukeyser was a student pilot at the time) with the world left on the ground: where 'our superiors, the voting men' sit 'around the committee-table', voting to disavow 'the eyes, and sex, and brain', the powers of perception, reproduction, and knowledge – and voting death, too, to all those who would liberate such powers, including poets and visionaries like Blake and Whitman. 'Now, in our time', wrote Rukeyser in the introduction to one of her volumes, 'many of the sources of power are obscured . . . or vulgarised . . . I have hoped to indicate some of the valid sources of power'. The piece with which she chose to begin her *Selected Poems* makes the point in another way. 'I set out once again', she says, 'From where I began: / Belief in the love of the world,/ Woman, spirit, and man'. 'I find love and rage', she adds:

Rage for the world as it is
But for what it may be
More love now than last year.
And always less self-pity
Since I know in a clearer light
The strength of the mystery.[56]

As these lines indicate, Rukeyser moved towards a greater clarity of diction, a more openly affirmative stance and an incantatory (and, on occasion, even declamatory) tone in order to unravel 'The strength of the mystery'. A poem like 'Boy with His Hair Cut Short' reveals her rage. The subject is simple enough: set in Chicago during the Thirties, it describes a boy having his hair cut by his sister in the hope that this might help him find a job. However, Rukeyser's elliptical style here, harsh diction, and suggestive imagery turn this into a vision of a shadow world where the machine rules ('The arrow's electric red always reaches its mark / successful neon!') and the human spirit is cowed. Brutally contemporary though the scene is ('Sunday shuts down on a twentieth-century evening. / The El passes. Twilight and bulb define / the brown room'), the ritual of hair-cutting cannot but recall the Biblical tale of Samson losing his strength with his hair: this is a society, evidently, that requires impotence as a sign of obedience. And, elsewhere, Rukeyser uses symbolic and mythic reference more openly on the grounds that, as she put it, 'The fear of symbol is linked with the fear of poetry in our culture. It is poetry's enemy, part of a great emotional wound'. This is particularly true of those poems more immediately concerned with 'love of the world' and the search for 'valid sources of power'. In her long poem, *Orpheus*, for instance, she uses the ancient Greek story of the death and resurrection of the poet-hero ('he has died the birth of the God') to celebrate the cycle of life and the creative spirit: 'There is only life', the poem tells us, and 'To live is to create'. In the poem-sequence, 'Ajanta', on the other hand, she uses another, Eastern tradition. The frescoes painted on the walls of the Ajanta caves in India become the occasion for celebrating 'The real world where everything is complete', where 'There are no shadows . . . / . . . no source of distortion' – and for lamenting this unreal world we now inhabit, 'World, not yet one . . ./ . . ./ A world of the shadow and alone'. Her approach to mythology is eclectic because, like Whitman, she encloses faiths ancient and modern in her search for truth. A poem like 'Mortal Girl', for example, uses three quite separate legends of the love of Zeus for mortal women to dramatise the idea of eternity intersecting with time. After the visitation of the god, the poem tells us, the girl 'stood in her naked room / Singing'. 'Make me more human', she sang:

> Give me the consciousness
> Of every natural shape, to lie here ready
> For love as every power
>
> . . .
>
> . . . make me mad
> With song and pain and waiting, leave me free
> In all my own shapes, deep in the spirit's cave
> To sing again the entrance of the god.[57]

Weaving together imagery of fire, sun, and light, Rukeyser suggests that what the girl's experience of divinity has given her, above all, is vision and expression, the power to see and the power to sing. It takes very little stretch of the imagination to realise that the 'mortal girl' is, among other people, Rukeyser herself, the poet as visionary singer, and that the songs she gives voice to include this one.

Laura (Riding) Jackson began from a very different base to Rukeyser and moved, eventually, in a very different direction, even though she too was guided by the visionary impulse. She was an honorary member of the Fugitive group for a while, sharing with them a strong commitment to poetic discipline and, with Tate in particular, a certain chilly intensity. However, she was hardly interested in their verbal variety and dexterity, and the very special character of her poetic aims is perhaps suggested by 'Incarnations':

> Do not deny
> Do not deny, thing out of thing.
> Do not deny in the new vanity
> The old, original dust.
>
> From what grave, what past of flesh and bone
> Dreaming, dreaming I lie
> Under the fortunate curse,
> Bewitched, alive, forgetting the first stuff . . .
> Death does not give a moment to remember in
>
> Lest, like a statue's too transmuted stone,
> I grain by grain recall the original dust
> And, looking down a stair of memory, keep saying:
> This was never I.

'A poem', Laura (Riding) Jackson wrote in the preface to her 1938 *Collected Poems*, 'is an uncovering of truth of so fundamental and general a kind that no other name besides poetry is adequate except truth'. Inspired by a passionate search for what she called 'an ultimate of perfect truth', she rejected metaphorical language, verbal ambiguity, or anything that as she saw it failed to illuminate the object or idea. Here, in these lines, the truth the poet is attempting to uncover concerns what she elsewhere termed 'the manifold totality' of things: in our life, the perception is, we are part of many lives, past, present, and future – in our many, different 'incarnations' we are all part of 'the first stuff', reality in its entirety. To uncover this truth, she adopts a characteristically stern, intense, approach. The language strives for absolute precision: in an almost compulsive way, the poet returns again and again to the same words so as to squeeze the last drop of exact meaning out of them. The verse is free and yet it has a formal, disciplined quality about it: she seems to be measuring everything she says, moving forward hesitantly, cautiously, as if uncovering the truth were like stalking a wild animal. The general feeling or tone issuing from all this is a mixture of the tightly buttoned-down and the incantatory, the cool and the hypnotic: (Riding) Jackson is trying to chart out spiritual geography and yet she is aware, as she does it, how slippery her tools are and just how difficult it is to draw a map. Here, the sense of difficulty is a matter of tone, but in other pieces it is made explicit: 'This is not exactly what I mean', she cries out anxiously at the beginning of one poem, 'What a world of awkwardness! / What hostile implements of sense!'[58]

'A most improbable one it takes / To tell what is so': this idea of the difficulty, perhaps the impossibility, of telling 'what is so' recurs throughout her poetry, even while she is attempting to tell it. Sometimes, it results in a desperate resort to paradox ('One self, one manyness'), oxymoron or simple self-contradiction ('The strangeness is not strange') as if the poet were trying to cancel definitions out as she uses them. Sometimes, and not unrelated to this, she narrows her focus down to one, very specific example of the difficulties of telling, as in 'Beyond':

> Pain is impossible to describe
> Pain is the impossibility of describing
> Describing what is impossible to describe
> Which must be a thing beyond description
> Beyond description not to be known
> Beyond knowing but not mystery
> Not mystery but pain not plain but pain
> But pain beyond but here beyond[59]

(Riding) Jackson wanted to 'describe' a reality that is as immediate and yet intangible, as searingly present but incommunicable as, from the experience of all of us, we know pain to be. In the end, she felt that poetry could not help, because, as she put it, 'truth begins where poetry ends'. 'My kind of seriousness', she said, 'in my looking to poetry for the rescue of human life from the indignities it was capable of visiting upon itself, led me to an eventual turning away from it as failing my kind of seriousness'. Her desire that poetry should tell the truth about 'the human reality . . . the reality of All, of which we are exponents': this, she believed, had been frustrated. The reason was simple: the currency in which poetry dealt was counterfeit. Far from providing 'for practical attainment of that rightness of word that *is* truth', it led only to 'a temporising less-than-truth (. . . eked out with illusions of truth produced by physical word-effects)'. So she turned her attention to a work of linguistics which would, she hoped, provide 'a single terminology of truth'. It was to be 'a work that would help dissipate the confusion existing in the knowledge of word-meanings': something in which, she insisted, 'all probity of word must start'. 'I was religious in my devotion to poetry', she said. 'But in saying this', she added, 'I am thinking of religion as it is . . . a will to know and to make known, the ultimate knowledge'; and that – or, rather, the equivalent of that – poetry had singularly failed to be.

Unlike (Riding) Jackson, Hart Crane never lost his belief in the religious possibilities of poetry. It became, and remained for him until his death, a means of absolute vision: 'the articulation', as he put it, 'of contemporary human consciousness *sub specie aeternitatis*'. Poems could and should, he felt, carry their author and readers alike 'toward a state of consciousness, an 'innocence' or 'absolute beauty': a condition in which 'there may be discoverable new forms, certain spiritual illuminations'. In this pursuit of what he termed 'a more ecstatic goal', Crane had little doubt about who his principal guide and mentor was. Walt Whitman, he insisted, 'better than any other, was able to coordinate those forces in America which seem most intractable, fusing them into a universal vision which takes on additional significance as time goes on'. In his letters, he admitted that he felt 'directly connected' to the Good Gray Poet; and he seems to have half-believed that, as one critic has put it, 'he was the "divine literatus" to whom in *Democratic Vistas* Whitman had played John the Baptist'. Much of his poetry is soaked in the imagery and symbolic devices of *Leaves of Grass*. Not only that, it alludes to Whitman with an almost obsessive frequency. 'Walt, tell me Walt Whitman', he implores in one poem, 'if infinity / Be still the same as when you walked the beach /Near Paumanok'. 'O Walt!' he cries out later, 'Ascensions of thee hover in me now / . . . / . . . O, upward from the dead / Thou bringest tally, and a pact, new bound / Of living brotherhood!' For Crane, in fact, Whitman was a still tangible presence, offering new possibilities of song, new openings beyond the commonplace, to him and to other visionaries:

> Thou, there beyond –
> Glacial sierras and the flight of ravens,
>
> .
>
> . . . thy wand
> Has beat a song, O Walt, – there and beyond![60]

Crane did not begin with this visionary impulse. His earlier work tends towards scepticism, detached wit and self-protective wryness. In 'Chaplinesque', for instance, the situation of the writer in modern times is sardonically compared to that of the little tramp, the disregarded fool, whom Charles Chaplin made famous in his films; while in 'Black Tambourine' what Crane called 'a description and bundle of insinuations bearing on the Negro's place somewhere between man and beast' turns into a serio-comic account of the poet, who tries to make something out of a radically delimited reality. Even here, however, some of the characteristics that were to mark his later verse are evident. 'Black Tambourine', for example, ends with these lines:

The black man, forlorn in the cellar,
Wanders in some mid-kingdom, dark, that lies
Between his tambourine, stuck on the wall
And, in Africa, a carcass quick with flies.[61]

This is not so much an argument, a paraphraseable conclusion, as a verbal collage; or, as Crane would have it, a complex of 'inter-relationships . . . raised on the organic principle of a "logic of metaphor" which antedates our so-called pure logic'. So the 'mid-kingdom, dark' does not define a specific area so much as take up meanings suggested and expectations aroused in previous lines: the cellar (and, by process of association, cell) of the black man is implied, the kingdom in exile of the black poet Aesop (mentioned at the beginning of the second stanza), and perhaps the world between heaven and hell generally. Similarly, 'tambourine' reminds us both of a degrading alternative (the minstrel stereotype imposed on the Negro, the poet as allowed fool), and a redemptive possibility (music, and all it signifies, as a means of escape from the 'cellar'); and 'Africa' describes a place that is at once literal (the home of the black man), imaginative (the Great Good Place of the poet) and, quite possibly, spiritual (heaven, the Absolute). The subtle play of allusion is sustained in the last four words. A 'carcass' (suggesting another alternative available to the black man) is a term normally used to describe the body of a dead animal: but here the very flies which are usually symptoms of death appear to be agents of life as well, since 'quick' means alive and vigorous. There is death-in-life here, we must infer, but there is the possibility of life-in-death too: suggestions of decay and recovery neatly balance one another. Further than this we cannot go when we try to paraphrase: because what the poem has done, Crane hopes, is supply us with 'a single new *word*, never before spoken, and impossible to enunciate but self-evident in the . . . consciousness henceforward'. It has, in effect, created a language rather than used one.

'As a poet', Crane declared, 'I may very probably be more interested in the so-called illogical impingements of the connotations of words on the consciousness (and their combinations and interplay in metaphor on this basis) than I am interested in the preservation of their logically rigid signification'. He saw each word, almost, as a cumulus of possibilities and latent associations many, but not all, of which could be fired into life by their verbal surrounds – by the words, and combinations of words, with which they were juxtaposed. The overtones of his language, consequently, tend to matter more than its strictly denotative meaning: what echoes in our minds forms an important part of what is being said. This is as true of the earlier poetry as it is of the later. But in the earlier, as those lines from 'Black Tambourine' illustrate, the positive overtones – the feelings of redemptive possibility generated by the words – tend to be tentative and partial. The ending of 'Chaplinesque' is slightly more affirmative, perhaps, but even here the affirmation is hedged about with numerous qualifications and ironies:

> The game enforces smirks: but we have seen
> The moon in lonely alleys make
> A grail of laughter of an empty ash can,
> And through all sound of gaiety and quest
> Have heard a kitten in the wilderness.[62]

The vision of the moon transforming an ash-can into a grail, and the enforced 'smirk' of daytime experience into a kind of holy laughter: this is certainly positive, suggesting as it does the imagination discovering in the desert of the actual a vessel of supernal beauty. But the vision is introduced suddenly, it is momentary; and, Crane implies, as a source of hope and help it is about as powerful as a kitten crying in the wilderness.

The reservations and irony that marked 'Chaplinesque' and 'Black Tambourine' gradually disappeared, as Crane went in search of what he called 'the metaphysics of absolute knowledge'. The immediate cause of this alteration was a personal experience. Like Whitman, Crane apparently enjoyed a moment of vision, or mystical seizure, which opened fresh possibilities in himself, and convinced him that 'we must somehow touch the clearest veins of eternity flowing through the crowds around us'. 'Did I tell you of that thrilling experience this last winter in the dentist's chair', Crane asked a friend:

> when under the influence of aether . . . my mind spiralled to a kind of seventh heaven and egoistic dance among the seven spheres – and something kept saying to me – "You have the higher consciousness"? . . . I felt the two worlds . . . Today I have made a good start on . ... 'Faustus and Helen'.[63]

As Crane indicates here, his long poem 'For the Marriage of Faustus and Helen' grew directly out of his mystical experience and, in a sense, tried to recover it, to make it and the knowledge it supplied available to every one of his readers. Faustus, Crane explained, is 'the symbol of . . . the poetic and imaginative man of all times', Helen the symbol of an 'abstract "sense of beauty"'; and the marriage between them is seen, not as an event really, but as a continuing possibility – the moment of communion between the soul and the spirit of essential

Beauty which illuminates all existence ever afterwards. 'Distinctly praise the years', Crane concludes the poem:

> whose volatile
> Blamed bleeding hands extend and thresh the height
> The imagination spans beyond despair
> Outpacing bargain, vocable, and prayer.[64]

The arc traced by the imagination, the poet affirms, reaches beyond the world of getting and spending, the world of ordinary language, and even the world conceived of in prayers; yet it irradiates those worlds, and our lives and 'years' beneath it, making everything that exists worthy of thanks and praise. By comparison with this, the affirmative note that sounds in the earlier poetry seems muted almost to the point of silence.

The poetry that followed 'Faustus and Helen' includes 'At Melville's Tomb', a hymn of praise to the prophetic author of *Moby Dick*, and 'Royal Palm', an evocative description of the 'green rustlings' of a palm tree that is also a symbolic account of the imagination climbing to discovery of the absolute, 'launched above / Mortality – ascending emerald-bright'. But perhaps the most powerful and moving expression of Crane's visionary impulse in his lyric poetry is to be found in 'Voyages'. A series of six poems written over three years, these are, as Crane explained at the time he was writing them, 'love poems' and 'sea poems' too: the sea appears in them as a threat to the poet-lover and as a rival, as a partner, an enemy, and eventually as a source of comfort and vision. One reason for the constant presence of the sea in the sequence is that the person to whom they were addressed was a sailor living temporarily in New York; another, that the poet and his lover stayed together in an apartment overlooking the harbour; and still another, that the sea was always a suggestive image for Crane. Like Whitman and Melville, he used the sea to describe both the cruelty of this 'broken' world and the mysterious 'answers' that ultimately might make the world whole again. Although the six poems can be read separately, they do have a – profoundly traditional – connecting argument. The poet begins with an earthly affection and experiences ecstasy: as the second poem indicates, Crane can be a memorably erotic poet ('Star kissing star through wave on wave unto / Your body rocking!'). Then, however, the poet loses his beloved, but discovers consolation for his loss in the love of heaven. The beauty of the passing world has been enjoyed for a time and then superseded by a vision of transcendent Beauty. And that vision offers the 'Word' that will give meaning to the poet's 'words':

The imaged Word, it is, that holds
Hushed willows anchored in its glow.
It is the unbetrayable reply
Whose accent no farewell can know.[65]

The 'Word', the poem tells us, perceived in vision and expressed in verse, transforms our given world; within its 'glow' the 'willows', emblems of change and death, are stilled. It also perfects the loves of this world: by giving them a permanent, 'unbetrayable' form, and by affording them a proper completion in love of the absolute – a condition, and affection, from which there is no 'farewell'.

Apart from 'Voyages', Crane's greatest achievement of his visionary years was his attempt at what he termed a 'Myth of America', *The Bridge*. 'I am concerned with the future of America', Crane wrote, 'not because I think America has any so-called par value as a state . . . It is only because I feel persuaded that there are destined to be discovered certain as yet undefined spiritual qualities . . . not to be developed so completely elsewhere'. It is the old problem of the American Dream the poet poses, in a series of eight poems that follow the westward thrust of the bridge into the body of the continent. The movement is one in time as well as space; and as Crane moves across the continent he continually presents the reader with the same question. How, he asks, can the ideal possibilities of people be liberated so as to recover the kingdom of heaven on earth? How can an arc or bridge be constructed between the world in which we live and the world of the imagination, so that the life of the individual may assume a fresh nobility and the forms of the community approximate to the divine? Having asked the question, he also tries to answer it. For Crane is no less like Whitman – that first great visionary in American poetry – in, that he sees himself as an agent of liberation, formulating in his work the new relation between consciousness and reality which will make the changes he requires possible. *The Bridge*, like so much of Crane's verse, offers us a series of visionary acts intended to alter our minds – to propose to us what Crane called 'a new hierarchy of faith' – as a preliminary to altering our surroundings. In the magnificent, 'Proem: To Brooklyn Bridge', for example, the opening poem in the sequence, the poet beseeches Brooklyn Bridge to act as a mediator between the actual and the ideal:

O Sleepless as the river under thee
Vaulting the sea, the prairies' dreaming sod,
Unto us lowliest sometimes sweep, descend
And of the curveship lend a myth to God.[66]

The poet is appealing to the bridge as a figure, of course, rather than a given object. He has transformed the *actual* bridge into an *ideal*, liberating symbol: uniting river and sea, land and sky in one revelatory 'myth', a single inviolate curve that leaps upward towards the absolute. In doing so, he has offered one small illustration of how the two dimensions, the mundane and visionary, can be related – and how, consequently, his prayers can be answered.

'Unless poetry can absorb the machine', Crane said, '. . . then poetry has failed of its full contemporary function'. In choosing Brooklyn Bridge for his 'myth', Crane was making a deliberate attempt to 'absorb the machine': to find a source of creativity in the industrial age. Traversing the same stretch of river, Whitman had used Brooklyn Ferry, with its perpetual ebb and flow of passengers, to symbolise what he called the 'eternal float of solution', the 'simple, compact, well-join'd scheme' to which all passing things belong. Crane had at his disposal a comparable, and yet significantly more contemporary, image: the bridge, that is a part of the technological age and yet somehow seems to 'condense eternity'. 'Thy cables breathe the North Atlantic still', exclaims the poet, 'And we have seen night lifted in thine arms'. Elliptical and allusive in texture, associative and even disjunctive in structure, *The Bridge* is clearly much more of a *modern* epic than 'Song of Myself'. Yet it is, finally, in that great tradition initiated by Whitman: in that it is, above all, an *American* epic, concerned with spiritual possibility rather than historical achievement, creating a hero or heroic consciousness instead of simply celebrating one. Like 'Song of Myself', and like all the other major attempts at American epic, *The Bridge* remains open, requiring the reader to complete it – by continuing the spiritual journey begun by the poet. The company and counsel Whitman had given him, Crane felt, he could now offer in turn to his successors. Together, he and the Good Gray Poet could walk along the road of spiritual discovery, in the hope that, one day, other visionaries and other Americans would follow:

Yes, Walt,
Afoot again, and onward without halt, –
Not soon, nor suddenly, – No, never to let go
My hand
in yours,
Walt Whitman –
so –[67]

Notes

1. See John Baxter, *Hollywood in the Thirties* (London, 1968); Richard H. Pells, *Radical Visions and American Dreams* (New York, 1973); Ralph Willett and

John White, 'The Thirties', in *Introduction to American Studies* edited by Bradbury and Temperley.

2. See Klaus Mann, 'Introduction' to Franz Kafka, *America* (New York, 1962), p. xii.
3. See Daniel Aaron, *Writers on the Left* (New York, 1965); Alfred Kazin, *On Native Grounds* (Garden City, N.Y., 1956); William Stott, *Documentary Expression and Thirties America* (New York, 1973).
4. Whitman, 'Song of Myself', section 51. See also, Ezra Pound, 'What I Feel about Walt Whitman', in *Walt Whitman: A Critical Anthology* edited by Francis Murphy (Harmondsworth, Middx., 1969), p. 184.
5. Carl Sandburg, 'Chicago', lines 1–5, 9–10, 22.
6. Carl Sandburg, 'Gone', line 16–17. See also, 'A Fence', lines 1, 4.
7. Robert Henri, *The Art Spirit* compiled by Margery A. Ryson (Philadelphia, 1923), p. 16. See also, Rose Henderson, 'Robert Henri', *The American Magazine of Art*, XXI (Jan. 1930), 10.
8. Carl Sandburg, 'More Country People', line 10. See also, 'Sunset from Omaha Hotel Window', lines 1, 3; 'Still Life', lines 3, 4.
9. Carl Sandburg, *The People, Yes* (New York, 1936), pp. 284, 286.
10. Vachel Lindsay, 'Bryan, Bryan, Bryan, Bryan', lines 3–9. See also, 'Abraham Lincoln Walks at Midnight', line 12; 'In Praise of Johnny Appleseed', section III, line 39; *Letters of Nicholas Vachel Lindsay* edited by A. Joseph Armstrong (Waco, Illinois, 1940), p. 93; Mark Harris, 'Introduction', to *Selected Poems of Vachel Lindsay* edited by Mark Harris (New York, 1963), pp. xiv, xix.
11. Edgar Lee Masters, 'Sersmith the Dentist', lines 24–5.
12. Kenneth Rexroth, 'New Objectives, New Cadres', lines 49–53, 58–61. See also, 'August 22, 1939', line 29; 'Unacknowledged Legislators and "Art Poor Art"' in *Bird in the Bush: Obvious Essays* (New York, 1959), p. 16; 'Introduction' to D. H. Lawrence, *Selected Poems* (New York, 1959); Whitman, 'An American Primer'; Tom Clark, review of *The Selected Poems of Kenneth Rexroth*, in *Rolling Stock* 9 (1985), 22.
13. Kenneth Rexroth, 'The Wheel Revolves', lines 47–49. See also, *An Autobiographical Novel* (New York, 1966), p. x; *Assays* (Norfolk, Conn., 1961), p. 57.
14. Kenneth Rexroth, 'Requiem for the Spanish Dead', lines 25–7. See also, lines 13, 14–15, 18–19, 20–22.
15. Ibid., lines 23–26. See also, *An Autobiographical Novel*, p. 14.
16. Rexroth, 'Requiem for the Spanish Dead', lines 28–31. See also, 'Introduction' to *The Phoenix and the Turtle* (New York, 1944), p. 9.
17. Kenneth Rexroth, 'August 22, 1939', lines 41–46. See also, 'Alienation', *Arts in Society*, VI (Spring–Summer, 1969), 59; 'The Signature of All Things', lines 14–15; Whitman 'Song of Myself', section 5.
18. Archibald MacLeish, 'American Letter', lines 36–39, 40. See also, lines 13, 26: *The Literary Fallacy* (New York, 1944), p. 47.

19. Archibald MacLeish, 'You, Andrew Marvell', lines 9–14. See also, lines 5–6; 'Ars Poetica', lines 23–24: Andrew Marvell, 'To His Coy Mistress', lines 21–22.

20. MacLeish, 'You, Andrew Marvell', lines 34–36.

21. Kenneth Fearing, 'Reception Good', lines 4–5.

22. Kenneth Patchen, 'The Fox', lines 10–12. See also, line 2; 'The Eve of St. Agony', line 36; 'Street Corner College', lines 3–4, 14.

23. W. E. B. Du Bois, *The Souls of Black Folk* (1903; New York, 1969 edition), p. 45. See also, James Baldwin, *Notes of a Native Son* (New York, 1955); Imamu Amiri Baraka (Leroi Jones), 'The Insidious Dr. Fu Man Chu'.

24. Langston Hughes, 'The Negro Artist and the Racial Mountain', *The Nation,* June 23, 1926, pp. 692–93. See also, p. 694.

25. Langston Hughes, 'Some Practical Observations: A Colloquy', *Phylon,* II (Winter 1950), 307. See also, 'The South', lines 1–2; 'Still Here', lines 1, 7–8.

26. Langston Hughes, 'The Weary Blues', lines 1–3, 18–22. See also, 'Jazz as Communication', in *The Langston Hughes Reader* (New York, 1958). pp. 492–94; Prefatory Note, *Montage of a Dream Deferred* (New York, 1950).

27. Langston Hughes, 'The Cat and the Saxophone', lines 1–13. See also, 'Children's Rhymes', lines 25–27.

28. Langston Hughes, 'Fire', lines 1–6. See also, 'Lenox Avenue: Midnight', lines 10–11.

29. Claude McKay, *A Long Way from Home* (1937: New York, 1970 edition), p. 28.

30. Langston Hughes, 'I, Too', lines 1–3, 8–10, 16–18.

31. Langston Hughes, 'The Negro Speaks of Rivers', lines 1–3. See also, 'Consider Me', lines 49–52.

32. James Weldon Johnson, 'The Creation', lines 84–91.

33. Countee Cullen, 'Heritage', lines 1, 7–10. See also, 'Yet Do I Marvel', lines 13–14; 'To Certain Critics', lines 6–8; George Schuyler, 'The Negro-Art Hokum', *The Nation,* June 16, 1926, pp. 662–63.

34. Robert Hayden, 'From the Corpse Woodpiles, From the Ashes', lines 1–3, 7–9. See also, 'Frederick Douglass', line 14; 'Monet's "Waterlilies"', line 1; *Kaleidoscope: Poems by American Negro Poets* edited by Robert Hayden (New York, 1967), p. 108.

35. Gwendolyn Brooks, 'Life for My Children Is Simple, and Is Good', lines 73–78.

36. See, '*The Art of Poetry*, An Interview with Donald Hall', in *Marianne Moore: A Collection of Critical Essays* edited by Charles Tomlinson (Englewood Cliffs, N.J., 1969), pp. 20–45.

37. Ibid.

38. Marianne Moore, 'The Steeple-Jack', lines 53–60. See also, Charles

Tomlinson, 'Introduction: Marianne Moore, Her Poetry and Her Critics' in *Moore: A Collection of Critical Essays*, p. 7.

39. Marianne Moore, 'Poetry', lines 1–3. See also, lines 17–18, 19.

40. Ibid., lines 20–25. See also, 'When I Buy Pictures', line 17.

41. Marianne Moore, 'The Frigate Pelican', lines 30–32. See also, lines 5, 10, 21–22. See also, William Carlos Williams, 'Marianne Moore', and John Crowe Ransom, 'On Being Modern With Distinction', in *Moore: A Collection of Critical Essays*.

42. Elinor Wylie, 'Velvet Shoes', lines 16–20. See also, 'The Eagle and the Mole', line 1; 'The Church-Bell', lines 21–2; 'Jewelled Binding', in *Collected Prose* (New York, 1946); 'Chimaera Sleeping', lines 9–10; 'Sunset on the Spire', lines 21–24; Marianne Moore, 'The Past Is the Present', lines 8–9.

43. Edna St. Vincent Millay, 'First Fig'. See also, 'Passer Mortuus Est', lines 5–6; 'What My Lips Have Kissed', lines 1–2; Elinor Wylie, 'Love Song', line 15.

44. Edna St. Vincent Millay, 'Thursday', lines 1–4.

45. Edna St. Vincent Millay, 'Second Fig'.

46. Josephine Miles, 'Grandfather', lines 9–12.

47. Louise Bogan, 'Portrait', lines 9–12.

48. Louise Bogan, 'Simple Autumnal', lines 9–14. See also, line 1; 'The Dream', line 1; 'Stanzas', lines 1–2.

49. Léonie Adams, 'Country Summer', lines 37–40. See also, 'April Mortality', line 15; 'Grapes Making', lines 23–24; 'Sundown', lines 14–15; Marianne Moore, 'Silence', lines 11–12; Emily Dickinson, 'Further in Summer than the Birds', line 11; Robert Frost, 'The Oven Bird', line 9.

50. e.e. cummings, *Selected Letters* edited by F. W. Dupee and George Stade (London 1972) p. 162. See also, p. 210; Norman Friedman, *e.e. cummings: The Art of His Poetry* (Baltimore, Md., 1960), ch. 1; Marianne Moore, 'A Penguin in Moscow' and 'e.e. Cummings, 1894–1962', in *The Complete Prose of Marianne Moore* edited by Patricia C. Willis (London, 1987), pp. 304, 562.

51. Ralph Waldo Emerson, 'Intellect'. See also, Marianne Moore, 'One Times One', in *Complete Prose*, p. 394.

52. e.e. cummings, 'my father moved through dooms of love', lines 1–4. See also, 'Buffalo Bill's defunct', lines 3, 4; Whitman, 'Song of Myself', section 2.

53. e.e. cummings, 'somewhere i have never travelled, gladly beyond', lines 5–8. See also, 'since feeling is first', lines 2–3.

54. e.e. cummings, 'enter no (silence is the blood whose flesh', lines 9–10, 13–16.

55. Whitman, 'Song of Myself', section 44. See also, sections 24, 43.

56. Muriel Rukeyser, 'This Place in the Ways', lines 13–18. See also, 'Theory of Flight'; preface to *Orpheus* (New York, 1949).

57. Muriel Rukeyser, 'Mortal Girl', lines 13–16, 24–27. See also, 'Boy with His Hair Cut Short', lines 1–3, 11–12; preface to *Orpheus; Orpheus*, sections 2, 3; 'The Broken World'; 'Ajanta', section 5.

58. Laura (Riding) Jackson, 'The World and I', lines 1, 5–6. See also, 'Original 1938 Preface: To the Reader', in *The Poems of Laura Riding* (Manchester, 1980), p. 407; *The Telling* (London, 1972), p. 23.

59. Laura (Riding) Jackson, 'Beyond'. See also, 'The Way It Is', lines 12–13; 'One Self', line 4; 'With The Face', line 4; 'Excerpts from the Preface to *Selected Poems* (1970)', in *Poems*, p. 416; 'Introduction' to *Poems*, pp. 2, 9; *The Telling*, p. 49.

60. Hart Crane, 'Cape Hatteras', section 4 of *The Bridge* (New York, 1930). See also, 'Modern Poetry' in *The Complete Poems and Selected Letters and Prose of Hart Crane* edited by Brom Weber (New York, 1966), pp. 260, 263; 'General Aims and Theories', ibid., p. 219; *The Letters of Hart Crane 1916–1932* edited by Brom Weber (Berkeley, Calif., 1965), p. 115; R. W. Butterfield, *The Broken Arc: A Study of Hart Crane* (Edinburgh, 1969), p. 129.

61. Hart Crane, 'Black Tambourine', lines 9–12. See also, *Letters*, p. 58: 'General Aims and Theories', p. 221.

62. Hart Crane, 'Chaplinesque', lines 19–23. See also, 'A Letter to Harriet Monroe', in *Complete Poems and Selected Letters and Prose*, p. 234.

63. Hart Crane, *Letters*, pp. 91–92. See also, p. 145.

64. Hart Crane, 'For the Marriage of Faustus and Helen', Section 3, lines 44–47. See also, *Letters*, p. 120.

65. Hart Crane, 'Voyages', poem 6, lines 39–42. See also, 'Royal Palm', lines 1, 12–13; 'The Broken Tower', line 17, 'Voyages', poem 3, lines 13–14; *Letters*, p. 192.

66. Hart Crane, 'Proem: To Brooklyn Bridge', lines 41–4. See also, 'General Aims and Theories', p. 219.

67. Crane, 'Cape Hatteras'. See also, 'Proem: To Brooklyn Bridge', lines 24, 35, 36; 'Modern Poetry', pp. 261–2; Whitman, 'Crossing Brooklyn Ferry', sections 2, 9.

Chapter 5

Formalists and Confessionals: American Poetry since the Second World War

From abundance to anger: the social and cultural tendencies of the first two decades after the War

Americans concluded the decade of the Thirties in an inward-looking mood, concerned with economic issues, unemployment, and the need to heal internal ideological divisions. By the close of the Second World War, however, that mood had changed: the United States had become a global superpower, committed to the international arena. In the new era of post-war, post-colonial politics, with its altered political and military alliances, it had come to stand for the 'American' way of capitalism, individualism, and the open market: opposed in every respect to the 'Russian' or 'Communist' way of collectivism and the organised economy. A war machine that had managed to treble munitions production in 1941, continued, if in a slightly lower gear. The cessation of conflict did not mean an end to arms production, now that the United States discovered a new threat in international socialism, and the next decade or so saw the rapid expansion of what one President was to term 'the military-industrial complex': a compact between military interests, eager to acquire ever newer and more powerful armaments, and industrial interests, just as eager to produce them, that was to prove satisfactory and very profitable to both. At the same time, the manufacturing industries catering to more peaceful demands began to expand rapidly. Construction boomed; the demand for the consumer durables of modern mass society – cars, television sets, refrigerators – grew among people suddenly released from the constraints of war; and unemployment only rose a little above the all-time low of 1.2. per cent created by a war economy. The only nation to emerge from World War II with its manufacturing plant intact and its economy strengthened, America presented itself to the rest of the world – and, in particular, to Europe – as an economic miracle. In 1949, the *per capita* income of the United States was twice that of

Britain, three times that of France, five times that of Germany, and seven times that of Russia. It had only six per cent of the world's population: yet it consumed forty per cent of the world's energy, sixty per cent of its automobiles, eighty per cent of its refrigerators, and nearly one hundred per cent of its televisions. This, evidently, was the society of abundance, appearing to prove an earlier President, Calvin Coolidge's claim that the business of America was business.

The business of America was also, perhaps, to dictate the terms of modern culture, at least to its Western allies, and to other parts of the globe where it claimed a right of intervention and control. As the Forties passed into the Fifties, America seemed to set the style in everything, from high art to advanced technology to popular culture. In Eisenhower, the President from 1952 until 1960, Americans also had someone at the head of state whose main aim seemed to be to preserve this economic abundance and cultural hegemony through a strategy of masterly inactivity. Gone were the frenetic commitments of the New Deal; and in their place was an administration that seemed intent on stopping things happening – on maintaining equilibrium by vetoing any legislation that seemed likely to promote radical change. To some commentators, it seemed a case of the bland leading the bland. Like Ronald Reagan thirty years later, Eisenhower made a dramatic exhibition out of not working too hard; as he apparently saw it, his job as President was to leave Americans alone to go about their business, and to discourage the state from any interference in the day-to-day life of the individual. If self-help was to be encouraged, then citizens had to be left to themselves: to work hard and then to enjoy the material comforts thereby earned. 'These are the tranquillized *Fifties*,' observed Robert Lowell; and for many Americans they were – a period when, after several decades of crisis, it was evidently possible to enjoy the fruits of their labour and exploitation of the earth's natural resources without any fear that, some day, those resources might run out. Many intellectuals and artists – although by no means all of them – participated in this era of consensus. This was the period of so-called 'value-free' sociology; much of the liberal intelligentsia acted on the assumption that it was possible to exercise the critical function untouched by social or political problems; and many poets, as we shall see, withdrew from active involvement in issues of public concern or ideology into formalism, abstraction, or mythmaking. One notable dissenter, Irving Howe, complained about this in an essay appropriately entitled 'This Age of Conformity'. 'Far from creating and subsidising unrest,' Howe observed:

> capitalism in its most recent stage has found an honoured place for the intellectuals; and the intellectuals, far from thinking of themselves as a desperate "opposition," have

> been enjoying a return to the bosom of the nation. . . .
> We have all, even the handful who still try to retain a
> glower of criticism, become responsible and moderate.
> And tame.[1]

No consensus, however, is quite as complete as it seems, just as no society – not even the most totalitarian one – is without its areas of dissent. Abundance breeds its own anxieties, not least the fear of losing the comforts one enjoys; in many ways, the calm society is the one most susceptible to sudden, radical fits of panic. This uneasiness that hovered beneath the bland surfaces of the times found its expression in many forms. In popular culture, for instance, it was expressed in a series of 'invaders from space' movies that uncovered a dark vein of public paranoia about the possible arrival of hostile forces, aliens who would rob Americans of their comforts and complacency. In poetry, as we shall see, related insecurities issued in a preoccupation with evil, the possible eruption of weariness, guilt, and remorse, into the rhythms of routine experience. In this respect, there was an almost willed dimension to the formalism of, say, the early Lowell or John Berryman: it was as if, like their fellow Americans (although, obviously, in a far more self-conscious and articulate way), they were trying to contain their anxiety by channelling it into socially established and accepted structures. And in the political life of the period, in turn, perhaps the most significant expression of this fear of invasion, subversion, or even destruction by covert agencies was the phenomenon known as McCarthyism. Joseph McCarthy was a young Senator from Wisconsin who had a self-appointed mission to wage war on anything he saw as Communist subversion. Exploiting his position on the Un-American Activities Committee, playing on popular anxieties about the growing power of Russia and the possible presence of an 'enemy within', he embarked on a modern-day witch-hunt: the result of which was that many people were sacked from their jobs and blacklisted on the mere suspicion of belonging to the Communist Party. Guilt was established by smear; loss of job followed on false witness; and a cast of characters that included Hollywood script-writers, intellectuals, and academics suddenly found themselves the subject of vicious public abuse. McCarthy declared that he was engaged in a battle that could not be ended 'except in victory or death for this civilisation';[2] and, during the period when he flourished, he managed to convince many Americans that the preservation of their material wealth and social health depended upon him rooting out enemies of the people wherever he could find or invent them.

One crucial fear that McCarthy exploited was the fear of the betrayal of atomic secrets. America had unleashed strange and terrible forces when it dropped atom bombs on Hiroshima and Nagasaki. The bomb cast its shadow over the immediate post-war decades, just as it has done ever since; and the discovery that certain people in the United States, Canada, and Britain had passed atomic secrets to the Russians, who could now explode nuclear weapons of their own, clearly exacerbated public anxieties about hidden enemies and conspiracies, and made it that much easier for McCarthy and his committee to flourish. Fear of the potential nuclear capability of the enemy, allied to this suspicion of a powerful enemy within, also increased the tensions of what Winston Churchill christened 'the Cold War': that policy of brinkmanship between the United States and Russia, their respective satellite states and allies, that was based on the premise that the two superpowers were engaged in a life-or-death struggle for global supremacy. Eisenhower's Secretary of State, John Foster Dulles, talked of 'the liberation of captive peoples' and the possibility of turning back the Communist tide. His Vice-President, Richard Nixon, who had first come to public attention while serving on the Un-American Activities Committee, announced that there would be no relaxation in the drive to root suspected subversives out of public service. And even Eisenhower himself, despite his evident mildness of manner, promised the American electorate, 'We will find out the pinks, we will find the Communists, we will find the disloyal.' The Red scare of the Eisenhower years was more than just a useful weapon in the hands of certain ambitious politicians, helping to generate policies of confrontation and containment. It was a clear symptom of the uneasiness, the nightmarish fears that haunted Americans at the time, despite their apparent satisfaction with themselves. There was abundance and some complacency, certainly, but there was also a scarcely repressed imagination of disaster, fuelled by the threat of nuclear war.[3]

By the late Fifties, this threat – and, more specifically, the bomb that embodied it – had become a potent symbol for the destructive potential of the new society: the dark side of those forces that had created apparently limitless wealth. Everywhere in the culture, there were signs of revolt, as the fears and phobias that had been lurking just below the 'tranquillized' surfaces of middle America began to bubble to the surface. There was a renewed spirit of rebelliousness, opposition to a social and economic order that had produced abundance, admittedly, but had also produced the possibility of global death. In music, the emergence of rock and roll, derived mainly from black musical forms, signalled a reluctance to accept the consensual mores, and the blandness, of white middle-class America: which is why, until they were absorbed into the mainstream, performers like Elvis Presley were perceived by political and religious leaders as such a potent threat, offering a gesture of defiance to 'civilised standards.' In the movies, similarly, new heroes appeared dramatising an oppositional stance to the dominant culture: James Dean, in films like *Rebel Without a Cause*, and Marlon Brando in, say, *The Wild One* seemed living monuments to the new spirit of alienation. And in literature, too, there were analogous developments. Two key fictional texts of the period were *The Catcher in the Rye* by J. D. Salinger and *On the Road* by Jack Kerouac. Radically dissimilar as these two books were, they had in common heroes at odds with modern urban-technological life: outsiders who moved between fragile mysticism and outright disaffiliation in their search for an alternative to the orthodox culture. They were willing, in effect, to say no, in thunder, just as earlier American heroes had been: which is also true, as we shall see, of many poets of the period. Poets as otherwise different as Robert Lowell and Allen Ginsberg bore witness to a gradual slipping away from the formalism and abstraction – and, to some extent, the conformism – of the post-war years and towards renewed feelings of freedom, individualism, and commitment. Recovering the impulse towards the personal, sometimes to the point of the confessional, and the urge towards an individual, perhaps even idiosyncratic beat, they gave voice to a growing sense of resistance to the social norms. Re-inventing the old American allegiance to the rebellious self, and weaving together personal and historical traumas, they sought in their line and language for a road to liberation: a way of realising their fundamental estrangement. No cultural development is seamless, of course, and it would be wrong to suggest that the story of the first two decades after the Second World War is one, simply, of abundance and anxiety merging into revolt and repudiation of fixed forms. But, in terms of a general bias of direction or tendency, this was the way that many American poets moved, along with their countrymen, as they saw one President, Eisenhower, who seemed 'pretty much for mother, home, and heaven,' succeeded by another, Kennedy, who preferred to talk in terms of 'a new generation of Americans' and of standing 'on the edge of a new frontier.'

From the mythological eye to the lonely "I": a progress of American poetry since the war

In the period immediately following the Second World War, many American poets wrote of their involvement in conflicts for which – as one of them, Randall Jarrell, put it – 'The soldier sells his family and his days'. 'It is I who have killed', declared Karl Shapiro, '/ It is I whose enjoyment of horror is fulfilled', and, for a while, this sense of having participated in a great historical crisis nurtured a poetry that was notable for its engagement, its direct address to public issues and events. In 1945, for instance, two substantial collections of war poems were published, *The War Poets* edited by the influential anthologist Oscar Williams and *War and the Poet* edited by Richard Eberhart. Not long after this, Louis Simpson produced work that spoke sardonically of 'war-heroes, . . . wounded war-heroes', 'packaged and sent home in parts', and that tried, too, to capture the tension, the actual experience of war:

> Most clearly of that battle I remember
> The tiredness in the eyes, how hands looked thin
> Around a cigarette, and the bright ember
> Would pulse with all the life there was within.[4]

Shapiro, for his part, produced plangent memorials for the unknown soldier ('Elegy for a Dead Soldier'), bitter accounts of a war machine in which 'Trains lead to ships and ships to death or trains' ('Troop Train'), and vivid descriptions of the life of an ordinary conscript during battles ('Full Moon: New Guinea'), the lulls between ('Sunday: New Guinea'), and on the return home ('Homecoming'). 'Lord, I have seen too much', begins one of Shapiro's poems; and that remark suggests the documentary accuracy, tinged with a bitter knowingness, a sense of having *seen* what life is really like at its worst, that characterises many of these pieces.

But if documentary accuracy was the primary aim of most of these poets, this did not necessarily preclude other ambitions. In particular, many writers were keen to see the war in mythological terms. 'Lord, I Have seen too much', for example, ends with the poet-combatant comparing himself to Adam 'driven from Eden to the East to dwell'; and the legend of the Fall became a favourite way of adding a further resonance to global conflict. This was especially true of Randall Jarrell. Innocence, and its loss, obsessed him; and the war became for him a powerful symbol of loss, a reversal of the westward myth in that his combatants invariably fall 'to the East' (as Shapiro puts it), from innocence to suffering and experience. This does not mean that his war poems are lacking in documentary detail. On the contrary, they give a vivid, particularised portrait of the life of pilots and gunners ('Eighth Air Force'), life aboard aircraft carriers ('Pilots, Man Your Planes'), in prisoner-of-war camps ('Stalag Luft'), in barracks, camp and field ('Transient Barracks', 'A Lullaby', 'Mail Call'). What is remarkable, however, is Jarrell's capacity for capturing the dual nature of the experience of war. As he presents it, war makes life more 'real' – in the sense that it brings people closer to the pressures of history and the physical facts of living and dying – and more 'unreal' – in that it cuts them off from everyday routine, propelling them into an unfamiliar realm, a world of potential nightmare. 'The soldiers are all haunted by their lives',[5] Jarrell remarks in one piece; and it is this feeling of moving through experience half-asleep and half-awake, together with imagery of a monstrous birth, of a fall in which innocence is violated, that distinguishes his most famous war poem, 'The Death of the Ball Turret Gunner':

> From my mother's sleep I fell into the State
> And I hunched in its belly till my wet fur froze.
> Six miles from earth, loosed from its dream of life,
> I woke to black flak and the nightmare fighters
> When I died they washed me out of the turret
> with a hose.

The work of Randall Jarrell in fact indicates the direction in which American poetry was to go within ten years after the end of the war: towards mythology, the use of dream and archetype. His poems are, certainly, intimate and idiomatic. 'What can be more tedious', he asked, 'than a man whose every sentence is a balanced epigram without wit, profundity and taste?' Particularly in his later pieces, where he turns from a taut, often strained voice to a richly varied use of iambics, he manages to capture the lively play of his speech and mind:

> . . . When they meet me they say:
> You haven't changed.
> I want to say: You haven't looked.[6]

In all his poems, however, and especially the earlier ones, the lively texture is complicated by the use of legends, dreams, and fairytale. 'All this I dreamed in my great ragged bed . . . / Or so I dreamed', he says in one piece; in another, he refers to a young girl reading in a library as 'An object among dreams'. Frequently, the dream convention or the structure of fairy-tale enables him to edge between the real and the surreal; soldiers mingle with figures from the Gospels in his work, ordinary people rub shoulders with angels, devils, corn kings, or characters from the Brothers Grimm. 'Behind everything', Jarrell insists, 'there is always / The unknown unwanted life'; and his extraordinary capacity for combining what he called 'the plain / Flat object-language of a child' with the vocabulary of dream registers this. The plain surfaces of a world where, so often, 'we miss our lives' and the 'inconceivable enchantment' beneath: they are both there, in the amphibious medium of his writing, recalling us constantly to his own sense that 'Living is more dangerous than anything'.

Writing in 1952, W. H. Auden commented on this interest in legends and archetypes that seemed to characterise a new generation of poets. Most poems, he observed, fall into one of two categories: those in which 'the historic occasion is . . . on the outside and the general significance on the inside' and those in which the reverse is the case. Auden called these, respectively, 'occasional' and 'mythological poetry', then added, 'it is impossible not to recognise . . . the increase of interest shown today, both by poets and critics, in myth, and a corresponding turning away, on the part of poets at least, from occasional subjects whether political or private'.[7] Auden's remarks were written as a preface to the first volume of W. S. Merwin; and Merwin, at least in his earlier work, illustrates this mythologising tendency even more clearly than Jarrell. With Jarrell, the impulse towards the legendary is tempered by his use of peculiarly fluent, even flat forms of speech and his professed commitment to the lives and dreams of ordinary people, their losses, their courage and their longing for change. In the early poetry of Merwin, however, the landscape is stylised and anonymous (there are, in fact, no references to the United States in the Fifties); the language is elevated and often archaic; and the tone is distanced, hieratic. The opening of 'Dictum: For a Masque of Deluge' is typical:

> There will be the cough before the silence, then
> Expectation; and the hush of portent
> Must be welcomed by diffident music
> Lisping and dividing its renewals;
> Shadows will lengthen and sway . . .

Exploiting traditional metres, populated by archetypal figures and ancient myths, this is a poetry that resolutely refuses any accommodation to the contemporary. Its subjects are the perennial ones of birth, death, and renewal, departure and return, and it deals with them in terms of allegory and parable, a vocabulary as old as the human race.

If the early poetry of Merwin reveals a characteristic feature of American poetry at the beginning of the Fifties, then the work of Richard Wilbur illustrates analogous ones. 'Most American poets of my generation', Wilbur has said, 'were taught to admire the English Metaphysical poets . . . and such contemporary masters of irony as John Crowe Ransom . . . Poetry could not be honest, we thought, unless it began by acknowledging the full discordancy of modern life . . . I still believe that to be a true view of poetry'. For Wilbur, the appropriate way of acknowledging discordancy in verse is to accommodate it within an elaborate formal structure. The poet, he argues, has to convert 'events' into 'experience', and he does this through a skilful application of form; the poet's forms supply a context, while his ironic, quizzical yet steady voice draws disparate elements together, relates them and holds them in equilibrium. The precision, the sense of control supplied by a traditional framework, is necessary: but so also is lightness of touch, wit, irony, and ambiguity, so as to prevent a hardening of the poetic arteries – to preserve nuances of feeling, the flash and play of this 'maculate, cracked, askew / Gay-pocked and potsherd world'. 'The strength of the genie', Wilbur declared, 'comes of his being confined in a bottle'; and, in saying this, he was speaking for many poets of his generation, with their belief in 'Beauty joined to energy',[8] the magical, liberating possibilities of form.

Few poets from this generation have demonstrated the potential of form more clearly than Wilbur has himself. 'So far as possible', he has said, 'I try to play the whole instrument'. These opening lines from one of his poems, 'Objects', suggest how cunningly he exploits the full range of any instrument available to him:

> Meridians are a net
> Which catches nothing; that sea-scampering bird
> The gull, though shores lapse every side from sight,
>   can yet:
> Sense him to land, but Hanno had not heard
>
> Hesperidean song
> Had he not gone by watchful periploi . . .

The basic conceit here is a navigational one. Wilbur is comparing sailing by chart ('meridians') or, like a gull, by 'sense' to Hanno's 'watchful' circumnavigations. Playing upon this conceit, his aim is to draw a contrast between different kinds of knowledge: the instinctive understanding of animals, abstractions that catch 'nothing', and that patient attentiveness to objects which enables voyages of discovery. 'Guard and gild what's common', Wilbur suggests later in the poem, '. . . forget / Uses and prices and names; have objects speak'. In doing this, the 'devout intransitive eye' of the observer can unlock mysteries, his ear can hear strange 'song'; by cherishing things, he releases them to new meaning. This is a common theme in Wilbur's work. Eyes and objects need each other, he insists ('Lamarck Elaborated'). Love calls us to the things of this world; we attend to them and so liberate them into a fresh ordering, the ordering of the imagination ('A World Without Objects Is a Sensible Emptiness'). Yet they always retain a certain strangeness, an otherness, he tells us: 'The beautiful changes as a forest is changed / By a chameleon's tuning his skin to it'[9]; eye and object are constantly altering, even as they incarnate themselves in each other, and so new incarnations, fresh couplings are constantly required. The theme is a common one, then, but what makes Wilbur's treatment of it uncommon, continually surprising, is the delicacy, the tact and poise he brings to it each time. As the passage just quoted illustrates: an evocative rhythm, an astute use of allusion, quickness of wit and verbal melody – all are directed towards a subtle development of the formal argument, so as to transmute an 'event' into 'experience', idea into music.

'Poems are not addressed to anybody in particular', Wilbur declared, 'The poem . . . is a conflict with disorder, not a message from one person to another'. To make a crude but serviceable distinction: he committed himself, early on in his career, to the idea of the poem as object, rather than vehicle of communication, an object with its own 'strictness of form'. Having made that commitment, he has stuck to it. Others of roughly his generation have done so too: among them, Stanley Kunitz, Weldon Kees, Reed Whittemore, Howard Nemerov, Anthony Hecht, Edgar Bowers, Donald Justice, X. J. Kennedy – and above all, in her own inimitable way, Elizabeth Bishop. After the early Fifties, however, many American poets actively rejected formalism, and the mythologising tendency, and went in search of other gods, new ways of turning the world into words. Some of those ways will be considered in the next chapter. The main one that concerns us here is the movement towards autobiography: poetry became, once again, not a flight from personality but a dramatisation, a reinvention of the personal. The first person, 'I', was restored to the centre of the poem. Recovering one of the major impulses, probably the major one, in the American tradition, poets began placing themselves squarely at the centre of the poem. The poet's private self became both subject and speaker, just as it had in 'Song of Myself'; the growth of the poet's mind informed the narrative or supplied whatever coherence there might be; and the poet addressed the reader directly, with an often unnerving intimacy, as if that reader were confessor, therapist, friend, or even lover. These lines, taken from some very different poems, illustrate the change – or, to be more exact, the rediscovery of what Whitman meant when he said, 'Who touches this book touches a man':

> I'm writing this poem for someone to see when
> I'm not looking. This is an open book.
> (Karl Shapiro, 'I'm writing this poem for someone to see')

> I am taking part in a great experiment –
> whether writers can live peacefully in the suburbs
> and not be bored to death.
> (Louis Simpson, 'Sacred Objects')

I was stamped out like a Plymouth fender
into this world.
First came the crib
with its glacial bars.

(Anne Sexton, 'Rowing')

I'm Everett Leroi Jones, 30 yrs. old.
A black nigger in the universe.

(Imamu Amiri Baraka (Leroi Jones),
'Numbers, Letters')

I must write for myself . . .
I look at my face in the glass and see
a halfborn woman

(Adrienne Rich, 'Upper Broadway')

I haven't read one book about
A book or memorised one plot.
Or found a mind I did not doubt.
I learned one date. And then forgot.

(W. D. Snodgrass, 'April Inventory')

I have no priest for now.
Who
will forgive me then. Will you?

(John Logan, 'Three Moves')

I am busy tired mad lonely & old.
O this has been a long long night of wrest.

(John Berryman, 'Damned')

I am only thirty.
And like a cat I have nine times to die.

(Sylvia Plath, 'Lady Lazarus')

I myself am hell,
– nobody's here.

(Robert Lowell, 'Skunk Hour')[10]

'Be guilty of yourself in the full looking glass', a poet of a slightly earlier generation, Delmore Schwartz, had said; and that injunction, to see and know the truth about oneself no matter how painful or embarrassing it might be, is clearly the enterprise, the heart of these poems.

Varieties of the personal: the self as dream, landscape, or confession

This rediscovery of the personal in American poetry has assumed many forms – as various, finally, as the poets involved. At one extreme are poets who attempt to plunge into the unconscious: in the work of Robert Bly, Robert Kelly, Galway Kinnell, and James Wright, for example, the poet dives down beneath the level of rational discourse, using subliminal imagery and a logic of association to illuminate the darker areas of the self, the seabed of personal feeling, dream and intuition. In Robert Bly's case, exploration of the subrational has led him towards 'tiny poems', in imitation of the Chinese, and prose poems that are, as he puts it, 'an exercise in moving against "plural consciousness"'. His aim is to uncover the 'dense energy that pools in the abdomen':[11] the fierce, mystical forces that unite him, at the deepest level, with the looser, livelier forms of the natural world. Kelly and Kinnell dip perhaps even further down. 'My wife is not my wife', Kelly insists in one of his poems, ' / *wife* is the name of a / process, an energy moving, / not an identity, / nothing in this world is / mine but my action'. To articulate the process, the activity that constitutes identity, Kelly has devised a poetry that is a haunting mixture of dream, chant, and ritual: his poems are an attempt to translate the interpenetration of things into intelligible (although not necessarily paraphraseable) signs and sounds. 'The organism / of the macrocosm', as he puts it, 'the organism of language, / the organism of *I* combine in ceaseless naturing / to propagate a fourth, / the poem, / from their trinity'.[12] Kinnell began from a rather different base from Kelly, in that his earlier poems were informed by a traditional Christian sensibility. But, while retaining a sacramental dimension, his later work burrows ferociously into the self, away from traditional sources of religious authority – and away, too, from conventional notions of personality. 'If you could keep going deeper and deeper', he has said:

> you'd finally not be a person . . . you'd be an
> animal; and if you kept going deeper and
> deeper, you'd be a blade of grass or
> ultimately perhaps a stone. And if a stone
> could read poetry would speak for it.[13]

The poems that issue from this conviction show Kinnell trying to strip away formal, verbal, and even surface emotional constructs, anything that might dissipate or impede the poet's continuing exploration of his deepest self and experience. 'How many nights', he asks, 'must it take / one such as me to learn / . . . / that for a man / as he goes up in flames, his one work / is / to open himself, to *be* / the flames?'[14] Short, chanting lines, a simple, declarative syntax, emphatic rhythms, bleak imagery and insistent repetition: all turn the poet into a kind of *shaman*, who describes strange, apocalyptic experiences in which he throws off the 'sticky infusion' of speech and becomes one with the natural world ('The Bear') or participates in the primal experiences of birth ('Under the Maud Moon') and death ('How Many Nights'). The tone of James Wright's work is quieter, less prophetic than this: but, he too, attempts to unravel from his own unconscious the secret sources of despair and joy. Of another poet whom he admired, Georg Trakl, Wright said this: 'In Trakl, a series of images makes a series of events. Because these events appear out of their 'natural' order, without the connection we have learned to expect from reading the newspapers, doors silently open to unused parts of the brain'. This describes the procedures of many of Wright's own poems, which evolve quietly through layers of images until they surface with the quick thrust of a striking final image or epiphany. For instance, in 'Lying in Hammock at William Duffy's Farm in Pine Island, Minnesota;' Wright carefully annotates his surroundings. 'Over my head', he begins:

> I see the bronze butterfly
> Asleep on the black trunk
> Blowing like a leaf in green shadow.
> Down the ravine behind the empty house
> The cowbells follow one another.

The vision of the butterfly suggests a being wholly at one with the world: entrusted, pliable, possessed of the stillness of a plant or even a mineral ('bronze'). This feeling persists into the following lines through the subtle harmonising of time and space ('the distances of the afternoon') and the sense of the cowbells as the musical measure of both. It is growing late, however, and as 'evening darkens' a succession of images toll the poet back to his sole self. The last two lines complete the series and confirm the discovery:

> A chicken hawk floats over, looking for home.
> I have wasted my life.[15]

The hawk, presumably, will find its home; it possesses the ease, the buoyancy and assurance, that characterise the other natural object in this landscape. But the poet will not. He can see in the things of this world only a vivid, subliminal reminder of ruin, his failure truly to live. Surprising though this last line may seem, it has been carefully prepared for by the hidden agenda of the poem; the images that constitute the argument, strange and emotionally precise as they are, have opened the doors to this revelation.

While writers such as Wright and Kinnell have tried to register the movements of the subconscious, others have dramatised the personal in more discursive, conscious forms. These include poets like Richard Hugo, Karl Shapiro, and Louis Simpson, who explore the self's discovery of the outer world and its reaction to it and, rather more significant, those, like John Logan, Adrienne Rich, Anne Sexton, and W. D. Snodgrass, who incorporate elements of their personal histories in their poems. In the poetry of Richard Hugo, the personal dimension is founded on the relationship between the private self of the poet and the bleak, lonesome world he describes. The setting he favours is the Far West: not the Far West of legend, however, but a far more inhospitable, emptier place. Looking at one decaying township in Montana, he asks himself, 'Isn't this your life?'; and his own poetic voice, sombre and laconic, seems to answer him in the affirmative. Yet he can also learn from his surroundings; their strength of spirit, 'rage' and endurance, have stamped their mark on him. 'To live good, keep your life and the scene', he concludes one piece, '/Cow, brook, hay: these are the names of coins':[16] the currency of the West has, in fact, saved him from moral bankruptcy, helped him pay his dues to himself and the world. Hugo's poetic stance has hardly shifted over the years: by contrast, Shapiro and Simpson began (as we have seen) as poets of public event, and only gradually changed their interests and allegiances. As the personal element in their poetry grew, so its shape and tone altered too. 'Sabotage the stylistic approach', Shapiro commanded in one of his later works, '. . . Get off the Culture Wagon. Learn how to walk the way you want'. Attacking 'the un-American-activity of the sonnet, writing pieces with titles like 'Anti-Poem', he adopted a long, flowing line somewhere between free verse and prose poetry. With this, he has explored himself and his surrounds with sometimes embarrassing frankness: 'When I say the Hail Mary I get an erection', he admits in 'Priests and Freudians will understand', adding wryly, 'Doesn't that prove the existence of God?'[17] The alteration in Simpson's work has been less radical: his verse, while becoming freer, has retained an iambic base. But he, too, wants to know what it is like to be him at this moment in history, 'an American muse / installed amid the kitchen ware'. Like Whitman, he is concerned with the representative status of his self, his Americanness; unlike Whitman, his landscapes are often suburban. 'Where are you Walt?' Simpson asks, observing sardonically '/ The Open Road goes to the used-car lot':[18] that observation measures the distance, as well as the kinship, between its author and the person addressed, the first, finest poet of national identity.

Of the four poets just mentioned who insert their own histories directly into their narratives, John Logan is the most apparently casual. His poems seem simple, informal: 'Three moves in six months', begins one, 'and I remain the same'. But, in fact, they are carefully organised, to allow for a subtle orchestration of theme and tone. In the poem just quoted, for instance, 'Three Moves', he graduates from startling colloquialism ('You're all fucked up') to moments of lyricism and grace:

> These foolish ducks lack a sense of guilt
> and so all their multi-thousand-mile range
> is too short for the hope of change.[19]

And although, as these lines imply, Logan himself suffers from 'a sense of guilt' from which the animal kingdom is blessedly free, he can occasionally participate in the vitality, the innocence of the natural world around him. 'There is a freshness / nothing can destroy in us –', he says:

> not even we ourselves
> Perhaps that
> *Freshness* is the changed name of God.[20]

The voice of W. D. Snodgrass, and his stance towards nature, is at once more controlled and intense. His finest work is 'Heart's Needle': a series of poems which have as their subject his daughter and his loss of her through marital breakdown. 'Child of my winter', begins the first poem:

> born
> When the new fallen soldiers froze
> In Asia's steep ravines and fouled the snows,
> When I was torn
>
> By love I could not still,
> By fear that silenced my cramped mind . . .

Cynthia, the poet's child, was born during the Korean War and she is, he gently suggests, the fruit of his own 'cold war': the static, frozen winter campaign that is getting nowhere is also Snodgrass's marriage. The allusions to the war, and descriptions of the season, are there, not because of any intrinsic interest they may possess, historical, geographical, or whatever, but because they image the poet's inner world, his personal feelings. 'We need the landscape to repeat us',[21] Snodgrass observes later: the measured, musical quality of his verse, and his frequent attention to objects and narrative, disguise an obsessive inwardness, a ferocious preoccupation with the subjective. It is characteristic that he should have insisted *The Waste Land* was 'about Eliot's insane wife and his frozen sex life' rather than the larger issues critics usually assume. After all, he seems to be saying, what else should a poem be about, despite its apparently objective paraphernalia, than the drives of the inner life?

'My poems . . . keep right on singing the same old song': the words could belong to Snodgrass, but in fact they were spoken by Ann Sexton. Even those pieces by Sexton that appear not to be concerned with herself usually turn out to be subjective, to have to do with her predicament as a woman. 'The Farmer's Wife', for instance, begins as a description of someone in rural Illinois, caught up in 'that old pantomime of love', and then concludes with these lines that suddenly switch the focus from farmer and wife to poet and lover:

>   while
> her young years bungle past
> their same marriage-bed
> . . . she wishes him cripple, or poet,
> or even lonely, or sometimes
> better, my lover, dead.[22]

Elsewhere, when the narrative mask is dropped, the tone can be painfully raw and open, and given a further edge by elaborate rhyme-schemes or tight stanzaic forms. 'All My Pretty Ones' is a good illustration of this. Addressed to the poet's father, the contrast between the passion and intimacy of the address and the strictness of the given measure only exacerbates the situation, intensifies the feeling of the poem. It is as if the disciplines of poetic form, which Sexton confronts in a half-yielding, half-rebellious fashion, were part of the paternal inheritance, something else that the father she both loves and hates has left her to deal with. However, she was not only concerned with the pain of being daughter, wife, mother, lover. She also sang, as she put it, 'in celebration of the woman I am'. Long before it was fashionable to do so, she wrote in praise of her distinctive identity, not just as an American poet, but as an American *female* poet. 'As the African says': she declares in one of her poems, 'This is my tale which I have told'; and for her this tale was, finally, a source of pride.

A similar pride in the condition of being a woman characterises the poetry of Adrienne Rich. Rich's early work is decorous, formal, restrained. But even here there is a sense of the subversive impulses that lie just beneath the smooth surfaces of life. In 'Aunt Jennifer's Tigers', for example, the character who gives the poem its title seems to be crushed beneath patriarchal authority: 'The massive weight of Uncle's wedding band / Sits heavily upon Aunt Jennifer's hand'. However, the tigers she has embroidered 'across a screen' suggest her indomitable spirit. Even after her death, 'The tigers in the panel that she made / Will go on prancing, proud and unafraid'. 'Sleek chivalric' and poised as they are, these animals nevertheless emblematise certain rebellious energies, turbulent emotions that will not be contained: polite on the surface, passionate beneath, Aunt Jennifer's art is, at this stage, Adrienne Rich's art. Gradually, though, Rich came to feel that she could 'no longer go to write a poem with a neat handful of materials and express these materials according to a prior plan'. 'Instead of poems *about* experience', she argued, 'I am getting poems that *are* experiences'. A work like 'Diving into the Wreck' measures the change. In it, the poet describes a journey under the sea, during which she has to discard all the conventional supports, the crutches on which she has leaned in the upper world. 'I came to explore the wreck', she says:

> The words are purposes.
> The words are maps . . . .
>
> the thing I came for:
> the wreck and not the story of the wreck
> the thing itself and not the myth.[23]

Diving deep into the inmost recesses of her being, exploring the 'wreck' of her own life, Rich feels compelled to jettison inherited techniques and fictions. A more open, vulnerable and tentative art is required, she feels, in order to map the geography of her self: a feeling that is signalled in this poem, not only by its argument, but by its directness of speech, its stark imagery and idiomatic rhythms, above all by the sheer urgency of its tone. The map, as it happens, is not just for her own use. 'We are confronted', Rich has declared, 'with . . . the failure of patriarchal politics'. 'To be a woman at this time', she goes on:

> is to know extraordinary forms of
> anger, joy and impatience, love and hope. Poetry,
> words on paper, are necessary but not enough;
> we need to touch the living who share . . . our
> determination that the sexual myths underlying
> the human condition can and shall be . . . changed.[24]

In Rich's later work, in fact, the confrontation with herself is inseparable from her broader, feminist purposes; her work has become intimate, confessional, but it is an intimacy harnessed to the service of community, the invention of a new social order.

From formalism to freedom: a progress of American poetic techniques since the war

The example of Adrienne Rich is interesting and symptomatic in several ways. In the first place, her later poetry shows how ready American poets have become to take risks. 'I have been increasingly willing', she has said, 'to let the unconscious offer its material, to listen to more than the one voice of a single idea'. This does not mean that she offers the reader unmediated psychic experience: as she is aware ('the words are maps'), such a thing is impossible and probably undesirable as well. Her aim, on the contrary, is like that of many of her contemporaries: to surrender to her material and then, in the act of writing, try to re-enact its complex rhythms – to turn activity, physical, emotional, or whatever, into speech and breath. In the second, she illustrates the particular triumph of the better poets of the personal. Her best work – 'Diving into the Wreck', for instance, or 'The Will to Change' – is squeezed out of her own intimate experience, it can be painfully straightforward and frank, but it can also be surreal or political. Personal experience, after all, includes dream and history: the fantasies of the inner life and also the facts of that larger world of war, work, and income tax to which every one of us, whether we like it or not, is subject. Rich's poetry acknowledges this. It absorbs the data of private events, the dramas of the public stage, and the fears and desires encountered in sleep. It incorporates the conscious and the subconscious levels, intimate confession and the historical imagination; as such, it bears comparison with the work of the finest poets of the personal mode over the last forty years – Theodore Roethke, John Berryman, Robert Lowell, and Sylvia Plath. Finally, Rich is representative in another, broader sense: in that she was far from alone in terms of her stylistic development from formal to freer verse forms. Not everyone ceased to be a formalist: as we have seen, Wilbur has been one among many to retain his old allegiances. Nor did those who changed their poetic voice necessarily do so as Rich – or, for that matter, Shapiro and Simpson did – as part of a commitment to a more confessional mode. But, whether interested in personal confessions or not, many poets turned at about the same time Rich did (that is, in the late Fifties or early Sixties) towards a more open and idiomatic poetry – in search of what one poet, Alan Dugan, has called 'words wrung out of intense experience and not constructed.'[25]

Among the poets who show this alteration is Donald Hall, who moved from traditional forms, as in 'My Son, My Executioner', to the more fluent and relaxed measures of poems like 'The Town of Hill' and 'Maple Syrup'. More important, there is Robert Bly, who began by writing short, quiet, carefully structured portraits of rural life and landscapes in the West, before graduating to a more sensuous, various and insinuating music – as in this passage from 'Looking into a Face':

> I have risen to a body
> Not yet born,
> Existing like a light around the body
> Through which the body moves like a sliding moon.[26]

Bly's later poetry of apocalypse, experiences at once mystical and erotic, in fact gains its impact from his mastery of very free verse forms. 'We must always reckon with the presence of things not yet discovered', Jung said; and the feeling of an experience that is simultaneously luminous and unknown – present but as yet undisclosed to the rational sense – is caught here, not only in the imagery of light and incantatory repetition, but in the movement of the verse. It edges forward on tip-toe, as it were, pausing in tentative excitement at 'Not yet born', creeping stealthily on again before finding release in the final, subtly assonanced line. The consciousness registered by this seems at once relaxed and passionate, as if the poet had allowed the urgencies of his own blood and senses to take control – hoping to write, as Rich said, 'poems that *are* experiences'. A similar transfiguration of restless life into mobile language is noticeable in the later work of W. S. Merwin. His earlier poetry – as that passage from 'Dictum: A Masque of Deluge', quoted earlier, illustrates – is formal and mythological, with the poet concealed behind the text paring his fingernails. From this, Merwin moved to more contemporary, sometimes personal subjects, although mostly written in fairly regular iambics ('Pool Room in the Lion's Cub', 'Grandmother Dying'), and then on, in turn, to the angular, radically disruptive rhythms of lines like these:

> The first morning
> I woke in surprise to your body
> for I had been dreaming it
> as I do[27]

This is certainly not confessional verse, but it does represent a startling departure from Merwin's earlier work. 'We are words on a journey', Merwin insists in one of his later poems, '/ not the inscriptions of settled people', and that remark alone serves to indicate the change: an interest in the more obviously permanent forms of human vision and voice has been replaced by a pursuit of the mobile and temporary – of life as it passes, in all its rapid disjunctive rhythms.

The change from formal to freer verse forms has not, however, always been a happy one. The earlier poems of Delmore Schwartz were predominantly iambic, and the relative strictness of the forms he employed seems to have exercised a useful discipline. Some of these poems present Schwartz as the engaged observer. 'A nervous conscience amid the concessions', the poet reflects on the 'banal dream' of the city, where most people 'live between terms' and 'death / Has his loud picture in the subway ride'; alternatively, he tries to picture some better world, 'soft-carpeted and warm', in which the self can become 'articulate, affectionate, and flowing'. Other pieces are more like an open wound: 'Shy, pale, and quite abstracted', Schwartz is confronted by the ineluctable, ugly fact of himself. 'I am I', one poem concludes; and to know who that 'I' is, Schwartz finds it necessary to deal with the accumulated debts of his past. 'The past is inevitable', he insists, and what the 'ghost in the mirror' – that is, the image of our past – tells us is that guilt is inseparable from the fact of living. 'Guilt is nameless', Schwartz says, '/ Because its name is death'; we are all burdened by 'the guilt of time' and so 'the child must carry / His father on his back'. There are many things to be said about this poetry but perhaps the most important is that it is, above all, a poetry of agony and transformation: in one poem, for instance, a man heard coughing in an upstairs apartment is transformed, in quick succession, into Christ (who has 'caught cold again'), 'poor Keats', and the archetypal figure of the victim, 'Longing for Eden, afraid of the coming war'. The formal and emotional dangers of this kind of verse are perhaps obvious: the transformations could easily become chaotic and unconvincing, while the sense of agony could degenerate into a maudlin, occasionally generalised self-pity. In his early work, though, Schwartz usually manages to skirt such dangers thanks to his adept handling of traditional forms; 'the subject of poetry', he said, 'is experience not truth', and he turns his own obsessive truths into imaginative experience with the help of inherited metres and conventional structures. In 'O City, City', for example, he uses the framework of the sonnet to focus a contrast between the quiet desperation of 'six million souls' in New York (established in the octave) and his own longing for a world of purity and passion, where 'in the white bed all things are made' (described in the sestet). It is a simple device, but it works beautifully. Unfortunately, in his later work, Schwartz adopted a long, rambling line, attempting to assimilate prose rather than speech rhythms. At its best, the verse that results is like higher conversation ('An adolescent girl holds a bouquet of flowers / As if she gazed and sought her unknown, hoped-for, dreaded destiny'). At its worst, and this is more frequent, it is slack and banal:

> If you look long enough at anything
> It will become extremely interesting.
> If you look very long at anything
> It will become rich, manifold, fascinating[28]

'I'd bleed to say his lovely work improved', John Berryman was to declare of Schwartz after his death, ' / But it is not so'. The enemies of free verse have always equated it with formlessness, a kind sprawling inertia, and sadly with Schwartz's later work they have a case.

As American poets gravitated, during this period, towards more flexible verse forms, they also, many of them, went in pursuit of a more idiomatic vocabulary. 'When you make a poem', William Stafford argued, 'you merely speak or write the language of every day'. 'Rather than giving poets the undeserved honour of telling us how . . . special poetry is', he went on,

> everyone should realise his own fair share
> of the joint risk and opportunity present in
> language: through the social process of language
> all of us should help each other to become
> more aware of what being alive means.[29]

This is a theme that recurs in the remarks of several recent American poets. 'I'm sick of wit and eloquence in neat form', Alan Dugan announced; while David Ignatow has insisted that he is 'antipoetic' – 'nothing', he has said, 'should be taken for more than it says to you on the surface'. The ideal, in effect, seems to be a virtual transparency of idiom. For John Ciardi, for instance, there is nothing worse than what he has termed 'the signatory way of writing': that is, language that is foregounded, calling attention to the distinctive 'signature' or style of its inventor. What he dreams of, Ciardi has said, is 'an act of language so entirely responsive to the poetic experience' that his 'habituated way of speaking' would be 'shattered and leave only the essential language called into being by the aesthetic experience itself'. The perfect poem would then be one that, as Ciardi puts it, 'seem[s] to declare not 'X spoke these words in his unique way' but rather 'man spoke these words of himself''. This is not, as it may appear at first sight, a desire for impersonality or anonymity, but for a language so simple and apparently inevitable that it seems to be the only possible way of expressing the subject. It is, in sum, another version of that commitment to authenticity – the precise application of word to event without superfluous gesture or ornament – that characterised so many earlier American poets from Whitman to Oppen and Williams.

Oppen and Williams were, of course, very different poets; and it has to be said that the search for an authentic language among recent writers has had some strikingly various consequences. With Alan Dugan, the result has been a tough, brittle, determinedly populist style. 'Here the world is', he declares in one piece, ' / enjoyable with whiskey, women, ultimate weapons, and class';[30] and he does his best to express that world as it is, together with all the *detritus* of contemporary life. John Ciardi also clearly likes the radicality of the colloquial, the voice of the plain-speaking, rough-and-tumble man who tolerates no nonsense, verbal or otherwise. The opening line of 'In Place of a Curse' is typical, in its candour and bluff wit: 'At the next vacancy for God, if I am elected'. Ciardi frequently tries to shock the reader into attention in this way, whereas the poems of William Stafford tend to open quietly ('Our car was fierce enough' 'They call it regional, this relevance – / the deepest place we have') and then move towards some muted discovery of a small truth, a partial explanation of things. 'The signals we give – yes or no, or maybe – / should be clear', Stafford says at the conclusion to 'A Ritual to Read to Each Other', adding 'the darkness around us is deep'.[31] Clarity of language, verbal modesty is for him, it seems, a stay against oblivion, something to illuminate or at least hold back the surrounding dark.

David Ignatow is just as verbally modest as Stafford, but not in entirely the same way. An avowed imitator of Williams's formal experiments, and concerned primarily with urban life, Ignatow has said that he has two main purposes: to remind other poets that 'there is a world outside' in the streets, and to reveal to people in general 'the terrible deficiencies in man'. 'Whitman spent his life boosting the good side', he has claimed, 'My life will be spent pointing out the bad' – although pointing it out, he adds, 'from the standpoint of forgiveness and peace'. The quarrel with Whitman, and by implication with the moral dimension of Williams's work, runs through Ignatow's poetry, generating a poignant contrast between method and message. The limpidity of diction and movement that those earlier writers had used to celebrate human innocence is now harnessed to a haunting vision of guilt:

Being a victim
I am the accuser. Being a human,
others feel my fallen weight
upon their thoughts and are oppressed –
as I am.[32]

A similar combination of verbal clarity and visionary sadness is notable in the work of Philip Levine. 'I was born / in the wrong year and in the wrong place', Levine has written; and many of his poems are in fact concerned with his childhood, spent in the Middle West during the Depression. The bleak cityscape of Detroit, the lonely farmlands of Illinois and Ohio, the sad, wasted lives of family and friends condemned to drudgery in factories and 'burned fields': all this is recounted with the strength and simplicity of idiom of Edgar Lee Masters, but without Masters's abiding feeling of waste. 'You / can pledge your single life, the earth / will eat it all', admits Levine. Nevertheless, his characters are marked by their courage in the face of the inevitable. In 'Animals are Passing from our Lives', for instance, Levine assumes the voice of a pig on its way to be slaughtered. 'The boy / who drives me along', says the pig, 'believes / that any moment I'll fall/ . . . / or squeal / and shit'. 'No', he swears defiantly, 'Not this pig'.[33] The jaunty obstinacy of this, framed as it is by our sense of the ultimate absurdity of such a gesture, allows for both humour and moral complexity. We are all going to the slaughterhouse, Levine intimates. Any defiance we show along the way is, *practically* speaking, useless, even ridiculous; still, it has its own, odd nobility – it is not *morally* insignificant. There is a subtle, disciplined sensibility at work behind poems like this: reminding us (if reminder is necessary) that simplicity of speech is not always synonymous with simplification of attitude.

'Dispossess me of belief: / between life and me obtrude / no symbolic forms': this request, made by another contemporary poet A. R. Ammons, repeats the aims of Levine and Ignatow, but in a different key. It also exposes a further, crucial way in which much recent American verse has removed itself from formalism: by dispensing, not only with conventional metres and 'signatory' language, but with the 'symbolic forms' of narrative closure. Revitalising the earlier American interest in 'organic form', Ammons is one among many current writers who want the radiant energy they perceive at the heart of the natural world to become the energy of the poem, 'spiralling from the centre' to inform every line. A poem like 'Corsons's Inlet' dramatises the details of this commitment. It opens in a characteristic way: 'I went for a walk over the dunes again this morning to the sea'. Few human bêings appear in Ammons's work, apart from the omnipresent 'I': who is there, however, not to impress but to observe. Ammons is preoccupied with what he calls 'amness', the intrinsic identity of things – which includes himself, of course, but also 'stars and paperclips' – and, in order to know this 'amness', he has to pay attention, 'losing the self' when necessary 'to the victory / of stones and trees'. In this instance, he tells us, the walk on which he embarks liberates him – from himself, as usual – and 'from the perpendiculars, / straight lines / of thought / into the hues, . . . flowing bends and blends of sight'. In particular, it releases him into knowledge of the inlet mentioned in the title. Watching its fluid, changing shape and the microscopic lives that animate it, Ammons perceives in it, not a symbol, but an example of what an appropriate form should be. 'In nature there are few sharp lines', the poet comments, and what he sees here is:

> an order held
> in constant change: a congregation
> rich with entropy: nevertheless, separable, noticeable
> as one event,
> not chaos[34]

The inlet opens up to him 'the possibility of rule as the sum of rulelessness': a form of knowing in which there is 'no forcing of . . . thought / no propaganda', and a form of expression, an aesthetic shape that is vital and kinetic, a ''field' of action / with moving incalculable centre'.

The notion of the 'field' was one that Williams cherished ('The poem is made of things – on a field') and that, as we shall see, Charles Olson developed. What such a notion resists, at all costs, is what Ammons calls 'lines' and 'boundaries': demarcations that exclude, hierarchies that prioritise, definitions that impose the illusion of fixity on the flux of experience. There are, Ammons suggests, 'no / . . . changeless shapes': the poet-seer must invent structures that imitate the metamorphic character of things. The organisms he creates must respond to life as particularity and process; they must be dynamic, unique to each occasion; above all, they must be *open*. 'There is no finality of vision', Ammons concludes (with deliberate inconclusiveness), '. . . I have perceived nothing completely, / . . . tomorrow a new walk is a new walk'. Echoing a whole series of great American texts, Ammons also speaks here for a new generation of poets: who respond to 'The wonderful workings of the world' with their own persistent workings and re-workings of the imagination. '*ecology* is my word', Ammons affirms in another, longer poem. 'Tape for the Turn of the Year', '. . . come / in there: / you will find yourself / in a firm-less country: / centres and peripheries / in motion'. 'My other word is *provisional*', he continues, '. . . you may guess / the meanings from *ecology* / . . . / the centre-arising / form / adapts, tests the / peripheries, draws in / . . . / responds to inner and outer / change.[35] Those lines could act as an epigraph to many volumes of American verse published over the past few decades: in which the poet tries to insert himself in the processes of life, and, in turn, the reader is asked to insert himself in the processes of the work.

The imagination of commitment: a progress of American poetic themes since the war

The emphasis Ammons places on ecology in his 'Tape for the Turn of the Year' brings into focus one aspect of contemporary American poetry that unites formalists, confessionals, and others: that is, a willingness to attend to social and political issues, and to the historical experience of the late twentieth century. On one, deep level, such attention is unavoidable: we are all historical beings and our participation in sociopolitical processes must necessarily feed into everything we do. Sylvia Plath clearly had this in mind when she said, 'the issues of the time which preoccupy me . . . are the incalculable genetic effects of fallout and . . . the terrifying . . . marriage of big business and the military in America'; however, she went on, 'my poems do not turn out to be about Hiroshima, but about a child forming itself finger by finger in the dark. They are not about the terrors of mass extinction, but about the bleakness of the moon over a yew tree in a neighbourhood graveyard'.[36] As it happens, this is not the whole truth about Plath's own work: her poems sometimes address social problems (notably, the position of women), and she is not afraid to link her personal intimations of disaster to the holocaust of world war and the apocalypse now threatened by nuclear weaponry. But, as a general point, it is still worth making: it is one thing to have a historical consciousness – and this nobody, not even the most abstracted writer, can avoid – and quite another to be historically involved, to have the imagination of commitment. One such form of commitment has already been touched on with reference to the work of Sexton and Rich: that is, the willingness of many poets to confront the questions of sexual identity and sexual politics. This is not, incidentally, a willingness confined to women poets. Robert Bly, among others, seems ready to blame the failures of American culture on its denial of what he sees as the inner-directed feminine principle ('the mother of solitude') in favour of the outer-directed masculine one ('the father of rocks'). Another kind of commitment will be considered in the next chapter: the continuing need Afro-American poets feel to give words to their identity, personal and communal. There are, of course, many others. Two further contemporary issues, in particular, have haunted poets and in one case at least continue to do so: the experience in Vietnam, which introduced America to defeat, and the possible destruction of the world by nuclear war.

The war in Vietnam stimulated an enormous amount of poetry, most of it of dubious quality. A representative collection is *Where is Vietnam? American Poets Respond*, which was published in 1967. For the most part, the poems published here and elsewhere rely on simple invective ('All your strength, America, is in your bombs!') or on equally simple documentation:

> On Thursday a Vietcong flag was noticed flying
> Above the village of Man Quang in South Vietnam.
> Therefore Skyraider fighter-bombers were sent in,
> Destroying the village school and other 'structures'.[37]

With the first kind of poetry, anger tends to lose its edge in generalised, unfocussed condemnation (American poets have, on the whole, been remarkably unsuccessful with satire and polemic). With the second, apart from the occasional gesture, very little seems to be added or gained by turning the experience into verse: in the passage just quoted, for instance, except for the parody of the neutral dehumanised tone of war communiqués ('structures') and the ordering of the data within a fairly rudimentary rhythmic pattern, the writer does nothing more than act the good journalist by handing us a series of received facts. It is worth adding perhaps that the poem from which these lines are taken has a footnote: 'This incident was reported from Saigon . . . by the Special Correspondent of the London *Times*'. This, presumably, is meant to stress the factual nature of the piece. However, it also serves to remind us that this poem, like the vast majority of those written about Vietnam, is by a non-combatant. The best poems of the Second World War were produced by people like Jarrell, Shapiro, and Simpson, who actually participated in it and, for the most part, saw it as nasty, brutish, but necessary. By contrast, the best poems about Vietnam have been by those who were not there but who had an *imaginative* involvement in it, and were committed to doing all they could to stop it. 'All wars are useless to the dead', Adrienne Rich insisted. 'Why are they dying?' Robert Bly asked. 'I here declare the end of the War',[38] announced Allen Ginsburg. Such pronouncements are typical. American poets felt that they had to participate; they were gripped by what they read about, what they saw on television, what they felt was happening in the streets and to the youth of their country. They also had the firm conviction – as poems like 'The Asians Dying' by W. S. Merwin and 'The Altar in the Street' by Denise Levertov suggest – that the war could be ended with the help of the language of poetry.

There were two kinds of poetic language that were particularly successful, if not in stopping the war, then at least in giving an adequate definition of its horror. The first is illustrated by the Vietnam poems of Robert Bly. Some of these poems, like *The Teeth-Mother Naked at Last*, are jeremiads, fierce prophecies of 'the end of the Republic' thanks to an increasingly authoritarian government. Others show him adopting the mask of some member of that business-dominated, power-oriented society which brought the war into being ('Counting Small-Boned Bodies'), or translating the obscene realities of war into a crazy, nightmarish surrealism:

> The bombers spread out, temperature steady
> A Negro's ear sleeping in an automobile tyre
> Pieces of timber float by saying nothing[39]

In all of these pieces, however, Bly relates the contemporary political crisis to a more general crisis of belief. Like Ginsberg, say, or Robert Duncan, he seeks an explanation for and answer to public events in terms that are, ultimately, mystical, erotic, and apocalyptic. The other strategy, adopted by Robert Lowell and a few other poets – Adrienne Rich, for instance –, is subtly different and, arguably, even more compelling. In poems like 'Waking Early Sunday Morning', Lowell links the godless militarism of his society and the bloody, futile conflict in South-East Asia to the sense of his own spiritual dereliction. Of all poets since the war, Lowell has the finest historical imagination, the most powerful capacity for juxtaposing past and present, public and private, and discovering significance in the juxtapositions. In his hands, autobiography becomes a spiritual biography of his times, he transforms his life into myth and that myth becomes emblematic, the story of a nation:

> Pity the planet, all joy gone
> from this sweet volcanic cone;
> peace to our children when they fall
> in small war on the heels of small
> war – until the end of time
> to police the earth, a ghost
> orbiting forever lost
> in our monotonous sublime.[40]

The final lines of 'Waking Early Sunday Morning', with their vision of the earth as 'a ghost / orbiting forever lost', recall another way in which American poets have felt compelled to think the unthinkable. After Auschwitz no poem could be written, Adorno insisted. Similarly, many writers have felt that no language is adequate before the possibility of global annihilation: the mind, perhaps, cannot encompass the destruction of mind, speech cannot speak of its own extinction. Still, poems have been written not only after Auschwitz but about it; and poets have tried to tell about the potential death of the earth. They suffer from the imagination of disaster and they struggle to give verbal shape to their imaginings in the hope that, this way, disaster may be forestalled. The quiet voice of William Stafford, in 'At the Bomb Testing Site', suggests one possible manoeuvre, to allow the obscene phenomenon to speak for itself. He simply describes 'a panting lizard' in the desert near a testing site that 'waited for history, its elbows tense'. Nothing seems to happen in the poem, it concludes with these lines:

> There was just a continent without much on it
> under a sky that never cared less.
> Ready for a change, the elbows waited.
> The hands gripped in the desert.[41]

It is what Stafford called the 'sleeping resources in language' that carry the message here: the sense of doom that occurs, as it were, in the spaces between the words. The unknown is presented as just that; the unspeakable becomes the only partially spoken; under a nuclear cloud, Stafford intimates, all we have is unnamed, unnameable dread. Galway Kinnell also uses the perspective of a primitive creature in his 'Vapour Trail Reflected in a Frog Pond', only in his case the frogs' eyes that keep 'The old watch' create a point of view that eerily resembles the Inhumanist Vision of Robinson Jeffers. These prehistoric creatures, with 'their / thick eyes' that 'puff and foreclose by the moon', make the vapour trail of an aircraft, and the power it emblematises, seem not only insane but inane: a passing cloud puffed by a race who have jettisoned the self-containment of the other animals in favour of self-absorption and self-destruction.

'The bomb speaks', said William Carlos Williams in one of his last poems, '. . . the bomb has entered our lives / to destroy us'.[42] Against the 'mere picture of the exploding bomb', he set the powers of love and the imagination: which, he said, were 'of a piece' since they both required a dedication to life, its beauties and possibilities. This is a theme on which James Merrill plays his own variations in his trilogy, *The Changing Light at Sandover*, where he tells us of conjured spirits who inform him, 'NO SOULS CAME FROM HIROSHIMA U KNOW'. Merrill, in effect, uses prophecy and magic to release his vision. The spirits he has met, he said, are 'HOPING AGAINST HOPE THAT MAN WILL LOVE HIS MIND & HIS LANGUAGE'; if man does not, then the 'WORLD WILL BE UNDONE' and 'HEAVEN ITSELF' will 'TURN TO ONE GRINNING SKULL'. If Merrill claims that he has become a medium for absolute truth, in order to voice his sense of the potential for mass destruction – and the redeeming power of love and language – then Sylvia Plath adopts similarly vatic tones in a poem like 'Nick and the Candlestick'. Here, the poet sets her fear of 'the incalculable effects of nuclear fallout' against her care for her as yet unborn child. 'Let the stars / Plummet to the their dark address', she declares:

> Let the mercuric
> Atoms that cripple drip
> Into the terrible well.
>
> You are the one
> Solid the spaces lean on, envious.
> You are the baby in the barn.[43]

Lines like these illustrate, again, how the poetry of the personal can become the poetry of prophecy. Universal annihilation and individual fertility are placed side by side: the poem is about both history and the body, the bomb and the womb, and manages to be at once oracular and intimate. In a very different sense, some of this is also true of a formalist piece on the nuclear threat, 'Advice to a Prophet' by Richard Wilbur. Wilbur adopts the modest pose of advising rather than being the prophet but the result is, in its own way, just as resonant – and just as personal. 'When you come . . . to the streets of our city', Wilbur advises, 'Speak of the world's own change'. 'We could believe', he goes on:

> If you told us so, that the white-tailed deer will slip
> Into perfect shade, grown perfectly shy,
> The lark avoid the reaches of our eye,
> The jack-pine lose its knuckled grip
>
> On the cold ledge, and every torrent burn . . .[44]

The beautiful objects of this world will be lost, Wilbur intimates: which means, too, the loss of ourselves. Unable to see or speak them, we shall also be unable to see and speak our own being; we, and our words, will 'slip / Into perfect shade'. 'Ask us, ask us', Wilbur repeats through the poem, 'Ask us, prophet, how we shall call / Our natures forth when that live tongue is all / Dispelled'. Formalists and confessionals alike retain their belief in the power of speech – the language that summons us to knowledge of our lives – even in the face of absolute silence.

The uses of formalism: Bishop, and others

There are many ways of being a formalist poet. One way is illustrated by the subtle, serious wit of Richard Wilbur. Another, by the passionate, metaphysical sensibility of Stanley Kunitz: in a poem like 'Foreign Affairs', for instance, Kunitz develops the conceit of lovers as 'two countries girded for war' to examine the intricacies, and erotic heat, of a relationship. The poem is at once cerebral and sensuous, turning what could have been little more than an intellectual *tour-de-force* into a sensitive analysis of the way 'fated and contiguous selves' can somehow be 'separated by desire'.[45] It represents, as it were, a peculiarly intense, mentally energetic kind of formalism: whereas the reverence for form that characterises, say, Howard Nemerov's work is calmer, more reflective, expressive of Nemerov's belief that a poem should mean as well as be: even great poems, he suggests, unlike the things of nature 'tell . . . rather than exemplify / What they believe themselves to be about'. Nemerov's 'Gulls' is characteristic in this respect. Carefully structured, written in a slightly formal, even abstract language, the poem nevertheless accommodates some powerful visual effects ('they glide / Mysterious upon a morning sea / Ghostly with mist'). It begins with an unsentimental vision of the birds – 'I know them at their worst', the poet tells us – and then gradually emblematises them, teases out moral inferences from their activities: 'Courage is always brutal', Nemerov insists, 'for it is / The bitter truth fastens the soul to God'. 'Bless the song that sings / Of mortal courage', he concludes, 'bless it with your form / Compassed in calm amid the cloud-white storm'.[46] What Nemerov wants, evidently, is a poetry that has the poise and assurance, and the bravery before the facts of life, possessed by the gulls; and in poems like this one, or 'Storm Window' and 'Death and the Maiden', he manages to achieve that aim.

Still other varieties of formalism, different in turn from those of Wilbur, Kunitz, and Nemerov, are illustrated by the idiomatic, often bizarre wittiness of Reed Whittemore ('I wish I might somehow / Bring into light the eloquence, say, of a doorknob'), the incisive, sardonic tones of Weldon Kees ('Sleep is too short a death') and the patent concern with getting it right, trying to put things properly, that characterises the work of Donald Justice ('I do not think the ending can be right'). At one extreme, perhaps, is the dispassionate, distanced reflectiveness of Edgar Bowers ('The enormous sundry platitude of death / Is for these bones, bees, trees, and leaves the same') or the equally dispassionate elegance of X. J. Kennedy ('She sifts in sunlight down the stairs / With nothing on. Nor on her mind'). At the other is the poetry of Anthony Hecht, whose measured, sometimes ironic voice (learned, in part, from his former teacher, Ransom) becomes a medium for passionate explorations of autobiography and history, the fear and darkness at the heart of things:

> We move now to outside a German wood.
> Three men are there commanded to dig a hole
> In which the two Jews are ordered to lie down
> And be buried alive by a third, who is a Pole.[47]

In recent times, however, perhaps the most memorable lesson in the uses of formalism has been given by Elizabeth Bishop. Of her good friend, Marianne Moore, Bishop once said, 'The exact way in which anything was done, or made, was poetry to her'.[48] Precisely the same could be said of Bishop herself: 'all her poems', Randall Jarrell once suggested, 'have written underneath, *I have seen it*'. Bishop's aim is to attend carefully to the ordinary objects around her; and then, through that gesture of attention, to catch glimpses of what she calls 'the always-more-successful surrealism of everyday life'. The more closely she observes something, the more it seems to become arrested in time, translated for a moment into a world of stillness and dream. This resembles Moore's habit of using close attention as a means of imaginative release. However, Bishop's poetic voice is quite unlike Moore's. Strongly musical rhythms, unexpected but inevitably recurring rhymes, wit and clarity of idiom, above all a use of inherited formal structures that is characterised by its elegance and tact: all help to create a poetry that balances itself between mellow speech and music, the lucidity of considered thought and the half-heard melodies appropriate to a more sensuous, magical vision.

The dream-like sharpness of sight and the alertness of tone that typify Bishop's best pieces are illustrated by a poem like 'The Map'. The subject is a favourite one: like so many American poets, Bishop is interested in space, geography rather than history, and she uses maps as both a figure and a medium for imaginative exploration. As these opening lines indicate, the poem has a fairly tight yet unobtrusive formal structure, enhanced by delicate tonalities and repetition:

Land lies in water; it is shadowed green.
Shadows, or are they shallows, at its edges
showing the line of long sea-weeded ledges
where weeds hang to the simple blue from green.

The picture Bishop paints is at once precise and surreal, in the sense that it is through a careful enumeration of the details of the map that she begins to unlock the mysteries of land and water, shadows or shallows, that it encloses. As the poet's imaginative voyage continues, so her feeling for potential magic grows. Sometimes, the tone is languorous, even sensual: 'Labrador's yellow', she murmurs, 'where the moony Eskimo / has oiled it. We can stroke these lovely bays . . .'. At other moments, Bishop allows her wit to play around the given particulars: 'These peninsulas take the water between thumb and finger', she observes mischievously, '/ like women feeling for the smoothness of yard-goods'. Neither the play of fancy, nor the feeling for mystery, is unrestricted, however: both are firmly yet quietly anchored to an awareness of the actual, the formal constraints of map and poem. The contours of the map are continually kept before our eyes, and the poet never strays too far from the original structure, the dominant rhythms and idiom. The closing four lines, in fact, return us to the frame established in the opening four, an emphatic rhyme contained within a simple, bell-like repetition:

Are they assigned, or can the countries pick their colours?
– What suits the character or the native waters best.
Topography displays no favourites; North's as near as
West.
More delicate than the historians' are the map-makers'
colours.[49]

By this stage, the arts of the map and the poem describing the map have become almost indistinguishable. A democratic eye that discloses the wonder nestling in everything, a lively imagination that denies limits, spatial or otherwise, in its efforts to reclaim the world for the mind: these qualities, Bishop intimates, characterise both the map-maker and the poet, as they attend to the sights we see, the signs we create.

The map for Bishop is like a poem because, above all, it is a symbolic journey, an excursion that is perhaps promising and perhaps not. Her poetry is full of travel, literal and otherwise. There are poems about travellers ('Crusoe in England'), poems that recall things seen while travelling ('Arrival at Santos'), poems that ask the question, 'Should we have stayed at home and thought of here?'. One of her pieces has as its epigraph a quotation from *Landscape into Art* by Kenneth Clark, 'embroidered nature . . . tapestried landscape'; and this suggests the peculiar ability she possesses to mingle landscapes literal with landscapes imagined, or to find the sources of art and inspiration in the most unpromising and apparently mundane of surroundings – in a filling station, for instance:

> Somebody
> arranges the row of cans
> so that they softly say:
> ESSO-SO-SO-SO
> to high-strung automobiles.
> Somebody loves us all.[50]

Typically, as here, the revelations her poetic journeys achieve are joyful but also sad: with the sadness of rootlessness, perhaps, and isolation. Bishop's watching eye and musing voice are kept at one remove, as it were, in this case, unable to determine who the 'somebody' might be – the arrangement is perceived, but not its shadowy creator. Whether peering through a map at the 'long sea-weeded ledges' it signifies, or looking at a landscape with the suspicion that there is something 'retreating, always retreating behind it', the quality of distance is there, enabling wonder certainly but also loss. As some of Bishop's personae learn, the solitude that is a prerequisite of attentiveness, and so imaginative discovery, promotes absence: to look and see is, after all, to stand apart.

One of Bishop's poems, 'In the Waiting Room', actually describes how the poet learned about this apart-ness. While sitting in a dentist's waiting-room, she recalls, 'I said to myself: three days / and you'll be seven years old'. 'I felt: you are an *I*', she goes on, 'you are an *Elizabeth*': 'I knew that nothing stranger / had ever happened, that nothing / stranger could ever happen'. The position realised here is the site of most of her work, whether she is attending to objects, people, or events. Her explorer's eye transforms ordinary creatures into extraordinary characters, the stuff of artifice and legend: a sandpiper, for instance, is metamorphosed into a fanatical investigator, 'final, awkward / . . . a student of Blake' in the sense that it evidently searches for the world in a grain of sand. The aim is not to be merely fanciful or whimsical, even in the more openly bizarre poems such as 'The Man-Moth'. On the contrary, what Bishop is after is a deeper realism. She is trying to reveal things that may be most available to the unhabituated eye: to uncover, perhaps, the peculiar strategies we and other animals use to confront and defy the forces that govern us ('The Armadillo'), or the strange communications that can occur between the different dimensions of life, the earth and the sea, waking and sleeping. One such communication is described in 'The Fish': where the poet remembers how oil that 'had spread a rainbow / around the rusted engine' of a fishing vessel led to sudden revelation. 'Everything / was rainbow, rainbow, rainbow!' the poet exclaims and, in that moment of illumination, 'victory filled up / the little rented boat'. Such insights are as bright, particular, and as fleeting as a mingling of oil, water, and light: objects, as Bishop shows them, brim with meaning that is vividly but only temporarily disclosed. In one of her most famous poems, 'At the Fishhouses', Bishop uses another image to convey the shock and the ephemerality of these revelatory experiences: not a rainbow this time, but the drinking of 'Cold dark deep and absolutely clear water' – so cold, in fact, that it seems to 'burn your tongue'. 'It is like what we imagine knowledge to be', she declares of such a draught:

> dark, salt, clear, moving, utterly free,
> drawn from the cold hard mouth
> of the world, derived from the rocky breasts
> forever, flowing and drawn, and since
> our knowledge is historical, flowing, and flown.[51]

It is surely not stretching a point to say that it is exactly this kind of knowledge that Bishop realises in her own work: where truth slips in, as it were, through the cold particularities of fact and then quietly slips away again.

The confessional 'I' as primitive: Roethke

Another poet who at least began as a formalist of sorts was Theodore Roethke. His first volume of poetry, published in 1941, used traditional verse structures and depended on the then fashionable mode of tough intellectualism. The opening lines of the first volume showed that this was no ordinary formalist, however:

> My secrets cry aloud.
> I have no need for tongue.
> My heart keeps open house,
> My doors are widely swung.[52]

Here, in a language that is stripped and bare, and rhythms that are driving and insistent, Roethke announces his intention of using himself as the material of his art. His major preoccupation was to be with the evolution and identity of the self: and these tight, epigrammatic verses cry that aloud. 'I'm naked to the bone', Roethke declares later in this poem, 'Myself is what I wear': that is almost, but not quite, true. He is still, after all, dressed in the uniform of an inherited poetics. But from the second volume on, this too was to be discarded in the search for the subrational, prehistorical roots of being. 'Cuttings (later)' bears witness to the change:

> I can hear, underground, that sucking and sobbing,
> In my veins, in my bones I feel it, –
> The small waters seeping upward,
> The tight grains parting at last.
> When sprouts break out,
> Slippery as fish,
> I quail, lean to beginnings, sheath-wet.[53]

Much of his verse after the first volume, Roethke explained, 'begins in the mire, as if man is [sic] no more than a shape writhing from the rock': a being, the birth and growth of whose consciousness can be fruitfully compared to the birth and growth of plants, trees, and all organic matter. There is a new rooting of poetry in sensuous experience here, the 'greenhouse' world or natural landscape of the poet's childhood (Roethke's father was a florist, joint owner of over twenty-five acres of greenhouses). Along with this, there is a new search for some dynamic concept of correspondence between the human and vegetable worlds. Roethke felt that he had to begin at the beginning, with primitive things: to journey into the interior of the natural order, and into himself as part of that order. This required, in turn, a more primitive voice. 'If we concern ourselves with more primitive effects in poetry', Roethke argued, 'we come inevitably to the consideration . . . of verse that is closer to prose . . . The writer must keep his eye on the object, and his rhythm must move as his mind moves'. So, in the passage just quoted, Roethke uses the free verse line, long, elaborately alliterated, with a preponderance of heavy stresses, open vowels, and participles, to create an effect of enormous effort and evolutionary struggle; instead of imposing order on experience (*all* experience, conscious, subconscious, and pre-conscious) he tries to discover the order latent in it. This ties in with an alteration of idiom. 'Approach these poems as a child would', Roethke instructed, 'naively, with your whole being awake, your faculties loose and alert'. As he dwelt on primeval life, so he naturally gravitated towards a more subliminal language: the intuitions of folktale, fairytale, and myth, shapes that lurk 'Deep in the brain, far back'. A simple but significant illustration of this imagery drawn from 'the gulfs of dream' is that haunting line, 'Slippery as a fish'. The fish is mentioned frequently in Roethke's verse ('My father was a fish', he says in another poem); and here the kind of life with which it is compared is left deliberately indeterminate. It might be the vegetation described in the preceding line, or the person, the 'I' of the following one; or it might, more likely, be both. It does not matter. What does matter is that, as one of the more primeval forms of sentient existence, the fish can act as a corresponding figure for the early, pre-conscious stages of human life and for the deeper, subconscious levels that remain a formative element in the psyche even after infancy has passed; it can remind us, in effect, that all forms of being are continuously present. As the poet leans towards his beginnings, still 'wet' with the mucus of the womb, chrysalis, or sheath, he is, as he will remain, part of an invincible process of becoming: in which (as Roethke put it in one of his very last pieces) 'everything comes to One / As we dance on, dance on, dance on'.[54]

Of growing up in the Midwest Roethke once said, 'sometimes one gets the feeling that not even the animals have been there before, but the marsh, the mire, the void is always there . . . It is America'. Roethke's poetry is a poetry of the self, certainly, but it is also very much a poetry of the West, in that it is concerned with the frontiers of existence, the ultimate, inchoate sources of being. This is particularly noticeable in some of the later work, where the poet lights out, beyond childhood and the natural world, for the unknown territory of racial memory: on a journey backward into unindividuated experience that then in turn becomes part of a general, evolutionary process forward. Talking of the poems that made up his third volume, for instance, Roethke said, 'Each . . . is complete in itself; yet each is a stage in a . . . struggle out of the slime'. 'The method is cyclic', he continued, 'I believe that to go forward as a spiritual man it is necessary to go back . . . There is a perpetual slipping-back, then a going-forward; but there is *some* "progress"'. Acting on this belief, Roethke modelled such poems as 'Where Knock is Open Wide' and 'Unfold! Unfold!' on an archetypal pattern: in which the heroic protagonist – in this case, the poet – travels into a nightworld, suffering perhaps a dark night of the soul, conquers the dangers he meets there, and then returns to lead a fuller, more inclusive life in the daylight realm of ordinary existence. Ancient and familiar as the tale may be, however, what gives it an air of unfamiliarity is Roethke's way of telling it. He compresses language and syntax into abrupt, dream-like units. At its most extreme, when the frontiers of individual consciousness are crossed and 'the dead speak' (that is, the inhabitants of the collective unconscious utter their communications), Roethke presents us with what he calls 'a whelm of proverbs', a speech as primitive as folk-saying, as sub-human, almost, as an animal cry:

> You're blistered all over
> – Who cares? The old owl?
> When you find the wind
> – Look for the white fire.[55]

Along with these mutterings of a rudimentary sensibility, Roethke telescopes imagery and symbols and employs rhythms that are primeval, even oracular in their effect. All this he does because, instead of simply reporting the journey to the frontiers of being as many other writers have done, he is trying to re-create it. He is inviting the reader to share in the departure into the interior and the return. If the reader accepts this invitation, then he or she can also share in the moments of revelation, that knowledge of the correspondences of life, on which each of these pieces ends:

> Sing, sing, you symbols! All simple creatures,
> All small shapes, willow-shy,
> In the obscure haze, sing![56]

'Often I think of myself as riding – ', observes the narrator of one of Roethke's later poems, '/ Alone, on a bus through western country'. 'All journeys, I think, are the same', she says a little later, 'The Movement is forward, after a few wavers'. The narrator here is an old woman, modelled partly on the poet's mother; and the poem from which these observations are taken, 'Meditations of an Old Woman', illustrates two ways in which the poet, even as he grew older, continued to change and grow. One way involved an intensified interest in the people around him. Having established a true sense of himself in poems like 'Unfold! Unfold!', Roethke turned outward to affirm his relationship with others: by adopting their voice and vision for a while, perhaps, as in 'Meditations' or 'The Dying Man', by celebrating the 'slow world' of erotic fulfilment where the lovers 'breathe in unison', or by a gently particularistic portrait of an individual – his father, it might be, 'Who lived above a potting shed for years', or 'a woman, lovely in her bones'. The other way in which Roethke moved was towards a creative analysis of ultimate questions: about God, Eternity – above all, about 'Death's possibilities' and their significance for the living. 'Old men should be explorers?' Roethke asked, echoing Eliot, ' / I'll be an Indian'; and he lived up to this promise in poems that sing of any person, like himself, who 'beats his wings / Against the immense immeasurable emptiness of things'. As the old woman meditates, she considers the imminence of her death ('What's left is light as seed'), and the disappointments of her past ('I have gone into the waste lonely places / Behind the eye'): but she remembers positive moments as well, when she achieved growth by realising a harmonious relationship with all that is. Such moments more than make up for others, she believes: they are blessed with a special perfection of their own, a sense of ecstasy that no deity can ever supply. 'In such times', she says, 'lacking a god / I am still happy'. It seems appropriate that even this poem, the product of 'an old crone's knowing' should end on a note of affirmation and possibility. For Roethke, life was a continual wayfaring, an expedition into the grounds of being that offered joy or wonder as a reward. It was a process of constant beginnings, 'many arrivals': whereby, the poet felt – as he put it in one of his most famous pieces – 'I learn by going where I have to go'.[57]

The confessional 'I' as historian: Lowell

'Alas, I can only tell my own story'. The words could be those of many American poets; in fact, they were written by the greatest poet of the self since the Second World War, Robert Lowell, and could be said to sum up his work. Despite the touch of regretfulness noticeable in this remark, Lowell did seriously believe that his story needed to be told; and for this his good friend Elizabeth Bishop envied him. 'I feel that I could write in as much detail about my uncle Artie, say', she wrote to Lowell:

> – but what would be the significance? Nothing
> at all . . . whereas all you have to do is
> put down the names! And the fact that it
> seems significant, illustrative, American etc., gives
> you, I think, the confidence you display . . . In
> some ways you are the luckiest poet alive.[58]

For Bishop, the source of this good fortune lay in the sheer splendour of Lowell's background, the fact that he was descended from two distinguished New England families. But two other things were quite as important: Lowell's characteristically American tendency to see himself as a representative of his culture, and his willingness, or rather his determination, to assume the role of scapegoat – to challenge and confront (or say 'No, in thunder!' as Herman Melville put it) and to expose himself, for the purposes of revelation and discovery, to the major pressures of his times.

In his early work, Lowell's painful awareness of self, together with his anxiety over a world that seemed to him to be corrupted by egotism, led him towards a consciously Catholic poetry. Poems like 'The Holy Innocents' and 'The Quaker Graveyard in Nantucket' juxtapose the self-absorption of the isolated individual with the selflessness of true faith. The introspective and fragmentary nature of the New England and American traditions is contrasted with the serenity and coherence of the Roman Catholic order. The short poem, 'Children of Light', illustrates this position. It is divided into two, densely imagistic passages, which offer the reader two historical examples of the crime of Cain, or violence committed against the brotherhood of man: first, the depredations of the early Puritan settlers, and then the horrors of the Second World War. The Puritans, Lowell argues, were 'Pilgrims unhouselled by Geneva's night'. They were deprived of the support of Catholicism, a system of beliefs founded on the community rather than the individual; and their imperialism of the self led them to slaughter the Indians ('Our fathers . . . / . . . fenced their gardens with the Redman's bones') and claim absolute possession of the land. World War II is the product of similar single-mindedness, prompting destruction even of the natural abundance of the earth in the pursuit of personal power; it, also, illustrates the primary truth that inwardness finds its issue, eventually, in the disruption of both the private life and the public. 'And here the pivoting searchlights probe to shock / The riotous glass houses built on rock', the poet concludes, in shocked response to global conflict:

> And candles gutter by an empty altar,
> And light is where the landless blood of Cain
> Is burning, burning the unburied grain.[59]

Lines like these suggest the characteristic voice of this early poetry: learned partly from Tate, it is notable for its cold passion, its icy bitterness and despair. The language is packed and feverish, the syntax often contorted, the imagery disruptive: all is barely kept in control by the formal patterns of the verse. Like an unwilling disciple, the poet seems to be trying to force himself into accepting the rigours of an inherited form and faith; he has to will his speech and his spirit into submission. For all the fierceness of his initial conversion, in fact, Lowell was too much and irrevocably a part of New England – too solitary, introspective, and individualist – to be comfortable as a Catholic or, indeed, stay a Catholic for very long; and it was only his rage for order that made him try for a while to compel himself into submission.

'It may be', Lowell wrote once, 'that some people have turned to my poems because of the very things that are wrong with me. I mean the difficulty I have with ordinary living'. By the time he wrote this, Lowell had had several nervous breakdowns and left the Catholic Church. More to the point, perhaps, this difficulty he had with 'ordinary living' had helped turn his poetry in a new direction: for in the hope, apparently, that he might resolve his problems he had begun writing, first in prose and then in poetry, about his life and family. In part, Lowell was prompted to take this change of course by his reading of other poets, notably William Carlos Williams: but in part it seemed a natural course for him to take, not only because of its possible therapeutic function but also because it enabled him to pursue his search for a satisfactory voice and place. In the event, in the poems that were eventually published in *Life Studies*, Lowell discovered not just a medium for expressing his immense, devouring inwardness but a way of fulfilling his desire for spiritual anchorage as well: something that, besides offering him the opportunity for emotional release, described a fleeting sense of stability and order. These lines, from 'Skunk Hour', the concluding poem in the volume, indicate the change in vision and idiom:

> One dark night
> my Tudor Ford climbed the hill's skull,
> I watched for love-cars. Lights turned down,
> they lay together, hull to hull
> where the graveyard shelves on the town . . .
> My mind's not right.[60]

As we compare poems like 'Skunk Hour', 'My Last Afternoon with Uncle Devereux Winslow' or 'Memories of West Street and Lepke', with the earlier work, the contrast could hardly be more striking. Gone is the Catholicism; in its place is a different, more muted and ironic kind of belief, in the imaginative and moral power of faithful speech. Gone, too, are the tortuous language and elaborate arrangements of line and rhythm; in *their* place are lines that are limpid and flexible, a syntax and idiom that play cunning variations on the colloquial, and rhymes that when they do occur are invariably unexpected and elusive. The poet, it seems, no longer begins with a predetermined structure for his material, but instead tries to discover structure of a kind, and immutability, in the actual processes of remembering and articulating. The only order now tolerated, we surmise, is the order of literature;

the poem re-creating the experience becomes the one acceptable means of refining and shaping it. The powerful closing lines of 'Skunk Hour', that give the poem its title, announce the new terms in which the poet will confront himself:

> I stand on top
> of our back steps and breathe the rich air –
> a mother skunk with her column of kittens
> swills the garbage pail.
> She jabs her wedge head in a cup
> of sour cream, drops her ostrich tail,
> and will not scare.[61]

The skunks are a figure for the actual, at once disgusting and amusing, to which the poet has returned. They are a figure, too, for the courage required to confront the actual: they 'will not scare' and neither will the poet while breathing in their 'rich air' (the rhyme underlining the analogy). Above all, they are a way of indicating how the poet can master his experience and evade despair: by transmuting it into poetry, the kind of condensed and controllable image that is illustrated here. Lowell continued to live life on the edge or, as he put it once, 'at the point of drowning', but at least now he had his own instrument for measuring the precipice: a raft of language, fashioned by his own hands, that could enable him, just about, to keep his head above water.

The success of *Life Studies* helped turn Lowell into a public figure, the most visible American poet of his generation. And it was partly in response to this enhanced status that he began taking a public stand on some of the major issues of the day, such as the war in Vietnam. At the same time, his poetry, while remaining profoundly personal, addressed problems of history and culture: in his own way, like Whitman he tried to consider what it was to be an American at mid-century. 'Waking Early Sunday Morning', discussed earlier, gives one illustration of how Lowell wedded his intense inwardness of impulse to historical event and contemporary crisis. Another is offered by 'For the Union Dead'. In this poem, the civic disorder of the present is contrasted with two alternative ideas of order. One is the public order of the past: old New England, conceived of in consciously mythological terms and figured in the statue of a Colonel Shaw, who commanded a black regiment during the Civil War. Shaw, the poet suggests, had 'an angry wrenlike vigilance, / a greyhound's gentle tautness' and rejoiced 'in man's lovely, / peculiar power to choose life and die'. He found perfect freedom in service to civic values, the values of a culture: the disciplines he accepted enabled him to live, and even to die, with grace and purpose. But, Lowell suggests, those disciplines are unavailable now. All that is offered by the present culture is anarchism and servility. 'Everywhere', declares the poet:

> giant finned cars move forward like fish
> a savage servility
> slides by on grease.[62]

In seeking to aggrandise themselves, people have lost themselves: the pursuit of power has generated the greatest betrayals of all – of humanity and of community. So the only possible order for the present and future is a personal one: registered here in the architecture of the poem. Shaw's statue, a monument to public principle, has to be replaced by acts of private judgement which, like this poem, may then furnish others with the vision and vocabulary necessary to change their own lives.

For many of the last years of his life, Lowell concentrated on a series of unrhymed and irregular sonnets, collected in books like *Notebook 1967–1968, The Dolphin*, and *History*. Talking about these sonnets, Lowell explained that they were 'written as one poem, intuitive in arrangement, but not a pile or sequence of related material'. They were, he added, 'less an almanac than the story of my life'. As a whole, they are further proof of their creator's belief in the power and efficacy of literature: in an almost manic way, the poet seems intent on metamorphosing all his life into art, on endowing his every experience, however trivial, with some sort of structure and durability. They are also proof of his Americanness; for, taken together, they constitute another epic of the self. Less openly responsive to the problems of political society than the *Cantos*, less deliberately preoccupied with the future of America than 'Song of Myself', *Notebook* and the succeeding volumes nevertheless share with those poems a concern with the life-in-progress of the protean poet, as representative of his time and place. Journeying over the blighted terrain of his own life, Lowell is also travelling over the waste land of his culture; measuring his personal feelings he is, too, taking the measure of larger events. Writing now becomes an existential act, a means of establishing presence: as Lowell puts it, the poem, the made work, 'proves its maker is alive'. By definition, it is also an act that must go on and on: 'this open book', the poet says, is his 'open coffin'.[63] An epic of personal identity, an epic that effectively *creates* identity, must remain unfinished, available to change. Lowell was continually composing new sonnets and revising old ones, then scattering the results through different volumes: because, like Whitman, Pound, and others, what he was after was not so much a poem as a poetic process – something that denied coherence, in the traditional sense, and closure.

After the sonnets, Lowell published only one further volume, *Day by Day*. The poems here, which show him returning to freer, more varied verse-forms, are elegiac, penitential, and autumnal, as if the poet were trying to resolve ancient quarrels and prepare himself for death. With storybook neatness, in fact, Lowell did die very shortly after the book was published: his life and his life's work were completed at almost exactly the same time. In reading these final poems, the reader is likely to be reminded once again just how much faith in the self provided the bedrock value, the positive thrust in all Lowell's writing: at times challenged, as in his earlier poetry, occasionally questioned or qualified, as in the later, but always, incontestably there. 'Sometimes everything I write', the poet admits at the end of *Day by Day*, '. . . seems a snapshot, / . . . / . . . paralysed by fact'. 'Yet', he continues, 'why not say what happened?':

> Pray for the grace of accuracy
> Vermeer gave to the sun's illumination
> stealing like the tide across the map
> to his girl solid with yearning.
> We are poor passing facts
> warned by that to give
> each figure in the photograph
> his living name.[64]

'I desire of every writer', Thoreau once said, 'a simple and sincere account of his own life'. 'Simple' and 'sincere' are not, perhaps, words that we normally associate with a poet as subtle and ironic as Lowell: but in his own way he tried to fulfil Thoreau's demand – by confronting his experience, pursuing the goal of self-discovery, and attempting to achieve some sense of order, however fragile and evanescent, through the activities of memory and reinvention. Like other great American poets, Lowell learned how to translate the poor passing facts of autobiography into the grace of an accurate language. Consequently, his story becomes history: he told true tales of his life which have, in turn, become true tales for all of us.

The confessional 'I' as martyr: Berryman

'Really we had the same life', Lowell wrote in his elegy for John Berryman, 'the generic one / our generation offered'. Lowell recognised in Berryman a fellow explorer of dangerous psychological territory: 'I feel I know what you have worked through', he declared, 'you / know what I have worked through . . . / . . . / John, we used the language as if we made it'. What is more, he learned from Berryman: *Notebook*, he acknowledged, bore the imprint of Berryman's *Dream Songs* – of which Lowell said, in an admiring review, 'All is risk and variety here. This great Pierrot's universe is more tearful and funny than we can easily bear'.[65] But *Dream Songs* was by no means Berryman's first work: like Lowell again, 'cagey John' (as he was later to call himself) began under the burden of alien influences, particularly Yeats and Auden. 'I didn't so much want to resemble [Yeats] as to *be* him', Berryman later admitted, 'and for several fumbling years I wrote . . . with no voice of my own'. 'Yeats . . . saved me from the then crushing influence of . . . Pound and . . . Eliot', he added, 'but he could not teach me to sound like myself'. Not that the earlier poetry is entirely lacking in intimations of self. Some poems, like 'Winter Landscape', manage to communicate personal feeling through apparently objective accounts of people, places, and things. Others, such as 'The Ball Poem', taught Berryman a crucial lesson: that, as he put it, 'a commitment of identity can be "reserved" . . . with an ambiguous pronoun'. In such cases, the 'he' of the poem becomes a mask for the poet: a means of dramatising the self but also displacing it and so making it available for wry, dispassionate scrutiny. On the whole, however, this poetry is constricted by its formal quality, attentiveness to established models. *Berryman's Sonnets*, for instance, start from an intensely personal base, an adulterous love affair the poet had with an unspecified woman. But everything is distanced by the use of the strict Petrarchan form, archaic language, and a conventional argument that leads us through love and loss to transference of affection from woman to muse ('my lady came not / . . . I sat down & wrote').[66] Only now and then do we get glimpses of the vain, sad, drunken, lustful, comic, and pathetic 'I' that dominates and distinguishes the later work.

'I want a verse fresh as a bubble breaks', Berryman declared in one of his sonnets; and the fresh style came in *Homage to Mistress Bradstreet*, which the poet called a 'drowning' in the past. In this long poem of fifty-seven stanzas, the 'benevolent phantom' of the seventeenth-century poet, Anne Bradstreet, is conjured from the grave; she speaks, through the voice Berryman gives to her, of her emigration to New England and her hard life there; in a moment of intense communion, at once spiritual and erotic, the two poets from different centuries engage with each other; then Bradstreet succumbs to the pull of the past, and she and Berryman are once more imprisoned in their own times. 'Narrative!' Berryman recalled himself thinking while he was writing the poem, 'Let's have narrative . . . and no fragmentation!' Along with the fundamental coherence of narrative, he was also aiming, he said, at poetic forms 'at once flexible and grave, intense and quiet, able to deal with matter both high and low'. The results of his efforts are perhaps suggested by this, the concluding stanza of the poem:

> O all your ages at the mercy of my loves
> together lie at once, forever or
> so long as I happen.
> In the rain of pain and departure, still
> Love has no body and presides the sun,
> and elfs from silence melody. I run.
> Hover, utter, still,
> a sourcing whom my lost candle like the firefly loves.[67]

The lines are highly compressed, packed with jagged rhythms, puns, repetitions, assonance, alliteration, rhetorical climaxes, rhymes and slant rhymes; the language is vividly eccentric, a mixture of archaisms and the quirkily demotic; the voice issuing out of this is by turns jokey, excited, elegiac, sensual, lyrical, grave. He did not choose Anne Bradstreet, Berryman claimed, she chose him; and she did so, 'almost from the beginning, as a woman, not much as a poetess'. It is not the author of 'bald / abstract didactic rime' he encounters, in other words, but a passionate rebel who resists the conventions of youth and age, the restrictions of her environment and culture, the limitations of her body and the apparent will of God. In each case, though, rebellion is followed by surrender: 'My heart rose', as she puts it, 'but I did submit'.[68] This pattern of defiance followed by submission, or reconciliation, is caught in each individual stanza, with its halting ebb-and-flow released in a long, last line; and it is the pattern of the poem as a whole – almost certainly because Berryman himself saw it as the basic rhythm of life. 'We dream of honour, and we get along', he was to say later: existence is a series of small, proud assertions made within the shadow of death, little victories in the face of ultimate defeat. Undoubtedly, *Homage* is a work of the historical imagination, in that Berryman re-creates the past, makes it alive in and for the present. But it is also a personal poem to the extent that it enables him to realise his own voice by making the dead speak and tell their story: 'Madame Bovary, c'est moi', observed Flaubert and Berryman might have said something very similar about his own Mistress Bradstreet.

'Man is entirely alone /may be', Berryman remarks just over midway through *Homage*, then adds, 'I am a man of griefs & fits / trying to be my friend'. This anticipates the tone and vision of

Berryman's major work, the *Dream Songs*: the first of which were published in 1964 and the last few of which he was still writing just before his death by suicide in 1972. 'I am obliged to perform in great darkness / operations of great delicacy / on my self', Berryman admits in one of these songs, and this suggests their essential thrust. Like *Notebook*, they document, in the manner of a journal or a diary, the chaotic growth of a poet's mind: the processes of his life, in all their absurdity, fear, pain, and wonder. Unlike *Notebook*, however, the story is told with the help of a character, a person called Henry who is 'at odds wif de world and its god'. Along with his creator, Henry is many things: transient, criminal, troubled and gone, wilful, lustful, tired, ridiculous, stricken. In the course of the poem, he dies ('I am breaking up' 'Henry's parts were fleeing') and then comes back to life ('others collected and dug Henry up'); and he is aided and abetted, particularly in the earlier songs, by another character called Tambo who speaks in a thick, stage-Negro dialect. If Henry, and by extension Berryman, is 'a divided soul', then Tambo helps to dramatise that division. Tambo talks to Henry like the end man in a minstrel show, calling him 'Mister Bones' or 'Brother Bones' ('Am I a bad man? Am I a good man? / – Hard to say, Brother Bones. Maybe you both, / like most of we'). And, as he does so, the reader is irresistibly reminded of earlier dialogues of self and soul, or mind and body: but with the suspicion that these dialogues have been transposed here into a more contemporary, fragmented and disjunctive key. The shifts of mood are kaleidoscopic: boredom ('Life, friends, is boring') slides into happiness ('moments of supreme joy jerk / him on'), then into guilt ('There sat down, once, a thing on Henry's heart'), then into stoic endurance ('We suffer on, a day, a day, a day'). Within this loose, baggy monster, Berryman can incorporate pain at the death of friends ('The high ones die, die. They die'), references to his casual lecheries or heavy drinking ('a little more whisky please'), irritation with whatever power rules the world ('I'm cross with god'), and horror at the lunacies of the twentieth century ('This world is gradually becoming a place / where I do not care to be any more'). Certain themes or obsessions recur, such as the suicide of his father then, later, the pleasures of his new marriage and the birth and growth of his child: but no particular theme is allowed to dominate. 'These Songs are not meant to be understood, you understand', warns Berryman, ' / They are only meant to terrify and comfort'.[69] They are '*crazy* sounds', intended to give tongue to life as it passes: hell-bent on resisting any notions of 'ultimate structure' (although 'assistant professors' will 'become associates' trying to find one, Berryman wryly observes), or any suggestion of a stable, unitary self.

At one point in *Dream Songs*, Berryman quotes Gottfried Benn, 'We are using our own skins for wallpaper and we cannot win'. Elsewhere, he refers to his verse as 'Henry's pelt put on sundry walls'. Both remarks invite us to see the poem as raw and immediate, made up, as it were, out of pieces of the poet. The flow of the bloodstream becomes a flow of language which, while the poet lasts, cannot stop: so the poem ends, appropriately, on a note of anticipation – its last words, 'my heavy daughter', looking towards a future burdened with promise. It is worth emphasising, however, that the immediacy of these songs is the product of craft. The calculated use of personae, a lively and variable idiom, a powerfully forced syntax and dense imagery, and a fairly tight formal structure ('18 – line sections', as Berryman put it, 'three six-line stanzas, each normally (for feet) 5-5-3-5-5-3, variously rhymed'): all these things enable the poet to displace and dramatise the play of feeling, translating the 'data' that is 'abundantly his' into objective imaginative experience. The tragedy of most of Berryman's last poems is that he forgot this. 'I wiped out all the disguises', he said of these poems, '. . . the subject was . . . solely and simply myself'. Their tone varies from the brashly self-confident ('I make a high salary & royalties & fees') to the desperate ('I'm vomiting. / I broke down today in the slow movement of K365'). There are some rather repellent litanies of sexual conquests ('shagging with a rangy gay thin girl / (Miss Vaughan) I tore a section of the draperies down'), statements of belief that range from the convincing ('Man is a huddle of need') to the banal ('Nobody *knows anything*'). And, as a whole, these poems chart a progress from skirt-chasing and self-promotion to humble religious faith ('I do not understand; but I believe'). The problem is that whether Berryman is declaring 'I fell in love with a girl, / O and a gash', or admitting, 'I fell back in love with you, Father', the poetic result remains the same: the rhythms are lumpen, the imagery thin, the idiom casual to the point of sloppiness. 'I am not writing autobiography-in-verse',[70] Berryman insists: unfortunately, he is at least trying to, and very little is added to the meanings or measure of his autobiography by the use of verse. This is not so much confessional poetry, in fact, as pure confession: moving, sometimes, in the way that the confidences of any stranger might be, but not something in which we can begin to share.

The confessional 'I' as prophetess: Plath

'I've been very excited by what is the new breakthrough that came with, say, Robert Lowell's *Life Studies*', said Sylvia Plath, 'This intense breakthrough into very serious, very personal emotional experience, which I feel has been partly taboo'. 'Peculiar and private taboo subjects I feel have been explored in recent American poetry', she went on, ' – I think particularly of the poetess Anne Sexton . . . her poems are wonderfully craftsmanlike . . . and yet they have a kind of emotional and psychological depth which I think is something perhaps quite new and exciting'. Plath's excitement grew, of course, from a sense of kinship. Even her earlier poems are marked by extremism of feeling and melodic cunning of expression, as these lines from 'Lorelei' indicate:

> O river, I see drifting
>
> Deep in your flux of silver
> Those great goddesses of peace.
> Stone, stone, ferry me down there.[71]

The compulsion to go inward and downward – to immerse oneself in 'the great depths', perhaps of death – is powerfully articulated here; and it is rendered at once piercing and mournful by the verbal pattern of thin 'i' ('drifting', 'in', 'silver') and tolling 'o' ('O', 'Stone, stone', 'down') sounds. But it was in the poems published after Plath's suicide, in *Ariel*, that the impulse towards oblivion, and the pain that generated that impulse, were rendered in inimitably brutal ways: in terms, at once daring and deliberate, that compel the reader to participate in the poet's despair. The suffering at the heart of her work has received ample attention; however, the craft that draws us into that suffering is sometimes ignored. Fortunately, Plath did not ignore it. 'I think my poems come immediately out of the . . . experience I have', she admitted, ' . . . but I believe that one should be able to control and manipulate experience, even the most terrifying . . . with an informed and intelligent mind'. Her later poetry is a poetry of the edge, certainly, that takes greater risks, moves further towards the precipice than most confessional verse: but it is also a poetry that depends for its success on the mastery of her craftmanship, her ability to fabricate larger, historical meanings and imaginative myth out of personal horror. And it is a poetry, as well, that draws knowingly on honoured traditions: the Puritan habit of meditation upon last things, the American compulsion to confront the abyss of the self – above all, the burning conviction felt by poets as otherwise different as Poe and Dickinson that the imagining of death is the determining, definitive experience of life.

A poem like 'Tulips' is a good illustration of Plath's passion and her craft. Its origins lie in personal experience: a time when the poet was taken into hospital and was sent flowers as a gift. The opening four stanzas recover her feelings of peace and release on entering the hospital ward. 'Look how white everything is', she exclaims:

how quiet, how snowed-in,
I am learning peacefulness, lying by myself quietly
As the light lies on these white walls, this bed, these hands,
I am nobody . . .[72]

The verse is nominally free but has a subtle iambic base; the lines, seven to each stanza, move quietly and mellifluously; and a sense of hidden melody ('learning' / 'lying', 'lying by myself quietly', 'light lies', 'white walls') transforms apparently casual remarks into memorable speech. What is more to the point, the almost sacramental terms in which Plath describes herself turn this experience into a mysterious initiation, a dying away from the world. 'I have given my name and my day-clothes up to the nurses', Plath says, ' / And my history to the anaesthetist and my body to the surgeons'. Everything that gives her identity, that imprisons her in existence, has been surrendered; and she sinks into a condition of utter emptiness, openness that is associated at certain times here with immersion in water – a return to the foetal state and the matrix of being. The only initial resistance to this movement comes from a photograph of her husband and children she has by her bedside: reminding her, evidently, of the hell of other people, who cast 'little smiling hooks' to fish her up out of the sea.

In the next four stanzas, the tulips – mentioned briefly in the first line and then forgotten – enter the scene with a vengeance:

The tulips are too red in the first place, they hurt me.
Even through the gift paper I could hear them breathe
Lightly, through their white swaddlings, like an awful baby.
Their redness talks to my wound, it corresponds.[73]

The flowers are all that is the opposite of the white, silent world of the hospital, carrying associations of noise and pressure, 'sudden tongues and . . . colour'. They draw Plath back to life, the conditioning forces that constitute existence. She feels herself 'watched', identified by 'the eyes of the tulips': their gaze commits her to a particular status or role. What is more, this contrary impulse drawing her back into the world and identification 'corresponds' to something in herself: it comes from within her, just as the earlier impulse towards liberation did. This probably explains why the conflict of the poem remains unresolved: the ninth and final stanza of the poem simply and beautifully juxtaposes images of imprisonment and escape, the blood of life and the salt sea of death. 'And I am aware of my heart', Plath concludes:

> it opens and closes
> Its bowl of red blooms out of sheer love of me,
> The water I taste is warm and salt, like the sea,
> And comes from a country far away as health.[74]

The alternatives here are familiar ones in American writing: either to live in the world and accept the identity it prescribes, or to flee into a state of absolute freedom. What is less familiar is that, here as elsewhere, Plath associates these two alternatives, traditionally figured in the clearing and the wilderness, with the absolute conditions of being and not-being. Fixity, in these terms, is life; flight is immolation; freedom is the immediate metaphor of the hospital and the ultimate metamorphosis of death.

'Dying / Is an art, like everything else', Plath remarks in 'Lady Lazarus', '/ I do it exceptionally well'. Her poetry is artfully shaped: setting stark and elevated imagery of the sea, fire, moon, whiteness, and silence – all suggestive of the purifying, peaceful nature of oblivion – against figures of domesticity and violence – the pleasures and the pains of living in the world. Everything is incorporated within a habit of intense personal meditation, conversation with the self: 'I've got to . . . speak them to myself', Plath said of these later poems, 'Whatever lucidity they may have comes from the fact that I say them aloud'. The poems concerning the affections that tie us to this world, like 'Morning Song' (about the birth of her daughter), are notable for their wry tenderness and wonder; those that describe the false self the world requires us to construct, such as 'The Applicant', are, on the other hand, marked by a corrosive wit; while the pieces that concentrate on the ambiguous nature of death ('Death & Co.') or the perfecting of the self in the experience of dying ('Fever 103°', 'Edge') are more rapt and bardic, singed by the fire of prophecy. What characterises all this work, however, despite evident differences of tone, is the sheer seductiveness of Plath's voice: she conjures up the roots of her own violence, and the reader is caught in the spell. In 'Ariel', for instance, she transmutes a morning ride on her favourite horse into an experience of dissolution: horse, rider, and surrounding landscape are rapidly dispersed as separate entities and then reunited as energy – 'the arrow / . . . that flies / Suicidal . . . / Into the red / Eye, the cauldron of morning'.[75] The poem is not just *about* the melting of distinctions, however; it enacts that process. It takes the individual objects that constitute its raw material and renders them 'substanceless', surreal. In effect, Plath drives the poem as she drives the horse, away from the cruel particularities of phenomenal life towards a world of pure, undifferentiated force; so, for a moment, the reader sheds the compulsion to perceive and distinguish, to see and to separate, just as the poet-narrator does.

The artful way in which Plath immerses the reader in her experience is also illustrated by 'Daddy': a poem that in addition measures the distance between her use of the confessional mode and, say, Lowell's. 'Daddy', Plath said, 'is spoken by a girl with an Electra complex'. More to the point, it is based on her own ambivalent relationship with her father, (who died when she was still young), her tendency to re-create aspects of that relationship in later, adult relationships, her attempts at suicide, and her desperate need to come to terms with all these things. The secret of the poem lies in its tension. There is the tension of the narrator's attitude to her father and other men, between fear and desire, resentment and tenderness. There is tension beyond this, the poet intimates, in all human connections: the victim both detests and adores the victimiser, and so is at once repelled and attracted by the brutal drama of life. Above all, there is tension in the poem's tone. The banal horrors of personal and general history that Plath recalls are rendered in terms of fairytale and folk story; while the verse form is as insistently jaunty as that of the nursery rhymes it invokes. This manic gaiety of tone, at odds with the bleak content, has a curiously hypnotic effect on the reader, who feels almost caught by a contagion, compelled to surrender to the irresistible litany of love and hate. Nor do the closing lines bring any release. 'Daddy, daddy, you bastard, I'm through', Plath concludes: but the impression is more that she is 'through' in the sense of being over and done with than 'through' to and with her father. Like scratching a wound, the speaking of her relationship seems only to have exacerbated the pain. 'Maybe it's an irrelevant accident that she actually carried out the death she predicted . . .' Lowell observed of Plath, 'but somehow the death is part of the imaginative risk'.[76] This captures perfectly the difference between the two poets. There is an art of reconciliation and an art of resistance. There are confessional poets who discover peace, therapeutic release in the disciplines of writing and those, equally disciplined, whose writing only pushes them further towards the edge. If Lowell is an example of the former, then Plath is clearly an illustration of the latter: in the interests of her art she committed herself, ventured to the point where there was nothing left but the precipice and little, if any, chance of a return.

New formalists, new confessionals: recent departures

Since the deaths of Plath, Berryman, and Lowell, a new generation has been busy redrawing the map of American poetry. Among this generation are some notable formalists, poets who necessarily derive their inspiration from personal experience but use a variety of means to distance things and disengage their work from autobiography. The personal stimulus and the desire for disengagement are particularly remarkable in the work of Charles Wright. 'I write poems to untie myself, to do penance and disappear / Through the upper right-hand corner of things', he declares in one poem; other typical lines are, 'I am weary of daily things', 'I'm going away now, goodbye'. If the first person enters Wright's poetry, it does so only to be erased. His poetry is poetry of an 'I' yearning for transcendence, and its own obliteration. It is a poetry of spiritual hunger, rather than fulfilment: expressed sometimes directly ('I want to be bruised by God . . . / . . . / I want to be entered and picked clean') and sometimes through symbolism of, say, a chrysalis turning into a mayfly or the Milky Way ('The spider, juiced crystal and Milky Way . . . / . . . looks down, waiting for us to ascend'). The structures Wright chooses – the three stanza form of 'Tattoos', for instance, or the twelve and fourteen line forms of *China Trace* and 'Skins' – are clearly a part of this larger project: seeking the still point of the turning world, he commits himself to spatial forms, a frozen moment, arrested motion. 'I'm talking about stillness',[77] Wright says; and that stillness is something he tries to imitate in his remote and severe lines.

Analogous but subtly different kinds of distancing are to be found in the work of Amy Clampitt and Louise Glück. Clampitt has a habit of weaving the phenomenal world into an artful piece of embroidery. In 'The Kingfisher', for example, the calculated play of imagery, a strict and quite complex stanzaic form, winding syntactical shapes and a feeling for words as distinctly odd artefacts: all help transmute the story of a love-affair into a tapestry, rich and strange – or, as Clampitt herself puts it, into 'an illuminated manuscript in which all the handiwork happens to be verbal'.[78] With Glück, the effects is not so much of a mosaic as of ritual, as these lines, from a poem describing a first day at school, memorably illustrate:

> And the teachers shall instruct them in silence
> and the mothers shall scour the orchards for a way out,
> drawing to themselves the gray limbs of the fruit trees
> bearing so little ammunition.[79]

Glück's poems deal with themes that are intimately personal in origin: family life ('Poem', 'Still Life'), motherhood and children ('All Hallows', 'The Drowned Children'), a lost sister ('Descending Figure'), love between a man and a woman ('Happiness'). But everything is rendered in an oblique, impersonal manner, seen as if through the wrong end of a telescope. The actors in these human dramas are usually anonymous; there is a timeless quality to their actions; and the terms in which they are rescued for our attention possess the stark inevitability of fable. This is the realm of divination, or myth: an oracular voice tells us of events that are dreamily repetitive, foreknown yet mysterious because they are attached at all times to certain rites of passage, the primal and traumatic experiences of birth, growing up, and death.

Along with these new departures in formalism, however, poetry of the personal has continued unabated. In several instances, recent writers have developed the tradition of relating identity to landscape. John Haines, for instance, connects the wintry surroundings of Alaska, and the Middle West 'with its trodden snow / and black Siberian trees', to harsh visions of himself and his culture: the natural world is seen in terms of internecine conflict ('Here too are life's victims', he exclaims), and so too is America ('There are too many . . . / . . . / columns of brutal strangers'). His aim, evidently, is to identify himself with these conflicts: to participate in a struggle that is at once elemental and political. The tone of this involvement is sometimes celebratory ('I believe in this stalled magnificence'), sometimes meditative ('I walked among them, / I listened and understood') and occasionally angry ('There will be many poems written in the shape of a grenade').[80] Whatever, it constantly recalls that great poet of participation, Whitman: for Haines shares with the Good Gray Poet not only a populist impulse and a feel for organic rhythms but also a radicalism that is both personal and political – a commitment to revolution in the self along with revolution in the state. Similar echoes of Whitman, tracing a correspondence between inner and outer worlds, are to be found in the work of Robert Pinsky: a poet who tries to capture what he calls the 'mothlike' life, 'the thin / Halting qualities of the soul' hovering behind 'The glazed surface of the world'. Pinsky's voice, quieter than Haines's, may sound ordinary, but that is precisely the point: like Whitman, he is obsessed with the heroism of the ordinary – or even of the apparently banal. So he describes 'the tyranny of the world visible', and in particular the suburban landscapes of New Jersey, and hints at the 'unique/Soul' beneath this, the 'hideous, sudden stare of self' that can be glimpsed by the sympathetic imagination. American life is marked for him by its doubleness: there is 'cash, tennis, fine electronics', certainly, but there is 'music, . . . yearning, suffering' as well. A favourite setting, the seashore, implies this duality of perspective. Set between the mysterious ocean and 'vast, uncouth houses', Pinsky and his characters inhabit a border area. They want the shock of vision and they want simply to make a living: they work 'For truth and for money' – two very different yet related 'stays /

Against boredom, discomfort, death and old age'.[81]

Dave Smith also secretes the poetry of the personal in the poetry of place: 'Grandfather', he declares in one poem, 'I wish I had the guts to tell you this is a place I hope / I never have to go through again'. Only in his case the place is Southern: the 'anonymous fishing village' where he lives, perhaps, the woods and rivers ('The Last Morning'), a disused railway ('Cumberland Station'), or a Civil War cemetery ('Fredericksburg'). His poetry is saturated in locality, focussing in particular on what most art, in its pursuit of an 'entirely eloquent peace', 'fails to see': the disinherited, those victimised by society and often excluded from its frames of reference. And through this plenitude of landscape moves the poet himself, trying to 'hold . . . obscure syllables / one instant.'[82] He, it seems, is given a local habitation and a name by these places: the 'I', or habit of being, is given presence by the 'eye', the observation of extrinsic detail. Another way of putting this would be to say that, for all his interest in the personal, Smith – like Haines and Pinsky – chooses to refract personality: to clothe the naked self in the warm details of circumstantiality. This, as we know, has not always been the case in American poetry; and it is not so now – as these lines, all from poems published since 1970, illustrate:

> If it resists me, I know it's real.
> I feel too much. I can't stand what I feel.
>
> (Frank Bidart, 'Happy Birthday')
>
> a ways off looking at you, my grandpa
> people listened to, I stand
> a ways off listening as I pour out soup
> young men with light in their faces
> at my table, talking love, talking revolution
>
> (Diane Di Prima, 'April Fool Birthday Poem for Grandpa')
>
> I, always slightly overweight according to Vogue standards,
> and living in the richest country in the world,
> would not be fairly using the material to hand
> were I not to speak of my own experiences[83]
>
> (Diane Wakoski, 'Greed, Part 3')

The poets responsible for these lines are, naturally, very different. Bidart splices disparate material together, forging a disjunctive, extremist art out of his feelings of rage, impotence, and alienation; Di Prima, by contrast, links bright, particular accounts of her life to an unashamedly optimistic vision of the political future ('America has not even begun as yet. / This continent is in seed'); whereas Wakoski is more exclusively confessional, favouring what she terms 'the completely personal expression'. The differences are, however, relatively insignificant; what matters is the original impulse, which is the same with each poet. This is poetry of the primal scream: speech that, in obedience to the most fundamental of American impulses, springs immediately out of the depths of identity, the innermost recesses of the self. It cries out in the anxiety and joy of the first person singular, and what it says simply is this: 'Here I am; the poem is me; listen'.

Notes

1. Irving Howe, 'This Age of Conformity,' *Partisan Review*, 1952. See also, Robert Lowell, 'Memories of West Street and Lepke', line 12. Also, Carl N. Degler, *Affluence and Anxiety* (Glenview, Ill., 1968); Eric Goldman, *The Crucial Decade and After: America, 1945–1960* (New York, 1960); David M. Potter, *People of Plenty: Economic Abundance and the American Character* (Chicago, 1954).
2. See Richard Rovere, *Senator Joe McCarthy* (New York, 1959).
3. See David Caute, *The Great Fear: The Anticommunist Purge Under Truman and Eisenhower* (London, 1978).
4. Louis Simpson, 'The Battle', lines 13–16. See also, 'The Heroes', lines 1, 14; Randall Jarrell, 'A Lullaby', line 2; Karl Shapiro, 'The Gun', lines 14–15; 'Troop Train', line 33; 'Lord, I Have Seen Too Much', line 1.
5. Randall Jarrell, 'Mail Call', line 5. See also, Shapiro, 'Lord, I Have Seen Too Much', line 13.
6. Randall Jarrell, 'The Face', lines 8–10. See also, line 25; 'A Note on Poetry', in *Kipling, Auden & Co.: Essays and Reviews 1935–1964* (Manchester, 1981), p. 49; 'The Island', lines 26–27; 'A Girl in a Library', lines 1, 60, 93; 'The Orient Express', lines 35–4; 'The Lines', lines 7–8.
7. W. H. Auden, 'Introduction' to W. S. Merwin, (*A Mask for Janus*) (New Haven, Conn., 1952), p. viii. See also, p. vii.
8. Richard Wilbur, 'Museum Piece', line 12. See also, *Responses: Prose Pieces, 1953–1976* (New York, 1976), pp. 19, 94; 'Objects', lines 27–28.
9. Richard Wilbur, 'The Beautiful Changes', lines 7–8. See also, 'Objects', lines 15–16.
10. Shapiro, 'I'm writing this poem for someone to see', line 1; Simpson, 'Sacred Objects', lines 1–3; Sexton, 'Rowing', lines 3–6; Baraka, 'Numbers, Letters', lines 29–30; Rich, 'Upper Broadway', lines 11, 19–20; Snodgrass, 'April Inventory', lines 26–28; Logan, 'Three Moves', lines 15–17; Berryman, 'Damned', lines 17–18; Plath, 'Lady Lazarus', lines 20–21; Lowell, 'Skunk Hour', lines 35–36. See also, Wilbur, *Responses*, p. 25.

11. Robert Bly, 'When the Wheel Does Not Move', line 1. See also, *Talking All Morning* (Ann Arbor, Mich., 1980), p. 116.
12. Robert Kelly, 'prefix:', lines 7–12. See also, 'Jealousy', section 5, lines 9–14.
13. Galway Kinnell, *Walking Down the Stairs: Selections from Interviews* (Ann Arbor, Mich., 1978), p. 79.
14. Galway Kinell, 'Another Night in the Ruins', section 7, lines 1–2. See also, 'The Bear', section 7, line 16.
15. Wright, 'Lying in a Hammock at William Duffy's Farm in Pine Island, Minnesota', lines 12–13. See also, line 6; *Twenty Poems of Georg Trakl* (Madison, Wisc. 1961).
16. Richard Hugo, 'Montgomery Hollow', lines 26–27. See also, 'Degrees of Gray in Philipsburg', lines 11, 19.
17. Karl Shapiro, 'Priests and Freudians will understand', line 5. See also, 'Lower the standard: that's my motto'; 'Why poetry small and cramped', line 1.
18. Louis Simpson, 'Walt Whitman at Bear Mountain', lines 8–9. See also, 'Sacred Objects', lines 4–5.
19. Logan 'Three Moves', lines 40–42. See also, line 36.
20. John Logan, 'Spring of the Thief', lines 95–9.
21. W. D. Snodgrass, 'Heart's Needle', poem 6, line 8: *In Radical Pursuit: Critical Essays and Lectures* (New York, 1975), p. 176
22. Ann Sexton, 'The Farmer's Wife', lines 27–32. See also, 'In Celebration of my Uterus', lines 44–5; 'Rowing', lines 45–46; *The Distinctive Voice: Twentieth Century American Poetry* edited by William J. Martz (Glenview, Ill., 1966), p. 297.
23. Adrienne Rich, lines 52–4, 61–63. See also, 'Aunt Jennifer's Tigers', lines 1, 4, 7–8, 11–12; *On Lies, Secrets and Silence: Selected Prose 1966–1978* (New York, 1979), p. 112.
24. Adrienne Rich, 'Foreword' to *Poems: Selected and New, 1950–1974* (New York, 1974), pp. xv–xvi.
25. Alan Dugan, in *Distinctive Voice*, p. 243.
26. Robert Bly, 'Looking into a Face', lines 7–10. See also C. G. Jung, *The Archetypes and the Collective Unconscious, Collected Works*, IX (Princeton, N.J., 1959), p. 279.
27. W. S. Merwin, 'The Morning', lines 1–4. See also, 'An Encampment at Morning', lines 13–14.
28. Delmore Schwartz, 'Seurat's Sunday Afternoon along the Seine', lines 55–58. See also, lines 35–36; 'Far Rockaway', line 23; 'Tired and Unhappy, You Think of Houses', lines 2, 12; 'O City, City', lines 1–2, 3, 12, 14; 'Parlez-Vous Français?', line 15; 'A Young Child and His Pregnant Mother', line 24; 'The Ballad of the Children of the Czar', lines 29–30, 64; 'Father and Son', lines 14–15, 63; 'Someone is Harshly Coughing as Before', lines 8, 10, 13; John Berryman, *The Dream Songs* (New York, 1969), songs 146–156.
29. William Stafford, *Distinctive Voice*, p. 190. See also, pp. 199, 243; David Ignatow, *The Notebooks of David Ignatow* edited by Ralph J. Mills, Jr. (Chicago, 1973), p. 9.

30. Alan Dugan, 'Prayer', lines 2–3. See also, John Ciardi, 'In Place of a Curse', line 1.
31. William Stafford, 'A Ritual to Read to Each Other', lines 19–20. See also, 'The Trip', line 1; 'Lake Chelan', lines 1–2.
32. David Ignatow, 'Waiting Inside', lines 3–7. See also, *Notebooks*, p. 134.
33. Philip Levine, 'Animals Are Passing From Our Lives', lines 14–16, 19–20, 24. See also, 'One for the Rose', lines 1–2; 'Ashes', lines 1, 15–17.
34. A. R. Ammons, 'Corson's Inlet', lines 82–86. See also, lines 1, 14–17, 93, 94–95, 115–16. See also, 'Gravelly Run', lines 3–4.
35. A. R. Ammons, *Tape for the Turn of the Year* (Ithaca, N.Y., 1965). See also, 'Corson's Inlet', lines 126–8; 'Cut the Grass', line 1.
36. Sylvia Plath, Interview and reading of poems for the British Council.
37. Denis Knight, 'Schoolday in Man Quang', lines 1–4. See also, Thanasis Maskaloris, 'Hecuba in Vietnam', line 1. Both poems are in *Where is Vietnam? American Poets Respond* edited by Walter Lowenfels (New York, 1967).
38. Allen Ginsberg, 'Wichita Vortex Sutra', section II. See also, Adrienne Rich, 'Implosions', line 12; Robert Bly, *The Teeth Mother Naked at Last*, section II.
39. Robert Bly, 'War and Silence', lines 1–3.
40. Robert Lowell, 'Waking Early Sunday Morning', lines 105–12.
41. William Stafford, 'At the Bomb Testing Site', lines 9–12. See also, lines 2–3; Galway Kinnell, 'Vapour Trail Reflected in the Frog Pond', lines 1–3.
42. William Carlos Williams, 'Asphodel, That Greeny Flower', book II, lines 70, 72–73. See also, line 41; 'Coda', line 17.
43. Sylvia Plath, 'Nick and the Candlestick', lines 37–42. See also, James Merrill, *The Changing Light at Sandover* (New York, 1982).
44. Richard Wilbur, 'Advice to Prophet', lines 16–21. See also, lines 26–27, 33.
45. Stanley Kunitz, 'Foreign Affairs', lines 1, 24, 30.
46. Howard Nemerov, 'The Gulls', lines 30–2. See also, lines 1, 9–11, 17–18; 'Trees', lines 16–17.
47. Anthony Hecht, 'More Light! More Light!', lines 13–16. See also, Reed Whittemore, 'Still Life', lines 18–19; Weldon Kees, 'January', line 20; Donald Justice, 'But That is Another Story', line 1; Edgar Bowers, 'The Mountain Cemetery', lines 11–12; X. J. Kennedy, 'Nude Descending a Staircase', lines 3–4.
48. Elizabeth Bishop, 'Efforts of Affection: A Memoir of Marianne Moore', in *The Collected Prose* edited by Robert Giroux (London, 1984), p. 149. See also, Jarrell, *Poetry and the Age*, p. 210.
49. Elizabeth Bishop, 'The Map', lines 24–27. See also, lines 10–11, 19–20.
50. Elizabeth Bishop, 'Filling Station', lines 36–41. See also, 'Questions of Travel', line 15; 'Brazil, January 1, 1502'.
51. Elizabeth Bishop, 'At the Fishhouses', lines 78–83. See also, line 60; 'In the Waiting Room', lines 54–55, 60–61, 72–74; 'Sandpiper', lines 3–4; 'The Fish', lines 66–67, 69–70, 74–75.

52. Theodore Roethke, 'Open House', lines 1–4. See also, lines 9, 11.
53. Theodore Roethke, 'Cuttings (later)', lines 5–11.
54. Theodore Roethke, 'Once More, the Round', line 12. See also, 'Night Crow', line 8; 'Open Letter', in *On the Poet and His Craft: Selected Prose of Theodore Roethke* edited by Ralph J. Mills, Jr. (Seattle, Wash., 1965), p. 10; 'Some Remarks on Rhythm', ibid., p. 181.
55. Theodore Roethke, 'Unfold! Unfold!', lines 12–13. See also, line 9; 'Open Letter', pp. 37–39.
56. Roethke, 'Unfold! Unfold!', lines 41–43.
57. Theodore Roethke, 'The Waking', line 24. See also, 'Meditations of an Old Woman: First Meditation', lines 18, 19, 20–21, 26, 74–75, 98–99; 'Memory', lines 1, 2; 'Otto', line 4; 'I Know a Woman', line 1; 'The Dying Man', lines 1, 102–3; 'The Longing', lines 57–58; 'The Manifestation', line 1.
58. Ian Hamilton, *Robert Lowell: A Biography* (London, 1983), p. 233. See also, p. 471.
59. Robert Lowell, 'Children of Light', lines 6–10. See also, lines 1, 4.
60. Robert Lowell, 'Skunk Hour', lines 25–30. See also, Hamilton, *Lowell: A Biography*, p. 309.
61. Lowell, 'Skunk Hour', lines 43–48. See also, Hamilton, *Lowell: A Biography*, p. 337.
62. Robert Lowell, 'For the Union Dead', lines 65–68. See also, lines 34–35, 37–38.
63. Robert Lowell, 'Reading Myself', lines 10, 14. See, Author's Note to *Notebook, 1967–1968* (London, 1969).
64. Robert Lowell, 'Epilogue', lines 15–23. See also, lines 8, 10, 13; Thoreau, *Walden*, ch. 1.
65. Robert Lowell, 'The Poetry of John Berryman', *New York Review of Books*, May 28, 1964. See also, 'For John Berryman', lines 9–11; 'For John Berryman: I', lines 1–3.
66. John Berryman, *Berryman's Sonnets* (New York, 1967), sonnet 115. See also, *Dream Songs*, song 51; 'The Art of Poetry XVI', *The Paris Review* (Winter 1972), 179.
67. John Berryman, *Homage to Mistress Bridstreet*, stanza 57. See also, stanza 33; *Berryman's Sonnets*, sonnet 23; 'One Answer to a Question: Changes', in *The Freedom of the Poet* (New York, 1976), p. 327.
68. Berryman, *Homage to Mistress Bradstreet*, stanza 7. See also, stanza 12; 'One Answer to a Question: Changes', p. 328; *Dream Songs*, song 42.
69. Berryman, *Dream Songs*, song 366. See also, songs 5, 14, 29, 36, 67, 78, 84, 91, 149, 153, 239, 271, 293, 325, 337, 373; *Homage to Mistress Bradstreet*, stanza 35.
70. John Berryman, 'Message', line 4. See also, *Dream Songs*, songs 16, 53, 148, 385; 'Art of Poetry XVI', 179; 'In & Out', lines 35–36; 'Despair', lines 7–8; 'My Special Fate', lines 13–14; 'A Huddle of Need', line 19; 'Have a Genuine American Horror-&-Mist on the Rocks', line 8; 'A Prayer for the Self', line 3; 'Her & It', line 1; 'Eleven Addresses to the Lord', no. 10, line 5.

71. Sylvia Plath, 'Lorelei', lines 33–36. See also, Interview for the British Council; *The Poet Speaks*, Argo Record Co., No. RG 455 (recorded, October 30, 1962).
72. Sylvia Plath, 'Tulips', lines 2–5. See also, lines 6–7.
73. Ibid., lines 36–39. See also, lines 41, 43.
74. Ibid., lines 60–63.
75. Sylvia Plath, 'Ariel', lines 27–31. See also, 'Lady Lazarus', lines 43–45; Interview for the British Council.
76. Cited by M. L. Rosenthal, 'Sylvia Plath and Confessional Poetry', in *The Art of Sylvia Plath: A Symposium* edited by Charles Newman (London, 1970), p. 74. See also, Introductory Notes to 'New Poems', a reading prepared for the B.B.C.
77. Charles Wright, 'Morandi', line 1. See also, 'Revision', lines 4–5; 'Next', line 1; 'Childhood', line 7; 'Clear Night', line 5; 'Spider Crystal Ascension', lines 1–2.
78. Amy Clampitt, Note to 'The Kingfisher'.
79. Louise Glück, 'The School Children', lines 11–14.
80. John Haines, 'A Poem Like A Grenade', lines 17–18. See also, 'In the Middle of America', lines 2–3, 30–31; 'In Nature', line 1; 'It Must All Be Done Over . . .', lines 8, 12; 'The Snowbound City', line 1.
81. Robert Pinsky, 'The Beach Women', lines 5–12. See also, 'To My Father', lines 1, 6–7, 38, 45; 'Poem About People', lines 21–22. 31; 'Essay on Psychiatrists', section XX1.
82. Dave Smith, 'On a Field Trip at Fredericksburg', lines 35–36. See also, 'Cumberland Station', lines 71–73; 'The Perspective and Limits of Snapshots', lines 8, 23.
83. Frank Bidart, 'Happy Birthday', lines 35–36; Diane Di Prima, 'April Fool Birthday Poem for Grandpa', lines 24–30; Diane Wakoski, 'Greed, Part 3', lines 4–7. See also, Diane Di Prima, 'Revolutionary Letter 10', lines 5–6; Diane Wakoski, Preface to *The Collected Greed: Parts 1–13* (Santa Barbara, Calif., 1984).

Chapter 6
Beats, Prophets, and Aesthetes: American Poetry since the Second World War

From the public to the personal: social and cultural tendencies of the Sixties and after

> Let the word go forth from this time and place, to friend and foe alike, that the torch has been passed to a new generation of Americans, born in this century, tempered by war, disciplined by a hard and bitter peace, proud of our ancient heritage, and unwilling to witness or permit the slow undoing of those human rights to which this nation has always been committed, and to which we are committed today at home and around the world.

The words are those of President John F. Kennedy, spoken at his Inaugural on 20th January, 1961. Kennedy had won the election by only the narrowest of margins: but, once elected, he brought with him to the office the expectation of great change, an optimism and confidence about the character of the United States and its role in the world that many Americans were eager to share. His words were ambiguous, to say the least. Did they anticipate the elimination of poverty and inequality or a renewed aggressiveness in foreign policy – or perhaps both? Despite that (or, it may be, even because of it), they struck a responsive chord in the heart of the nation. 'We stand today on the edge of a new frontier,' Kennedy declared, '. . . a frontier of unknown opportunities and perils . . . I am asking each of you to be pioneers on that New Frontier.' The appeal to the apparently timeless myth of the West, pioneering and conquest, was echoed in the words of Robert Frost at the Inaugural. Frost had been invited to the ceremony as America's unofficial poet laureate, and as an emblem of Kennedy's belief that he could, among many other things, preside over a revitalisation of the nation's cultural life. The poet, eighty-six years old now, had prepared some verses especially for the occasion. However, the sun was particularly bright that day (as if nature itself was aware of the symbolic character of the occasion, heralding the hope of a new dawn!). Blinded by the light, Frost was unable to read the words he had written; and so, instead, he recited from memory another of his poems, 'The Gift Outright.' Just like Kennedy's speech, it caught the confidence, the ambition, the sense of potential, and, some might say, the arrogance of a 'new generation of Americans' and wedded all this to the ideology of a long-vanished frontier:

> This land was ours before we were the land's.
> She was our land more than a hundred years
> Before we were her people . . .
> . . .
> Such as we were we gave ourselves outright
> (The deed of gift was many deeds of war)
> To the land vaguely realising westward,
> But still unstoried, artless, unenhanced,
> Such as she was, such as she would become.[1]

The America to and for which both poet and President spoke was a constellation of many new attitudes and forces: a nation of 180 million people, a growing number of whom were white suburbanites living in quiet comfort on the edge of the older, urban areas, buying their goods in out-of-town shopping malls, and working in white-collar service-sector industries. Nine out of ten families, by this time, owned a television, and six out of ten of them a car. The gross national product seemed to move inexorably upward, from 285 billion dollars in 1950 to 503 billion in 1960, and so too did the population index: during the Fifties, the population had risen by 18.5 per cent. Most of this increase was due to the rapid rise in the birth-rate and a prolonged life-expectancy, rather than to immigration; and the result was that nearly half of the population now was either under eighteen or over sixty-five, too young or too old to participate in the economic life of the nation. To those excluded by youth or age from full participation in the nation's growing wealth could be added those excluded by race or situation: fruitpickers in California, say, black sharecroppers in the South, and the different ethnic groups comprising the urban poor. While the income of middle-class Americans of working age continued to improve, that of the bottom 20 per cent showed hardly any advance at all. There was conspicuous abundance, certainly, but there was equally conspicuous poverty: the rhetoric of the President possibly acknowledged this but it tended to be forgotten amidst the general euphoria, the sense of irresistible expansion and movement forwards towards a 'New Frontier.' And it was only in the later Sixties that the seeds of discontent and dissension sowed by this conspicuous contrast between haves and have-nots began to be harvested.[2]

In the meantime, in the early Sixties, optimism and the promise of adventure were in the air. Responding to the sense of new frontiers to be conquered, many artists of the period, of every kind, were notable for their willingness to experiment. A decade is, of course, an artificial measure and, in this respect as in many others, 'the Sixties' had really begun in the middle to late Fifties: when the popular arts were revivified by a new sense of energy and anger, and a lively *avant-garde* embarked on challenging conventional mores and forms. Happenings, festivals, multi-media performances became commonplace events; readings of poetry and prose, often to jazz accompaniment, attracted dedicated audiences. In poetry, the wars between the different 'schools,' the confessionals and the beats, the Black Mountain poets and the New York group, generated publicity and created the sense that a thousand new poetic blooms were flowering in a genuine renaissance. There was a sense of *risk*, of venturing beyond the formalism, the preoccupation with craftsmanship of the earlier decade. Poems became more open, rawer, alert to the possibility of change and the inclusion of random factors. Whether it was Charles Olson exploring the notion of 'projective' verse or Frank O'Hara celebrating 'personism,' there was a renewed emphasis on chance, arbitrariness, impermanency, a new willingness to see the artistic object as shifting, discontinuous, part of the flux and variety of things. 'this country might have/been a pio/neer land. once,' declared the black poet Sonia Sanchez, 'and it still is.'[3] For poets like Sanchez, confessionalism, spontaneity, and free form were another way of tuning into the aggressive confidence of the times and tapping the energies of the American tradition. They were a way of saying that poetry, too, was on the edge of a new frontier.

If the Inauguration of President Kennedy acted as a catalyst for the optimism of the early Sixties, then his assassination in Dallas in November, 1963, served as a focus for energies of another kind. The belief in the possibility of radical change persisted but it was now contained within a harsher, more abrasive and confrontational sense of the social realities. The divisions and discontent that had always been there – in a society still painfully split between rich and poor, white and black, suburbanite and ghetto-dweller – now came to the surface; the violence that brought the President's life to an end was echoed in the national life, at home and abroad. Of course, there was and is an honoured tradition of protest in American life, ever since the Puritan settlement, and a spirit of unease had been particularly notable in the culture since the late Fifties, symbolised by popular heroes like James Dean and poetic heroes like Allen Ginsberg. But now the protest became more widespread and exacerbated, and the uneasiness burgeoned into open revolt. The Civil Rights movement, for example, grew more militant. Instead of merely boycotting segregated businesses and services, black and white activists began to use them, challenging the authorities to enforce iniquitous segregationist laws. Confrontations occurred in several Southern townships, between civil-rights workers and white authorities: in Little Rock, Arkansas, for instance, in Selma, Alabama, and Oxford, Mississippi. In August, 1963, there was a massive demonstration in Washington D.C., involving over a quarter of a million people, who heard Martin Luther King, the movement's inspired leader, talk of his dream of a multi-racial society. The demonstration was notably and triumphantly peaceful: but, in this respect, it marked the end of an era. Within a few years, King himself had been assassinated, and the ghettoes of Los Angeles, Detroit, New York, Washington, and many other cities were aflame. During the late Sixties, it seemed as if rioting in the streets of the cities had become an annual event, as black people expressed their anger with a social and economic order that tended to deprive them of their basic rights. At the same time, the nation's universities were the scene of almost equally violent confrontations, as students expressed their resistance to local university authorities and the power of the state.

For university students, as for many other protest groups of the time, the central issue was the Vietnam War. In the summer of 1964, President Lyndon Johnson persuaded Congress to give him almost unlimited powers to wage war against what was perceived as the Communist threat from North Vietnam. American troops were committed to a massive land war against an indigenous guerilla movement; the American military was involved in saturation bombing and what was euphemistically known as 'defoliation' – that is, destruction of the forests, the vegetation and plant life of a country situated about 12,000 miles from Washington; and American policy was, effectively, to bleed the nation's human and economic resources in support of what was little more than a puppet government in South Vietnam. By 1967, millions of Americans were beginning to feel that the war was not only useless but obscene, and took to the streets in protest: these included novelists, like Norman Mailer, and poets like Robert Lowell and Allen Ginsberg. Simultaneously with this, in response to what looked like the obscenity of the official culture, a vigorous alternative culture developed. Much of this alternative culture was specifically political in its direction. Young men burned their draft cards; and, when the Democratic Party met in Chicago in 1968 to nominate their candidate for President, young people upstaged the proceedings by engaging in pitched battles with police in the streets. But much of it, too, had to do with styles of life and styles of art. Hair was worn unconventionally long, skirts unconventionally short; hallucinogenic drugs, psychedelic art, hugely amplified rock concerts all became part of an instinctive strategy for challenging standard versions of social reality, accepted notions of behaviour and gender. The analytical mode was supplanted by the expressive, the intellectual by the imaginative; and artists as a whole went even further towards embracing a sense of the provisional, a fluid, unstructured reality. Poets like Ginsberg and Ferlinghetti howled their protests to large and enthusiastic audiences or, like Gary Snyder or Ed Dorn, explored new forms of consciousness and perception. And artistic eclecticism became the norm, as writers in general hit upon unexpected aesthetic mixtures: mingling fantasy and commitment, myth and social protest, high and popular art.

One of the paradoxes of the year 1968 was that it witnessed alternative culture at its zenith *and* the election of Richard Nixon, self-proclaimed spokesman for the 'silent majority' of white, middle-class Americans, to the office of President. To the extent that 'the Sixties' have become a convenient label for a particular frame of mind – radical, experimental, subversive, and even confrontational – they did not end in 1970 any more than they began in 1960. Many aspects of the alternative culture survived well into the next decade; and some, like the feminist and ecological movements, effectively became part of the cultural mainstream. Nevertheless the election of such an un-alternative, un-radical President as Nixon, and his re-election in 1972, did signal a shift in the national mood that was gradually confirmed throughout the Seventies and beyond. The Vietnam War was brought to an ignominious end, removing one of the major sources of confrontation and revolt. Black Americans remained economically dispossessed, but the Civil Rights movement did increase their electoral power, and so gave them the opportunity of expressing their dissatisfaction through the ballot-box rather than taking to the streets. The children of the post-war 'baby boom', who had fuelled the fires of apparent revolution, began to enter the workforce and take on the responsibilities of jobs, homes, and families. And, while the United States continued to prosper – the gross national product had risen to 974 billion in 1970 – there were worrying signs of possible economic crisis. Inflation was worse than in most Western European countries; the balance of payments deficit began to grow to frightening proportions; while the dollar steadily lost its purchasing power. As the economic situation grew harsher, especially after the oil crisis of the early Seventies, more and more Americans narrowed their horizons, devoting their attention and energies to the accumulation and preservation of personal wealth. One commentator christened the Seventies 'the me decade'; another referred to the culture of narcissism.[4] And these significant tendencies did not alter with the resignation of Nixon. First Gerald Ford, and then later Jimmy Carter and Ronald Reagan, offered notable alternatives to the radicalism of the Sixties. With Carter, for instance, there was a new emphasis on the limits to growth and power and a new, introspective moralism: 'Your strength,' he told the American public at his Inaugural in 1977, 'can compensate for my weakness, and your wisdom can help minimise my mistakes.' More recently, the rhetoric of Reagan may sound similar, at times, to that of Kennedy: when, for instance, he talks about building a shining city upon a hill or declares that the best years of America are yet to come. But this rhetoric occurs within structures of beliefs and assumptions that are quite different from those of the assassinated President. For Reagan, the crucial appeal is to the past, the mythical American past of stable, familial, and to an extent pastoral values, that, as he sees it, it is the duty of Americans to recover; and to this predominantly backward-looking impulse is added a strong sense of personal responsibility, a feeling that each American should look after himself or herself, which finds little room for accommodating the communal vision of an earlier decade.

Culturally, this renewed emphasis on the personal and, to some degree, inherited values of self-help and self-improvement has found its expression in such otherwise different texts as *Zen and the Art of Motorcycle Maintenance* by Robert M. Pirsig, *The Presentation of the Self in Everyday Life* by Erving Goffman, and *Jane Fonda's Work-Out Book.* There has been a notable drift, at every level, away from public affairs and commitment and towards introspection, the cult of the personal. Writers have, for the most part, turned away from immediate history, the pressures of the times, and devoted their imaginations to the vagaries of consciousness, the deeper forms of myth, ritual, and fantasy, the imagery figured and the language articulated by the isolated mind. Inevitably, there are exceptions to this, such as the novelist E. L. Doctorow or the poets John Haines and Ed Dorn. Equally inevitably, even the most personal of contemporary poets have to devote some of their attention to problems of class, race, and gender – and even, sometimes, to such crucial social and political issues as ecology or the bomb. But the drift, or tendency, is clear. There is a recovery of intimacy in, say, the more recent poems of John Ashbery and James Merrill, an almost painful investigation of the self in the work of Frank Bidart, Diane Di Prima, and Diane Wakoski, a withdrawal into worlds of resonant abstraction or hieratic distance in the writings of Louise Glück or Amy Clampitt: in short, there is a renewed emphasis on the central, organising, and private consciousness in the poems of the past two decades that marks, not a break with the work of the Sixties, but nevertheless a significant shift of stress. The personal has always been there in American poetry. But it is there, perhaps, more clearly now than at any time since the War. Certainly, it is there with a strength of feeling and an exclusiveness of focus that has been unmatched for some time.

Rediscovering the American voice: the Black Mountain poets (Olson, J. Williams, Levertov, Blackburn, Wieners, Creeley, Dorn, Duncan)

In 1950, Charles Olson began his essay on 'Projective Verse' in this way:

> (projectile (percussive (prospective
>
> *vs.*
>
> The NON-Projective[5]

With these words, he declared war on both the formalists and the confessionals; and he announced the emergence of new and powerful forces in post-war American poetry. 'Closed' verse, the structured and metered writing 'which print bred' was to be jettisoned, Olson declared: so too was 'the private-soul-at-any-public-wall', the lyricism and introspection of the strictly personal approach. What was required was an 'open' poetry. A poem, he announced, was 'a high energy-construct', the function of which was to transfer energy 'from where the poet got it' in experience 'to the reader'. This transfer could be achieved by means of 'FIELD COMPOSITION': 'FORM IS NEVER MORE THAN AN EXTENSION OF CONTENT', Olson insisted, writing the words large (as he often did) to register the importance of what he was saying. And in his view the ideal form would consist of a steady, dense stream of perceptions: 'ONE PERCEPTION', as he put it, 'MUST IMMEDIATELY AND DIRECTLY LEAD TO A FURTHER PERCEPTION', so that the poem could become more 'the act of the instant' than 'the act of thought about the instant'. The 'smallest particle' in this form, or rather field, would be the syllable, 'the king and pin of versification': the poet should always pay attention to the sound of the syllables as they unrolled from the mind and appealed to the ear. 'It is by their syllables that words juxtapose in beauty', Olson said; and these syllables, energetically constructed, should in turn rule and hold together the lines, which constituted 'the larger forms' of the poem. 'The line comes . . . from the breath, from the breathing of the man who writes', Olson argued, 'at the moment he writes'; it was therefore unique to the poet and the occasion. Breath reified experience by creating an awareness of bodily 'depth sensibility': the poet responded to the flow and pressure of things, he registered this in his diaphragm, and he then compelled his readers, by sharing his breathing rhythms, to feel the same pressures and participate in the flow of the moment.

Several points could be made about Olson's notions of 'projective' or 'open' poetry. In the first place, they clearly have antecedents in the theory and practice of the Imagists and Objectivists. Fundamental to Olson's approach is a belief in the process, particularity, and instantaneity of things. 'There is only one thing you can do about kinetic, reenact it'; 'things, and present ones, are the absolute conditions'; 'if there is any absolute, it is never more than this one, you, this instant in action':[6] such remarks recall earlier ones by Pound and Williams, just as Olson's emphasis on the syllable and breath echo Pound's references to the 'sequence of the musical phrase' and Williams's experiments with the variable foot. In the second, Olson's several statements of artistic intent are at the very least symptomatic of a wider revolution in the post-war arts. 'While I am *in* my painting', Jackson Pollock suggested, 'I'm not aware of what I'm doing'; 'the painting has a life of its own', he went on, 'I try to let it come through'. Pollock's interest in art as action, participation, and chance was echoed by a number of musicians, including John Cage: like Olson, they were all committed to what the poet called 'the *kinetics* of the thing', 'the PLAY of the mind' – as indeed were and are many other writers, some of whom Olson has influenced and some of whom have just happened to share his feelings. And, in the third place, it has to be emphasised that, despite all these connections past and present, Olson was still *sui generis*, engaged in a passionate process of discovery that was his and nobody else's. His poetics were ultimately *his*, and they were so principally because they grew out of *his* metaphysics: a theoretical system that represented a sustained, radical attack on traditional Western notions of a separate self, and a world of subjects and objects. Against such notions, Olson set what he termed 'Objectism', which involved 'getting rid of the lyrical interference of the individual as ego' and seeing man 'as a creature of nature' no different from 'those other creations of nature which we may, with no derogation, call objects'. The world is not a discrete series, he argued, it is a continuous process: man is a part of that process, 'a thing among things'; and it should and could be the aim of poetry to substantiate this. The breath of the poem should liberate the self from the mind and place it firmly in physical movement, because 'he who possesses rhythm possesses the universe'. The language of the poem should remind us that 'things / . . . don't carry their end any further than / their reality in themselves': it should be *of* reality rather than referential to it, predicated on involvement not separation. And the field of the poem, in turn, should enact a process consonant with natural processes: it should dramatise the primary intuition that 'What does not change / is the will to change'. 'Art is the only twin life has', Olson declared; it is 'the only valid metaphysic' since it 'does not seek to describe but to enact'. Its aesthetic shapes rehearse ontological truths, supply an access to the real. Not only that, they add to the stock of available reality: for, like the men and women who devised them, they are a part of what Olson once referred to as 'the world's / businesses' – or, on another occasion, termed 'the absolute condition of present things'.

'I have had to learn the simplest things / last', Olson wrote in one of his poems, 'Which made for difficulties'. The problem, as he saw it, was not that truth was intrinsically difficult: on the contrary, earlier civilisations like the Mayan had acted upon it with instinctive ease. It was that habits of mind and language that had been entrenched for centuries had to be *un*learned: man had become 'estranged / from that which was most familiar', and he had to turn his consciousness against itself in order to cure the estrangement. The process of unlearning, and then making a new start, began with books like *Call Me Ishmael*, his extraordinary critical work on Melville which opens with the ringing assertion, 'I take SPACE to be the central fact to man born in America . . . I spell it large because it comes large here': a belief that was to be developed in his preoccupation with spatial, rather than linear, forms as well in his later, direct explorations of 'American space' (where there is 'nothing but what is', Olson claimed, 'no end and no beginning'). It was also initiated in some of the earlier poems published in the Forties, which celebrate the movement of nature in 'Full circle' and attack the tendency to perceive life and literature in closed terms ('The closed parenthesis reads: the dead bury the dead, / and it is not very interesting'). However, it was in the work published after this, through the Fifties and beyond, that his sense of poems as performative moral acts was fully exercised: in shorter pieces like 'The Kingfishers', 'In Cold Hell, In Thicket', 'The Lordly and Isolate Satyrs', 'As the Dead Prey Upon Us', and 'Variations Done for Gerald Van de Wiele' as well as in the *Maximus Poems*, written over several decades, which represent Olson's own version of the American epic. A poem such as 'The Kingfishers' powerfully expresses Olson's belief in serial, open forms:

Not one death but many,
not accumulation but change, the feed-back proves, the feed-
back is the law
Into the same river no man steps twice[7]

But it not only expresses it in the literal sense, it enacts it: working on the assumption that nothing can be said exactly and finally, Olson uses repetition, parenthesis, and apposition. 'To be in different states without a change', the poet suggests, '/ is not a possibility'; and so recurring figures metamorphose according to the altered conditions in which they are placed. As they change, the line changes, too, in lively responsiveness: rapid, energetic, constantly varying in pace, it denies any attempt to receive the discourse and experience of the poem as anything other than a continuous flow. Nor does the flow end with the nominal end of the poem: as the last line, 'I hunt among stones', indicates, it is simply stepped aside from, not staunched. The poet remains committed to the activities of attention and discovery. With Rimbaud – whom he alludes to here – Olson continues to fix his gaze upon phenomena, 'la terre et les pierres', and to dedicate himself to the search for 'honey / where maggots are': the lively possibilities that surge even through apparent decay.

Undoubtedly, though, Olson's major poetic achievement is the *Maximus Poems*. The Maximus who gives these poems their title is an 'Isolated person in Gloucester, Massachusetts', the poet's home town, who addresses 'you / you islands / of men and girls': that is, his fellow citizens and readers. A 'Root person in root place', he is, like Williams's Paterson, a huge, omniscient version of his creator. The poet is the hero here, as he normally is in the American epic, and this poet is notable as an observer, correspondent (many of the poems are described as 'letters'), social critic, historian, pedagogue and prophet. The poems that constitute this serial epic vary in stance and tone. The ones in *Maximum IV, V, VI*, for example, published in 1968, are more clearly mythic, more openly preoccupied with convincing their audience that 'the world / is an eternal event' than are the pieces in *The Maximus Poems*, published eight years earlier. Nevertheless, certain themes recur, supplying a stable centre to this constantly shifting work. Olson's aim is a specific reading of the history of Gloucester, and the surrounding area by land and sea, that will enable a revelation of truth: one particular 'city' will then become the 'City', an 'image of creation and of human life for the rest of the life of the species'. The opening lines of the first poem announce the quest: 'the thing you're after / may be around the bend'. The voyage of discovery is, in effect, in search of the near, the familiar: 'facts' or particulars which must be dealt with 'by ear', spontaneously and as if for the first time. Such a goal is not easy, Olson suggests, at a time when 'cheapness shit is / upon the world' and everything is measured 'by quantity and machine'. Nothing valid is easy, not even love, when 'pejorocracy is here', the degradations of capitalism and consumerism – and where the familiar has been contaminated by the 'greased slide' of 'mu-sick', the evasions of modern mass culture. But it is still possible to live *in* the world, achieving the recognition that:

> There are no hierarchies, no infinite, no such
> many as mass, there are only
> eyes in all heads,
> to be looked out of[8]

It is still possible, in fact, to resist the myopic barbarism of 'Tell-A-Vision' and 'the several cankers of profit-making' so as to pay reverent attention to the real ('The real / is always worth the act of / lifting it'), to realise contact with particular places and moments ('there is no other issue than the moment'), and to build a new community or 'polis' based upon humility, curiosity, and care:

> Eyes
> & polis,
> fishermen
> & poets
> or in every human head I've known is
> both:
> the attention, and
> the care.[9]

Like many other American epics, the *Maximus Poems* juxtapose America as it is – where 'The true troubadours / are CBS' and 'The best / is soap' – with America as it might be. 'The newness / the first men knew', the poet informs us, 'was almost / from the start dirtied / by second comers'. But 'we are only / as we find out we are', and perhaps Americans can 'find' a new identity and society; Gloucester itself, we are told, is a place 'where polis / still thrives', and it may be that enough will be found there to promote a 'new start'.[10] Certainly, Olson hoped so and worked hard, in both his art and his life, to realise that hope: he had something of the evangelical fervour of Pound, which came out in particular during the years he taught at Black Mountain College in North Carolina. Among his colleagues and pupils there were a number of poets who shared at least some of his aims. They and a few others found an outlet for their work in *Origin* and then later *Black Mountain Review*. As a result, they have become associated as a group: a loose constellation of people who, for a while at least, found in Olson a guide, example, and father figure. These poets include Jonathan Williams, whose Jargon Press became an important publisher of *avant garde* writing, and Denise Levertov, an Englishwoman who emigrated to America – where, she claimed, she found 'new rhythms of life and speech', and was transformed into 'an American poet'. 'These poems decry and exalt', Williams has said of his work; and he has added elsewhere that 'being a mountaineer', he has 'a garrulous landscape nature' and yet at times can be 'as laconic . . . as a pebble'. Whether sprawling or succinct, though, satiric or lyrical, his poems are marked by their radical innovations of language and line ('Credo'), their affection for the Appalachian Mountains and English rural landscapes ('Reflections from Appalachia', 'Two Pastorals for Samuel Palmer at Shoreham, Kent') and by a constant desire to see 'not with / but *thru* / the eye!'[11] – to couple perception with vision. Levertov has a similar obsession with seeing, coupling this with the use of open forms and idiomatic language. But for her 'Honesty / isn't so simple'. She tends to be more deliberate, painstaking, more hesitant in her unravelling of theme. The poetic 'I' here is quieter, more tentative, as these few lines from 'Beyond the End' illustrate:

> maybe
> a gritting of teeth, to go
> just that much further, beyond the end
> beyond whatever end: to begin, to be, to defy.[12]

Two other poets whose work has registered the impact of the Black Mountain experience are Paul Blackburn and John Wieners. Wieners studied at the college briefly, Blackburn published work in *Origin* and the *Review*; and both poets have acknowledged the influence of Olson – which would in any event be clear from their use of the poem as an open field, their preoccupation with 'breath' and typographical experiment. It is there, however, that the resemblance ends. Blackburn is much the more expansive, outgoing of the two. His poem, 'The Continuity', for example, begins as an overheard conversation ('The bricklayer tells the busdriver / and I have nothing to do but listen'), moves into a skilful imitation of street speech ('Th' holdup at the liquor store, d'ja hear?'), and then concludes with a celebration of community. 'A dollar forty – /two that I spent . . .', the poet says, ' / is now in a man's pocket going down Broadway'.[13] 'Thus far the transmission is oral', he adds, referring to the conversation he has just heard: but his own writing is about to change that. The message is clear: exchanges, financial, conversational, literary, are all a way of maintaining 'the continuity'. They are all acts of communion, no matter how small, and that includes this poem. The work of John Wieners could not be more opposed to this idea of communality: he has even referred to public poetry reading as 'a shallow *act*'. For him, an audience is a dangerous thing, a 'wild horde who press in / to get a peek at the bloody hero', and seem not only to violate but to feed off his privacy. Intense, edgy, his poetry withdraws from nightmare landscapes ('America, you boil over / The cauldron scalds') and presses in upon his inner life: where, however, he discovers other kinds of horror. For him, in effect, the poem is not an act of communion but an authentic cry of pain: or, as he puts it, 'a man's / struggle to stay with / what is his own, what / lives within him to do'.[14]

Apart from Olson, however, the most important poets connected with the Black Mountain group are Robert Creeley, Ed Dorn, and Robert Duncan. In Creeley's case, an interest in open forms and the belief that 'words are things too' has combined with two quite disparate but in a way complementary influences. There is, first, his involvement with the free-flowing experiments of Abstract Expressionism and modern jazz. 'To me', Creeley has said, 'life is interesting insofar as it lacks intentional "control"';[15] and it is clear that the example of painters like Jackson Pollock and musicians like Charlie Parker and Miles Davis has encouraged him to see the artist as someone immersed in the work he creates, experiencing its energy, involved in its movement, and limited in terms of how he expresses himself only by 'the nature of the activity'. Along with this, there is what Creeley has termed his 'New England temper'. New England has given Creeley many things, including a tendency to be 'hung up', to suffer from pain ('I can / feel my eye breaking') and tension ('I think I grow tensions / like flowers . . .'). Above all, though, what it has given him is two things, one to do with perception, the other with expression. 'Locate *I*', declares Creeley in one of his poems; elsewhere, he insists, 'position is where you / put it, where it is'. He is fascinated, in effect, by the perceptual position of the speaker, how the poem grows out of the active relationship between perceiver and perceived. The preoccupation with the limits of vision that earlier New Englanders demonstrated is consequently translated into cool, modernist terms: the aim being not an 'ego-centred' verse but precisely its opposite, words that reveal how our eyes and minds 'are not separate . . . from all other life-forms'. At the same time, New England habits have, Creeley says, given him a 'sense of speech as a laconic, ironic, compressed way of saying something to someone', the inclination 'to say as little as possible as often as possible'. So the forms of his saying have become, as he believes they should, an extension of content. His purpose is 'a realisation, a reification of what is': 'a process of discovery' that turns out to be a matter of vocabulary as well as vision. 'What's the point of doing what we already know?' Creeley has asked, and his writing continually illustrates this belief in experiment. His poems evolve on both a sequential grammatical level and a cumulative linear level; each line reaffirms or modifies the sense of the sentence and the total argument, each word exists in contrapuntal tension with all the others. There is risk here, in fact, a taste for the edgy and subversive, of a kind that would be equally familiar to Thelonious Monk and Emily Dickinson.

The difficulties of seeing and knowing, the tendency of the ego to be 'locked in itself', and the related problems of location and expression, are all thoughtfully registered in these lines from Creeley's poem, 'The Pattern':

> As soon as
> I speak, I
> speaks. It
>
> wants to
> be free but
> impassive lies
>
> in the direction
> of its
> words.[16]

Given the habit 'I' or self-consciousness has of getting in the way of revelation, Creeley tries to strip poetry of all its more obtrusive, interfering devices: easy generalisations, abstractions, and colourful comparisons are eschewed in favour of patient attentiveness, a tendency to approach things and words as if they were small bombs set to explode unless carefully handled. To capture the 'intense instant' what is needed is caution, perhaps ('The Innocence'), surprise ('Like They Say'), spontaneity ('To Bobbie'): above all, a willingness to follow the peculiar shape and movement of an experience, however unpredictable it may be. This last point is nicely dramatised in 'I Know a Man', where the unnamed narrator talks to his friend 'John' about what they might do, or where they might drive, to escape 'the darkness' that surrounds them. 'John''s reply is short and to the point:

> drive, he sd, for
> christ's sake, look
> out where yr going[17]

As Creeley has observed, 'you can drive to the store with absolute predetermination to get the bread and return home'. Alternatively, 'you can take a drive, as they say . . . where the driving permits you certain information you can't anticipate'. To plan is one thing: it has its advantages, but it inhibits discovery, 'the delight of thought as a possibility of forms'. To take a chance is quite another, and it is clearly what 'John' and his creator prefer: to go off in an unpremeditated way and simply to watch, to 'look out' where one is going. 'I want to range in the world as I can imagine the world', Creeley has said, 'and as I can find possibility in the world'. This he has done in sparse, brittle poems that use their silences just as effectively as their speech and that ('true / Puritan' as the poet is, he admits) present the cardinal sin as cowardice: a reluctance to resist the several forces that would imprison us in habit – the fear of the challenge thrown out to us by the, as yet, unseen and unarticulated.

If Creeley's work represents a peculiarly Eastern, and more specifically New England form of 'open' verse, then the poetry of Ed Dorn draws much of its point, wit, and power from his attachment to the American West. This is not simply because some of his poems, like 'The Rick of Green Wood', are situated in Western landscapes or, like 'Vaquero' or *Slinger*, play with popular mythic versions of the frontier. It is also because Dorn adopts a poetic voice that in its expansiveness, cool knowingness, ease, and wry humour seems to belong to wide open spaces. Additionally, it is because he adopts an alert political stance that depends on an understanding of the different possibilities of American 'know-how', mobility, and energy: the same forces that could be positive, humane, and liberating – and have been, sometimes, in his own personal history and the story of the West – have also, he realises, generated the 'North Atlantic Turbine' of mass production, conscienceless power, and the destruction of people and the planet for profit. 'From near the beginning', Dorn has said, 'I have known my work to be theoretical in nature and poetic by virtue of its inherent tone'.[18] He is not afraid of speculation and direct, unmetaphorical speech; however, he is saved from simple didacticism by his 'tone' – which is the combined product of rapid transitions of thought, subtle tonalities of rhythm and phrasing, and an astute use of personae, irony ('a thing I've always admired', he has said), comedy, and sarcasm.

'The Sundering U.P. Tracks' is an example of Dorn's political poetry at its best. It opens with a witty, idiomatic recall of black speech and music – but softened, in both cases, to cross the line to the white world:

I never hear the Supremes
but what I remember Leroy.

Then, suddenly, the poem switches to a more formal diction and stance:

> McLucas came
> to Pocatello the summer of 1965 . . .

The use of the surname suggests that white narrator and black character may not be as intimate as first suggested: there may be a 'sundering' or division that is more than skin deep. Having suggested this, Dorn then explores different forms of 'sundering', separation where there should be communion. The crucial figure here – or, rather, illustration, since it is meant quite literally – is the 'U.P.' or Union Pacific Railway tracks mentioned in the title. Leroy McLucas, we learn, took rooms on the other side of those tracks, 'in that part of town owned / by Bistline, the famous exploiter'. The memory of that leads the poet into an attentive account of the railway that brought McLucas there, and its tracks that divide so many different places ('Every little bogus town / on the Union Pacific bears the scar / of an expert linear division'). Swiftly, with wit and passion, Dorn follows the trajectory of the Union Pacific across the spaces and times of North America: the geographical 'sundering' has now clearly become an historical one as well, exemplified by the profiteers who made their fortunes from the railroads – and repeated, now, every day of every American's life. The conclusion to the poem is as sardonic, and as emotionally charged, as the lines that precede it:

> You talk of colour?
> Oh cosmological america, how well
> and with what geometry
> you teach your citizens[19]

The humour of these lines depends on Dorn's perception that the 'geometry' of 'america' has been more concerned with division than unity; their passion, on his sympathy for the impulses consequently betrayed. The echoes of Whitman here, the delicate harmonies of phrasing (notable, especially, in the play of 'o', 'l', 'w', and 'y' sounds), the lilt and drive of the free verse: all these things remind us that the energy Americans have directed towards cutting a 'shining double knife' 'through the heart' of the continent is a potentially creative force. The power that has destroyed conscience and community could also create – among other things, poems like this one.

Apart from political works such as this, or 'The Stripping of the River', Dorn has written many lyrical poems: explorations of human sentiment, like 'The Air of June Sings' or 'Song', that demonstrate, with especial clarity, what Creeley has called Dorn's '*Elizabethan* care for the sound of syllables'. More recently, he has favoured epigrams, tight, aphoristic pieces which he has labelled 'dispatches'. Light and essential enough, Dorn hopes, to be accepted 'in the spirit / of the Pony Express', they carry his commitment to alertness of perception and precision of speech to a new extreme. In between, he has produced *Slinger*, a long anti-heroic poem of the American West that enacts its significances through radical variations of idiom, surreal imagery, puns, personifications, and jokes. Constantly allusive, packed with a range of characters that includes – besides the eponymous Slinger – a madam of a brothel, a refugee from a university, and Howard Hughes, it explores questions of thought and culture (Lèvi-Strauss is invoked, both the anthropologist and the jeans manufacturer) and the use and abuse of power, money, words, and weaponry, in 'cosmological america'. As far as his 'personal presence' in the poem is concerned, Dorn has said, 'It's omnipresent, absolutely omnipresent', then added, 'Actually, I'm absolutely uncommitted except to what's happening'. In its own way, in fact, *Slinger* is another version of the American epic, a song of the self in which the self becomes dispersed, problematic, part of the matter for attention. Asked what the meaning of the poem's actions are, at one stage, Slinger laughs and replies:

> Mean?
> Refugee, you got some strange
> obsessions, you want to know
> what something *means* after you've
> seen it, after you've been there.[20]

That makes the point. Meaning and identity inhere in the actual processes, the activities of the lines; like Olson and Creeley, Dorn seems to be recalling what Williams meant when he said 'the poet thinks with his poem'.

'I like to wander about in my work writing so rapidly that I might overlook manipulations and design':[21] that remark of Robert Duncan's suggests that he, too, sees the poem as a process, of being and knowing. However, another remark of his illustrates the mystical strain that helps to distinguish him from his Black Mountain colleagues: 'Poetry is the very life of the soul: the body's discovery that it can dream'. With a background as a romantic and a theosophist, Duncan has said that he experienced from the first an 'intense yearning, the desire for something else'. 'I knew the fullest pain of longing', he declared '. . . to be out of my being and enter the Other'. Consumed with a desire for 'identification with the universe', he was still quite young when he recognised in poetry his 'sole and ruling vocation';

'only in this act', he felt, could his 'inner nature unfold'. His feeling for verse and its constituent language was, in fact, prophetic, cabalistic. Language, he believed, we drink in with our mother's milk, possessed by its rhythmic vibrations; we acquire it 'without / any rule for love of it / "imitating our nurses"' and hardly aware of its 'vacant energies below meaning'. Poems spring from this nurture, and from our dim recognition of the 'metaphorical ground in life'. A metaphor, Duncan has claimed, 'is not a literary device but an actual meaning . . . leading us to realise the coinherrence of being in being': it reveals correspondences in that world of forms 'in which . . . spirit is manifest', and it offers glimpses of 'the wholeness of what we are that we will never know'. Language, rhythm, metaphor: all these, then, Duncan began by seeing as a means of transcendence, an access to revelation. What the Black Mountain experience added to this was the liberating influence of open forms. Duncan took the notion of the poem as field and coloured it with his own original impulses: so that it became for him, the idea of the poem as a 'Memory-field' in which 'all parts . . . co-operate, co-exist' in mystical union. Past and future are folded together within the present in his vision, in one 'company of the living'. Similarly, they are woven together in the 'one fabric' of his verse: with the result that what the reader sees, ideally, is 'no first strand or second strand' but the 'truth of that form', the timeless 'design' as a whole.

Just how Duncan pursues this synchronicity is illustrated by a poem like 'Often I Am Permitted To Return to A Meadow'. The title of the piece is also its first line, and it then continues:

> as if it were a scene made-up by the mind
> that is not mine, but is a made place
>
> that is mine, it is so near the heart,
> an eternal pasture folded in all thought
> so that there is a hall therein
>
> that is a made place . . .

'There is a natural mystery in poetry',[22] Duncan has written. In these lines, and elsewhere (in pieces like 'A Poem Beginning with a Line by Pindar' or 'Passages'), Duncan uses plangent repetition of word and phrase, subtle verbal melody, and a serpentine syntax that seems to fall back upon itself, all to announce the presence of the mystery: to create a verse that is, in equal portions, magic, ritual, and incantation. Above all, there is the metaphor of the 'eternal pasture' here, which gradually accumulates associations that are pagan ('ring a round of roses'), Platonic ('light/wherefrom the shadows that are forms fall'), and Christian ('likenesses of the First Beloved / whose flowers are flames lit to the Lady'). Like the figures of H.D. (a poet whom Duncan admired), this metaphor is at once precise and resonant, exact and strange; and, while it is possible to 'see' it and gather some of its reverberations (omens and celebrations that are at once sacred and sensual, the 'pure spirit' that 'grows beneath the skin of stones', the holy place that links 'being' and 'Other'), it is precisely its point that it should remain unparaphraseable, a 'releasing/word' that releases us simply into a dim awareness of the 'god-step at the margins of thought'. The last line of the poem, 'everlasting omen of what is', in a way takes us no further than the first. Yet that, surely, is because Duncan makes us feel that we have always been in the 'meadow' he describes. Like a suddenly remembered dream, an experience of *déjà vu* or a half-recovered melody, its appeal depends on our suspicion that it has always been there below 'the currents of language' – and still is, even if we cannot quite grasp it.

Restoring the American vision: the San Francisco poets (Ferlinghetti, Everson, Spicer, Lamantia, Whalen, McClure, Snyder)

Duncan gradually moved, he claimed, from 'the concept of a dramatic form to a concept of musical form in poetry'. This does not tell the whole truth, if only because his poetry written after his initial involvement with the Black Mountain group *is* capable of dramatic statement: it incorporates vigorous attacks on 'The malignant stupidity of statesmen', vivid accounts of homoerotic experiences ('my Other is not a woman but a man'), and careful descriptions of how 'The poem / feeds upon thought, feeling, and impulse'. As a broad brushstroke portrait of the impact that Olson and others had on him, though, it is reasonably helpful – and handy, since it brings into focus a second group of poets who reacted, in their own way, against the formalist and confessional establishments. The 'dramatic form' Duncan refers to is the one he favoured when he emerged as a leading poet in the late Forties, as part of what has become known as the San Francisco Renaissance. For the San Francisco poets, drama and performance were primary. One of them, Lawrence Ferlinghetti, put it this way:

> the kind of poetry which has been
> making the most noise here . . . is what should

> be called street poetry . . . It amounts to getting
> poetry back into the street where it once
> was, out of the classroom, out of the speech
> department, and – in fact – off the printed
> page. The printed word has made poetry
> so silent.[23]

Ferlinghetti is speaking here for a more demotic, populist poetry than the kind preferred by many of the San Franciscans – including Duncan, even in his early years – but he still speaks for more than himself. Immediacy, drama, above all language and a line shaped by the *voice*, in conversation or declamation: these were the priorities of a group of otherwise different poets who wanted to liberate poetry from the academy.

Ferlinghetti's own poems illustrate this interest in oral impact: many of them were, in fact, conceived of as 'oral messages' and have been performed to a jazz accompaniment. Their flavour, and the sense of the poet's role that informs them, is perhaps caught in these lines from 'A Coney Island of the Mind':

> Constantly risking absurdity
>   and death
>   whenever he performs
>   above the heads
>   of his audience
> the poet like an acrobat
>   climbs on rime
>   to a high wire of his own making
> . . .
> For he's the super realist
>   who must perforce perceive
>   taut truth
>   before the taking of each
>   stance or step.[24]

The line is long and flowing, often as here using Williams's 'variable foot' to govern the pace; the language is strongly idiomatic; the imagery colourful to the point of theatricality. As Ferlinghetti sees him, the poet is at once a performer, 'a charleychaplin man', and a pedagogue, a 'super realist' who is willing to risk absurdity as he strives not only to entertain but to instruct. 'Balancing . . . / above a sea of faces', he uses all the tricks at his disposal, 'entrechats' and 'high theatrics', to perceive and communicate 'taut truth'. 'Only the dead are disengaged', Ferlinghetti has insisted and his poetry, while indulging in slapstick and corny jokes, is seriously engaged with the issues of the day: the 'engines / that devour America', the absurdities of institutional life, the humourless collectives called nation-states. The energy of his voice, in fact, expresses the coherence of his vision: which is that of the anarchic individualist, who waits hopefully for 'the final withering away / of all governments' – and the day when 'lovers and weepers / . . . lie down together / in a new rebirth of wonder.'

Someone else from the San Francisco area who uses roaming verse forms and a declamatory style is Brother Antoninus: a writer who, since his departure from the Dominican Order in 1970, has published under the name of William Everson. Like Ferlinghetti, Everson has also favoured such devices as incremental repetition and a paratactic syntax. In his case, though, the poetry that results has a rugged, flinty quality to it, an austere intensity. None of his work has the flat speech rhythms that characterise so much contemporary verse. On the contrary, it fluctuates between a long, wavering line that can approach the stillness of a moment of contemplation, and a line that tightens together into an abrupt, insistent rhythmic unit. Whether recording the harsh landscapes of the West Coast and the 'wild but earnest' forms of life that inhabit them, or rehearsing more immediately personal experiences of love, religious faith and doubt, his work is notable for a diction that ranges between the brutally simple and the lofty, imagery that can be at once primitive and apocalyptic, frequently incantatory rhythms and a general tone that recalls the work of Robinson Jeffers (a poem to whom Everson has professed an allegiance). 'A Canticle to the Waterbirds' is exemplary, in many ways. It opens with an invocation to the birds, inviting them to 'make a praise up to the Lord'. The Lord they are asked to praise is no gentle Jesus, however, but the creator and overseer of a 'mighty fastness', 'indeterminate realms' of rock, sea, and sky. And the praise they are asked to give is not so much in the saying as the being. 'You leave a silence', the poet declares, 'And this for you suffices, who are not of the ceremonials of man'. 'Yours is of another order of being, and wholly it compels', he goes on, '/ But may you, birds, . . . / . . . / Yet . . . teach a man a necessary thing to know'. For:

> God has given you the imponderable grace to
> *be* His verification,
> Outside the mulled incertitude of our forensic choices;
> That you, our lessers in the rich hegemony of Being,
> May serve as testament to what a creature is,
> And what creation owes.[25]

What Everson celebrates, in fact, is the capacity these creatures possess for living in the Now; they have none of the human taint of self-consciousness, no compulsion to look before and after. They act with purity, simplicity, and instinctive courage, as part of the processes of creation. To live beyond evasions and inwardness: this is the lesson taught by the waterbirds. For that matter, it is the lesson taught by Everson's tough yet oracular poetry, which represents a sustained assault on the idea of a separate self – and which is insistently reminding us of 'the strict conformity that creaturehood entails, / . . . the prime commitment all things share'.

'I would like to make poems out of real objects', another poet associated with the San Francisco area, Jack Spicer, has declared, '. . . The poem is a collage of the real'.[26] This sounds like Ferlinghetti and Everson, in their commitment to what Williams called 'things – on a field'; and Spicer does certainly share with those poets an interest in the irreducible reality of objects as well as a preference for open-ended structures and a flexible line – in effect, the poem as process. Just as Ferlinghetti and Everson are not entirely alike, however, Spicer is different from both of them in turn in that his commitment (as the phrase 'collage of the real' intimates) is to a more surreal medium; the materials of his work seem to come from the subconscious, even though the organising of those materials is achieved by a conscious poetic intelligence. His 'Imaginary Elegies', for instance, begin by asking if poetry can mean that much if all it deals with is visible phenomena, 'like a camera', rendering them 'alive in sight only for a second'. Then working through a complex association of imagery – that leads from the eye of the camera to the eye of God, to the eyes of the moon and the sun and the moving earth and sea over which they both preside – Spicer answers his own question simply by dramatising his own sense of the potentials of poetry. 'This much I've learned', Spicer says, '. . . / Time does not finish a poem': because a poem is a fluid, changing medium that actively imitates the equally fluid, changing stream of life. It is a matter, not of perception, but of correspondence; 'Poet, / be like God', Spicer commands, that is create 'not . . . an image or a picture but . . . something alive – caught forever in the structure of words'. This alertness to poetry as active translation, a carrying across of 'real objects' called things into other 'real objects' called words, also characterises the writing of another poet from the Bay Area, Philip Lamantia. Lamantia has claimed that he 'broke with surrealism in 1946': but it is clear that, like Spicer, he retains the essential surrealist quality of revealing the inner life via explosive patterns of imagery. So, a poem like his 'Terror Conduction' uses disjunctive rhythms and an ecstatic tone, as well as kaleidoscopic images, to create an atmosphere of dread, unparaphraseable feelings of menace:

FACES
FACES
going by
like icebergs
like music
like boats
like mechanical toys
LIKE
RAINING
SWORDS![27]

In this sense, just as much as Spicer he reveals the more extremist tendencies of the San Francisco area group.

A similar extremism is to be found in the work of two other poets more loosely associated with the Bay Area, Philip Whalen and Michael McClure. 'This poetry', Whalen has said of his writing, 'is a picture or graph of a mind moving',[28] and his poem, 'The Same Old Jazz', shows what he means. For him, as he insists in this piece, there is 'A one-to-one relationship' between inner and outer, 'The world inside my head and the cat outside the window'. His aim is to dramatise that relationship: to write a kind of abstract expressionist diary in which abrupt, syncopated rhythms, a pacey idiom, and images that are continually deliquescing into other images are all harnessed to the re-creation of experience as a mixed media event. Something that McClure says of his own work could, in fact, also be applied to Whalen's poetry: 'I am the body, the animal, the poem / is a gesture of mine'.[29] With McClure, however, the 'gesture' is a much more unnerving one because he chooses to confront and challenge the reader and, whenever necessary, uses violence as a means of revelation. 'The poem . . . is black and white', says McClure in 'Hymn to St. Geryon', 'I PICK IT UP BY THE TAIL AND HIT / YOU OVER THE HEAD WITH IT'. What McClure wants, he has said, is to 'BREAK UP THE FORMS AND FEEL THINGS', to 'Kick in the walls', literary, social, and psychological – and that includes the conventional 'walls' or barriers between writer and reader. This is, perhaps, Thoreau's and Whitman's notion of self-emancipation through writing carried about as far as it can go: 'my viewpoint is ego-centric'. McClure has admitted, 'The poem is as much of me as an arm'. But while favouring 'the direct emotional statement from the body', like those earlier writers McClure is also intent on addressing and embracing the body, or identity, of his audience. 'Self-dramatisation is part of a means to belief and Spirit', he claims; and 'hopefully . . . the reader' will learn about this by challenge and model – from the emancipation enacted by the 'loose chaos of words / on the page'.

'THIS IS THE POWERFUL KNOWLEDGE', says McClure in

'Peyote Poem, Part I', '/ we smile with it'. Like many writers associated with the counter-culture of the Sixties, McClure locates his 'powerful knowledge' in extreme states and subversive forms, and in particular in the drug experience. His work is not simply irrational but anti-rational, responding as he puts it to 'WHAT I HEAR IN HEARTS NERVES LUNGS'. If the reader feels threatened by this, then that is part of the point. Vivid, ejaculatory rhythms, a language that is sometimes fiercely idiomatic and sometimes startlingly fantastic, and structures that are 'not predestined or logical but immediate' are all directed at breaking through the customary social and psychic defences so as to enable contact and vision. The passion and intimacy that result are illustrated by these lines, taken from 'Ode for a Soft Voice':

> I am a shape and meet you
> at our skins edge.
> We change and speak and make our histories. I am all I feel
> and what you see and what you touch
> There are no walls but ones we make.
> I AM SICK CONFUSED AND DROP IT FROM ME[30]

'I put my hands / to you', says McClure in another poem, ' – like cool jazz coming'. This is a poetry of the solitary 'I' searching for words that are an extension of the poet's body and a bridge to the body of the reader; it yearns to touch, to tear down the barriers that constitute verbal and moral *apartheid*. The violence of its attack may seem strange to us, but it is rooted in the American tradition: the tradition, that is, which seeks to 'pass/ from ancestral myth to myth of self' and sees the poet as 'THE SELF'S FREE HERO', offering exemplary gestures for the 'self-liberation' of everyone.

Liberation is also an impulse at the heart of the work of Gary Snyder, who was born in San Francisco and has worked as a logger, forester, and farmer in the Northwest. 'As much as the books I've read the jobs I've done have been significant in shaping me', Snyder has said, 'My sense of body and language and the knowledge that . . . sensitivity and awareness are not limited to educated people'.[31] Most of his poems are direct and simple, characterised by an elemental reverence for existence and salvaging poetry from the most primitive human experiences. Unmarked by the normal tensions of language, they depend on lucidity and specificity, open forms and the 'rhythms of physical work . . . and life' for their impact. The simplicity of Snyder's work is not simplification, however. It derives in part from his devotion to Zen Buddhism; and it reflects his need to fill the

'Intricate layers of emptiness' where 'Human tenderness scuttles / Down dry endless cycles' with the peace of enlightenment, purification, and quiet. Zen encourages the active appreciation of the natural world as an agent of vision, transcendence and elimination of the self; and its art of deft brushstrokes dispenses with calculated technique and structured reasoning in favour of immediate, spontaneous attention to living things. 'A poet faces two directions', Snyder suggests, 'one is the world of people and language and society, and the other is the non-human, non-verbal world . . . the inner world, as it is itself, before language . . . custom, . . . culture'. Zen has helped Snyder to bridge the gap between these two worlds, to achieve 'a new sense' via a passionate encounter with objects; it has enabled him to find 'the way of activity' through 'activity', positive silence through the movements of body and speech.

The opening lines of one of Snyder's best poems, 'Riprap', reveal his characteristic voice:

Lay down these words
Before your mind like rocks,
        placed solid, by hands
In choice of place, set
Before the body of the mind
        in space and time:
Solidity of bark, leaf, or wall
        riprap of things:
Cobble of milky way . . .

A 'riprap', Snyder tells us elsewhere, is 'a cobble of stones laid on steep slick rock to make a trail for horses in mountains';[32] it provides sure footing for a literal ascent just as poetry, 'a riprap on the slick rock of metaphysics', provides sure footing for a metaphorical one. Like some Imagist poetry, these lines are as remarkable for what they omit as for what they exclude: there are no elaborate figures, no close-woven argument, no irony or introspection. As the poet intimates, the words here have the substance and weight of rocks; and the poet himself is the good craftsman, who works with not against the grain of things, allowing them to express their nature. There is no forcing of the material: the voice is clear and quiet, cleaving faithfully to the enacted experience. And there is no insistence of feeling: the emotions are not denied but neither are they insisted on, rather they are distilled into significant activity. Just as 'torment of fire and . . . / Crystal and sediment linked hot' has eventuated in stone and pebble, so passions encountered and then refined into language have generated the firm, particular surfaces of this poem. Energy has produced matter, cool, solid, and specific; and that matter in turn invites us into mystery, the 'preternatural clearness' that can issue from being 'Attentive to the real-world flesh and stone'.

'I hold the most archaic values on earth', Snyder insists, 'They go back to the Paleolithic'; 'I try to hold history and the wilderness in mind', he has added, 'that my poems may approach the true nature of things, and stand against the unbalance and ignorance of our times'.[33] For him, identification with 'that other totally alien, non-human' can be experienced in tilling the soil, shaping word or stone, 'the lust and ecstasy of the dance', or 'the power-vision in solitude'. And it has led him on naturally to a hatred of human assumptions of power and 'the ancient, meaningless / Abstractions of the educated mind'. His work celebrates such primary rituals as hunting and feasting ('Eating each other's seed / eating / ah, each other') and the mysteries of sex and birth ('How rare to be born a human being!'): but, with its commitment to participation in nature rather than possession of it, it is equally capable of polemic, an unremitting radicalism of consciousness – something that is especially noticeable when Snyder directs his attention to the ecology and the 'Men who hire men to cut groves / Kill snakes, build cities, pave fields'. It is at this point, in particular, that the Eastern and Western strains in his writing meet and marry. Snyder has learned about 'the buddha-nature', the intrinsic vitality lurking in all things, not just from Zen but from poets like Whitman; just as his habit of meditation rather than appropriation has been borrowed from Thoreau as well as the Buddhist tradition, and his belief in renewal springs from the spirit of the frontier as much as from oriental notions of the eternal cycle. 'First day of the world', begins one of Synder's poems describing a morning in the Sierras:

White rock ridges
                        new born
Jay chatters   the first time
Rolling a smoke by campfire
New! never before.[34]

In his eyes, enlightenment remains perpetually available, a fresh start can always be made. As Thoreau said at the end of *Walden* – and Snyder borrows the line for one of his poems – 'The sun is but a morning-star': each day represents a new opportunity to recover the nobility of life, another chance to turn aside from use to wonder.

Re-creating American rhythms: the Beat poets (Ginsberg, Corso) and Bukowski

Snyder, Ferlinghetti, and many of the other San Francisco poets were also involved in the activities of another group that rose to prominence and notoriety in the Fifties, commonly known as 'the beat generation'. The term 'beat generation' seems to have been coined by one of the most famous members of the group, Jack Kerouac; and it has several relevant connotations. In a musical sense, the word 'beat' suggests keeping the beat, being in the groove or harmony with others. More specifically, it implies the jazz beat: beat poetry is, as one of the group has termed it, 'typewriter-jazz', aimed at catching the abrupt, syncopated rhythms, the improvisational dash and *bravura* of jazz, bebop, and swing. In a social, psychological and vaguely political sense, 'beat' connotes the 'beaten' condition of the outsider, who is down perhaps but certainly not out. Like so many Romantic and American writers, the beats cherished the stance of the alienated, the dispossessed and even the nominally insane: those who look at normal, 'square' society from the periphery and reject its discipline and codes. As Allen Ginsberg put it, echoing a whole line of poets from Blake to Whitman and Dickinson, 'The madman is holy as you my soul are holy'.[35] Finally, in a spiritual sense, 'beat' is related to 'beatitude' and describes the innocence, blessedness, and raptness of what Ginsberg called 'angelheaded hipsters burning for the ancient heavenly connection': the pursuit of 'visionary consciousness' through music or meditation, drugs, mantras, or poems. 'The only poetic tradition is the voice out of the burning bush', insisted Ginsberg, and that sums up an impulse shared by most of the beat generation. They were, undoubtedly, a remarkable social phenomenon: part of a decade that seemed suddenly to have invented adolescence and rebellion. More important, though, they were and are part of a great tradition that identifies poetry with prophecy.

The beat generation was initially associated with New York, but it first attracted the interest of a larger public when, in 1956, Ginsberg, Kerouac, and Gregory Corso joined Ferlinghetti, Snyder, Whalen, and others in public reading appearances in the coffeehouses and colleges of San Francisco. And national fame was almost guaranteed with the confiscation of copies of Ginsberg's *Howl* by the San Francisco police in the same year – on the grounds that, as the Collector of Customs put it, 'The words and the sense of the writing are obscene'. *Howl*, Ginsberg's first published book of poems (although by no means his first stab at poetry), then sold over 50,000 copies within a relatively brief period of time. Along with Kerouac's *On the Road*, it became what Kenneth Rexroth, something of a father-figure for some of the beats, called 'the confession of faith of the generation that is going to be running the world in 1965 and 1975 – if it's still there to run'.[36] For a while, the figure of the beat or beatnik even attracted national media attention, although he (and it was usually a 'he' rather than a 'she') tended to be considered only to be mocked and dismissed. *Time* magazine, for instance, referred to the beat as 'a rebel without a cause who shirks responsibility on the ground that he has the H-bomb jitters'. The liberal establishment was hostile, too: Norman Podhoretz, for example, declared, 'No new territory is being staked out by these writers', while Diana Trilling sniffily observed, 'there is no more menace in 'Howl' or *On the Road* than there is in the Scarsdale P.T.A.' What such commentators seemed to object to was that, while the beat generation was anti-establishment, it was not involved with the kind of programmatic leftism that characterised many of the writers of the Thirties. Rather, it was committed to what Norman O. Brown has termed 'metapolitics': the politics of Blake, that is, in which psychological or spiritual freedom is the only sure warrant for political freedom.

There is, perhaps, no surer exponent of 'metapolitics' than the greatest poet of the beat generation, Allen Ginsberg. When he took part in a demonstration against American involvement in Vietnam, for instance, he carried a placard that declared simply, 'War is black magic'. With him, as he has said, poetry is 'a catalyst to visionary states of mind'; and he has been assisted in his pursuit of a visionary goal by a mystical experience he had while still quite young. As he describes it, he was reading Blake's poem, 'Ah, Sun-Flower!' when he heard Blake's voice reciting the lines; it seemed to him, listening, as if 'God had a human voice'. He then had, he says, 'the consciousness of being alive unto myself, alive myself unto the creator'; more than that, he became convinced that he was 'the son of the Creator – who loved me . . . or who responded to my desire'. 'My first thought was this was what I was born for', he insists:

> . . . and second thought . . . Never deny the
> voice . . . don't get lost mentally wandering in . . .
> American or job worlds . . . or war worlds or earth
> worlds . . . I suddenly realized . . . what Blake was
> talking about . . . a breakthrough from ordinary habitual
> quotidien consciousness into consciousness that was really
> seeing all of heaven in a flower.[37]

This experience goes to the heart of Ginsberg's work, even though in recent years he has tended to devalue its importance. For it implicates him in what he has called the 'messianic thing': the sense, inherited from Whitman, that he is a 'chosen, blessed, sacred poet' whose vocation it is to prophecy to America. 'The spirit of the universe was what I was born to realise', he has claimed; and part of that birthright, as he sees it, involves breaking down 'everybody's masks and roles', the self-consciousness and fear that actively inhibit vision. Everywhere are 'lack-love and cold war', people in 'horrible grotesque masks, grotesque because *hiding* the knowledge from each other': that is Ginsberg's first point, accounting for his jeremiads against the 'Moloch' that is contemporary America. But everywhere, too, are the possibilities of 'depth of consciousness . . . cosmical awareness', 'the knowledge' available to all those willing to learn: that is Ginsberg's second, and for him more significant, point, explaining why the naturalist perceptions in his poetry are so often shot through with spiritual emotion – the firm belief that, as he has put it, 'existence itself' is 'God'.

At first, Ginsberg attempted to insert his prophetic vision into what he later termed 'overwritten coy stanzas, a little after Marvell, a little after Wyatt'. This came to an end when William Carlos Williams commented, 'In this mode, perfection is basic, and these are not perfect'. He then took to imitating Williams, writing 'poetry adapted from prose seeds, journals, scratchings, arranged by phrasing or breath into little short-line patterns': until, that is, he realised that what he should imitate was not Williams's specific forms but his example. He needed, he saw, to do what Williams and before him Whitman had done, 'to adapt . . . poetry rhythms out of . . . actual talk rhythms'; and he now recognised Whitman's long line as an appropriate precedent, a possible vehicle for what he called 'my romantic – inspiration – Hebrac-Melvillian bardic breath'. 'My breath is long', Ginsberg declared, 'that's the Measure, one physical-mental inspiration of thought contained in the elastic of breath'. *His* breath, *his* speech was to be the organiser of the line, a perception to which he was helped, not only by Whitman and Williams, but by the advice of Jack Kerouac. A jazz musician, Kerouac observed – and especially a saxophone player when improvising – is 'drawing in a breath and blowing a phrase . . . till he runs out of breath, and when he does, his sentence, his statement s been made'. This sense of drawing in the breath, in a way that reminds the reader at once of Charlie Parker and a prophet of the Old Testament, is what is perhaps most noticeable about the famous opening lines of 'Howl':

> I saw the best minds of my generation destroyed
> by madness, starving hysterical naked,

dragging themselves through negro streets at dawn
looking for an angry fix . . .
. . .
who poverty and tatters and hollow-eyed and high
sat up smoking in the supernatural darkness
of cold-water flats floating across the tops
of cities contemplating jazz . . .[38]

Having established the basic beat in the opening lines, Ginsberg then relied, he has said, on the word 'who' to retain it, to supply 'a base to keep the measure, return to and take off from again onto another stream of invention'. It offered a theme on which he could improvise, a rhythm he could twist and turn in response to what he once termed 'the actual movie of the mind'.

'Mind is shapely': that remark of Ginsberg's suggests how much a piece like 'Howl' is committed to the discontinuities of consciousness and its sudden revelations. What he is after, he has suggested, is 'the poem *discovered* in the mind and in the process of writing it out on the page'. The long line is the base, but what organises and sustains it, over the distance, is a strategy of association and juxtaposition. 'It's natural inspiration that keeps it moving', Ginsberg has said of his poetry, 'disparate things put down together': which is a notion that he has learned partly from the surrealists (he once described himself as wearing 'the black cloak of French poetry'), in part from the example of *haiku*, like Pound – and partly from his enthusiasm for the painter Paul Cézanne. In Cézanne's paintings, Ginsberg has noted, 'it's just juxtaposition of one colour against another' that supplies 'visual structuring'. And this has given him the idea of juxtaposing 'one *word* against another' so that a *gap* between the two words' is created, 'like the space gap in the canvas', which the mind can then 'fill in with the sensation of existence'. Ginsberg offers as examples of what he aims at two phrases from 'Howl': 'hydrogen jukebox' and 'winter midnight smalltown streetlight rain'. The aim behind juxtapositions such as these is to 'reach different parts of the mind' that exist simultaneously ('hydrogen jukebox', for instance, immediately suggests jazz, jukebox all that' and 'politics, hydrogen bomb'), and then force them together to create a temporary suspension of habitual thought. The result is (or should be) an ellipsis, a disjuncture that stops mind-flow, arrests normal consciousness, and creates a temporary void. This void is what Buddhists call *Sunyata*, the absence of rational, controlled mind, intuitive knowledge. Also it is clearly what Ginsberg himself has in mind when, in one brief passage in 'Howl', he refers to those:

Who dreamt and made incarnate gaps in Time & Space
through images juxtaposed, and trapped the archangel

of the soul between 2 visual images and joined the
elemental verbs and set the noun and dash of
consciousness together jumping with sensation of Pater
Omnipotens Aeterna Deus[39]

In these circumstances, the reader is enlightened by the discontinuous activities of the poem; he, or she, learns not so much from what it says as from how it says it.

For all that, though, Ginsberg's poems do also have paraphraseable arguments – or, if not that exactly, certain structures of feeling and assumption that are more immediately assimilable than those that animate earlier exercises in the ideogrammic method, like the *Cantos* and *Paterson*. 'Howl', for instance, is a grimly serious and yet comically surreal account of the betrayal of a generation. The first part explores the denial of the visionary impulse by forces like 'the narcotic tobacco haze of Capitalism' and celebrates its continuance in such subversive elements as 'angelheaded hipsters', 'saintly motorcyclists', and 'the madman bum and angel beat in Time'. In the second part, the poet denounces 'Moloch the loveless', the god of power and 'pure machinery' in a way that recalls earlier prophets like Isaiah. It suggests what Richard Eberhart meant when he said the poem was 'profoundly Jewish in temper'; and it demonstrates Ginsberg's peculiar ability to combine the disjunctures of modernism with melancholy, an ancient sense of apocalypse. Finally, the third part concentrates on the destiny of one man, Carl Solomon, whom the poet identifies with as an archetype of suffering. Fired by this identification, Ginsberg then projects an imaginary liberation for them both, where they 'wake up electrified out of coma' to their 'own souls' airplanes roaring over the roof'. The planes have 'come to drop angelic bombs', the poet announces:

imaginary walls collapse O skinny legions
run outside O starry spangled shock of mercy
the eternal war is here O victory forget your
underwear you're free[40]

That last, jubilant remark illustrates the mixture of religious intensity and wry realism which is one of Ginsberg's most memorable gifts. Poems like 'Howl', 'In Back of the Real' or 'A Supermarket in California', work precisely because they walk a tightrope between acknowledgement of the grubby particulars of everyday life and proclamation of the immanent presence of the ideal. Even moments of annunciation, statements of vision and purpose, can be tempered with a wise and sufficient irony – a measured appreciation of what, in 'Sunflower Sutra', the poet calls the 'skin of grime' covering 'all beautiful golden sunflowers inside'. And this is because, as Ginsberg sees it, the two, skin and sunflower, are inseparable. For him (as his visionary experience while reading Blake indicates) that 'battered old thing' known as the soul announces itself through the 'dread bleak dusty' apparitions of the body; the joy of the spirit is incarnated in the sadness of the flesh.

'It occurs to me that I am America, / I am talking to myself again'. These lines are another example of Ginsberg's capacity for being intimate and prophetic, comic and serious, at one and the same time. And they also express his very American desire to celebrate and sing himself as representative man: to present his poems as what he has called 'a complete statement of Person'. As part of this statement, Ginsberg has written some extraordinarily powerful accounts of personal grief, like 'Kaddish', his fugue-like elegy to his mother. He has also produced poems of passionate sexual encounter, such as 'Love Poem on Theme by Whitman' and other pieces, including 'The Reply' and 'The End', that describe his experience of drugs in terms that recall earlier, prophetic accounts of wrestling with God. In the Sixties, in particular, Ginsberg made his wanderings over America and the globe his subject: in poems that are, as he has put it, 'not exactly poems nor not poems: journal notations put together conveniently, a mental turn-on'.[41] Often spoken into a tape-recorder rather than composed on the page, they carry his commitment to 'mind-flow', 'jumps of perception from one thing to another', to a new extreme. 'All contemporary history', Ginsberg says, 'whatever floated into one's personal field of consciousness and contact' is drawn together here, 'like weave a basket, basket-weaving'. Some of these poems of the late Sixties and early Seventies reveal a greater commitment to the specifics of history; nevertheless, they do so from the standpoint of Ginsberg's root concerns. In 'Wichita Vortex Sutra', for instance, the poet denounces the Vietnam War. But 'The war is language', he insists: that is, the Vietnam conflict is product and symptom of something deeper – the 'Black magic language' or 'formulas for reality' with which corporate America has blinded itself. Ginsberg's answer to this problem is to construct a model of 'language known / in the back of the mind': a true vocabulary, enabling true vision, of the kind once sculpted by Whitman and Pound and now constituted by this poem as a whole. Like the *Cantos*, in effect, 'Wichita Vortex Sutra' situates moral and political failure in a failure of words and proposes itself as 'the right magic / Formula' for recovering the good of body, spirit, and the body politic. 'I lift up my voice aloud', announces Ginsberg, '/ Make mantra of American language now, /pronounce the words beginning my own millenium, / I here declare the end of the War!' A new language will promote a new vision and a new society: it is a noble aim and one that has haunted American writing ever since what Ginsberg refers to as 'the prophecy of the Good Grey Poet'.

In more recent years, Ginsberg has gravitated closer to Buddhism. The idea of 'an awakened emptiness' or 'no Self' that was always lurking in his earlier work has now assumed more importance, promoting what the poet himself has termed 'a less attached, less apocalyptic view'. He is now trying hard, he says, to 'Avoid that mountain of ego vision!'; 'not even great Whitman's universal self', he claims, suits him any longer. One side result of this is that the Blake epiphany interests him less than it used to. Another is that many of his poems in recent collections direct gentle mockery at his own egotism, or survey the nightmares of contemporary history and his own story with a sense of acceptance, even distance. His poem about the death of his father, 'Don't Grow Old', charts the alteration: unlike 'Kaddish' it responds to loss, not with rage, but with a grave, melancholy quietude. 'What's to be done about Death?' Ginsberg asks and then softly, with sad resignation, answers his own question '/ Nothing, nothing'. This is not to say that such poems are unfeeling: but they place human emotion within the measureless scope of 'a relatively heavenly emptiness' and they aim to 'set surpassing example of sanity as measure for late generations'. Nor is it to ignore the continuities that underpin the evident change. The long line remains in evidence; so do humour, fits of exuberance, lust, or anger, and the impulse to transmute verse into vision. Only very recently, Ginsberg said this:

> . . . because the mind is continuously active, and is also
> discontinuous, . . . there's an endless variety of impression
> . . . language flowing through the head, pictures flashing,
> somewhat like MTV . . . The presentation of actual mind
> in public . . . reveals the fakery . . . of false mind, false
> language – and of all attempts to make up public speech
> acts . . . out of things you don't really think of, but
> would like other people to think you think of.[42]

Apart from the modish reference to MTV, this could have been said by Ginsberg thirty years ago. It indicates that, behind the Buddhist mask, the authentic American rebel is still at work; the voice of the prophet is still there, demanding to be heard.

Among the other Beat poets, the most memorable is probably Gregory Corso. The writings of Peter Orlovsky are too slight to constitute a distinctive body of work; and, although Jack Kerouac wrote some interesting poems, like his variations on black musical forms

'Mexico City Blues', it was, as Ginsberg has suggested, in his 'inspired prose' that he created 'really a new poetry'.[43] Corso, on the other hand, has evolved a distinct identity out of his poems: or, perhaps it would be more accurate to say, identities. For his best poetry is mobile, protean, above all disaffiliated. 'Should I get married? Should I be good?' begins one of his most famous pieces, 'Marriage', which then presents him trying out possible marriages, inventing potential selves, only to discard each one of them in turn. Jokey at times, at others wildly surreal, the poet is like Whitman's 'essential Me': standing apart from the game of life, and the roles and rules it prescribes, refusing to commit himself to a fixed, definite status. The rapidity of Corso's verse line is, in this sense, part of his message, as are his subversive humour and unpredictable alterations of pace and tone: the poet will not, it seems, be tied down by any of the institutions or forms that we use to organise life, whether they involve metre, stability of mood, or marriage. Chameleonlike, his is the voice of fluidity and change, the American as underground or confidence man. In his own way, in fact, Corso has tried to do what the novelist Ken Kesey has attempted in prose: to 'go with the flow', as Kesey puts it, to 'exist in the moment itself – Now!' – and to do this by means of mockery of other people's 'movies', conventional notions of the serious and the significant.

The loose forms and cool, anarchic voice favoured by so many of the Beats were not confined to them. Charles Bukowski, for instance, a writer associated with the urban sprawl of Los Angeles, uses a cryptic, free-floating line and an off-hand, casual idiom to describe the other America: life among the underclass, the bums, dropouts, and dispossessed who cast a cold eye on the national dream of success. 'I am not aiming high', Bukowski admits in one of his poems, ' / I am only trying to keep myself alive / just a little longer'. This is true enough, in a sense. There are no large gestures in his work: he simply tries to record things as they pass in a downbeat, laconic or even sardonic, way. However, this commitment to the notion of the writer as recording instrument does not inhibit judgement. Bukowski is a frustrated moralist, slyly reminding us of what Rexroth has called 'the unfulfilled promises of "Song of Myself" and *Huckleberry Finn*'. Nor does it limit the range of his voice. His poems are sometimes documentaries, alive with grubby detail ('Men's Crapper'), and at others strange and bizarre to the point of surrealism ('the catch'). This reflects a common impulse among contemporary writers: the sense that the extraordinary landscapes of post-war America can only be accommodated by a vision ready to use both fact and fantasy – the eye of the camera, with its disposition for empirical detail, and the inner eye of the fabulist, alert to nightmares and magic. 'Our history has moved on two rivers', the novelist Norman Mailer has observed:

> one visible, the other underground; there has been the history of politics which is concrete, practical . . . and there is the subterranean river of untapped, ferocious, lonely and romantic desires, that concentration of ecstasy and violence which is the dream life of the nation.[44]

How can American writers now navigate these two rivers? Mailer asks. How can they invent a language adequate to a reality that incorporates Harlem and Hollywood, the Vietnam War and MTV, Richard Nixon, Charles Manson, and Colonel Oliver North? The answer, suggested by a writer like Bukowski, is a mixture of naturalism and surrealism: demonstrating a willingness to write the facts down *and* to attend to the 'ecstasy and violence' that generated those facts, to gravitate between outer space and inner, documentary and dream.

Resurrecting the American rebel: black poetry (Baraka, Kaufman, Joans, Evans, Sanchez, Giovanni, Mahubuti, Karenga, Nelson)

Nobody has had more to navigate, as far as the two rivers of recent American history are concerned, than black writers, among them many poets. On the level of the 'visible' river, there has been the trauma of the assassinations of Malcolm X and Martin Luther King, the 'second American Revolution' of the Civil Rights movement and its aftermath, and, more recently, the emergence, within the framework of conventional party politics, of leaders like Jesse Jackson and, outside it, of the followers of Elijah Muhammed and the Black Muslim movement. And on the level of the 'subterranean' river, there has been the slow, painful, but triumphant growth of black pride: the sense that, as Leroi Jones – who subsequently renamed himself Imamu Amiri Baraka – puts it, 'the black man is the future of the world'. 'Let Black people understand that / they are the lovers and the sons of lovers', Baraka has declared, ' / and warriors and sons of warriors Are poems / poets & all the loveliness here in the world'. 'We are unfair, and unfair', he says elsewhere, turning from exhortation to incantation, ' / we are black magicians, black art / & we make in black labs of the heart. / . . . / . . . we own / the night'.[45] Appropriating the mythic power that Western symbolism habitually imputes to blackness, black poets have been in the vanguard of those aiming to turn those symbols inside out, so as to make them a source of pride for black people and a source of fear and wonder for whites. Absorbing black cultural influences as ancient as Islam and as modern as the music of John Coltrane, they have pushed Langston Hughes's commitment to cultural separateness to a fresh extreme. As far as forms and performance are concerned, this has involved the frequent adoption of the 'preacher style' of public speaking, endemic to the African and Afro-American traditions: where the poet/leader recites at a rapt, rapid pace and the audience/chorus dance, shout, and sing in response to the nervous fire of his words and the contagious nature of his rhythms. And as far as concerns content, this has had as one consequence a new assertiveness of tone and aggression of gesture: a renewed eagerness to see poetry as, to use the words of one recent black poet, 'survival motion set to music' – or, to borrow a phrase from another, 'magic . . . spells, to raise up / return, destroy, and create'.

'The Black Artist's role in America is to aid in the destruction of America as he knows it'.[46] The author of this remark is Imamu Amiri Baraka and it powerfully summarises a presiding aim that he shares with many other recent black writers: another one, Ron Karenga, for example, has put it this way, 'all our art must contribute to revolutionary change and if it does not, it is invalid'. To such remarks, however, it is worth adding a gloss. Not all recent black poets feel this way. Some even seem content to follow the path of Countee Cullen, by producing work that is virtually indistinguishable from the white tradition. David Henderson, for instance, writes poems like 'Sketches of Harlem' that resemble those of the white street poets of New York; while, in a different key, the woman poet G.C. Oden chooses to be closer in much of her writing to Louise Bogan ('The Carousel') or Elizabeth Bishop ('A Private Letter to Brazil') than to other black writers, male or female. Even the poets who have committed themselves to a specifically black revolutionary art cannot be entirely separated from the white tradition. Rebellion is hardly a black monopoly, after all; and much of the most trenchant white American poetry has also been preoccupied by the gap between performance and promise: America as the poet 'knows it' – which invites destruction – and America as he dreams of it – which begs to be realised, first in words and then in deeds. A gloss of this kind may be necessary, then, but it should not take away from the vital fact: at its best, recent black poetry *is* different. The difference can even be measured in terms of Baraka's own progress: as he has moved over the past thirty years from imitation of white forms, however innovative or subversive, to the formulation of a purely black aesthetic.

In the earlier stages of his career, while he was still known as Leroi Jones, Baraka was clearly influenced by those white American poets who, like him, saw themselves as alienated from the cultural mainstream. There are several poems that recall the work of Frank O'Hara: in 'Epistrópbe', for instance, Baraka uses the random, chancey rhythms of casual speech and imagery assembled by a mobile vision to capture the oddity of a familiar vista, 'what you see (here in New York)'. The figure of Charles Olson, in turn, hovers behind 'How You Sound??', Baraka's announcement of his aesthetic published in 1959. '"How You SOUND??" is what we recent fellows are up to', he declared:

> There must not be any preconceived *design* for what the *poem* ought to be . . . The only 'recognisable tradition' a poet need follow is himself . . . & with that, say, all those things out of tradition he can use . . . to broaden his *own* voice with.[47]

Baraka's principal involvement at this time, however, was not with the Black Mountain poets (although some of his earlier poems, such as 'In Memory of Radio', do resemble projectivist poetry) but with the beats. There have been a number of black writers associated with the beat generation. Among them is Bob Kaufman, who has used the long, sweeping line favoured by Ginsberg to announce that 'no man is our master', and address the possibility of universal brotherhood 'On this shore'. There is also Ted Joans, whose claim, 'Jazz is my religion', is catchily illustrated by poems like 'Voice in the Crowd' that imitate the abrupt, syncopated movement and startling dissonances of Ornette Coleman. But Baraka was, at least for a while, the most innovative and accomplished of the black beat poets, blending influences as disparate as European surrealism and dadaism, the jazz poetry of Vachel Lindsay and Langston Hughes, the Afro-American oral tradition, and the music of Charlie Parker. With these he fashioned poetry that, in marked contrast to his later work, was determinedly autobiographical, preoccupied with sex and death, and shaped by an existential despair.

Definition of self is, in fact, the overriding aim of this earlier writing. Unlike, say, Ginsberg's, the voice of this poetry is muted and introspective, susceptible to guilt and self-laceration. 'It's impossible to be an artist and a bread/winner at the same time', Baraka insists in one poem, and elsewhere, 'If I think myself / strong, then I am / not true to the misery / in my life'. Occasionally, there are traces of the rage that was to be such a significant force, for destruction and creation, in his later life and writing: 'There is something / in me so cruel, so / silent', he admits in 'The New Sheriff', 'It hesitates / to sit on the grass / with the young white virgins'. But there is, as yet, no firm sense of a connection with an African past, no clear recognition of blackness as the determinant of identity. 'African blues / ' does not know me', Baraka laments:

Their steps, in sands
of their own
land . . . Does
not feel
what I am . . .
. . .
My colour
is not theirs. Lighter, white man
talk. They shy away. My own
dead souls, my, so called
people. Africa
is a foreign place.[48]

The alteration in Baraka's vision and voice came in the Sixties: when, like many black nationalists, he dispensed with his white 'slave name' Leroi Jones and adopted a title more in keeping with his new self and his new mission. The function of his art now became prophetic and social. 'We want 'poems that kill',' he announced:

Assassin poems. Poems that shout
guns. Poems that wrestle cops into alleys
and take their weapons leaving them dead
with tongues pulled out and sent to Ireland.
Knockoff poems for dope selling wops or slick
halfwhite politicians . . .
. . .
Poem scream poison gas on beasts in green berets
Clean out the world for virtue and love,
Let there be no love poems written
until love can exist freely and
cleanly.[49]

What Baraka anticipates is nothing less than a 'jihad' or holy war of believers against unbelievers, black against white ('Come up, black dada / nihilismus. Rape the white girls / Rape the fathers. Cut the mother's throats'). From this holocaust, this ritual bloodletting of all that is false and dead – that is, specifically, white Christian civilisation – little will survive. But creation will nevertheless follow destruction. Primal innocence and energy will be restored; and a new nation will emerge out of the union between black power in America and anticolonialist movements in Africa. 'It's nation time eye ime', Baraka sings triumphantly:

> it's nation ti eye ime
> chant with bells and drum
> its nation time[50]

In a way, this is the American Dream in bright new pan-African robes: liberation from the present tyranny, the poet hopes, will be accompanied by a recovery of the perfection of the past and its restitution for an imagined future. There is no place for whites here, certainly: 'white people', we are told, '. . . are full of, and made of / shit'. But, ironically, Baraka still reflects the millenial tendencies of a culture he is determined to reject.

As for that determination itself, Baraka's conscious need to reject Western culture: that is real enough, and retains one of his dominating motives. He cannot entirely unlearn his American education, or excise those portions of himself that have been shaped by white culture, but he has tried painfully hard to do so. 'When I die', he has written,

> the consciousness I carry I will to
> black people. May they pick me apart and take the
> useful parts, the sweet meat of my feelings. And leave
> the bitter bullshit rotten white parts
> alone.[51]

The process of excision is, in effect, to be continued after his death: the few, lingering traces of white identity are to be left to decay while the rest, 'the sweet meat' of the black self, is to achieve a strictly carnal resurrection, growing in and through the bodies of others. As far as active practice is concerned, this insistence on 'Black feeling, Black mind, Black judgement' has led Baraka not only to political involvement but to the promotion of black community theatre. And, on the level of theory, it has encouraged the formulation of a black poetics. 'I think of the artist as a moralist', Baraka has said, '. . . demanding . . . a cleaner vision of the world'; 'we are spiritual', he goes on, . . . we must see ourselves again, as black men, as the strength of the planet, and rise to rebuild . . . what is actually good'. Even the rage that characterises so much of his work has been defended by him in terms of his moralist/nationalist aesthetics: 'What I'm after is a sense of clarity', he claims, 'if it sounds like anger, maybe that's good in a sense'. And anger is not, in any case, his only mode. His writing is also punctuated by cries for help ('calling all black people, come in, black people, come on / in'), friendly persuasion ('I want you to understand the world / as I have come to understand it'); above all, by respect for the energy of black people – something that he identifies with the ultimate agent of creativity ('God . . . is energy') and as an instrument of change, to be mobilised by force if necessary:

> Dynamite black girl
> swingin in the halls
> the world cant beat you
> and my slaps are love[52]

As part of this exorcism of his white self, Baraka now dismisses his earlier writing as 'a cloud of abstraction and disjointedness'. 'That was just whiteness', he has said of it, 'European influence . . . from the dead minds the dying morality of Europe'. The sense of disjuncture between his own present and the African past that characterised his first poems has been replaced by a feeling of continuity: 'We are beautiful people with african imaginations', he declares:

> full of masks and dances and swelling chants
> with african eyes, and noses, and arms
> though we sprawl in grey chains in a place
> full of winters, when what we want is sun.[53]

As these lines indicate, the self-consciousness and *angst* of the previous poetic voice has disappeared too, and in its place something more other-directed has been substituted: a faith and pride in *collective* identity, the belief that black people 'are all beautiful'. Shuffling off the burdens of the Western tradition, Baraka now seeks to harness the 'ancient images' and 'magic' of the African inheritance to his cause, coupling this with the verve he finds in all black cultural forms, from the speeches of Malcolm X to the music of Muddy Waters. 'What will be / the sacred words?' he asks. His aim, which he sees himself as sharing with other black writers, is to unravel a new language and line, 'sacred words, that will liberate him, his poetry, and in the process the hearts and minds of all his 'black family'. 'We have been captured, / brothers', he proclaims, 'And we labour / to make our getaway'. A new song that will generate a new self and, eventually, a new society: it is an ambition at least as old as *Leaves of Grass*, but it has been rendered almost unrecognisable here. For this is song in the service of, if necessary, violent revolution: designed, as Baraka has put it, to 'teach White Eyes their deaths, and teach the black man how to bring these deaths about'.

The work of Amiri Baraka, and the black power movement in general, has inspired a number of other poets who came to prominence in the sixties and after, among them Mari Evans, Sonia Sanchez, Nikki Giovanni, Don L. Lee / Haki R. Mahubuti, Ron Karenga, and David Nelson. These writers share with Baraka the belief that, as Sonia Sanchez puts it:

> this country might have
> been a pion
>   eer land. once.
>   and it still is
> check out
>   the falling
> gun / shells
>   on our blk / tomorrows.[54]

In other words, they have rejected the white American Dream ('The white man's heaven is the Black man's hell', a young writer has proclaimed): but they are also trying to restore the pioneer values of liberation and mobility, originally so fundamental to that Dream, in and for their own people. This necessarily involves them in a commitment to revolutionary struggle: 'change-up', one black poet commands, 'let's go for ourselves / . . . / change-up and yr children will look at u differently / than we looked at our parents'. The aim is to achieve an irreversible shift of power: 'I'm / gonna make it a / crime to be anything BUT black', Mari Evans has announced, 'gonna make white / a twenty-four hour / lifetime / J.O.B.' Formally, this aligns them with all those trying to 'write black', to realise a verbal approximation of the frantic energy, the hip rhythms, of black speech and music – as these lines, from a poem by Don L. Lee / Haki R. Mahubuti, attest:

> he didnt know
> after detroit, newark, chicago &c.,
> we had to hip
>   cool-cool / super-cool / real cool
>   that
> to be black
> is
> to be
> very-hot[55]

This is a poetry of *exhortation*, primarily: that, rather than dwell on personal suffering, insists on the abolition of communal suffering. 'Don't Cry, Scream', Lee/Mahubuti tells his audience and then obeys his own instructions, in a wild, typographical imitation of modern jazz:

scream – eeeeeeeeeeee – ing
SCREAM – EEEeeeeeeeeee – ing
loud &
SCREAM – EEEEEEEEEEEEEE – ing long with
feeling – [56]

Two further points need to be made about these other disciples of a black poetics. In the first place, the women among them have been keen to combat not just the racism of white culture but the latent sexism of the black: even revolutionary poets like Baraka tend to talk in generic terms about 'the black man' and to identify black women mainly with the sexual and reproductive functions. 'i wish i knew how it would feel / to be free', says Nikki Giovanni, and then goes on to link her historical imprisonment as a black with her cultural imprisonment as a woman:

its a sex object if you're pretty
and no love
or love and no sex if you're fat
get back fat black woman be a mother
grandmother strong thing but not a woman[57]

In the second place, many of these poets, women and men, are selective in their treatment of black culture. They want to jettison those elements in it which, they believe, impede the revolutionary momentum. Among these elements, the most notable are the music and spirit of the blues which, as Ron Karenga explains it, are 'not functional . . . because they do not commit us to the struggle of today and tomorrow'. Blues are 'a very beautiful, musical, and psychological achievement of our people', he admits, but 'they . . . keep us in the past' and 'whatever we do we cannot remain in the past'.[58] So no more blues, Sonia Sanchez insists, 'blues ain't culture / they sounds of oppression / against the white man's shit'. 'We ain't blue, we are black'. Lee/Mahubuti argues, and clearly David Nelson would agree with him: 'Blues was for waking and enduring and suffering / We need a new BLACK thing'. This 'new BLACK thing' will be the opposite of the old, a 'music . . . for the senses' that is 'fast an' happy an' mad!!!!!' Reversing the vicious cycle of oppression breeding despair breeding further oppression, it will be a 'song above horror', alive with 'black rhythm energy' and alert above all to the necessity to 'change-up'.

A significant aspect of the new black writing is that it is often aimed at performance. Like the work of the beats, as well as the San Francisco and Black Mountain groups, it relies as much on the spoken word as the written. And just as significant is the fact that it defies conventional distinctions between 'high' and 'popular' culture. Intended to be immediately accessible, and nurture feelings of community, it is a poetry of and for the street. So the four-man group known as The Last Poets (both the originals and the subsequent groups of that name) have exploited ghetto culture, rapping and hip-hop, to get their message across to their Harlem neighbours; while some of the recordings of David Nelson, Nikki Giovanni, and more recently Gil Scott-Heron, have become popular hits on a national scale. This bridging of the gap between 'high' and 'popular' is just as remarkable in, say, the work of Ginsberg: his haunting mix of surreal vision and social comment finds its equivalent in the songs of Bob Dylan. Ginsberg even invokes 'Angelic Dylan singing across the airwaves',[59] in 'Wichita Vortex Sutra', as the prophet of a redemptive language, needed to subvert the dominant vocabulary of war and waste. Few other white poets have pushed things quite as far as this. It is worth noting, though, that Ferlinghetti was among those who appeared at the farewell concert for The Band, Dylan's former backing group, along with Joni Mitchell and Muddy Waters. And it is also worth pointing out that echoes of the line and language of the beats are to be found in the songs of the Grateful Dead and Bruce Springsteen – along with those twin preoccupations of beat poets, the vastness of American space and the sadness or strangeness of much American life. The reasons for this alliance between rock, jazz, and poetry are not difficult to fathom: all are seen as weapons of the counterculture. Beats, prophets, aesthetes, and rock musicians can all come together at least on this: the dream of an alternative America.

Reinventing the American self: the New York poets (O'Hara, Guest, Schuyler, Berrigan, Koch, Ashbery) and Merrill

Another, rather different vision of alternative America surfaces in the work of a group whose main connections have been with the visual arts, both 'high' and 'popular': the New York poets, among them Frank O'Hara, Kenneth Koch, Ted Berrigan, and John Ashbery. 'Poetry was declining', wrote the leading member of this group, Frank O'Hara, in one of his poem-painting collaborations with the painter Larry Rivers, ' / Painting advancing / we were complaining / it was

'50'.[60] O'Hara felt at odds with most of the poetry that was being written in America in the 1950s. He deeply disliked the confessional poets, complaining that Lowell's 'confessional manner' let him 'get away with things that are just plain bad': 'but you're supposed to be interested', he added. 'because he's supposed to be so upset'. Ginsberg was a personal friend, but O'Hara studiously avoided the beat poet's revolutionary fervour and prophetic assumptions: politics and metaphysics were not among his immediate interests – 'I don't believe in god', he said, '. . . You just go on your nerve'. As for the Black Mountain group: O'Hara was wary of what he saw as their programmatic approach. Of Olson he remarked, with a characteristic blend of sympathy and acumen, 'I don't think that he is willing to be as delicate as his sensibility may be emotionally and he's extremely conscious . . . of saying the important utterance'. He was less generous towards Creeley and Levertov, however: observing that they 'pared down the diction' to the point that what came through was 'the experience of their paring it down' rather than 'the experience that is the subject'. All these poets had too palpable a design on the reader, he believed: at some point, no matter how circuitous the route, they began to spin off beyond the hard material surfaces and processes of their purported subject. 'The objective in writing is to reveal', O'Hara insisted, 'It is not to teach, to advertise, not to see, not even to communicate . . . but to reveal'. Too often this objective was ignored: succumbing to the 'symbols of an over-symbolic society', writers assumed an aesthetics of transcendence rather than what should be the case – an aesthetics of immediacy, of presence.

'I am needed by things', O'Hara declared, 'as the sky must be above the earth'. His aim was to 'defamiliarise' the ordinary, even what he felt was the 'sheer ugliness in America': and, in order to do this, he wanted to be as attentive as possible to the world around him. It was the artist's 'duty to be attentive', he felt: so the artists he cherished were those like his friend Larry Rivers who, as he put it, 'taught me to be more keenly interested while I'm still alive'. 'Perhaps this is the most important thing art can say', he suggested, and as a way of saying this himself – a means of assuring recognition of the lively details of the now – he pursued a poetic structure that was changing, shifting, quirky, quick, and immediate. His literary mentors were people like Whitman, with whom O'Hara shared a belief in the multiple nature of identity ('Grace / to be born and live as variously as possible') and Williams, whose commitment to seeing and mobility O'Hara appreciated ('How I hate . . / . . . all things that don't change'). There was also Pound, whom he called 'the father of modern poetry in English'. More to the point, O'Hara clearly learned much from the 'charming artifice' of French poets like Apollinaire and Reverdy ('My heart is in my / pocket. It is Poems by Pierre Reverdy'), and from the Surrealists and Dadaists, who taught him how to capture the simultaneity of the instant. On a strictly literary level, in fact, O'Hara's development could be charted from his early experiments in what might be termed 'straight Surrealism' ('Chez Jane') and, rather different, his imitations of Americanist writers such as Williams ('Les Etiquettes Jaunes'), to the mature poetry of the late Fifties where the two modes are wedded. The result of this union – between a surreal understanding of the elusive, metamorphic nature of things and a toughly empirical American idiom – is poetry that can shift, with astonishing speed, from flat literalism to fantasy and then back again. These opening lines, from a poem called 'Music', show just how sudden the transitions can be:

> If I rest for a moment near the Equestrian
> pausing for a liver sausage sandwich in the Mayflower Shoppe
> that angel seems to be leading the horse into Bergdorf's
> and I am naked as a table cloth, my nerves humming.

But to talk in strictly literary terms about O'Hara or the other New York poets is only to tell half the story. 'After all', O'Hara mischievously remarked, 'only Whitman and Crane and Williams, of the American poets, are better than the movies.'[61] He, and his friends, were interested in an art fired into life by the moment; and that meant, certain kinds of poetry certainly, but also all forms of dance, the *motion* picture and *action* painting.

'We . . . divided our time between the literary bar, the San Remo, and the artists', the Cedar Tavern', O'Hara later said of his early days together with Ashbery and Koch, '. . . the painters were the only generous audience for our poetry'.[62] A *rapport* was quickly established between the poets, and painters as diverse as Jasper Johns, Larry Rivers, Robert Rauschenberg, Grace Hartigan, and Willem de Kooning. All of them shared the excitement of New York City: which was, as they saw it, a model of simultaneity, the place where more was happening at one moment than anywhere else in the world. By comparison, the rest of the country, and especially the countryside, seemed stale: 'I can't even enjoy a blade of grass', O'Hara claimed, 'unless I know there's a subway handy, or a record store or some other sign that people do not totally *regret* life'. The shared excitement issued in collaborative work, poem-paintings and mixed media performances, and in mutual appreciation: O'Hara was and Ashbery still is a distinguished art critic, while O'Hara was also a curator at the Museum of Modern Art. Above all, it generated a common aesthetic: one that perceived the surface of the poem or painting as a field on which the physical energies of the artist could operate, without mediation of metaphor or symbol. 'Now please tell me', wrote O'Hara in a letter to Larry Rivers, in which he enclosed some of his work, 'if you think these poems are filled with disgusting self pity . . . if the surface isn't "kept up" . . . or if they don't have "push" and "pull"'. That request signals his priorities, those imperatives of artistic creation that he shared with other members of the New York group. The surface is to be '"kept up"': that is the first imperative. The artwork should not be 'reflective, or self-conscious', there should be nothing *behind* it. A successful relation of verbal imagery or visual planes should create a lively, depthless microcosm of the artist's world, as empirically verifiable as a street map yet also surreal, fantastic – since it involves mind as well as scene, the *active* engagement of the artist with subject matter and materials. In turn, the audience responding to the work should 'travel over the complicated surface exhaustively': that is the second imperative. The audience, in effect, should be no more self-indulgent than the artist is, and no more detached: they should give themselves up to the lively play of figuration, the 'marvellous burgeoning into life', that constitutes the work, continually refreshing their instinctive sense of what it 'says'. 'The best of the current sculpture', O'Hara insisted, 'didn't make me feel I wanted to *have* one, they made me feel I wanted to *be* one'. And it is precisely this surrendering of the self to surface, not interpreting but participating, that he aimed for in his own work. If the poem or painting creates presence, he believed, and if the audience is as attentive to presence as the artist has been, then the process of identification is complete.

O'Hara's own term for this aesthetic he shared with other poets and painters was 'Personism'. He even wrote his own 'manifesto' for this 'Personism'. Characteristically, this is both an act of comic bravado (he had an instinctive distrust of programmes of any kind and this, in part, is a witty parody of them) and a serious statement of intention. 'Personism', the poet tells us, 'puts the poem squarely between the poet and the person . . . The poem is at last between two persons instead of two pages'. True to this credo, there is a quality of intimate conversation to much of O'Hara's poetry – of talk 'between two persons' that is at once familiar and fantastic:

It is 12.10 in New York and I am wondering
if I will finish this in time to meet Norman for lunch
ah lunch! I think I am going crazy
what with my terrible hangover and the weekend coming up . . .

The voice talking here, however, is not a confessional but a responsive one, eager to attend to the continuum of things and ready for immersion in the processes it contemplates. O'Hara does not reflect in a traditional way nor try to extrapolate significances. Instead, he swims in the medium of his feeling and being: inviting us to come into momentary awareness of things just as he does. He traces, say, the disjunctive movements of his sensibility ('In Memory of my Feelings', 'Ode (to Joseph Le Sueur) on the Arrow that Flieth by Day'). Or he compels us into attention to the total environment of the city: its noises ('a faint stirring of that singing seems to come to me in heavy traffic'), its shifting qualities of light ('the cool graced light / is pushed off the enormous glass piers'), its discontinuities, surprises, and the 'strange quiet excitement' it can generate. As he does so, he alerts us to his own instinctive belief that 'the slightest loss of attention leads to death'. Life, in these terms, has an immanent rather than transcendent value: it is, as O'Hara himself put it once, 'just what it is and just what happens'. 'I'm not going to cry all the time, /nor shall I laugh all the time', O'Hara announces in 'My Heart', ' / I don't prefer one strain to another'. 'I want my face to be shaven', he continues, 'and my heart – / you can't plan on the heart, but / the better part of it, my poetry, is open'. How does O'Hara achieve this 'openness', and so dodge the habitual? On a larger scale, he does so by opting for a range of tone and form. There are his 'I do this, I do that' poems, like 'Joe's Jacket', 'Personal Poem', and 'Lana Turner has Collapsed!'; and there are also more intensely surreal pieces, such as 'Second Avenue', Whitmanesque odes like 'To the Film Industry in Crisis', and powerfully erotic lyrics, the most striking of which perhaps is 'You are Gorgeous and I'm Coming'. On the more local level of the individual poem, O'Hara's discomposing mix of literalism and surrealism works with other strategies to strip away the veneer of habituation. His lineation, for instance, with its ambivalent positioning of words, constant breaks and compulsive enjambement, generates tension, a sense of breakneck speed. At the same time, an elaborate system of syntactical ambiguity, based on non-sequiturs, pseudo-connectives, ellipses and dangling, incomplete sentences: all this helps turn the poem into an instantaneous performance, denied conventional divisions of beginning, middle, and end. Like a Cubist or Abstract Expressionist painter, O'Hara scrambles his representational clues, preferring complex effects of simultaneity, the clash of surfaces, to the illusions of depth and coherence. There are constant temporal and spatial dissolves too; the poet shifts rapidly from one place or moment to another without the usual semantic props, such as 'when', 'after', or 'before'. Everything, as a result, is absorbed into an undifferentiated stream of activity, the flow of the now – as in these lines, where an elevator ride in Manhattan becomes a trip to heaven becomes a voyage into a Hollywood jungle:

515 Madison Avenue
door to heaven? portal

stopped realities and eternal licentiousness
or at least the jungle of impossible eagerness
your marble is bronze and your lianas elevator cables
swinging from the myth of ascending
I would join . . .[64]

O'Hara is not only the major poet of the New York group: he is also the one who, both before and after his tragically early death in 1966, has acted as the main inspiration to others. Ted Berrigan spoke for these others when he said that 'in one brief poem' O'Hara could 'create a whole new kind of awareness of feeling, and by this a whole new kind of poetry': a poetry, Berrigan added, 'in which everything could be itself and still be poetry'. The particular poem Berrigan had in mind when he said this was one of O'Hara's most famous pieces, 'The Day Lady Died', an elegy dedicated to the blues singer Billie Holiday, who was known by those who loved her – friends and audiences alike – as 'Lady Day'. The tenderly jokey way in which O'Hara reverses her nickname in the title epitomises the quirky and yet passionate nature of his approach – here and elsewhere. This is an elegy, certainly, but it is an unconventional one, not so much lamenting the fact of the singer's death as enacting the process whereby the poet comes to learn of it. 'It is 12.20 in New York, a Friday', the poem begins:

three days after Bastille day, yes
it is 1959 and I go get a shoeshine
because I will get off the 4.19 in Easthampton
at 7.15 and then go straight to dinner
and I don't know the people who will feed me

This is vintage O'Hara, in its use of the chancey rhythms of American speech and its meandering, apparently casual syntax. So is it, too, in its specificity of person and place: 'and in the GOLDEN GRIFFIN', the poet tells us, 'I get a little Verlaine / for Patsy'. As usual in O'Hara's work, the name-dropping has a curiously ambivalent effect. It helps situate the 'I' of the poem in a particularised space, but, because of the avoidance of explanation (who is Patsy?), it insists on our, the readers' alienation from his inner life: all we are permitted is the surface details. This is a mobile, depthless landscape, marked by feelings of anonymity, disconnection, and incipient melancholy ('I don't know the people who will feed me'). As such, it is distinctively urban; and it finds its distillation in the strangeness and sadness of the figure, and songs, of Lady Day, towards whom the poet moves in the closing lines:

and I am sweating a lot now and thinking of
leaning on the john door in the 5 SPOT
while she whispered a song along the keyboard
to Mal Waldron and everyone and I stopped breathing[65]

'Everyone and I stopped breathing': the process that leads to the discovery of Billie Holliday's death has been rendered in such an immediate, authentic way that, when we come to these final words, we actually participate in the poignant memory of her performance. The last line 'stops breathing' just as the name of Lady Day is about to be uttered: the announcement of the wonder of her song and the absolute finality of her death is caught there, in the last two words and the blank, unpunctuated space that follows them. 'It may be that poetry makes life's nebulous events tangible to me', O'Hara observed once, 'and restores their specific detail; or conversely, that poetry brings forth the intangible quality of incidents that are all too concrete and circumstantial'.[66] 'The Day Lady Died' illustrates perfectly what he meant. The minutiae of one day are restored here in all their random particularity, their bright, material surfaces. But this sequence of meaningless moments is cast into a different shape, irradiated by an 'intangible quality' of apparent meaning, by the moment of recollection that concludes it. Everyone, so the cliché goes, remembers what they were doing when they first heard that President Kennedy had been shot: an otherwise unremarkable day has been rendered remarkable, engraved on our minds, by this most arbitrary of connections. By the same token, what O'Hara was doing one Friday in 1959 has been rescued from oblivion by his catching sight of a newspaper headline and glimpsing the news of another death. Time collapses at the end of this poem, in more ways than one. The remembered song of Billie Holliday, we are told, inspired a moment of epiphany, when the normal compulsion to breathe seemed to be suspended; and the song of the poet now identifies the present with the past in one seamless series, as circumstantiality is redeemed by memory. The details of O'Hara's day have not changed: they are still without intrinsic meaning, they are unburdened by what the poet himself called 'symbolic aura'. But they have been thrown into new configurations by the presence of a momentous fact: they are surfaces suddenly shining with revelation.

'O'Hara's poetry has no programme', John Ashbery has insisted, 'and therefore cannot be joined'.[67] This is perfectly true. Nevertheless, many poets have felt an affinity with him, and shared at least some of his purposes. Their personal affection for him has been expressed in the numerous elegies that appeared after his death: the most notable of which, perhaps, are 'Strawberries in Mexico' by Ron Padgett,

'Buried at Springs' by James Schuyler, and 'Frank O'Hara' by Ted Berrigan. And the sense of aesthetic kinship is evident not only from what members of the New York group have said about O'Hara but from particular poetic habits. The attention to surface, the unexpected line-breaks and gamey, casual idiom, the switchback movement between the literal and surreal, an almost voyeuristic attention to empirical detail and an expressionist involvement in the poem as field of action: all, or at least some, of these characteristics help to mark out writers like Schuyler, Berrigan, Barbara Guest, Kenneth Koch, and Ashbery himself. But of course such writers are not possessed of a corporate mind and, as Ashbery points out, were not following a formulated programme; so, inevitably, very clear differences have emerged between them. The poetry of Barbara Guest, for instance, is edged with delicacy of feeling and a frail exoticism:

> In the golden air, the risky autumn
> leaves on the piazza, shadows by the door
> on your chair the red berry
> after the dragon fly summer[68]

Schuyler similarly recomposes landscape in a painterly manner, finding new shapes and patterns, but he possesses an intrinsic reverence for nature that is rare among the group. These lines taken from his elegy to O'Hara are a poignant illustration, not only of tenderness, but of difference of sensibility between their author and their subject (who once claimed that 'One need never leave the confines of New York to get all the greenery one wishes'):

> Delicate day, setting the bright
> of a young spruce against the cold
> of an old one with unripe cones
> each exuding at its tip
> gum, pungent, clear as a tear . . .[69]

Some of the poems of Ted Berrigan are embarrassingly derivative of O'Hara: 'Today I woke up / bright and early', one begins, '/ Then I went back to sleep / I had a nice dream'. What is more, they imitate O'Hara's reverence for detail while missing his extraordinary modulations of tone, his split-second dissolves and syntactic displacements; as a result, the mood is slack, tending towards a simple empiricism, a catalogue of particulars that do not really add up. At its best, though, Berrigan's work has a memorable clarity that issues from his willingness to put the 'I'/ eye of the poet at the centre of things: as he says of New York, 'it's only here you can turn around 360 degrees / And everything is clear from the centre / To every point along the circle of the horizon'. This clarity can sometimes be the clarity of consciousness (he can create hallucinatory effects out of the condition of 'Sleep half sleep half silence'), the clarity of American speech (many of his poems, like Williams's, are vignettes of urban life and idiom), or simple clarity of feeling – as in these lines from the epitaph he wrote for himself:

Love, & work,
Were my great happiness, that other people die the source
Of my great, terrible, & inarticulate one grief. In my time
I grew tall & huge of frame, obviously possessed
Of a disconnected head, I had a perfect heart. The end
Came quickly & completely without pain . . .[70]

Kenneth Koch is less immediately serious than this: 'I think I have three souls', he has announced. ' / One for love one for poetry and one for acting out my insane self'.[71] His poems are alive with wild, surreal comedy, rambunctious rhythms and verbal inventiveness; it is as if they were written by a Kafka with a slapstick sense of humour. His aim, he says, is to 'recreate the excitement', the spontaneity and exuberance, he has found in French poetry; and the main object of his aesthetic loathing are what he calls the 'castrati of poetry', 'Young poets from the universities' who write 'elegant poems' in 'stale pale skunky pentameters'. At the heart of his writing is an absurdist sense that poets and readers alike are victims of 'an absolute and total misunderstanding (but not fatal)'; and the result is that nearly everything he has written, from parodies of other poets ('Variations on a Theme by William Carlos Williams') through surrealistic love poems ('To You') to autobiography ('Alive for an Instant') is edged with a verbal grin that is simultaneously playful and grim.

Apart from O'Hara, however, the most significant poet associated with the New York group is neither Koch nor Berrigan, Schuyler nor Guest, but John Ashbery. Ashbery first met O'Hara at Harvard, and when O'Hara moved to Manhattan in 1951 the two met regularly. 'Frank got me interested in contemporary music', Ashbery has recalled. 'American painting seemed the most exciting art around', he added, '. . . and . . . much of my feeling for Rothko and Pollock came through Frank'.[72] The enthusiasms the two poets shared generated at least some similar tendencies in their poetry. There is the same commitment to the work as personal idiom, for instance, the discontinuous activities of individual experience: 'I know that I braid too much my own / snapped-off perceptions as they come to me', admits Ashbery in one piece, ' / They are private and always will be'. There is, too, a similar estrangement from simple mimesis, a shared belief that poetry does not reflect reality it constitutes it: which leads, in turn, to a relentless opposition to systematics ('there's no excuse / For always deducing the general from particulars'), consistency ('I often change my mind about my poetry', he has said) and the illusion of meaning. 'What does it mean ??????????????' he asks of one of his poems, during the course of writing it; and the fourteen question marks slyly subvert the assumptions, the need for cause and explanation, that lie behind the question. 'Most of my poems are about the experience of experience'. Ashbery has remarked, in one of his rare moments of elucidation, '. . . and the particular experience is of lesser interest to me than the way it filters through me'. 'I believe this is the way in which it happens with most people', he declares, 'and I'm trying to record a king of generalised transcript of what's really going on in our minds all day long'. According to these terms, if the poem is a verbal graph of the consciousness, then the poet is a transparent medium through which the experiences of the day flow; and the words of the poem, in turn, constitute the notations, the signs that cease to apply as quickly and imperceptibly as the experiences they signify, and the moment of consciousness that acted as signifier.

Another way of putting all this, and signalling the difference between Ashbery and O'Hara, is to say that Ashbery's is a poetry of absence. Ashbery has said as much himself. 'The carnivorous / way of these lines is to devour their own nature', he confides in one of his poems, 'leaving / Nothing but a bitter impression of absence, which as we know involves presence'. 'Nevertheless', he adds, 'these are fundamental absences, struggling to get up and be off themselves'. There are various influences at work here, to which O'Hara was more or less immune: among them Poe, with his belief in a poetry that disappears as it is read, and Stevens, with his interest in epistemology, the mind's baffling encounter with the objects it contemplates. Also, the example of Gertrude Stein is not to be discounted. Stein was trying, she said, to write the way Picasso painted or an infant sees: in terms of fragments (one side of a mother's face, for example), and without trying to reconstitute some memory or inference of the whole. Her ultimate ambition was 'a continuously moving picture', like a series of cinematic frames: works enacting a perpetually developing present, for which there is 'no memory,' and so no 'assembling' or 'relating', no increasing density of significance. 'After all', she argued, 'the natural way to count is not that one and one make two but to go on counting by one and one'. 'Counting by one and one' is what Ashbery does. His poetry deflates our expectation of sense, of presence, by offering us always the playful, fluid zone of deferred sense, suspended meaning. 'Someday I'll explain', he promises jokily in 'Ode to Bill,' 'Not today though'.[73] The 'I' that shadows his writing consequently resembles Sartre's existential man: in whom, as Sartre puts it, 'acts, emotions, and ideas suddenly settle . . . and then disappear'. 'You cannot say he submits to them', Sartre points out, 'He experiences them. There seems to be no law governing their appearance'.

Ashbery's earliest published poems, such as 'Some Trees', are mainly concerned with the operations of the sleeping consciousness, and are activated by the belief that the function of the poet is, as he puts it, to 'give fullness / To the dream'. These were followed by his experimenting, at roughly the same time as O'Hara, in 'straight surrealism'. In poems like 'Europe' and 'They Dream Only of America', fractured images, jumbles of non-sequiturs, and techniques of verbal collage are used to dramatise the humiliating and reifying aspects of modern life. But it has been from the later Sixties on that Ashbery has hit his real stride, with poems such as 'The Skaters', 'Self-Portrait in a Convex Mirror' and 'A Wave' as well as prose pieces like 'The System'. No one work can adequately demonstrate the nature of his mature writing, since each new one tends to constitute an act of renewal. These few lines from 'Grand Galop', though, offer a characteristic realisation of what Ashbery himself has called 'the quirky things that happen to me':

> Still, that poetry does sometimes occur
> If only in creases in forgotten letters
> Packed away in trunks in the attic – things you forgot you had
> And what would it matter anyway,
> That recompense so precisely dosed
> As to seem the falling true of a perverse judgement.[74]

An irresolute syntax, the casual use of slang, cliché and apparent redundancies ('still', 'anyway'), the false starts and back-tracking, the free associations, the occasional opacity of phrasing and the equally occasional hard, focussed image: all are the verbal weapons of a mind in process – or, rather, a mind that *is* process, a medium in which quite disparate objects meet and merge. The long, serpentine verse paragraphs hold the different elements in close physical contiguity, as if the writer were trying to create a multidimensional space, a 'seamless web' in which everything could be folded into everything else. This is a poetry which insists that structures are always virtual, always to-be-known or more exactly always to-be-inferred: as Levi-Strauss has said, a structure is a vital object whose shadow alone is real. And this is a poet who insists on the disjunctive nature of history and personality. Historical experience, evidently, is a 'tangle of impossible resolutions and irresolutions', what happens outside the neat demarcations of sages and storytellers: 'The sagas purposely ignore how better it was the next day', Ashbery observes, ' / The feeling in between the chapters', and it is clear that he does not wish to imitate them. Personality, in turn, is stripped of conclusive choices: 'I cannot decide in which direction to walk', the poet admits in 'Grand Galop', adding happily, ' / But this doesn't matter to me'. Lacking such determinants, the co-ordinates of a particular road taken, it too becomes shadowy, as shifting and irresolute as the language that enacts its absence, its baffling and blank contingency.

'All was strange': the closing remark in 'A Wave' sounds a theme that resonates through Ashbery's poetry and the work of other contemporary American poets, not all of them necessarily identified with the New York group. The metamorphoses of consciousness, the absolute ravishment of the senses by the radiant surfaces of the world are, for instance, the primary intuitions of a writer who is in many respects hauntingly different from Ashbery or O'Hara, James Merrill. Merrill is commonly associated with the disciples of the New Critical school and, in a strictly formal sense, there is some truth to this association: much of his work is characterised by a delicate, ironic verbal wit, formal prosody, careful crafting of syntax and metaphor, and a baroque sense of decor. He betrays traces of the confessional tendency too, in that some of his poems deal with painful autobiographical material: his tangled erotic involvement with his mother, say ('The Broken Home', 'The Emerald'), his fiercely oedipal relationship with his father ('Scenes from Childhood'), or the pleasures and pains of being a homosexual ('Days of 1964', 'Mornings in a New House'). That said, however, it has to be added that Merrill begins and ends where Ashbery and O'Hara do: with what Merrill himself, in 'Transfigured Bird', calls 'the eggshell of appearance'. There may be a perilous abyss beneath *this* surface, perhaps, but what Merrill senses always is the inevitability and necessity of masks, screens, fictions. In fact, the eye that attempts to peer beneath the 'glassen surface' of things is for him a kind of predator – a monster:

> coaxed out by lusters
> Extraordinary, like the octopus
> From the gloom of its tank half-swimming half-drifting
> Toward anything fair . . .
> . . .
> Till on glass rigid with his own seizure
> At length the sucking jewels freeze.[75]

Life, in Merrill's view, is 'fiction in disguise'. As poets and as people, our function is to skim over the surfaces that constitute our known world 'with an assurance of safety – the thoughtful ease of someone 'skating upon a sheet of ice . . . formed above a black torrent'. This may be 'a form of flight', Merrill admits, 'but it is also a form of healing': the surfaces we stay poised above are 'protecting' ones, sheltering us from waste and anxiety, unconditional surrender to the void.

An early and relatively simple expression of Merrill's belief in the healing nature of artifice is the poem, 'For Proust'. In it, the poet describes Marcel Proust going home after a painful encounter with his lover and writing about the event: 'What happened', we are told, 'is becoming literature'. By the end of this process, and the poem that portrays it, 'The world will have put on a thin gold mask': the brute experience will have been shaped and contained within a gilded artefact that is simultaneously Proust's art and Merrill's. In this sense, the lacquered finish of the poem is an essential part of its point: the cool, poised surfaces of lines like the following – describing Proust's lover – enact the aestheticising of experience that they also celebrate:

> She treats you to a look you cherished, light,
> Bold, "*Mon ami*, how did we get along
> At all, those years?" But in her hair a long
> White lock has made its truce with appetite.[76]

As these lines indicate, perhaps, the poem is a mask in several senses: in that it is written in praise and imitation of masking, in that it accepts Proust's masking of his homosexuality in heterosexual terms, and in that Merrill uses this, in turn, as a mask or disguise for his own sexual preferences. Masking, or masquerade, operates in all human activity, as Merrill perceives it: love, for instance, he sees as founded on mutual deception and projection, 'the erotic mask / Worn the world over by illusion / To weddings of itself and simple need'. In another poet, this might be a motive for tragic discontent. With Merrill, however, the premise is that appearances *are* our realities, and that it is neither wise nor prudent to question them. The experiential consequences of this are that morality is for Merrill a matter of behaviour, manners. 'Manners', he has said, 'are the touch of nature, an artifice in the very bloodstream'. 'They are as vital as all appearances', he adds, 'and if they deceive us they do so by mutual consent'. And in literary terms, the result is a painterly approach to things. Issuing from a different source from the painterliness of Ashbery, and radically different in its formal details, his poetry demonstrates the same wilful refusal to penetrate below its own 'cool web / And stinging song', the same determined rejection of inwardness.

If Merrill's lyric poems aestheticise autobiography, reflecting what he calls 'the dull need to make some kind of house / Out of the life lived, and out of the love spent',[77] then his epic trilogy, *The Changing Light at Sandover*, expresses a larger desire to create an aesthetic for survival. Written in a variety of poetic forms, the trilogy is the result, Merrill claims, of a communion with spirits: into it he has poured his beliefs and fears, spread among passages of revelation that were spelled out to him on an ouija board. 'The design of the book swept me along', he has said: this is an epic as formless and personal, as locked into process and possibility, as all other American epics. It can sometimes be as absurd or narcissistic as, say, 'Song of Myself': as, for instance, when the poet tries to argue that homosexuals are the ultimate triumph of evolution, the true creators of poetry and music, 'THOSE 2 PRINCIPAL LIGHTS OF GOD BIOLOGY'. Equally, it can be as obscure as the *Cantos* or the *Maximus Poems* occasionally are, as prosaic as passages in *Paterson* or *Notebook*, as fragmented and bewildering as *The Bridge* or *Dream Songs*. Along with these and other experiments in this genre, though, it is also possessed of a fierce energy, the animating conviction that there is still time to choose between the apocalypse and the millenium. On the one hand, Merrill points out, there is the danger of global destruction wrought by 'ANIMAL SOULS', the passive victims of technology and their own destructive impulses. On the other, there is the opportunity of a new life, a paradise on earth springing from the liberation of the imaginative intelligence and its discovery of a redemptive fiction. 'Stevens imagined the imagination / And God are one', Merrill observes:

> the imagination, also
> As that which presses back, in parlous times
> Against "the pressure of reality".[78]

Merrill is clearly in agreement with this: the words and artefacts fashioned by feeling are for him, as for so many other American writers, an access to a saving knowledge of our predicament. They are as necessary, he implies, as breath and bread; and in this sense the true opposite of poetry is, not prose or science, but annihilation.

Postscript: America a poem

'This poem is concerned with language on a very plain level', begins one of Ashbery's more recent pieces,

Look at it talking to you. You look out a window
Or pretend to fidget. You have it but you don't have it
You miss it, it misses you. You miss each other.[79]

This is the authentic American voice, still talking over a hundred years after Whitman published the first edition of *Leaves of Grass*. The tone is intimate, immediate, even confrontational. As so often in American writing, the 'you', the direct address to the reader, appears even before the 'I' does. 'What's a plain level?' the voice of the poem asks, and then answers:

It is that and other things,
Bringing a system of them into play. Play?
Well, actually, yes . . .[80]

The poem, evidently, requires playfulness, the sprightly mobility of words and rhythms announcing that life is motion; and it needs to be 'Open-ended', so susceptible to change as to be protean, 'lost in the steam and chatter of typewriters'. Also, the poet intimates, it should generate a sense of unease, something that is a necessary consequence of a commitment to potential, the 'dreamed role-pattern' of the future rather than the prescriptive structures of the past. As Ashbery draws to a conclusion in which very little is concluded, he seems to be speaking not only for his own perception of things but for generations of American poets who have made the direct encounter with process and particularity their shaping aim. The 'I' is more shifting and shadowed here than it is in 'Song of Myself', or for that matter the work of Pound and Williams (let alone, the poetry of Frost or Robinson). Still, there is a feeling as always of a specific consciousness, however metamorphic its nature, at work on the real and the reader. Ashbery's closing point is, in fact, one that links the elusive character of his own identity to the equally elusive character of his audience. 'It has been played once more', Ashbery says of the casual yet graceful sense of experience he has been celebrating, and the poetic instrument used to celebrate it. And he then adds this, almost as a gesture of challenge:

I think you exist only
To tease me into doing it, on your level, and you aren't there
Or have adopted a different attitude. And the poem
Has set me softly down beside you. The poem is you.[81]

These last words express a belief that fires every American poem into life. The poem is the identity of the poet, realised in the act of writing; it also, Ashbery insists, enacts identity for the reader, as he or she participates in the re-creative process of reading; in doing so, it achieves a brief moment of communion. Poet and audience are caught, for a moment, in a fragile web of words; together, they are compelled into a recognition that the liberation of being and the realisation of communal meaning dreamed of by the first colonisers of America – if they are to be found anywhere at all – are to be found there.

Notes

1. Robert Frost, 'The Gift Outright,' lines 1–3, 10–14.
2. See, Michael Harrington, *The Other America* (New York, 1962).
3. Sonia Sanchez, 'Right on: white America,' lines 11–12. See also, Morris Dickstein, *Gates of Eden: American Culture in the Sixties* (New York, 1977).
4. See, Christopher Lasch, *The Culture of Narcissism: American Life in an Age of Diminishing Expectations* (New York, 1978).
5. Charles Olson, 'Projective Verse', in *The New American Poetry 1945–1960* edited by Donald M. Allen (New York, 1960), p. 386. See also, pp. 387, 388, 389; 'Human Universe', in *Selected Writings of Charles Olson* edited by Robert Creeley (New York, 1967), p. 54.
6. Charles Olson, 'Human Universe', pp. 55, 61; 'Equal, That Is, To the Real Itself', *Selected Writings*, p. 52. See also, 'Projective Verse', pp. 387, 395; 'Human Universe', pp. 61, 118; *The Maximus Poems* (New York, 1960), pp. 42, 52; 'The Kingfishers', section I, line 1; Jackson Pollock, 'Problems of Contemporary Art', *Possibilities*, I (1947–8).
7. Charles Olson, 'The Kingfishers', section I, 4, lines 1–4. See also, section I, 4, lines 16–17, section III, lines 18, 19; *Maximus Poems*, p. 52; *Call Me Ishmael* (New York, 1947), p. 1; 'To Gerhardt, There, Among Europe's Things . . .', section 4, lines 3, 6; 'La Preface', line 11.
8. Charles Olson, *Maximus Poems*, p. 29. See also, pp. 1, 2, 3, 10, 12, 134. *Maximus Poems IV, V, VI* (London, 1968), p. 37; '"I know a man for whom everything matters": Charles Olson in conversation with Herbert A. Kenny', *Olson*, 1 (Spring, 1974), 9.
9. Charles Olson, *Maximus Poems*, p. 28. See also, pp. 42, 71, 72, 92, 125.
10. Charles Olson, *Maximus Poems*, p. 22. See also, pp. 71, 95, 134–45.
11. Jonathan Williams, 'Dirge for Seer-Scrivener, Prince-Plangent of Gormenghast', lines 8–10. See also, Notes to 'From: Elegies and Celebrations' and 'Sank-Aunt-Sank Shows', in *An Ear in Bartram's Tree: Selected Poems 1957–1967* (Chapel Hill, N.C., 1969); Denise Levertov, 'Biographical Note', in *New American Poetry*, p. 441.
12. Denise Levertov, 'Beyond the End', lines 30–33. See also, 'The Third Dimension', lines 8–9.

13. Paul Blackburn, 'The Continuity', lines 14–16. See also, lines 1–2, 3, 17.
14. John Wieners, 'A Poem for Painters', section 6, lines 5–8. See also, section 4, lines 1–2; 'From a Journal', in *New American Poetry*, p. 425.
15. Robert Creeley, 'Brendan O'Regan and Tony Allan: An Interview with Robert Creeley', in *Robert Creeley, Contexts of Poetry: Interviews 1961–1971* edited by Donald Allen (Bolinas, Calif., 1973), p. 131. See also, pp. 127, 132, 155; 'Linda W. Wagner: A Colloquy with Robert Creeley', ibid., pp. 100, 117; 'The Window', lines 1–2, 23–24; 'The Flower', lines 1–2; 'The Language', line 1; 'The Writer's Situation', in *Interviews*, p. 180; 'David Ossman: An Interview with Robert Creeley', ibid., p. 10.
16. Robert Creeley, 'The Pattern', lines 1–9.
17. Robert Creeley, 'I Know a Man', lines 9–12. See also, line 5; 'Wagner: A Colloquy', p. 110; 'O'Regan and Allan: An Interview', pp. 127, 167; 'On Vacation', lines 12–13.
18. Edward Dorn, 'Preface' to *Collected Poems 1956–1974* (Bolinas, Calif., 1975), p.v. See also *Views* edited by Donald Allen (San Francisco, 1980), p. 12.
19. Edward Dorn, 'The Sundering U.P. Tracks', lines 55–58. See also, lines 1–4, 13–14, 21–23, 33.
20. Edward Dorn, *Slinger*, Book I. See also, Robert Creeley, 'Preface' to *Selected Poems* edited by Donald Allen (Bolinas, Calif., 1978), p. vii; Donald Wesling, 'The Poetry of Edward Dorn' in *Modern American Poetry*, pp. 229–30.
21. Robert Duncan, 'Pages from a Notebook', in *New American Poetry*, pp. 401–2. See also, p. 401; *The H.D. Book*, 'Rites of Participation', in *A Caterpillar Anthology* (New York, 1974), p. 24; 'Source', in *Derivations* (London, 1968); *Dante* (New York, 1974), n. pag.; 'Biographical Note', in *New American Poetry*, pp. 432, 436; 'Preface to a Reading of Passages 1–22', *Maps*, vol. 6, edited by John Taggart (Pennsylvania, 1974); 'Passages I', line 11.
22. Robert Duncan, 'Pages for a Notebook', p. 407. See also, 'Often I Am Permitted to Return to a Meadow', lines 6–7, 9–10, 18, 23; 'Such is the Sickness of Many a Good Thing', lines 7–8; 'A Poem Beginning with a Line by Pindar', line 2.
23. Lawrence Ferlinghetti, 'Note on Poetry in San Francisco', in *Pictures of the Gone World* (San Francisco, 1955). See also, Robert Duncan, 'Ingmar Bergman's *Seventh Seal*', line 26; 'Passages 18', line 53; 'Poetry, A Natural Thing', lines 6–7.
24. Lawrence Ferlinghetti, 'A Coney Island of the Mind', section 15, lines 1–2, 6–7. See also, section 1, line 14; section 15, lines 3, 4, 5, 10; (Statement on Poetics), in *New American Poetry*, p. 413; "I Am Waiting," lines 82–4.
25. Brother Antoninus/ William Everson, 'A Canticle to the Waterbirds', lines 65–9. See also, lines 20, 21, 22, 57, 59–60, 62, 63–64.
26. Jack Spicer, 'Letter to Lorca', in *New American Poetry*, p. 413. See also, p. 414; 'Imaginary Elegies', section I, lines 1, 2; section III, lines 45–46; section IV, lines 7, 9.
27. Philip Lamantia, 'Terror Conduction', lines 18–20. See also, 'Biographical Note', in *New American Poetry*, p. 440.

28. Philip Whalen, ('Statement on Poetics'), in *New American Poetry*, p. 420. See also, 'The Same Old Jazz', lines 13, 14.
29. Michael McClure, 'Hymn to St. Geryon, I', lines 93–94. See also lines 72, 74–75; 'The Flowers of Politics', line 14; 'From a Journal', in *New American Poetry*, p. 423; 'Peyote Poem, Part I', lines 74–75.
30. Michael McClure, 'Ode for Soft Voice', lines 19–24. See also, 'Peyote Poem, Part I', lines 81–82; 'The Flowers of Politics, II', lines 5, 24–25; 'From a Journal', p. 427; 'The Rag', lines 5–6; 'Hymn to St. Geryon, I', line 23.
31. Gary Snyder, *Earth House Hold: Technical Notes and Queries to Follow Dharma Revolutionaries* (New York, 1969), p. 211. See also, (Statement on Poetics), in *New American Poetry*, p. 420; 'Burning', poem 2, lines 7, 10–11; poem 8, line 19; poem 11, lines 6, 7.
32. Gary Snyder, epigraph to *Riprap* (Kyoto, Japan, 1959). See also, 'Riprap', lines 12–13; 'Burning', poem 2, line 5; poem 8, line 17; poem 17, line 9.
33. Gary Snyder, *Earth House Hold*, p. 73. See also, 'Burning', poem 2, line 2; poem 16, line 23; 'Song of the Taste', lines 15–17; 'Hunting', poem 15, line 1; 'Logging', poem 15, lines 19–20.
34. Gary Snyder, 'Hunting', lines 1–6. See also, 'Burning'; 'the myth', line 20.
35. Allen Ginsberg, 'Footnote to Howl', line 4. See also, 'Howl', section 1; Richard Howard, *Alone With America: The Art of Poetry in the United States Since 1950* (London, 1970), p. 146.
36. Kenneth Rexroth, 'San Francisco Letter', in *On the Poetry of Allen Ginsberg* edited by Lewis Hyde (Ann Arbor, Mich., 1984), p. 32. See also, Lawrence Ferlinghetti, 'Horn on "Howl"', ibid., p. 43; 'The Disorganisation Man', ibid., p. 55; Norman Podhoretz, 'A Howl of Protest in San Francisco', ibid., p. 35; Diana Trilling, 'The Other Night at Columbia', ibid., p. 64.
37. Allen Ginsberg, 'A Blake Experience', in *On the Poetry of Allen Ginsberg*, pp. 122–5. See also, pp. 126, 128, 129; Lewis Hyde, 'Introduction', ibid., p. 4.
38. Allen Ginsberg, 'Howl', section 1. See also, *Allen Verbatim: Lectures on Poetry, Politics, Consciousness* edited by Gordon Ball (New York, 1974), p. 139; 'Notes for "Howl" and Other Poems', *New American Poetry*, pp. 414–15; 'A Talk with Allen Ginsberg', *Partisan Review*, 38 (1971), 295–6; 'Craft Interview with Allen Ginsberg', in *The Craft of Poetry* edited by William Packard (New York, 1969), p. 58; Jack Kerouac, 'Interview', *Paris Review*, 43 (Summer 1968), 83.
39. Ginsberg, 'Howl', section 1. See also, 'Notes for "Howl"', p. 415; 'Craft Interview', pp. 28, 29, 57; 'Interview', *Paris Review*, 37 (Spring 1966), 28–29).
40. Ginsberg, 'Howl', section III. See also, sections I and II; 'Sunflower Sutra', lines 10, 22; Richard Eberhart, 'West Coast Rhythms', in *On the Poetry of Allen Ginsberg*, p. 25.
41. Howard, *Alone with America*, p. 151. See also, Ginsberg, 'America', lines 45–6; 'Wichita Vortex Sutra', sections I and II.
42. Allen Ginsberg, 'Poetry or Fiction?', *Margin*, 2 (Spring 1987), 22–23. See also, 'From an Interview', in *On the Poetry of Allen Ginsberg*, p. 320; *To*

Eberhart from Ginsberg (Lincoln, Mass., 1976), p. 172; 'Don't Grow Old', poem VII, lines 1–2; 'Ego Confession', line 32; Paul Portugés, *The Visionary Poetics of Allen Ginsberg* (Santa Barbara, Calif., 1978), p. 110.

43. Ginsberg, 'Notes for "Howl"', p. 415. See also, Gregory Corso, 'Marriage', line 1; Tony Tanner, *City of Words: American Fiction 1950–1970* (London, 1971), p. 384.

44. Norman Mailer, *The Presidential Papers* (New York, 1963), p. 221. See also, Charles Bukowski, 'don't come round but if you do . . .', lines 20–22; Rexroth, 'San Francisco Letter', p. 32.

45. Leroi Jones / Imamu Amiri Baraka, 'Black Art', lines 25–28; 'State / Meant', *Home: Social Essays* (New York, 1966), p. 252. See also, 'It's Nation Time', line 17; D. L. Graham, 'Soul', line 13; Carl Wendell Himes Jr., 'Two Jazz Poems', I, lines 7–8.

46. Baraka, 'State / Meant', p. 251. See also, Ron Karenga, 'Black Cultural Nationalism', in *The Black Aesthetic* edited by Addison Gayle (New York, 1971), p. 36.

47. Baraka, 'How You Sound??', *New American Poetry*, pp. 424–45. See also, Bob Kaufman, 'To My Son, Parker, Asleep in the Next Room', line 19; Ted Joans, author's note to *Beyond the Blues* (London, 1962).

48. Baraka, 'Notes for a Speech', lines 1–6, 10–15. See also, 'Hymn for Lanie Poo', lines 1–2; 'The Insidious Dr. Fu Man Chu', lines 1–4; 'The New Sheriff', lines 1–6.

49. Baraka, 'Black Art', lines 11–16, 20–4. See also, 'Black Dada Nihilismus', lines 7–10; 'Who Will Survive America?', lines 1, 3–5.

50. Baraka, 'It's Nation Time', lines 16–17. See also, 'A School of Prayer', lines 5–6.

51. Baraka, 'Leroy', lines 1–5. See also, 'The Legacy of Malcolm X', *Home*, p. 248; 'An Explanation of the Work', *Black Magic: Poetry 1961–1967* (New York, 1969); 'SOS', lines 1–2; 'Goodbye!', lines 1–2; *Black Music* (New York, 1967), p. 193; Theodore R. Hudson, *From Leroi Jones to Amiri Baraka: The Literary Works* (Durham, N.C., 1973), p. 46.

52. Baraka, '20th-Century Fox', lines 1–4.

53. Baraka, 'Ka ' Ba', lines 9–12. See also, lines 15–17, 18, 20, 22–3; 'Explanation of the Work'; 'State / Meant', p. 252.

54. Sonia Sanchez, 'Right on: white america', lines 11–14. See also, Marvin X, *The Black Bird*, in *New Plays from the Black Theatre* edited by Ed Bullins (New York, 1969), pp. 109–18; Don L. Lee / Haki R. Mahubuti, *We Walk the Way of the New World* (Detroit, 1970), p. 71; Mari Evans, 'Vive Noir!', lines 1–6.

55. Don L. Lee / Haki R. Mahubuti, 'But He Was Cool', lines 23–31.

56. Haki R. Mahubuti, 'Don't Cry, Scream', lines 7–9.

57. Nikki Giovanni, 'Woman Poem', lines 18–22.

58. Ron Karenga, 'Black Cultural Nationalism', p. 36. See also, Sonia Sanchez, 'Liberation Poem', lines 3–5; Haki R. Mahubuti, 'Don't Cry, Scream', line 3; David Nelson, 'No Time for Blues Now', lines 1, 5, 7–8; Baraka, *Black Music*, p. 160.

59. Ginsberg, 'Wichita Vortex Sutra', section II.
60. Marjorie Perloff, *Frank O'Hara: Poet Among Painters* (New York, 1977), p. 9. See also, 'An Interview with Frank O'Hara', in *Standing Still and Walking in New York* edited by Donald Allen (Bolinas, Calif., 1975), pp. 13, 23 ; 'The Sorrows of the Youngman, John Rechy's *City of Night*,' ibid., p. 162; 'Art Chronicle', ibid., p. 132; 'Personism: A Manifesto', in *The Collected Poems of Frank O'Hara* edited by Donald Allen (New York, 1971), p. 498.
61. Frank O'Hara, 'Personism', p. 498. See also, 'Meditations in an Emergency', line 7; 'Larry Rivers: A Memoir', in *Collected Poems*, p. 515; 'In Memory of My Feelings', section 4, lines 19–20; 'To Hell with It', lines 10, 14; 'A Step Away from Them', lines 44–45; Perloff, *Frank O'Hara*, pp. 61, 74.
62. Frank O'Hara, 'Larry Rivers: A Memoir', p. 512. See also, 'Meditations in an Emergency', line 6. See also, 'Notes on "Second Avenue"'; 'David Smith: The Colour of Steel', in *Standing Still and Walking*, pp. 123, 125; 'Growth and Gaston', in *Art Chronicles 1954–1966* (New York, 1975), p. 141; Perloff, *Frank O'Hara*, p. 22.
63. Frank O'Hara, 'Adieu to Norman, Bon Jour to Joan and Jean-Paul', lines 1–4. See also, 'Personism', p. 499; 'Ode to Michael Goldberg ('s Birth and Other Births)', line 4; 'Poem (Kruschev is coming on the right day!)', lines 2–3; 'Poem (Light clarity avocado salad in the morning)', line 10; 'Joe's Jacket', line 52.
64. Frank O'Hara, 'Rhapsody', lines 1–7. See also, 'My Heart', 1–3, 13–15.
65. Frank O'Hara, 'The Day Lady Died', lines 25–28. See also, Perloff, *Frank O'Hara*, p. 180.
66. Frank O'Hara, (Statement on Poetics), in *New American Poetry*, p. 420.
67. John Ashbery, 'Frank O'Hara's Question', *Book Week*, 26 (25 September, 1966), 6.
68. Barbara Guest, 'Piazzas', lines 1–4.
69. James Schuyler, 'Buried at Springs', section II, lines 16–20.
70. Ted Berrigan, 'Last Poem', lines 21–26. See also, 'Today in Ann Arbor', lines 1–4; 'Whitman in Black', lines 8–10; '(Sonnet) XXXVIII', line 1.
71. Kenneth Koch, 'Alive for an Instant', lines 19–20. See also, 'Fresh Air', sections 2, 5; 'Biographical Note', in *New American Poetry*, p. 439.
72. John Ashbery, 'How to be a Difficult Poet', *New York Times Magazine* 23 (May 1976), 19–20. See also, 'The One Thing That Can Save America', lines 24–26; 'All and Some', lines 22–23; 'Idaho'; *Contemporary American Poetry* edited by A. Poulin Jr. (Boston, 1971), p. 519.
73. John Ashbery, 'Ode to Bill', line 12. See also Gertrude Stein, *Picasso* (Boston, 1959), p. 15; *Lectures in America* (New York, 1935), p. 227; Jean-Paul Sartre, *Literary and Philosophical Essays* (London, 1955), p. 91.
74. John Ashbery, 'Grand Galop', lines 231–36. See also, lines 88–89, 121; 'Le Livre Est Sur La Table', lines 7–8; 'Plainness in Diversity', lines 14–15.
75. James Merrill, 'The Octopus', lines 1, 7–10, 25–26. See also, 'Transfigured Bird', line 1; 'Days of 1935', line 105; Judith Moffett, *James Merrill: An Introduction to the Poetry* (New York, 1984), p. 18.

76. James Merrill, 'For Proust', lines 25–28. See also, lines 40, 44; 'Days of 1964', lines 41–43; 'Interview', *Contemporary Literature*, 9 (Winter 1968), 10–11; 'Scenes of Childhood', lines 94–95.

77. James Merrill, 'An Urban Convalescence' lines 86–87.

78. Merrill, *Changing Light at Sandover*.

79. John Ashbery, 'Paradoxes and Oxymorons', lines 1–4.

80. Ibid., lines 6–8.

81. Ibid., lines 13–16.

Appendix

The problem of literary nationality: the case of T. S. Eliot

The question to be asked, whenever American writing – or, more specifically, the writing of the United States – is concerned is, What do we mean by a national literature? This is easily answered in respect of, say, Albania whose language is coextensive with history and territory; it is not so easily answered as regards Italy and Greece, whose historical continuity is denied by the change from a classical language to a modern one and, in Italy certainly, by a large number of dialects that have full linguistic status – where, too, the very concept of a nation is of fairly recent manufacture. With the United States of America, limits have to be artificially imposed. The major problems here are of finding a dividing line between the literature of a colonial people and that of an emancipated one, and – of greater relevance to this book – of dealing with the modern reversal whereby someone like T. S. Eliot ceased to be American and became British while Christopher Isherwood and W. H. Auden abandoned England and became, respectively, a Californian and a New Yorker. It is probably not enough to limit the literature of the United States to what has been written in English on American soil below the Great Lakes and the forty-ninth parallel. It is better, and more appropriate to any attempt to chart a national literature, to look for a definable American quality, though prepared to see it shade off into recidivistic Britishry or expand into internationalism. Which is what, in however a faltering manner, this study has attempted to do.

The case of a poet just mentioned, T. S. Eliot, is symptomatic here. Born in St. Louis, Missouri, Eliot was descended on both sides of his family from early English settlers in New England. Andrew Eliot emigrated from the village of East Coker in 1667, and T. S. Eliot's maternal ancestor Isaac Stevens was one of the original settlers in the Massachusetts Bay Colony in 1630. The memory of that place from which the Eliot family had departed, over two hundred years before the poet's birth, was to inform the second of the *Four Quartets*: where Eliot, realising that 'In my beginning is my end', returns in imagination to the home of his ancestors. 'In that open field' near East Coker, he says:

> If you do not come too close, if you do not come too close,
> On a summer midnight, you can hear the music
> Of the weak pipe and the little drum
> And see them dancing around the bonfire . . .[1]

It was natural that a writer for whom the immanence of the past in the present was an obsessive theme should register his English and American Puritan origins in his lines and his consciousness; and equally natural, perhaps, that his Mid-Western upbringing should appear so often, though through a glass darkly, in his work. 'A writer's art must be racial', Eliot wrote in 1917, ' – which means, in plain words, that it must be based on the accumulated sensations of the first twenty-one years'. And what we know of his childhood shows that it became the source of insistent images in his poetry. Close to the family house in St. Louis, for instance, was a school founded by Eliot's grandfather and attended by his sisters, and he preserved a vivid memory of it throughout his life. It had 'a high brick wall', he later recalled, and 'concealed our back garden from the schoolyard'; from the garden he could listen to the children playing in the yard, and after school hours he could play in the empty schoolyard himself and even venture into the school. In this, we have the source for the laughter of hidden children that recurs in Eliot's poetry. In 'Burnt Norton', for example, there are these lines: 'Go said the bird, for the leaves were full of children, / Hidden excitedly, containing laughter'. As Helen Gardner has put it, 'this . . . symbol of the laughter . . . of children heard playing was not only a symbol of the happiness that the childless Eliot was never to know, but a memory of childish loneliness, hearing the "others" . . . and longing to be "one of them"'.

When Eliot was just nine, his father built a summer home for the family by the sea at Gloucester, Massachusetts; and here the boy was to spend his summer vacations. So another source of vivid imagery and mythic allusion was initiated. Memories of the sea pervade his poetry. 'What seas what shores what grey rocks and what islands', proclaims the speaker in 'Marina':

> What water lapping the bow
> And scent of pine and woodthrush through the fog
> What images return.[2]

Elsewhere, in *Ash Wednesday*, the reader is offered a glimpse 'from the wide window towards the granite shore' of 'The white sails' that 'still fly seaward, seaward flying / Unbroken wings'; while Eliot's expertise at sailing, acquired during these summer visits, is invoked in the brief, memorable reference, towards the end of *The Waste Land*, to the boat that 'responded / Gaily, to the hand expert with sail and oar'. Mingled imagery of fog and water was, in any case, something that Eliot could associate with his childhood homeplace for the spring, autumn, and winter months. St. Louis itself, with its mists and 'the sunsets and the dooryards and the sprinkled streets' seems to be the setting for 'The Love Song of J. Alfred Prufrock'. And Eliot's recollections of the 'strong brown god' of the Mississippi River, which flows by the city, were to be captured in the third of the *Four Quartets*, 'The Dry Salvages'. 'I think I was fortunate to have been born here', Eliot declared of St. Louis, 'rather than in Boston, or New York, or London'. Certainly, his birthplace added to the sense of the complexity of his fate, the mixed nature of his background: particularly since he himself tended to see St. Louis, not so much as a Mid-Western, but as a Southern town. 'Some day I want to write an essay about the point of view of an American who wasn't an American', he said in 1928:

> because he was born in the South and went to school in
> New England as a small boy with a nigger drawl, but
> who wasn't a southerner in the South because his people
> were northerners in a border state and looked down on all
> southerners . . ., and who so was never anything
> anywhere and who therefore felt himself to be more a
> Frenchman than an American and more an Englishman
> than a Frenchman and yet felt that the U.S.A. up to a
> hundred years ago was a family extension.[3]

Southerner, northerner – and, surely, mid-westerner – by birth and background, Eliot transmogrified himself into 'a Frenchman' and 'an Englishman' by a subtle and yet strenuous act of will. After a thorough reading of poets like Laforgue, Rimbaud, and Verlaine, and a year studying at the Sorbonne, he succeeded in assimilating the achievements of French symbolism into English-speaking poetry. 'Prufock', for example, employs the Laforgian dramatic monologue, unfolding the fragmentary consciousness of its narrator (whose name, it turns out, is borrowed from a firm of furniture wholesalers in St. Louis) in a way that locates him, as Hugh Kenner has finely said, as 'a name plus a Voice' rather than a character. Like so many poems derived from the symbolist experience, the poem offers us not a verifiable description of the world, nor the depiction of a 'real' character but (to quote

Kenner again) 'a zone of consciousness' which each of us, as readers, has to pass through for himself or herself. The scene is, perhaps, initially American but it, and the narrator who dissolves into it, are presented in those radically disintegrative, dream-like terms that characterise many of the best French poets of the late nineteenth century. The name and voice that Kenner refers to are, in this sense, unlocated: the 'one-night cheap hotels / And sawdust restaurants'[4] that are recalled – with traces of the wry self-deprecation of Laforgue, and the febrile intensity of Baudelaire – could be part of any unreal city, Paris or London as much as (or perhaps even more than) St. Louis.

After his stay in Paris, from which he returned 'perceptibly Europeanised' according to Conrad Aiken, Eliot spent three more years in the United States before embarking for England in the summer of 1914. Apart from a brief trip back a year later, he did not revisit the United States until 1932; and, although Eliot was to continue these visits almost annually from the late 1940s until his death in 1965, he came to look on England as his home. This was confirmed in 1927 when, in the same year that he announced his conversion to Anglo-Catholicism, Eliot became a British citizen. Gradually, he assimilated a particular concept of the English tradition: his dress, speech, and manners all became impeccably English although, if anything, excessive in their perfection. He was, he declared, in a famous formulation, 'classicist in literature, royalist in politics, and anglo-catholic in religion'. Almost from the beginning, he had been convinced of the necessity of a literary tradition: something that, as he put it in 'Tradition and the Individual Talent', 'compels a man to write not merely with his own generation in his bones, but with a feeling that the whole of literature of Europe from Homer . . . has a simultaneous existence and composes a simultaneous order'.[5] Slowly, this idea of a specifically literary tradition enlarged so as to acquire social, political, and theological implications. The individual was to shuffle off the constraints of the self, was to find perfect freedom in service to his culture, just as the poet, he had once said, was to 'escape from personality' in obedience to the demands of an impersonal art. It is not within the terms of this brief account to chart Eliot's development from *The Waste Land*, where he uses a cunning mixture of symbolist, imagist, and dramatic strategies to expose the rootless, sterile nature of his own, immediate culture, through the spiritual voyagings of *Ash Wednesday* to the more achieved, if still tentative, spiritual wisdom of the *Four Quartets*. It is worth noting, however, that this development, and the beliefs that generated it, raise in a particularly sharp way, the problem of Eliot's literary nationalism.

The problem can be stated simply, although as with most literary expatriates the simplicity of the statement conceals a host of difficulties.

Eliot 'became' an Englishman and an English poet: but he did so in a fashion that is characteristically American, that betrays his origins in the New World. His earlier poetry demonstrates that concern with the isolate self, the lonely 'I' which is perhaps *the* predominant theme in American poetry. Only it demonstrates it in what was to become known as a characteristically Eliotic way: refracted through a fragmented *persona*, the self being dissolved into a series of objective correlatives. At its most obvious – in, for example, the opening line of 'Prufrock' – 'I' becomes 'you and I' to dramatise the narcissism of isolation; and the narcissistic ego translates the blank stare of reality into, alternatively, a mirror of its own concerns or a threat to its purity, or even its existence. So 'Gerontion' concludes with the narrator internalising his surroundings, denying them any referential reality: the various cosmopolitan characters that populate his meditations cease to be people, 'Tenants of the house', and become figments of his imagination, 'Thoughts of a dry brain in a dry season'. And 'Prufrock' offers one among many illustrations of Eliot's recurrent imagery of eyes, the gaze of the other that reduces the self to shivering ineptitude, a merely nominal existence:

> And I have known the eyes already, known them all –
> The eyes that fix you in a formulated phrase,
> And when I am formulated, sprawling on a pin,
> When I am pinned and wriggling on the wall,
> Then how should I begin
> To spit out all the butt-ends of my days and ways?[6]

In a very real sense, *The Waste Land* continues this lonely drama of the self. Of course, any genuinely imaginative reading of Eliot's most famous poem is likely to yield larger cultural inferences. Like the *Cantos*, *The Waste Land* uses a form of the ideogrammic method, dense patterns of imagery and a disjunctive narrative sequence, a radical juxtaposition of different perspectives and languages, to solicit an active response, a collaboration in the creation of meanings; and the meanings so created will probably include commentary on the decay of contemporary civilisation. It is, however, worth recording Eliot's own comment here:

> Various critics have done me the honour to interpret the poem in terms of criticism of the contemporary world, have considered it, indeed, as an important bit of social criticism. To me it was only the relief of a personal and wholly insignificant grouse against life; it is just a piece of rhythmical grumbling.[7]

Eliot was probably reacting, when he said this, against that school of criticism that turns *The Waste Land* into a social document or an anthropological exercise and, in doing so, he tends to overstate the case. 'I wrote *The Waste Land* simply to relieve my own feelings', he said elsewhere; and there can be little doubt that a sense of sterility is so powerful in the poem precisely because its ultimate source is personal. At its inception, *The Waste Land* was a poem of the self: a cry from the heart from a man who had been haunted since childhood by the 'hidden laughter of children', whose own marriage was childless, and who, at the time of writing, was acutely troubled by feelings of sexual unhappiness. Characteristically, Eliot then transformed this cry into a dramatic, imagistic, objective work of art that each reader could experience and interpret according to his or her own terms of reference, personal *and* cultural.

'Poetry is not a turning loose of emotion, but an escape from emotion', Eliot insisted in 'Tradition and the Individual Talent', 'it is not the expression of personality, but an escape from personality'. 'But of course', he added, 'only those who have personality and emotions know what it means to escape from these things'. Poems like 'Prufrock', 'Gerontion', and *The Waste Land* demonstrate the point Eliot is making here, and in a particularly pressing fashion. They are intensely inward in terms of their initial emotional sources. But that inwardness is resisted: formally, in the sense that the poet seeks to impersonalise the personal, to escape from the 'I' *via* his poetic masks and manoeuvrings, and argumentatively, to the extent that each poem assures us of the limits, vulnerability, and utter unreliability of the self, the simple, separate person. As such they represent an assault on the American Adamic mode, the celebration of individuality, of a kind that perhaps only an American could make. And as Eliot developed, both as a man who suffered and a mind that created, this assault only grew the more concentrated, deliberate, and comprehensive. Something of this development has been alluded to already. Removing himself to the Old World, he became in effect more English than the English. He was a royalist, but his royalism seemed more the product of a spiritual devotion to Elizabeth I and the Stuarts than any allegiance to the impeccably bourgeois House of Windsor. He was a Tory, but his Toryism was largely based on a hopeless misunderstanding of the intellectual potential of the English aristocracy (a misunderstanding he shared with James and many other American expatriates); and, in any event, he himself admitted that it had nothing to do with that contemporary '"Conservatism"' which has been overrun first by deserters from Whiggism and later by business men'. He was, too, an Anglican, or more precisely an 'Anglo-Catholic': but his religious feeling, too, aligned him with an imagined past rather than an actual present – 'the

English Church under the Stuarts', to use his own phrase, the sanctuary of poets, preachers, and divines like Laud and Andrewes, Herbert and Donne. In his own way, he was discovering a tradition for himself that was a product of a mythopoeic view of history, just as some Southern writers like Ransom and Tate were. Unlike those Southerners, however, he could not discover it within the confines of the United States: even though he would sometimes claim that he could trace 'some recollection of a "tradition" in the South' and discern 'the chances for the re-establishment of a native culture'[8] there. For him, otherness had to be found elsewhere, on another continent.

The search for otherness, some order that denies and disciplines the self, is also at the heart of Eliot's later poetry. Consider, for instance, these lines from *Ash Wednesday*:

> And the lost heart stiffens and rejoices
> In the lost lilac and the lost sea voices
> And the weak spirit quickens to rebel
> For the bent golden-rod and the lost sea smell
> Quickens to recover
> The cry of quail and the whirling plover
> And the blind eye creates
> The empty forms between the ivory gates
> And smell renews the salt savour of the sandy earth[9]

This passage occurs towards the end of the poem, when the narrator has come to believe what he has only sensed up until then: that the only way he can redeem himself is to surrender himself, that the only means of finding his being is to lose it. Only the blind eye sees the true forms of liberation, the intimation is; only the spirit that rebels against its own devouring inwardness can begin to tap the sources of salvation and creativity. There is repetition in these lines, and parallelism, of a kind that hauntingly recalls Whitman, and a sense of natural bounty, the fruits of earth, sea, and sky, that is reminiscent of the later Williams. But the formal echoes of these other poets only emphasise the utter difference of tone and sensibility. If anything, the Whitman style is adopted here in order to deny the cogency and truth of all that Whitman, and Williams, said; memories of the American Adamic mode are evoked only so as to be slyly mocked and rejected.

Writing in 1928, Eliot dismissed the content of Whitman's poetry as in 'large part . . . clap-trap'; two years earlier, he insisted that Whitman's animating convictions were 'negligible'. Harsh words, perhaps: but they were a way of distancing himself, even at this relatively early stage in his development, from the dominating figure in the American poetic tradition, just as he was distancing himself from what he saw as the thin soil of American culture. It was no wonder, really, that from his own standpoint Williams saw *The Waste Land* as such a betrayal. 'To me especially it struck like a sardonic bullet', Williams confessed in his *Autobiography*:

> I felt at once that it had set me back twenty years, and I'm sure it did. Critically Eliot returned us to the classroom just at the moment when I felt that we were on the point of an escape to matters much closer to the essence of a new art form itself – rooted in the locality which should give it fruit. I knew at once that in certain ways I was most defeated.[10]

'Eliot had turned his back on the possibility of reviving my world', Williams added; and Williams's world, he realised, was above all an American one. This is not to say, of course, that Williams saw *The Waste Land* as being specifically, or even mainly, concerned with American culture, or that he objected in principle to casting a cold eye on modern society. What he was profoundly disconcerted by, in the first instance, was Eliot's academicism: his commitment, as Williams saw it, to a complexly allusive, highly wrought poetics that dismissed the pleasures of the local, the pressures of the particular and the personal. Allied to this, what frightened Williams in a way was Eliot's fiercely articulated yearning for otherness: for more traditional forms of culture, and stricter, more prescriptive codes of being, than anything his American inheritance could supply. Formally and intellectually, Williams realised, *The Waste Land implied* a rejection of its creator's birthplace, even if it did not actively state one; this might not have been the sole reason for its existence, but it was there as part of its structure of assumptions. Inscribed as a subtext of the poem, as it were, was a denial of the New World, both as a fact and a possibility, imaginative space.

The difference between Eliot and a poet of the American local such as Williams is inevitably extreme: Williams could, as he put it, 'stagger . . . under the blast of Eliot's genius' but he could also be appalled by it, because it was so obviously foreign to him. But the difference between Eliot and a less clearly dissimilar man and writer like Pound is, in its own way, no less radical. Williams instinctively recognised this himself: so that, although he criticised Pound for running off to Europe after strange gods, he remained firmly of the belief that he and 'Ez' were working along similar lines. 'Ezra . . . was the hero', he was to say of their youthful friendship; and, while Williams would have nothing to do with Pound's later political and intellectual commitments, and was horrified by Pound's espousal of Fascism, there remained always a feeling of aesthetic brotherhood between them. Other, more recent poets have responded to this feeling, to the extent that they have benefited from the shared influence of the two poets. Writers like Ginsberg, Olson, and Lowell may have little enough in common, but what they do have is the belief in a Pound-Williams axis, the conviction that the two men *together* represent something crucial – for them individually, and for the American tradition in general. In short, for all his expatriatism, Pound remained a distinctively and even aggressively American poet: not just in the sense that he retained United States citizenship but because his peculiar characteristics *as poet* marked him out from his European contemporaries. This is not the place to rehearse those characteristics again: the interested reader can, if he or she wishes to, refer to the second chapter of this book. It is perhaps enough to point out that, unlike Eliot, Pound responded to history in a self-evidently personal and eclectic way. Like most American poets, he insisted on inventing a tradition for himself – a mythology that was his and his alone, a personal 'Kulchur' – out of the wealth of historical possibilities available to him. This is why, as was suggested earlier, the *Cantos* belong in the great line of the American epic: because they involve the poet in re-creating himself as hero and making rather than recording the cultural framework that gives him presence, a local habitation and a name. 'I make a pact with you Walt Whitman', Pound had said, '. . . / I am old enough now to make friends'[11]; and he proved his friendship, among other ways, by writing his own great song of the self.

By contrast, Eliot grew sufficiently sure of his grounding in another, and established, tradition to be able to measure himself against the Whitman line. Already by the time of *Ash Wednesday* he was beginning to do this, as a passage quoted earlier indicates. When it came to the last poems, however, the opposition was scarcely veiled at all. In these lines from 'East Coker', for instance, there is not only an echo of Whitman's phrasing but also a recall of the earlier poet's metrical arrangement of syntax – and both seem to be there openly so as to establish moral, emotional, and imaginative distance:

>   You say I am repeating
> Something I have said before. I shall say it again.
> Shall I say it again? In order to arrive there,
> To arrive where you are, to get from where you are not,
>   You must go by a way wherein there is no ecstasy.
> In order to arrive at what you do not know
>   You must go by the way which is the way of ignorance.
> In order to possess what you do not possess
>   You must go by the way of dispossession.
> In order to arrive at what you are not
>   You must go through the way in which you are not.
> And what you do not know is the only thing you know

And what you own is what you do not own
And where you are is where you are not.[12]

Whereas Whitman would absorb everything into the image of himself, Eliot organises everything – and denies the presence, or at least knowledge, of himself – so as to catch a hint, or a glimpse, of otherness. The 'I' in this passage is not, as it is in Whitman and so much American writing, the active and re-active core of the poem, its vital centre and source of creative energy. It is, at best, a linguistic convenience, a way of locating the initial source of these perceptions and, at worst, a kind of spiritual undertow that those following the 'way of dispossession' must resist. Here, Roy Harvey Pearce has acutely observed, 'a wholly personal style takes on a grand impersonality': the language and line of Whitman are used against themselves. To which it might be added that here, too, the illusion of personality is raised for a moment only to be dismissed as just that, an illusion: the words 'you' and 'I' become floating signifiers, which can never be anchored in any meaningful, moral reality.

Whitman does not represent all of American poetry, of course. And the principle of definition by rejection has to be acknowledged, at some point: writers, like other people, are defined by the things they reject (or try to reject) as much as anything else – and, to this extent, Americanism seems to have been as important to Eliot as, say, Catholicism was to James Joyce. Nevertheless, the basic point remains the same: Eliot was not an American poet, in the *relatively* simple and straightforward sense in which the writers considered in this book were – and are. He was an American by birth and an Englishman by choice, or rather force of will. Brought up in St. Louis, where the South meets the Mid-West, deeply affected by the introspective inheritance of New England, he became a European, and more specifically, an English poet. Yet, while doing all this, he retained the marks of his American upbringing, as he had to, on his imagination and his memory. Commonly identified with the British tradition as he now is (his work is included in just about all anthologies of modern British poetry), all he has written can nevertheless be seen in terms of a fierce, irreconcilable conflict with his birthplace – and what he believed were the limited terms of American culture. There is no easy definition of the place of Eliot, as there cannot be of any poets of mixed nationality like him. And not only of such poets: others, some of whom never even left their native shores, have to be perceived within frames of reference other than the American eventually, if only because no frame is adequate, absolute or terminal. No critical approach can do more than offer notes towards an understanding of the particular texts to which it attends; and that includes one such as this, that tries to see writers in terms of their national identity. In sum, Eliot poses a problem in his own right, because he slips across cultural boundaries with such consummate and calculated skill. In doing so, though, he reminds us of a larger problem: that every attempt to mediate literature carries with it its own losses as well as gains. To see American writing as American is necessary, perhaps, if we are ever to understand how writers such as Williams and Pound, Stevens and Lowell, have engaged with their homes and histories. But there are always other terms of reference, other forms of critical discourse just as valid as this one. And there is always, or should be, the compulsion to return to the single, separate poem.

Notes

1. T. S. Eliot, 'East Coker', section I, lines 24–28. See also, line 1; 'Burnt Norton', section I, lines 40–41; Bernard Bergonzi, *T. S. Eliot* (London, 1972), p. 2; Helen Gardner, 'The Landscapes of Eliot's Poetry', *Critical Quarterly* (Winter 1968).
2. T. S. Eliot, 'Marina', lines 1–4. See also, 'Ash Wednesday', section VI, lines 8–10; *The Waste Land*, section V; 'The Love Song of J. Alfred Prufrock', line 101; 'The Dry Salvages', section I, line 2.
3. T. S. Eliot, *T. S. Eliot: The Man and His Work* edited by Allen Tate (New York, 1966), p. 15.
4. Eliot, '. . . Prufrock', lines 6–7. See also, Bergonzi, *Eliot*, p. 17.
5. T. S. Eliot, 'Tradition and the Individual Talent', in *Selected Essays* (London, 1934), p. 14. See also, p. 21; preface to *For Lancelot Andrewes* (London, 1928).
6. Eliot, 'Prufrock', lines 54–59. See also, 'Generation', lines 74–75.
7. T. S. Eliot, *The Waste Land: A Facsimile and Transcript of the Original Drafts Including the Annotations of Ezra Pound* edited by Valerie Eliot (London, 1971), p. 1.
8. T. S. Eliot, *After Strange Gods* (London, 1934), pp. 15–16. See also, 'Tradition and the Individual Talent', p. 21; 'John Bramhall', in *For Lancelot Andrewes*; Bergonzi, *Eliot*, p. 125.
9. Eliot, 'Ash Wednesday', section VI, lines 11–19.
10. Williams, *Autobiography*, p. 174. See also, T. S. Eliot, 'Introduction' to *Selected Poems of Ezra Pound* (London, 1928), p. 10; Roy Harvey Pearce, *The Continuity of American Poetry* (Princeton, 1961), p. 305.
11. Pound, 'A Pact', lines 1, 5. See also, Williams, *Autobiography*, p. 68.
12. Eliot, 'East Coker', section III, lines 34–47. See also, Pearce, *Continuity of American Poetry*, p. 304.

Chronology

DATE	WORKS OF POETRY	OTHER WORK	HISTORICAL/CULTURAL EVENTS
1900		Dreiser, Theodore *Sister Carrie* Baum, Frank, *The Wizard of Oz*	Population 75 million
1901	Moody, William Vaughn, *Poems*	Norris, Frank, *The Octopus* Washington, Booker T., *Up From Slavery*	President Mckinley assassinated; Theodore Roosevelt's administration (1901–9)
1902	Robinson, *Captain Craig*	James, Henry, *The Wings of the Dove* James, William, *Varieties of Religious Experience* Wister, Owen, *The Virginian*	U.S coal strike (May–Oct.)
1903		James, Henry, *The Ambassadors* London, Jack, *The Call of the Wild*	New York Stock Exchange completed Wright brothers' flight
1904		James, Henry, *The Golden Bowl* London, *Sea-Wolf*	Pacific cable completed Panama canal begun

DATE	WORKS OF POETRY	OTHER WORK	HISTORICAL/CULTURAL EVENTS
1905	Stickney, Trumbull, *Poems*	Dixon, Thomas, *The Clansman* Wharton, Edith, *The House of Mirth*	Founding of Rotary clubs and International Workers of the World
1906		Sinclair, Upton, *The Jungle* Traubel, Horace, *With Walt Whitman in Camden*	San Francisco earthquake Pure Food and Drugs Act
1907		Adams, *The Education of Henry Adams* James, William, *Pragmatism*	Georgia and Alabama adopt prohibition
1908		Fox, John, *Trail of the Lonesome Pine*	Agreement with Japan restricts immigration
1909	Pound, *Personae*	Stein, Gertrude, *Three Lives*	Taft's administration (1909–13) Henry Ford's Model 'T' car initiates mass production of automobiles Freud lectures in U.S.
1910	Robinson, *The Town Down the River*	James, William, *A Pluralistic Universe* Lomax, Alan, *Cowboy Songs*	Population 91 million
1911		Bierce, Ambrose, *Devil's Dictionary* *Masses* (later, *New Masses*, 1911–53)	Standard Oil and American Tobacco trusts dissolved
1912	Lowell (Amy) *A Dome of Many-Coloured Glass* *Poetry: A Magazine of Verse* (1912–)	Grey, Zane, *Riders of the Purple Sage* Johnson, James W., *The Autobiography of an Ex-Coloured Man*	F. W Woolworth Company incorporated Progressive Party (1912–46)

DATE	WORKS OF POETRY	OTHER WORK	HISTORICAL/CULTURAL EVENTS
1913	Frost, *A Boy's Will* Lindsay, *General William Booth Enters Heaven* Williams, *The Tempers*	Cather, Willa, *O, Pioneers!*	Wilson's administration (1913–21) Armoury show Charlie Chaplin signs contract with Mack Sennett
1914	Dickinson, *The Single Hound* Frost, *North of Boston* Lowell (Amy), *Sword Blades and Poppy Seeds* Lindsay, *The Congo and Other Poems*	Little Review (1914–29) *New Republic* (1914–)	Panama Canal opened Provincetown and Washington Square Players begin
1915	Masters, *Spoon River Anthology* Pound, *Cathay; Some Imagist Poets*	Brooks, Van Wyck, *America's Coming of Age*	*Lusitania* sunk D. W. Griffith's film, *Birth of a Nation*
1916	Aiken, *The Jig of Forslin* H. D., *Sea Garden* Frost, *Mountain Interval* Robinson, *The Man Against the Sky* Sandburg, *Chicago Poems*	O'Neill, Eugene, *Bound East for Cardiff*	*Saturday Evening Post* publishes its first Norman Rockwell illustration Coca-Cola adopts distinctively shaped bottle
1917	Eliot, *Prufrock and Other Observations* Lindsay, *The Chinese Nightingale and Other Poems* Robinson, *Merlin*	*Cambridge History of American Literature* (1917–20)	U.S. enters World War I First jazz record, 'The Darktown Strutters Ball'
1918	Sandburg, *Cornhuskers*	Cather, *My Antonia*	End of World War I

DATE	WORKS OF POETRY	OTHER WORK	HISTORICAL/CULTURAL EVENTS
1919	Ransom, *Poems About God*	Anderson, Sherwood, *Winesburg, Ohio* Mencken, H. L., *The American Language*	Alcock and Brown fly the Atlantic
1920	Eliot, *Poems* Millay, *A Few Figs from Thistles* Pound, *Hugh Selwyn Mauberley* Robinson, *Lancelot* Sandburg, *Smoke and Steel* Williams, *Kora in Hell*	Fitzgerald, F. Scott, *This Side of Paradise* Lewis, Sinclair, *Main Street*	Population 105 million Prohibition of sales of alcohol in U.S. First commercial radio broadcasts Women get the vote
1921	Moore, *Poems* Robinson, *Collected Poems* Wylie, *Nets to Catch the Wind*	Dos Passos, John, *Three Soldiers*	Harding's administration (1921–3)
1922	Eliot, *The Waste Land* Williams, *The Fugitives* (1922–5)	cummings, *The Enormous Room*	Coal and railway strikes
1923	Frost, *New Hampshire* Millay, *The Harp-Weaver and Other Poems* Stevens, *Harmonium* Williams, *Spring and All*	Lawrence, D. H., *Studies in Classic American Literature*	Coolidge's administration (1923–9) *Time* magazine begins
1924	Dickinson, *Complete Poems* Jeffers, *Tamar and Other Poems* Moore, *Observations* Ransom, *Chills and Fever*	Melville, Herman, *Billy Budd, Sailor* Hemingway, Ernest, *in our time*	New immigration quotas First performance of Gershwin's 'Rhapsody in Blue'

DATE	WORKS OF POETRY	OTHER WORK	HISTORICAL/CULTURAL EVENTS
1925	H. D., *Collected Poems* Jeffers, *Roan Stallion and Other Poems* Pound, *Cantos I–XVI*	Dos Passos, John, *Manhattan Transfer* Fitzgerald, *The Great Gatsby* Williams, *In the American Grain*	Tennessee forbids teaching of evolution in schools
1926	Crane, *White Buildings* Hughes, *The Weary Blues*	Hemingway, *The Sun Also Rises* Sandburg, *Abraham Lincoln: The Prairie Years*	Translantic wireless telephone Execution of Sacco and Vanzetti
1927	Davidson, *The Tall Men* Marquis, *archy and mehitabel* Robinson, *Tristram* Sandburg, *The American Songbag*	Aiken, *Blue Voyage*	Lindbergh flight, New York to Paris Transatlantic telephone
1928	Frost, *West-Running Brook* MacLeish, *The Hamlet of A. MacLeish* Sandburg, *Good Morning, America*	*American Literature* (1928–)	Pan-American conference First 'Mickey Mouse' cartoon
1929	Aiken, *Selected Poems*	Faulkner, William, *The Sound and the Fury* Hemingway, *A Farewell to Arms*	Hoover's administration (1929–33) Wall Street Crash Museum of Modern Art opens
1930	Crane, *The Bridge* Eliot, *Ash Wednesday* MacLeish, *New Found Land*	*I'll Take My Stand*	Over four million unemployed

DATE	WORKS OF POETRY	OTHER WORK	HISTORICAL/CULTURAL EVENTS
1931	Aiken, *Preludes for Memnon*	O'Neill, *Mourning Becomes Electra*	Ford's twenty-millionth automobile Scottsboro trial
1932	Jeffers, *Thurso's Landing and Other Poems* MacLeish, *Conquistador* *An 'Objectivist's' Anthology*	Caldwell, Erskine, *Tobacco Road* Farrell, James T., *The Young Manhood of Studs Lonigan*	War veterans' march in Washington
1933	Crane, *Collected Poems* MacLeish, *Frescoes for Mr. Rockefeller's City* Robinson, *Talifer*	Stein, *Autobiography of Alice B. Toklas* West, *Miss Lonelyhearts*	Franklin Roosevelt's administration (1933–45) End of Prohibition James Joyce's *Ulysses* ruled acceptable for U.S. publication
1934	Hughes, *The Ways of White Folks* Oppen, *Discrete Series* Williams, *Collected Poems* Zukofsky, *First Half of 'A'-9*	Miller, Henry, *Tropic of Cancer* Pound, *Jefferson and/or Mussolini* *Partisan Review* (1934–)	Gangster John Dillinger shot dead by F.B.I.
1935	cummings, *No Thanks* Moore, *Selected Poems* Robinson, *King Jasper* Stevens, *Ideas of Order*	Odets, Clifford, *Waiting for Lefty* Wolfe, Thomas, *Of Time and the River*	New Deal social security legislation
1936	Frost, *A Further Range* Sandburg, *The People, Yes* Tate, *The Mediterranean and Other Poems*	Dos Passos, *U.S.A.* Faulkner, *Absalom, Absalom!* Mitchell, Margaret, *Gone With the Wind*	Federal Theatre Project Frank Lloyd Wright's 'Kauffman House' built

DATE	WORKS OF POETRY	OTHER WORK	HISTORICAL/CULTURAL EVENTS
1937	Jeffers, *Such Counsels You Gave Me* Stevens, *The Man With the Blue Guitar*	Hemingway, *To Have and Have Not* Williams, *White Mule*	Supreme Court validates National Labour Relations Act
1938	cummings, *Collected Poems* Riding Jackson, *Collected Poems* Schwartz, *In Dreams Begin Responsibilities*	Pound, *Culture*	Largest peace-time naval bill in U.S. history *Snow White and the Seven Dwarfs*, film by Walt Disney
1939	Frost, *Collected Poems* Patchen, *First Will and Testament*	Steinbeck, John, *The Grapes of Wrath*	Regular translantic air service
1940	Winters, *Poems*	Hemingway, *For Whom the Bell Tolls* MacLeish, *The Irresponsibles* Wright, Richard, *Native Son*	Population 131 million Over eight million unemployed Limited state of national emergency; first peacetime conscription
1941	Bogan, *Poems and New Poems* Moore, *What Are Years?* Roethke, *Open House* Zukovsky, *55 Poems*	Agee, James, *Let Us Now Praise Famous Men*	Japanese bomb Pearl Harbour and U.S.A enter World War II *Citizen Kane*, film by Orson Welles
1942	Jarrell, *Blood for a Stranger* Shapiro, *Person, Place and Thing* Stevens, *Parts of a World; Notes Toward a Supreme Fiction*	Wilder, Thornton, *The Skin of Our Teeth*	U.S. forces surrender in Philippines: General MacArthur commands forces in Southwest Pacific

DATE	WORKS OF POETRY	OTHER WORK	HISTORICAL/CULTURAL EVENTS
1943	Eliot, *Four Quartets* Fearing, *Afternoon of a Pawnbroker*	Smith, Betty, *A Tree Grows in Brooklyn* Thurber, James, *Men, Women and Dogs*	Eisenhower becomes Allied commander in Europe; Italian armistice: Roosevelt and Churchill agree on policy of unconditional surrender
1944	H. D., *The Walls Do Not Fall* Rexroth, *The Phoenix and the Tortoise* Shapiro, *V-Letter and Other Poems* Warren, *Collected Poems 1923–43*	Jackson, Charles, *The Lost Weekend* Smith, Lillian, *Strange Fruit*	'D-Day' invasion of Europe Supreme Court rules an American cannot be refused vote on grounds of colour
1945	Brooks, *A Street in Bronzeville* Frost, *A Masque of Reason* Jarrell, *Little Friend, Little Friend* Shapiro, *Essay on Rime*	Williams, Tennessee, *The Glass Menagerie* Wright, *Black Boy*	World War II ends in Europe Roosevelt dies and is succeeded by Truman U.S. drops atom bombs on Japan; Japan surrenders
1946	Bishop (Elizabeth), *North and South* Jeffers, *Medea* Lowell, *Lord Weary's Castle* Merrill, *The Black Swan and Other Poems* Williams, *Paterson: Book I* Zukofsky, *Anew*	McCullers, Carson, *The Member of the Wedding* Warren, *All the King's Men*	First meeting of United Nations Returning veterans increase college enrollments to two million

DATE	WORKS OF POETRY	OTHER WORK	HISTORICAL/CULTURAL EVENTS
1947	Duncan, *Heavenly City, Earthly City* Frost, *A Masque of Mercy* Wilbur, *The Beautiful Changes and Other Poems*	Miller, Arthur, *All My Sons* Williams (Tennessee), *A Streetcar Named Desire*	Truman doctrine of aid to countries considered threatened by communism
1948	Berryman, *The Dispossessed* Bishop (John Peale), *Collected Poems* Pound, *The Pisan Cantos* Roethke, *The Lost Son and Other Poems*	Faulkner, *Intruder in the Dust* Mailer, Norman, *The Naked and the Dead*	Truman recognises state of Israel 'Number One', painting by Jackson Pollock
1949	Brooks, *Annie Allen* Rexroth, *The Signature of All Things* Simpson, *The Arrivistes*	Miller, *Death of a Salesman*	American Communist Party leaders convicted of conspiracy
1950	Duncan, *Poems 1948–9* Williams, *Collected Later Poems*	Eliot, *The Cocktail Party* Olson, 'Projective Verse'	Population 150 million Korean War begins
1951	Hughes, *Montage of a Dream Deferred* Lowell, *The Mills of the Kavanaughs* Moore, *Collected Poems* Roethke, *Praise to the End!* Rich, *A Change of World* Williams, *Collected Earlier Poems*	Jones, James, *From Here to Eternity* Salinger, J. D., *The Catcher in the Rye*	First performance of Symphony No. 2 by Charles Ives CBS broadcasts colour television First power-producing nuclear reactor built

DATE	WORKS OF POETRY	OTHER WORK	HISTORICAL/CULTURAL EVENTS
1952	Creeley, *Le Fou* MacLeish, *Collected Poems* Merwin, *A Mask for Janus* O'Hara, *A City Winter and Other Poems*	Hemingway, *The Old Man and the Sea* Malamud, Bernard, *The Natural*	Eisenhower defeats Stevenson in presidential election Investigation into 'un-American' activities
1953	Creeley, *The Immoral Proposition* Olson, *In Cold Hell, In Thicket; The Maximus Poems 1–10* Roethke, *The Waking* Shapiro, *Poems 1940–53*	Baldwin, James, *Go Tell It On the Mountain* Bellow, Saul, *The Adventures of Augie March* Ellison, Ralph, *Invisible Man* Warren, *Brother to Dragons*	Ethel and Julius Rosenberg executed Korean War ends *Playboy* magazine begins publication
1954	Jeffers, *Hungerfield and Other Poems* Pound, *Rock-Drill Cantos* Stevens, *Collected Poems* Williams, *The Desert Music*	Faulkner, *A Fable* Pound, *The Classic Anthology* Welty, Eudora, *The Ponder Heart*	Supreme Court rules segregation in schools is unconstitutional
1955	Corso, *The Vestal Lady of Brattle* Ferlinghetti, *Pictures of the Gone World* Rich, *The Diamond Cutters* Williams, *Journey to Love*	Ferlinghetti 'A Note on Poetry in San Francisco' Nabokov, Vladimir, *Lolita*	Rosa Parks of Montgomery, Alabama, refuses to give up her bus seat to a white man Bill Haley's 'Rock Around the Clock' a number one hit for eight weeks Film, *Rebel Without a Cause*, starring *James Dean*

DATE	WORKS OF POETRY	OTHER WORK	HISTORICAL/CULTURAL EVENTS
1956	Ashbery, *Some Trees* Berryman, *Homage to Mistress Bradstreet* Ginsberg, *Howl and Other Poems* Wilbur, *Things of This World*	Barth, John, *The Floating Opera* H. D., *Tribute to Freud* O'Neill, *Long Day's Journey into the Night*	Lerner and Lowe's *My Fair Lady* 'Heartbreak Hotel' recorded by Elvis Presley
1957	Levertov, *Here and Now* Stevens, *Opus Posthumous*	Cheever, John, *The Wapshot Chronicle* Kerouac, Jack, *On the Road*	School integration riots at Little Rock, Arkansas Civil Rights Commission instituted Leonard Bernstein's *West Side Story* Roger Session's Symphony No. 3
1958	Ferlinghetti, *A Coney Island of the Mind* Kunitz, *Selected Poems 1928–58* Roethke, *The Waking*	Albee, Edward, *The Zoo Story* Capote, Truman, *Breakfast at Tiffany's*	John Birch Society founded Launch of first U.S. satellite
1959	Lowell, *Life Studies* McClure, *Hymns to St. Geryon* Snodgrass, *Heart's Needle*	Burroughs, William, *The Naked Lunch* Roth, Philip, *Goodbye, Columbus*	Alaska and Hawaii admitted to U.S. as 49th and 50th states Eisenhower says economy is 'on a rising curve of prosperity'

DATE	WORKS OF POETRY	OTHER WORK	HISTORICAL/CULTURAL EVENTS
1960	Duncan, *The Opening of the Field* Jarrell, *The Woman at the Washington Zoo* Kinnell, *What a Kingdom it Was* O'Hara, *Second Avenue* Olson, *The Distances* Plath, *The Colossus* Sexton, *To Bedlam and Part Way Back*	Barth, *The Sot-Weed Factor* Shapiro, *In Defence of Ignorance* Updike, John, *Rabbit, Run*	Population 180 million Kennedy defeats Nixon in presidential election
1961	Baraka, *Preface to a Twenty Volume Suicide Note* H. D., *Helen in Egypt* Ginsberg, *Kaddish and Other Poems* Wilbur, *Advice to a Prophet and Other Poems*	Baldwin, *Nobody Knows my Name* Heller, Joseph, *Catch-22*	U.S. severs relations with Fidel Castro's Cuba Bay of Pigs invasion Berlin Wall erected First U.S. manned space expedition
1962	Ashbery, *The Tennis Court Oath* Bly, *Silence in the Snowy Fields* Oppen, *The Materials* Reznikoff, *By the Waters of Manhattan* Williams, *Pictures from Breughel*	Albee, *Who's Afraid of Virginia Woolf?* Porter, Katherine Anne, *Ship of Fools*	Cuban missile crisis U.S aids South Vietnam against Vietcong guerillas

DATE	WORKS OF POETRY	OTHER WORK	HISTORICAL/CULTURAL EVENTS
1963	Ginsberg, *Reality Sandwiches* Rich, *Snapshots of a Daughter-in-Law* Roethke, *Sequence, Sometimes Metaphysical* Williams, *Paterson: Books I–V*	Friedan, Betty, *The Feminine Mystique* Pynchon, Thomas, *V* Vonnegut, Kurt, *Cat's Cradle*	Assasination of Kennedy; Johnson sworn in as successor Civil Rights march on Washington: Martin Luther King's 'I have a dream' speech
1964	Baraka, *The Dead Lecturer* Berryman, *77 Dream Songs* Lowell, *For the Union Dead* O'Hara, *Lunch Poems* Rexroth, *Natural Numbers: New and Selected Poems* Reznikoff, *Testimony* Roethke, *The Far Field*	Baraka, *Dutchman* Bellow, *Herzog* Selby, Hubert, *Last Exit to Brooklyn*	Johnson re-elected U.S. bombs bases in North Vietnam Race riots in Harlem and Philadelphia Student 'free speech' movement at the University of California
1965	Ammons, *Tape for the Turn of the Year* Bishop (Elizabeth), *Questions of Travel* Plath, *Ariel* Zukofsky, *All: The Collected Short Poems 1923–58*	Malcolm X, *The Autobiography of Malcolm X*	U.S. formally allies with South Vietnam Civil rights demonstrations in Selma, Alabama, and Chicago Race riots in Los Angeles Malcolm X killed
1966	Duncan, *Of the War: Passages 22–27* Rich, *Necessities of Life* Roethke, *Complete Poems*	Baraka, *Home: Social Essays* Capote, *In Cold Blood*	Race riots in Cleveland, Chicago, and Atlanta

DATE	WORKS OF POETRY	OTHER WORK	HISTORICAL/CULTURAL EVENTS
1967	Baraka, *Black Magic: Poetry 1961–7* Bly, *The Light Around the Body* Creeley, *Words* Dorn, *The North Atlantic Turbine* Lowell, *Near the Ocean*	Brautigan, Richard, *Trout Fishing in America* Styron, William, *The Confessions of Nat Turner*	Anti-Vietnam demonstrations Race riots throughout country
1968	Berryman, *His Toy, His Dream, His Rest* Dickey, *Poems 1957–67* Ginsberg, *Planet News* Olson, *The Maximus Poems IV, V, VI*	Cleaver, Eldridge, *Soul on Ice* Mailer, *Armies of the Night* Vidal, Gore, *Myra Breckinridge*	Robert Kennedy and Martin Luther King assassinated Riots in Chicago, Boston, and other cities My Lai Village massacre Nixon elected president
1969	Bishop, *Complete Poems* Jarrell, *Complete Poems* Lowell, *Notebook 1967–8* Merrill, *The Fire Screen* Pound, *Drafts and Fragments of Cantos CX–CXVII*	Roth, *Portnoy's Complaint* Vonnegut, *Slaughterhouse Five*	U.S. moon landing Woodstock music festival
1970	Baraka, *It's Nation Time* Dickey, *The Eye-Beaters Blood, Victory Madness, Buckhead and Mercy* Duncan, *Tribunals: Passages 31–5* Olson, *Collected Poems*	Brown, Dee, *Bury My Heart at Wounded Knee* Millett, Kate, *Sexual Politics*	Population 203 million National Guard kill four protesting students at Kent State University

DATE	WORKS OF POETRY	OTHER WORK	HISTORICAL/CULTURAL EVENTS
1971	Mahubuti, *Directionscore* Merwin, *The Miner's Pale Children* O'Hara, *Complete Poems* Rich, *The Will to Change* Sexton, *Transformation*	Doctorow, E. L., *The Book of Daniel*	Vietnam War increases inflation rate 18-year-olds get the vote
1972	Ammons, *Collected Poems 1951–71* Ashbery, *Three Poems* Berryman, *Love & Fame* Plath, *Winter Trees* Zukovsky, *'A' 24*	Barth, *Chimera*	Watergate affair begins; *Washington Post* initiates investigation
1973	Lowell, *The Dolphin; For Lizzie and Harriet; History* Giovanni, *Black Judgement* Rich, *Diving into the Wreck* Sanchez, *A Blues Book for Magical Black Women*	Pynchon, *Gravity's Rainbow* Vidal, *Burr*	Cease-fire in Vietnam; bombing of Cambodia
1974	Creeley, *Thirty Things* Snyder, *Turtle Island* Wakoski, *Trilogy*	Heller, *Something Happened*	Nixon resigns over Watergate scandal; Ford succeeds him

DATE	WORKS OF POETRY	OTHER WORK	HISTORICAL/CULTURAL EVENTS
1975	Ashbery, *Self-Portrait in a Convex Mirror* Dorn, *Collected Poems; Slinger* Olson, *The Maximus Poems, Volume Three* Pinsky, *Sadness and Happiness*	Doctorow, *Ragtime* Wolfe, Tom, *The Painted Word*	Watergate trials American's 'Apollo 16' docks in space with Russia's 'Soyuz 19'
1976	Merrill, *Divine Comedies* Warren, *Selected Poems 1923–75* Wilbur, *The Mind-Reader*	Haley, Alex, *Roots*	Bi-centennail celebrations 'Viking II' lands on Mars
1977	Bidart, *The Book of the Body* Ginsberg, *Mind Breaths* Lowell, *Day by Day* Smith, *Cumberland Station* Snodgrass, *The Führer Bunker*	Coover, Robert, *The Public Burning*	Carter becomes president and pardons all draft-evaders Gary Gilmore executed
1978	Dorn, *Hello, La Jolla* Ferlinghetti, *Landscapes of Living and Dying* Levertov, *Collected Earlier Poems* Lord, Audre, *The Black Unicorn* Merrill, *Mirabell: Books of Number*	Irving, John, *The World According to Garp*	Strikes in mining and fire services lead to widespread violence Indians demonstrate against violation of treaty rights

DATE	WORKS OF POETRY	OTHER WORK	HISTORICAL/CULTURAL EVENTS
1979	Bly, *This Tree Will Be Here for a Thousand Years*	Mailer, *The Executioner's Song* Roth, *The Ghost Writer*	U.S. recognises new government in Iran Carter supports production of new MX missile
1980	Berrigan, *So Going Around Cities* Dickey, William, *Moon Under Saturn* Glück, *Descending Figure* Goedicke, Patricia, *Crossing the Same River* Kearney, Lawrence, *Kingdom Come* Manley, Frank, *Resultances*	Doctorow, *Loon Lake* Toole, John Kennedy, *A Confederacy of Dunces*	Reagan elected president U.S. hostages held in Iran
1981	Ashbery, *Shadow Train* Bowers, *Witnesses* Bronk, William, *Life Supports* Crase, Douglas, *The Revisionist* Sorrentino, Gilbert, *Selected Poems 1958–80* Stewart, Susan, *Yellow Stars and Ice*	Irving, *Hotel New Hampshire* Updike, *Rabbit is Rich*	U.S. hostages freed by Iran Reagan wounded in attempted assassination 'Columbia' space shuttle in orbit

DATE	WORKS OF POETRY	OTHER WORK	HISTORICAL/CULTURAL EVENTS
1982	Bukowski, *Love is a Dog from Hell* Cooper, Jane, *Scaffolding* Forché, Carolyn, *The Country Between Us* Haines, *News from the Glacier* Merrill, *The Changing Light at Sandover* Ostriker, Alicia, *A Woman Under the Surface*	Bellow, *The Dean's December* Fiedler, Leslie, *What Was Literature?*	In his first State of the Union address Reagan denies that 'America's best days are behind her'
1983	Clampitt, *The Kingfisher* Eigner, Larry, *Waters/Place/Time* Malanga, Gerard, *This Will Kill That* Piercy, Marge, *Stone, Paper, Knife* Pietri, Pedro, *Traffic Violations*	Didion, Joan, *Salvador* Walker, Alice, *The Colour Purple*	Reagan proposes a five-year military budget for over two trillion dollars; plans for 'star wars' are announced
1984	Clark, Tom, *Paradise Resisted* Elon, Florence, *Self-Made* Ginsberg, *Collected Poems 1947–80* Grosholz, Emily, *The River Painter* Matthias, John, *Northern Summer* Wakoski, *The Collected Greed, Parts 1–13* Wright (Charles), *The Other Side of the River*	Heller, *God Knows* Phillips, Jayne Anne, *Machine Dreams*	Reagan wins landslide victory in presidential election

DATE	WORKS OF POETRY	OTHER WORK	HISTORICAL/CULTURAL EVENTS
1985	Ashbery, *A Wave* Clampitt, *What the Light Was Like* Glück, *The Triumph of Achilles* Gregor, Debora, *And* Merrill, *Late Settings* Piercy, Marge, *My Mother's Body*	Ellis, Brett Easton, *Less Than Zero* Keillor, Garson, *Lake Woebegon Days*	U.S. military involvement in Nicaragua grows Increasing threat of A.I.D.S. Reagan and Gorbachev meet at Geneva

General Bibliographies

Note: Each section is arranged alphabetically. The books marked with an asterisk are of particular use and importance.

(i) Bibliographies and Reference Guides

Bradbury, Malcolm, Franco, Jean and Mottram, Eric (eds.) *The Penguin companion to Literature: United States and Latin America (1971)* (Especially strong on poetry although now rather dated.)

Elliott, Emory (ed.) *Columbia Literary History of the United States* (1988) (A new reference work offering a variety of critical attitudes and reflecting recent developments in literary theory and approaches to the canon.)

* Gohdes, Clarence and Marovitz, Sanford (eds.) *Bibliographical Guide to the Study of the Literature of the U.S.A.* (1954; 5th revised edn., 1984) (The most thorough guide for American literature in general.)

Greiner, Donald (ed.) *American Poets Since World War II* (1980). Vol. 5 of *Dictionary of Literary Biography* (A standard reference work for biographical information.) Other volumes in this series may be of use to some readers: e.g. vol. 16, *The Beats: Literary Bohemians in Postwar America*, edited by Ann Charters (1983), and vol. 41, *Afro-American Poetry Since 1955* edited by Thadious M. Davis and Trudier Harris (1985).

Hart, James *The Oxford Companion to American Literature* (1941; 5th revised edn., 1983) (A standard reference work, although poor on recent poetry.)

Leary, Lewis *American Literature: A Study and Research Guide* (1976); *Articles on American Literature* (1954–71) (Two invaluable reference tools for more advanced research.)

* Salzman, Jack (ed.) *The Cambridge Handbook of American Literature* (1986) (Some surprising omissions, but the best reference work for anyone new to American literature.)

Schweik, Robert C. and Riesner, Dieter *Reference Sources in English and American Literature: An Annotated Bibliography* (1977) (Useful for more advanced research.)

* Spiller, Robert et al. (eds.)	*Literary History of the United States* (1948; 4th revised edn., 1974) (A standard reference work, with useful essays and bibliographies.)
Woodress, James, and Robbins, J. Albert (eds.)	*American Literary Scholarship: An Annual* (1965–) (A comprehensive annual survey of books and articles on American literature.)

(ii) Literary, historical, and cultural backgrounds

Aaron, Daniel	*The Unwritten War: American Writers and the Civil War* (1973); *Writers on the Left: Episodes in American Literary Communism* (1961) (Two important books by a major critic on American writers' historical and political commitments.)
Aldridge, John	*After the Lost Generation: A Critical Study of the Writers of Two Wars* (1951) (The standard study of war and post-war writing.)
Anderson, Paul and Fisch, Max	*Philosophy in America from the Puritans to James* (1965) (A valuable survey.)
Anderson, Quentin	*The Imperial Self: An Essay in American Literary and Cultural History* (1971) (Useful analysis of the American preoccupation with selfhood.)
Bercovitch, Sacvan	*The American Puritan Imagination: Essays in Revaluation* (1974); *Puritan Origins of the American Self* (1975) (Invaluable for an understanding of Puritan influence.)
Berthoff, Werner	*The Ferment of Realism: American Literature 1884–1915; A Literature Without Qualities: American Writing Since 1945* (1980) (Two interesting, if necessarily compressed, surveys).
* Bewley, Marius	*The Complex Fate: Hawthorne, James, and Some Other American Writers* (1952); *The Eccentric Design: Form in the Classic American Novel* (1959) (Two influential books on the 'Americanness' of American writing.)
Bigsby, C. W. E.	*The Second Black Renaissance: Essays in Black Literature* (1980) (On recent Afro-American writing.)
Boynton, Percy	*The Rediscovery of the Frontier* (1931) (A useful summary of other books and arguments concerning the frontier.)
Bradbury, John	*Renaissance in the South: A Critical History of the Literature 1920–60* (1963) (A thorough survey of writing in the South, including poetry.)

Bradbury, Malcolm, and Temperley, Howard (eds.) — *Introduction to American Studies* (1981) (Essays on general themes and topics, with some helpful annotated bibliographies.)

Bridgeman, Richard — *The Colloquial Style in America* (1966) (Critical examination of the vernacular mode in American writing.)

Brogan, Hugh — *The Pelican History of the U.S.A.* (1986) (The best introduction to American history.)

Brookeman, Christopher — *American Culture and Society since the 1930s* (A lively account of more recent developments, particularly in the visual arts.)

Brooks, Van Wyck — *Makers and Finders: A History of the Writer in America* (1937–52) (Anecdotal and informative, although the different volumes vary considerably in quality.)

* Chase, Richard — *The American Novel and its Tradition* (1957) (One of the most helpful introductions to the 'Americanness' of American writing.)

Cohen, Hennig (ed.) — *The American Culture: Approaches to the Study of the United States* (1968); *The American Experience: Approaches to the Study of the United States* (1968) (Of particular use to anyone new to American writing.)

Conn, Peter — *The Divided Mind: Ideology and Imagination in America, 1898–1917* (1987) (A useful account of political, economic, and cultural contexts.)

Cowley, Malcolm — *After the Genteel Tradition: American Writing 1910–30* (1964); *Exile's Return* (1951); *A Second Flowering: Works and Days of the Lost Generation* (1973) (Three lively accounts of the Twenties and expatriatism, by a critical participant.)

Cunliffe, Marcus — *The Literature of the United States* (1954; 4th revised edn., 1986) (The best one-volume survey of American writing.)

Curti, Merle — *The Growth of American Thought* (1963) (A brief but very helpful account of major intellectual movements.)

Dickstein, Morris — *Gates of Eden: American Culture in the Sixties* (1977) (An enjoyable and informative account of this significant period.)

Douglas, Ann — *The Feminization of American Culture* (1977) (Indispensable for anyone interested in feminist approaches to American culture.)

Fender, Stephen — *Plotting the Golden West: American Literature and the Rhetoric of the California Trail* (1982) (An interesting examination of the literary effects of the westward movement.)

Ferguson, Robert A.	*Law and Letters in American Culture* (1984) (Intriguing analysis of a significant and neglected theme.)
Fiedelson, Charles S.	*Symbolism and American Literature* (1953) (One of the pioneering discussions of the 'Americanness' of American writing.)
⋆ Fiedler, Leslie	*Love and Death in the American Novel* (1960); *The Return of the Vanishing American* (1968) (Two indispensable books, one on the 'Americanness' of American writing, the other on ideas of the frontier, the West, and the Indian.)
Frank, Waldo	*Our America* (1919) (A lively, prophetic protest against American philistinism; like Williams's work, it is both symptomatic (of the forces that helped shape modern American poetry) and informative.)
Fussell, Edwin	*Frontier: American Literature and the American West* (1965) (A standard survey concentrating on major nineteenth-century writers.)
Galinski, Hans (ed.)	*The Frontier in American History and Literature* (1960) (Helpful approaches towards the idea and impact of the frontier.)
Gates, Henry L. (ed.)	*Black Literature and Literary Theory* (1984) (Useful for anyone interested in black aesthetics.)
Gray, Richard	*The Literature of Memory: Modern Writers of the American South* (1977); *Writing the South: Ideas of an American Region* (1986) (Two discussions of the South by the author of this book.)
Gross, Seymour L. and Hardy, John E.	*Images of the Negro in American Literature* (1964) (Useful for anyone interested in attitudes towards the black experience.)
⋆ Hamburger, Michael	*The Truth of Poetry: Modern Poetry from Baudelaire to the 1960s* (1972) (The finest account of the international contexts of modern American poetry.)
Hazard, Lucy	*The Frontier in American Literature* (1929) (Demonstrates how the idea of the frontier permeates American literature.)
Hoffman, Daniel	*Form and Fable in American Fiction* (1961) (On the 'Americanness' of American literature.)
Hoffman, Frederick	*The Twenties: American Writing in the Postwar Decade* (1955) (A standard account of the period, literary and cultural.)
Hofstadter, Richard	*Social Darwinism in American Thought* (1944) (A powerful analysis of one of the major impulses in American writing.)

Homberger, Eric — *American Writers and Radical Politics 1906–39: Equivocal Commitments* (1985) (A lively and opinionated examination of writers on the left.)

Howard, John — *Our American Music: A Comprehensive History from 1620 to the Present* (1968) (The best introduction to the subject.)

Huggins, Nathan — *Harlem Renaissance* (1971) (A discussion of black culture in the earlier part of this century.)

Jones, Howard M. — *O Strange New World: American Culture, the Formative Years* (1964) (On major themes in American thought and writing.)

Kazin, Alfred — *An American Procession* (1984); *On Native Grounds: An Interpretation of American Prose Literature* (1942) (Two books by a major critic, mainly on American prose but relevant to poetry.)

King, Richard H. — *A Southern Renaissance: The Cultural Awakening of the Modern South 1930–55* (1980) (A controversial account of the backgrounds to Southern writing.)

Klein, Marcus — *Foreigners: The Making of American Literature 1900–40* (1981) (One of the more useful recent books on cultural nationalism.)

Keledny, Annette — *The Land Before Them: Fantasy and Experience of the American Frontier 1630–1860* (1984); *The Lay of the Land: Metaphor as Experience and History in American Life and Literature* (1975) (On the impact of American geography on American writing.)

Larkin, Oliver — *Art in America* (1960) (The best brief introduction.)

* Lawrence, D. H. — *Studies in Classic American Literature* (1920) (A characteristically provocative, and inspiring, account of the 'Americanness' of American writing.)

Lears, T. J. — *No Place of Grace: Antimodernism and the Transformation of American Culture, 1886–1920* (1981) (Useful for the cultural backgrounds to modern American poetry.)

* Lewis, R. W. B. — *The American Adam: Innocence, Tragedy, and Tradition in the Nineteenth Century* (1955) (A brilliant discussion of the Adamic theme in American writing.)

Lindberg, Gary — *The Confidence Man in American Literature* (1982) (A stimulating examination of a recurrent type, and its implications.)

Margolies, Edward — *Native Sons: A Critical Study of Twentieth-Century Negro American Authors* (1968) (A helpful survey of black writing.)

* Matthiessen, F. O. — *American Renaissance: Art and Expression in the Age of Emerson and Whitman* (1941) (A brilliant,

	pioneering examination of cultural nationalism and the 'Americanness' of American writing.)
Martin, Jay	*Harvests of Change: American Literature 1865–1914* (1967) (One of the best general accounts of the period.)
★ Marx, Leo	*The Machine in the Garden: Technology and the Pastoral Ideal in America* (1964) (A major account of the impact of technology on the pastoral ideal.)
McKay, David	*American Politics and Society* (1983) (A useful survey of the subject.)
★ Miller, Perry	*The New England Mind from Colony to Province* (1953); *Nature's Nation* (1967) (Two books by a major critic, one on Puritanism and the other on cultural nationalism.)
Miller, Ruth	*Backgrounds to Black American Literature* (1971) (Indispensable for anyone interested in the subject.)
Mumford, Lewis	*The Golden Day: A Study in American Literature and Culture* (1926) (An early but still useful book on American ideology.)
Nye, Russell B.	*The Unembarrassed Muse: The Popular Arts in America* (1970) (A helpful introduction to the subject.)
O'Brien, Michael	*The Idea of the American South 1920–41* (1979) (A rigorous analysis of the intellectual contexts of Southern writing.)
Pells, Richard H.	*Interpretations of American Literature from the Beginnings to 1920* (1927–30) (Useful for an understanding of Americans' attitudes towards their own literature.)
★ Poirier, Richard	*A World Elsewhere: The Place of Style in American Literature* (1966) (A brilliant, persuasive approach to the 'Americanness' of American writing.)
Rourke, Constance	*American Humour: A Study of the National Character* (1931) (An early and still indispensable account of humour in America.)
Seelye, John	*Prophetic Waters: The River in Early American Life and Literature* (1977) (A thoughtful analysis of the image of the river, and its implications.)
Singal, Daniel J.	*The War Within: From Victorian to Modernist Thought in the South 1919–45* (1982) (A painstaking examination of cultural change in the South.)
Sklar, Robert	*Movie-Made America* (1975) (A general account of the relationship between American film and culture.)
Slotkin, Richard	*Regeneration Through Violence: The Mythology of the American Frontier 1600–1860* (1973) (A stimulating examination of the idea of the frontier.)

* Smith, Henry Nash — *Virgin Land: The Amerian West as Symbol and Myth* (1950) (The standard book on the idea and experience of the West.)

Spindler, Michael — *American Literature and Social Change: William Dean Howells to Arthur Miller* (1983) (Useful for anyone interested in the relationship between the writing and the socio-political context.)

Stepto, Robert — *From Behind the Veil: A Study of Afro-American Literature* (1979) (Indispensable account of black writing.)

Sundquist, Eric (ed.) — *American Realism: New Essays* (1982) (Some stimulating approaches to the 'realistic' strain in American writing.)

* Tanner, Tony — *The Reign of Wonder: Naivety and Reality in American Literature* (1965) (An indispensable examination of the innocent eye and the vernacular style in American writing.)

Taylor, Gordon O — *Chapters of Experience: Studies in Twentieth-Century American Autobiography* (1983) (Relevant for those concerned with the autobiographical strain in American writing.)

Taylor, William R. — *Cavalier and Yankee: The Old South and the American National Character* (1961) (An informative analysis of attitudes towards the South.)

Walker, Marshall — *The Literature of the U.S.A.* (1983) (A brief but helpful survey, particularly good on this century.)

Welland, Dennis (ed.) — *The United States: A Companion to American Studies* (1974) (A useful reference work for those new to the subject.)

Williams, Williams Carlos — *In the American Grain* (1925) (On the 'Americanness' of American literature: lively, controversial, and (like Waldo Frank's book) at once symptomatic and informative.)

Young, James O. — *Black Writers of the Thirties* (1973) (An informative account of the period.)

Ziff, Larzer — *Literary Democracy: The Declaration of Cultural Independence in America* (1981) (A thoughtful examination of cultural nationalism.)

(iii) History and criticism

Allen, Donald and Tallman, Warren (eds.) — *The Poetics of the New American Poetry* (1973) (Statements about poetics, chiefly by writers discussed in chapter 6.)

Alvarez, A. *Stewards of Excellence: Studies in Modern English and American Poets* (1958) (Intelligent, if now rather dated, account of some modern poets.)

Altieri, Charles *Enlarging the Temple: New Directions in American Poetry During the 1960s* (1979); *Self and Sensibility in Contemporary American Poetry* (1984) (A brilliant, if sometimes difficult, critic, particularly perceptive about the problems and possibilities of postmodernist poetry.)

Bellamy, Joe D. (ed.) *American Poetry Observed: Poets on their Work* (1984) (A useful collection of observations by the poets themselves.)

Berke, Roberta *Bounds out of Bounds: A Compass for Recent American and British Poetry* (1981) (A very helpful account, by a practising poet.)

Bernstein, Michael *The Tale of the Tribe: Ezra Pound and the Modern Verse Epic* (1980) (Detailed analyses of the *Cantos, Paterson,* and the *Maximus* poems.)

Blasing, Mutlu K. *American Poetry: The Rhetoric of its Forms* (1987) (Particularly good on O'Hara and Ashbery.)

Bloom, Harold *The Anxiety of Influence: A Theory of Poetry* (1973); *Figures of Capable Imagination* (1976) (By a major critic of modern American poetry. Both books are sometimes difficult, always stimulating.)

Boroff, Marjorie *Language and the Poet: Verbal Artistry in Frost, Stevens, and Moore* (1978) (A careful examination of the use of language, particularly good on Stevens.)

Boyers, Robert (ed.) *Contemporary Poetry in America: Essays and Interviews* (1974) (On a wide selection of poets, including Lowell, Jarrell, Plath, Rich, Olson, Merwin, Nemerov, and Dickey.)

Bradbury, John *The Fugitives: A Critical Account* (1958) (A critically painstaking account of the Fugitives' theories and practice.)

Breslin, J. E. *From Modern to Contemporary: American Poetry, 1945–65* (1980) (Excellent on the principal movements and some major poets associated with them.)

Brooks, Cleanth *Modern Poetry and the Tradition* (1939); *The Well Wrought Urn: Studies in the Structure of Poetry* (1947) (Studies of some of the more important modernist and traditionalist poets by one of the most interesting of the New Critics.)

Butterfield, R. W. (Herbie) (ed.) *Modern American Poetry* (1986) (Essays on various poets from Whitman to Dorn.)

Cambon, Glauco *The Inclusive Flame: Studies in American Poetry* (1963); *Recent American Poetry* (1962) (Two useful, fairly wide-ranging, studies.)

Carroll, Paul — *The Poem in its Skin* (1968) (A stimulating account of more recent poets' resistance to the generation of Eliot.)

Charters, Samuel — *Some Poems/Poets: Studies in American Underground Poetry Since 1945* (1968) (Brief, helpful essays on some of the poets discussed in chapter 6, including Olson, Duncan, Snyder, and Ferlinghetti.)

Coffman, Stanley K. — *Imagism: A Chapter for the History of Modern Poetry* (1951) (A lucid and thorough summary, with particularly good chapters on Pound and on 'Amygism'.)

Cowan, Louise — *The Fugitive Group: A Literary History* (1959) (Less critically rigorous than Bradbury's book on the group, but more informative.)

Dembo, L. S. — *Conceptions of Reality in Modern American Poetry* (1966) (A very useful account of notions of, and stances towards, reality favoured by various major poets.)

Donoghue, Denis — *Connoisseurs of Chaos: Ideas of Order in Modern American Poetry* (1956) (Excellent essays on various poets; the pieces on Robinson, Cunningham, Lowell, on Stevens and on Roethke, are particularly good.)

Duberman, Martin — *Black Mountain: An Exploration in Community* (1974) (The most thorough account available of the Black Mountain poets, and others associated with Black Mountain College.)

Ehrenpreis, Irvin (ed.) — *American Poetry* (1965) (Essays of variable merit on very different subjects, including Imagism, 'the age of Lowell', and Stevens.)

Faas, Ekbert (ed.) — *Towards a New American Poetics: Essays and Interviews* (1978) (A valuable collection.)

Fussell, Edwin — *Lucifer in Harness: American Metre, Metaphor, and Diction* (1973) (An incisive discussion of American poets' frustrated and rebellious response to inherited forms and traditions.)

Gelpi, Albert — *A Coherent Splendour: The American Poetic Renaissance 1910–50* (1988) (An important new book on major authors: recommended for advanced research.)

Gould, J. — *Modern American Women Poets* (1985) (A lively and idiosyncratic discussion.)

Gregory, Horace and Zaturenska, Maya — *A History of American Poetry 1900–40* (1946) (An able, if now fairly dated, survey.)

Hollander, John (ed.) — *Modern Poetry: Essays in Criticism* (1968) (An attempt to outline some of the ways in which modern poetry has been read by drawing on the essays of many of its finest critics.)

Homberger, Eric *The Art of the Real: Poetry in England and America Since 1939* (1977) (A discussion of the relationship between the poetry and society, expressed as an 'art of the real'.)

Howard, Richard *Alone with America: Studies in the Art of Poetry in the United States Since 1950* (1970) (Brief essays on over forty poets from Ammons to James Wright.)

Hughes, Glenn *Imagism and the Imagist: A Study in Modern Poetry* (1960) (Informative discussion of the cultural background, and individual chapters on seven poets, including H.D. and Pound.)

Hungerford, Edward B. (ed.) *Poets in Progress: Critical Prefaces to Thirteen Modern American Poets* (1962) (A series of very helpful introductions.)

Jarrell, Randall *Poetry and the Age* (1955) (A collection of reviews and essays, many of them outstanding, on such poets as Frost, Ransom, Stevens, and Moore.)

Jordan, June (ed.) *Soulscript: Afro-American Poetry* (1970) (Essential reading for those interested in black poetry.)

Juhasz, Suzanne *Naked and Fiery Forms: Modern American Poetry by Women: A New Tradition* (1976) (Indispensable for those interested in the subject.)

Kalstone, David *Five Temperaments* (1977) (Analyses the ways poets find to write about their lives, focussing on E. Bishop, Lowell, Merrill, Rich, and Ashbery.)

Keller, Lynn *Re-Making It New: Contemporary American Poetry and the Modernist Tradition* (1986) (A provocative re-reading of recent poetry.)

Kenner, Hugh *A Homemade World: The American Modernist Writers* (1975); *The Pound Era* (1971) (Two books on modernism by one of its most influential critics.)

Lansing, George, and Moran, Ronald *Four Poets and the Emotive Imagination: Robert Bly, James Wright, Louis Simpson, and William Stafford* (1976) (Useful discussions of often neglected poets.)

Leiberman, Lawrence *Unassigned Frequencies: American Poetry in Review, 1964–77* (1978) (A large collection of reviews, nearly all of recent poetry.)

Lutyens, David *The Creative Encounter* (1966) (A bold attempt to analyse the work of writers like Jeffers, Crane, and Lowell in terms of a creative encounter with the crisis of modern life.)

McNally, Dennis *Desolate Angel: Jack Kerouac, the Beat Generation, and America* (1979) (A lively and involving account of the Beats.)

Malkoff, Karl *Crowell's Handbook of Contemporary American Poetry: A Critical Handbook of American Poetry Since*

1940 (1973); *Escape from the Self: A Study in Contemporary American Poetry and Poetics* (1972) (The first book offers a useful introduction, the second a more advanced analysis of attitudes to the self in contemporary poetry.)

Martin, Robert K. — *The Homosexual Tradition in American Poetry* (1979) (Crane, Ginsberg, Duncan, Merrill among those discussed.)

Mazzaro, Jerome — *Postmodern American Poetry* (1980) (An attempt to isolate recurrent patterns in the work of seven poets, including Jarrell, Berryman, and Plath.)

Mazzaro, Jerome (ed.) — *Modern American Poetry: Essays in Criticism* (1970) (A collection of essays of varying quality.)

Meltzer, David (ed.) — *The San Francisco Poets* (1971) (A useful introduction.)

Mersman, James — *Out of the Vietnam Vortex: A Study of Poets and Poetry Against the War* (1974) (A lively account of an important and relatively neglected topic.)

Miller, J. Hillis — *Poets of Reality* (1965) (By one of the more astute critics of modern poetry, particularly good on Williams.)

Mills, Ralph J. — *Contemporary American Poetry* (1965); *Creation's Very Self: On the Personal in Recent American Poetry* (1969); *Cry of the Human: Essays on Contemporary American Poetry* (1974) (Some brilliant discussions, particularly of the increasing presence of the 'personal element' in contemporary American poetry.)

Molesworth, Charles — *The Fierce Embrace: A Study of Contemporary American Poetry* (1979) (An interesting and useful study.)

Nemerov, Howard — *Reflexions on Poetry and Poetics* (1972) (Thoughts on poetry by a practising poet.)

Nemerov, Howard (ed.) — *Poets on Poetry* (1961) (Valuable collection, that includes the comments of, among others, Aiken, Eberhart, Duncan, Berryman, Wilbur, and Corso.)

Ossman, David — *The Sullen Art: Interviews by David Ossman with Modern American Poets* (1967) (Interviews with Rexroth, Bly, Creeley, and Ginsberg, among others.)

Ostriker, Alicia S. — *Stealing the Language: The Emergence of Women's Poetry in America* (1986) (Especially strong on poetry since the 1960s.)

Ostroff, Anthony (ed.) — *The Contemporary Poet as Artist and Critic* (1964) (A valuable collection of comments.)

Packard, William (ed.) — *The Craft of Poetry: Interviews from the New York Quarterly* (1974) (Lively collection of interviews.)

Parkinson, Thomas (ed.) *A Casebook on the Beats* (1961) (The most useful introduction to the subject.)

* Pearce, Roy Harvey *The Continuity of American Poetry* (1961) (A brilliant and indispensable account of the American tradition in poetry, concentrating on the major writers.)

Perloff, Marjorie *The Dance of the Intellect: Studies in the Poetry of the Pound Tradition* (1986); *The Poetics of Indeterminacy: Rimbaud to Cage* (1981) (Some trenchant analyses of Pound, Oppen, Williams, and the relation of poetry to other arts.)

Perkins, David *A History of Modern Poetry* (1976) (A useful survey.)

Phillips, Robert *The Confessional Poets* (1973) (A thoughtful account of Lowell, Plath, and others.)

Pinsky, Robert *The Situation of Poetry: Contemporary Poetry and its Traditions* (1977) (By a practising poet, this is particularly good on the impact of the Emersonian tradition.)

Redmond, Eugene *Drumvoices: The Mission of Afro-American Poetry, A Critical History* (1976) (An indispensable discussion.)

Rexroth, Kenneth *American Poetry in the Twentieth Century* (1973) (A wide-ranging survey, relating poetry to larger questions of culture.)

* Rosenthal, M. L. *The New Poets: American and British Poetry since World War II* (1967) (An indispensable book, containing a particularly good discussion of the confessional poets.)

Rubin, Louis D. *The Wary Fugitives: Four Poets and the South* (1978) (The best and most comprehensive book on the subject.)

Scully, James (ed.) *Modern Poets on Modern Poetry* (1966) (Reprints statements by Pound, Frost, Williams, Ransom, Crane, Lowell, and Olson, among others.)

Shaw, Robert (ed.) *American Poetry Since 1960: Some Critical Perspectives* (1974) (A varied selection including pieces on Lowell, O'Hara, Rich, and the poetry of protest.)

Simpson, Louis *A Revolution in Taste: Studies of Dylan Thomas, Allen Ginsberg, Sylvia Plath, and Robert Lowell* (1978) (Interesting for its discussions of its subjects and for the indirect light it throws on Simpson's own work.)

Stanford, Donald *Revolution and Convention in Modern Poetry: Studies in Ezra Pound, T. S. Eliot, Wallace Stevens, Edwin Arlington Robinson, and Yvor Winters* (1983) (Thorough and often stimulating.)

Stauffer, Donald B. *A Short History of American Poetry* (1974) (A comprehensive if sometimes hurried account; stronger on individuals than on general developments.)

Stepanchev, Stephen *American Poetry Since 1945: A Critical Survey* (1965) (A brief, informal discussion of general developments and a mixed bag of individuals (e.g. Olson, Ashbery, Stafford.))

Sutton, Walter *American Free Verse: The Modern Revolution in Poetry* (1978) (Particularly useful for those interested in problems of form.)

Thurley, Geoffrey *The American Moment: American Poetry in the Mid-Century* (1977) (A combative account, arguing that American poetry only came of age in the late 1950s.)

Tytell, John *Naked Angels: The Lives and Literature of the Beat Generation* (1986) (A lively introduction to the subject.)

Vendler, Helen *Part of Nature, Part of Us: Modern American Poets* (1980) (A collection of essays and reviews by one of the leading critics of American poetry.)

von Hallberg, R. *American Poetry and Culture 1945–80* (1984) (Of variable quality, but good on Merrill, Lowell, Dorn, Bowers,Bidart, and Pinsky.)

Waggoner, Hyatt H. *American Poets from the Puritans to the Present* (1968; revised edn., 1984); *American Visionary Poetry* (1982); *The Heel of Elohim: Science and Values in American Poetry* (1950) (Three wide-ranging surveys, concerned in part with poetry and belief; the first book cited here offers the most useful introduction.)

Wagner, Jean *Black Poets of the United States: From Paul Laurence Dunbar to Langston Hughes* (1978) (Useful for an understanding of the earlier poets of this century.)

Watts, Emily J. *The Poetry of American Women from 1832 to 1945* (1977) (Another indispensable book, for those interested in poetry by American women.)

Winters, Yvor *On Modern Poets* (1959) (Characteristically trenchant and opinionated: a book to argue with.)

Woodward, Kathleen *At Last, the Real Distinguished Thing: The Late Poems of Eliot, Pound, Stevens, and Williams* (1980) (Links the later work of these poets to the problems of modernism, post-modernism, endings, and the process of ageing.)

(iv) Some useful anthologies

Aduffi, Arnold (ed.) *Black Out Lord: An Anthology of Modern Poems by Black Americans* (1975) (A lively, useful selection.)

* Allen, Donald (ed.) *The New American Poetry 1945–60* (1960) (A landmark anthology, containing work by most of the poets discussed in chapter 6.)

Allen, Gay Wilson et al. (eds.) *American Poetry* (1965) (A reasonably wide selection, from Bradstreet to Berry.)

Bass, Ellen, and Howe, Florence (eds.) *No More Masks! An Anthology of Poems by Women* (1973) (A wide selection, beginning with Amy Lowell.)

Baym, Nina et al. (eds.) *The Norton Anthology of American Literature* (1971; revised edn., 1985) (A college textbook, with a good selection from the major modernist writers.)

Carruth, Hayden *The Voice that is Great Within Us: American Poetry of the Twentieth Century* (1978) (An exciting collection of the work of well over a hundred poets, beginning with Frost.)

Collier, Eugenia, and Long, Richard A. (eds.) *Afro-American Writing: An Anthology of Prose and Poetry* (1972) (A very useful selection.)

Cooper, Dennis *Coming Attractions: An Anthology of American Poets in their Twenties* (1980) (A taste of things to come . . .)

DeLoach Allen (ed.) *The East Side Scene: American Poetry 1960–5* (1972) (A lively collection, but difficult to obtain.)

Ellman, Richard (ed.) *The New Oxford Book of American Verse* (1976) (Some remarkable omissions, but nevertheless a thoughtful selection from Bradstreet to Baraka.)

Eshleman, Clayton (ed.) *A Caterpillar Anthology* (1971) (A collection from one of the most important little magazines of the 1960s.)

Germain, Edward (ed.) *English and American Surrealist Poetry* (1978) (Includes work by Fearing, Patchen, Kees, O'Hara, Duncan, Ashbery, Bly, Haines, McClure, and others.)

Gray, Richard (ed.) *American Poetry of the Twentieth Century* (1976) (Edited by the author of this book.)

* Hall, Donald (ed.) *Contemporary American Poetry* (1962; revised edn., 1971) (Concentrates on some of the poets discussed in chapter five: to be read in conjunction with the Allen anthology.)

Harmon, William (ed.) *The Oxford Book of American Light Verse* (1979) (A particularly strong selection of writers from the twentieth century, including the work of many major poets.)

Haydon, Robert (ed.) *Kaleidoscope: Poets by American Negro Poets* (1967) (An interesting and reasonably wide selection, concentrating on this century.)

Hughes, Langston (ed.) *New Negro Poets: U.S.A.* (1964) (A very wide selection of relatively recent poetry.)

Johnson, James Weldon (ed.) *The Book of American Negro Poetry* (1922) (Interesting for the light it sheds on the controversy concerning the proper aims of black poetry.)

* Jones, Peter (ed.) *Imagist Poetry* (1972) (An excellent anthology, offering the best possible introduction to the subject.)

Martz, William J. (ed.) *The Distinctive Voice: Twentieth-Century American Poetry* (1966) (A thoughtfully arranged selection of the work of thirty poets, from Frost to Sexton, with copious notes.)

* Moore, Geoffrey (ed.) *The Penguin Book of American Verse* (1977) (A very astute and varied selection.)

Mohr, Bill (ed.) *'Poetry Loves Poetry': An Anthology of Los Angeles Poets* (1985) (A lively selection of very recent work.)

Padgett, Ron, and Shapiro, David (eds.) *An Anthology of New York Poets* (1970) (A useful introduction.)

Poulin, A. (ed.) *Contemporary American Poetry* (1971; 3rd revised edn., 1980) (A large and varied selection from forty very different poets, with excellent critical commentaries.)

* Pratt, William (ed.) *The Fugitive Poets* (1965) (An intelligent selection, with commentary, and an excellent introduction to the group.)

Quasha, George, and Rothenberg, Jerome (eds.) *America a Prophecy* (1974) (A lively selection, offering a radical re-reading of the American poetic tradition.)

Strand, Mark (eds.) *The Contemporary American Poets: American Poetry since 1945* (1969) (Contains brief selections from the work of over ninety poets.)

Vendler, Helen (ed.) *The Harvard Book of Contemporary American Poetry* (1985) (Interesting if highly selective, concentrating on poets in the Stevens tradition.)

Individual Authors

Notes on biography, major works, and criticism

ADAMS, Léonie (1899–), born in New York City, and taught English at New York University and Bennington College. Her major books are *Those Not Elect* (1925), *High Falcon* (1929), *This Measure*, and *Poems* (1954).

See: Deutsch, B. *Poetry in Our Time* (1952; revised edn., 1963)
Vinson, J. (ed.) *Contemporary Poets* (1975)

AIKEN, Conrad (1889–1973), born in Savanna, Georgia. While he was still young, his father killed his mother and committed suicide. Lived with relatives in Massachusetts and graduated from Harvard in 1912 where he was part of the class that included Eliot and Van Wyck Brooks. Lived for a time in England from 1923, where he was a friend of John Gould Fletcher. His first book of poetry, *Earth Triumphant*, published in 1914 and his first collection of critical writing on contemporary poets, *Scepticisms*, published in 1919. The poetic volumes that followed include *Turns and Movies* (1916), *The Jig of Forslin: A Symphony* (1916), *Nocturnal of a Remembered Spring* (1917), *The House of Dust* (1920), *Punch: The Immortal Liar* (1921), *The Pilgrimage of Festus* (1923), *Preludes for Memnon* (1931), *And in the Human Heart*, a sequence of love sonnets (1940), *The Soldier*, a poem tracing the common soldier through history (1944), *The Kid*, based on the legend of William Blackstone (1942), and *Thee*, a book-length poem (1967). His *Selected Poems* (1929), won a Pulitzer Prize; *The Divine Pilgrim*, a long work evolved out of earlier poems, appeared in 1949; and a *Collected Poems* was published in 1954. Apart from criticism and short-stories (see *A Reviewer's ABC* (1958) and *Collected Short Stories* (1950)) he wrote five novels, notably *Blue Voyage* (1927), brought together in *Collected Novels* (1964), and an autobiographical piece, *Ustant* (1952). A *Selected Letters* was also published in 1978.

See: Denny R. *Conrad Aiken* (1964)
Hoffman, F. *Conrad Aiken* (1962)
Martin, J. *Conrad Aiken: A Life of His Art* (1962)

AMMONS, A [rchie] R [andolph] (1926–), born in Whiteville, North Carolina and educated at Wake Forest College and the University of California, Berkeley. His first collection, *Ommateum, with Doxology* appeared in 1955, but it was his second, *Expressions of Sea Level* (1964) that established his reputation. Subsequent volumes include *Corsons Inlet* (1965), *Tape for the Turn of the Year*, a long poem (1965), *Collected Poems: 1951–71* (1972), *The Snow Poems* (1977), *Worldly Hopes: Poems* (1982), and *Lake Effect Country: Poems* (1983). *The Selected Poems 1951–77* was published in 1977, and *The Selected Longer Poems* in 1980. Since 1964, he has taught at Cornell University.

See: Holder A., *A. R. Ammons* (1978)

ANTONINUS, Brother [EVERSON, William] (1912–), born in Sacramento, California. During World War II, he was a conscientious objector and was a member of a group of writers whose Untide Press produced influential protest poetry. In 1948, his *The Residual Years: Poems 1934–48* collected together poems previously published privately; and in the following year he became a Catholic and began a term with the Catholic Worker Movement. In 1951, he entered the Dominican Order as a lay brother; then, after six years of monastic withdrawal, he re-emerged as a member of the San Francisco Renaissance. *The Crooked Lines of God: Poems 1949–54* (1960) and *The Hazards of Holiness: Poems 1957–60* (1962) describe his spiritual experiences; *The Rose of Solitude* (1967) concerns his love for a young woman; *The City Does Not Die* (1969) recalls the San Francisco earthquake. Left the Dominicans in 1970. More recent books include *Archetype West: The Pacific Coast as a Literary Region* (1976), and *The Masks of Drought* (1980).

See: Charters, S. *Some Poems/Poets* (1971)
Gelpi, A. *The Poet in America* (1973)
Kherdian, D. *Six San Francisco Poets* (1969)
Stafford, W. (ed.) *The Achievement of Brother Antoninus* (1967)

ASHBERY, John (1927–), born in Rochester, New York and educated at Harvard and Columbia. He worked in publishing until 1955, when a Fulbright Scholarship enabled him to go to Paris. There, he became art critic for the European edition of the *New York Herald Tribune*. Returned to New York in 1965 and served on the editorial panel of *Art and Literature* (1964–67) and *Locus Solus* (1961–62). Became involved with the New York school of poets, including Frank O'Hara, Kenneth Koch, and James Schuyler. His first collection, *Turandot and Other Poems*, was published in 1953. This was followed by *Some Trees* (1956), *The Poems* (1960), *The Tennis Court Oath* (1962), *Rivers and Mountains* (1966), *Sunrise in Suburbia* and *Three Madrigals* (1968), *Fragment* (1969), *The Double Dream of Spring* and *The New Spirit* (1970), *Three Poets* (1972), *The Vermont Notebook* (1975, with Joe Brainard), *Self-Portrait in a Convex Mirror*, which won a Pulitzer Prize (1975), *Houseboat Days* (1971), *As We Know* (1979), *Shadow Train* (1981), and *A Wave* (1984). A *Selected Poems* appeared in 1985. He has also written plays and collaborated on a novel, *Nest of Ninnies* (1969), with James Schuyler. Now teaches at Brooklyn College.

See: Howard, R. *Alone With America: The Art of Poetry in the United States Since 1950* (1969)
Lehman, D. (ed.) *Beyond Amazement: New Essays on John Ashbery* (1980)
Shapiro, D. *John Ashbery: An Introduction to the Poetry* (1979)

BARAKA, Imamu Amiri (1934–), born Leroi Jones in Newark, New Jersey and educated at Rutgers, Howard, the New School of Social Research, and Columbia. After serving in the airforce, he began his career in 1956 as writer and activist. Establishing his reputation under his given name, he converted to Islam in 1965, changing his name to Imamu Amiri Baraka and moving to a black ghetto in Newark, where he founded the Spirit House Theatre. His other activities include founding *Yugen* magazine, Totem Press (which prints the works of contemporary poets), and the Black Arts Repertory Theatre in Harlem. His political commitments have led him to serve as a member of the Congress of Afrikan Peoples and secretary-general of the National Black Political Assembly; and he has taught at Columbia, the New School for Social Research, and the State University of New York at Buffalo. First collection was *Preface to a Twenty Volume Suicide Note* (1961). Subsequent volumes of poetry include *The Dead Lecturer* (1964), *Black Art* (1966), *It's Nation Time* (1920), *Spirit Reach* (1972), and *Hard Facts* (1975). Has written many notable plays, among them *Dutchman* (1964), and a novel, *The System of Dante's Hell* (1965). His many books of non-fiction include *Blues People: Negro People in White America* (1963), *Home: Social Essays* (1966), *Raise, Race, Rays, Raze: Essays Since 1965* (1971), and *Daggers & Javelins: Essays* (1984).

See: Benston, K. *Baraka: The Renegade and the Mask* (1976)
Benston, K. (ed.) *Imamu Amiri Baraka (Leroi Jones): A Collection of Critical Essays* (1978)
Brown, L. *Amiri Baraka* (1980)
Hudson, T. R. *From Leroi Jones to Amiri Baraka: The Literary Works* (1973)
Sellers, W. *Amiri Baraka / Leroi Jones: The Quest for a 'Populist Modernism'* (1978)

BERRIGAN, Ted (1934–83), born in Providence, Rhode Island. After serving in the army, he studied at the University of Tulsa and then moved to New York in 1960. Founded *'C' Magazine* (1963), which helped establish a new group of poets centred in New York, and taught at the University of Iowa and Essex University in England. Among his books are *Sonnets* (1964), *In the Early Morning Rain* (1970), and *So Going Around Cities: New and Selected Poems, 1958–79* (1980).

See: Vinson, J. (ed.) *Contemporary Poets* (1975)

BERRY, Wendell (1934–), born in Louisville, Kentucky. After graduating from the University of Kentucky, he taught at Stanford and New York University. Now lives and farms in Kentucky. His ecological interests are reflected in such essay collections as *A Continuous Harmony* (1980) and *The Gift of Good Land* (1981); other collections include *Standing by Words* (1983). His interest in the South is registered in his novels *Nathan Coulter* (1960), *A Place on Earth* (1968; revised edn., 1983), and *The Memory of Old Jack* (1974). Among his books of poetry are *The Broken Ground* (1963), *Openings* (1969), *Findings* (1969), *A Part* (1980), and *The Wheel* (1982).

See: Vinson, J. (ed.) *Contemporary Poets* (1925)

BERRYMAN, John (1914–72), born in McAlester, Oklahoma, he graduated from Columbia and Clare College, Cambridge, and taught at Brown,

Harvard, and Princeton. At the time of his suicide, he was teaching at the University of Minnesota. His work first appeared in little magazines and then in *Five American Poets* (1940). After *Poems* (1942) and *The Dispossessed* (1948), widespread recognition came with *Homage to Mistress Bradstreet* (1956). In 1965, awarded the Pulitzer Prize for *77 Dream Songs* (1964); with *His Toy, His Dream, His Rest* (1968), this became part of *The Dream Songs* (1969). Other published volumes are *His Thoughts Made Pockets & The Plane Buckt* (1958), *Short Poems* (1967), *Berryman's Sonnets*, a sequence of love sonnets written in the 1940s (1968), *Love & Fame* (1970; revised edn., 1972), *Delusions, Etc.* (1972), and *Henry's Fate & Other Poems* (1977). Also wrote the first major critical work on Stephen Crane and an autobiographical novel, *Recovery* (1973). *The Freedom of the Poet*, a collection of essays, appeared in 1976.

Haffenden, J. *The Life of John Berryman* (1982)

See: Conarroe, J. *John Berryman: An Introduction to the Poetry* (1977)
Haffenden, J. *John Berryman: A Critical Commentary* (1980)
Linebarger, J. M. *John Berryman* (1974)
Martz, W. J. *John Berryman* (1969)

BIDART, Frank (1939–). His books include *Golden State* (1973), *The Book of the Body* (1977), and *The Sacrifice* (1983).

See: Vendler, H. *Part of Nature, Part of Us: Modern American Poets* (1980)
von Hallberg, R. *American Poetry and Culture 1945–80* (1984)

BISHOP, Elizabeth (1911–79), born in Worcester, Massachusetts, her childhood was marred by the death of her father and the mental breakdown of her mother. Raised by grandparents, in Worcester and Nova Scotia, she was educated at Vassar where she met the novelist, Mary McCarthy. Much of her life was spent travelling and living in Brazil, the setting of some of her poems. Her reputation established with her first volume, *North and South* (1946). This was followed by *Poems: North and South – A Cold Spring*, which won her the Pulitzer Prize (1955), *Questions of Travel* (1965), *The Ballad of the Burglar of Babylon* (1968), *The Complete Poems* (1969), *Geography III* (1976). *The Collected Prose* (1984) includes several short stories, autobiographical and travel sketches and a memoir of Marianne Moore.

See: Estess, S. P. and *Elizabeth Bishop and Her Art* (1983)
Schwartz L. (eds.) *On the Poetry of Elizabeth Bishop*
Kalstone, D. M. *Five Temperaments: Elizabeth Bishop, Robert Lowell, James Merrill, Adrienne Rich, John Ashbery* (1977)
Stevenson, A. *Elizabeth Bishop* (1966)

BISHOP, John Peale (1892–1944), born in West Virginia and educated at Princeton, where he became a friend of F. Scott Fitzgerald. Lived in a chateau near Paris from 1926 until 1933, then stayed in New Orleans for a year before settling on Cape Cod. Apart from temporary residence in New York and Washington, remained there until his death. His volumes of poetry are *Green Fruit* (1917), *The Undertaker's Garland*, written with Edmund Wilson (1922), *Now With His Love* (1933), and *Minute Particulars* (1935). Also wrote a collection of stories, *Many Thousands Gone* (1931), and a novel, *Act of Darkness* (1935). *Collected Poems* and *Collected Essays* were both published in 1948.

See: Spindler, E. *John Peale Bishop* (1980)
Tate, A. (ed.) *A Southern Vanguard: The John Peale Bishop Memorial Volume* (1947)

BLACKBURN, Paul (1926–71), born in St. Albans, Vermont and brought up in New Hampshire, South Carolina, and New York. Served in the army and attended New York University and Wisconsin before spending a year at the University of Toulouse. Lived in Spain for much of 1953–7. Established a reputation as a translator of Spanish and Provençal poetry. His many volumes include *The Dissolving Fabric* (1955), *The Nets* (1961), *The Cities* (1967), *In. On. Or About These Premises* (1968), *Halfway Down the Coast* (1975), and *The Journals* (1975). *The Collected Poems* was published in 1985.

See: Rosenthal, M. L. *The Modern Poets: American and British Poetry After World War II* (1967)

BLY, Robert (1926–), born in Madison, Minnesota and brought up on a neighbouring farm. Served in the navy, then educated at Harvard and the University of Iowa. Founded the journal, *The Fifties*, in 1958, subsequently named *The Sixties* and then *The Seventies*. Involved in the movement against the Vietnam War, he gave his National Book Award prize money for *The Light Around the Body* (1967) to aid those trying to 'defy the draft authorities'. His books of poetry and translations include *Silence in the Snowy Fields* (1962), *Sleepers Joining Hands* (1973), *This Body Is Made of Camphor and Gopherwood* (1977), *The Eight Stages of Translation* (1983), and *Four Ramages* (1983). Now lives on a farm in his native state.

See: Nelson, H. *Robert Bly: An Introduction to the Poetry* (1984)

BOGAN, Louise (1897–1970), born in Maine and educated at Boston University, she spent most of her life in New York City where, from 1931, she was the regular poetry reviewer for *The New Yorker*. Her first book of poems was *Body of This Death* (1923). *Collected Poems 1923–53* was published in 1954 and her finest volume, *The Blue Estuaries: Poems 1923–68*, in 1968. Her *Achievement in American Poetry 1900–50* (1951) is a useful introduction, and *Journey Around My Room* (1980) is a 'mosaic' of autobiographical materials. There is also a *Selected Criticisms* (1958) and a prose collection, *A Poet's Alphabet* (1970)

See: Frank, E. *Louise Bogan: A Portrait* (1985)
Pope, D. *A Separate Vision: Isolation in Contemporary Women's Poetry* (1984)

BOWERS, Edgar (1924–), born in Rome, Georgia and educated at the University of North Carolina, Chapel Hill and Stanford. Served in the U.S. Army and teaches at the University of California, Santa Barbara. His first book of poetry was *The Form of Loss* (1956); others include *The Astronomers* (1965), *Living Together: New and Selected Poems* (1973), *Paroxisms: A Guide to the Isms* (1974), and *Witnesses* (1981).

See: Howard, R. *Alone With America: The Art of Poetry in the United States Since 1950* (1969)
von Hallberg, R. *American Poetry and Culture 1945–80* (1984)
Winters, Y. *Forms of Discovery* (1967)

BROOKS, Gwendolyn (1917–), born in Topeka, Kansas and brought up in Chicago. Began her professional career in 1941, by attending a poetry workshop at the South Side Community Art Centre in Chicago. Her first volume, *A Street in Bronzeville*, was published in 1945 and her second, *Annie Allen* (1949), won the Pulitzer Prize. *Selected Poems* appeared in 1963 and subsequent collections include *The Wall* (1970) and *Aloneness* (1971). Named 'Poet Laureate of the State of Illinois' in succession to Carl Sandburg, she published *For Illinois 1968: A Sesquicentennial Poem* (1968). The first volume of her autobiography, *Report from Part One* was published in 1972, the second, *The Tiger Who Wore White Gloves*, in 1974.

See: Bigsby, C. W. E. (ed.) *The Black American Writer* (1969)
Melhelm, D. H. *Gwendolyn Brooks: Poetry and the Heroic Voice* (1987)
Shaw, H. B. *Gwendolyn Brooks* (1980)

BUKOWSKI, Charles (1920–), born in Germany and brought to the United States by his parents when he was two. Grew up in Los Angeles, where he now lives, and attended Los Angeles City College. His prolific output began when he was thirty-five and he has written some thirty volumes of poetry, among them *Drowning in Flame: Selected Poems 1955–73* (1976), *Love is a Dog from Hell* (1977), *Dangling in the Tournefortia* (1981), and *Hot Water Music* (1987). He has also produced novels, such as *Post Office* and *Ham on Rye* (1982); *Notes of a Dirty Old Man*, a prose record of his underground life (1969); and a remarkable collection of stories, *Erections, Ejaculations, Exhibitions, and General Tales of Ordinary Madness* (1972).

See: Vinson, J. (ed.) *Contemporary Poets* (1975)
Webb, J. E. (ed.) 'Charles Bukowski Issue', *The Outsider*, I (1963)

CLAMPITT, Amy (1920–), born in New Providence, Iowa and educated at Grinnell College. Her poems began appearing in magazines in 1978. *The Kingfisher*, her first volume, was published in 1983, and *What the Light Was Like* in 1985. A third book, *Archaic Figure*, appeared in 1987. She lives in New York City.

See: Perloff, M. 'The Case of Amy Clampitt', *Sulfur*, 10 (1983), 167–78

CORSO, Gregory (1930–), born in Greenwich Village, New York, the son of poor immigrants, and raised by foster parents. His youth marked by poverty and violence and he spent three years in prison for attempted robbery. Allen Ginsberg and other beat poets encouraged his gift for poetry, and his first collection, *The Vestal Lady*, appeared in 1955. Later collections include *Gasoline* (1958), *The Happy Birthday of Death* (1960), *Long Live Man* (1962), and *Elegiac Feelings American* (1970). More recent volumes, like *Egyptian Cross* (1971) and *Earth Eggs* (1974), reflect his interest in Egyptology. Has also written a play, *This Hung-Up Age* (1955), and a prose memoir, *The American Express* (1961).

See: Howard, R. *Alone With America: The Art of Poetry in the United States Since 1950* (1969)
Vinson, J. *Contemporary Poets* (1975)

CRANE, [Harold] Hart (1899–1932), born in Garrettsville, Ohio and grew up in the neighbouring city of Cleveland. His parents separated while he was still young, his mother was admitted to a sanatorium, and he lived with his grandparents. Began to write poetry when he was thirteen. When sixteen, he stayed with his mother at his grandparents' plantation on the Isle of Pines, south of Cuba: a crucial experience of exotic nature. Leaving Cleveland for New York City, he worked briefly in his father's business, then as a labourer, munitions worker, and advertising agent. Became acquainted with other writers in the city, and his work began appearing in *The Little Review*, *Poetry*, and *The Dial*. His first volume, *White Buildings*, published in 1926. Before that, while living in Brooklyn in 1924, he had already conceived of a 'Myth of America': which subsequently became *The Bridge*, published privately in 1929 and in a general edition in 1930. Awarded a Guggenheim Fellowship in 1931, to go to Mexico to write a poem on Montezuma. But increasingly dogged by a sense of failure, alcoholic dependency, and a breakdown in personal relationships. Disappeared from the ship returning him from Vera Cruz to New York, presumably having committed suicide by leaping into the sea. *Collected Poems* published in 1933. Two collections of letters have also appeared: *The Letters of Hart Crane, 1916–32* (1952) and *The Letters of Hart Crane and his Family* (1974).

Unterecker, J. *Voyager: A Life of Hart Crane* (1970)

See: Brunner, E. *Hart Crane and the Making of "The Bridge"* (1984)
Butterfield, R. W. *The Broken Arc: A Study of Hart Crane* (1969)
Giles, P. *Hart Crane: The Contexts of 'The Bridge'* (1986)
Lewis, R. W .B. *The Poetry of Hart Crane: A Critical Study* (1967)
Liebowitz, H. A. *Hart Crane: An Introduction to the Poetry* (1968)
Weber, B. *Hart Crane: A Biographical and Critical Study* (1948)

CREELEY, Robert (1926–), born in Arlington, Massachusetts and attended Harvard. In 1954, joined the faculty of Black Mountain College, where he founded the *Black Mountain Review*. After the closure of the college in 1956, he moved to San Francisco, where he met Allen Ginsberg, Jack Kerouac, and other Beat writers. Has also taught at the University of New Mexico and more recently at the State University of New York in Buffalo. *Le Fou* (1952) was his first collection of poetry. Other collections include *You* (1956), *For Love: Poems 1950–60* (1962), *Words: Poems* (1967), *Divisions and Other Early Poems* (1968), *St. Martin's* (1971). *The Collected Poems of Robert Creeley, 1945–75* (1982), and *Mirrors* (1983). Among other works, there is a novel, *The Island* (1963) and a collection of short stories, *The Gold Diggers* (1954). *The Collected Prose of Robert Creeley: A Story* appeared in 1984.

See: Altieri, C. *Self and Sensibility in Contemporary American Poetry* (1984)
Edelberg, C. D. *Robert Creeley's Poetry: An Introduction* (1978)
Ford, A. L. *Robert Creeley* (1978)
Fredman, S. *Poet's Prose: The Crisis in American Verse* (1983)
Howard, R. *Alone With America: The Art of Poetry in the United States Since 1950* (1969)
Paul, S. *The Lost America of Love: Reading Robert Creeley, Edward Dorn, and Robert Duncan* (1981)

CULLEN, Countee (1903–46), born in Harlem, New York and raised by foster parents. Educated at New York University and Harvard. First book, *Colour*, published in 1925, followed by *Copper Sun* (1927), *The Ballad of the Brown Girl* (1928), *The Black Christ* (1929), *The Medea and Some Poems* (1935), and *On These I Stand* (1947). He wrote one novel, *One Way to*

Heaven (1931), besides editing a magazine for black writers, *Opportunity*, and an anthology of black poetry, *Caroling Dusk* (1927)

See: Dinger, H. J. *A Study of Countee Cullen* (1953)
Ferguson, B. E. *Countee Cullen and the Negro Renaissance* (1966)

CUMMINGS e[dward] e[stlin] (1894–1962), born in Cambridge, Massachusetts, where his father was a teacher and church minister. Enrolled at Harvard, he contributed poetry to the college magazines and, shortly after he graduated in 1916, some of this appeared in *Eight Harvard Poets*. Serving in an ambulance unit in World War I, he was imprisoned through bureaucratic error: this imprisonment became the subject of his first book, *The Enormous Room* (1922). After the War, he returned to New York to devote himself to poetry and painting then, in 1920, moved to Paris. These cities were his principal bases for the rest of his life. His poetry began to appear in *The Dial*, when it started in 1920. His first collection of poetry, *Tulips and Chimneys*, was published in 1923, followed by *XLI Poems* (1925), & (1925), and *is 5* (1925). Many more volumes followed, brought together eventually in *Poems 1923–54* (1954). After this came *Ninety-Five Poems* (1958), *73 Poems* (1963), and *Complete Poems 1912–62* (1972). He also published two plays, one of which, *HIM*, was produced by the Provincetown Players in 1927. Other work includes *EIMI*, a critical account of travels in Russia (1933), *Six Non-Lectures*, which he gave while Charles Eliot Norton Professor of Poetry at Harvard (1957), and *CIOPW*, a collection of drawings and paintings (1931). A *Selected Letters* was published in 1969.

Kennedy, R. *Dreams in the Mirror: A Biography of e. e. cummings*

See: Baum, V. (ed.) *EΣTI:eec: e. e. cummings and the Critics* (1962)
Friedman, N. *e. e. cummings: The Art of His Poetry* (1962): *e. e. cummings: The Growth of a Writer* (1964)
Kidder, R. M. *e.e. cummings: An Introduction to the Poetry* (1979)
Lane, C. *I Am, A Study of e. e. cummings' Poems* (1976)
Norman, C. *The Magic-Maker: e. e. cummings* (1969)

CUNNINGHAM, J[ames] V[incent] (1911–65, born in Cumberland, Maryland and educated at Stanford. Taught at the universities of Hawaii, Chicago, Virginia, and Brandeis. His volumes of poetry are *The Helmsman* (1942), *The Judge is Fury* (1947), *Doctor Drink* (1950), *Trivial, Vulgar, & Exalted: Epigrams* (1957), *The Exclusions of a Rhyme: Poems and Epigrams* (1960), *To What Strangers, What Welcome: A Sequence of Short Poems* (1964), and *Some Salt: Poems and Epigrams* (1967). *The Collected Poems and Epigrams* appeared in 1971, and *Collected Essays* in 1976.

See: Butterfield, R. W. (Herbie) (ed.) *Modern American Poetry* (1984)
Winters, Y. *The Poetry of J. V. Cunningham* (1961)

DAVIDSON, Donald (1893–1968), born in Tennessee and eventually a teacher at Vanderbilt University, Nashville, he helped found and edit *The Fugitive*. His poems were published in *An Outland Piper* (1924), *The Tall Men* (1927), *Lee in the Mountains, and Other Poems* (1938), *The Long Street* (1961), and *Poems 1922–61* (1966). Other work includes *Attack on the Leviathan: Regionalism and Nationalism in the United States* (1938), *Still Rebels, Still Yankees, and Other Essays* (1957), *Southern Writers in the Modern World* (1958), and *The Spyglass: Views and Reviews, 1924–30* (1963). To his death, he remained the most militant defender of Southern traditionalism among former Fugitives.

See: Bradbury, J. M. *The Fugitives: A Critical Account* (1958)
Gray, R. *The Literature of Memory: Modern Writers of the American South* (1977)
Rubin, L. D. *The Wary Fugitives: Four Poets and the South* (1978)

DICKEY, James (1927–), born in Atlanta, Georgia, and educated at Vanderbilt University, Nashville, Tennessee. In addition to work in advertising, has taught at Rice University, the University of South Carolina, and other colleges. *Into the Stone and Other Poems*, his first volume, was published in 1960. Other volumes include *Drowning with Others* (1962), *Helmets* (1964), *Buckdancer's Choice* (1965), *Poems 1957–67* (1968), *The Eye-Beaters, Blood, Victory, Madness, Buckhead and Mercy* (1970), and *The Central Notion: Poems 1968–79* (1979). His most recent publications are *The Early Notion* (1981) and *Puella* (1982). Has also produced a collection of criticism, *Babel to Byzantium* (1968), and a best-selling novel, *Deliverance* (1970).

See: Calhoun, R. (ed.) *James Dickey: The Expansive Imagination* (1973)
Howard, R. *Alone with America: The Art of Poetry in the United States Since 1950* (1969)
Lieberman, L. *The Achievement of James Dickey* (1968)

DI PRIMA, Diane (1934–), born in New York City and educated at Swarthmore College, Pennsylvania. Has been a contributing editor to *Kulchur*, editor with Leroi Jones of *Floating Bear*, and publisher and editor of the Poets Press, New York. Among her books of poetry are *Earthsong's Poems 1957–9* (1968), *Revolutionary Letters* (1969), *So Fine* (1971), and *Luba, Part I* (1973).

See: Vinson, J. (ed.) *Contemporary Poets* (1975)

D[oolittle] H[ilda] (1886–1961), born in Bethlehem, Pennysylvania and educated at Bryn Mawr, where she met Marianne Moore and – from the University of Pennysylvania – Ezra Pound and William Carlos Williams. Moved to Europe in 1911 where she became one of the Imagist group. Pound, to whom she had been briefly engaged, arranged for the publication of her work in *Poetry* and then in *Des Imagistes* (1914). First volume, *Sea Garden* (1916), appeared in England, where she stayed throughout World War I. After her marriage to the English writer Richard Aldington dissolved, she began a life-long relationship with Bryher (Winifred Ellerman), an English novelist and patron of the arts. Volumes of poetry that followed include *Hymen* (1921), *Heliodora and Other Poems* (1924), and the *Collected Poems* of 1925 and 1940. Her analysis by Freud and her experience of the blitz in London during World War II helped inspire her long poem *Trilogy*, which consisted of *The Walls Do Not Fall* (1944), *Tribute to the Angels* (1945) and *The Flowering of the Rod* (1946). Among her many other works are *Helen in Egypt*, an epic re-creation of the story of Helen of Troy (1961); the prose works *Hedylus* (1928) and *Bid Me To Live* (1960); the memoirs, *Tribute to Freud* (1956), *End to Torment: A Memoir of Ezra Pound* (1979), and *The Gift* (1982); and several prose pieces dealing with explicitly lesbian themes, published in 1981 as *Hermione*. A final series of poetic sequences, *Hermetic Definitions*, appeared in 1972 and *Collected Poems 1912–44* in 1983.

Guest, B. *Herself Defined: The Poet H. D. and Her World* (1984)

See: Friedman, S. S. *Psyche Reborn: The Emergence of H. D.* (1981)
Quinn, V. *Hilda Doolittle (H. D.)* (1967)
Robinson, J. *H. D.: The Life and Work of an American Poet* (1982)
Swann, T. B. *The Classical World of H. D.* (1962)

DORN, Edward (1929–), born in Illinois and educated at Illinois University and Black Mountain College. Edited the magazine *Wild Dog* and has taught, among other places, at Idaho State University and the University of Essex, England. *The Newly Fallen* (1961) was his first volume. Subsequent collections include *Gloucester Out* (1964), *Geography* (1965), *The North Atlantic Turbine* (1967), *Hello, La Jolla* (1978), and *Yellow Lola, formerly titled Japanese Neon* (1981). His anti-epic, *Slinger*, and a *Collected Poems 1956–74* both appeared in 1975. Among his most recent books is *Captain Jack's Chaps or Houston/MLA* (1983).

See: Butterfield, R. W. (Herbie) ed. *Modern American Poetry* (1984)
Paul, S. *The Lost America of Love: Reading Robert Creeley, Edward Dorn, and Robert Duncan* (1981)
von Hallberg, R. *American Poetry and Culture 1945–80* (1984)
Wesling, D. *Internal Resistances: The Poetry of Edward Dorn* (1985)

DUGAN, Alan (1923–), born in New York City and a graduate of Mexico City College, his first book, *Poems* (1961) won the Pulitzer Prize. Later volumes include *Poems 2* (1963), *Poems 3* (1967), *Collected Poems* (1969), *Poems 4* (1974), and *Sequence* (1976).

See: Howard, R. *Alone With America: The Art of Poetry in the United States Since 1950* (1964)
Vinson, J. (ed.) *Contemporary Poets* (1975)

DUNCAN, Robert (1919–1988), born in Oakland, California, and orphaned shortly after his birth. Named after his adoptive father, Robert Edward Symmes, he took the name Robert Duncan in 1941. After graduating from the University of California, Berkeley, he began publishing poetry in *Phoenix* and served as co-editor of *Experimental Review*. First volume, *Heavenly City, Earthly City* was published in 1947, followed soon after by *Medieval Scenes* (1950), *Poems 1948–9* (1950), and *The Song of the Border-Guard* (1951). After first emerging as a leading poet in the San Francisco Renaissance, he moved to Black Mountain College, where he taught during 1956–7 and became associated with the Black Mountain school. The later writing can be found in *Caesar's Gate: Poems 1949–50* (1956), *Letters* (1958), *Selected Poems 1942–50* (1959), *The Opening of the Field* (1960), *Roots and Branches* (1964), and *Bending the Bow* (1968). After a break of fifteen years, *Ground Work: Before the War* appeared in 1984. Among his other writings are plays, a collection of pieces on Gertrude Stein, and a commentary on H. D.

See: Bertholf, R. J., and Reid, I. W. *Robert Duncan: Scales of the Marvellous* (1979)
Butterfield, R. W. (Herbie) (ed.) *Modern American Poetry* (1984)
Faas, E. *Young Robert Duncan: Portrait of the Artist as a Homosexual in Society* (1983)
Paul, S. *The Lost America of Love: Reading Robert Creeley, Edward Dorn, and Robert Duncan* (1981)

EBERHART, Richard (1904–), born in Minnesota and educated at Dartmouth and Harvard. Has had a variety of jobs, including tutoring a Siamese prince, teaching naval gunnery, and serving as poet-in-residence at several universities. The first of his almost thirty volumes of poetry, *A Bravery of Earth*, was published in 1930. Among the subsequent volumes are *Reading the Spirit* (1936), *Poems New and Selected* (1944), *Burr Oaks* (1947), *Undercliff: Poems 1946–56* (1956), *The Quarry* (1960), *Selected Poems 1930–65*, which won the Pulitzer Prize (1965), *Fields of Grace* (1972), *Collected Poems 1930–76* (1976), and *The Long Reach: New and Uncollected Poems 1948–84* (1984). His *Collected Verse Plays* appeared in 1962.

See: Engel, B. F. *The Achievement of Richard Eberhart* (1968)
Roache, J. *Richard Eberhart: The Progress of an American Poet* (1971)
Mills, R. J. *Richard Eberhart* (1966)

ELIOT, T[homas] S[tearns] (1888–1965), born in St. Louis, Missouri and descended on both sides of the family from early English settlers in New England. Family encouraged him to write poetry and trained him in the classics before sending him to Harvard in 1906. After graduating, spent a year at the Sorbonne then returned to Harvard to write a doctoral dissertation on the philosopher F. H. Bradley; chose, however, not to take the degree. Returned to Europe in 1914, settling in London, and did not revisit the United States until 1932. Joined the Church of England and became a British citizen in 1927. Worked as a schoolmaster, in banking, and then finally as an editor and publisher. His literary career initiated by some youthful attempts at verse, published eventually as *Poems Written in Early Youth* (1967). Completed 'The Love-Song of J. Alfred Prufrock' by 1911; it appeared in *Poetry* in 1915 and *Prufrock and Other Observations* in 1917. This followed by *Ara vos prec*, which includes 'Gerontion' (1920) and *The Waste Land*, which was dedicated to Ezra Pound and appeared in the first number of *The Criterion* (1922), of which Eliot had become editor. In 1925 *Poems 1909–25* appeared, including 'The Hollow Men', and in 1936 *Collected Poems 1909–35*, including 'Ash Wednesday'. *Four Quartets* was published in 1943, consisting of 'Burnt Norton' (1935), 'East Coker' (1940), 'The Dry Salvages', and 'Little Gidding' (1942). *Collected Poems 1909–62* was published in 1963. Also wrote verse dramas, including *Murder in the Cathedral* (1935), and influential literary and cultural criticism, some of which is to be found in *Selected Prose* (1975). Awarded the Nobel Prize in 1948.

Ackroyd, P. *T. S. Eliot* (1984)

See: Bergonzi, B. *T. S. Eliot* (1972)
Bush, R. *T. S. Eliot: A Study in Character and Style* (1984)
Frye, N. *T. S. Eliot* (1950)
Gardner, H. *The Art of T. S. Eliot* (1950)
Kenner, H. *The Invisible Poet: T. S. Eliot* (1960)
Kenner, H. (ed.) *T. S. Eliot: A Collection of Critical Essays* (1962)
Matthiessen, F. O. *The Achievement of T. S. Eliot* (1947)
Moody, A. D. *Thomas Stearns Eliot, Poet* (1979)
Williamson, G. *A Reader's Guide to T. S. Eliot* (1953)

EVANS, Mari (1927–), born in Toledo, Ohio and educated at the University of Toledo. Has taught at several universities, including Purdue, Cornell, and the State University of New York, Buffalo, and produced and directed *The Black Experience*, an important television programme.

Among her collections are *Where Is All the Music?* (1968), *I Am a Black Woman* (1970), and *Nightstar: 1973–80* (1981).

See: Evans, M. (ed.) *Black Women Writers (1950–80): A Critical Evaluation* (1984)

FEARING, Kenneth (1902–61), born in Oak Park, Illinois. After graduating from the University of Wisconsin, he moved to New York City working at various jobs then becoming a freelance writer. Commercial work appeared under several pseudonyms, while poetry first collected in *Angel Arms* (1929). Other volumes include *Dead Reckoning: A Book of Poetry* (1938), *Afternoon of a Pawnbroker and Other Poems* (1943), and *New and Selected Poems* (1956) Wrote a number of novels, among them *The Big Clock* (1946).

See: Millett, F. B. *Contemporary American Authors* (1940)

FERLINGHETTI, Lawrence (1919–), born in New York City and studied at the University of North Carolina, Columbia, and the Sorbonne. As cofounder of City Lights Bookshop in San Francisco and a publisher of City Lights Books and the Pocket Book series, he helped make available the work of poets like Allen Ginsberg and Gregory Corso. His own public readings and publication of poems as broadsides helped create a wider audience for poetry. First book of poetry was *Pictures from the Gone World* (1955). Among the collections that followed are *A Coney Island of the Mind* (1958), *Starting from San Francisco* (1961; revised edn., 1967), *The Secret Meaning of Things* (1969), *Open Eye, Open Heart* (1973), *Landscapes of Living and Dying* (1979), and *Endless Life: The Selected Poems* (1981). Has also produced a novel, *He* – (1960), translations, 'political-satirical tirades', and experimental plays.

See: Smith, L. *Lawrence Ferlinghetti: Poet-at-Large* (1983)

FLETCHER, John Gould (1886–1950), born in Little Rock, Arkansas and educated at Harvard. Travelled to Italy in 1908, then settled in London in 1909. Five volumes of his poetry published at his own expense in 1913. Met Ezra Pound and became associated with the Imagists. Disquieted by the radical implication of Pound's approach, associated himself with Amy Lowell's breakaway group, his work appearing in her *Some Imagist Poets* (1915). Best-known volume, *Irradiations: Sand and Spray*, published in 1915 followed by *Goblins and Pagodas* (1916). Remained in Europe until 1933, with brief visits to the United States. Became acquainted with the Fugitives and, at the request of Allen Tate, contributed to the Southern Agrarian anthology, *I'll Take My Stand* (1930). Later volumes include *The Epic of Arkansas* (1936), *Selected Poems*, which received the Pulitzer Prize (1938), *South Star* (1941), and Arkansas (1947). An autobiography, *Life is My Song*, appeared in 1937.

See: de Chasca, E. S. *John Gould Fletcher and Imagism* (1978)

FROST, Robert (1874–1963), born in San Francisco into a family from New England. His father died in 1884, and the family returned to New England, living first with the paternal grandparents and then in small apartments in or near Lawrence, Massachusetts. First poem published when he was nineteen. Went to Dartmouth and Harvard, and between 1900 and 1905 worked making shoes, editing a country newspaper, teaching school, and farming. Deaths of son, mother, and daughter led to deep depression and thoughts of suicide. Moved to England in 1912, where he found a publisher for his first volume, *A Boy's Will* (1913). Introduced to Pound while in London and, through Pound, to other writers; Pound helped him have his work published in *Poetry*. Settling in Gloucestershire, became friendly with the 'Georgian' group, particularly Edward Thomas. *North of Boston* (1914), his second volume, a best-seller. Returned to the United States in 1915, settling his family on a small farm near Franconia, New Hampshire, and made New England his home for rest of his life. Third collection, *Mountain Interval* (1916), attracted national attention. Accepted posts of poet-in-residence at several universities and taught for twenty years at Amherst College, Massachusetts. *New Hampshire* (1923) won a Pulitzer prize; so, too, did *Collected Poems* (1930), *A Further Range* (1936), and *A Witness Tree* (1942). Other volumes are *West-Running Brook* (1928), *A Masque of Reason* (1945), *A Masque of Mercy* (1947), *A Steeple Bush* (1947), and *In the Clearing* (1962). Invited to give public readings all over the world; and, in 1961, read one of his poems at the inauguration of President Kennedy.

Thompson, L. *Robert Frost: The Early Years, 1874–1915* (1966); *The Years of Triumph, 1915–38* (1972); (and Winnick, R. H.), *The Later Years, 1938–63* (1976)

See: Brower, R. *The Poetry of Robert Frost: Constellations of Intention* (1963)
Cox, J. M. (ed.) *Robert Frost: A Collection of Critical Essays* (1962)
Gibbs, K. (ed.) *Robert Frost: Studies of the Poetry* (1979)
Isaacs, E. *Robert Frost: An Introduction to the Poetry* (1962)
Kemp, J. C. *Robert Frost and New England: The Poet as Regionalist* (1979)
Lynen, J. F. *The Pastoral Art of Robert Frost* (1964)
Poirier, R. *Robert Frost, The Work of Knowing* (1977)
Pritchard, W. H. *Frost: A Literary Life Reconsidered* (1980)
Squires, R. *The Major Themes of Robert Frost* (1963)

GINSBERG, Allen (1926–), born in Newark, New Jersey. His father. Louis Ginsberg, a poet and teacher, his mother a Russian immigrant and a political activist. After studying at Columbia, he took up various jobs, including dish-washer, seaman, welder, night porter, and book reviewer for *Newsweek*. Embarked on intense study of Whitman and Blake, and experimented with drugs to explore alternative states of consciousness. First collection, *Howl* (1956), established him as a major poet and a leader of the Beats. Later collections include *Kaddish and Other Poems* (1961), *Reality Sandwiches* (1963), *Planet News* (1964), *The Fall of America: Poems of these States, 1965–71* (1972), *First Blues: Ragas, Ballads, and Harmonium Songs, 1971–4* (1975), and *Poems All Over the Place: Mostly Seventies* (1978). A *Collected Poems 1947–80* appeared in 1984. Has also travelled extensively, giving talks on poetry and politics as well as poetry readings: some of these talks are brought together in *Allen Verbatim* (1974).

See: Hyde, L. (ed.) *On the Poetry of Allen Ginsberg* (1986)
Kramer, J. *Allen Ginsberg in America* (1969)
Merrill, T. E. *Allen Ginsberg* (1969)
Milosz, C. *Visions from San Francisco Bay* (1975)
Portuges, P. *The Visionary Poetics of Allen Ginsberg* (1978)

GIOVANNI, Nikki (1943–), born in Knoxville, Tennessee and educated at Fisk University. Her first two volumes *Black Feeling, Black Talk* (1968) and *Black Judgement* (1969), closely related to the civil rights movement. Among her subsequent collections are *Recreation* (1970), *My House* (1972), *Ego-Tripping and Other Poems for Young People* (1974), *Cotton Candy on a Rainy Day* (1980), and *Those Who Ride the Night Winds* (1983). Also of interest is *Gemini: An Extended Autobiographical Statement on my First Twenty-Five Years of Being a Black Poet* (1971).

See: Gibson, D. B. (ed.) *Modern Black Poets: A Collection of Critical Essays* (1973)
Lee, D. L. *Dynamite Voices: Black Poets of the 1960s* (1971)

GLUCK, Louise (1943–), born in New York City and educated at Sarah Lawrence College and Columbia. Her collections are *Firstborn* (1969), *The House on the Marshland* (1976), *Descending Figure* (1980), and *The Triumph of Achilles* (1985).

See: Vendler, H. *Part of Nature, Part of Us: Modern American Poets* (1980)

GUEST, Barbara (1923–), born in Wilmington, North Carolina and educated at the University of North Carolina, Los Angeles and Berkeley. Her collections include *Poems: The Location of Things, Archaics, the Open Skies* (1962), *The Blue Stairs* (1968), *I Ching: Poems and Lithographs* (1969) and *Moscow Mansions* (1973)

See: Vinson, J. (ed.) *Contemporary Poets* (1975)

HAINES, John (1924–), born in Norfolk, Virginia and educated at art schools in Washington D.C. and New York City. Served in the U.S. Navy (1943–46). Lived as a homesteader in Alaska, 1947–9. Has taught at Universities of Alaska, Washington, and Montana. First volume, *Winter News: Poems*, published in 1966. Subsequent volumes include *The Mirror* (1971), *The Stone Harp* (1971), and *Leaves and Ashes: Poems* (1974).

See: 'John Haines Issue', *Stinktree* (Memphis, Tenn.) November, 1972.
Vinson, J. (ed.) *Contemporary Poets* (1975)

HALL, Donald (1928–), born in New Haven, Connecticut and a student at Phillips Exeter Academy, Harvard, Oxford, and Stanford. Taught at the University of Michigan for ten years before returning to his father's farm in Danbury, New Hampshire. Has been poetry editor for *The Paris Review*, compiled thirteen anthologies (including *Contemporary American Poetry* (1962; revised edn., 1971)), and written extensively on modern poetry. His books of poetry include *Exiles and Marriages* (1955), *The Alligator Bride: Poems New and Selected* (1969), and *The Toy Bone* (1979).

See: 'Donald Hall Issue', *Tennessee Poetry Journal* (Martin) Winter, 1971
Vinson, J. (ed.) *Contemporary Poets* (1975)

HAYDEN, Robert (1913–), born in Detroit and educated at Wayne State University and the University of Michigan. Has taught at Fisk, Louisville, Washington, and Michigan universities. His first collection, *Heart-Shape in the Dust* (1940), was followed by *The Lion and the Archer* (1948), *Figures of Time: Poems* (1955), *A Ballad of Remembrance* (1962), *Selected Poems* (1966), *Words in the Mourning Time* (1970), *The Night-Blooming Cereus* (1972), *Angle of Ascent: New and Selected Poems* (1975), and *American Journal* (1978; expanded edn., 1980). Has also edited *Kaleidoscope* (1967), an important anthology of Afro-American poetry, and is one of the editors of *Afro-American Literature: An Introduction* (1971).

See: Baxter Miller, R. (ed.) *Black American Poets Between Worlds 1940–60* (1986)
Bigsby, C. W. E. *The Second Black Renaissance* (1980)
Gibson, D. G. (ed.) *Modern Black Poets: A Collection of Critical Essays* (1973)
Litz, A. W. (ed.) *American Writers: A Collection of Literary Biographies: Supplement II* (1981)

HECHT, Anthony (1923–), born in New York City and educated at Bard College and Columbia. Served in the U.S. Army in World War II. Has taught at several colleges and universities, including Kenyon College and the State University of New York, Rochester. First volume, *A Summoning of Stones*, appeared in 1954. Among his other collections are *The Seven Deadly Sins: Poems* (1958), *The Hard Hours: Poems*, which won a Pulitzer Prize in 1968, *Aesopic: Twenty Four Couplets* (1967), and *The Venetian Vespers* (1979).

See: Howard, R. *Alone With America: The Art of Poetry in the United States Since 1950* (1969)
Vinson, J. (ed.) *Contemporary Poets* (1975)

HENDERSON, David (1942–), born in Harlem and raised there and in the Bronx. Attended the New School for Social Research, Bronx Community and Hunter Colleges, and the East-West Institute, Cambridge, Massachusetts. A founder of *East Village Other*, out of which grew the Underground Press Service, and *Umbra*. His collections include *Felix of the Silent Forest* (1967), *De Mayor of Harlem* (1970), and *The Low East* (1980). Also wrote *Jimi Hendrix: Voodoo Child of the Aquarian Age* (1978).

See: Davis, T. M., and Harris, T. (eds.) *Afro-American Poets Since 1955* (1985)

HUGHES, Langston (1902–67), born in Joplin, Missouri and spent his boyhood in various Midwestern towns. During his youth he taught in Mexico, farmed on Staten Island, served as a seaman, and worked as a cook in a Montmartre night-club and a bus-boy in a Washington hotel. Becoming part of the Harlem Renaissance, he wrote poetry that first appeared in *The Crisis* (1923–42) and an influential anthology, *The New Negro* (1925). First collection, *The Weary Blues*, published in 1926, the same year he wrote an important essay, 'The Negro Artist and the Racial Mountain', for *The Nation*. After his second volume, *Fine Clothes to the Jew* (1927), he began an extensive speaking tour of the South. Later volumes are *Shakespeare in Harlem* (1942), *Fields of Wonder* (1947), *Montage of a Dream Deferred* (1951) and *Ask Your Mama* (1961). Also founded black theatre groups in Harlem, Chicago, and Los Angeles and his play, *The Mulatto*, was produced on Broadway in 1935. There are several collections of short stories, numerous books and essays on social, historical, and cultural subjects, and two autobiographies, *The Big Sea* (1940) and *I Wonder as I Wander* (1956). Edited collections of black folklore and poetry; and spent much of his later life on the 'Simple Stories', concerning a supposedly slow-witted character who invariably outwits other people. His first novel, *Not Without Laughter*, appeared in 1930, and his second, *Tambourines To Glory*, in 1958.

Emanuel, J. *Langston Hughes* (1967)

See: Rampersad, A. *The Life of Langston Hughes* (1986–8)
Barksdale, R. K. *Langston Hughes: The Poet and His Critics* (1977)
Haskins, J. S. *Always Movin' On: The Life of Langston Hughes* (1976)
Jemie, O. *Langston Hughes: An Introduction to the Poetry* (1976)
O'Daniel, T. B. (ed.) *Langston Hughes, Black Genius: A Critical Evaluation* (1972)
Rollins, C. *Black Troubadour* (1970)

HUGO, Richard (1923–), born in Seattle and educated at the University of Washington. A bombardier in the U.S. Army Air Corps during World War II, then worked for the Boeing Company for twelve years, before becoming a teacher at the University of Montana. Among his volumes are *A Run of Jacks* (1961), *The Lady in Kicking Horse* (1973), and *Road Ends at Tahola* (1978). A *Selected Poems* was published in 1979.

See: Howard, R. *Alone With America: The Art of Poetry in the United States Since 1950* (1969)
Myers, J. (ed.) *A Trout in the Milk: A Composite Portrait of Richard Hugo* (1982)
Vinson, J. (ed.) *Contemporary Poets* (1975)

IGNATOW, David (1914–). born in Brooklyn. Has worked as a salesman, public relations writer, shipyard handyman, and in a bindery firm. Took up full-time teaching in 1965, first at the New School for Social Research and Columbia, then at York College. Coeditor of the *Beloit Poetry Journal* (1945–59) and poetry editor of *The Nation* (1962–63). His first collection was *Poems* (1948); *Poems 1934–69* (1970) contains previously uncollected and unpublished material; more recent volumes include *Facing the Tree: New Poems* (1975), *Tread the Dark: New Poems* (1978), and *Sunlight: A Sequence for My Daughter* (1979). *The Notebooks of David Ignatow* was published in 1973, and *Open Between Us: Essays, Reviews, and Interviews* in 1980.

See: Vinson, J. (ed.) *Contemporary Poets* (1975)

JARRELL, Randall (1914–65), born in Nashville, Tennessee, and spent much of his childhood in California. Studied at Vanderbilt University, taught at Kenyon College, then served in the U.S. Army Air Corps from 1942 until 1946. After World War II, taught at the University of Texas, Sarah Lawrence College, Princeton, and the Women's College of the University of North Carolina. After contributing to *Five Young American Poets* (1940), his volumes of poetry began with *Blood for a Stranger* (1942) and continued with *Little Friend, Little Friend* (1945), *Losses* (1948), *The Seven-League Crutches* (1951), *Selected Poems* (1955: revised edn., 1964), *Uncollected Poems* (1958), *The Woman at Washington Zoo* (1960), and *The Lost World* (1965). *Complete Poems* (1969) and *Jerome: The Biography of a Poem* (1971) were published after his sudden death in a traffic accident. His extensive critical writing includes *Poetry and the Age* (1953) and *Kipling, Auden & Co.: Essays and Reviews 1935–64* (1979). Also wrote books for children, fables (see, *A Sad Heart at the Supermarket* (1962)), and a novel, *Picture from an Institution* (1954).) *Letters: An Autobiographical and Literary Selection* appeared in 1985.

See: Ferguson, S. *The Poetry of Randall Jarrell* (1971)
Quinn, Sister B. *Randall Jarrell* (1981)
Lowell, R., Taylor, P., and Warren, R. P. W. (eds.) *Randall Jarrell, 1914–65* (1967)
Rosenthal, M. L. *Randall Jarrell* (1972)

JEFFERS, [John] Robinson (1887–1962), born in Pittsburgh, Pennsylvania. His father a student of the Bible, a classicist and stern Calvinist: he supervised the boy's education for seven years. Then tuition at private schools in the neighbourhood, Switzerland, and Germany. Enrolled at the University of Pittsburgh and, within a year, at Occidental College when his family moved to California. After graduating from Occidental, studied at the Universities of Zurich, Switzerland, California, and Washington. After marrying, went to live at Carmel on the California coast, then sparsely populated, where he built a granite house and tower on cliffs, facing the sea. Two volumes of conventional poetry published privately, in 1912 and 1916. But poetic career really initiated with *Tamar and Other Poems* (1924). Published privately, reaction to *Tamar* enthusiastic; and a commercial edition with new poems added, *Roan Stallion, Tamar, and Other Poems*, published in 1925. Many other volumes followed, among them *The Women at Point Sur* (1927), *Cawdor and Other Poems* (1928), *Thurso's Landing and Other Poems* (1932), *Give Your Heart to the Hawks and Other Poems* (1933), *Be Angry at the Sun* (1941), *The Double Axe* (1948), and *Hungerfield, and Other Poems* (1954). Suffered critical attacks during World War II, partly because of his espousal of isolationism. Reputation recovered a little afterwards: a free adaptation of *Medea* produced on Broadway in 1947. But, in general, attitudes towards the work hostile or indifferent. After his wife's death in 1950, he lived quietly and alone.

See: Antoninus, Brother *Robinson Jeffers: Fragments of an Older Fury* (1968)
Beilke, M. *Shining Clarity: God and Man in the Works of Robinson Jeffers* (1977)
Brophy, R. *Robinson Jeffers: Myth, Ritual and Symbol in His Narrative Poems* (1973)
Carpenter, F. I. *Robinson Jeffers* (1962)
Coffin, A. B. *Robinson Jeffers: Poet of Inhumanism* (1971)
Powell, L. C. *Robinson Jeffers: The Man and His Work* (1940)
Squires, R. *The Loyalties of Robinson Jeffers* (1956)
Sterling, G. *Robinson Jeffers: The Man and His Work* (1926)
Zaller, R. *The Cliffs of Solitude: A Reading of Robinson Jeffers* (1983)

JOANS, Ted (1928–), born in Cairo, Illinois, the son of a riverboat entertainer and educated at Indiana University. Moved to Greenwich Village, New York, where he became associated with the Beats, reading at the Seven Arts Coffee Gallery; then to Paris, Copenhagen, Amsterdam, Tangiers, and Morocco. His books include *Jazz Poems* (1959), *All of Ted Joans and No More* (1961), *Black Pow-Wow: Jazz Poems* (1969), *Afrodisia* (1970), and *A Black Manifesto in Poetry and Prose* (1971)

See: Davis, T. M., and Harris, T. (eds.) *Afro-American Poets Since 1955* (1985)

JOHNSON, James Weldon (1871–1938), born in Jacksonville, Florida and the first black admitted to the Florida Bar since Reconstruction. An executive director of the N.A.A.C.P. and professor at Fisk University, his best poetry is to be found in *God's Trombones: Seven Negro Sermons in Verse* (1927), although more volumes followed this one, among them *Fifty Years and Other Poems* (1917) and *Saint Peter Relates an Incident at the Resurrection Day* (1930). Also wrote *Autobiography of an Ex-Coloured Man* (1912).

See: Redding, J. S. *To Make a Poet Black* (1939)
Wagner, J. *Black Poets of the United States: From Paul Laurence Dunbar to Langston Hughes* (1973)

JUSTICE, Donald (1925–), born in Miami, Florida and educated at the Universities of Miami, Iowa, North Carolina, and Stanford. Has taught at Iowa and Syracuse Universities and the University of California, Irvine. His collections of poetry include *The Summer Anniversaries* (1960), *A Local Storm* (1963), *Night Light* (1967), *From a Notebook* (1972), *Departures* (1974), and *Selected Poems* (1979). A more recent book is *The Sunset Maker* (1987).

See: Howard, R. *Alone With America: The Art of Poetry in the United States Since 1950* (1969)
Vinson, J. (ed.) *Contemporary Poets* (1975)

KAUFMAN, Bob (1925–), born in New Orleans, the eleventh of thirteen children. Raised in Catholic Church but eventually identified with Buddhism. Went to work at sea at age of thirteen and served twenty years in Merchant Marine. Settled in California in late 1950s, where he became one of the founders of West Coast literary movement. His collections include *Abomunist Manifesto* (1959), *Does the Secret Mind Whisper* (1959), *Solitudes Crowded with Loneliness* (1965), *Golden Sardine* (1967), *Watch My Tracks* (1971), and *The Ancient Rain: Poems 1956–78* (1981).

See: Jordan, J. (ed.) *Soulscript: Afro-American Poetry* (1970)
Redmond, E. *Drumvoices: The Mission of Afro-American Poetry, A Critical History* (1976)

KEES, Weldon (1914–55), born in Beatrice, Nebraska and spent most of his early life in New York City, writing for *Time*, making documentary films, and exhibiting paintings. Moved to San Francisco in 1951 and disappeared four years later, presumed dead. His poems in *The Last Man* (1943), *The Fall of the Magicians* (1947), *Poems 1947–54* (1954), and *Collected Poems* (1960).

See: Justice, D. Preface to *Collected Poems* (1960)

KELLY, Robert (1935–), born in Brooklyn and educated at the City College of New York and Columbia. Helped launch *Chelsea Review* and *Trubar*, an influential poetry magazine; has taught at several colleges; and with seven other poets formed The Blue Yak, a poets' co-operative, in New York in 1961. Some of his best poetry in *Finding the Measure* (1968). Other volumes include *Avon Dendron Tree* (1967), *A California Journal* (1969), and *Kali Yuga* (1970).

See: 'Robert Kelly Issue' *Vort* (Bloomington, Indiana), 1974
Stepanchev, S. *American Poetry Since 1945: A Critical Survey* (1965)

KENNEDY, X. J. [Joseph Charles] (1929–), born in Dover, New Jersey and studied at Columbia and the Sorbonne. Served in the U.S. Navy and has taught at Tufts and other universities. His first collection was *Nude Descending a Staircase* (1961); others include *Growing into Love* (1969),

Breaking and Entering (1972), *Emily Dickinson in Southern California* (1974), and *Cross Ties: Selected Poems* (1985).

See: Vinson, J. (ed.) *Contemporary Poets* (1975)

KINNELL, Galway (1927–), born in Providence, Rhode Island and studied at Princeton and the University of Rochester. Served in U.S. Navy, then visited Paris on a Fulbright Fellowship. Has worked for the Congress of Racial Equality, travelled widely in the Middle East and Europe, and taught at various colleges. Now teaches at New York University. His first collections, *What a Kingdom It Was* (1960), *Flower Herding on Mount Monadnock* (1964), and *Body Rags* (1968), established his reputation. Among later volumes are *First Poems 1946–54* (1970), *The Book of Nightmares* (1971), *Mortal Acts, Mortal Words* (1980), *Selected Poems*, which won a Pulitzer Prize (1982), and *The Past* (1985). Also a novel, translations, and a collection of interviews, *Walking Down the Stairs* (1978).

See: Howard, R. *Alone With America: The Art of Poetry in the United States Since 1950* (1969)
Vinson, J. (ed.) *Contemporary Poetry* (1975)

KNIGHT, Etheridge (1931–), born in Corinth, Mississippi and raised in Kentucky. Served in the U.S. Army 1947–51, including active service in Korea. Imprisoned for robbery 1960–68. First book, *Poems from Prison*, published in 1968. Others are, *Belly Song and Other Poems* (1977), and *Born of a Woman: New and Selected Poems* (1986).

See: Davis, T. M., and Harris, T. (eds) *Afro-American Poetry Since 1955* (1985)

KOCH, Kenneth (1925–), born in Cincinnati, Ohio and educated at Harvard and Columbia. Became a leading member of the New York school in the 1950s. Has taught at the New School for Social Research, Rutgers, and Columbia, and taught creative writing to children and the elderly. His books of poetry include *Poems* (1953), *Ko, or a Season on Earth* (1959), *Sleeping With Women* (1969), *The Duplications* (1977), *Sleeping on the Wing* (1981), and *Selected Poems* (1985). A collection of his dramatic work, *Bertha and Other Plays*, appeared in 1969.

See: Howard, R. *Alone With America: The Art of Poetry in the United States Since 1950* (1969)
Vinson, J. (ed.) *Contemporary Poets* (1975)

KUNITZ, Stanley (1905–), born in Worcester, Massachusetts and graduated from Harvard. Has taught at Bennington, Brandeis, Columbia, and Yale. First volume, *Intellectual Things*, published in 1930, but did not achieve recognition until *Selected Poems, 1928–58*, which won a Pulitzer Prize (1958). Among later volumes are *The Poems of Stanley Kunitz, 1928–78* (1979) and *The Wellfleet Whale & Companion Poems* (1983).

See: Orr, G. *Stanley Kunitz: An Introduction to the Poetry* (1985)

LAMANTIA, Philip (1927–), born in San Francisco and educated at public schools there. Published at the age of fifteen and praised by André Breton. Assistant Editor, *View* magazine. Among his publications are *Selected Poems 1943–66* (1967), *The Blood of Air* (1970), *Erotic Poems* (1986), and *Meadowland West* (1986).

See: Tyler, P. Preface to Lamantia, *Touch of the Marvellous* (1966)
Vinson, J. (ed.) *Contemporary Poets* (1975)

LEVERTOV, Denise (1923–), born in Essex, England. First collection, *The Double Image*, published there in 1946. Moved to New York City with her American husband in 1948. Lived in Mexico before returning to New York. Has taught at Vassar, Drew, City College of New York, M.I.T., and Tufts, and served as poetry editor of *The Nation*. Poems showing influence of Black Mountain and Beat poets first collected in *Here and Now* (1957). Increasingly political and feminist themes in such later volumes as *O Taste and See* (1964), *To Stay Alive* (1971), *The Freeing of the Dust* (1975), and *Wanderer's Daysong* (1981). *The Poet in the World* (1973) contains analyses of her own creative process.

See: Howard R. *Alone With America: The Art of Poetry in the United States Since 1950* (1969)
Pope, D. *A Separate Vision: Isolation in Contemporary Women's Poetry* (1984)
Wagner, L. W. *Denise Levertov* (1967)
Wagner, L. W. (ed.) *Denise Levertov: In Her Own Province* (1979)

LEVINE, Philip (1928–), born in Detroit and educated at Wayne State and Iowa Universities. Held a fellowship in poetry at Stanford and, since 1958, has taught at California State University, Fresno. His first volumes, among them *On the Edge* (1961) and *Not This Pig* (1968), established his reputation. More recent volumes include *5 Detroits* (1970), *Ashes: Poems Old & New* (1979), and *One for.the Rose* (1981). A *Selected Poems* appeared in 1983.

See: Vinson, J. (ed.) *Contemporary Poets* (1975)

LINDSAY, Vachel (1879–1931), born in Springfield, Illinois. Parents wanted him to become a minister but he left college to study art in Chicago and New York. Taught social settlement and Y.M.C.A. programmes then, at the age of thirty, tramped across much of the United States trading 'rhymes for bread'. His third collection of poetry, *General William Booth Enters Into Heaven and Other Poems* (1913) won him widespread recognition; the title poem had already appeared in *Poetry*. Followed by *The Congo and Other Poems* (1914) and *The Chinese Nightingale and Other Poems* (1917). Associated with the Chicago school of poetry, he gave popular public readings across the country. Four later volumes of poetry of poorer quality; audience at poetry readings diminished; disappointed and exhausted, he committed suicide. *Collected Poems* appeared in 1929. Also wrote *The Golden Book of Springfield*, anticipating a utopia founded on a 'Gospel of Beauty', and a book of political essays, *The Litany of Washington Street* (1929). A collection of *Letters* appeared in 1979.

Ruggles, F. *The West-Going Heart: A Life of Vachel Lindsay* (1959)

See: Massa, A. *Vachel Lindsay: Fieldworker for the American Dream* (1970)

LOGAN, John (1923–), born in Red Oak, Iowa, and studied at Coe College, Iowa, Georgetown, and the University of California, Berkeley. Has taught at various universities and acted as poetry editor for *The Nation*. Among his collections are *Cycle for Mother Cabrini* (1955), *Spring of the Thief: Poems 1960–2* (1963), *The Zig-Zag Walk: Poems 1963–8* (1969), and *The Bridge of Change: Poems 1974–9* (1980).

See: Carroll, P. *The Poem in its Skin* (1968)
Howard, R. *Alone With America: The Art of Poetry in the United States Since 1950* (1969)
Vinson, J. (ed.) *Contemporary Poets* (1975)

LORD, Audre (1934–), born in New York City and educated at Hunter College, National University of Mexico, and Columbia. Worked as a librarian 1961–8. Currently active in promotion of Kitchen Table: Women of Colour Press, of which she is a founding member. First poetry book, *The First Cities*, issued in 1968. Among others are, *From a Land Where Other People Live* (1973), *New York Head Shop and Museum* (1974), *Coal* (1976), *The Black Unicorn* (1978), and *Chosen Poems, Old and New* (1982). Also prose works, including *Sister Outsider: Essays and Speeches* (1984).

See: Bigsbee, C. W. E. (ed.) *The Black American Writer* (1969)
Evans, M. (ed.) *Black Women Writers (1950–80): A Critical Evaluation* (1984)

LOWELL, Amy (1874–1925), born in Brookline, Massachusetts and descended from a prominent New England family. Educated privately and travelled abroad during her youth. First volume, *A Dome of Many-Coloured Glass*, published in 1912. After meeting Ezra Pound in London in 1913, became an enthusiastic disciple of Imagism. Pound, breaking with the group, dismissed her own diluted form of Imagism as 'Amygism'. *The Complete Poetical Works of Amy Lowell* appeared in 1955.

See: Gregory, H. *Amy Lowell: Portrait of the Poet in Her Time* (1958)

LOWELL, Robert (1911–77), born in Boston, Massachusetts, into same distinguished New England family as Amy Lowell. Mother a Winslow, a descendant of the first woman to step off the *Mayflower*. Taught by Richard Eberhart at St. Mark's School, and met Robert Frost while at Harvard. After two years at Harvard, completed his formal education at Kenyon College, Ohio, where he was a student of John Crowe Ransom and became a friend of Allen Tate. Converted to Roman Catholicism and married to writer Jean Stafford. Moved to Louisiana State University, then to Greenwich Village. Drafted during World War II, he declared himself a conscientious objector and was imprisoned during 1943–44. Moved to Maine after imprisonment. *Land of Unlikeness* published in a limited edition in 1944, followed by *Lord Weary's Castle*, containing poems from first volume and additions (1946). Left Catholic Church. Divorced in 1948; re-married twice, to the writers Elizabeth Hardwick and Caroline Blackwood. After *The Mills of the Kavanaughs* (1951), *Life Studies* (1959) helped initiate the confessional school of poetry. Together with *For the Union Dead* (1964) and *Near the Ocean* (1967), this confirmed status as a major poet. Taught at Harvard and elsewhere, and continued to be politically active, in protest against the Vietnam War. *Notebook 1967–8* (1969; augmented edition as *Notebook* (1970)) marked new stage. Moved to England in 1970, teaching for a while at Essex University. Spent much of his time in England until his death. Later volumes are *For Lizzie and Harriet* (1973), *History* (1973), *The Dolphin* (1973), and *Day by Day* (1977). Other work includes plays and translations and a version of *The Oresteia* (1978). A *Selected Poems* appeared in 1976.

Hamilton, I. *Robert Lowell: A Biography* (1983)

See: Axelrod, S. *Robert Lowell: Life and Art* (1978)
Axelrod, S., and Deese, H. (eds.) *Robert Lowell: Essays on the Poetry* (1986)
Cooper, P. *The Autobiographical Myth of Robert Lowell* (1970)
Mazzaro, J. *The Poetic Themes of Robert Lowell* (1965)
Parkinson, T. (ed.) *Robert Lowell: A Collection of Critical Essays* (1968)
Perloff, M. *The Poetic Art of Robert Lowell* (1973)
Rudman, M. *Robert Lowell: An Introduction to the Poetry* (1983)
Williamson, A. *Pity the Monsters: The Political Vision of Robert Lowell* (1974)
Yenser, S. *Circle to Circle: The Poetry of Robert Lowell* (1974)

MacLEISH, Archibald (1892–1982), born in Glencoe, Illinois and graduated from Yale. Served in World War I, studied law at Harvard and practised briefly before becoming an expatriate in Paris from 1923 to 1928. Later served as editor of *Fortune* (1929–38), Librarian of Congress (1939–44), Assistant Secretary of State (1944–45), and Professor of Rhetoric at Harvard (1949–62). Also represented the United States at U.N.E.S.C.O. First collection, *Tower of Ivory*, appeared in 1917. Other poetry books include *The Hamlet of A. MacLeish* (1928), *New Found Land* (1930), *Conquistador*, an epic poem which won a Pulitzer Prize (1932), and *Frescoes for Mr. Rockefeller's City* (1933). His *Collected Poems 1917–52* (1952) won him a second Pulitzer. Other work includes verse plays and a collection of essays, *A Continuing Journey* (1968).

See: Falk, S. L. *Archibald MacLeish* (1965)
Smith, G. *Archibald MacLeish* (1971)

MAHUBUTI, Haki R. (1942–), born Don L. Lee in Little Rock, Arkansas and raised in 'black bottom' region of Detroit, Michigan. Educated at Chicago City College, Roosevelt University, and University of Iowa. Many jobs include cleaner, apprentice curator, stock clerk, and post office clerk. Since late 1960s, has taught at various universities, including Cornell, Howard, and Central State. Founder and editor of *Black Books Bulletin* and Third World Press, Chicago-based operations providing outlet for new black writers. Among his books are *Think Black* (1967), *Don't Cry, Scream* (1969), *We Walk the Way of the New World* (1970), *Directionscore: New and Selected Poems* (1971), *Book of Life* (1973), and *Earthquakes and Sun Rise Missions: Poetry and Essays of Black Renewal 1973–83* (1984).

See: Davis, T. M., and Harris, T. (eds.) *Afro-American Poetry Since 1955* (1985)
Mosher, M. *New Directions from Don L. Lee* (1975)

MARQUIS, Don (1878–1937), born in Walnut, Illinois and humorous columnist on New York *Sun* and New York *Tribune*. Wrote a sequence of humorous books beginning with *archy and mehitabel* (1927), purporting to be the work of a cockroach, archy, who had earlier existence as *vers libre* poet.

See: Anthony, E. *O Rare Don Marquis: A Biography* (1962)

MASTERS, Edgar Lee (1868–1950), born in Kansas and raised in rural Illinois. Practised law in Chicago from 1891 to 1920. Published over fifty volumes of biography, fiction, and poetry. Most famous work, *Spoon River Anthology* (1915), associated with renaissance of literature in Chicago. Never repeated this success, although he attempted to do so in books like *The New Spoon River* (1924). An autobiography, *Across Spoon River*, appeared in 1924.

See: Duffy, B. *The Chicago Renaissance in American Letters* (1954)
Flanagan, J. T. *Edgar Lee Masters: The Spoon River Poet and His Critics* (1974)
Primeau, R. *Beyond Spoon River: The Legacy of Edgar Lee Masters* (1981)

McCLURE, Michael (1937–), born in Maryville, Kansas and has spent most of his life in San Francisco. Among his many volumes of poetry are *Passage* (1956), *For Artaud* (1959), *Hymns to St. Geryon* (1959), *A New Book / A Book of Torture* (1961), *Ghost Tantras* (1964), *Thirteen Mad Sonnets* (1964), *Poisoned Wheat* (1965), *Little Odes and Raptors* (1969), *The Book of Joanna* (1973), *September Blackberries* (1974), *Solstice Blossom* (1974), *Antechamber and Other Poems* (1978), and *Selected Poems* (1986). Among his other works are the plays, *The Blossom, or Billy the Kid* (1967) and *The Beard* (1967), and *Meat Science Essays* (1963).

See: Meltzer, D. *Six San Francisco Poets* (1969)
Vinson, J. (ed.) *Contemporary Poets* (1975)

MERRILL, James (1926–), born in New York City and educated at Amherst. Divides his time between living in Greece and Connecticut. His first book, *The Black Swan*, published in 1946. Subsequent volumes are *First Poems* (1951), *Short Stories* (1954), *The Country of a Thousand Years of Peace and Other Poems* (1959; revised edn., 1970), *Water Street* (1966), *The Fire Screen* (1969), *Braving the Elements* (1972), *The Yellow Pages* (1974), *Divine Comedies* (1976), *Mirabell: Books of Number* (1978), and *The Changing Light at Sandover* (1982). A selection, *From the First Nine*, appeared in 1983, and *Late Settings* in 1985. Has also written two novels.

See: Berger, C., and Lehman, D. *James Merrill: Essays in Criticism* (1983)
Moffett, J. *James Merrill: An Introduction to the Poetry* (1984)
Yenser, S. *The Consuming Myth: The Work of James Merrill* (1987)

MERWIN, W[illiam] S[tanley] (1927–), born in New York City and studied at Princeton. Since 1951, has devoted most of his time to writing, poetry readings, and translating. Has lived in the United States, England, Mexico, and France. First book, *A Mask for Janus* (1952) won the Yale Series of Younger Poets Award. Among his other books are *The Dancing Bears* (1954), *The Drunk in the Furnace* (1960), *The Moving Target* (1963), *The Carrier of Ladders*, which won a Pulitzer Prize (1970), and *Feathers from the Hill* (1978).

See: Davis, C. *W. S. Merwin* (1981)
Howard, R. *Alone With America: The Art of Poetry in the United States Since 1950* (1969)
Jones, P. *A Reader's Guide to Fifty American Poets* (1980)
Shaw, R. (ed.) *American Poetry Since 1960: Some Critical Perspectives* (1973)

MILES, Josephine (1911–), born in Chicago, Illinois and educated at the University of California, Los Angeles and Berkeley. Taught English at the University of California, Berkeley. Has written extensively on poetic vocabulary in such books as *The Continuity of Poetic Language* (1951). Her collections of poetry include *Lines at Intersection* (1939), *Poems 1930–60* (1960), *Kinds of Affection* (1968), and *To All Appearances: New and Selected Poems* (1974).

See: Vinson, J. (ed.) *Contemporary Poets* (1975)

MILLAY, Edna St. Vincent (1892–1950), born in Rockland, Maine and educated at Vassar. In 1912 published her first poem, 'Renascence', which became the title poem in her first collection, *Renascence and Other Poems* (1917), consisting of pieces written while she was a student. Moved to Greenwich Village, New York City, after graduating. Second volume, *A Few Figs from Thistles* (1920) established her as one of the poet laureates of the Jazz Age; while her third, *The Harp-Weaver and Other Poems*, which was awarded a Pulitzer Prize (1923), revealed a new maturity. Settled in the Berkshires after 1923. Later books of poetry include *The Buck in the Snow and Other Poems* (1928), *Fatal Interview*, a sonnet sequence (1931), *Conversation at Midnight* (1937), and *Make Bright the Arrow* (1940). The *Collected Poems* appeared in 1956.

See: Atkins, E. *Edna St. Vincent Millay* (1967)
Brittin, N. A. *Edna St. Vincent Millay* (1967)

MOORE, Marianne (1887–1972), born near St. Louis, Missouri. After her father suffered a nervous breakdown, rest of family went to live with the maternal grandfather and then moved to Carlisle, Pennsylvania. Graduated from Bryn Mawr in 1909, then spent four years teaching at the Indian School in Carlisle. Two poems published in 1915, in *The Egoist* and *Poetry*. Moved with her mother to Chatham, New Jersey in 1916, and began visiting New York City, where she met the group of poets associated with the magazine *Others*, among them William Carlos Williams and Wallace Stevens. Moore and her mother then moved to Greenwich Village, New York, in 1918. Lived there until her death, working during the early years as a secretary, private tutor, and library assistant. Her first volume, *Poems*, published in 1921 in London without her knowledge by two friends, H. D. and Robert McAlmon. Second collection, *Observations* (1924) won the *Dial* award. Became editor of *The Dial* (1924–9). Other collections include *Selected Poems* (1935), *The Pangolin and Other Verse* (1936), *What Are Years?* (1941), *Nevertheless* (1944), *Collected Poems*, which won a Pulitzer Prize (1951), *Like a Bulwark* (1956), *O, To Be a Dragon* (1959), *Tell Me, Tell Me: Granite, Steel, and Other Topics* (1966). Among her other works are a volume of essays, *Predilections* (1955) and verse translations of *The Fables of La Fontaine* (1954), *The Complete Poems of Marianne Moore* appeared in 1967.

See: Costello, B. *Marianne Moore, Imaginary Possessions* (1981)
Engel, B. F. *Marianne Moore* (1964)
Hall, D. *Marianne Moore: The Cage and the Animal* (1970)
Martin, T. *Marianne Moore: Subversive Modernist* (1986)
Nitchie, G. W. *Marianne Moore: An Introduction to the Poetry* (1969)
Slatin, J. M. *The Savage's Romance: The Poetry of Marianne Moore* (1986)

Stapleton, L. *Marianne Moore: The Poet's Advance* (1978)
Tomlinson, C. (ed.) *Marianne Moore: A Collection of Critical Essays* (1970)

NASH, Ogden (1902–71), born in Rye, New York and educated at Harvard. Among his many volumes of comic verse are *Cricket of Cavador* (1925), *I'm a Stranger Here Myself* (1938), *Versus* (1949), *Marriage Lines* (1964), and *A Penny Saved Is Impossible* (1981).

See: Bier, J. *The Rise and Fall of American Humour* (1968)

NEMEROV, Howard (1920–), born in New York City and studied at Harvard. Associate editor of the magazine *Furioso* from 1946 to 1951, and has taught at Hamilton and Bennington colleges. First collection of poetry was *The Image and the Law* (1947). Volumes that followed include *Guide to the Ruins* (1950), *New and Selected Poems* (1960), *The Blue Swallows* (1967), and *The Western Approaches: Poems 1973–5* (1975). Has also written fiction, drama, and criticism.

See: Duncan, B. *The Critical Reception of Howard Nemeron* (1971)
Labrie, R. *Howard Nemerov* (1981)

NIEDECKER, Lorine (1903–70), born in Wisconsin and educated at Beloit College. Various jobs, including working in a library, radio station, and hospital. Spent most of her life in the lakes region of Wisconsin. Work first appeared in *New Directions* in 1936 and her first book, *New Goose*, published in 1946. Among her books are *My Friend Tree* (1961), *North Central* (1968), and *My Life by Water: Collected Poems 1936–68* (1970).

See: Dent, P. (ed.) *The Full Note: Lorine Niedecker* (1983)

O'HARA, Frank (1926–66), born in Baltimore, Maryland and educated at the New England Conservatory of Music, Harvard, and the University of Michigan. Spent most of his life in New York City and was one of the leading members of the New York school of poets. Joined the Museum of Modern Art in 1951, resigned to spend more time on his writing, and rejoined it in 1955, remaining there as assistant curator and then curator until his sudden death in an accident. Responsible for the organisation of major exhibitions by David Smith, Reuben Nahian, Robert Motherwell, and Jackson Pollock; wrote books on painting, among them *Jackson Pollock* (1959) and *Robert Motherwell* (1965); and published a number of his poems in collaboration with artists. Wrote several plays, many of them produced in *avant-garde* theatres, and worked as playwright in residence at the Poet's Theatre, Cambridge, Massachusetts. First book of poetry, *A City Winter and Other Poems*, published in 1952. Other volumes are *Oranges* (1953), *Meditations in an Emergency* (1952), *Second Avenue*, a long poem published as a pamphlet (1960), *Odes* (1960), *Lunch Poems* (1964), *Love Poems: Tentative Title* (1965), *In Memory of My Feelings* (1967), *The Collected Poems of Frank O'Hara* (1971), *The Selected Poems of Frank O'Hara* (1974), and *Poems Retrieved* (1977). *Art Chronicles 1954–66* appeared in 1974, and *Selected Plays* in 1978.

See: Blasing, M. U. *American Poetry: The Rhetoric of its Forms* (1987)
Feldman, A. *Frank O'Hara* (1980)
Howard, R. *Alone With America: The Art of Poetry in the United States Since 1950* (1969)
Perloff, M. *Frank O'Hara: Poet Among Painters* (1977)

Shaw, R. (ed.) *American Poetry Since 1960: Some Critical Perspectives* (1973)

OLSON, Charles (1910–70), born in Worcester, Massachusetts and educated at the Universities of Harvard, Yale, and Wesleyan. Taught at Clark University in Worcester and Harvard from 1936 to 1939. Took a position at Black Mountain College in 1948 and from 1951 to 1956 was rector there. Joined by other poets, including Robert Creeley, Ed Dorn, Robert Duncan, and Denise Levertov. Their prose and poetry published in *Black Mountain Review*. In 1952, studied Mayan hieroglyphics in Yucatan. Also taught in the Department of Further Studies at the State University of New York, Buffalo. During much of his life, lived in Gloucester, Massachusetts, the setting for many of the Maximus poems. Influential essay, 'Projective Verse', published in 1950. First book of poems, *To Corrado Cagli*, appeared three years before this. Other books of poetry include *y & x* (1948). *In Cold Hell, in Thicket* (1953), *O'Ryan 2 4 6 8 10* (1958; expanded edn. *O'Ryan 1 2 3 4 5 6 7 8 9 10*, 1965), *The Distances: Poems* (1960), and *Archaeologist of Morning: The Collected Poems Outside the Maximus Series* (1970). *The Maximus Poems 1–10* appeared in 1953. Followed by *The Maximus Poems 11–22* (1956), *The Maximus Poems*, a single edition of poems 1–22 (1960), *Maximus from Dogtown* (1961), *Maximus Poems, IV, V, VI* (1968), and *The Maximus Poems: Volume Three* (1975). First complete edition, *The Maximus Poems*, published in 1983. Volumes of poetry and prose include *Selected Writings* (1967), *Causal Mythology* (1969), and *Poetry & Truth: The Beloit Lectures and Poems* (1971). Among the prose works are *Call Me Ishmael: A Study of Melville* (1947), *Projective Verse* (1959), *The Mayan Letters* (1953), *The Human Universe and Other Essays* (1967), *The Special View of History* (1970), *Letters for Origin 1950–55* (1970), and *Charles Olson and Robert Creeley: The Complete Correspondence* (1984).

See: Butterick, G. F. *A Guide to the Maximus Poems of Charles Olson* (1978)
Byrd, D. *Charles Olson's 'Maximus'* (1980)
Charters, A. *Olson/Melville: A Study in Affinity* (1968)
Christensen, P. *Charles Olson: Call Him Ismael* (1979)
Merrill, T. F. *The Poetry of Charles Olson: A Primer* (1982)
Paul, S. *Olson's Push: Origin, Black Mountain, and Recent American Poetry* (1978)
von Hallberg, R. *Charles Olson: The Scholar's Art* (1978)

OPPEN, George (1908–84), born in Rochelle, New York and educated in California. Closely associated with Objectivist school. Founded 'To Publishers' with his wife, which provided a publishing outlet for new poets (1930–33). Member of the Objectivist Press Co-op in New York (1934–36). First book of poems, *Discrete Series*, published in 1934. Poems also appeared in Thirties in the *Objectivists Anthology* edited by Pound, *Poetry*, and *Hound and Horn*. Became political activist. Worked in factory in Detroit, and as a cabinet maker in Los Angeles, and was a member of Worker's Alliance in Brooklyn and Utica, New York. Joined Communist Party in 1935; moved to Mexico in 1950 to escape political pressure. Second collection, *The Materials*, appeared in 1962. Followed by *This in Which* (1965), *Of Being Numerous*, which won a Pulitzer Prize (1968),

Alpine (1969), *Seascape: Needle's Eye* (1972), and *Primitive* (1978). *The Collected Poems of George Oppen 1929–75* published in 1975.

See: Butterfield, R. W. (Herbie) (ed.) *Modern American Poetry* (1984)
Hatlen, B. (ed.) *George Oppen: Man and Poet* (1981)

PATCHEN, Kenneth (1911–72), born in Niles, Ohio. Attended Alexander Meiklejohn's Experimental College, University of Wisconsin, for one year and Commonwealth College, Arkansas, for one semester. Worked in a steel mill at age of seventeen. Seriously incapacitated after major spinal surgery in 1950. First volume of poetry, *Before the Brave*, published in 1936. Among his other volumes are *The Teeth of the Lion* (1942), *Pictures of Life and Death* (1946), *Because It Is* (1960), *Collected Poems* (1968), *There's Love All Day: Poems* (1970). Prose poems collected as *Panels for the Walls of Heaven* (1947) and *The Famous Boating Party* (1954). Prose works include *The Journal of Albion Moonlight* (1941) and *Memoirs of a Shy Pornographer* (1945).

See: Nelson, R. *Kenneth Patchen and American Mysticism* (1984)
Rexroth, K. *American Poetry in the Twentieth Century* (1973)

PINSKY, Robert (1940–). His collections include *Sadness and Happiness* (1975), *An Explanation of America* (1979), and *History of My Heart* (1984).

See: Vendler, H. *Part of Nature, Part of Us: Modern American Poets* (1980)
von Hallberg, R. *American Poetry and Culture 1945–80* (1984)

PLATH, Sylvia (1932–63), born in Boston, Massachusetts and educated at Smith College and Newnham, Cambridge. Married the English poet, Ted Hughes, in 1957. Taught for a year at Smith (1957–58), then returned to England in 1960. Committed suicide in 1963. First collection, *The Colossus and Other Poems*, published in England in 1960 and in United States in 1962. Posthumous volumes include *Ariel*, which established her as a leading poet of the confessional school (1966), *Uncollected Poems* (1965), *Crossing the Water: Transitional Poems* (1971), *Crystal Gazer and Other Poems* (1971), *Lyonesse: Poems* (1971), and *Winter Trees* (1971). Also wrote a novel, *The Bell Jar* (1963). *Letters Home* appeared in 1975, and her prose is collected in *Johnny Panic and The Bible of Dreams: Short Stories, Prose, and Diary Excerpts* (1979).

Wagner Martin, L. Sylvia Plath: A Biography (1988)

See: Barnard, C. K. *Sylvia Plath* (1978)
Bundtzen, L. K. *Plath's Incarnations: Woman and the Creative Process* (1983)
Kroll, J. *Chapters in a Mythology* (1976)
Lane, G. (ed.) *Sylvia Plath: New Views on the Poetry* (1979)
Lehrer, S. *The Dialectics of Art and Life: A Portrait of Sylvia Plath as Woman and Poet* (1985)
Newman, C. (ed.) *The Art of Sylvia Plath: A Symposium* (1970)
Rosenblatt, G. *Sylvia Plath: The Poetry of Initiation* (1979)

POUND, Ezra (1885–1972), born in Hailey, Idaho. Family moved to Wyncote, Pennsylvania, when he was four. Entered University of Pennsylvania at age of sixteen, studying Romance languages there and at Hamilton College, New York. Became friend of William Carlos Williams and H. D. Taught briefly at Wabash College, Indiana. Left for Venice in 1908, then to London where he renewed acquaintance with W. B. Yeats. Also a friend of Ford Madox Ford, James Joyce, and Wyndham Lewis. As European correspondent of *Poetry*, promoted careers of T. S. Eliot, Robert Frost, and Marianne Moore. First collection, *A Lume Spento*, published in Venice in 1908. Followed by *Personae* (1909), *Exultations* (1909), *Provenca* (1910), and *Canzoni* (1911). Translations of Cavalcanti (1912) and *Ripostes* (1912) marked beginning of association with Imagist school, which he founded with T. E. Hulme, H. D., and Richard Aldington. By 1914, abandoned Imagism for Vorticism, contributing to Vorticist journal, *Blast* (1914–15). Studies of Chinese poetry led to *Cathay* (1915), followed by *Homage to Sextus Propertius*, a major series of imitations from Latin (1917), and two collections, *Lustra* (1916) and *Quia Pauper Amavi* (1919). *Hugh Selwyn Mamberley* appeared in 1920; in same year, left London for Paris, where he met Gertrude Stein and Ernest Hemingway and worked on first draft of *The Waste Land* with Eliot. Settled in Rapallo, Italy in 1924. *Personae: The Collected Poems of Ezra Pound* published in 1926. Had been working on *The Cantos* since before the Vorticist period, and *A Draft of XVI Cantos* appeared in 1925. Epic continued in *A Draft of XXX Cantos* (1930), *Eleven New Cantos* (1934), *The Fifth Decad of Cantos* (1937), and *Cantos LII–LXXI* (1940). Met Mussolini in 1933 and impressed by him. Began broadcasting from Rome for the Axis in 1941. Arrested by partisans in 1945; imprisoned by American military authorities; then transferred to Washington, where he was declared unfit to stand trial for treason on grounds of insanity. Confined in St. Elizabeth's until 1958. Returned to Italy and died in Venice. Later *Cantos* in *The Pisan Cantos* (1948), *Section: Rock-Drill* (1956), *Thrones* (1959), *Drafts and Fragments of Cantos CX–CXVII* (1969). *The Cantos of Ezra Pound* (I–CXVII) appeared in 1970, and *Collected Early Poems* in 1976. Among his many prose works are *The Spirit of Romance* (1910), *Instigations* (1920), *How to Read* (1931), *ABC of Reading* (1934), and *A Guide to Kulchur* (1938). Adaptation from the Chinese, *The Classic Anthology Defined by Confucius*, his finest translation, published in 1954. Other publications include *The Literary Essays of Ezra Pound* (1954) and *The Letters of Ezra Pound* (1950).

Stock, N. *The Life of Ezra Pound* (1970)

See: Brooke-Rose, C. *A ZBC of Ezra Pound* (1971)
Cookson, W. *A Guide to the Cantos of Ezra Pound* (1985)
Davie, D. *Ezra Pound: The Poet as Sculptor* (1965)
Dekker, G. *Sailing After Knowledge: The Cantos of Ezra Pound* (1963)
Jackson, T. H. *The Early Poetry of Ezra Pound* (1968)
Kenner, H. *The Poetry of Ezra Pound* (1951); *The Pound Era* (1972)
Sutton, W. (ed.) *Ezra Pound: A Collection of Critical Essays* (1963)
Terrell, C. F. *A Companion to the Cantos of Ezra Pound* (1980–4)
Wilhelm, J. J. *The American Roots of Ezra Pound* (1985)
Witemeyer, H. *The Poetry of Ezra Pound: Forms and Renewal, 1908–20* (1969)

RANSOM, John Crowe (1888–1974), born in Pulaski, Tennessee. Enrolled at Vanderbilt University, Nashville, at age of fifteen. In 1913 studied at Oxford as Rhodes Scholar. On return to United States, taught at preparatory school for a year, then taught at Vanderbilt until 1927. First collection, *Poems About God*, published in 1919. Became member of the Fugitive group and helped edit *The Fugitive* (1922–25). Nearly all his mature poetry written during Fugitive period, much of it collected in *Chills and Fever* (1924) and *Two Gentlemen in Bonds* (1927). After 1927, committed only four new poems to print. Concentrated on public affairs and aesthetics in books like *God Without Thunder: an Unorthodox Defence of Orthodoxy* (1930), *The World's Body*, a collection of critical essays (1938), and *The New Criticism* (1941). Moved to Kenyon College, Ohio, in 1937, and founded the *Kenyon Review*, an influential organ of the New Criticism. Retired in 1958, and continued revising and rearranging his poetry for such volumes as *Selected Poems*, published in 1945, 1963, and 1970, and *Poems and Essays* (1955).

Young, T. D. *Gentleman in a Dustcoat: A Biography of John Crowe Ransom* (1976)

See: Buffington, R. *The Equilibrists: A Study of John Crowe Ransom's Poems* (1967)
Knight, K. F. *The Poetry of John Crowe Ransom: A Study of Diction, Metaphor, and Symbol* (1964)
Parsons, T. H. *John Crowe Ransom* (1969)
Stewart, J. L. *John Crowe Ransom* (1962)
Williams, M. *The Poetry of John Crowe Ransom* (1972)
Young, T. D. (ed.) *John Crowe Ransom: Critical Essays and a Bibliography* (1968)

REXROTH, Kenneth (1905–82), born in South Bend, Indiana and spent much of childhood in Midwest. Orphaned at age of thirteen and largely self-educated at first. Travelled around country, working in wide variety of jobs. Then, in his twenties, studied at the New School, the Arts Students League, and the Chicago Art Institute. Moved to San Francisco in 1927, where he became active in union and left-wing movements and established himself as a central figure in literary community. Early poems in *In What Hour* (1940), *The Phoenix and the Tortoise* (1944), *The Art of Worldly Wisdom* (1949), and *The Signature of All Things* (1949). Briefly associated with the Beats, organising the San Francisco poetry centre with Allen Ginsberg and Lawrence Ferlinghetti and participating in the group's 'Six Gallery' reading in 1955. Later collections are *Poems* (1955), *Natural Numbers* (1963), *The Collected Shorter Poems* (1967), *The Collected Longer Poems* (1968), *New Poems* (1974), *The Silver Swan* (1976), and *The Morning Star: Poems and Translations* (1979). Also published translations, four verse plays entitled *Beyond the Mountains* (1951), and *An Autobiographical Novel* (1966). Critical essays collected in *The Bird in the Bush* (1959) and *Assays* (1961).

See: Beach, J. W. *Obsessive Images* (1960)
Gibson, M. *Kenneth Rexroth* (1972)
Lipton, L. *The Holy Barbarians* (1959)
Parkinson, T. *A Casebook on the Beats* (1961)
Rosenthal, M. L. *The Modern Poets* (1960)

REZNIKOFF, Charles (1894–1976), born in Brooklyn, educated at the University of Missouri and received a law degree from New York University. Associated with the Objectivist movement of the 1930s. First collection, *Rhythms*, published in 1918. Many volumes followed but did not establish reputation until *By the Waters of Manhattan: Selected Verse* (1962). *Testimony: The United States, 1885–90*, a documented poetic meditation on American history, appeared in 1965, and a sequel,

Testimony: The United States, 1891–1900, in 1968. A complete edition, *Testimony: The United States, 1885–1915*, including previously unpublished material, appeared in two volumes in 1978 and 1979. *Poems 1918–36: Volume One of the Complete Poems* published in 1976, and *Poems 1937–75: Volume Two of the Complete Poems* in 1977.

See: Hindus, M. *Charles Reznikoff: A Critical Essay* (1977)

RICH, Adrienne (1929–), born in Baltimore, Maryland and attended Radcliffe College. First book of poems, *A Change of World* published in 1951, followed by *The Diamond Cutters* (1955). *Snapshots of a Daughter-in-Law* (1963) marked a change to freer verse forms and more openly feminist themes. Later volumes are *The Necessities of Life* (1966), *Selected Poems* (1966), *Leaflets: Poems 1965–8* (1969), *The Will to Change: Poems 1968–70* (1971), *Diving into the Wreck: Poems 1971–2* (1973), *Poems: Selected and New 1950–74* (1975), *The Dream of a Common Language: Poems 1974–7* (1978), *A Wild Patience Has Taken Me This Far: Poems 1978–80* (1981), *Sources* (1983), and *The Fact of a Doorframe: Poems Selected and New 1950–84* (1984). *Of Woman Born: Motherhood as Experience and Institution* (1976) established her as a radical feminist critic; *On Lies, Secrets, and Silence: Selected Prose 1961–78* (1979) is a collection of essays.

See: Cooper, J. R. (ed.) *Reading Adrienne Rich* (1984)
Gelpi, B. C. and Gelpi, A. (eds.) *Adrienne Rich's Poetry* (1975)
Kalstone, D. M. *Five Temperaments: Elizabeth Bishop, Robert Lowell, James Merrill, Adrienne Rich, John Ashbery* (1977)
Keyes, C. *The Aesthetics of Power: The Poetry of Adrienne Rich* (1986)
Martin, W. *An American Triptych: Anne Bradstreet, Emily Dickinson, Adrienne Rich* (1984)
Pope, D. *A Separate Vision: Isolation in Contemporary Women's Poetry* (1984)

(RIDING), Laura Jackson (1901–), born in New York City and educated at Cornell. Associated with the Fugitive group in 1920s, but her early work mostly written during fifteen years spent in Majorca, England, and Switzerland. During this period, also wrote several books with the English poet, Robert Graves. What came to be known as the "New Criticism" was based on a critical method introduced in *A Survey of Modernist Poetry* (1927) of which (Riding) was first author. First collection, *The Close Chaplet*, published in 1926. Followed by *Love as Death, Death as Death* (1928), *Poems: A Joking Word* (1930), *Twenty Poems Less* (1930), *Poet: A Lying Word* (1933), and other volumes including *Collected Poems* (1938). Renounced poetry in the 1940s and began work with second husband, Schuyler Jackson, on *Rational Meaning: A New Foundation for the definition of Words*, which is still unpublished. A *Selected Poems: In Five Sets* appeared in 1970. Other works include *Progress of Stories* (1935; new edition 1982), *A Trojan Ending* (1937; new edition 1984), *Lives of Wives* (1939; new edition, 1988), and *The Telling* (1972).

See: Wexler, J. P. *Laura Riding's Pursuit of Truth* (1979)

ROBINSON, Edwin Arlington (1869–1935), born in Head Tide, Maine. Shortly after his birth, family moved to Gardiner which was to supply basis for 'Tilbury Town', the setting of many of his poems. Enrolled at Harvard in 1891, but summoned home after two years by death of father. Other family problems, including death of mother in ghastly circumstances, helped make life 'a living hell' for him at this time. First collection, *The Torrent and the Night Before*, published privately in 1896.

Left Gardiner for New York City in 1897 and in same year a second, revised, and expanded collection, *The Children of Night*, appeared. Followed by *Captain Craig*, a novel in verse (1902). After several years of menial employment and near destitution, Theodore Roosevelt became interested in his work and, in 1905, obtained sinecure for him at New York Customs House. *The Town Down the River* (1910) successful enough to allow him to give up job and devote himself to writing. In 1911, began spending summers at the MacDowell Colony, New Hampshire and returning to New York for rest of year. *The Man Against the Sky* (1916) brought him his first real critical acclaim, and in 1917 *Merlin*, first in a trilogy of poems based on Arthurian legend, confirmed his reputation. *Collected Poems* (1921) awarded a Pulitzer Prize. *Tristram*, third book in Arthurian series (1927), a bestseller. Other volumes include *The Three Taverns* (1920), *Avon's Harvest* (1921), *The Man Who Died Twice*, which won a Pulitzer Prize (1924), *Collected Poems* (1927), *Sonnets 1889–1927* (1928), *Cavender's House* (1929), *Collected Poems* (1929), *Talifer* (1933), *Amaranth* (1934), *King Jasper* (1935), and *Collected Poems* (1937).

See: Anderson, W. L. *Edwin Arlington Robinson: A Critical Introduction* (1968)
Barnard, E. *Edwin Arlington Robinson: A Critical Study* (1952)
Barnard, E. (ed.) *Edwin Arlington Robinson: Centenary Essays* (1969)
Coxe, L. *Edwin Arlington Robinson: The Life of Poetry* (1969)
Franchere, H. C. *Edwin Arlington Robinson* (1968)
Fussell, E. *Edwin Arlington Robinson: The Literary Background of a Traditional Poet* (1954)
Murphy, F. (ed.) *Edwin Arlington Robinson: A Collection of Critical Essays* (1970)
Neff, E. *Edwin Arlington Robinson* (1948)
Robinson, W. R. *Edwin Arlington Robinson: A Poetry of the Act* (1967)
Smith, C. P. *Where the Light Falls: A Portrait of Edwin Arlington Robinson* (1965)
Winters, Y. *Edwin Arlington Robinson* (1946)

ROETHKE, Theodore (1908–63), born in Saginaw, Michigan, where his family had successful business as florists. Attended University of Michigan and Harvard. Taught at several universities, for the longest period at the University of Washington (1946–63). First volume, *Open House*, appeared in 1941. Followed by *The Lost Son and Other Poems* (1948), *Praise to the End!* (1951), *The Waking: Poems 1933–53*, which won the Pulitzer Prize (1953), *Words for the Wind: The Collected Verse* (1957), *I Am! Says the Lamb* (1961), *Sequence, Sometimes Metaphysical* (1963), *The Far Field* (1964), and *The Collected Poems of Theodore Roethke* (1966). The *Selected Letters of Theodore Roethke* was published in 1968 and there are also two collections of prose: *The Contemporary Poet as Artist and Critic* (1964) and *On the Poet and His Craft: Selected Prose* (1965). A selection from his notebook, *Straw for the Fire*, appeared in 1972.

See: La Belle, J. *The Echoing Wood of Theodore Roethke* (1976)
Malkoff, K. *Theodore Roethke: An Introduction to the Poetry* (1966)
Martz, W. J. *The Achievement of Theodore Roethke* (1966)
Parini, J. *Theodore Roethke: An American Romantic* (1979)
Stein, A. (ed.) *Theodore Roethke: Essays on the Poetry* (1965)
Sullivan, R. *Theodore Roethke: The Garden Master* (1975)
Wolff, G. *Theodore Roethke* (1981)

RUKEYSER, Muriel (1913–80), born in New York City. Her first collection, *Theory of Flight* (1935), concerns researches at the Roosevelt School of the Air; while her second, *U.S.1* (1938), reflects her involvement in the social movements of the 1930s. Later volumes include *The Turning Wind* (1939), *The Green Wave* (1948), *Body of Waking* (1958), *The Speed of Darkness* (1968), and *The Gates* (1976). *The Collected Poems of Muriel Rukeyser* was published in 1979. She also produced a work of fiction, two biographies, and translations.

See: Kertesz, L. *The Poetic Vision of Muriel Rukeyser* (1980)

SANCHEZ, Sonia (1934–), born in Birmingham, Alabama and educated at Hunter College. Graduate work in poetry with Louise Bogan. Involved in radical activities since 1960s, including black studies movement. Has taught at several universities, including Rutgers, Pennsylvania, and Temple. Among her books of poetry are *Homecoming* (1969), *We a BaddDDD People* (1970), *I've Been a Woman: New and Selected Poems* (1981), and *homegirls and handgrenades* (1984).

See: Evans, M. (ed.) *Black Women Writers (1950–80): A Critical Evaluation* (1984)
Davis, T. M., and Harris T. (eds.) *Afro-American Poetry Since 1955* (1985)

SANDBURG, Carl (1878–1967), born in Galesburg, Illinois, the son of Swedish immigrants. Left school at the age of thirteen, working in Galesburg and then travelling across the West taking a variety of jobs. Served in the Spanish-American War. Enrolled at Lombard College, Galesburg and began writing poetry, some of which privately printed in *In Reckless Ecstasy* (1904). Withdrew before studies completed, finding work as a journalist and advertising copywriter. Moved to editorial position on a Chicago newspaper. After marriage in 1908, lived briefly in Milwaukee, Wisconsin, working as secretary to the socialist mayor. Returned to Chicago in 1913. Some of his poetry published in *Poetry* in 1914. *Chicago Poems* (1916) and *Cornhuskers* (1918) established him as a major poet of Midwest and important part of Chicago renaissance. Appointed assistant editor on Chicago *Daily News* in 1918; left in 1932 to devote himself to writing. Later volumes of poetry include *Smoke and Steel* (1920), *Slabs of the Sunburnt West* (1922), *Good Morning, America* (1928), *The People, Yes*, an epic poem (1936), and *Complete Poems*, which won a Pulitzer Prize (1950; revised edn., 1970). Also wrote a two-volume biography of Abraham Lincoln, several books for children, a novel, a study entitled *Steichen the Photographer* (1929) and an account of his youth, *Always the Young Strangers* (1952). Edited a collection of folk songs, *The American Songbag* (1927). A selection of *Letters* appeared in 1968.

See: Allen, G. W. *Carl Sandburg* (1972)
Callan, N. *Carl Sandburg: Lincoln of Our Time* (1970)
Crowder, R. *Carl Sandburg* (1964)
Durrell, H. *The America of Carl Sandburg* (1965)
Sutton, W. A. *Carl Sandburg Remembered* (1979)
Van Doren, M. *Carl Sandburg* (1969)

SCHUYLER, James (1923–), born in Chicago, Illinois and educated at Bethany College, West Virginia. Has lived in Italy, and worked in the

Museum of Modern Art, New York City. First collection, *Salute* (1960); others include, *May 24th or So* (1966), *The Crystal Lithium* (1972), and *Hymn to Life: Poems* (1974). Collaborated with John Ashbery on a novel, *Nest of Ninnies* (1969).

See: Vinson, J. (ed.) *Contemporary Poets* (1975)

SEXTON, Anne (1928–74), born in Newton, Massachusetts and grew up in neighbouring Wellesley. Claimed to have had 'no visible education', but did attend seminars taught by Robert Lowell and W. D. Snodgrass, and from 1961 until 1963 was a scholar at the Radcliffe Institute. Committed suicide. First collections, *To Bedlam and Part Way Back* (1960) and *All My Pretty Ones* (1962) established her reputation as confessional poet. Subsequent volumes are *Selected Poems* (1964), *Live or Die* (1966), *Love Poems* (1969), *Transformations* (1971), *The Book of Folly* (1973), *O Ye Tongues* (1973), *The Death Notebooks* (1974), *The Awful Rowing Towards God* (1975). There are also two posthumous collections, *45 Mercy Street* (1976) and *Words for Dr. Y: Uncollected Poems with Three Stories* (1978).

See: George, D. H. *Oedipus Anne: The Poetry of Anne Sexton* (1987)
McClatchy, J. P. (ed.) *Anne Sexton: The Artist and Her Critics* (1978)

SHAPIRO, Karl (1913–), born in Baltimore, Maryland and attended the University of Virginia and Johns Hopkins University. Poetry first appeared in *Five Young American Poets* (1941). First volume was *Person, Place, and Thing* (1942). Served in the U.S. Army in World War II. *V-Letter and Other Poems* (1944) won him a Pulitzer Prize. Served as poetry consultant to the Library of Congress (1946–47), editor of *Poetry* (1950–56), and *The Prairie Schooner* (1956–66), and taught at various colleges. Later volumes include *Essay on Rime* (1945), *Trial of a Poet* (1947), *Poems of a Jew* (1958), *The Bourgeois Poet* (1964), *White-Haired Lover* (1968), and *Adult Bookstore* (1976). Has also written several critical works; *The Poetry Wreck: Selected Essays 1950–70* was issued in 1975.

See: Reino, J. *Karl Shapiro* (1981)
Stepanchev, S. *American Poetry Since 1945* (1965)

SIMPSON, Louis (1923–), born in Jamaica and came to the United States in 1940. Attended Columbia University for three years, then served in the U.S. Army. Returned to Columbia after the war; and since then has taught at several universities, including the State University of New York at Stony Brook. First collection, *The Arrivistes: Poems 1940–9*, published in Paris in 1949. Among his subsequent volumes are *A Dream of Governors* (1959), *At the End of the Open Road: Poems*, which won a Pulitzer Prize (1963), *Searching for the Ox* (1976), and *The Best Hour of the Night* (1983). Has also written extensively on poetry.

See: Moran, R. *Louis Simpson* (1972)

SMITH, Dave (1942–), born in Virginia. His books of poetry include *Cumberland Station* (1976), *An Apology for Loving the Old Hymns* (1982), *Gray Soldiers: Poems* (1983), and *The Roundhouse Voices: Selected and New Poems* (1985).

See: Vendler, H. *Part of Nature, Part of Us: Modern American Poets* (1980)

SNOD GRASS, W[illiam] D[eWitt] (1926–), born in Wilkinsburg, Pennsylvania and attended the University of Iowa, where he studied with Robert Lowell in the Writer's Workshop. Has taught at various universities. His first book of poems, *Heart's Needle* (1959), won a Pulitzer Prize and helped establish him as a leading confessional poet. Later books include *After Experience: Poems and Translations* (1968), *The Führer Bunker: A Cycle of Poems in Progress* (1977), and *Six Minnesinger Songs* (1983). His discussions of poetry were published in *In Radical Pursuit* (1975).

See: Gaston, P. *W. D. Snodgrass* (1978)

SNYDER, Gary (1930–), born in San Francisco and raised in Oregon and Washington. Studied at Reed College, then at University of California, Berkeley, where he read oriental languages and met Jack Kerouac, Allen Ginsberg, and other Beats. Later studied Zen Buddhism in a monastery in Kyoto, Japan. Has worked as a seaman, logger, forester, and farmer, and taught at Berkeley. First collection, *Riprap*, published in 1959. Other collections include *Myths and Texts* (1960), *Six Sections from Mountains and Rivers Without End* (1965), *A Range of Poems*, a collection of earlier and new work (1966), *The Back Country* (1968), *Regarding Wave* (1969), *Turtle Island*, which contains prose and poetry (1974), and *Axe Handles* (1983). *Earth House Hold* (1969) and *The Old Ways* (1972) are collections of his prose.

See: Almon, B. *Gary Snyder* (1979)
Howard, R. *Alone With America: The Art of Poetry in the United States Since 1950* (1969)
Kherdian, D. *Six San Francisco Poets* (1969)
Steuding, B. *Gary Snyder* (1976)

STAFFORD, William (1914–), born in Kansas and educated at Kansas, Wisconsin, and Iowa universities. Conscientious objector during World War II and active in pacifist organisations. Taught at Lewis and Clark College (1956–79). His collections include *West of Your City* (1960), *Stories That Could Be True: New and Collected Poems* (1977), and *Things That Happen Where There Aren't Any People* (1980).

See: Holden, J. *The Mark to Turn: A Reading of William Stafford's Poetry* (1976)

STEVENS, Wallace (1879–1955), born in Reading, Pennsylvania. Enrolled at Harvard as a special student in 1897. Contributed prose and verse to college magazines and came into contact with philosopher, George Santayana, who was to influence his work. Worked on editorial staff of *The New York Tribune* and *The World's Work*, then entered New York Law School in 1901. Admitted to the Bar in 1904, and engaged in general practice in New York. Four poems appeared in *Poetry* in 1914. Became acquainted with Marianne Moore, e.e. cummings, William Carlos Williams and other writers living in New York. In 1916, moved to Hartford, Connecticut, to join legal staff of Hartford Accident and Indemnity Company. Remained there until his death, becoming vice-president of company in 1934. First collection, *Harmonium*, published in 1923. A few good reviews, but sold less than one hundred copies. No new poems published for seven years. Then second, revised edition of *Harmonium* appeared in 1931. Followed by *Ideas of Order* (1935), *Owl's Clover* (1936),

The Man With The Blue Guitar (1937), *Parts of a World* (1942), *Notes Toward a Supreme Fiction* (1942), *Esthétique du Mal*, (1944), *Transport to Summer* (1947), and *The Auroras of Autumn* (1950). A *Selected Poems* appeared in 1953; *Collected Poems* (1955) won a Pulitzer Prize. *The Necessary Angel: Essays on Reality and the Imagination* (1956) is a collection of essays and lectures; *Opus Posthumous* (1957) contains poems, essays, and plays. *The Letters of Wallace Stevens* was issued in 1966.

See: Beckett, L. *Wallace Stevens* (1974)
Bloom, H. *Wallace Stevens: The Poems of Our Climate* (1977)
Doggett, F. *Stevens' Poetry of Thought* (1966); *Wallace Stevens: The Making of the Poem* (1980)
Fuchs, D. *The Comic Spirit of Wallace Stevens* (1963)
Gelpi, A. (ed.) *Wallace Stevens: The Poetics of Modernism* (1985)
Litz, A. W. *Introspective Voyager: The Poetic Development of Wallace Stevens* (1972)
Miller, J. H., and Pearce, R. H. (eds.) *The Act of the Mind: Essays on the Poetry of Wallace Stevens* (1965)
O'Connor, W. V. *The Shaping Spirit: A Study of Wallace Stevens* (1950)
Sukenick, R. *Wallace Stevens: Musing the Obscure* (1967)
Vendler, H. *On Extended Wings: Wallace Stevens's Longer Poems* (1967); *Wallace Stevens: Words Chosen Out of Desire* (1984)

TATE [John Orley] Allen (1899–1979), born in Winchester, Kentucky and in 1922 graduated from Vanderbilt University, Nashville, Tennessee, where he met John Crowe Ransom, Robert Penn Warren, and Donald Davidson and became a member of the Fugitive group. Lived in New York (1924–8) and Paris (1928–9), taught at several universities, and edited *Hound and Horn* (1931–4), *The Kenyon Review* (1938), and *The Sewanee Review* (1944–6). First collection, *The Golden Mean and Other Poems* (1923), published privately. Subsequent collections include *Mr. Pope and Other Poems* (1928), *Poems 1928–31* (1932), *The Mediterranean and Other Poems* (1936), *Selected Poems* (1937), *Poems 1922–47* (1948), *Poems* (1960), *The Swimmers and Other Selected Poems*, and *Collected Poems* (1977). His many critical volumes include *Collected Essays* (1959) and *Essays of Four Decades* (1968). A novel, *The Fathers*, appeared in 1938.

Squires, R. *Allen Tate: A Literary Biography* (1971)

See: Dupree, R. S. *Allen Tate and the Augustinian Imagination: A Study of the Poetry* (1983)
Hemphill, G. *Allen Tate* (1964)
Meiners, R. K. *The Last Alternatives: A Study of the Works of Allen Tate* (1963)
Squires, R. (ed.) *Allen Tate and His Work* (1972)

WAKOSKI, Diane (1937–), born in Whittier, California and educated at the University of California, Berkeley. Taught school in New York City and at several universities, including Michigan State University. First book of poetry, *Coins and Coffins*, appeared in 1962. Over thirty books of poetry since, including *The George Washington Poems* (1967), *Looking for the King of Spain* (1974), and *The Collected Greed, Parts 1–13* (1984).

See: Gemmell, R., and Gerber, R. *A Terrible War: A Conversation with Diane Wakoski* (1970)

WARREN, Robert Penn (1905–), born in Guthrie, Kentucky and in 1921 entered Vanderbilt University where he met John Crowe Ransom, Allen Tate, and Donald Davidson and became a member of the Fugitive group. After graduation from Vanderbilt, studied at the University of California, Berkeley, Yale, and Oxford as a Rhodes Scholar. Taught at Southwestern College, Tennessee, Vanderbilt, Louisiana State University, University of Minnesota, and Yale. First poems published in small pamphlet published by the Verse Guild, *Driftwood Flames* (1923) and in *The Fugitive* (1922–25). First collection, *Thirty-Six Poems*, issued in 1935. Among his many subsequent volumes are *Selected Poems, 1923–43* (1944), *Brother to Dragons: A Tale in Verse and Voices* (1953; revised edn., 1979), *Promises: Poems 1954–6*, which won a Pulitzer Prize (1957), *Selected Poems 1923–75* (1976), *Now and Then: Poems 1976–8*, which also won a Pulitzer (1978), and *Chief Joseph of the Nez Perce* (1983). Has written two collections of short stories and nine novels, one of which, *All the King's Men* (1946), won a Pulitzer Prize. His numerous books of non-fictional prose include *Segregation: The Inner Conflict in the South* (1956), *Selected Essays*, a collection of critical pieces (1958), *Who Speaks for the Negro?* (1965), *Democracy and Poetry* (1975), and *Jefferson Davis Gets His Citizenship Back* (1980). With Cleanth Brooks, he founded the *Southern Review* in 1935, and produced two influential college textbooks, *Understanding Poetry* (1938; revised edns., 1950 and 1960) and *Understanding Fiction* (1943; revised edn., 1958).

See: Bedient, C. *In the Heart's Last Kingdom: Robert Penn Warren's Major Poetry* (1984)
Gray, R. (ed.) *Robert Penn Warren: A Collection of Critical Essays* (1980)
Justus, J. H. *The Achievement of Robert Penn Warren* (1981)
Strandberg, V. H. *A Colder Fire: The Poetry of Robert Penn Warren* (1965); *The Poetic Vision of Robert Penn Warren* (1977)
Walker, M. *Robert Penn Warren: A Vision Earned* (1979)

WHALEN, Philip (1923–), born in Oregon, served in the U.S. Air Force (1943–6), studied at Reed College, and was associated with the San Francisco poetry revival. First volume, *Three Satires* (1951). Other collections include *Self-Portrait from Another Direction* (1960), *On Bear's Head: Selected Poems* (1969), *Severance Pay: Poems 1967–9* (1970), *Scenes of Life at the Capital* (1971), *Decompression: Selected Poems* (1978), and *Heavy Breathing: Poems 1967–83* (1984).

See: Vinson, J. (ed.) *Contemporary Poets* (1975)

WHITTEMORE, Reed (1919–), born in New Haven, Connecticut and educated at Yale and Princeton. Served in the U.S. Air Force (1941–5) and has taught at Carleton College, Minnesota, and the University of Maryland. Edited *Furioso* and *Carleton Miscellany*. First collection, *Heroes and Heroines: Poems* (1947); others include, *The Self-Made Man and Other Poems* (1956), *Poems, New and Selected* (1967), *The Mother's Breast and the Father's House* (1974), and *The Feel of Rock: Poems of Three Decades* (1982).

See: Vinson, J. (ed.) *Contemporary Poets* (1975)

WIENERS, John (1934–), born in Boston and educated at Boston College and Black Mountain College, and the State University of New York, Buffalo. Has worked as a library clerk, stage manager and actor, and bookkeeper. First volume, *The Hotel Wentley Poems* (1958; revised edn., 1965) established his reputation. Other collections include *Pressed Wafer* (1967), *Asylum Poems* (1969), *Nerves* (1970), *Youth* (1970), and *Selected Poems* (1972), and *Selected Poems: Nineteen Fifty-Eight to Nineteen Eighty-Four* (1986). More recent books include *A Superficial Estimation* (1987) and *Conjugal Contraries* (1987).

See: Vinson, J. (ed.) *Contemporary Poets* (1975)

WILBUR, Richard (1921–), born in New York City and educated at Amherst and Harvard. Served in the U.S. Army in World War II. Has taught at Harvard, Wellesley, and Wesleyan where he was an editor of the Wesleyan University Press poetry series. First collection, *The Beautiful Changes and Other Poems*, appeared in 1947. Among other collections are *Ceremony and Other Poems* (1950), *Things of this World: Poems*, which won a Pulitzer Prize (1956), *Advice to a Prophet and Other Poems* (1961), *The Poems of Richard Wilbur* (1963), *Walking to Sleep: New Poems and Translations* (1968), and *The Mind-Reader: New Poems* (1976). Also published several translations and a collection of essays, *Responses: Prose Pieces 1957–76* (1976).

See: Cummins, P. F. *Richard Wilbur* (1971)
Hill, D. L. *Richard Wilbur* (1967)

WILLIAMS, Jonathan (1929–), born in Asheville, North Carolina and attended Princeton, Chicago Institute of Design, and Black Mountain College. A conscientious objector, he served in the U.S. Army Medical Corps from 1952 until 1954. Has divided his time between the mountains of North Carolina and Yorkshire, England. First collection, *Red/Gray*, published in 1951. Subsequent collections include *An Ear in Bartram's Tree: Selected Poems 1957–67* (1969), *The Loco Logodaedalist in Situ: Selected Poems 1968–70* (1972), *Imaginary Postcards* (1973), *Elite-Elate Poems* (1974), and *Get Hot or Get Out: A Selection of Poems 1957–81* (1982). A more recent book is *In the Azure over the Squalor, Ransackings & Shorings* (1985).

See: Vinson, J. (ed.) *Contemporary Poets* (1975)

WILLIAMS, William Carlos (1883–1963), born in Rutherford, New Jersey. Parents both immigrants, father from England and mother from Puerto Rico. Entered University of Pennsylvania Medical School in 1902. Met Ezra Pound in Philadelphia. Received M.D. in 1906 and then began internship in New York City. First collection, *Poems*, published privately in Rutherford in 1906. After studying paediatrics in Leipzig and visiting Pound in London, returned to become a general practitioner in Rutherford. Poetry began appearing in *Poetry* and *The Dial*; second-volume, *The Tempers*, appeared in 1913; became acquainted with Marianne Moore, Wallace Stevens, and other poets in New York. Involved with the Imagist movement, he contributed to *Des Imagistes* (1914): new poems in third book, *Al Que Quiere!* (1917), bore witness to new commitment. *Kora in Hell* (1920) and *Spring and All* (1923) helped establish reputation. In 1930s, allied with George Oppen, Louis Zukofsky and others in Objectivist movement. Among his subsequent volumes are *An Early Martyr* (1935), *Adam and Eve and the City* (1936), *The Clouds* (1948), *Collected Later Poems* (1950), *Collected Earlier Poems* (1951), *The Desert Music and Other Poems* (1954). *Journey to Love* (1955), and *Pictures from Bruegel and Other Poems*, which won a Pulitzer Prize (1962). Between 1946 and 1958, published five books of his great epic poem, *Paterson*: issued in one volume in 1963, together with fragments of a projected sixth book. Published four novels, including *White Mule* (1937), a collection of short stories, *The Farmer's Daughter* (1961), and a collection of plays, *Many Lives and Other Plays*. Works of non-fiction include *In the American Grain* (1925), *The Autobiography of William Carlos Williams* (1951), and *I Wanted to Write a Poem* (1958).

Manani, P. *William Carlos Williams: A New World Named* (1981)

See: Breslin, J. E. *William Carlos Williams: An American Artist* (1970)
Cushman, S. *William Carlos Williams and the Meanings of Measure* (1985)
Doyle, C. *William Carlos Williams and the American Poem* (1982)
Guimond, J. *The Art of William Carlos Williams: A Discovery and Possession of America* (1968)
Lloyd, M. G. *William Carlos Williams's 'Paterson': A Critical Reappraisal* (1980)
Miller, J. H. (ed.) *William Carlos Williams: A Collection of Critical Essays* (1966)
Riddel, J. F. *The Inverted Bell: Modernism and the Counter-Poetics of William Carlos Williams* (1974)
Sankey, B. *A Companion to William Carlos Williams's 'Paterson'* (1971)
Wagner, L. W. *The Poems of William Carlos Williams: A Critical Study* (1963)
Weaver, M. *William Carlos Williams: The American Background* (1971)

WINTERS [Arthur] Yvor (1900–68), born in Chicago and studied at Chicago, Colorado, and Stanford Universities. Taught at Stanford. First collection of poems, *Poetry: The Immobile Wind*, published in 1921. Among other volumes are *Magpie's Shadow* (1922), *The Bare Hills* (1927), and *To the Holy Spirit* (1947). The *Collected Poems* appeared in 1952. A distinguished critic, his critical books include *In Defence of Reason* (1947), *The Function of Criticism* (1957), *Yvor Winters on Modern Poets* (1959), and *Forms of Discovery* (1967).

See: Comito, T. *In Defence of Winters: The Poetry of Yvor Winters* (1986)
Isaacs, E. *An Introduction to the Poetry of Yvor Winters* (1981)
Powell, G. *Language as Being in the Poetry of Yvor Winters* (1980)

WRIGHT, Charles (1935–), born in Pickwick Dam, Tennessee and educated at Davidson College and the State University of Iowa. Selections from first four volumes appeared in *Country Music* (1982). Since then, has published *The Southern Cross* (1981) and *The Other Side of the River* (1984).

See: Vendler, H. *Part of Nature, Part of Us: Modern American Poets* (1980)

WRIGHT, James (1927–80), born in Martin's Ferry, Ohio and educated at Kenyon College and the University of Washington. Served in the army in World War II. Taught at Hunter College, New York City, from 1966 until his death. His first volume, *The Green Wall*, was issued in 1957. The *Collected Poems* (1971) won a Pulitzer Prize. Followed by *Two Citizens* (1973), *Moments of the Italian Summer* (1976), *To a Blossoming Pear Tree* (1977), and *This Journey* (1982). Also published several translations.

See: Howard, R. *Alone With America: The Art of Poetry in the United States Since 1950* (1969)

Lensing, G. S., and Moran, R. *Four Poets of the Emotive Imagination: Robert Bly, James Wright, Louis Simpson, and William Stafford* (1976)

WYLIE, Elinor (1885–1928), born in New Jersey and educated in Philadelphia. *Incidental Numbers* (1912) published anonymously and privately. *Nets to Catch the Wind* (1921) established her reputation. Followed by *Black Armour* (1923), *Trivial Breath* (1928), and *Angels and Earthly Creatures* (1928). *Collected Poems* appeared in 1932, *Collected Prose* in 1937, and *Last Poems* in 1943.

See: Farr, J. *The Life and Art of Elinor Wylie* (1983)

ZUKOFSKY, Louis (1904–78), born in New York City and educated at Columbia. Lived in New York for most of his life. Taught at the University of Wisconsin, San Francisco State College, and Brooklyn Polytechnic Institute. Associated with the Objectivist school, and his poetry first appeared in *An 'Objectivists' Anthology* (1932), which he edited. Among his later collections of shorter poems are *55 Poems* (1941), *Anew* (1946), *Some Time* (1956), *Barely and Widely* (1958), *After I's* (1964), and *I Sent Thee Late* (1965). *All: The Collected Shorter Poems* appeared in 1966. In 1940, he published *First Half of 'A'–9.* Other sections of the ambitious long poem, *'A'*, appeared over the next thirty-eight years. Expanded eventually to twenty-four sections, and published in complete form in 1978. Among his other publications are *A Test of Poetry* (1948), *Bottom: On Shakespeare* (1963), *Arise, Arise* a play (1965), *Prepositions* (1967), and *Little: A Fragment for Careenagers*, a novel (1970).

See: Ahearn, B. *Zukofsky's 'A': An Introduction* (1983)
Terrell, C. F. (ed.) *Louis Zukofsky: Man and Poet* (1979)

Index

Adams, Henry, 29–31, 33, 38, 76, 79
Adams, John, 13
Adams, Léonie, 191, 193–94
Adler, Alfred, 71
Adorno, Theodor, 241
Aesop, 203
Agee, James, 160
Aiken, Conrad, 69, 70–72, 339
Aldington, Richard, 52–53
Ammons, A. R., 236–38
Andrewes, Lancelot, 342
Antoninus, Brother, 293–94
Aquinas, Thomas, 37
Arensberg, Walter, 39
Aristotle, 37
Ashbery, John, 38, 41, 278, 315, 317, 321, 323–26, 327, 328–30
Auden, W. H., 221, 257, 336

Bach, J. S., 63
Baldwin, James, 176
Band, The, 315
Baraka, Imamu Amiri, 177, 224, 307, 308–12, 314
Baudelaire, Charles, 116, 339
Benn, Gottfried, 259–60
Berrigan, Ted, 315, 320, 322–23
Berry, Wendell, 123–24
Berryman, John, 216, 224, 231, 234, 256–60, 264
Bidart, Frank, 267, 278
Bishop, Elizabeth, 223, 244–47, 251, 308
Bishop, John Peale, 121, 123, 129, 152
Blackburn, Paul, 284–85
Blackmur, R. P., 107
Blake, William, 13, 89, 200, 246, 299, 300, 304
Bly, Robert, 41, 225, 232, 238–239, 240
Bogan, Louise 191, 192–93, 308
Bohr, Niels, 32
Bowers, Edgar, 223, 244
Bradstreet, Anne, 11, 257–58
Brando, Marlon, 218
Brooks, Cleanth, 110
Brooks, Gwendolyn, 183–84
Brooks, Van Wyck, 8, 105
Brown, Norman O., 300
Bruegel, Pieter, 88
Bryan, William Jennings, 105, 167
Bukowski, Charles, 306–7
Burke, Kenneth, 35
Byron, Lord, 190

Cage, John, 280
Cantwell, Robert, 159
Carter, Jimmy, 278
Cather, Willa, 105–6
Cézanne, Paul, 42, 302
Chaplin, Charles, 204
Ciardi, John, 234–35
Clampitt, Amy, 265–78
Clark, Kenneth, 246
Coleridge, Samuel Taylor, 89
Coltrane, John, 308
Confucius, 79, 80
Conroy, Jack, 159
Coolidge, Calvin, 102, 215
Cooper, James Fenimore, 137
Corse, Gregory, 305–6
Crabbe, George, 142
Crane, Hart, 1, 8, 11, 13, 16, 34–35, 39, 40, 41, 51, 55, 57, 113, 114, 160, 203–9, 317
Creeley, Robert, 41, 45, 285–87, 289, 316
Crèvecoeur, St. Jean de, 1
Crockett, Davy, 118
Cullen, Countee, 182–83, 308

cummings, e. e., 51, 57, 60, 194–99
Cunningham, J. V., 127–29

Dante, 73
Darrow, Clarence, 105
Darwin, Charles, 32, 33, 34, 38
Davidson, Donald, 106, 107, 117–18
Davis, Miles, 285
Dean, James, 218, 275
Descartes, René, 10
Dickey, James, 123, 124–25, 139
Dickinson, Emily, 15, 16, 24, 25, 26–28, 38, 45, 57, 69, 93, 105, 130, 135, 193, 261, 286, 299
Di Prima, Diane, 267–68, 278
Doctorow, E. L., 278
Donne, John, 342
D[oolittle] H[ilda], 39, 52–53, 57–60, 70, 73, 80, 96–97, 109, 291
Dorn, Edward, 277, 278, 285, 287–89
Dostoevsky, Fyodor, 9
Dreiser, Theodore, 164
DuBois, W. E. B., 177
Duchamp, Marcel, 42
Dugan, Alan, 232, 234, 235
Duller, John Foster, 217
Duncan, Robert, 60, 240, 285, 289–91, 292
Dürer, Albrecht, 186, 187
Dylan, Bob, 342

Eberhart, Richard, 129–31, 219, 303
Einstein, Albert, 32, 33, 35, 38
Eisenhower, Dwight D., 215, 217, 218
Eliot, Andrew, 336
Eliot, T. S., 39, 51, 52, 60 70, 73, 84, 106, 109, 113–14, 116, 173, 183, 229, 250, 257, 336–46
Emerson, Ralph Waldo, 1, 10, 12, 15, 23, 29, 32, 40, 45, 55, 135, 137, 196
Epstein, Jacob, 76
Evans, Hiram Wesley, 103–4
Evans, Mari, 313
Everson, William, *see* Antoninus, Brother

Faulkner, William, 10, 106, 160
Fearing, Kenneth, 174–75
Fenollosa, Ernest, 77
Ferlinghetti, Lawrence, 277, 291–93, 294, 299
Fitzgerald, F. Scott, 101, 121, 160, 191
Fletcher, John Gould, 69–70, 108–9
Flint, F. S., 52, 53, 54, 55, 56
Fonda, Jane, 278
Ford, Ford Madox, 44, 53
Ford, Gerald, 278
Ford, Henry, 63
Franklin, Benjamin, 3, 10, 11, 14
Freud, Sigmund, 33–34, 35, 38, 70, 71
Frost, Robert, 15, 29, 40, 55, 73, 131–38, 139, 147, 152, 193, 273–74, 329

Galbraith, J. K., 158
Gardner, Helen, 337
Gaudier-Brezska, 76
Ginsberg, Allen, 1, 73, 218, 239, 240, 275, 276, 277, 299–305, 315, 316, 344
Giovanni, Nikki, 313, 314, 315
Glück, Louise, 265–66, 278
Goffman, Erving, 278
Grateful Dead, The, 315
Guest, Barbara, 322, 323

Haines, John, 266, 278
Hall, Donald, 232
Harding, Warren, 103
Hartigan, Grace, 317
Hawthorne, Nathaniel, 10
Hayden, Robert, 183
Hecht, Anthony, 223, 244
Heisenberg, Werner, 32–33
Hemingway, Ernest, 51, 160
Henderson, David, 308
Henri, Robert, 164–65
Herbert, George, 342
Hirsch, Sidney, 106, 107
Holliday, Billie, 320–21
Hoover, Herbert, 157–58
Howe, Irving, 215–16
Hughes, Howard, 289
Hughes, Langston, 177–81, 182, 183, 184, 308, 309
Hugo, Richard, 227
Hulme, T. E. 52, 55

Ignatow, David, 234, 235–36
Isherwood, Christopher, 336

Jackson, Andrew, 167
Jackson, Jesse, 307
Jackson, Laura Riding, *see* Riding, Laura

Jakobson, Roman, 36–37
James, Henry, 10, 161, 341
Jarrell, Randall, 135, 186, 219–21, 239, 244
Jeffers, Robinson, 16, 17, 57, 147–52, 170, 241, 293
Jefferson, Thomas, 22, 79
Joans, Ted, 309
Johns, Jasper, 317
Johnson, James Weldon, 181–82
Johnson, Lyndon, 276
Jolas, Eugene, 41
Jones, Leroi, *see* Baraka, Imamu Amiri
Josephson, Matthew, 105
Joyce, James, 38, 78, 345
Jung, Carl, 71, 137, 232
Justice, Donald, 223, 244

Kafka, Franz, 158–59, 161
Kant, Immanuel, 37
Karenga, Ron, 308, 313, 314
Kaufman, Bob, 309
Keats, John, 20, 52, 88, 182, 233
Kees, Weldon, 223, 243–44
Kelly, Robert, 224
Kennedy, John F., 218, 273, 321
Kennedy, X. J., 223, 244
Kenner, Hugh, 338, 339
Kerouac, Jack, 218, 299, 301, 305–6
Kesey, Ken, 306
King, Martin Luther, 276, 307
Kinnell, Galway, 224–25, 227, 241
Koch, Kenneth, 315, 317, 322, 323
Kooning, William de, 317
Kreymburg, Alfred, 39, 41
Kunitz, Stanley, 223, 243

Laforgue, Jules, 338, 339
Lamantia, Philip, 294–95
Last Poets, The, 315
Laud, Archbishop, 342
Lawrence, D. H., 33, 38, 43
Lee, Don, *see* Mahubuti, Haki R.
Levertov, Denise, 56, 240, 284, 316
Levine, Philip, 236
Lèvi-Strauss, Claude, 289, 325
Lincoln, Abraham, 166, 167
Lindbergh, Charles, 101–102
Lindsay, Vachel, 39, 167–68, 178, 309
Linton, Ralph, 102
Locke, John, 10, 37
Loeb, Harold, 41
Logan, John, 224, 227, 228
Lowell, Amy, 40, 53–54, 56, 57, 70
Lowell, James Russell, 10
Lowell, Robert, 8, 24, 215, 216, 218, 224, 231, 240–41, 251–56, 257, 264, 276, 316, 344 346
Lowes, John Livingstone, 56–57

Mahubuti, Haki R., 184, 313–14
Mailer, Norman, 8, 276, 306–7
Malcolm X, 307, 312
Manson, Charles, 307
Marquis, Don, 197
Marvell, Andrew, 174, 301
Marx, Karl, 32, 33, 34, 38
Masters, Edgar Lee, 168, 236
Mather, Cotton, 3, 10, 12–13, 14
Melville, Herman, 10, 252
Meredith, George, 57
Merrill, James, 38, 241–42, 278, 326–28
Merwin, W. S., 221, 232–33, 240
Miles, Josephine, 191
Millay, Edna St. Vincent, 190–91
Mitchell, Joni, 315
Monk, Thelonious, 286
Monroe, Harriet, 39, 42, 52, 56, 168
Moore, Marianne, 15, 39, 52, 56, 57, 60, 82, 162, 184–89, 193–95, 197, 244
Muhammed, Elijah, 307
Muir, Edwin, 192
Mukarovsky, Jan, 36, 37
Mumford, Lewis, 8
Munson, Gorham B., 41
McAlmon, Robert, 40
McCarthy, Joseph, 216, 217
McClure, Michael, 295–96
McKay, Claude, 180
McLeish, Archibald, 41, 173–74

Nabokov, Vladimir, 38
Nash, Ogden, 197
Nelson, David, 313, 314, 315
Nemerov, Howard, 223, 243
Niedecker, Lorine, 66, 67–69
Nixon, Richard, 217, 277, 278, 307
North, Oliver, 307
Norton, Charles Eliot, 10

Oden, G. C., 308
O'Hara, Frank, 275, 309, 315–21, 322, 323, 326
Olson, Charles, 17, 22, 41, 73, 237, 275, 279–84, 289, 309, 316, 344

Oppen, George, 60, 64–66, 67, 73, 235
Oppenheim, James, 39
Orlovsky, Peter, 305
Ovid, 79

Padgett, Ron, 321
Parker, Charlie, 285, 301, 309
Patchen, Kenneth, 174, 175–76
Pearce, Roy Harvey, 345
Picasso, Pablo, 42, 324
Pinsky, Robert, 266–67
Pirsig, Robert M., 278
Plath, Sylvia, 224, 231, 238, 242, 260–64
Podhoretz, Norman, 300
Poe, Edgar Allan, 4, 14, 16, 28, 29, 38, 45, 57, 70, 84, 93, 191, 261, 324
Pollock, Jackson, 280, 285
Pound, Ezra, 13, 17, 18, 19, 25–26, 27, 29, 33, 35, 39, 40, 41, 44–45, 51, 52–57, 59, 60, 61, 69–70, 73–81, 84, 97, 108, 109, 159, 160, 173, 255, 257, 280, 302, 304, 316, 329, 343–4, 346
Presley, Elvis, 217
Proust, Marcel, 327

Rakosi, Carl, 60
Ransom, John Crowe, 15, 40, 57, 106, 107, 109–13, 114, 116–117, 118, 119, 121, 122, 125, 129, 150, 152, 189, 221, 342
Rauschenberg, Robert, 317
Reagan, Ronald, 278
Reverdy, Pierre, 316
Rexroth, Kenneth, 60, 169–173, 300, 306
Reznikoff, Charles, 60, 66–67
Rich, Adrienne, 224, 227, 229–32, 238, 239, 240
Riding, Laura, 107, 108, 200, 202–3
Rimbaud, Arthur, 282, 338
Rivers, Larry, 316, 317
Robinson, Edwin Arlington, 15, 138–45, 147, 152, 329
Roethke, Theodore, 57, 231, 247–51
Roosevelt, Franklin, 158, 159
Roosevelt, Theodore, 42
Rosenthal, M. L., 163
Roth, Henry, 160
Rukeyser, Muriel, 200–1
Russell, Bertrand, 10

Salinger, J. D., 218
Sanchez, Sonia, 275, 313, 314
Sandburg, Carl, 30, 39, 40, 56, 162–67, 168, 178
Santayana, George, 91
Sapir, Edward, 36
Sartre, Jean-Paul, 325
Saussure, Ferdinand de, 35–36, 38
Schoenberg, Arnold, 72
Schuyler, George, 182
Schuyler, James, 322, 323
Schwartz, Delmore, 224, 233–34
Scopes, John, 104–5
Scott-Heron, Gil, 315
Sexton, Anne, 224, 227, 229, 238, 261
Shapiro, Karl, 218–19, 223, 227, 231, 239
Shelley, Percy Bysshe, 12, 190
Shklovsky, Victor, 22–23
Simpson, Louis, 219, 223, 227–28, 231, 239
Smith, Dave, 267
Snodgrass, W. D., 224, 227, 228–29
Snyder, Gary, 277, 296–98, 299
Socrates, 70
Solomon, Carl, 303
Spicer, Jack, 294
Springsteen, Bruce, 315
Stafford, William, 234, 235, 241
Steffens, Lincoln, 164
Stein, Gertrude, 40, 51, 106, 324
Steinbeck, John, 159–60
Stevens, Wallace, 16, 19, 33, 37, 39, 52, 56, 60, 88–97, 144, 324, 346
Strauss, Richard, 72
Synge, J. M., 192

Tate, Allen, 40, 41, 106, 107, 108, 109, 113–16, 117, 118, 121, 122, 125, 150, 152, 191, 202, 342
Taylor, Edward, 11
Thoreau, Henry David, 6, 256, 298
Tocqueville, Alexis de, 5, 14–15, 16–17, 18
Tolson, Melvin B., 183
Tomlinson, Charles, 186
Trakl, Georg, 226
Trilling, Diana, 300
Trilling, Lionel, 34, 136
Turner, Frederick Jackson, 8
Twain, Mark, 196

Van Gogh, Vincent, 42, 83
Verlaine, Paul, 338

Wakoski, Diane, 267, 268, 278
Ward, John, 101
Warren, Robert Penn, 107, 117, 118–21
Waters, Muddy, 312, 315
West, Nathanael, 160
Whalen, Philip, 295
Whitman, Walt, 1, 4–5, 7, 8, 10, 11, 13, 15, 16, 18, 19–25, 27, 28, 29, 32, 33, 38, 45, 55, 57, 59, 73, 79, 81, 84, 88, 92, 93, 105, 128, 130–31, 135, 137, 158–59, 161–62, 163, 164, 168, 169, 171, 172, 176, 177–78, 180, 181, 185, 187–88, 194, 196, 199, 200, 203–4, 206, 207, 209, 227, 235, 254, 255, 266, 288, 299, 300, 304, 305, 306, 316, 317, 329, 342, 344–45
Whittemore, Reed, 223, 243
Whorf, Benjamin Lee, 17–18, 35
Wieners, John, 285
Wilbur, Richard, 221–23, 231, 242–43
Williams, Jonathan, 284
Williams, Oscar, 219
Williams, William Carlos, 13, 16, 19, 29, 34–35, 38–39, 40, 43–44, 45, 51, 52, 53, 55, 56, 60, 61–62, 67, 69, 73, 82–88, 97, 169, 172, 186, 189, 235, 237, 241, 253, 280, 292, 294, 301, 316, 317, 329, 343–44, 346
Wilson, Edmund, 121
Wilson, Woodrow, 51
Winters, Yvor, 125–27, 152, 191
Wittgenstein, Ludwig, 37–38
Wordsworth, William, 13, 22, 52
Wright, Charles, 264
Wright, James, 225, 226–27
Wright, Richard, 160
Wylie, Elinor, 189–90

Yeats, W. B., 38, 73, 188, 257

Zukofsky, Louis, 60, 61, 62–64, 67, 69, 73